HIKING
WESTERN DEATH VALLEY NATIONAL PARK

PANAMINT, SALINE, AND EUREKA VALLEY

Second Edition

Michel Digonnet

First edition: March 2009
Second edition: February 2023

Maps, illustrations, and book design by the author
Photographs by the author, unless otherwise specified

Volume Editor: Susan Cole
Cover Designer: Karen Frankel

Published in Palo Alto, California
Printed and bound in the United States of America

Library of Congress Control Number: 2022921045

ISBN: 978-0-9659178-5-8

Cover: (clockwise from right)
Beveridge Canyon, Inyo Mountains
Prickly-pear in bloom
Petroglyph panel, Nelson Range
Salt Tramway control tower, Inyo Mountains
Hidden Dunes, Eureka Valley

Back cover: Saline Valley from Salt Tramway Trail
Wild burros, Panamint Mountains

By the same author:
Hiking Death Valley (second edition)
Hiking the Mojave Desert (second edition)
Mojave Desert Peaks
Hiking Joshua Tree (in preparation)
Mojave Trails National Monument (in preparation)

To my mother

WARNING

Many of the hikes suggested in this book are potentially dangerous. They involve hours of strenuous physical activity across often rugged terrain, with no water, little to no shade, in a hot desert. They should be attempted only by hikers in excellent physical condition, with prior experience in desert hiking and good route-finding skills. Although many of the dangers of specific routes are mentioned in the text, all of them cannot possibly be covered. The information contained in this book should not be considered a substitute for common sense. The author declines all responsibilities for any injuries, physical or otherwise, anyone might sustain while hiking any of the routes suggested herein.

ACKNOWLEDGMENTS

Several people have made significant contributions to the first edition of this book, and I extend to them my sincere appreciation. First of all, I would like to thank my wife Susan Cole for letting me take the time to carry out this six-year project, although it meant spending many evenings and long weekends apart; and for diligently editing the manuscript in various stages of completion. I would also like to thank my many friends who occasionally accompanied me on my trips to the desert—Francie Allen, Michael Closson, Marc Fermigier, Bruno Marchon, Mae "Taj Majal Kita" Pomfret, David and Hélène Pureur, Debra Schlueter, as well as Susan of course, and my indefatigable mother, who still treks over thorns and rocks with a smile at the venerable age of 82. There was also that one heroic "trip with the girls," when I took five women friends on a hiking spree to the desert—Melanie Brady, Karen Frankel, Leslie Murphy-Chutorian, Helen Rakove, and Susan—and was chastised by some of their hopeful husbands for bringing them back. In spite of this regrettable error on my part, this was one of my most enjoyable trips. In your own and different ways, you have all greatly enhanced my appreciation of the desert and made my experience so much more meaningful. A special acknowledgement goes to my non-blood-relative cousin but nevertheless friend Jeff Weintraub, who came along on more trips than anyone else besides Susan. He was the only person foolish enough to join me on the toughest hikes, in snow storms or three-digit temperatures, including our memorable backpacking trips to the remote ghost towns of Beveridge and Panamint City. I am well aware that he did this mostly to see his name cited in print; but we still had a lot of fun.

I am indebted to Bill Graham of Panamint Springs Resort for pointing out over the years a few delightful places in Panamint Valley, and for serving me on numerous occasions rejuvenating dinners at the end of tiring days in the wild; to Keith Seal, long-time waiter at Panamint Springs, for always welcoming me as a friend; to David Rogers for sharing the history of the Saline Valley's talc mines, which have been in his family for several decades; to former Willow Creek Camp caretaker Steve Wyatt, who entertained me on a few occasions with his passionate accounts of Saline Valley's history; and to former Ballarat caretaker Lightfoot Louie and former Chris Wicht Camp resident Rocky Novak for sharing some of their precious knowledge of the Panamint Mountains. I would also like to thank Bill Michael, Beth Porter, Roberta Harlan, and Jon Klusmire of the Eastern California

Museum in Independence for supplying archival material on some of the region's pioneers, including the Shepherd family, and for their assistance in identifying the historic photographs that appear in this volume.

Many of Death Valley National Park's staff members have spent a lot of time and effort reviewing this book and providing information and suggestions in their respective areas of expertise, and I acknowledge their valuable contributions: Linda Greene, Chief of Resources Management, who said some kind words about *Hiking Death Valley* and the manuscript of this book; Corky Hays, former Chief of Interpretation; Park Superintendent James T. Reynolds; Kelly Turner, former Park Archaeologist; and Vicki Wolfe, former Interpretive Ranger. A very special thank you goes to Charlie Callagan, who has been an Interpretive Ranger in Death Valley for many years. Charlie's in-depth knowledge of the park backcountry and patient responses to my numerous detailed inquiries were instrumental throughout this review process. I would also like to acknowledge the assistance of David Blacker, Executive Director of Death Valley Natural History Association.

Several people at the Bureau of Land Management should be mentioned for reviewing portions of this manuscript: Wilderness Coordinator Marty Dickes, who also provided useful maps of the wilderness boundaries, former Archaeologist Judyth Reed, Supervisory Resource Management Specialist Joe Pollini, and Archaeologist Donald Storm.

For the second edition, I would like to thank again my wife for proofreading the manuscript; and for joining me on some of the hikes that were added to this edition, as did our friend Alice Fermigier. I am again indebted to Karen Frankel for the cover design and for her attention to details in the selection of the photographs. I thank Death Valley National Park superintendent Mike Reynolds and park rangers April Stiltz and Matthew Lamar for their patience in answering my many questions about road conditions, park regulations, and private properties in the park. I also want to acknowledge and thank Katrina Meyer at the Ridgecrest Bureau of Land Management Field Office for clarifying the status of mining claims in the Inyo Mountains, and for taking the time to drive out to the Talc City Hills to determine which roads were closed to motor vehicles.

CONTENTS

Narrow-gauge rail on ore-loading bridge, White Swan Mine, Talc City Hills

FOREWORD

Part of the emblematic Basin and Range province, the desert region of eastern California sandwiched between Death Valley to the east and Owens Valley to the west is a vast playground of stunning beauty and proportions. Encompassing Eureka Valley, Saline Valley, and Panamint Valley, this 130-mile-long corridor is defined by a formidable topography of deep hydrological basins enclosed by majestic mountain ranges that rise up to two miles above sea level. Shielded from development by this sheer geography, it is still largely in a pristine state, far from cities and major throughways, much of it accessed by rough primitive roads that discourage casual travel. The region's extreme range of elevations has spawned a wealth of ecosystems that elicits both our incredulity and admiration. This 2,700-square-mile wilderness is home to scorched salt flats and alpine summits covered in snow in winter, peaceful oases and evergreen forests, sand dunes and meandering canyons, cool streams and cactus gardens, and an equally diverse wildlife. Almost all of it enjoys the highest level of federal protection: more than half is part of Death Valley National Park, and the rest is either designated and *de facto* wilderness. Collectively, it is one of the world's largest blocks of preserved desert land.

When it first appeared in print in 2009, this was the first book dedicated entirely to this special region, and this second edition still is. It is remarkable that since then, and in contrast to other desert parks where visitation has exploded, this area has not changed. There has been no new resorts, campgrounds, signed trails, high-speed highways, or outhouses desecrating the middle of nowhere. There are still only two main roads in Eureka Valley and Saline Valley, all unpaved. If you camp along the Saline Valley Road, chances are that no one will drive at night. There is still not a single artificial light in all of Eureka Valley. In Saline Valley, the only places where people might be found are the undeveloped campground at Warm Springs and the former mining outpost of Willow Creek Camp. Panamint Valley is a little more developed, but not by much: it has a few paved roads, two small settlements, and it remains one of California's largest and wildest desert valleys. In an era where many parks are being loved to death and constrained by red tape, this *status quo* is a rare blessing.

Although all three valleys hold incomparable recreational value, each one offers its own set of unique attractions and a different overall outdoor experience. Eureka Valley, least visited of the three, is a haven of solitude. It is famous for its desert dunes, which are the tallest in the country, and, surprisingly, not anything else. Yet it is brimming with visual treasures, from hidden dunes to the well-preserved ruins of historic talc, sulfur, copper, and mercury mines. In Saline Valley, you are in a lost world, isolated by two hours of driving on bone-rattling roads. The rugged Inyo Mountains, which loom over the valley's west side, are the site of gold-mining ghost towns dating back to the 1880s. One of them, Beveridge, is possibly the most remote in the American West, and it has become a legend. Many canyons in the Inyos are prized for their year-round streams and idyllic oases. They also rank among the best and most challenging canyoneering destinations in the California desert. Being more accessible, Panamint Valley sees more visitation, although only a tiny fraction of Death Valley's most popular spots. The Panamint Range and Argus Range, which frame this long valley, are a mecca for rough canyon hikes and four-wheeling expeditions to remote springs, abandoned mines, and dusty ghost towns.

Having explored in the intervening years many of California's other desert parks and wilderness, I have come to realize that none of them holds a candle to the greater Death Valley region. Here the mountains are bigger, the scenery is grander, the silence deeper, and the sense of space and isolation more intense. This is unquestionably our most spectacular desert land. Paradoxically, it is also so relatively poorly known that a curious hiker can still discover something no one has seen in decades, or possibly ever.

In an era where most of us spend a good portion of our awake time staring at a screen for work, communication, or entertainment, exploration of the natural world is hardly on anyone's agenda. The desire may never have been taught, or the psychological need may have faded through disuse. More than anything else, this book is an attempt to induce, or rekindle, this longing for adventures in nature—arguably the only true adventures. As I wrote in the first edition's foreword, this book is meant for all of you who love the desert, and all of you eager to discover it; to learn to cherish the brilliant light, the tormented rocks, the silence, the billion-year-old dust, the wind howling between canyon walls, the pungent smell of creosote after a rain, the mysteries and legends of departed cultures, the shriek of the lonesome hawk pinned high against infinity, the thirst and the prickles, the scorching days and frigid nights, and the rivers of weathered stones that snake forever into the mountains. May it entice you to live a thousand adventures, and fill your mind with your greatest memories.

Paris, France
October 20, 2022

ABOUT THIS BOOK

General Organization

This book has ten main sections. The first three sections provide general background information. Part 1 gives a synopsis of the region's natural and human history. Part 2 covers safety tips, regulations, and ethics of backcountry use, and Part 3 local facilities. The remaining seven sections describe hikes in specific geographic areas, arranged generally from north to south and east to west: Eureka Valley, the western slopes of the Last Chance Range, Saline Valley, the eastern slopes of the Inyo Mountains, the western slopes of the Panamint Range, Panamint Valley, and finally Darwin Plateau and the Argus Range. Each section starts with a general overview of the area's main features (location, access and backcountry roads, geology, hiking, etc.), summary tables of suggested road trips and hikes, and a shaded-relief map. The rest of each section consists of descriptions of individual driving and/or hiking destinations, organized in the same cardinal order. At the end of the book, an index of destinations provides a quick reference to most of the destinations, categorized by type, and identifies the places I found most special.

To avoid potential ambiguities, this chapter explains the purpose of these subsections, the definitions that were used, and the assumptions that were made.

Tables of Suggested Hikes

For out-and-back hikes, the distance that is listed is the *one-way* distance, and the elevation change is the *total* elevation gain on the *round-trip* hike. For loop hikes, the figures listed are the *total* distance and again the *total* elevation gain.

Organization of Individual Driving/Hiking Area Descriptions

Each individual area description contains six common sections: a summary of highlights, three sections titled "General Information," "Location and Access," and "Route Description," a distance and elevation chart, and a topographic map. When warranted, additional sections are included, such as "Geology" or "History."

About "General Information." This section provides a synopsis of the most important facts about the hikes/road trips. It includes the following entries.

Road status mentions first whether the hike is done on a road, a trail, or cross-country, then the type of road that gives driving access to the area (paved graded, or primitive), and the vehicle requirement (standard-clearance, high clearance (HC), or four-wheel drive (4WD)).

Hikes: The next entry lists the distance, elevation gain, and difficulty of the main hike(s) in the area. For out-and-back hikes, distances and elevations are one-way figures from the starting point defined by mile 0 in the chart. For loop hikes, the figures listed are the *total* distance and the *total* elevation gain.

Difficulty rates the overall hiking difficulty (this is often the only place where the level of difficulty is mentioned). Importantly, ratings assume that the entire round-trip hike is done in one day (breaking up a long hike into a two-day backpacking trip usually lowers its difficulty). They also assume cool to warm weather. In very hot weather, the difficulty of hiking anywhere worsens considerably, and these ratings underestimate the difficulty. The following scale is used:

- Very easy: a fairly short stroll on nearly level terrain.
- Easy: involves relatively short, easy cross-country walks on gentle grades, or longer walks on trails or roads, and no obstacles that cannot be avoided by walking around them; accessible to most people.
- Moderate: a longer hike (3-6 miles each way), with steeper grades and/or a few obstacles; anyone in reasonably good shape should pass this level.
- Difficult: steep grades (500–1,000 feet per mile) over moderate distances (~6 miles), rough terrain, uneasy footing, and/or obstructions to bypass or climb. Good physical condition is imperative.
- Strenuous: implies a combination of several of the following: steep grades (1,000 feet per mile or more) over long distances (8 miles or more each way), large rocks, high falls to climb or circumvent, and very steep and rough terrain; requires excellent physical condition and recent practice.

This scale is subjective. However, I did my best to use it consistently throughout this and other books. So even if you disagree with it, use it as a relative scale. For example, you may find after trying a few hikes that what I rate moderate is usually easy for you.

Ratings of technical climbs are estimates based on personal evaluations and are subjective too. The following five classes are used:

- Class 1: Walking with no need for hands.
- Class 2: Use of hands for scrambling or balance, or on short easy walls or dry falls with little exposure.

MAP LEGEND

Symbol	Meaning	Symbol	Meaning
190	Highways/Paved road		Contour line
	Unpaved road (2WD)		Contour line (every fifth line)
	4WD-HC road	3200	Elevation, in feet
	Hiking trail		Wash
	Cross-country route		Broad gravel or sand wash
	Wilderness area boundary		Wash distributary
	National Park boundary		Fall/Boulder jam/Chockstone
To Darwin (25 mi)	Mileage from edge of map		Sand dunes
			Natural bridge/Arch
	Pass		Summit
	Gate		Grotto
	Manmade structure		Pond/Lake
	Ruin		Spring
	Grave		Well
	Campground		Water tank
	Ranger station		Mine adit
	Picnic area		Collapsed adit
	Guzzler		Mine shaft
	Corral		Open pit/Surface mine
			Prospect
-N-	North Star		Windmill
		•S	Starting point of a hike

• Class 3: Use of hands on somewhat exposed rock surfaces; beginners may need a rope. From this class on up, a fall could be fatal.

• Class 4: Simple climbing moves with high exposure; natural protection can be found, although a rope may be required.

• Class 5: Technical climbing on sheer or overhanging rock faces with small footholds and handholds; requires skill and training, and on high climbs a rope and other hardware for safety.

USGS topographic maps lists the USGS 7.5' maps that cover the entire hiking/driving area. When several maps are required, the most useful maps are identified with an asterisk.

Maps indicates, in this order, the page location of:

(1) the main contour map(s) for the hike, marked by an asterisk;

(2) in some cases, other contour maps (no asterisk) showing the area in relation to adjacent areas;

(3) the shaded-relief map of the area's general location, in italics.

About "Location and Access." This section gives driving directions to the starting point of a hike. They are meant to be clear enough without consulting a map. The type of road is mentioned, and the vehicle requirement for unpaved roads *assuming dry weather*. Vehicle requirement is *very subjective,* and it reflects only my own experience. When I need to get there, I tend to be tolerant of rocks, bushes, and the possibility of getting stuck. Not everyone feels this way. *So be aware that on most of the primitive roads that I claim can be driven with a passenger vehicle, the NPS and BLM recommend a four-wheel-drive vehicle. If you have little experience driving desert roads, follow their recommendations.*

About "Route Description." This is the main section. It describes the natural features, main attractions, and challenges of the hike and/or drive. When necessary, route finding and specific difficulties are discussed. All cardinal directions are referenced to the true north (North Star), except on a few stated instances where they refer to the magnetic north. The magnetic declination is 14.5°–15.5° east.

About the Distance and Elevation Charts. Each description contains a chart of key features along the route, their elevations, and their distance from the starting point (mile 0). For features reached by a side trip, the one-way distance from the preceding entry is shown in parentheses. For example, under Pleasant Canyon, 7.1 miles from Ballarat the canyon road reaches the side road to the World Beater Mine. This road leads 0.5 mile to the Word Beater Mine. The next entry in the table is then "Word Beater Mine (0.5)." The entry after this, Ratcliff Mine, is 1.8 miles beyond the World Beater Mine, and is shown as "Ratcliff Mine (2.3)." The next entry, "Stone Corral 8.5," has no parenthesis, which means that it is measured from mile 0, assuming that you did *not* take the side trip to the World Beater Mine.

About the Maps. Each description includes a topographic map of either the entire area or the most important portion of it (in a few cases the map is shared with a nearby section). All maps were hand drawn from USGS topographic maps. North (North Star) is parallel to one edge of the map. Although not as densely contoured as USGS maps, they are accurate enough for most hikes. They also often show features (falls, springs, trails, names, ruins, etc.) not shown elsewhere. Not all obstacles are shown, especially in canyons with many falls and in less traveled areas. However, on more extensive hikes, especially requiring orienteering, they should not be used as a substitute for USGS maps.

■

— 1 —

NATURAL AND HUMAN HISTORY

The Region

The backcountry drives and hikes suggested in this book are located within the hydrologic basins of Eureka, Saline, and Panamint valleys, in eastern California. Roughly aligned in a northwestern direction, these desert valleys form a narrow corridor nearly 120 miles long sandwiched between Owens Valley to the west and Death Valley to the east. All three valleys are part of the northern Mojave Desert, which is itself part of the Great Basin. Each valley is a northwest-trending sink completely enclosed by high mountain ranges, and with no outlet to the sea. To the east they are bounded by the Sylvania Mountains, the Last Chance Range, and the Panamint Range, and to the west by the Inyo Mountains, the Saline Range, the Nelson Range, the Argus Range, and the Slate Range. All of these mountains are formidable barriers towering thousands of feet above the valley floors. Covering approximately 2,700 square miles, most of it a dry desert, this vast region is characterized by wild extremes in elevations, often occurring over short distances. Its lowest point, the southern playa of Panamint Valley (1,033'), lies just a few air miles from 11,049-foot Telescope Peak in the Panamint Mountains. Its highest point, Waucoba Mountain (11,123') in the Inyo Mountains, reaches more than 10,000 feet above the floor of Saline Valley a few miles to the south. Because of this wide range of elevations, this region offers an extraordinary contrast of terrains, climates, and ecosystems. It holds biomes ranging from sterile low-desert salt pans to grasslands, dune fields, Joshua tree forests, lush riparian canyons, and temperate pine woodlands. One usually has to travel an entire continent to sample such profound diversity.

Since passage of the California Desert Bill in October 1994, much of this region is part of Death Valley National Park, of which it forms approximately the western half. The northern half of Panamint Valley, all of Saline Valley, and the southern half of Eureka Valley, are part of the park. Much of the rest of it, in particular the ranges west of all three valleys, is protected as wilderness areas under the jurisdiction of the Bureau of Land Management (BLM) and National Forest Service (NFS). The glaring exception is the floor of central and southern Panamint Valley, which is still mostly non-wilderness BLM land.

Thanks to its ruggedness, this region has been spared from extensive development, and it is crossed by only a few paved roads. The main one is Highway 190, which provides access to Panamint Valley. From its start in Olancha, at the foot of the Sierra Nevada, it crosses Owens Valley eastward, skirts the southern edge of the Inyo Mountains, then drops into and crosses Panamint Valley on its way to Death Valley. Panamint Valley can also be reached from Mojave to the south via Trona on the Trona-Wildrose Road, then the Panamint Valley Road. The region's only other paved road is the western section of the Big Pine Road, which connects Big Pine in Owens Valley to northern Death Valley via Eureka Valley. It is paved to the edge of Eureka Valley, and graded the rest of the way. Saline Valley is the only valley that is free of asphalt. It is reached primarily via the Saline Valley Road, a graded road that links Highway 190 west of Panamint Valley to the Big Pine Road west of Eureka Valley, a distance of 78 miles.

Weather

Temperature. By and large, the weather here is not dramatically different from what it is in Death Valley. In the summer, when it is as hot as hell in Death Valley, Eureka, Saline, and Panamint valleys are also as hot as hell. When Death Valley goes through a cold winter snap, all three valleys are just as cold. The main difference is that being higher and located further west and/or north, they are almost always a little cooler.

The following table lists the mean minimum temperature and mean maximum temperature (in °F) for each month of the year near the lowest (and thus generally warmest) point in each valley. Data for January and July were obtained from isotherms averaged between 1931 and 1952. Data for other months were computed by assuming the same annual temperature evolution as in Death Valley. I have put these figures to the test often and found them reasonably accurate.

These are average temperatures. No official long-term record exists for the absolute lowest and highest temperatures. However, based on

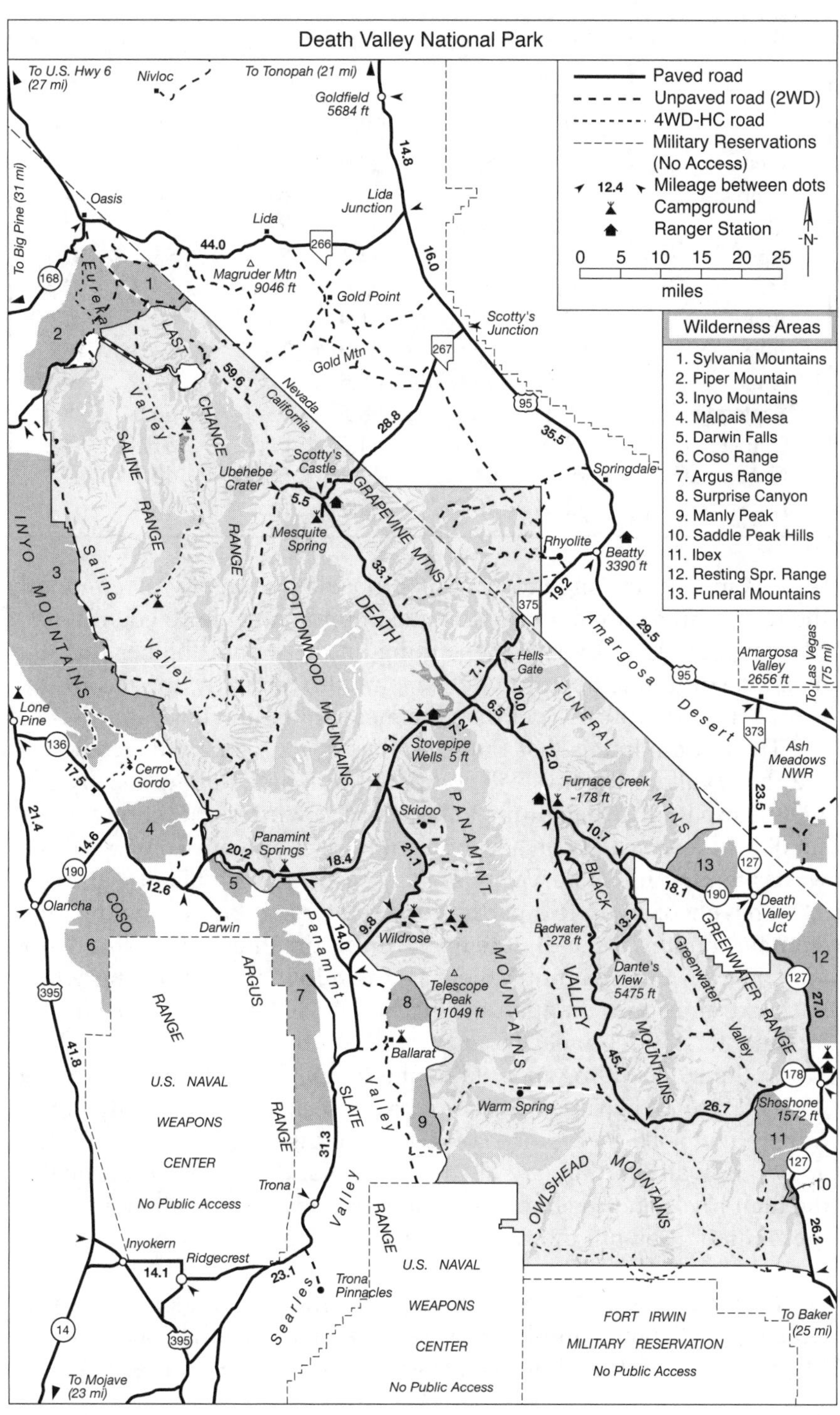
Death Valley National Park
Paved road
Unpaved road (2WD)
4WD-HC road
Military Reservations (No Access)
12.4 Mileage between dots
Campground
Ranger Station
N
0 5 10 15 20 25
miles
Wilderness Areas
1. Sylvania Mountains
2. Piper Mountain
3. Inyo Mountains
4. Malpais Mesa
5. Darwin Falls
6. Coso Range
7. Argus Range
8. Surprise Canyon
9. Manly Peak
10. Saddle Peak Hills
11. Ibex
12. Resting Spr. Range
13. Funeral Mountains
To U.S. Hwy 6 (27 mi)
Nivloc
To Tonopah (21 mi)
Goldfield 5684 ft
To Big Pine (31 mi)
Oasis
Lida
Lida Junction
Magruder Mtn 9046 ft
Gold Point
Gold Mtn
Scotty's Junction
Eureka
LAST CHANCE RANGE
Valley
SALINE RANGE
Saline Valley
INYO MOUNTAINS
Nevada
California
Scotty's Castle
Ubehebe Crater
Mesquite Spring
GRAPEVINE MTNS
COTTONWOOD MOUNTAINS
DEATH VALLEY
Springdale
Rhyolite
Beatty 3390 ft
Amargosa Desert
Amargosa Valley 2656 ft
To Las Vegas (75 mi)
Hells Gate
FUNERAL MTNS
Lone Pine
Cerro Gordo
Stovepipe Wells 5 ft
Furnace Creek -178 ft
Ash Meadows NWR
Skidoo
PANAMINT MOUNTAINS
Panamint Springs
Olancha
COSO
Darwin
Panamint
Wildrose
Badwater -278 ft
BLACK MOUNTAINS
Dante's View 5475 ft
Greenwater Valley
GREENWATER RANGE
Death Valley Jct
ARGUS RANGE
Telescope Peak 11049 ft
Ballarat
SLATE RANGE
Valley
Warm Spring
Shoshone 1572 ft
U.S. NAVAL WEAPONS CENTER
No Public Access
Trona
OWLSHEAD MOUNTAINS
Inyokern
Ridgecrest
Trona Pinnacles
Searles Valley
FORT IRWIN MILITARY RESERVATION
No Public Access
To Baker (25 mi)
To Mojave (23 mi)
168
266
267
95
375
136
190
373
127
178
395
14
44.0
14.8
16.0
59.6
28.8
35.5
5.5
33.1
19.2
29.5
7.1
10.0
6.5
7.2
9.1
12.0
10.7
17.5
21.4
14.6
20.2
18.4
21.1
12.6
9.8
14.0
13.2
18.1
23.5
27.0
45.4
26.7
41.8
31.3
26.2
14.1
23.1

Month	Eureka Valley (sand dunes)		Saline Valley (Salt Lake)		Panamint Valley (Ballarat)	
	Min.	Max.	Min.	Max.	Min.	Max.
January	21.5	55.0	24.0	57.2	32.5	60.1
February	27.8	62.5	30.3	64.4	38.4	67.7
March	34.8	69.5	37.2	71.2	44.9	74.8
April	41.8	76.7	44.1	78.2	51.4	82.1
May	50.7	86.9	52.9	88.2	59.7	92.5
June	59.8	96.1	61.9	97.3	68.3	102.0
July	66.0	102.0	68.0	103.0	74.0	108.0
August	63.5	99.6	65.5	100.7	71.6	105.6
September	56.4	92.7	58.5	93.9	65.0	98.5
October	42.0	79.3	44.3	80.8	51.6	84.8
November	29.8	64.7	32.2	66.5	40.3	69.9
December	22.5	56.1	25.0	58.1	33.4	61.1

records in surrounding valleys it is probable that in any given month the record high temperature—the maximum temperature you can possibly expect—is 15 to 25°F (depending on the month) higher than the mean maximum temperature for this month. Similarly, the record low is probably 20 to 40°F lower than the mean minimum temperature.

The bottom line is that Eureka Valley is consistently the coolest of the three valleys, by 2 to 3°F compared to Saline Valley, and by 5 to 12°F compared to Panamint Valley. In the winter and summer this small difference can have a significant impact on your comfort. When winter tenting in Saline Valley, I often need an extra blanket at night, and I have woken up to a partly frozen water jug. But during the three summer months, three-digit temperatures, sometimes exceeding 110°F, are common in Panamint Valley. The window of time during which such extremes may happen in Eureka and Saline valleys is shorter. Summer heat is definitely easier to handle there.

In the surrounding mountains the temperature drops by 4 to 5°F per 1,000 feet of elevation gain up to 5,000 feet, and at a slightly higher rate above 5,000 feet. Since some mountains reach over 10,000 feet above the valleys, they are always significantly cooler. In particular, the high Inyos and the high Panamints provide a pleasant escape from the summer heat, but they are miserably cold in the winter.

Precipitation and wind. The region's main source of winter precipitation is the moisture-laden westerly winds from the Pacific Ocean. Most of this moisture, however, is captured by the Sierra Nevada and the Inyo Mountains, which explains the aridity of the desert valleys lying in their rain shadow. Annual rainfall at Panamint Springs averages a meager 3.5 inches. It is a little higher in Saline and Eureka valleys, but probably not more than 6 inches a year. The rainiest months are January and February. Precipitation increases with elevation by about 0.5 inch per 1,000 feet of elevation gain up to about 5,000 feet, a little more above 5,000 feet. The mean annual precipitation probably does not exceed 10 inches in the high Panamints and 16 inches in the high Inyos. Snowfalls are common in both ranges and in the Argus Range, even as late as May. Occasional thundershowers occur in the summer, fueled by moisture from the Gulf of Mexico. Although they tend to be brief, lasting often just a few hours and hardly ever more than a couple of days, they can be the region's most violent atmospheric perturbations.

The region is notorious for its strong winds and sand storms. In all three valleys, wind storms can occur several times a month, especially in the spring. They generally prevail at lower elevations and for a few hours only, although on occasion they can persist for a few days. Wind storms can generate impressive walls of yellow dust hundreds of feet tall in which visibility is close to nil. During one of my best desert storms ever, just outside of Ridgecrest, it was actually *raining* stones. For a few minutes, gravel bounced off my car like hail, eventually coating it so thickly that one could not tell its original color!

Geology

Panamint, Saline, and Eureka valleys share much the same geologic history as Death Valley. During the latter part of the Precambrian (about 1,140 to 541 million years ago) and the Paleozoic (541 to 252 million years), the region lay under an early rendition of the Pacific Ocean, much of this time a few hundred miles or less west of a continental shore. For 600 million years, layer upon layer of sediments were deposited on the ocean floor, eventually cumulating more than 7 *miles* of rock. The composition of the sediment varied rapidly westward, away from the continent. Heavier particles washed into the ocean by rivers and storms, such as sand, settled closer to shore, whereas lighter particles such as silt were carried further out to sea. As a result, the composition of the sedimentary rocks changes markedly from east to west across the region. The transition takes place across a narrow north-northeast-trending zone that extends along the length of the three valleys, and across the northern Last Chance Range. The strata east of this zone tend to be terrigenous and contain more quartzite and sandstone—rocks derived from sand. The equivalent west-side

Deformed limestone beds of the Keeler Canyon Formation, Ophir Mountain

sequences contain more siltstone and shale (derived from silt or clay) and limestone and dolomite (derived from organic matter), and they are generally more fossiliferous.

Geologists group sequences of strata into formations, units defined by either relatively homogeneous deposition conditions, repetitive sequences, well-defined upper and lower boundaries, or other criteria. The sequence of formations encountered in a given region is tabulated in what is called a stratigraphic column. The stratigraphic column of the Saline-Eureka-Panamint region is shown on pp. 14–21. Each pair of facing pages covers one of the four geological eras—Cenozoic, Mesozoic, Paleozoic, and Precambrian—each of which is subdivided into epochs. The vertical axis is time, each era with its own (approximately linear) scale. Formations are listed in the order they were deposited, younger towards the top. Even pages (pp. 14, 16, 18, and 20) represent the west side of the three valleys: the Inyo Mountains and the Saline, Nelson, and Argus ranges. The facing pages (pp. 15, 17, 19, and 21) represent the east side: the Sylvania Mountains, the Last Chance Range, and the Panamint Range. The east-west evolution in lithology mentioned earlier is clearly reflected in facing pages: with few exceptions, the east-side and west-side formations are different. The east-side formations are essentially the same as in Death Valley. The west-side formations have different names and compositions, but

STRATIGRAPHIC COLUMNS LEGEND			
————	Comformable formations	□	Thickness of formation
- - - - - -	Uncomformability	(*Corals*)	Main fossils
....	Unknown comformability	Q. M.	Quartz monzonite
L	Late	?	Approximate age
M	Middle		
E	Early		

they are all matched to one or more formations of equivalent age on the east side. For example, the Paleozoic Eureka Quartzite, found exclusively on the east side, has been correlated to the west-side Johnson Spring and Barrel Spring formations. Most of the Precambrian and Paleozoic formations were derived from fine sediment. The only exceptions are formations in the Late Devonian–Early Mississippian and Late Permian, when mountain building took place on the edge of the continent. The formations from these epochs contain large amounts of gravel, rocks, and boulders washed down from these mountains.

When two consecutive formations were deposited without a hiatus, they are said to be conformable. In the stratigraphic columns, the horizontal line separating them is then solid (as between most middle-Paleozoic formations). When there was a time lag between two consecutive formations, for example due to erosion or discontinued deposition, they are called unconformable. The separation is then a dashed line (as between Cenozoic formations). In some cases, the nature of the contact is not known, for example when it is buried or when intermediate strata were removed by erosion. The line is then dotted (as between most east-side Cambrian formations). The stratigraphic columns also list the average thickness of each formation and the main rocks it contains, in chronological order, younger towards the top.

Just after the end of the Paleozoic, as a result of continental drift the ocean withdrew and sedimentation stopped. Until then, throughout the region Precambrian and Paleozoic rock formations lay essentially flat and undeformed. The Mesozoic (252 to 66 million years ago) changed all that: the neatly laid strata were first folded and faulted by intense tectonic activity, then pushed aside and distorted by multiple intrusions of granitic masses. The first and perhaps most extensive crustal deformation occurred along the Last Chance thrust, a nearly horizontal fault plane that stretched from the Inyo Mountains to the Nevada border. In the Triassic, this entire area was shoved eastward over the thrust plane for more than 20 miles. Similar events took place in the late Jurassic along the Argus Sterling Thrust Fault in the Argus

West side: Inyo Mountains to Argus Range					
	EPOCH		AGE Million years	FORMATION	LITHOLOGY
CENOZOIC	Pleistocene		2.6	?	• Fluvial, lacustrine, and fan deposits
	Pliocene	L	3.6		
		E	5.3	?	• Olivine basalt flow □ 0–560 ft • Quartz olivine basalt □ 430 ft • Fanglomerate and breccia □ >7,800 ft • Rhyolite tuff □ 0–150 ft • Lacustrine limestone and travertine
	Miocene	L	11.6		
		M	16.0		
		E	23.0	?	• Rhyolite and rhyodacite • Fluvial gravels • Landslide breccia
	Oligocene	L	30.0		
		E	33.9		
	Eocene	L	41.2		
		M	47.8		
		E	56.0		
	Paleocene	L	61.6		
		E	66.0		

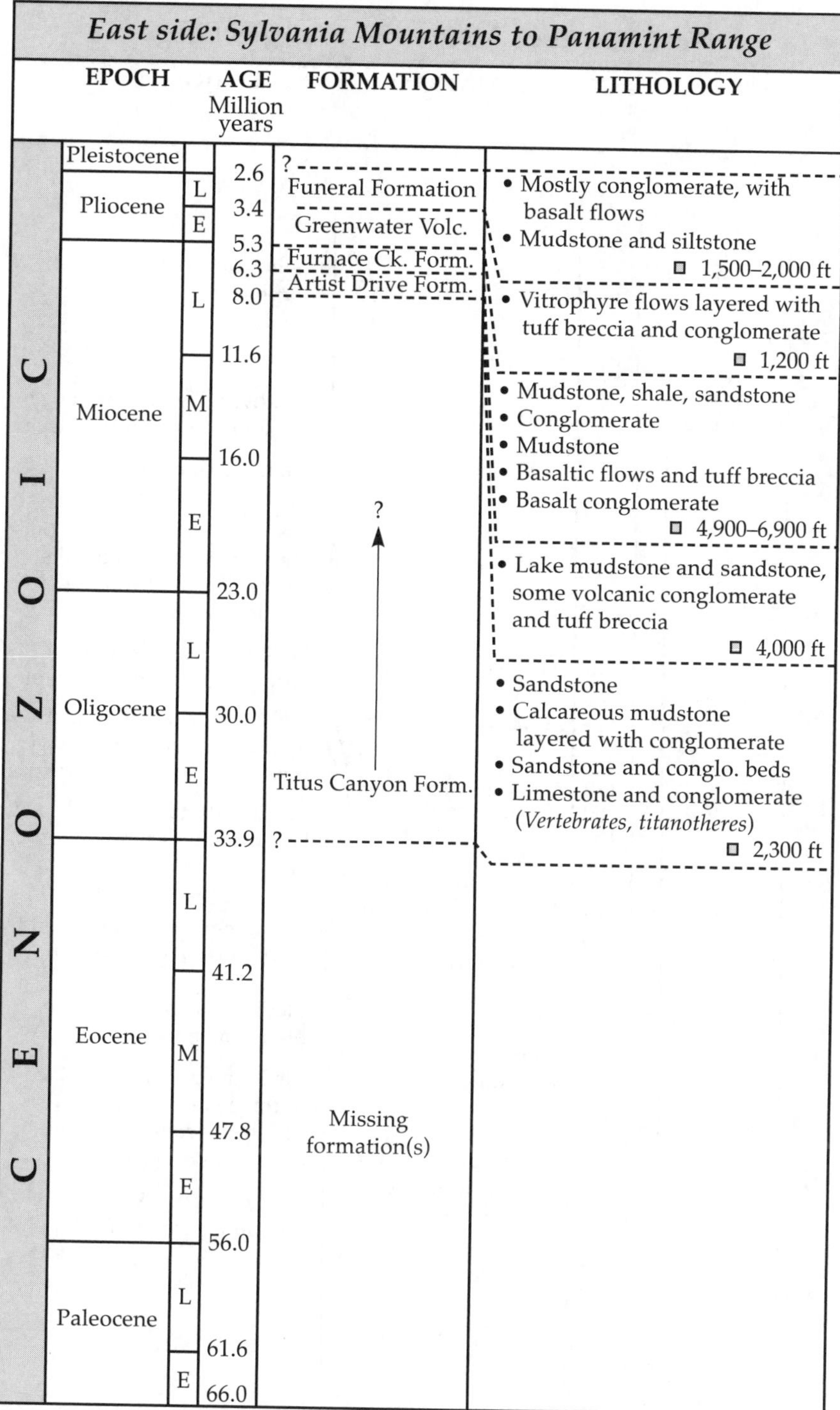
East side: Sylvania Mountains to Panamint Range
EPOCH
AGE Million years
FORMATION
LITHOLOGY
C E N O Z O I C
Pleistocene
Pliocene
L
E
Miocene
L
M
E
Oligocene
L
E
Eocene
L
M
E
Paleocene
L
E
2.6
3.4
5.3
6.3
8.0
11.6
16.0
23.0
30.0
33.9
41.2
47.8
56.0
61.6
66.0
?
Funeral Formation
Greenwater Volc.
Furnace Ck. Form.
Artist Drive Form.
?
Titus Canyon Form.
?
Missing formation(s)
• Mostly conglomerate, with basalt flows
• Mudstone and siltstone
1,500–2,000 ft
• Vitrophyre flows layered with tuff breccia and conglomerate
1,200 ft
• Mudstone, shale, sandstone
• Conglomerate
• Mudstone
• Basaltic flows and tuff breccia
• Basalt conglomerate
4,900–6,900 ft
• Lake mudstone and sandstone, some volcanic conglomerate and tuff breccia
4,000 ft
• Sandstone
• Calcareous mudstone layered with conglomerate
• Sandstone and conglo. beds
• Limestone and conglomerate (Vertebrates, titanotheres)
2,300 ft

West side: Inyo Mountains to Argus Range					
	EPOCH		AGE Million years	FORMATION	LITHOLOGY
MESOZOIC	Cretaceous	L	66.0		
			80	Q. M. of Papoose Flat	Light-gray, coarse-grained, porphyritic, biotite quartz monzonite
			100		
		E	?	Q. M. of Anthony Mill	Porphyritic biotite quartz monzonite with pink feldspar
			140	Alaskite of Bendire C.	Coarse-grained biotite alaskite
			145		
	Jurassic	L	148	Q. M. Maturango Pk.	Medium-grained, mostly porphyritic biotite-hornblende quartz monzonite and granodiorite, w/ pink perthite
			157	Q. Monz. of Beer Cr.	Medium to coarse-grained porphyritic quartz monzonite
			160	Paiute Monum't Q. M.	Light-gray, coarse-grained quartz monzonite with large pink to red orthoclase crystals
			163		
		M	167		
			170	Hunter Mtn Q. M.	Mostly quartz monzonite, w/ borders of monzonite, diorite, syenodiorite, and hornblende gabbro
			174	Monz. of Eureka Val.	Medium-grained augite- and olivine-bearing monzonite
		E	178	Monzonite of Joshua Flat	Medium-gray, hornblende, biotite, monzonite
			?	Diorite of Marble Canyon	Medium-gray, med.-grained hornblende and augite diorite w/ some monzonite and granodiorite
			201		
	Triassic	L	?	Diorite of N.Y. Butte	Medium- to dark-gray, medium-grained diorite
			?	Diorite porphyry	
			?	Volcanic flows	
			?	Silicic tuff	
			?	Sedimentary rocks	
			237		
		M			
			247		
		E	252		

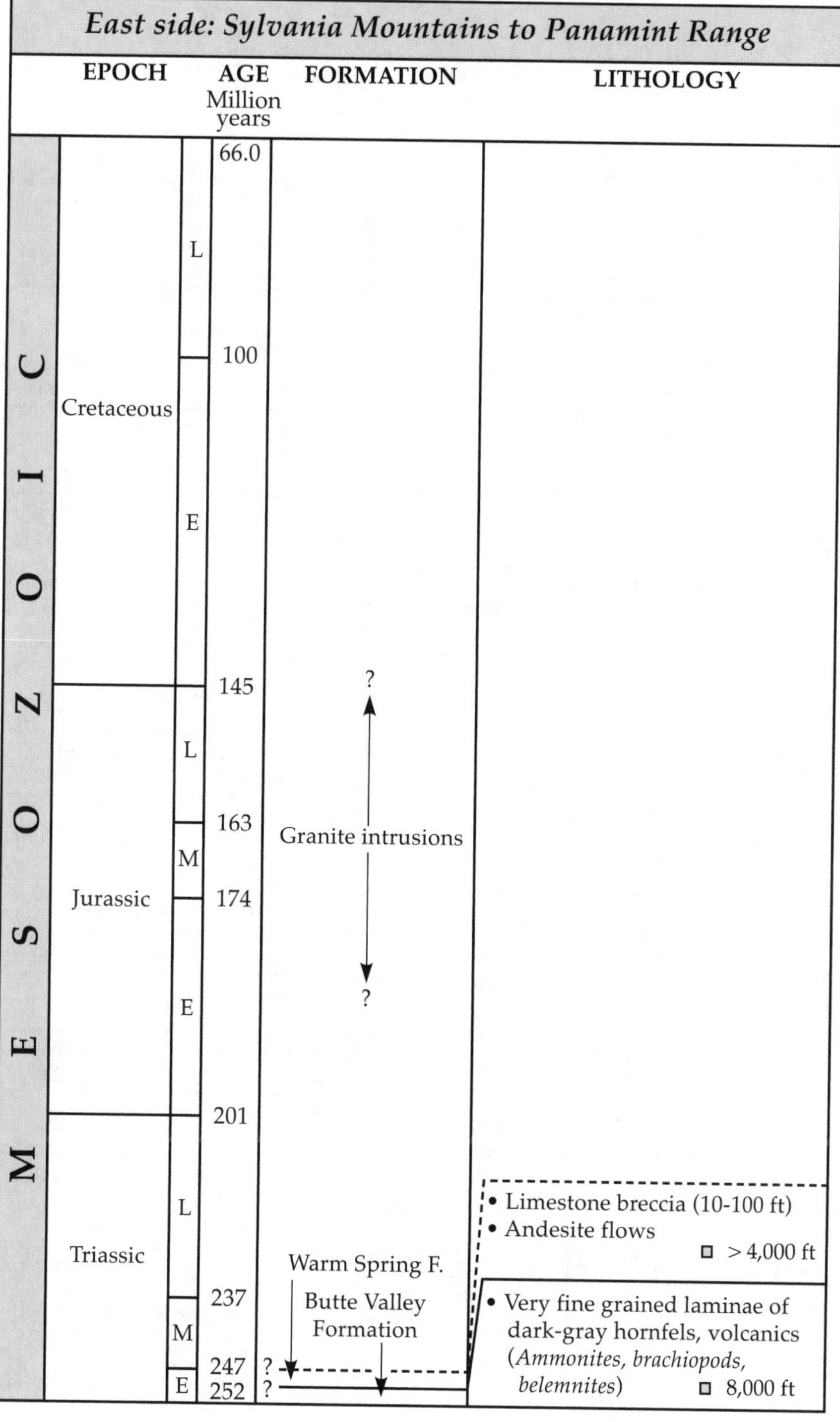
East side: Sylvania Mountains to Panamint Range
EPOCH
AGE Million years
FORMATION
LITHOLOGY
MESOZOIC
Cretaceous
Jurassic
Triassic
L
E
L
M
E
L
M
E
66.0
100
145
163
174
201
237
247
252
?
Granite intrusions
?
Warm Spring F.
Butte Valley Formation
?
?
• Limestone breccia (10-100 ft)
• Andesite flows
> 4,000 ft
• Very fine grained laminae of dark-gray hornfels, volcanics (*Ammonites, brachiopods, belemnites*)
8,000 ft

West side: Inyo Mountains to Argus Range				
	EPOCH		**AGE** Million years	**FORMATION**
P A L E O Z O I C	Permian	L	252	Owens Valley Formation
		M	259	
		E	273	
	Pennsyl.		299	Keeler Cyn Form.
				Lee Flat Limestone
	Mississip.		323	Perdido Formation
				Tin Mtn. Limestone
	Devonian	L	359	Lost Burro Formation
		M	383	
		E	393	Hidden Valley Dolomite
	Silurian	L	419	
		E	433	
	Ordovician	L	444	Ely Springs Dolomite
		M	458	Johnson Spring F.
				Barrel Spring F.
		E	470	Badger Flat Lim.
				Al Rose Form.
	Cambrian	L	485	Tamarack Cyn Dolo.
				Lead Gulch Formation
		M	497	Bonanza King F.
				Monola Formation
		E	521	Mule Spring Lim.
				Saline Valley Formation
				Harkless Formation
				Poleta Formation
				Campito Formation
			541	Deep Spring Formation

LITHOLOGY
• Interlayered limestone, shale, sands., & conglomerate ◘ 1,800-3,100 ft
• Gray limestone • Calcarenite and silty limestone, cherts near base ◘ 1,800-2,700 ft
• White marble, locally altered to dolomitic marble ◘ 650 ft
• Siltstone, shale, limestone, chert, and conglo. (*Spirifers, goniatite*) ◘ 600 ft
• Limestone with thin beds of shale and chert nodules (*Spirifers, corals, crinoids, brachio.*) ◘ 500 ft
• Sands., quartzite, dolo. (*Cyrtospirifer*) • Dolomite ◘ 1,500 ft • Layered dolom. and lim. (*Corals*)
• Dolomite (mostly light gray) (*Crinoids, favosites*) • Dolomite with chert ◘ 1,400 ft
• Massive dolomite (black) (*Corals*) ◘ 400-900 ft
• Interbedded limestone, dolomite, and quartzite ◘ 160-380 ft
• Sandstone, shale, and limestone ◘ 100-150 ft
• Fossiliferous silty lim., siltstone, and chert ◘ 600 ft
• Thin beds of siltstone, limestone, and shale ◘ 450 ft
• Laminated to thick-bedded dolomite ◘ 910 ft
• Interlayered lim., siltstone, dolomite, chert, and shale ◘ 280 ft
• Limestone, shale, silt beds • *Trilobite trash beds* ◘ 1,200 ft
• Siltstone, lim., and shale ◘ 1,200 ft
• Massive lim. (*Girvanella*) ◘ 850 ft
• Sandstone, lim., and shale ◘ 850 ft
• Shale, sands., siltstone ◘ 3,600 ft
• Sequence of shale & lim. (*Scolithus*) • Mass. lim. (*Archeocyathids*) ◘ 900 ft
• Sandstone, siltstone, and shale (*Trilobites*) ◘ 3,500 ft

East side: Sylvania Mountains to Panamint Range

ERA	EPOCH		AGE Million years	FORMATION	LITHOLOGY
PALEOZOIC	Permian	L M	252 259	Anvil Spr. Form.	• Limestone, light gray-white with thinner dark-gray beds ◻ 3,600-4,100 ft
		E	273	Owens Valley Formation	• Interlayered limestone, shale, sandstone, and conglomerate ◻ 1,800-3,100 ft
	Pennsyl.		299	Tihvipah Form.	• Mostly light-gray limestone with calcareous shale ◻ 200 ft
				Rest Spring Shale	• Siltstone, shale (olive gray) • Shale with concretions ◻ 200-750 ft
	Mississip.		323	Perdido Formation	• Siltstone, shale, limestone, chert, conglomerate (*Spirifers, goniatite*) ◻ 600 ft
				Tin Mtn. Limestone	• Limestone with thin beds of shale and chert nodules (*Spirifers, corals, crinoids, brachiopods*) ◻ 500 ft
	Devonian	L M E	359 383 393	Lost Burro Formation	• Sandstone, quartzite, dolomite (*Cyrtospirifer*) • Dolomite ◻ 1,500 ft • Layered dolom. & lim. (*Corals*)
	Silurian	L E	419 433	Hidden Valley Dolomite	• Dolomite (mostly light gray) (*Crinoids, favosites*) • Dolomite with chert ◻ 1,400 ft
	Ordovician	L	444	Ely Springs Dolomite	• Massive dolomite (black) (*Corals*) ◻ 400-900 ft
		M	458	Eureka Quartzite	• Massive quartzite (white) ◻ 350 ft
		E	470	Pogonip Group	• Dolom. with limest. (*Gastropods*) • Thin-bedded shale ◻ 1,500 ft • Dolomite (*Gastropods*)
	Cambrian	L	485	Nopah Formation	• Shale (*Gastropods*) • Mostly black/light 100-ft bands of dolomite ◻ 1,200-1,500 ft
		M	497	Bonanza King F.	• Mostly thick beds of dark dolomite ◻ 2,000-3,000 ft
			521	Carrara Formation	• Limestone, shale, silt beds • *Trilobite trash beds* ◻ 1,200 ft
		E		Zabriskie Quartzite	• Quartzite, mostly massive and granulated ◻ 150 ft
			541	Wood Cyn Form.	• Dolomite • Quartzite, shale, quartzite beds ◻ 2,600 ft

West side: Inyo Mountains to Argus Range					
	EPOCH		AGE Million years	FORMATION	LITHOLOGY
PRECAMBRIAN	Proterozoic	L	541	Deep Spring Form.	• Limestone, quartzite, sandstone, dolomite, and shale (*Stromatolites, microbial mats*) ▫ 1,800 ft
				Reed Dolomite	• Thick dolomite beds ▫ 2,000 ft
				Wyman Formation ?	• Argilite, quartzitic sandstone, siltstone, dolomite ▫ 3,700 ft
				Crystalline basement (not exposed)	• Gneiss and schist
		M	1,000		
		E	1,600		

East side: Sylvania Mountains to Panamint Range					
	EPOCH		AGE Million years	FORMATION	LITHOLOGY
PRECAMBRIAN	Proterozoic	L	541	Stirling Quartzite	• Quartzite, shale ▫ 4,900 ft
			580	Johnny Formation	• Mostly shale (*stromatolites*) ▫ 2,400 ft
			615	Noonday Dolomite	• Dolomite and limestone (*stromatolites*) ▫ 500-2,000 ft
			635 ?	Kingston Peak Formation	• Sandstone and siltstone • Limestone • Diamictite (*stromatolites, oncolites, microbiota*) ▫ 1,600-9,000 ft
			720	Beck Spring Dolomite	• Dolomite (*stromatolites*) ▫ 1,000-1,600 ft
		M	1,300 ?	Crystal Spring Formation	• Thick-bedded dolomite and diabase • Thin-bedded dolomite (*stromatolites*) • Shale (purple) • Quartzite • Conglomerate ▫ 2,300-3,900 ft
			1,140 ?	Crystaline basement	• Gneiss and schist
		E	1,600		
			1,700 ?		

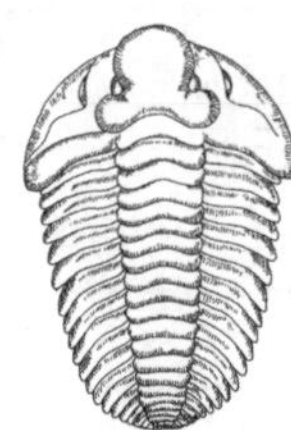
Trilobite

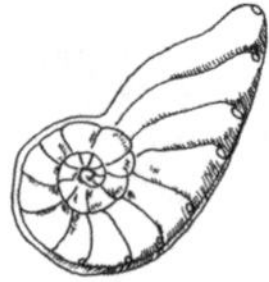
Foraminifer

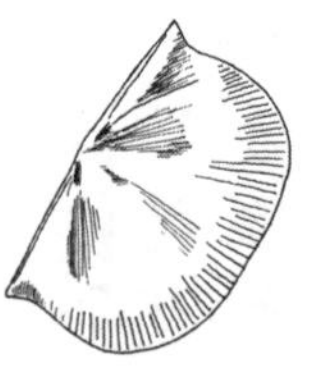
Strophomenid

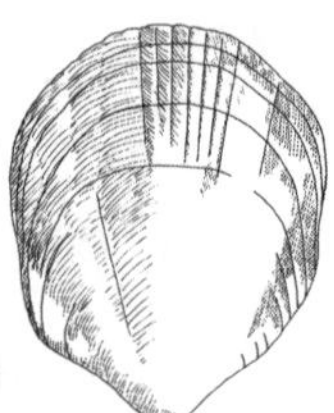
Brachiopod

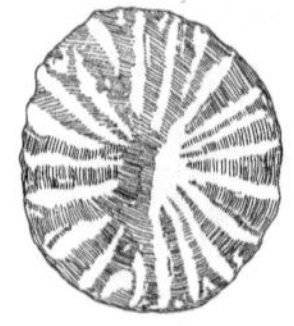
Coral

Range, along the Racetrack Thrust Fault north of Hunter Mountain, and at several other locations. The Mesozoic plutonic events that followed were even more devastating. Over a period of 130 million years, more than a dozen granitic plutons forcefully intruded the region's sedimentary formations. From the Slate Range to the Sylvania Mountains, rising bubbles of molten magma up to tens of miles across slowly broke through the crust, folding, baking, and metamorphizing the adjacent stratified rocks up as far as 3 miles from the contact zone.

The names, approximate ages, and compositions of the Mesozoic plutons are tabulated in the stratigraphic columns (pp. 16 and 17). Most plutons are made of quartz monzonite, a rock of similar composition and appearance as granite. Later uplifted by tectonic movements, they constitute about one third of the region's mountains. The largest one, the Hunter Mountain Quartz Monzonite, is over 70 miles long and outcrops intermittently from the Slate Range to the central Inyo Mountains. All these plutons are considered to be eastern extensions of the considerably larger Sierra Nevada batholith. This relationship explains why plutons are more numerous and generally larger on the west side, closer to the Sierra. Metal deposits often occur in veins associated with plutons or in skarns formed by contact metamorphism at pluton boundaries. Some of the east-side mountains, especially the Last Chance Range, were intruded by only a few small plutons, and they are devoid of large metal deposits. This explains why mining was so much less extensive in the east-side ranges, and why the region's richest mines—Cerro Gordo, the Darwin mines, and the Modoc District—were all on the west side.

During the Cenozoic (66 million years to present), the region was periodically under sea and received a few more coatings of sedimentary rocks. These formations have been since partly eroded, and they are now exposed only over small, scattered areas. On numerous occasions, sedimentation was interspersed with brief but violent volcanic events. Starting about

12 million years ago, volcanoes opened up on the region's western fringe and belched out great flows of basalt, latite, and andesite. Around 5 million years ago, a thick volcanic field spread out from the Inyo Mountains eastward across the Saline Range to Dry Mountain. About 3 million years later, in the Late Pliocene and Pleistocene, the Darwin Plateau was blanketed under thousands of feet of lava and ash. These and many other Mesozoic eruptions created most of the colorful tuffs, rhyolite, and basalt that crop out throughout the region's mountains.

Eureka, Saline, and Panamint valleys did not begin to take shape until as recently as about 4.5 million years ago. Their genesis was fueled by the same extensive faulting that created the Basin and Range province to which they belong. Extensional stresses broke the land into long north-northeast-trending blocks bound by major fault zones (see figure next page). These blocks then suffered complex relative displacements, both vertical and horizontal, one earthquake at a time. In general, each block was rotated about its long axis, its west side being uplifted and its east side pushed down. The west side thus became a mountain and the east side a valley. In the figure, the side of a fault that moved down is indicated by hatches. For example, the Panamint Range block (east of the Hunter Mountain Fault Zone) was tilted down to the east, sinking into what became Death Valley, and its west side was uplifted to form the Panamint Mountains. In addition, the blocks were transported northward, the blocks located further west generally moving further than eastern blocks. This relative motion of facing blocks is indicated in the figure by facing arrows. The largest fault is the Hunter Mountain Fault Zone (see figure). More than 100 miles long, it bisects the entire region like a giant scar, and it is responsible for much of today's topography. Starting at the south end of the Panamint Valley, it follows the western base of the Panamint Mountains, then swings northwest between Hunter Mountain and the Nelson Range, and continues north along the west side of Saline Valley. It is believed that Panamint Valley and Saline Valley were formed concurrently as the result of paired extensional movements along this fault. Except for minor differences (the Inyo Mountains, for example, were uplifted on both sides), all of the region's mountains were created by similar fault-block movements. The Saline Range is the only anomaly: out of alignment with the other ranges, it obviously does not fit the general topography. The current theory is that this range had a different genesis. In the early stages of faulting, there was no Saline Range. Saline Valley and Eureka Valley were connected and formed a single depression. The broad dome of Saline Range was

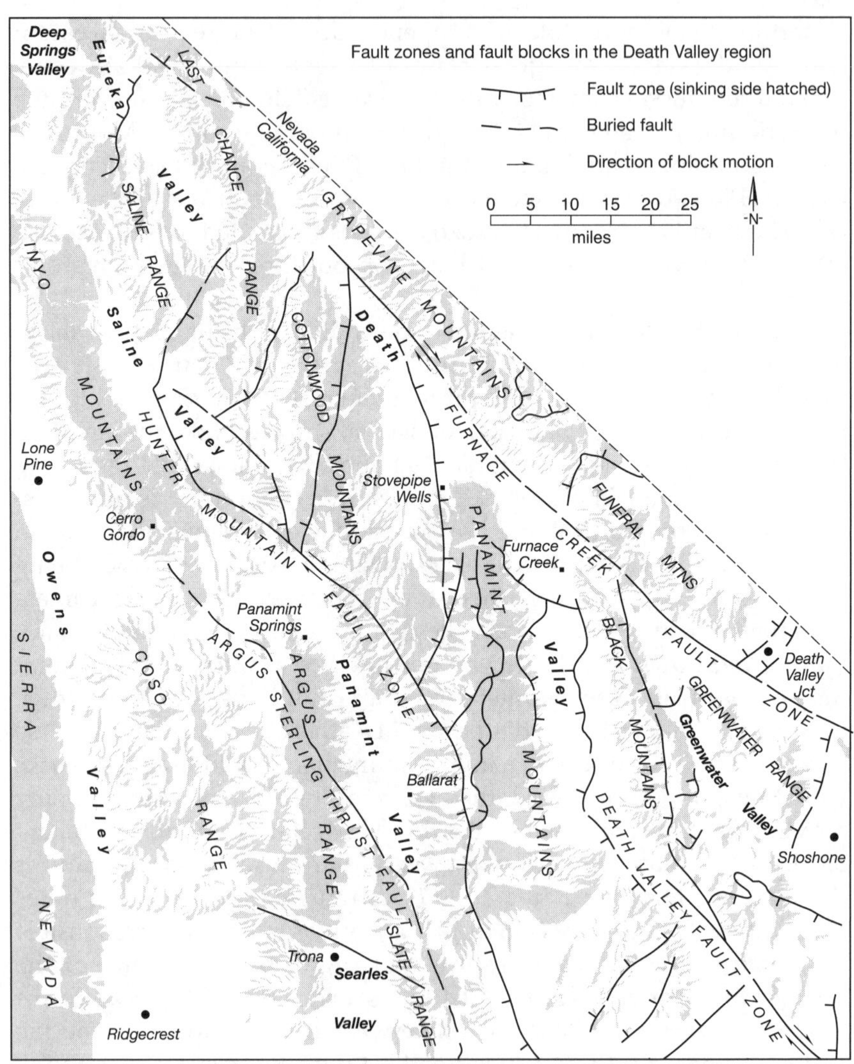

formed later on, when basalt originating from deep magma sources was released by extensional deformations and erupted. As the Saline Range pushed its way up, it split the early depression into the Saline and Eureka valleys we know today.

Flora

The topography of the region is one of high insular mountains isolated by deep basins. This diversity provides habitats for a wide range of plant species. The plant communities in Eureka, Saline, and

Panamint valleys and in the surrounding ranges have a great deal in common with the flora of nearby Death Valley. I refer the reader to *Hiking Death Valley* for a brief description of these communities and their most common plants. For more in-depth information, Roxana Ferris' *Death Valley Wildflowers* is an invaluable beginner's field guide applicable to much of the western Death Valley National Park region. More exhaustive descriptions of local plants can be found in two other, more technical classics, Edmund Jaeger's *Desert Wild Flowers* and Mary DeDecker's *Flora of the Northern Mojave Desert, California*.

The plant that is arguably the region's strangest and most emblematic is the Joshua tree. In a land where weird plants are commonplace, Joshua trees manage to be a few notches weirder. Their spiny trunks are topped by crooked, dagger-tipped branches stretched out skyward like frozen humanoids. You cannot walk through a Joshua-tree landscape without being constantly aware of their unsettling presence. Joshua trees live almost exclusively in the Mojave Desert: if you traced the perimeter of their territory, you would closely follow the Mojave Desert's boundary. However, they are fussy about their habitat, and they do not grow everywhere within this boundary. They generally need loamy alluvial soils and 3 to 12 inches of annual precipitation. They cannot stand the sweltering summer of the low desert or the harsh winters of the high country. They also grow very slowly. Given these constraints, they do not abound in the region. They are fairly common only on the Darwin Plateau, and over limited areas in the Cottonwoods Mountains, the northern Inyo Mountains, and the Argus Range, usually on gravel slopes between 4,200 and 5,800 feet.

As in Death Valley, the spring wildflower displays are one of the greatest gifts this region has to offer. The blooming season usually begins on the alluvial fans and lower canyon washes between mid-March and early April (earliest in Panamint Valley, latest in Eureka Valley). As the season progresses, the flower show moves up to higher elevations, eventually reaching the highest mountain peaks in the midsummer. If you look around a little, it is difficult not to spot a few wildflowers any time of the year.

Over time, the insularity of both the ranges and the basins has fostered the evolution of several rare and even endemic plant species—plants that grow here and nowhere else on the planet. Some endemics exist over a very limited area, such as dune grass, found only on the Eureka Valley dunes. Others have somewhat broader distributions, like the beautiful Panamint daisy, which grows in a few canyons of the western Panamints, or Telescope Peak bedstraw, which grows at elevations above 10,825 feet. Even so, their distributions are so limited that

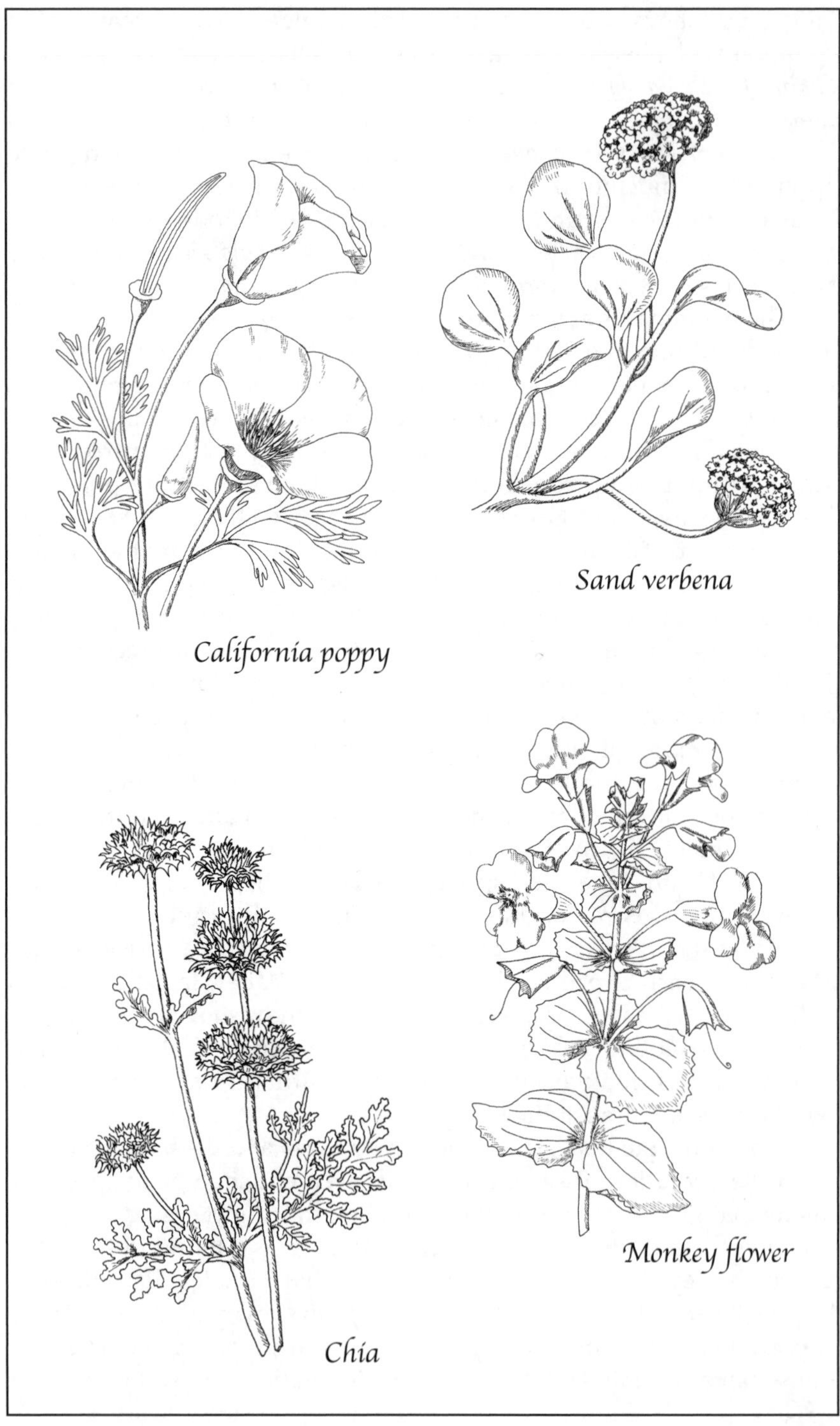
California poppy
Sand verbena
Chia
Monkey flower

Selected Rare and/or Endemic Plants of Western Death Valley		
Species	**Common name**	**Locations**
Astragalus atratus mensanus	Darwin Mesa milk-vetch	Darwin Plateau
Astragalus lentiginosus micans	Shining milk-vetch	Eureka Valley
Caulostramina jaegeri	Cliffdweller	Inyo Mountains
Dedeckera eurekensis	July gold	Panamints, Last Chance R., Inyos
Dudleya saxosa saxosa	Panamint dudleya	West. Panamints
Enceliopsis covillei	Panamint daisy	West. Panamints
Eriogonum eremicola	Wildrose Cyn buckwheat	Inyos, Western Panamint Mtns
Eriog. microtecum panamintense	Panamint Mtns buckwheat	Inyos, Panamints
Galium hypotrichium tomentellum	Telescope Peak bedstraw	Panamint Mtns
Hulsea vestita inyoensis	Inyo Hulsea	Inyos, Panamints
Oenothera californica eurekensis	Eur. D. evening-primrose	Eureka Dunes
Perityle inyoensis	Inyo rock daisy	Inyo Mountains
Phacelia amabilis	Saline Valley phacelia	Inyo Mountains
Swallenia alexandrae	Eureka Valley dune grass	Eureka Dunes

their chance of survival is low and many of these plants have been listed federally as endangered species. The table above lists some rare or endemic plants, as well as their bioregional distributions.

Fauna

The fauna in and around Eureka, Saline, and Panamint valleys is similar to Death Valley's fauna. Again I refer the reader to *Hiking Death Valley*, which describes the region's most common wildlife.

Mammals. Bighorn sheep and deer are the area's largest native mammals. The former occur in several bands, generally confined to remote mountain areas, in particular the Inyo Mountains, the Last Chance Range, and the Panamint Range. Deer live almost exclusively in the forested areas of the high Inyos and Panamints, which are the only places where they can find the water and forage they need.

Feral burros are the largest non-native mammals. Native to northeastern Africa, they were first introduced in the 1870s by prospectors, who used them as beasts of burden. Burros proved to be well adapted to the arid climate, and they multiplied into large populations. The main problem is that they compete for forage and water with globally threatened native bighorn sheep. They eat and drink more, congregate around springs, contaminate the water, scare away other wildlife, create extensive networks of trails, often uproot plants and increase soil erosion, and reproduce at the alarming rate of 20-25% a year. Since 1939, NPS has humanely removed some 10,000 burros from the Death Valley region. Burros are still doing quite well on BLM and U.S. Forest Service desert lands, where, ironically, they are protected. Over time, they are drifting out of these protected areas into NPS units. Sightings are common in many areas, in particular in the Argus Range, the western Panamint Mountains, Saline Valley, and the Inyo Mountains.

Although less often seen than heard, coyotes are fairly numerous in all three valleys, and if you camp under the stars you are likely to hear their eerie calls. Coyotes live over a wide range of elevations, from valley floors to forest belts. Being as lazy as *homo sapiens,* in more heavily visited areas they have learned that visitors will feed them for a closer look, and they are beginning to beg for food from passing cars. Do not feed coyotes, or any other wildlife. For their own good, scare them away instead. We must try to teach them that humans are their worst enemy, and to stay away from us.

Other mammals are represented by numerous species, with habitats covering all elevations. At lower elevations you might encounter kit foxes, badgers, ringtail cats, bobcats, antelope and roundtail ground squirrels, and several species of rabbits, woodrats, kangaroo rats, mice, and bats. Kit foxes are occasionally spotted near campgrounds, especially at night. Higher elevations support some of the same species as well as scattered populations of pocket gopher, porcupine, mule deer, and gray fox. Mountain lions have also been reported, although extremely rarely.

Reptiles. The region is home to many species of snakes and lizards. Snakes are generally shy, often nocturnal, and you will need a keen eye to detect them. Common snakes include the gopher snake, king snake, red racer, and the shovel-nosed snake. There are also several species of rattlesnakes, including the Mojave and Panamint rattlesnakes, and the sidewinder. Snakes being cold-blooded, they do not fare well in high temperatures and they are more common at higher elevations. Sightings of lizards, on the other hand, are frequent over a wide range of elevations. The most common lizards are the western whiptail, side-blotched, zebra-tailed, horned, and collared lizards. The

Wild burros, Pleasant Canyon, Panamint Mountains

chuckwalla, largest of them all, is more occasionally seen in rocky areas. Less common species include the banded gecko, the beautiful leopard lizard, and the desert iguana. The Panamint alligator lizard, a large lizard with a tail nearly twice its body length and brown cross-bands on the body, is known from only 16 disjunct localities in Inyo County, including Surprise, Pleasant, Grapevine, and Daisy canyons.

Desert tortoises inhabit semi-arid grasslands, gravelly washes, and rocky hillsides from about 1,500 to 3,500 feet. They live in burrows which they dig to escape temperature extremes. They come out mostly in the spring and fall to build up their fat and water reserves for the rest of the year. Because they are uncommon and spend much of their time underground, they are rarely encountered. The desert tortoise is a threatened species. If you see one, approach it slowly and enjoy it from a distance. Do not touch it, as you may pass on fatal diseases.

Birds. Although an actual count has never been published, it is likely that several hundred species of birds live in or pass through the Eureka Valley-Panamint Valley corridor. Bird sightings are common at almost all elevations. The most commonly encountered species are ravens, turkey vultures, wrens, sparrows, hummingbirds, hawks, thrashers, and Gambel quail. More occasionally you might spot owls, ducks, finches, and larks. The largest and most diverse populations are found around springs and at higher elevations, especially in pinyon pine-juniper forests.

Native American History

Comparatively little is known about the prehistory of the Native Americans who inhabited Panamint Valley. We know that over time, groups of various sizes lived in different parts of the valley, either permanently or seasonally. Northern Panamint Valley was populated by Shoshone Indians, and the southern valley by Kawaiisu Indians. In spite of their ethnic differences, the two groups probably had very similar subsistence and settlement strategies and differed mainly in details of organization and styles. The earliest known occupation sites were in the vicinity of Lake Hill around 10,000–10,500 years ago. Lake Panamint, a shallow body of water, then covered the north Panamint basin, and native populations had settled near marshes on the prime lake-front property near Lake Hill. Residents had mastered the fine art of carving stone tools out of basalt, which they quarried in local mountains. Although this cultural trait is believed to be the expression of a widely distributed Western tool-making tradition, it was so prominent in the northern Panamint Valley that archaeologists have coined it the Panamint Basalt Industry. It is likely that these same people also created the giant stone alignments found today on the valley's alluvial fans. This period overlapped with the earliest known occupation of Death Valley (Nevares Spring Culture), which also enjoyed a comparatively wetter climate and the presence of Lake Manly.

As a result of worldwide climate changes, between about 10,000 and 9,000 years ago the lake slowly dried up, and some of the springs that the natives had been relying on probably lost some of their flow as well. The Lake Hill communities did not survive this drastic change in hydrology. They dispersed and adopted a more nomadic lifestyle, settling in the warmer valleys in winter and moving to the cooler mountains in summer. That prehistoric hunter-gatherers continued to visit or live in Panamint Valley is supported by many, more recent archaeological sites. The patterns of these settlements, in particular their location and human occupancy, were most likely dictated at least in part by the proximity and reliability of springs. At some locations in the valley, dozens of prehistoric sites spanning the last 9,000 years have been identified, with intensified occupation over the last 3,000 years.

Saline Valley to the north also exhibits long sequences of human occupation. Like Death Valley, it hosts today and probably hosted in prehistoric times many resources not found in such abundance in Panamint Valley. Both Saline Valley and Death Valley were in fact more densely populated in historic times than Panamint Valley. Eureka Valley to the north, like Saline Valley, never had a pluvial lake; the passes surrounding it are too high for the neighboring lakes to spill into it. It also has extremely few springs, none of them much heavier than a trickle. We can only surmise that Eureka Valley was probably more scarcely populated, and perhaps visited mostly seasonally.

Much of the natives' lives was spent gathering food. The primary food in their diet was pinyon nuts. In historic times, and probably in recent prehistoric times as well, they collected, stored, and prepared the nuts in much the same ways as other southern Great Basin native groups. Their diet also included seasonal plants such as rice grass, cactus, ephedra, berries, mesquite, yucca, and various greens, which were harvested by ranging far and wide throughout the valleys and surrounding mountains.

The archaeological record is too scant, and studies too limited, to reveal social structures and behavior of prehistoric natives. But we know that the inhabitants of Panamint Valley had social relationships with groups living in Saline Valley, Death Valley, and the Coso Range, although the frequency of contact and the level of interaction are unknown. The inhabitants of Panamint and Saline valleys spoke a similar language. They fashioned stone tools out of obsidian, a rock that does not occur naturally in Panamint Valley but is found in the southern Coso Range and in the Saline Range. This suggests economic contacts with the residents of these areas. In historic times, the residents of both valleys harvested pinyon nuts in the Cottonwood Mountains. During the few weeks of harvest, the two groups probably engaged in various forms of trade and perhaps social activities.

Little is known, also, about the life of the Panamint Valley and Saline Valley Indians in early historic times, in part because they were very few of them to transmit their history to us, in part because these valleys were far away from emigration routes. Then as in prehistoric times, the scarcity of water and sparsely distributed food resources were prime reasons for the Indians' extremely low populations, which numbered at most in the hundreds. Because water was both so critical and so scarce, many of the perennial springs in and around Panamint Valley and Saline Valley were inhabited. This was the case of the warm springs and the springs in Little Hunter Canyon in Saline Valley. In Panamint Valley, the springs in Wildrose Canyon were a favorite winter camp. The village of Ha:uta at Warm Springs, near Indian Ranch, was perhaps the only major residential area in northern Panamint Valley. In the late 1890s, a famous Panamint Indian named Indian George had a camp at Indian Ranch and supplied Ballarat residents with fruit. Some of the population then still followed the ages-old nomadic pattern of migration, wintering in the valleys and moving to higher elevations in the summer. In the early 1890s, explorers reported observing groups of Panamint Indians still harvesting pinyon nuts high in the Panamints and on Hunter Mountain. There was a winter encampment at the low dunes just south of Indian Ranch. Rock shelters, perhaps old seasonal summer camps, have been excavated in the Panamint Range. Old base camps and stone-chipping grounds are still relatively common in the high Inyo Mountains out of both Saline Valley and Eureka Valley.

An ethnographic report from 1891 mentioned about 100 inhabitants living in northern Panamint Valley. Another one, a year later, described a group of 25 up on the western slopes of the Panamint Mountains. By then the heavy mining booms of the 1870s in the Panamint Mountains, the Argus Range, and the Inyos had introduced alternative crops, wage labor, and a cash economy, and all these traits had been adopted by the local inhabitants to varying degrees. The last native resident of Panamint Valley moved out of Indian Ranch in the late 1990s. Neither Saline Valley nor Eureka Valley have supported a permanent native population in decades. The descendants of the region's prehistoric inhabitants now live in the Timbisha Shoshone village near Furnace Creek and in scattered reservations in Owens Valley.

After years of legal battles, in November 2000 the Timbisha Shoshone tribe won access to some of its ancestral homeland when President Clinton signed into law the Timbisha Shoshone Homeland Act. The Furnace Creek village was increased to 314 acres, and about 7,440 acres of tribal land were created outside the park near Lida, Scotty's Junction, Death Valley Junction, and Centennial Flats. A huge land area called the Timbisha Shoshone Natural and Cultural Preservation Area was also earmarked within the park for the tribe to perform low-impact, ecologically sustainable, traditional practices. It includes the Panamint Range and portions of Mesquite Flat, Saline Valley, and Eureka Valley. The tribe uses these areas, in particular traditional camps at Wildrose and on Hunter Mountain, for cultural and religious activities.

Modoc Mine furnaces, ca. 1915 (Courtesy of Eastern California Museum)

Mining History

Panamint, Saline, and Eureka valleys have had a long history of mining, which dates back to the 1860s and continues into the present. Eclipsed by the popularity of their neighbor Death Valley to the east, they never gained nearly as much notoriety. But they did have far more valuable deposits, and over the years they produced a much greater wealth than Death Valley ever dreamed of. A superb lesson we learn from their mining past is that even 150 years ago, long before plate tectonics and satellite surveying, prospectors were amazingly good at their trade. In all of this huge unchartered territory there were only a few exceptional lodes, yet prospectors zoomed in on them almost right away. In spite of the ruggedness of the local mountains, in just 10 years the richest metal deposits had been discovered. By 1875, most of the best ore had been taken out.

The very first mine to be put on the map was the Christmas Gift Mine in Wildrose Canyon, in 1861. It exploited antimony, which was not in great demand, and the local Indians were making the area unsafe. The property was soon abandoned and remained undeveloped for five decades. But during World War I, the Christmas Gift and a few other local mines were re-opened to fill the need for strategic metals, and they produced close to one million dollars in antimony.

The first mine that actually made a profit was Cerro Gordo, nearly 50 years earlier—and it turned out to be by far the richest. This huge silver-lead-zinc lode was discovered in 1865, up on the crest of the Inyo Mountains, nearly a mile above the turquoise waters of Owens Lake. In just a few years, half a dozen mines had been opened, and this figure had doubled by 1871. It was a tremendous enterprise, which involved large smelters to reduce the ore, pipelines to bring water to the town, armies of woodcutters, a continuous stream of mule-drawn wagons to transport the silver to southern California, and a real mining town of a few thousand people. For a while the mines' output was so high that transportation could not keep up with it, and pure silver bars had to be stockpiled by the lakeshore. The historic production up to 1876 was 7 million dollars. When the last significant mining operation ended in 1933, Cerro Gordo had returned about 17 million dollars, more than all other mines combined.

In 1872, while Cerro Gordo was booming, another silver strike occurred, in the forested upper reaches of Surprise Canyon. It was to be the first of many mining ventures in the rich Panamint Mountains. There was no way of telling the size of the deposit, but everyone wanted so much to believe it was another Cerro Gordo that it triggered an unprecedented rush. The town of Panamint City sprouted overnight as thousands of fortune seekers and merchants flocked to the site. Over the next few months, numerous mining companies were formed, dozens of tunnels were sunk all over the canyon slopes, and miles of trails and tramways were developed. Much of this frantic activity was controlled by three prominent crooks, including two Nevada senators, who saw in this madness a perfect opportunity to get richer, not from silver but from gullible investors. Their scam made national news, but Panamint City never paid up. By 1876, all it had produced was a few hundred thousand dollars. It was not even half of what had been invested, and there was not enough ore left to pay for the difference. It spelled the end of what was the region's most glamorous mining frenzy, although its near success continued to attract miners for decades.

After the Inyos and the Panamints, it was the Argus Range's turn to be thrown in the limelight with three significant silver discoveries back to back: Darwin in 1874, the Modoc Mine the following year, and the Minnietta Bell Mine in 1876. Darwin soon had a few well-developed properties, including the famous Defiance Mine, which yielded $750,000 in silver and gold by 1883, plus a huge tonnage of lead. The lode was extensive, and Darwin remained active for over a century, eventually taking second place behind Cerro Gordo, with a total production in excess of 7 million dollars. The Modoc and the Minnietta Belle did not come close to this figure, but they did very well—2.4 and nearly 1 million dollars, respectively. The town of Lookout, erected above the mines on a high ridge overlooking Panamint Valley, was an active frontier town, a social center, and the site of two smelters that also treated the ore from neighboring mines. A series of large stone kilns was erected in Wildrose Canyon across the valley to produce the charcoal that fueled the smelters. For many years prior to 1900, the district contributed greatly to southern California's budding economy, and it enjoyed a sporadic but productive life until the 1980s.

The eastern slopes of the Inyo Mountains were last to be exploited—not that they lacked valuable minerals, but their inaccessibility deterred all but the staunchest prospectors. Their main resource was gold, and there was plenty of it. The first claims were filed as early as 1866, but mining did not start until richer deposits were discovered in Hunter Canyon (Bighorn Mine) in 1877, then in Keynot Canyon (Keynot Mine) the following year. The ore looked so good that a new district was organized—the Beveridge Mining District—and as usual camps, arrastres, smelters, a small town, and other developments were introduced in due course. The eastern Inyos were also blessed with plenty of water and wood, precious assets most desert mining districts could only envy. But they also suffered from two major difficulties that completely hindered large-scale mining. First, the terrain was so rough that the construction of access roads was unthinkable. For their entire history, the mines could only be reached by long and strenuous trails. Transportation of the ore to market was so expensive that only the highest grade ore was worth hauling out. Unfortunately—and this was the second difficulty—only a tiny percentage of the huge gold reserve was high grade. The district remained active until around 1906, under conditions even more unfavorable than in the rest of the desert. The richest property, the Keynot Mine, had nearly 2 miles of tunnels and a cyanide mill, as well as several buildings, and it produced an honorable $420,000. All the other mines combined—there were dozens—only came up with a fraction of this amount.

These early mines were the region's most prosperous historic metal producers. By the turn of the previous century, most of the richest metal deposits had been opened and the easiest veins exhausted. Every acre of land that could be walked on had also probably been thoroughly examined. The odds of a prospector stumbling upon a valuable outcrop that had been overlooked were slim. But prospectors live in a world of hope, oblivious to the lessons of history. Until the 1960s, they returned in great numbers, lured by earlier mining successes, and they combed the region over and over. Many claims were filed, but as time went on, the remaining deposits became poorer and more scarce, and new mines were generally less and less prosperous. The

Main Historic Mines of Western Death Valley				
Discovery date/Name		Commodity	Main period of activity	Approx. total production
1860	Wildrose Canyon mines	Antimony	1915–1918	$1,000,000
1864	Saline Valley salt mine	Salt	1911–1933	>30,000 tons
1865	Cerro Gordo mines	Silver-lead	1865–1933	$17,000,000
1870s	Gavalan Mine	Gold	1870s–1900	$50,000
1872	Panamint City mines	Silver-lead	1872–1882	$600,000
1874	Darwin mines	Silver	1875–1970s	>$7,000,000
1874	Conn & Trudo Borax Wks	Borax	1875–1907	Unknown
1875	Modoc Mine	Silver-lead	1875–1890	$2,400,000
1876	Minnietta Mine	Silver-lead	1875–1915	$1,000,000
1877	Bighorn Mine	Gold	1877–1930s	$40,000
1878	Keynot Mine	Gold	1878–1906	$420,000
1880s	Loretto Mine	Copper	1907–1915	Unknown
1880s	St. George Mine	Gold, silver	1883–1930s	Unknown
1882	Marble Cyn gold placers	Gold	1934–1960	>$12,000
1883	Thorndike Mine	Lead-silver	1920s–1944	Unknown
1890s	Snow Flake Mine	Talc	1940s–1980s	5,000 tons
1896	Ratcliff Mine	Gold	1896–1903	$530,000
1896	World Beater Mine	Gold	1896–1905	$180,000
1899	Corona Mine	Gold	1890s–1950s	Unknown
1900s	Big Silver Mine	Silver	1920s–1940s	$4,000
1902	Blue Jay Mine	Copper	1914–1915	4,000 lbs
1903	Anton and Pobst Mine	Copper	1916	>82,000 tons
1906	Lippincott Mine	Lead–silver	1942–1952	$80,000
1906	Ubehebe Mine	Lead–silver	1906–1930	>$120,000
1907	Blue Monster Mine	Lead-silver	1907–1911	Unknown
1910	Santa Rosa Mine	Lead-silver	1911–1950	~$1,000,000
<1912	Keystone Mine	Gold	1930s–1950s	>$32,000
<1915	Talc City Mine	Talc	1914–1950	250,000 tons
1915	Crater mines	Sulfur	1929–1969	>50,000 tons
<1917	Zinc Hill Mine	Zinc	1910s–1949	>$170,000
<1920s	Bunker Hill Mine	Lead-silver	1920s–1930s	Unknown
1940s	Nikolaus-Eureka Mine	Talc	1945–1970	75,000 tons
1941	White Eagle Mine	Talc	1941–1980s	<50,000 tons
1966	El Captan Mine	Mercury	1968–1970	$1,500,000
<1970s	Up and Down Mine	Mercury	1970s	Unknown

Ratcliff Mine, in the western Panamints, was one of the last operations that was almost rich. Between 1896 and 1903 it returned $450,000, the largest historic gold production in the district. Its neighbor, the World Beater Mine, produced $180,000 over the same period. The region's two main lead properties, in the Last Chance Range above Saline Valley, peaked even later. The Ubehebe Mine was operated from 1906 to 1930 and produced around $120,000. Its neighbor the Lippincott Mine, active mostly in the 1940s, returned less than $100,000. All other mines were much poorer—the Lotus, the Corona, and Gold Bug in the Panamints, the St. George and the Golden Lady in the Argus Range, the Blue Jay and the Big Silver in Saline Valley, the Loretto Mine and Marble Canyon's gold placers in Eureka Valley, and dozens of others.

In these difficult times, a few entrepreneurs managed to make a living by re-working the tailings of historic mines. Old tailings often had tons of medium-grade ore that was too poor in historic times to bother hauling out. After the mid-1930s, as the market value of metals increased and transportation improved, these derelict treasures became very attractive. Lee Foreman and William Skinner were among the most itinerant of these tailing scavengers. In the 1940s and 1950s, they cleaned out several lead-silver mines around Panamint Valley and retrieved an estimated $500,000, most of it from the Modoc Mine.

The region also had valuable non-metallic resources, including borax, salt, sulfur, and talc, which all sparked exciting mining ventures of their own. The first one was borax, which was discovered on Saline Valley's lake bed in 1874. This was the first report of "white gold" in the Death Valley region. Two enterprising men, Conn and Trudo, jumped on the opportunity to cash in on it. By 1875, seven years before Coleman made Death Valley famous with his Harmony Borax Works and twenty-mule teams, the Conn and Trudo Borax Works were already refining borax out in Saline Valley. Their little operation survived the harsh desert environment for more than 20 years. It was even for a while the largest borax producer in the country.

A few years later, the same area became active again when the salt flats on the Saline Valley playa were opened to large-scale exploitation. By 1913, a sizable infrastructure had been erected on the lakeshore, including small evaporation ponds on the edge of the playa and pipelines to flood them with fresh water. As surprising as it may be, this turned out to be the region's grandest enterprise. What made it so remarkable, besides the foolhardy concept of mining such a cheap commodity in such a harsh place, was the salt mine's spectacular tramway. Rather than transporting the salt to market by road, a gigantic, 13.5-mile tramway was built over the Inyo Mountains, 7,700 feet up to their crest, then nearly one vertical mile down the other side to Owens Valley. Against all odds, the enterprise was a success. Operated off and on for 12 years until around 1933, this marvel of mining engineering hauled 30,000 tons of high-purity salt out of Saline Valley.

Eureka Valley was the poorest of the three valleys. Every corner of it was probed for gold, silver, and copper with no success. It was two more prosaic resources—talc and sulfur—that eventually brought mining to Eureka Valley. Talc occurred in large veins on the eastern slopes of the Inyo Mountains, high above the valley floor. Known by the early 1900s, these outcrops remained unexploited until the 1940s, when the higher demand for talc in cosmetics and pharmaceuticals boosted its market value and made mining profitable. Eureka Valley's most successful talc mine was by far the Nikolaus-Eureka. Operated intermittently from the mid-1940s to 1970, its extensive tunnels and quarry produced about 75,000 tons of steatite-grade talc.

But it was sulfur, not talc, that ended up being Eureka Valley's true claim to fame. In 1915, an enormous deposit covering several square miles was discovered in the Last Chance Range east of the valley. Containing three million tons of exceptional ore, it was one of the biggest sulfur lodes in the country. Mining began in 1929 on many claims, and continued nearly continuously for 40 years. A small town named Crater was erected near the center of the lode, as well as fancy retorts that refined the ore to high-purity sulfur before it was trucked to market. By the mid-1950s, the area had produced nearly 30% of California's native sulfur, and over 50,000 tons of pure sulfur when it closed down in 1969. In the great alchemy of Earth, sulfur often goes hand in hand with mercury, and the Crater area had plenty of this liquid metal as well. The El Captan Mine, just north of Crater, was the only good mercury mine in all of greater Death Valley. Between 1968 and 1971 it returned about $1.5 million of mercury. So it was that the grand finale of the region's long tradition of mining ended in Eureka Valley, the poorest of them all—not with a whimper but with a bang.

Very few mines are still operating today. Since 2018 lime is produced at a small quarry in the Argus Range foothills. Every so often a little high-grade talc might still be shipped out of Saline Valley. In the Panamint Mountains, a small-scale private outfit reopened the Ratcliff Mine in the early 2010s. If it weren't for the C. R. Briggs Mine still chewing the edge of the national park, and the Panamint Valley Limestone at the foot of Revenue Canyon, the mining days would be over.

■

— 2 —

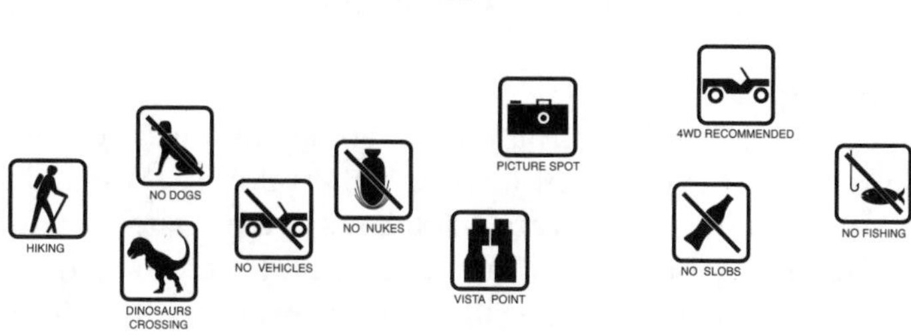

BACKCOUNTRY USE: TIPS, ETHICS, AND REGULATIONS

This chapter summarizes the features, hazards, ethics, and regulations of hiking and driving in and around Eureka, Saline, and Panamint valleys. For more information, refer to the equivalent chapter in *Hiking Death Valley*, which treats some of these topics in greater detail, and to desert survival books (see *Bibliography*).

Best Seasons to Visit

Because the region's elevation covers a huge range (from 1,033 to 11,123 feet), the temperature varies substantially with location. Also, at any one place the temperature variations from winter to summer can exceed 100°F. Between these extremes, there is a long time period and a vast geographic area over which the temperature is comfortable. Year-round there are pleasant places to explore. Consult the temperature chart in Part 1 to select the best times to visit.

The comfort zone for lower lying areas extends approximately from mid-October to mid-June, depending on your tolerance for heat and cold. March-April and October are the ideal months. They offer fairly balanced diurnal and nocturnal temperatures, and longer days. Early spring is best: the days are longer and the desert blooming season is at its peak.

The peak tourist seasons of Death Valley National Park fall during Easter week, Thanksgiving, and Christmas/New Year. If you like your deserts people-free, avoid these time windows. However, their impact on Eureka, Saline, and Panamint valleys is considerably lower than on Death Valley. These three valleys are very lightly visited year-round.

Should this situation change in the future, remember that most people dislike walking. It is easy to find solitude if you are willing to hike.

Winter Hiking

Winter hiking can be fairly cold, even at the lowest elevations. If possible, select your hikes on or near valley floors. Winter days can also be quite windy. Bring warm clothes (sweaters and down jackets are in order!), sleeping bags, insulating pads, and a tent. Rain is uncommon but a definite possibility. Take rain gear with you. At higher elevations, especially in the Inyos and Panamints, the climate is just like in any other mountain. Expect snow, ice, unpredictable weather, and frigid nights. Your drinking water needs should be comparable to what they are when hiking in temperate regions. Count on one to two quarts a day for any reasonable amount of ground you cover. Winter days are short (in December, sunset is around 4 PM). This significantly reduces sightseeing time and how far you can hike in a day. Get an early start. Bring a flashlight, in case you finish your hike after dark.

Summer Hiking

Water needs. Because of the extreme heat, summer hiking can be dangerous and should be attempted only with great care and adequate preparation. The two most important rules are to always take water with you, even on an intended short walk, and to always drink plenty of it. Your water needs depends mostly on the temperature and how far you walk. It also depends on the amount of shade and wind, the level of physical activity and the terrain difficulty, your metabolism, and your clothing. On level ground in 100°F weather, drink at least one quart per hour while walking, about one or two cups per hour while resting in the shade. On steeper terrain, you may need two quarts per hour. A common mistake is to think that you can personally get by with less and to become dehydrated. Unless you have serious reasons for rationing your water (for example if you are lost), do not stockpile it in your canteen. Drink it! To make up for your body's loss of minerals and salts, take multi-vitamin/mineral tablets, or drink a mineralized drink instead of straight water. Thirst lags behind your body's need for water, so do not wait until you are thirsty to drink. In hot weather, drink every 15 to 30 minutes, even if you think you do not need it. Refer to *Hiking Death Valley* for tips on water caching.

Spring water. With few exceptions, the only perennial creeks and water holes in the region are confined to canyons in the Inyo and Panamint mountains, and in the Argus Range. Low-lying areas are almost destitute of fresh water. *Carry your own water on all hikes, year-round.* Do not plan on using springs for drinking water. They are often either unreliable or dry, and most of them have never been tested. If, as a last resource, you must drink spring water, be aware of the dangers to which you are exposing yourself. Spring water and even running creeks are likely to be biologically contaminated, particularly with giardia. Always treat the water first, by boiling, filtering, and/or chemical treatment. Carry a vial of iodine pills for such emergency, and learn how to use it properly. Spring water can also be heavily mineralized, a problem that the above treatments do not fix. It may upset your stomach. If your situation is not so desperate as to warrant taking a chance at drinking spring water, use it to soak your clothes to cool you down.

Clothing. Other obvious tricks help make summer hiking safer. Wear a wide-brimmed hat. It will reduce water loss through your head and exposure to harmful ultraviolet radiation. Dress lightly, but do wear a light-colored long-sleeved shirt and long pants. Covering your skin reduces water loss by insulating your body from the heat source. Avoid hiking around midday. Get an early start to take advantage of the cooler morning hours. By mid-morning, find shade and rest. Resume hiking in the shadier late afternoon. Stay away from the wind, which may make you feel better but at the cost of accelerated water loss. If this is not possible, keep a thin layer of clothing on to cut down the drying power of the wind.

Hiking Time

In the text I seldom mention hiking time, a variable that depends too strongly on individual strength and traveling conditions to be universal. To fill this gap, here is a rough guideline. On fairly level cross-country terrain, count on hiking at about 80% of your usual speed on established trails—from a typical 3 mph to 2.5 mph. With a light daypack, expect to cover 12 to 14 miles in an eight-hour day, including breaks. Allow for additional time when traveling uphill, about 15 minutes per 1,000 feet, and for handling difficult obstacles. With a heavier backpack, count on 1.5 to 2 mph, including breaks, a little less in hot weather, when you might need to rest 10 minutes or so every hour.

Hazards

Mines. Many of the mine tunnels and shafts in the region are old, unsupported, and treacherous. Potential dangers include collapsing ceiling or ground, concealed shafts, holed-up rattlesnakes, pockets of deadly gases, and sharp rusted objects. To stay out of trouble, keep out of tunnels. If you decide to break this rule, do not go in without a flashlight. In particularly dangerous mining areas, the NPS has posted warning signs and blocked off some openings with wiring, fences, or grates. While browsing through mining areas, also stay clear of suspicious drums, bags, or chemical odors.

Wildlife. To avoid contact with dangerous wildlife, especially rattlesnakes, scorpions, black widow and brown recluse spiders, do not put your hands or feet anywhere you cannot see. Mountain lions are rare, but they have been sighted, and they do constitute a potential hazard. If you encounter a lion, do not approach it, and do not run from it either, or you may trigger a chase. Do all you can to appear as large as possible: spread out your arms, open your jacket or shirt. Do not crouch or bend over. Speak firmly in a low voice. If attacked, fight back, for example by throwing stones.

Hantaviruses. In recent years there have been increasing reports of hantavirus infections in the United States, especially in rural areas in the West. Hantaviruses can cause hantavirus pulmonary syndrome, a fairly uncommon but potentially deadly disease. They are carried by rodents, especially deer mouse, but also cotton rat, marsh rice rat, and white-footed mouse. They shed the virus in their urine, droppings, and saliva. The virus is transmitted mainly when breathing contaminated air. You may also get the virus by touching something contaminated, then touching your nose or mouth; by eating contaminated food; or by receiving a bite from an infected rodent (which is very rare). The areas most likely to be contaminated are cabins and mine tunnels, in which rodents often squat. Minimize your stay in these places. Avoid rodent-infested areas in high winds, which spread the virus around. If you have been touching rocks, plants, or soil, make a habit of washing your hands before eating (or picking your nose).

Flashfloods. Flashfloods are common in the desert. Even though it may not be raining where you are, torrents of water from a nearby mountain can appear with lightning speed, washing out roads and killing unwary people. Never set up camp in a wash. If a flashflood occurs, move to high ground.

Backcountry Regulations in Death Valley National Park

More than 50% of the region covered in this book is under the protection of the National Park Service, and the rest under that of the BLM and National Forest Service. To protect the land under their jurisdiction, its environment, its resources, and its visitors, these agencies impose a number of similar regulations for backcountry use, summarized in this section (NPS) and the next section (BLM). Regulations change over time; obtain updated information before heading out.

Backcountry camping. Camping is permitted 1 mile beyond any developed area, paved road, and "day use only" dirt road. The latter includes the Wildrose Canyon Road, where backcountry camping is prohibited. Camping is prohibited within 200 yards of all water sources to protect them for wildlife use. Avoid camping near mines, for your safety and to protect these fragile resources. Overnight groups are limited to a maximum of 12 people and six vehicles.

Backcountry permits. A permit is not required for overnight backcountry use (except for the Marble/Cottonwood Canyon loop), but it is recommended by the NPS for safety reasons. This policy may change: check before your trip. Permits are available at the park Visitor Center and on-line. You just need to indicate where you intend to travel, for how long, and provide basic information about your party. A permit can be used for a multiple-day trip or just for a day hike.

Off-road driving. Driving off roads is prohibited. Stay on established roadways to spare the land and prevent vehicle damage.

Mountain bikes. Bicycles are allowed on all paved and open dirt roads. They are *not* allowed off roads, on trails, or in wilderness areas.

Horseback riding. Horse use is allowed except in developed campgrounds and on paved roads. Overnight horseback-riding groups in the wilderness and at backcountry campsites are limited to a maximum of 12 people and eight pack animals.

Garbage. Pack out all garbage; do not bury any of it, biodegradable or not. Bury human waste at least six inches deep.

Wildlife. Feeding all wildlife is prohibited. When wild animals are fed by humans, they become dependent on this unreliable food source rather than forage for their natural diet.

Pets. Pets are permitted only in developed areas and on roads. They must be leashed and restrained at all times. Pets are not allowed off roads, on trails, and in the wilderness areas of the park.

Natural environment. The removal of rocks, plants, or animals is strictly prohibited. Leave the park and wilderness areas undisturbed for others to enjoy. The use of metal detectors is prohibited.

Cultural resources. All cultural resources, historical and prehistorical, are protected on all federal and state lands, and it is illegal and punishable by law to disturb or remove them.

Weapons. Weapons are strictly prohibited. This applies to firearms, air guns, bows and arrows, slingshots, and similar weapons.

Campfires. To prevent wildfires and conserve the scant supply of desert wood, ground fires are not allowed in the backcountry, even in portable fire pits. For the same reasons, the gathering of native wood, dead or alive, as well as lumber from historical structures, is unlawful. If you intend to cook, bring a stove and your own fossil fuel. Fires are not allowed inside any backcountry cabins. However, fires are allowed in metal fire rings wherever they have been installed by the NPS, including outside of backcountry cabins.

Private lands. Please respect all private properties, including the many mining claims located within the park boundaries.

BLM Regulations on Public Lands

Road classification. All of the BLM land within the three hydrological basins of Eureka, Saline, and Panamint valleys are classified as either Closed Areas or Limited Use Areas. There are *no* Open Areas, which means that *no cross-country vehicle travel is allowed anywhere.* Limited Use Areas are clearly marked. Any area that is unmarked should be considered as a Closed Area.

In a Closed Area, no motor vehicles of any kind are allowed. Hiking, biking, horseback riding, and other forms of non-motorized transportation are permitted. Closed routes do not allow motor vehicles, but hiking, biking, and horseback riding are allowed.

In Limited Use Areas, motor vehicles are restricted to *approved* routes of travel only. A route of travel is a road that shows significant evidence of prior vehicle use. It can be designated as either open or limited. On open routes, all types of motor vehicles are permitted. Limited routes are open to motor vehicles subject to certain restrictions, including, but not limited to, special season of use and limitations on the number or types of vehicles.

The classification of BLM roads is clearly posted. Even if a road classification sign has been removed (usually by vandals), it is your responsibility to know whether the road is open, limited, or closed. Violations are punishable by law. Call the BLM office in Bishop, Lone Pine, or Ridgecrest to inquire about the status of a particular road

Mechanized or motorized vehicles are strictly prohibited in all BLM wilderness areas. Vehicles must be parked outside the wilderness boundary, which is set back 30 feet on unmaintained roads and 300 feet on paved roads, unless posted otherwise.

Camping. On BLM public lands, you can pitch your tent any distance from a road, paved or otherwise. However, your vehicle must be parked within 30 feet of an unmaintained open route. Use existing campsites rather than making new ones. Do not camp within 200 yards of a water source. Leave your campsite as clean as or cleaner than you found it. Pack out all your trash; never bury it, and avoid burning it. Camping at a given location is limited to 14 days within any 28-day period. Campers must then relocate at least 25 miles from the previous site. These rules also apply to BLM wilderness.

Wildfires. When parking by a road, avoid stopping in tall grass or brush. Hot catalytic convertors or exhaust pipes can ignite dry material and cause wildfires. Fireworks are not allowed on public lands, including the safe-and-sane type. Follow campfire regulations.

Campfires. Campfires, barbecues, and gas stoves are allowed in all desert lands without permits during the winter months, and in the summer in low-elevation areas. During fire season, (1) in forested and brush-covered lands campfires are not allowed, and gas stoves are allowed by permit only, and (2) in the high country, campfires and barbecues are allowed by permit only, and gas stoves are allowed without permits. Contact the BLM to see whether these rules have changed.

Be as careful with campfires in the desert as in a forest. When building a campfire or using a stove, do so in an area clear of flammable material for a minimum radius of five feet to prevent fire escape. Never build a campfire in high wind, and never leave it unattended. Extinguish it completely before leaving, using a shovel and water. You can be held liable for the cost of suppression and damages caused by a wildfire that starts through negligence on your part.

Springs. Limit your stay at water holes and springs to 30 minutes or less to minimize wildlife disturbance.

Private lands. Please respect private properties. Obtain permission from a private landowner before trespassing. Do not assume that personal property left on the desert, such as equipment or camping gear, has been abandoned.

Pets. Pets are permitted on BLM lands and wilderness, but they should be kept under control in consideration of other visitors.

Plant collection. Plant collection is allowed by permit only, except for small-scale collection of annual flowers and dead or dry plant material (other than firewood) for personal use.

Rock hounding. Unless otherwise posted, rocks, minerals, gemstones, and common invertebrate fossils may be removed by hand or with simple hand tools in reasonable quantities for personal use. Removal for commercial sale, in large quantities, or with mechanical equipment, all require a permit.

Cultural resources. Any object or structure made or modified by people may have historical or archaeological value. Destruction or mere disturbance of such cultural resources not only deprives others of a unique experience, but it also undermines future efforts of analysis by researchers. Do not disturb historical or archaeological sites. Do not collect artifacts. It is punishable with fines and/or imprisonment.

Backcountry Driving

Road conditions. Road conditions in western Death Valley cover the whole spectrum, from 65-mph highways to beat-up tracks. Road conditions are generally detailed in the text. However, road conditions can change dramatically. After a good rain, unpaved roads can become impracticable for a few days until they dry out. So if you are several miles out on a primitive road with a passenger car and it starts pouring, do not hang around too long or you may not be able to drive back for some time. Over longer periods of time, storms and wear take their toll and perfectly good roads become impassable. So bear in mind that the road conditions mentioned in the text may have become incorrect.

Even if you are used to driving desert backcountry roads, inquire about road conditions beforehand. Rangers will tell you if a road is closed, washed out, or snowed in, and suggest alternate routes, possibly saving you a lot of needless driving. In the winter, some roads may be closed for a few days due to snow, especially the Big Pine Road over the Inyos, and the Saline Valley Road at South Pass or North Pass.

Vehicle requirements. The region's maintained roads are generally in decent enough shape for standard two-wheel-drive vehicles. Unmaintained roads often require high clearance, more rarely four-wheel drive. This is an important point: clearance is often more critical than power. Four-wheel-drive sedans often do not fare much better than normal vehicles because their clearance is only marginally higher.

That said, many of the primitive roads can be negotiated with a standard-clearance two-wheel-drive vehicle. Since passenger cars are most prevalent, I indicate in the text whether access roads can be driven with such vehicles. However, such estimations are *very subjective.* Whether they apply to you depends in part on how determined and skilled you are. Be aware that on most of the primitive roads I claim can be driven with a passenger car, the NPS and BLM recommend a sturdier vehicle. If you do not want to push either your car or your luck too hard, follow the NPS or BLM recommendations, *not mine.*

Flat tires. The most common breakdown on primitive roads is flat tires, which are often caused by nothing bigger than a tiny sharp pebble that gets rammed into the treads. The incidence of flat tires gets rapidly worse with increasing speed. The best advice to minimize the risk of a flat tire is never to drive faster than 15 mph, even on decent roads. Owners of SUVs should not feel exempt. In fact, they may be more prone to flat tires, because most SUVs are equipped with city tires too thin for primitive roads. SUV drivers are generally unaware of this, have a false sense of safety, and thus tend to drive faster. Take a flat tire kit with you; it may fix your tire long enough to get you back to town. A second spare tire may also prevent a ruined trip.

Getting unstuck. If you are driving on a dirt road and you feel your wheels spinning and sinking into the ground, stop feeding gas as soon as your car is stuck. If you are on a slope, push your vehicle out of the bad spot and try again. On level ground, try to drive the car forward and backward repeatedly and slowly to acquire momentum and get out of the ruts. If it does not work, the best remedy is to jack up the buried tire, slip a few flat rocks underneath it, and slowly drive out.

If you cannot get unstuck, or if your vehicle breaks down and you cannot fix it, stay with your vehicle and wait for help to come to you. It is a lot easier for rescuers to spot a stranded vehicle than a wandering human being. Open all doors to make your vehicle more visible and to provide shade. Use the horn and headlights for signals. Leave your vehicle only if you are certain you can walk to help safely.

Be prepared for such emergencies. Always keep in your vehicle plenty of water and food, a flashlight, matches, a rope, jumper cables, and tool box. Inspect your spare tire before each trip.

Wilderness Ethics: Leave No Trace

Be considerate to others. When other hikers are nearby, speak quietly, or not at all. Do not play music out of a speaker; use earphones instead, leaving one ear free to listen to rattlesnakes and other possible imminent dangers. Avoid hiking in large groups. It violates the wilderness spirit, and it has a negative impact on the fragile desert environment. Large groups are also more noisy and visible, which is unfair to other visitors. Do not beep your car when locking or unlocking it in campgrounds or at trailheads. Close each car door only once while getting ready in the morning or late at night. Respect quiet hours.

Minimize the traces you leave behind: walk softly, on rocks rather than gravel, and on gravel rather than plants. Most perennial desert plants are slow growers and slow healers, and important fodder or habitat for wildlife. Avoid stepping on or near them.

Practice low-impact camping. Pack out what you pack in. Do not discard organic matter, which often takes months to decompose.

Cairns are often resented by others as a blemish on nature. In DVNP, building cairns and rock sculptures is considered as vandalism. On BLM lands build cairns only when necessary for *your* benefit, and destroy them on your way back. They may otherwise mislead other hikers. Do not build rock sculptures; they are also intrusive.

Summit registers are an endearing tradition, but they are also an intrusion. Like litter and graffiti, they violate the old adage—leave only footprints. Do not put up new registers. In DVNP, they are prohibited except on the 47 peaks in Andy Zdon's *Desert Summits*.

Leave everything where you find it for others to enjoy. The bits of metal scattered around mines and camps have historical value and are irreplaceable. If every visitor was to take away even just one of them, they would be all gone in a few years.

The prehistoric archaeological sites found in the region are strongly tied to the heritage of local contemporary Native American tribes. They are very important to their traditions, and many of them are sacred. Treat them with respect. They are also protected by law. Do not disturb, touch, or remove anything. This applies to rock art (which tarnishes and wears under repeated contact), stone alignments (which lose their significance when disturbed), artifacts, and camps.

■

— 3 —

FACILITIES

WE LOVE TO ROUGH IT, but after a while, sometimes not so long a while, most of us crave a bit of comfort. This section goes over the facilities you will almost certainly look for while traveling through the western Death Valley region—motels, restaurants, campgrounds, public showers, places to buy groceries and gas up, to fix a flat tire, or to have your disabled vehicle towed. The two tables in the following pages list the locations of these facilities and phone numbers that might come in handy when preparing your trip or in case of an emergency.

Eureka Valley

Of the three valleys covered in this book, Eureka Valley is the least developed. Its only facility is the small campground at the north end of the Eureka Dunes. The outhouse is a chemical pit, and there is no shade and no tap water. Nowhere in the valley's approximate 575 square miles is there a single restaurant, motel, gas station, grocery store, or public shower. In fact, the campground's outhouse is the valley's only modern structure.

When it comes to backcountry camping, on the other hand, choices are plentiful. Unless otherwise posted, camping is permitted off any primitive road where driving is allowed. Follow the regulations of the agency in charge (generally the NPS south of the Big Pine Road and the BLM north of it), outlined in Part 2. In particular, remember that most of Eureka Valley's hydrologic basin is part of the federal wilderness system: you can set a tent any distance from an open road, but you must keep your vehicle on the road and off vegetation.

The closest restaurant and lodging are in Big Pine, a distance of about 49 miles from the Eureka Dunes. The town of Bishop, 15 miles north of Big Pine on Highway 395, has a much greater selection of restaurants and accommodations. Independence to the south has a few motels. If you are after a good meal, this quaint little town also happens to boast Owens Valley's greatest French restaurant, the Still Life Cafe, a little corner of France where you can enjoy such traditional fare as paté, steak frite, salade niçoise, and the occasional rabbit, duly accompanied with a smooth glass of Bordeaux. The closest towing services are in Bishop and Lone Pine (Miller's Towing). The latter bailed me out on a couple of critical occasions. For a small extra fee, someone will even come and rescue you on a Sunday.

Saline Valley

Just like Eureka Valley, Saline Valley has no restaurants, no lodging, no grocery stores, no service stations—and it is even more remote. The one place with any kind of public facilities is Saline Valley's famous hot springs. *Homo sapiens* being by and large highly gregarious, this is where visitors tend to gravitate. There are two primitive campgrounds at the springs, a partly shaded one at Lower Warm Springs and a more open, smaller one at Palm Spring. Set on a beauti-

Abandoned gas station, Darwin, 1999

Facilities in and around Death Valley National Park	Restaurants	Groceries	Lodging	Campgrounds	Gas stations	Auto repair	Towing
Bishop	✓	✓	✓	✓	✓	✓	✓
Big Pine	✓	✓	✓	✓	✓	✓	
Independence	✓	✓	✓	✓	✓	✓	
Lone Pine	24 h	✓	✓	✓	✓	✓	✓
Olancha	✓	✓	✓		✓		
Panamint Springs	✓	Snacks	✓	✓	✓		
Trona	✓	24 h	✓		✓		
Ridgecrest	✓	✓	✓	✓	✓	✓	✓
Scotty's Castle		Snacks					
Stovepipe Wells	✓	✓	✓	✓	✓		
Beatty, Nevada	✓	✓	✓	✓	✓	✓	
Furnace Creek	✓	✓	✓	✓	✓	✓	✓
Death Valley Jct	✓		✓				
Pahrump, Nevada	✓	✓	✓	✓	✓	✓	✓
Shoshone	✓	✓	✓	✓	✓		
Baker	✓	✓	✓		✓	✓	✓
Mojave	✓	✓	✓	✓	✓	✓	✓

ful travertine shelf overlooking the valley, these idyllic sites offer running water, hot pools, pit toilets, open-air public showers, picnic tables, and plenty of shade. A camp host lives in a trailer at Lower Warm Springs. In case of emergency, medical or mechanical, this is a good place to seek assistance. The camp host has a radio telephone, a few basic tools to cure minor automotive traumas, and he has even been known to fix the odd flat tire. Even if he is out, which is infrequent and usually brief, the hot springs are the only place in Saline Valley where you have the greatest chance of finding a fellow human being. The only other quasi-permanently inhabited settlement in the valley is Willow Creek Camp, which is the residence of the caretaker of Saline Valley's talc mines. However, this is private property, so try the warm springs first and only contact Willow Creek Camp in a true emergency.

The regulations for backcountry camping in Saline Valley are much the same as in Eureka Valley. There are no paved roads, so unless otherwise posted camping is permitted off any open road. This includes the short access roads that head west from the Saline Valley Road towards the Inyo Mountains Wilderness (BLM land), such as the Hunter Canyon Road, the Lead Canyon Road, and other roads in between. You can also camp off any open road on NPS land (generally off the Saline Valley Road), in particular the Big Silver Mine Road and the Lippincott Road. Again, make sure your vehicle is parked on the road, and obey all other regulations.

If you get desperate for a real meal or a bed, you will have to drive out of the valley, which is a long haul. If you are north of approximately Salt Lake, it is fastest to drive out northbound to Big Pine and Bishop (see *Eureka Valley* above). If you are south of Salt Lake, the closest accommodations are south at Panamint Springs, or in Olancha and Lone Pine on Highway 395 (see *Panamint Valley* below).

Panamint Valley

For many repeat visitors to Panamint Valley, Panamint Springs is their home away from home. This funky resort is nothing short of the legendary cafe in the middle of the desert. After a long drive on empty roads, its hacienda-style restaurant, shaded by fan palms and pepper trees during the day, twinkling with cheerful lights at night, beams like a way station waiting for wary travelers. Panamint Springs offers year-round more amenities than can reasonably be expected in such an out-of-the-way location—a bar to socialize, a restaurant for country-style meals, the only lodging in the valley, quite possibly the most expensive gas in the state, basic groceries and ice, and a campground for tents and trailers across the road. And, sweetest of all, hot showers.

The resort was built in 1937 by William Reid and Agnes Cody Reid. A cousin of William "Buffalo Bill" Cody, Agnes had moved at an early age with her family from Jackson Hole to the Death Valley area. Her husband was a long-time prospector and miner. For many years, the couple catered to both locals and visitors on their way to Death Valley. Agnes became famous for her warm hospitality and fine food, which she served in dinnerware with a custom-designed Panamint logo. A few famous locals became regulars and close friends of the owners, including Death Valley Scotty, Albert Johnson, who financed Scotty's Castle, and his wife Bessie. Over time, the Reids owned and either operated or leased several small mines, including the Big Four Mine up the valley, and the Lee Mine on the way to Saline Valley. After her husband's death in 1945, Agnes continued running the resort on her own until 1959, thus becoming one of the few historic woman innkeepers of the Death Valley region.

For the following three decades, the property went through several owners. It was off and on open and boarded up, slowly falling apart. Jerry Graham acquired it in 1992, and he and his family restored it to a verdant desert resort with good food, a friendly staff, and a convivial

Telephone Numbers

Area code 760 unless otherwise specified

Emergency	
24 hours	911
Dispatch office for outside the park	786-2330
Fire Department	911
Towing services	
A-1 All Night Service, Baker	733-4380
Ken's Towing, Baker	567-2850
M & S Towing, Mojave	(800) 978-1869
Miller's Towing, Lone Pine	876-4600
Paul & Sons, Ridgecrest	371-9116
Pearson's Towing, Ridgecrest	377-4585
St. Clair Auto and Towing, Ridgecrest	375-4456
Sporstman Towing, Bishop	873-4430
Two Star Towing, Pahrump	(775) 727-5197
Auto repair	
A&L Tire Co., Ridgecrest	499-2575
Lone Pine Auto Care	876-4600
Paul & Sons, Ridgecrest	371-9116
Lodging	
Amargosa Hotel	852-4441
Cerro Gordo	876-5030
Panamint Springs	(775) 482-7680
Stovepipe Wells Village	786-7090
The Inn at Death Valley	786-2345
Reservations	(800) 297-2757
The Oasis at Death Valley	786-2345
Reservations	(800) 297-2757
Visitor centers/Information	
BLM field office, Ridgecrest	384-5400
DVNP general information	786-2331
Furnace Creek Visitor Ctr.	786-3200
Interagency Visitor Center, Lone Pine	876-6200
Ranger stations	
Furnace Creek Headquarters	786-3200
Stovepipe Wells	786-2342
White Mtn R. S., Bishop	873-2500
Campground reservations	
Death Valley Nat'l Park	(877) 444-6777
Panamint Springs	(775) 482-7680
Stovepipe Wells	786-7090

ambiance. The Cassell family purchased and took over the business in 2006. On a warm morning—that would be most every morning—it is a delightful place to start off the day with a hearty breakfast on the veranda, or out on the lawn overlooking the valley. In the springtime, sparrows nesting in the rafters hop about to pick off vagrant crumbs. In the evening, after a jostling ride or a hard day's hike, you can kick back in front of a glass of wine or a rejuvenating meal and swap desert adventures with fellow travelers—hikers, jeepers, casual travelers, cowboys, miners, kid-toting couples, German students, and little old ladies in purple hats. You may even get to meet some of the funky locals if, perchance, they come out of hiding for a bite to eat. Over the years, I have had the good fortune to meet great people here, and even seal a few long-lasting friendships.

The cottages are small and rustic but cozy, and just about every room is different. One has a four-poster bed, some sleep two people, others six, and all have the last thing you need here—TV. Being the only motel for 30 miles in any direction, it is often booked up. Avoid dropping in without a reservation, although it does sometimes work. Reserve as much as a few months in advance if you are targeting a long week-end or the high season (Christmas-New Year to Easter).

There are three year-round campgrounds in Panamint Valley: in Ballarat, in Panamint Springs, and in Wildrose Canyon (Wildrose Campground). The first two are privately owned and have showers. The third one is run by the NPS. Ballarat also has a small general store with emergency food and water, a few tools, and a compressor for minor repairs, but its hours are erratic. In addition, there are two smaller NPS campgrounds in upper Wildrose Canyon (Thorndike and Mahogany Flat campgrounds). They are open from March through November, when the weather is cooperating, and they do not accommodate trailers, campers, or motor homes.

If you prefer to set up camp in the wild, Panamint Valley has plenty of space to offer. Camping is permitted along any open road on BLM lands, which include the valley floor from Highway 190 south to the China Lake Naval Weapons Center, the access roads to the Argus Range Wilderness, and the lower portion of most of the canyon roads into the western Panamint Mountains. The areas of Panamint Valley within Death Valley National Park (in particular the valley floor north of Highway 190 and the upper Panamint Mountains) are subject to different camping regulations. To stay out of trouble, the main rule you need to follow is camping at least 1 mile from a developed area, a paved road, or a "day use only" primitive road. This regulation does not restrict camping in the western Panamints. It does mean, however, that you cannot camp along the first 1 mile of the Big Four Mine Road. Again, refer to Part 2 for more detailed camping and campfire regulations on BLM and NPS lands.

Panamint Valley has a few other small settlements: Indian Ranch, the C. R. Briggs Mine, and the Diversified Minerals limestone quarry. None of these have public services. The same is true of the half-ghost, half-alive town of Darwin. Again, respect the privacy of their residents and contact them only in case of an emergency.

■

— 4 —

EUREKA VALLEY

EUREKA VALLEY LIES at the western edge of the Basin and Range province, in the remote northern corner of the California desert. Few Californians have ever heard of it. Even fewer know exactly where it is. Hidden between the intricate folds of high mountains, far away from major throughways, it is in fact easy to miss. You have to make special efforts to get to Eureka Valley: you do not just happen to go through it on your way somewhere else.

About 28 miles long and 9 miles wide at its widest, it is a relatively small basin. It is completely enclosed by imposing ranges: the Last Chance Range to the east, the Sylvania Mountains to the northeast, the Inyo Mountains to the north and west, and the Saline Range to the south. What differentiates it from the park's other basins is that all of it is high desert. The elevation of Eureka Dry Lake, the valley floor's lowest point, is 2,870 feet, more than half a mile higher than its neighbor Death Valley to the east. The basin's high points—the Last Chance Mountain (8,456 ft) on the east side, and Waucoba Mountain (11,123 ft) on the west side—rise more than one mile above the valley floor.

One of the first immigrants to set foot in Eureka Valley was Lieutenant D. A. Lyle, who commanded one of the two detachments of the historical Wheeler Survey of 1871. Lyle failed to find water in it and called it Termination Valley. The name was changed to Eureka in 1888. We do not know whether it was applied in derision or because something, perhaps water, was actually found there.

Eureka Valley is a desolate place. Left relatively untouched by the mining frenzy of the 1900s, it never attracted large enough crowds to warrant the development of any infrastructure. Ephemeral mining camps were the only settlements it ever had. Today, Eureka Valley is crossed by only a handful of roads, all of them unpaved. This relatively pristine condition made it a prime candidate for conservation: with the exception of two small mining areas, almost all of the valley's hydrologic basin is now preserved as a natural biosphere. The northern half, north of the Big Pine Road, is protected by two wilderness areas (Piper Mountain and Sylvania Mountains). The southern half is part of Death Valley National Park. The two exceptions are the sulfur claims around the site of Crater in the Last Chance Range, and the talc and copper claims in the foothills of the Inyo Mountains to the west, which were excluded because of their mineral potential. All of it—some 570 square miles of spectacular desert land—is yours to explore.

There are no services of any kind in Eureka Valley. Other than the roads, the only tribute to modern comfort is the stuffy outhouse at the Eureka Dunes. The only campground, also at the dunes, is primitive. There are no grocery stores, no gas stations, no lodging, no telephone, no domestic water supplies, no junk-food dealers. The way the world was, the way a park should be. Whatever you need you must bring.

Access and Backcountry Roads

The Big Pine Road. The main access to Eureka Valley is the Big Pine Road—also known as the Death Valley Road. From Highway 168 just east of Big Pine in Owens Valley, this scenic byway climbs the long western flank of the Inyo Mountains to a high pass above timberline. On the east side of the mountains it winds down through forested slopes to a shallow sink called Little Cowhorn Valley, then through the long tilted valley of Joshua Flats, before descending several more miles through mountainous terrain to Eureka Valley.

Until around 2000 this section was unpaved. Unfortunately, while nobody was watching, and without asking anyone's opinion, Inyo County officials had it paved to the western edge of Eureka Valley. From there the Big Pine Road crosses the valley eastward, climbs the Last Chance Range through Hanging Rock Canyon, then crosses many dusty miles down the northern arm of Death Valley to meet asphalt again at the Ubehebe Crater Road. Other than a short stretch in Hanging Rock Canyon, this segment is still unpaved, though mostly graded and usually suitable for a passenger car. About 41 miles long, it is one of the longest and wildest unpaved roads around Death Valley, and driving it is a rare experience.

Backcountry roads. There are three primitive access routes to Eureka Valley. The northern route is the Piper Road, which starts on

Suggested Backcountry Drives in Eureka Valley					
Route/Destination	Dist. (mi)	Lowest elev.	Highest elev.	Road type	Pages
Andrews Mountain (saddle)	4.6	7,040'	8,940'	F	129
Cucomungo Canyon Road	12.8	4,611'	7,130'	P	63-68
Dry well	2.4	2,974'	2,990'	P	91
El Captan Mine	3.2	5,180'	6,520'	H	74
Harlis and Broady Mine Rd	2.3	5,400'	5,995'	F	119-120
Lead Peak Road	1.9	5,155'	5,740'	F	75-76
Loretto	0.7	4,757'	5,230'	H	115-116
Marble Canyon	1.6	5,500'	~5,900'	H	123-125
Nikolaus-Eureka Mine Road	2.0	5,150'	5,880'	F	121-122
North Eureka Valley Road	20.9	3,276'	5,520'	G	63
Piper Road	14.3	3,415'	6,374'	H	97-98
South Eureka Valley Road	10.2	2,871'	3,317'	G	85
Steel Pass Road	29.3	1,475'	5,091'	F	191-195
Key: G=Graded H=Primitive (HC)	P=Primitive (2WD) F=Primitive (4WD)				

Highway 168 at Gilbert Summit and cuts south through northern Eureka Valley, where it meets the Big Pine Road (see *The Piper Road*). The second route is from the east on the North Eureka Valley Road. It starts on Highway 168 near the Nevada state line, traverses Fish Lake Valley southeastward, then crosses the Cucomungo Hills and drops along the east side of Eureka Valley to the Big Pine Road just below Hanging Rock Canyon. This road can also be reached from Nevada Highway 266 via the Cucomungo Canyon Road (see *Cucomungo Canyon*). The southern route is the rough Steel Pass Road from Saline Valley (see *The Steel Pass Road*). These roads generally require a high-clearance and/or four-wheel-drive vehicle.

The selection of backcountry roads in Eureka Valley is limited. Not that roads have been closed to motorized traffic: there just were never many in the first place. Other than the Big Pine Road, the only main roads are the South Eureka Valley Road (graded) down to the Eureka Dunes, and the North Eureka Valley Road, which follows the valley's east side and eventually crosses the low divide into Fish Lake Valley to the north. For easy four-wheeling, try the Piper Road and the Horse Thief Canyon Road in the north valley, the short roads around Crater, or the Cucomungo Canyon Road on the northeast side. The toughest roads in Eureka Valley are the roads to the talc mines on the west side, and the Steel Pass Road to Saline Valley.

Mining History

Mining never made it big in Eureka Valley. No fabulous gold mine, no lost silver lode, no giant lead deposit. But it was not for want of trying. Here as most everywhere in the desert, prospectors and miners put their luck to the test for decades, poking and burrowing feverishly, hitting pay dirt only occasionally, until they called it quits with, in most cases, nothing to show.

The earliest recorded mining venture in the valley was the Loretto Mine, in the eastern foothills of the Inyo Mountains. Discovered around the 1880s, this copper deposit was first developed in 1907, but like all other copper mines in the Death Valley region it turned out to be a dead loss, and it shut down in 1915. Talc was also discovered in the same area around 1909. Though not a great lode, it was large enough to sustain several decades of sporadic mining. The area's wealthiest, the Nikolaus-Eureka Mine, produced around 75,000 tons of talc between 1945 and 1970.

Eureka Valley's only mining claim-to-fame was high-purity native sulfur. It came out of a rich hydrothermal zone on the east side of the valley, high up in the Last Chance Range. Known as Crater, this area was developed extensively between 1929 and 1969 and produced record quantities of sulfur, as well as some mercury—and most of it is still in the ground. There were other mining efforts—gold placer mines in Marble Canyon, a revival of the Loretto Mine in 1975, and small-time prospecting of marginal gold and silver-lead deposits in the northwest corner of the valley. All of them were uneventful failures. Since its preservation as a wilderness and a national park in 1994, Eureka Valley has resumed its peaceful four-million-year snooze.

Weather

From November through February, daytime temperatures can be quite low and the weather changeable, due to the proximity of the Inyo Mountains. Expect mean valley floor temperatures in the 50s or under during the day and near or below freezing at night. Bring warm clothes, and a warm sleeping bag and a tent if you are planning on camping. Snow down to the valley floor as early as November is not uncommon. If it snows in the mountains while you are in the valley and you don't have chains to get out over the high passes, your best chance is to drive the Big Pine Road east over the Last Chance Range and out through Death Valley. That pass rarely gets much snow.

Inyo Mountains from the Harlis and Broady Road in Eureka Valley

From late June through early September the mean temperature on the valley floor is far more comfortable, in the range of about 60°F to 100°F, and it rarely runs into three digits. The surrounding high country is also significantly cooler than further south in the region.

Springs

In spite of its high elevation, the majority of the Eureka Valley hydrologic basin is utterly dry. The reason is again that it lies in the rain shadow of three formidable mountain ranges—the Sierra Nevada, the Inyo Mountains, and the White Mountains—which divert almost all of the moisture brought in by winter storms from the Pacific Ocean. As a result, this basin supports virtually no perennial streams and very little surface water except for snow in the winter and a handful of isolated springs on the high slopes of the Inyos and the Last Chance Range. The floor of Eureka Valley does not have a single mesquite tree, a record that even Death Valley does not match.

Hiking

Though not always easy, most of the hiking in and around Eureka Valley is generally easier than in the region's highest mountain ranges, such as the Panamint Mountains or the Inyo Mountains in Saline Valley. Because of its higher mean elevation, this valley is on average noticeably cooler than the other valleys in the park. The best time to

Suggested Hikes in and Around Eureka Valley					
Route/Destination	Dist. (mi)	Elev. gain	Mean elev.	Access road	Pages
Short hikes (under 5 miles round trip)					
Andrews Mtn (north route)	2.2	2,140'	8,200'	P/1.5 mi	130
Andrews Mtn (west route)	2.4	1,820'	8,500'	P/1.5 mi	129
April Fool Prospect	2.3	1,380'	3,630'	Graded	84
Crater Mine loop	0.6	~50'	5,180'	P/0.1 mi	71-72
Dedeckera Canyon narrows	0.9	380'	3,850'	P/6.0 mi	194-195
Easy Pickings Mine	1.8	510'	5,660'	Graded	126
Eureka Dunes summit	1.3	670'	3,200'	Graded	87-88
Harlis and Broady Mine	2.4	1,650'	5,670'	Paved	119-121
Lead Pk (from Big Pine Rd)	2.1	780'	5,590'	Graded	75-77
Loretto Mine (quarry)	1.0	580'	5,060'	Paved	116-117
Nikolaus-Eureka Mine					
via Big Pine Road	2.0	1,050'	5,560'	Paved	121-122
via Loretto	2.0	1,440'	5,360'	Paved	118, 121
Rebecca No. 2 Mine Camp	1.0	1,150'	5,250'	F/1.5 mi	77-78
Sugarloaf Mountain	1.6	950'	6,000'	P/2.7 mi	99-102
Sulphur Queen Mine					
from Lead Peak Road	1.5	1,360'	4,930'	F/1.5 mi	78
Tule Spring	1.3	680'	4,920'	H/8.8 mi	98-99
Up and Down Mine	2.3	1,690'	3,710'	Graded	79-82
White Cliff Canyon narrows	0.9	490'	5,410'	P/10.2 mi	64-65
Intermediate hikes (5-12 miles round trip)					
Andrews Mountain loop	6.1	2,230'	8,160'	P/1.5 mi	129-132
Deep Sprs. College overlook	3.6	1,620'	4,730'	P/5.3 mi	104-105
Deep Springs Lake overlook	4.7	2,530'	6,820'	Paved	112-114
Deep Sprs. Valley overlook	5.0	2,280'	7,040'	Paved	110-111
El Captan Mine	3.2	1,400'	5,810'	Graded	72-74
Eureka Dunes southern loop	~7.0	~1,500'	3,160'	Graded	90
Hidden Dunes				P/2.4 mi	
first dune	3.3	520'	3,150'		91-92
highest dune	5.3	1,690'	3,440'		91-94
Joshua Flats/Rainbow Mine	2.9	1,310'	6,530'	Paved	110-111
Marble Canyon lower gorge	4.0	1,160'	4,940'	H/1.6 mi	125-128

Key: P=Primitive (2WD) H=Primitive (HC) F=Primitive (4WD)
Distances: one way for out-and-back hikes, round-trip for loops
Elev. gain: sum of all elevation gains on round-trip or loop hike

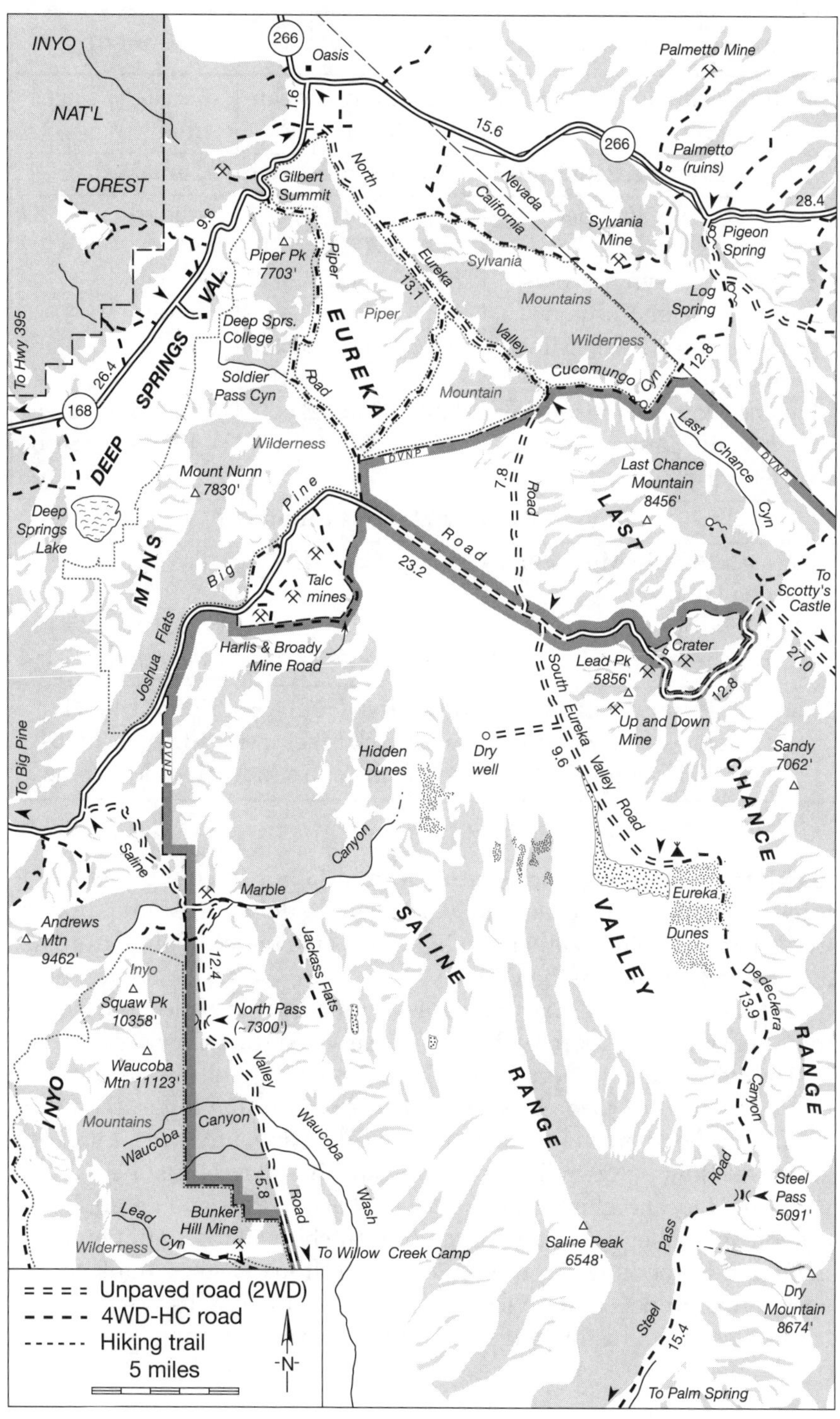
INYO
NAT'L
FOREST
Oasis
266
Palmetto Mine
Palmetto (ruins)
Pigeon Spring
Sylvania Mine
Gilbert Summit
Piper Pk 7703'
Deep Sprs. College
Soldier Pass Cyn
Mount Nunn 7830'
Deep Springs Lake
DEEP SPRINGS VAL
MTNS
EUREKA
Sylvania Mountains Wilderness
Piper Mountain Wilderness
North Eureka Valley Road
Piper Road
Log Spring
Cucomungo Cyn
Last Chance Cyn
Last Chance Mountain 8456'
LAST CHANCE RANGE
Big Pine Road
Talc mines
Harlis & Broady Mine Road
Joshua Flats
Crater
Lead Pk 5856'
Up and Down Mine
To Scotty's Castle
Sandy 7062'
Hidden Dunes
Dry well
South Eureka Valley Road
Saline Canyon
Marble Canyon
Andrews Mtn 9462'
Jackass Flats
Inyo
Squaw Pk 10358'
North Pass (~7300')
Waucoba Mtn 11123'
INYO Mountains Wilderness
Waucoba Canyon
Waucoba Wash
Valley Road
Bunker Hill Mine
Lead Cyn
SALINE RANGE
EUREKA VALLEY
Eureka Dunes
Dedeckera Canyon
Steel Pass 5091'
Steel Pass Road
Saline Peak 6548'
Dry Mountain 8674'
To Willow Creek Camp
To Palm Spring
To Hwy 395
To Big Pine
168
DVNP
Nevada
California
1.6
15.6
28.4
9.6
13.1
26.4
12.8
7.8
23.2
27.0
12.4
15.8
13.9
15.4
= = = = Unpaved road (2WD)
- - - - 4WD-HC road
------ Hiking trail
5 miles
N

Suggested Hikes in and Around Eureka Valley (Cont'd)					
Route/Destination	Dist. (mi)	Elev. gain	Mean elev.	Access road	Pages
Intermediate hikes (5-12 miles round trip) (Cont'd)					
Mercury Knob Prospect	3.8	2,800'	4,050'	Graded	82
Piper Peak Trail	3.0	1,700'	6,970'	P/0.5 mi	102
Soldier Pass Cyn narrows	3.4	1,450'	4,670'	P/5.3 mi	106
Sulphur Queen Canyon				Graded	
to Sulphur Queen Mine	3.2	1,600'	3,680'		78
to Lead Peak	5.2	2,960'	4,210'		76, 78
Up and Down Mine loop	8.6	2,560'	3,680'	Graded	80-84
White Cliff Canyon Trail	2.7	1,220'	6,160'	P/13.9 mi	64-68
Wyler Spring cabin	3.0	850'	4,520'	P/5.3 mi	106-108
Long hikes (over 12 miles round trip)					
Harlis & Broady Mine loop	13.7	3,070'	4,440'	Paved	62
Hidden Dunes					
via Marble Canyon	8.1	2,180'	4,390'	H/1.6 mi	125-128
Mount Nunn	6.3	3,540'	6,950'	Paved	109-114
Key: P=Primitive (2WD) H=Primitive (HC) F=Primitive (4WD) Distances: one way for out-and-back hikes, round-trip for loops Elev. gain: sum of all elevation gains on round-trip or loop hike					

hike here is from mid-spring through mid-fall. If three-digit temperatures bother you, this is definitely the place to do your summer hiking. Conversely, if cold weather hinders your enjoyment of the outdoors, avoid Eureka Valley in the winter.

Of the few longer hikes available around Eureka Valley, the largely forgotten 13.7-mile loop road that once serviced the valley's talc mines ranks high on the scenery meter. From its south end on the Big Pine Road, the beat-up road climbs east over a spur of the Inyos, then dips steeply to the interesting Harlis and Broady Mine. From there it drops 2,500 feet down a gravelly canyon to Eureka Valley, skirts the valley's western edge, and climbs up a rocky fan back to the paved road. In the canyon and valley, the road is a random stitchery of discontinuous segments. Side roads climb the spur's precipitous eastern flank to the abandoned tunnels of the Victor Consolidated Mine. This is wild country suffused with history, ideal for a quiet overnight outing.

■

CUCOMUNGO CANYON

If you are looking for a fun and (usually) easy primitive road trip out of Eureka Valley, try Cucomungo Canyon. This long and scenic canyon will take you over the Sylvania Mountains into Nevada, climbing from wrinkled badland hills dotted with Joshua trees to beautiful high-desert country forested with majestic pinyon pines. This route gives access to springs and abandoned cabins, mills, gold, talc, and copper mines, and a canyon with several narrow passages carved out of striking porphyritic granite to explore on foot.

General Information
Jurisdiction: DVNP, Sylvania Mountains Wilderness
Road status: Road through canyon, often 2WD
White Cliff Canyon narrows: 0.9 mi, 420 ft up, 70 ft down one way / easy
White Cliff Canyon Trail: 2.7 mi, 470 ft up, 750 ft down one way / moder.
Main attractions: Long scenic canyon drive, narrows, mines, and cabins
USGS 7.5' topo maps: Horse Thief Canyon, Last Chance Range*, Sylvania Mountains
Maps: pp. 67*, 61

Location and Access

Cucomungo Canyon is located in northwestern Eureka Valley, at the northern tip of the Last Chance Range. To get to it, start from the Big Pine Road and drive the North Eureka Valley Road north 7.1 miles, at which point it enters Cucomungo Canyon. Continue 0.7 mile to a Y junction and make a right on the Cucomungo Canyon Road. From there it follows the canyon wash up to the head of the canyon just inside Nevada. It then drops north into another drainage to eventually end at Nevada Highway 266 15.6 miles east of the town of Oasis.

The Cucomungo Canyon Road is graded and generally good. In the summer 2000, it had just been bladed and was as smooth as a pool table. Two years earlier, violent summer storms had completely wiped out several wash crossings, and for months only four-wheelers could drive through. At the canyon mouth, it had been redesigned into a roller coaster of dry mud hummocks, and it took a hair-raising balancing act to make it without rolling over. When this sort of thing happens, Inyo County officials make sure to take all the fun out of backcountry driving and iron out the washouts to boring perfection. So it is hard to say what the road will be like in the future. Go find out.

Route Description

The lower canyon. This is a beautiful canyon, filled with a great diversity of scenery and imbued with pastoral charm. If the road is in decent shape, the ride through it is one of the most relaxing in all of Eureka Valley. Along the broad canyon bottom, platoons of Joshua trees poke their ruffled heads above a fragrant sea of sagebrush, cliffrose, buckwheat, and other shrubs. In the warm season, carpets of wildflowers line the road, especially prince's plume and desert prickle-poppy. Cucomungo Canyon traces the boundary between two dissimilar geologic terrains, and its facing walls are remarkably different. To the north rise the plutonic Sylvania Mountains. This side is a high sweep of Jurassic quartz monzonite wildly dissected into a salt-and-pepper wonderland of cracks, ravines, buttresses, and spires. In contrast, the Last Chance Range to the south is almost entirely sedimentary. That side is a colorful juxtaposition of shale, sandstone, siltstone, quartzite, dolomite, and fanglomerate from the Cambrian, eroded into steep taluses crowned by short cliffs. Early and late in the day, this wrinkled landscape fills with dark shadows. The drama of Joshua trees against this intriguing background is a photographer's paradise.

White Cliff Canyon. Confronted with this inviting landscape, it is difficult to resist the urge to pull over and take a walk. Anywhere will do: the north side of the road is a wilderness (Sylvania Mountains), and the south side is national park land. But save a little time for a more structured hike up the side canyon called White Cliff. It is one of the best around. Look for it 2.2 miles from the North Eureka Valley Road, on the north side. The canyon is a short distance up the wash. It is not overly impressive at first, until you reach a wide amphitheater a few hundred yards in and the sheer 35-foot fall that blocks the way just past it. The most exciting stretch is, of course, above this unscalable fall. Fortunately, a short trail bypasses it up the crumbly talus to the left of the fall. After a few switchbacks it tops a sharp ridge, from which you can scramble down the steep far side into the wash.

The payoff is a series of shallow, U-shaped trenches lined with sand that wiggles up the canyon for the next 0.6 mile. The polished bluffs that frame the trenches, whitish in color, probably inspired this canyon's name. They are made of Quartz Monzonite of Beer Creek, about 157 million years old and part of the Sylvania Mountains Pluton. This rock is porphyritic: it cooled down slowly enough to develop large crystals, which now sparkle all along the bluffs. Past the last trench the canyon splits into unexpectedly green and scenic forks. The washes are covered with Joshua trees and high-desert plants, and the

Joshua trees and buttressed slopes along lower Cucomungo Canyon

hills with dark-green pinyon pines. If you go up the right fork, and the right fork after it, you will get to the lower end of a road that climbs east to a small gold mine (see *Upper Cucomungo Canyon* below).

Willow Spring. Like most springs in Eureka Valley, this one is so small that it is easy to miss. It is 4.7 miles into Cucomungo Canyon. A short ramp on the north side of the road climbs 30 feet to a decrepit wooden cabin hidden amongst tall sagebrush, then drops back to the road. Willow Spring is just beyond: an open swamp of grass and watercress drained by a rivulet of water. USGS maps optimistically show a stream called Willow Creek flowing through Cucomungo Canyon. The reality is that except during rare flashfloods, this meager runoff *is* the creek. Barely strong enough to cross the road, it usually dries up a few yards down canyon. Its underground flow is piped into a cattle trough filled with gelatinous algae. Chukars often come here for a drink, sometimes in surprisingly large flocks. On the hillside near the upper end of the spring there is an abandoned hopper, and Willow Spring's sole willow.

Upper Cucomungo Canyon. Over the next few miles, as the road winds higher up the wash, sneaks into Nevada, and climbs through rolling hills to the head of the canyon, the Joshua-tree woodland sweeps up into a beautiful pinyon-pine forest. This quasi-miracle is one of Cucomungo Canyon's greatest assets. On a hot day, it is a cool retreat to escape from the low-desert madness. Wildlife abounds on this unexpected island in the sky. You are likely to spot chipmunks and rabbits frantically hopping across the road; blackbirds flying about at the springs; zebra-tailed lizards sprinting for cover; or a killdeer feigning a broken wing to lure you away from its nest.

In the upper canyon, several side roads branch off to small gold prospects (see map). All of them were a dead loss, and most of them are fabulously boring, but they are still worth poking around—you never know what you will find. Even if you do not care for mines, these side roads are fun to explore. They provide easy foot access to forested places where you can cool off, have a picnic in a field of sagebrush, or camp under large shady pines. The two open cuts at the Midway Group show lots of hematite and blue-green coatings of malachite and chrysocolla. The road up to the Nev-Cal Copper Prospect is badly overgrown. You will have to walk the steep final pitch in and out of Nevada to its high open cut (~6,740'), bladed in the 1970s, to enjoy the views of the canyon. Shortly past the state line, another road veers left up a fork in the canyon to Cucomungo Spring, a grassy slope irrigated by a film of surface water and sometimes used by cattle.

Cucomungo Canyon

	Dist.(mi)	Elev.(ft)
N. Eureka Val. Rd/Big Pine Rd	0.0	3,276
Canyon mouth (dip into wash)	7.1	4,440
Jct with Cucomungo Cyn Rd	7.8	4,611
White Cliff Canyon (hike)	10.0	5,230
Top of narrows	(0.9)	5,580
Cabin	11.7	~5,760
Willow Spring	11.8	5,780
White Cliff Canyon Trail (hike)	13.9	6,330
Pass into White Cliff Canyon	(0.5)	6,520
Mine's open cuts	(2.7)	6,050
Road to Cucomungo Spring	15.2	6,705
Cucomungo Spring	(0.3)	6,805
Pass	~16.3	~7,130
Log Spring Cabin	18.1	6,725
Pigeon Spring	19.9	6,430
Nevada Highway 266	20.6	6,377

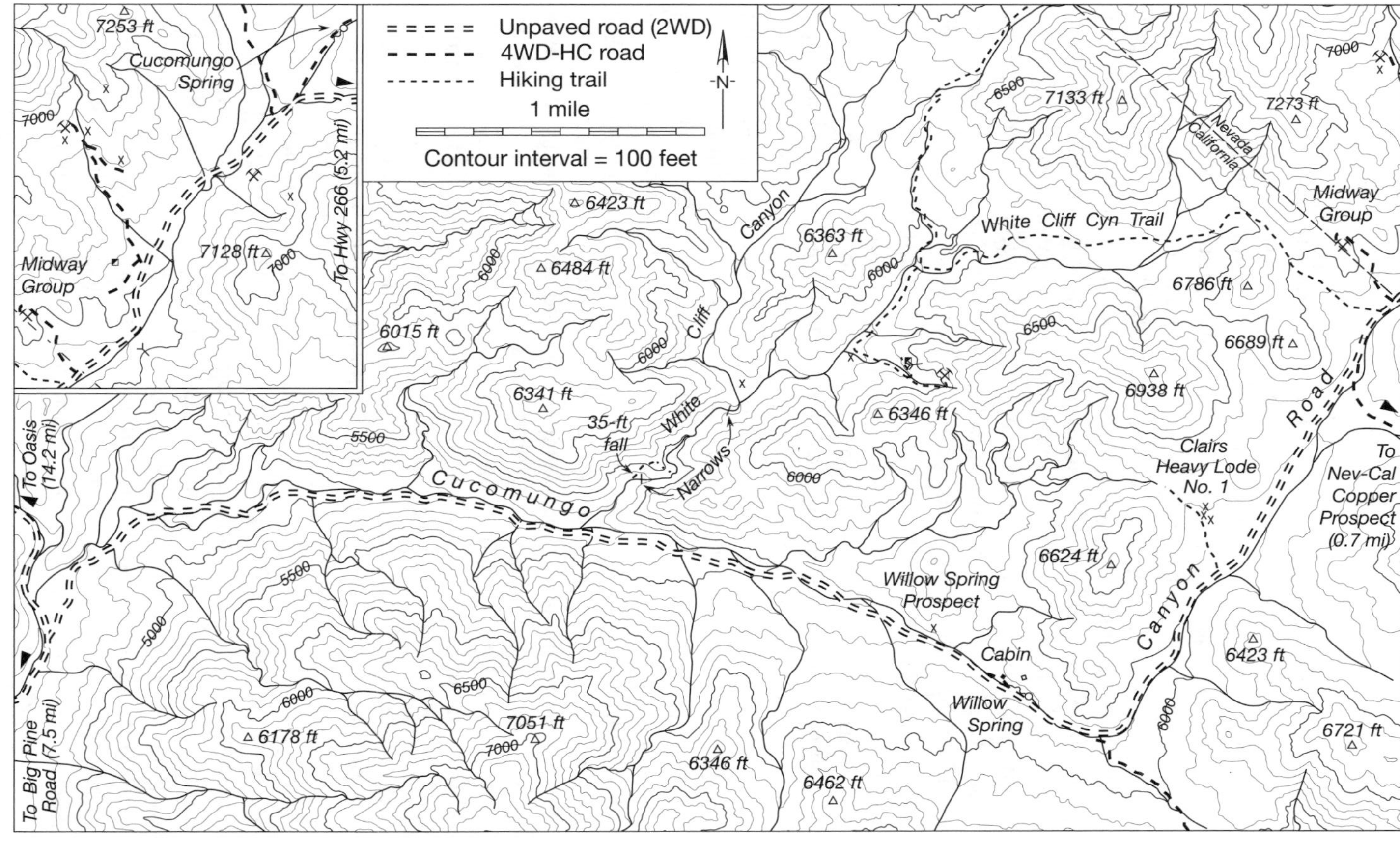
7253 ft
Cucomungo Spring
Midway Group
7128 ft
To Hwy 266 (5.2 mi)
Unpaved road (2WD)
4WD-HC road
Hiking trail
1 mile
Contour interval = 100 feet
N
6423 ft
Canyon
6363 ft
6484 ft
Cliff
6015 ft
6341 ft
35-ft fall
White
Narrows
Cucomungo
To Oasis (14.2 mi)
To Big Pine Road (7.5 mi)
6178 ft
7051 ft
6346 ft
6462 ft
7133 ft
7273 ft
Nevada
California
Midway Group
White Cliff Cyn Trail
6786 ft
6689 ft
6938 ft
6346 ft
Clairs Heavy Lode No. 1
Road
To Nev-Cal Copper Prospect (0.7 mi)
6624 ft
Willow Spring Prospect
Cabin
Willow Spring
Canyon
6423 ft
6721 ft

The side road on the north side just before the Nevada state line (the White Cliff Canyon Trail), now a foot trail, is one of the longest and most scenic. It drops 2.3 miles into the green upper drainage of White Cliff Canyon, then angles sharply into a steep ravine. It ends in 0.5 mile at a recent gold mine. What kept me entertained was not its workings, which are largely barren, but the fauna cleverly re-using them. Birds congregated near the rain-fed pool that collected inside the short inclined tunnel, while a lonesome rat had set up residence at the bottom of the 50-foot shaft.

Nevada State Line to Highway 266. The canyon road eventually climbs to a long pass out of Cucomungo Canyon. It then descends into the Palmetto Creek watershed in Fish Lake Valley, winding down through thickly forested hills along a series of washes broadening to open valleys. It is only 4.3 miles to Nevada Highway 266, but points of interest are so numerous that this stretch may well occupy the rest of your day. This area has been extensively probed for minerals, and the road is lined with abandoned cabins, gold mills, and mines. Do not miss the wooden cabin below Log Spring; the run-down but well-built white-stone house 500 feet north of it; the two deep ponds on the east side of the road, dug down to the water table and now filled with aquatic plants; and the smooth light-green soapstone at the small talc mine on the hilltop east of Log Spring.

The most interesting area is Pigeon Spring, the site of a historic mill that processed for a brief time gold ore from the local hills. The spring itself is a row of venerably old cottonwoods along the right side of the road, 3.6 miles north of the pass. The mill is 0.3 mile further down the road. Built in 1890, it was a proud 10-stamp installation erected on three levels shored by 5-foot stone walls. The long retaining walls are still there, as is a small portion of the mill's wooden frame, upright on its concrete pilings and studded with the original bolts. When the mill was active, a small community lived at the spring, in a town so small that in 1899 its application for a post office was declined. The ghost town is now reduced to a dugout, mortared foundations, and stone walls overwhelmed by shrubs. Oblivious to the vagaries of human affairs, the spring's tiny creek of clear water continues to keep alive a timeless community of brittlebush and big sagebrush.

If you return via Oasis, check out the historic ghost town of Palmetto, 2.2 miles down Highway 266. Its huge stone walls are quite photogenic in the late afternoon sun.

■

CRATER

Whether your heart goes to hiking or four-wheeling, you will enjoy roaming the dirt roads that crisscross Crater, a hilly region at the top of the Last Chance Range that holds one of the largest sulfur deposits in the West. This is a rare opportunity to explore sulfur and mercury mines. Look forward to old camps, unusual geology, minerals, and diggings, and one-of-a-kind ore processing equipment.

General Information

Jurisdiction: BLM and NPS
Road status: Hiking on old mining roads; graded access road
Crater Mine: 0.6 mi, ~50 ft up loop/very easy
El Captan Mine: 3.2 mi, 1,340 ft up, 60 ft down one way/easy
Main attractions: Sulfur and mercury mines, geology, history, minerals
USGS 7.5' topo map: Hanging Rock Canyon
Maps: pp. 73*, *61*

Location and Access

Crater is located at the crest of the Last Chance Range north of the Eureka Valley Dunes. To get to it, drive the Big Pine Road 5.0 miles east from the South Eureka Valley Road to the pass. Refer to the text below for directions to the four main sites. The area north of the road is privately owned; treat it with respect. Keep out if mining resumes.

Geology: Quicksilver and Volcanic Sulfur

Sulfur is one of the few elements that occur in a native state. In this form it is known as brimstone, "the stone that burns," and it has been used since antiquity. Although sulfur is common in the earth's crust, it is mostly combined with other elements and rarely in its elemental state. In California, native sulfur is found at only ten locations. Of these, the Crater deposit is the second largest. It also stands out for having a volcanic origin, which it shares with only a few percent of the world's native-sulfur deposits. This is also one of only two sites in the region with known deposits of mercury, also called quicksilver.

This joint occurrence of sulfur and mercury is connected to a complex fault system called the Last Chance Thrust Fault. In the Mesozoic, movements along the fault produced an extensive zone of fractured rocks. During the last 4,000,000 years, hydrothermal solutions associated with magmatic activity rose through this permeable zone, known as a breccia pipe, and filled its fractures with mercury and iron. The presence of gypsum supports this hydrothermal origin. Sulfur was probably formed by reduction of the gypsum by organic matter and water rich in carbonic acid. This reaction produced hydrogen sulfide—the gas responsible for the delicate fragrance of rotten eggs—which was then oxidized to sulfur. The gas could also have originated from buried magma, and been delivered by the breccia pipes. This mineralization produced a huge and unusually rich deposit—about three square miles of veins up to tens of feet thick assaying 30 to 80% sulfur.

Mining History: The Crater Mines

Mining at Crater began in 1917, two years after its discovery, but no sulfur was shipped because of difficulties in refining it, a problem that hindered production until 1929. Some 200 claims were filed and eventually developed, but only three—the Crater, the Gulch, and the Fraction and Southwest Sulphur—became large producers.

Crater was operated by far the longest and the most consistently. In June 1929, the Pacific Sulphur Company took an option on the Crater and Southwest Sulphur claims. It carried out extensive development, sinking a 200-foot inclined shaft and drill holes to map the deposits, before interrupting its activities in December 1930. This was the first of a long list of owners, leasers, and sub-leasers. Over the next 10 years alone, at least six outfits took turns working at Crater. Each one produced a few thousand tons of sulfur. The West Coast Sulphur Company was the most successful: in two years it shipped 12,000 tons of 83% pure sulfur. No operation had sustainable production due to the high cost of shipping and the lack of water for refining. Some companies hauled their ore to a refinery near Big Pine. Others erected their own on-site retort. The thousands of gallons of water needed daily to run a retort had to be trucked 30 miles from Oasis. Both approaches were costly and extremely dangerous. At least two retorts were destroyed by sulfur-dust explosions, one of them at Crater in 1953.

The Crater ore was originally mined from shafts. To reduce the risk of explosion, shafts were later supplanted by open pits. By 1938 Crater's main pit was more than 20 feet deep and covered half an acre, and the exposed veins were tapped by several galleries. Mining peaked until 1943, and it continued intermittently until 1969.

The Fraction and Southwest Sulphur claims were developed in the late 1930s. Three men were employed to mine the shafts and refine the ore in three on-site stone ovens. The Gulch claims were exploited by an open pit, tunnels, and a shallow shaft. Mining continued off and on for many years on both properties, until at least 1955 on the Gulch claims.

Retort and tumbler at the Crater Mine

Crater was the richest. It had produced nearly 30% of California's native sulfur by the mid-1950s, and over 50,000 tons of pure sulfur when it closed down in 1969. Yet the surface has been barely scratched. The hills adjoining Crater still contain an estimated 3 million tons of sulfur, which was the reason for excluding this area from the park.

Route Description

Crater. This is the area's most interesting site. To visit it, drive the road on the north side of the pass 100 yards to the edge of an expansive open playa on the right. The playa has been graded to give local plants a chance to heal the mining scars, so do not drive on it. Park and walk the Crater loop instead; it is only 0.6 mile and almost level.

Crater's mood is strangely unsettling. The landscape is subdued and unusually bleak. The ground is nearly white and as blinding as snow. And then there is all the sulfur. Myriad small pieces dot the ground. As soon as you step out of your car you are assaulted by noxious sulfur fumes. In the intense summer heat, this is a closer approximation to hell than to your dreamed vacation spot. The ruins of Crater's last refinery are visible at the east end of the playa, in front of a knoll. Before mining, the playa was a slight circular depression, and it inspired the name of Crater. Walk across it, aiming left of the ruins, to the north end of the trench-like pit that wraps around the knoll (see map). The pit's outer walls are quite colorful, light gray and topped with red and yellow bluffs. The ground is littered with cobbles and small boulders of bright yellow sulfur laced with light-green twirls. Some samples are coated with tiny translucent sulfur crystals.

Just past the east end of the pit, loop back to the ruins of Crater's refinery. This is one of very few ruins of a sulfur retort in the West. The complex metal contraption is a tumbler. It crunched the ore to expose as much sulfur as possible. Next to it, the pointed cylinder that looks like Apollo's Command and Service Module is the retort. In operation, it stood upright on three legs, nose down. It was loaded with sulfur ore and high-pressure steam was injected into it. The refractory bricks lining its inner wall provided thermal insulation. Sulfur has a low melting point; it was liquefied while other rocks remained solid. Pure molten sulfur was then drawn off through one of the openings at the bottom of the retort. Samples of refined sulfur are still lying around. Other equipment includes water tanks, the boiler that generated the steam, and the charred remains of the ore chute that delivered the ore.

After completing your loop walk, drive or walk 0.3 mile up the road to the ghost town of Crater, at the next road junction. Most of the cabins have collapsed into piles of bleached lumber. When I last visited in 2008, the only standing structures were a water tank, a one-of-a-kind two-door cooler, and a curious dugout—perhaps the only house in the country with chunks of sulfur in its walls!

The El Captan Mine. Mercury mines are a rarity. The El Captan Mine was the largest producer in the Death Valley region, which makes it even more of a rarity. First discovered as a sulfur deposit in 1952, it remained unexploited until 1966 when mercury was accidentally uncovered while digging for sulfur. The following year, the property and its mill in Tehachapi were acquired by the El Captan Mercury Company. Between January 1968 and May 1970 it produced 260,000 pounds of mercury worth about $1.5 million. The mine shut down in 1971 after the price of mercury dropped below $4 per pound.

Crater		
	Dist.(mi)	Elev.(ft)
Big Pine Road	0.0	5,230
Crater Mine (leave road)	0.05	5,215
Crater Mine pit	(~0.3)	~5,210
Crater	0.4	~5,300
El Captan Mine (tunnel)	2.8	6,410
Glory hole	3.2	6,485

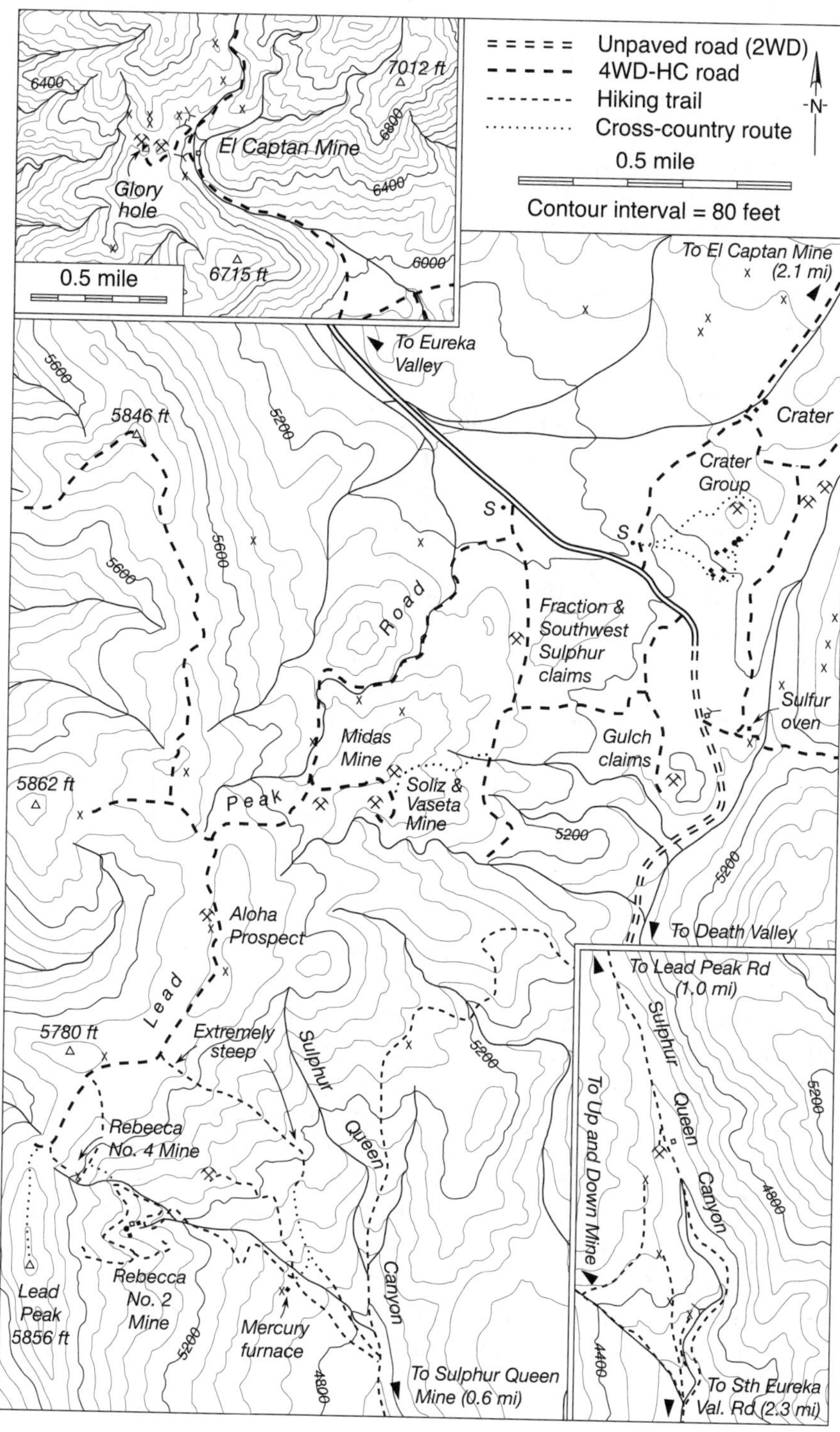
Unpaved road (2WD)
4WD-HC road
Hiking trail
Cross-country route
N
0.5 mile
Contour interval = 80 feet
El Captan Mine
Glory hole
7012 ft
6715 ft
6400
6800
6000
0.5 mile
To El Captan Mine (2.1 mi)
To Eureka Valley
Crater
Crater Group
5846 ft
5600
5200
Road
Fraction & Southwest Sulphur claims
Gulch claims
Sulfur oven
Midas Mine
Soliz & Vaseta Mine
5862 ft
Peak
Aloha Prospect
Lead
To Death Valley
5780 ft
Extremely steep
Sulphur Queen Canyon
Rebecca No. 4 Mine
Rebecca No. 2 Mine
Lead Peak 5856 ft
Mercury furnace
To Sulphur Queen Mine (0.6 mi)
4800
To Lead Peak Rd (1.0 mi)
To Up and Down Mine
To Sth Eureka Val. Rd (2.3 mi)
4400

To get to the El Captan Mine, from Crater drive north on the same road 1.4 miles to a Y junction and bear left. This high-clearance road soon angles west into a narrow gulch. The mine is 1 mile past the Y junction. Perhaps only a desert lover will find beauty in this unadorned landscape of tumbled rocks and gnarled Joshua trees enclosed by low hills. The main workings are on the west side of the road. The first one, by far the largest, was the main producer. For a small mine, its proportions are remarkable. Its long inclined tunnel shoots 800 feet straight underground. The short side road just past it on the left climbs to a 300-foot long, sheer-walled trench and a gaping shaft past it that drops 120 feet to the end of the tunnel. The shaft's opening was widened into a glory hole to generate additional ore, which was simply tossed down the shaft and trucked out of the tunnel. Be extremely careful, as the glory hole has vertical, crumbly walls.

In this alchemist's lair that produced liquid metals and burning stones, one expects extraordinary things. The wild collection of minerals exposed at El Captan certainly fits the bill. The trench's distorted walls are crusted with dark-red cinnabar—mercury sulfide. The shaft goes straight down a breccia pipe. Cinnabar smears its walls like dried blood on a giant carotid. Adjoining prospects still contain as much as 10 pounds of quicksilver per ton. The second tunnel north bores through flaky, light-cream jasper. Near the end of the road, tailings sparkle with brown crystals of silicified dolomite. Elsewhere there is calcite, gypsum, hematite, alunite, and opaline. One of the workings contains translucent rocks filled with rare realgar—arsenic sulfide. In the beam of a flashlight they transmit an ethereal pink glow, but if taken out into the sunlight their magical radiance withers and dies.

The Gulch and Fraction sulfur mines. To get to the Gulch claims, take the side road 0.1 mile east of the pass on the south side. After 300 yards, the road splits; the left fork ends in 0.2 mile at the Gulch claims' pit. For the Fraction and Southwest Sulphur claims, take the side road 0.25 mile west of the pass and follow it 0.25 mile south to the mine's slender trench. At both sites, sulfur is ubiquitous: the ground is peppered with small pieces of it, and bright yellow outcrops line the walls of the pits. The Gulch ore contained a high percentage of crystalline sulfur. The light-gray inclusions locked in the sulfur are pieces of the original breccia pipe within which the deposit was formed. A short walk from the Big Pine Road (see map) will take you to the mine's old three-compartment oven. In use in the 1930s, it is an exceedingly rare piece of mining equipment, and perhaps the area's most interesting.

■

LEAD PEAK

The Lead Peak area, just south of Crater, has something to offer for everyone. Four-wheelers will enjoy the tortuous road to the vicinity of the peak and its spectacular views of Eureka Valley. From there hikers can tackle the short peak climb, descend a precipitous old road to a well-preserved mercury mine camp, push on into a colorfully banded canyon to a small sulfur mine, or continue down the sulfur-smelling wash to the South Eureka Valley Road near the dunes.

General Information

Jurisdiction: Death Valley National Park
Road status: Access by rough road (HC/4WD); roadless beyond
Lead Peak: 2.1 mi, 730 ft up, 50 ft down one way/easy
Rebecca No. 2 Mine: 1.0 mi, 800 up, 350 ft down one way/easy–moder.
Sulphur Queen M.: 1.5 mi, 1,330 ft up, 30 ft down one way/easy–mod.
Main attractions: Easy peak climb, panoramas, mines and camps
USGS 7.5' topo map: Hanging Rock Canyon
Maps: pp. 73*, 83, 61

Location and Access

Lead Peak is the long, razor-sharp summit bordering the east side of Eureka Valley a few miles north of the dunes. The easiest approach is from Crater at the crest of the Last Chance Range, where the Lead Peak Road ascends to within a quarter of a mile of Lead Peak. From Eureka Valley, drive the Big Pine Road 4.7 miles east of the South Eureka Valley Road to a primitive road on the right side. If you reach the pass, you have gone 0.25 mile too far. Drive this road 120 yards to a fainter road on the right, which is the Lead Peak Road.

Route Description

The Lead Peak Road. This road first follows the windy course of a shallow gulch, then climbs steeply out of it to the high spine of the Last Chance Range overlooking Eureka Valley. It then traces this ridge, roughly southward, to within a short distance of Lead Peak. In the gulch this road has a high crown of vegetation, but it can be negotiated with a run-of-the-mill sub-compact car. However, the grade up to the ridge is quite steep and requires either a four-wheel drive or good legs.

This road passes by several small mercury prospects. Part way up the grade, a short road cuts east to the three 30-feet deep, 150-foot long trenches of the Midas Mine and the Soliz and Vaseta Mine. They explored a low-grade sulfur, mercury, hematite, and gold deposit in fractured Zabriskie Quartzite. The next one is the Aloha Prospect, on the open ridge. Its shallow 100-foot trench shows traces of cinnabar in shale and quartzite, and a little onyx. The Rebecca No. 4 Prospect, near the end of the road, has a 100-foot open cut. These mines are small, and only geology-oriented minds are likely to find them of interest. For lay-people, the main reward is the expansive views from the ridge over Eureka Valley to the west and a colorful canyon to the east. In the late spring and summer the area is graced with striking wildflowers, from scented cryptantha to phacelia, globemallow, Indian paintbrush, purple owl's clover, and many others.

Lead Peak. The first hike in this vicinity is the peak climb. From the end of the road just climb the ridge southward. Although this route involves a little scrambling, it is very short (0.25 mile, 110 feet up) and deserves a special award for providing such spectacular views at the cost of so little effort! The local rock is quartzite of the Carrara Formation and Zabriskie Quartzite, approximately 510 million years

Lead Peak

	Dist.(mi)	Elev.(ft)
Lead Peak Road (drive)		
Big Pine Road	0.0	5,155
Jct with Lead Peak Road	~0.1	5,180
Midas Mine Jct	0.8	5,540
Midas Mine	(0.2)	~5,500
Crest/Road junction	1.1	5,740
Trail to Sulphur Queen Mine	1.5	5,740
End of road	1.85	5,740
Lead Peak (hike)	(0.25)	5,856
Rebecca Mine and Sulphur Queen Canyon (hike)		
Trail to Sulphur Queen Mine	0.0	5,740
Junction to Rebecca No. 2 Mine	0.6	4,940
Rebecca No. 2 Mine Camp	(0.4)	5,290
Canyon wash	0.8	4,740
Sulphur Queen Mine cabin	1.5	4,435
Canyon mouth	3.3	3,540
South Eureka Valley Road	4.6	2,900

Mining camp and mill at the Rebecca Mine

old. Along the ridge the quartzite layers have been upturned and eroded into natural stairways. From the narrow peak the land falls off abruptly to the west, down to eerie badlands drained by serpentine canyons 2,000 feet below, as black as if they had been torched. Eureka Valley sprawls beyond, framed by the high Inyo Mountains and a fringe of the high Sierra. To the south, the scenery is dominated by the colorfully banded Last Chance Range, the crisp outline of the Eureka Dunes, and the somber volcanic mass of the Saline Range.

The Rebecca No. 2 Mine. This mercury mine, hidden in a crease of Lead Peak, is a small gem. A road goes partway to it, starting in the left bend 0.35 mile north of the end of the Lead Peak Road. To call it a road is an exaggeration. It is nothing more than a bladed track, rocky and canted, that plunges down a 40% ridge and ends at a washout. It is closed to vehicles: even if you made it down you might have to abandon your car at the bottom! Hike down the road 0.4 mile to the washout, then down a wash 0.15 mile, and cut southwest 100 yards to a road junction marked by an interesting mercury furnace. The camp is 0.4 mile up the leftmost road. There are shorter routes near the end of the Lead Peak Road (see map), but they are even steeper...

The camp's modest plywood cabin is the most impeccably kept backcountry cabin I have come across. It is furnished with a bed, shelves, cabinets, a table and chairs. The owner obviously left with the intention to return. Next to it are a ramshackle tool shed, an elevated water tank, and a few mining implements. Like many local mines, this was a latecomer that employed only one or two men, ran on a shoestring budget for a time, and became idle in the 1980s.

The ore is cinnabar-stained quartzite with traces of gold. It was extracted from trenches further up the slope, then crushed to a half-inch size and screened. Two of the screens are still there; one of them is a curious homemade contraption vibrated with an electric motor. The ore was then roasted in the brick furnace just west of the cabin. This is a rare and well-preserved structure, still topped with its two slender smokestacks. The two low concrete tanks next to the large screen may have been used to extract gold with cyanide.

Sulphur Queen Canyon. The last segment of this hike drops along Sulphur Queen Canyon east of Lead Peak to the South Eureka Valley Road (4.0 miles). From the Rebecca No. 2 Mine, follow the steep grade below the camp down to the wash of Sulphur Queen Canyon, passing by the mercury brick furnace, then continue down the road in the wash. This is not the most spectacular spot on Earth, but it is wild and remote, and there is a road, now closed to motor vehicles, most of the way. Comparatively wide and shallow, the canyon is dominated by the colorfully banded Carrara Formation, a Cambrian mixture of blue-gray limestone, light-green to brown shale, sandstone, and quartzite. After 1.3 miles you will reach the Sulphur Queen Mine. Until the 1990s a good-size cabin stood on the canyon's east bank. The relentless local winds have now reduced it to a heap of lumber. The 80-foot open cut across the wash was the mine's only substantial working. Active mostly prior to the 1950s, it produced only a little sulfur. The cut exposes low-grade sulfur and gypsum. The other workings, 0.4 mile down canyon, are shallow and uninteresting exploratory trenches.

The rest of Sulphur Queen Canyon slices through a colorful mosaic of older Cambrian rocks, from cavernous limestone spurs to rust-stained bluffs and wrinkled outcrops of yellow and green mudstone. The wash is littered with pieces of sulfur that fell off the Sulphur Queen Mine trucks. Decades later, their strong smell still permeates the air. Down to the canyon mouth the road is largely gone; it resumes on the fan, where it bounces down to the South Eureka Valley Road, 6.0 miles south of the Big Pine Road. This final stretch commands beautiful views of Eureka Valley, from the lonesome dome of Saline Peak to the Eureka Dunes and the sand-dusted Saline Range to the west.

■

THE UP AND DOWN MINE

This exciting loop hike follows an abandoned mining road half way up the Last Chance Range, through eerie narrows and sculpted badlands of black shale, to the Up and Down Mine and two other mercury mines. The ore and geology are unusual, the views of Eureka Valley from the high road absolutely breathtaking, and the mine's surreal retorts rank among the most interesting cultural remains in Eureka Valley.

General Information

Jurisdiction: Death Valley National Park
Road status: Roadless; hiking on old road closed to motorized traffic
Up and Down Mine: 2.3 mi, 1,620 ft up, 70 ft down one way / moderate
Mercury Knob Prospect: 3.8 mi, 2,130 ft up, 670 ft down one way / moder.
April Fool Prospect: 2.3 mi, 1,350 ft up, 30 ft down one way / moderate
Up and Down Mine loop: 8.6 mi, 2,560 ft up loop / difficult
Main attractions: Mercury mines and camp, panoramas, geology, trail
USGS 7.5' topo map: Hanging Rock Canyon
Maps: pp. 83*, *61*

Location and Access

The Up and Down Mine is located high on the western slope of the Last Chance Range, north of the Eureka Dunes. It was once reached from the South Eureka Valley Road by a four-wheel-drive road that climbed up a short canyon to the mine and returned down a different canyon. Today, long segments of this road are washed out, and the road is closed to motorized traffic. To see the mine you will have to walk. The north end of the road is 3.45 miles south of the Big Pine Road, on the east side. This end is very faint. It used to be right across from the road to the dry well. Look for that road instead: it is easier to spot. The south end of the road is 1.5 miles further south. It is clearly visible climbing the fan east to the Last Chance Range.

There are several ways to hike to the Up and Down Mine. You can start from either end of the mining road and return the same way. The northern route, though mostly cross-country, is the fastest: it takes a short day. Alternatively, you can hike the whole road and loop back along the South Eureka Valley Road. Including visits to all three mines, this loop takes a full day. The following section describes the loop hike starting from the northern end of the road.

Route Description

The northern approach. From the South Eureka Valley Road, hike up the fan west-northwest towards a low knoll at the foot of the range, three quarters of a mile away, crossed by a visible segment of the old road. Up to this knoll the road is completely gone. At the knoll the road resumes, climbs east across it to the mouth of a canyon, and ends on the edge of the canyon wash. The rest of the way is up the wash.

Together with its three southern neighbors, this relatively narrow canyon holds truly unique scenery. For half a mile it cuts through rare badlands nearly black in color, as if the sun had baked them to charcoal. The rock that created this stark landscape is shale of the Perdido Formation, about 340 million years old. Shale this dark is rare in the region, but here it makes up a whole mountainside. In spite of its darkness, this is a colorful canyon, relieved by white quartzite boulders in the wash and the brilliant ochres of the sheer bluffs looming high above it. You will pass by the mining property gate, hanging road segments blasted into the walls, soft flows of crumbly shale, and a water tank stranded in the wash. The road resumes shortly below the tank (0.3 mile into the canyon), on the north side of the wash. After a few steep curves it tops a high bench above the shale exposure and reaches the Up and Down Mine.

The Up and Down Mine. The first remains are two small plywood cabins, united by a shady veranda and nestled in a small roadside opening. In the main cabin, a shelf protected by wire mesh still holds salt, tea bags, rancid oil, and peanut butter baked solid by the heat. Vandalism has taken its toll, but the cabins are still standing, thanks, in no small measure, to the road closure.

The mine had two retorts, erected 200 yards south of the cabin, and they are guaranteed to set off your sensory overload. In seconds you will be confronted with both the most curious mining remains in Eureka Valley and breathtaking views of the valley. The smaller retort is precariously balanced on the edge of the bench, overlooking Eureka Valley. The long metal box in its corrugated-metal shed is a rotary furnace. Its role was to heat the crushed mercury ore and liberate mercury as vapor. The electric motor that rotated the furnace for uniform heating, the drive chain, gauges, insulation, electrical switches and wiring are all in place. The array of vertical pipes just outside the shed is a condenser. Air circulating around the pipes cooled the vapor to liquid mercury, which dripped into the metal trough under the far end of the pipe. The main retort, 200 feet east, is larger and even more striking. Except for its rotary furnace, all of it—ore screen, hopper, catwalk, lad-

One of the two mercury retorts at the Up and Down Mine

der, and the fantastic organ pipes of the condenser—was welded from scrap metal. They are the brainchild of a forgotten miner, both a master welder and a talented sculptor, whose legacy bespeaks silently of his struggles against nature.

There is something disconcerting about this site, an almost palpable strangeness. These extraordinary objects on display in the middle of nowhere add a surreal dimension to the land and create an illusionistic scene. In an eerie way they amplify the absence of life and the stillness of the space. They put you face to face with your own isolation. If you stay put long enough, you will hear the silence.

Just past the main plant the road climbs by a short tunnel and a small open cut above it. There are larger open cuts further up the road, but this one has the best exposures of cinnabar—dark red masses in pale brecciated quartzite from the Wood Canyon Formation. Here as at Crater, the mercury was delivered by hydrothermal solutions that rose through a breccia pipe and filled its fractures with metals. Hematite and limonite (iron ore), gypsum, alunite, and apatite are also exposed. Although it has no known production, the Up and Down Mine may well have yielded a fair amount of quicksilver: its sizable workings still contain up to 10 pounds of mercury per ton. If you harbor any illusion about the joys of mining, read the hand-written notes left in the cabin by J. A. Johnson, who worked here in the 1970s. They recount in vivid details his hardship, from fruitless gold panning to failed retorting runs and endless maintenance of the furnaces.

The high road. The road continues south for 1 mile, nearly level, teetering high on an exposed bench of brilliant earth tones. The scenery alone makes this hike. Just below the road, the entire mountainside is a steep exposure of black shale carved into a fairyland of sharp, pointed ridges and twisted canyons, oddly refractory to sunlight. Two thousand feet below, the dark hills merge into the blinding emptiness of Eureka Valley, framed in the far distance by the majestic Inyo Mountains. You may have, as I did, a hard time resisting the temptation to forget the road, the mines, the desert light, and to drop along one of the enticing canyons into this nightmarish landscape.

The Mercury Knob Prospect. At a ridge crossing just before the road descends to the valley, a dim road drops west into a wide ravine. In 250 yards it reaches the ruins of two cabins, now wall-less floorboards piled deep with broken appliances. Originally known as the Mercury Knob Prospect, this site was later relocated as the Storm Cloud claims. Its 30-foot deep open cut and short tunnel are just a little further. They show traces of turquoise, plus a little chrysocolla, wavellite, and cinnabar. Mining fixtures are few but worth searching for. My favorite was an ingenious crusher custom-made with a cut-off oil barrel, a washing-machine door, and an electric motor.

The Up and Down Mine

	Dist.(mi)	Elev.(ft)
South Eureka Valley Road	0.0	2,990
Canyon mouth	1.15	3,620
Up and Down Mine (retorts)	2.3	4,540
Junction (to Eureka Prospect)	3.05	4,740
Eureka Prospect	(0.45)	~5,100
Jct to Mercury Knob Prospect	3.25	4,620
Mercury Knob's last open cut	(0.5)	4,450
Jct to April Fool Prospect	3.55	4,310
April Fool's (third trench)	(0.25)	4,340
Top of narrows	3.9	3,980
Bottom of narrows/falls	4.4	3,600
South Eureka Valley Rd	5.6	2,915
Back to starting point	7.1	2,990

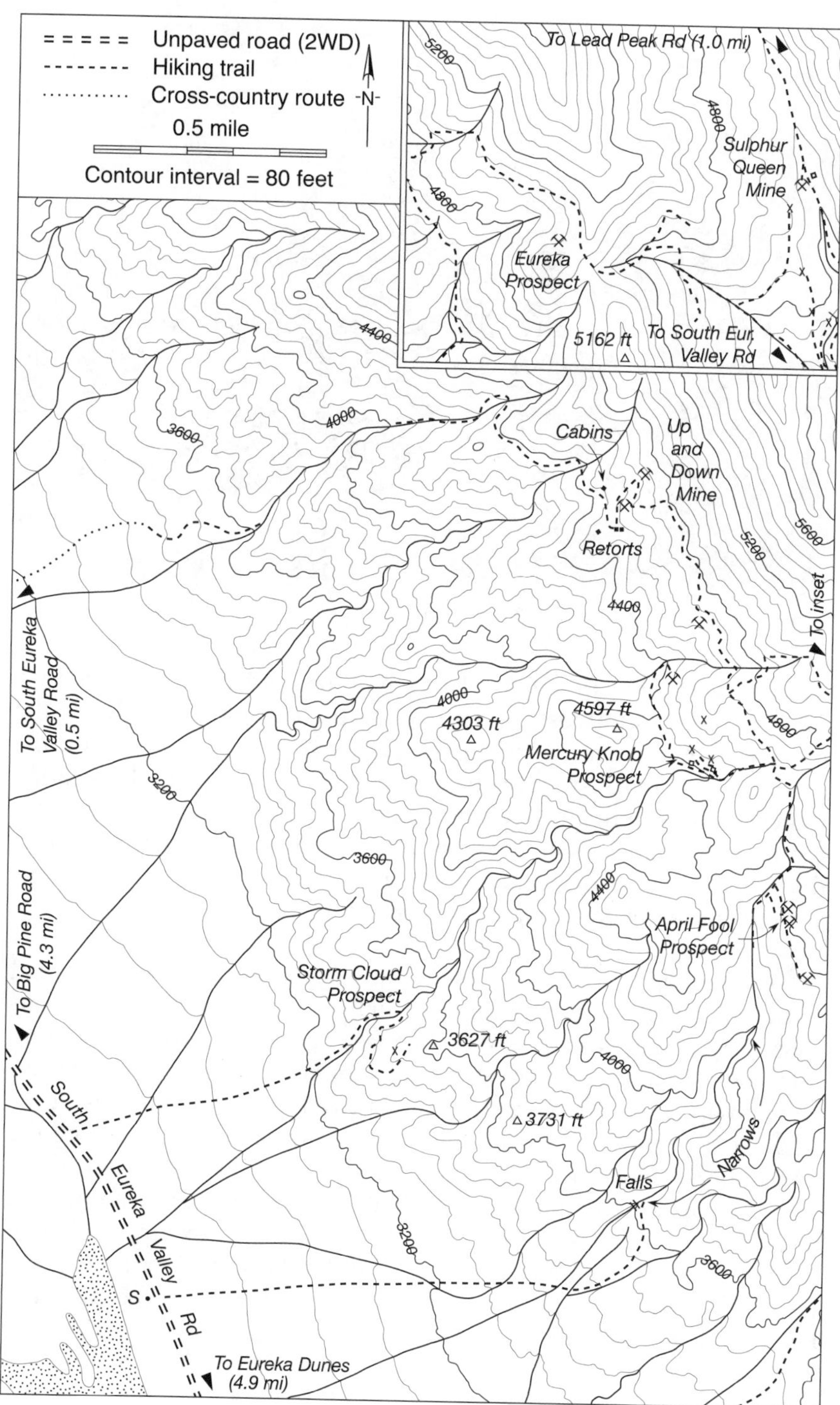

Unpaved road (2WD)
Hiking trail
Cross-country route
N
0.5 mile
Contour interval = 80 feet
To Lead Peak Rd (1.0 mi)
Sulphur Queen Mine
Eureka Prospect
5162 ft
To South Eur. Valley Rd
Cabins
Up and Down Mine
Retorts
To inset
To South Eureka Valley Road (0.5 mi)
4303 ft
4597 ft
Mercury Knob Prospect
April Fool Prospect
To Big Pine Road (4.3 mi)
Storm Cloud Prospect
3627 ft
3731 ft
Narrows
Falls
South Eureka Valley Rd
S
To Eureka Dunes (4.9 mi)
5200
4800
4400
4000
3600
3200
5600

Black-shale badlands below the Up and Down Mine

The April Fool Prospect. This small mercury mine is located 0.3 mile further (southwest) along the main road, part way down the canyon that funnels the road back to the valley. A side road on the south side wavers steeply up and down past its three long open trenches. None of them shows very much cinnabar, which may explain the mine's tongue-in-cheek name. Interesting mining equipment was discarded below the workings and further down the road, including a jaw crusher, early gas refrigerators, and stone-age heaters.

The southern exit route. Below the April Fool Prospect the road continues down canyon to the final highlight: a half-mile strip of narrows snaking between low walls of limestone and quartzite. All along this angular corridor, flashfloods have dumped piles of rocks and completely wiped out the road. The canyon walls and the boulders in the wash bear ripple marks from the Early Cambrian ocean in which the limestone (Wood Canyon Formation) was deposited. At their lower end, the narrows are abruptly terminated by two impressive polished falls that cascade back-to-back about 50 feet down to the upper edge of the fan. The road resumes at the head of the falls. It curves widely to the south to bypass them, reaches the foot of the range, and crosses the fan 0.9 mile to the South Eureka Valley Road.

■

THE EUREKA DUNES

> *If I had to choose one place to show a friend how beautiful the Great Basin is, I might well pick the Eureka Dunes. Towering more than 650 feet above pristine Eureka Valley, framed by surreal desert ranges, they are a desert fantasy. Climbing the Eureka Dunes' spellbinding mountain of sand or crossing the extensive southern dunes are unique experiences you will remember for years.*

General Information

Jurisdiction: Death Valley National Park
Road status: Roadless; easy access from graded road
Sand mountain: 1.3 mi, 670 ft up, 0 ft down one way/moderate
Southern dunes: ~7.0 mi, ~1,500 ft up loop/difficult
Main attractions: Spectacular high dunes in a remote desert valley
USGS 7.5' topo maps: Hanging Rock Canyon, Last Chance Range SW*
Maps: pp. 89*, *61*

Location and Access

The Eureka Dunes are nestled in the shallow basin at the south end of Eureka Valley. To get there, from the Big Pine Road drive the South Eureka Valley Road 9.8 miles to the small campground at the northwest corner of the dunes. Standard-clearance vehicles can usually make this graded road without difficulty. Being closest to the highest dunes, this starting point is a favorite among hikers. You can also drive and start hiking from further along this road, which circumvents the east side of the dunes. This road is usually sandy, as well as muddy after a rainstorm, and at times it requires a four-wheel drive.

Natural History

Like most dunes in the region, the Eureka Dunes are located in a dry lake bed, near the bottom of a valley that has no outlet to the sea. They were formed after the shallow lake that filled Eureka Valley dried up at the end of the Pleistocene. All that is left of the lake today is Eureka Dry Lake, the small playa northwest of the dunes.

Unique for their striking beauty, the Eureka Dunes are also special in many other ways. Some 670 feet high, they are the tallest sand dunes in the Great Basin. No one knows why they are so high. By preventing the sand from spreading out, the relatively abundant plants that live on the dunes may help them to stay that way. How does the

Long rippled slope down the side of the sand mountain

vegetation get its water? Although they do not look like it, compared to most dunes the Eureka Dunes are wet. Being close to the Last Chance Range, they receive some of the moisture captured by these high mountains and have stored a huge reserve of water. It is this underground water which, as it slowly percolates to the surface, feeds the plants.

The Eureka Dunes are home to over 50 species of plants, including common dune vegetation like creosote and indigo bush. Three of these species are so rare that they live on these few square miles of sand and nowhere else on Earth. One endemic is a species of locoweed that bears striking white and purple flowers. The Eureka evening primrose, more rare, blooms only in the spring after a wet winter, producing large, white showy flowers. The third and most common endemic is the Eureka Valley dune grass (*Swallenia alexandrae*), uniquely adapted to survival in shifting sands. It is an ancient plant whose closest relatives are found in the Mediterranean region. Its range has shrunk considerably: it is believed to be a relict of the sub-tropical grasslands that covered western North America more than 20 million years ago, which was then much wetter. But it has beautifully adapted to this dry, sandy environment, in part by growing rapidly between March and November to keep from becoming buried by drifting sand, in part by having spiny leaves to reduce evaporation and for protection against herbivores. It is one of the easiest local endemics to locate: you will find it growing at the top of small sand hummocks on the unstable upper slopes of the dunes.

The fauna is as unusually rich as the flora. Dozens of species of birds and mammals, nine species of reptiles, and countless species of insects, including four endemic beetles, inhabit the dunes. Most of the mammals are rodents, like the kangaroo mouse and rat, which have adapted to the hot and arid dune environment by living in burrows and metabolizing their own water from fats. Rodents prefer to burrow in the sheets of sand surrounding the dunes. At places the density of burrows is so high that it is almost impossible to walk without breaking through the sand. If you run into one of these rodent condos, turn around and look for another way through—no need to force the little creatures to remodel.

Another unusual feature of the Eureka Dunes is that they are one of the very few booming dunes in North America. When sand blown over the crest of a dune exceeds the angle of repose, it slips down the slope in an avalanche. The flowing sand produces a low humming vibration that has been compared to the sound of an airplane or a bass viol. The noise is thought to be generated by the grains of sand rubbing against each other in a coherent fashion. However, it is not clear what determines the low frequency of the boom. One thing is clear: the sound itself, which is unmistakable.

Topographic maps show that back in the 1950s, the Eureka Dunes were 40 feet taller than they are today. Although this could be the result of erroneous mapping or natural evolution, another possible explanation is human abuse. Up until the late 1970s, the dunes were occasionally assaulted by dune buggies, motorcycles, and even trucks, which slowly broke down the high points and killed the plants that hold the sand together. Half a century after the off-road ban, the highest dune has grown back 20 feet. Since this area is bound to witness increasing visitation, unruly foot traffic may ultimately cause the same problems. Tread lightly on the dunes: walk on the stronger ridges, and stay away from unstable steep slopes and plants. No sand boarding or skiing is allowed.

Route Description

As you approach the Eureka Dunes along the road, they rise tall and sharp above the flat valley floor, shimmering white and strangely delicate against the background of rugged desert mountains. The contrast between sand and the spectacularly banded range is stunning. When you reach their base you realize they are not really dunes but a mountain of sand, hundreds of feet high. The north face is truly a sand wall, chiseled by the wind into long arcuate ramps that snake up gracefully to the keen edge of the distant summit. In the winter, the ranges are sometimes covered with snow, and the mind struggles to adjust to yet another incongruous element.

The Eureka Dunes cover an oblong area pointing north, about 3.5 miles by 1 to nearly 2 miles wide. The sand mountain occupies roughly the northern half (about 3.2 square miles). The southern half is composed of smaller dunes, and an extensive sheet of sand almost completely surrounds the dunes.

Climbing the sand mountain. The top of the sand mountain is a popular destination. With slopes exceeding 45% at places, the abrupt northern and western walls make uphill progress almost hopeless, and hiking here is visually damaging. Instead, climb the more moderate northwestern ridge. It is still hard going, and slipping one step down for every few steps up is par for the course. The soft sand underfoot, the rhythmic patterns of the dunes, and the shifting horizon all add up to a rare experience. Many imprints are stamped in the sand by the locals—rodents, lizards, snakes, birds, and sometimes larger mammals. In the early morning when the tracks are clearest, it is a delight to follow them up and down hills of sand and try to reconstruct their owners' nocturnal activities.

The sand mountain has four summits, three at about the same elevation, and a fourth one a little lower. The views of the empty valley and desert ranges from the highest ridge are truly awe-inspiring. At the south end of the Eureka Dunes, where the Saline Range and the Last Chance Range converge and the valley floor tapers down to a V, they break down into a sea of basins and swells. The sand seems to flow out of the V, as if the dunes were spawned by the mountain. Bring binoculars to spot the shoreline of the Pleistocene lake northwest of the dunes, and visually explore the Last Chance Range canyons.

The Eureka Dunes

	Dist.(mi)	Elev.(ft)
Road	0.0	2,875
Top of sand mountain	1.3	3,545
Saddle	2.5	3,040
South end of dunes	4.6	~3,000
Return via east or west side	~7.0	2,875

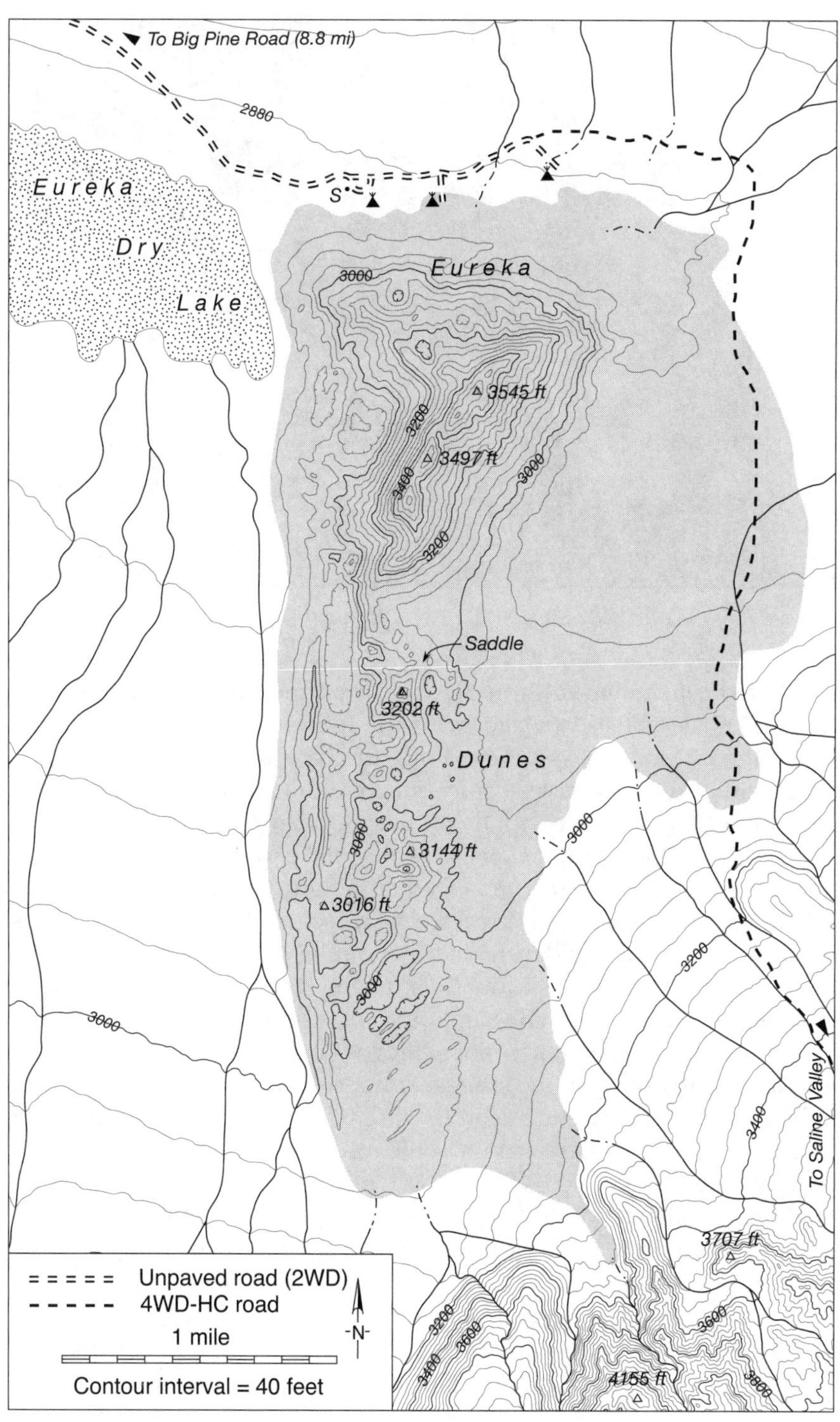
To Big Pine Road (8.8 mi)
2880
Eureka Dry Lake
S
Eureka
3000
3545 ft
3200
3497 ft
3000
3400
3200
Saddle
3202 ft
Dunes
3000
3144 ft
3000
3016 ft
3000
3000
3200
3400
To Saline Valley
3707 ft
3200
3600
3400
4155 ft
3600
3800
Unpaved road (2WD)
4WD-HC road
1 mile
N
Contour interval = 40 feet

The Eureka Dunes in a late afternoon summer storm

The southern dunes. From the fourth summit the sand crest snakes down 500 steep feet to a saddle at the foot of the next tallest dune. From there it is an easy return along the base of the sand mountain, along either the east or west side, but continuing south into the southern dunes is far more exciting. Smaller in height, the southern dunes are oceanic in their proportions, and they make up in grace and magnitude what they lack in stature. Freed of the constraints of canyon walls or abrupt ridges that limit travel to one direction, the landscape invites aimless, unbridled wandering, like swimming in a tropical lagoon. The experience is liberating, intimate, strangely intoxicating. The sunrise side ripples in sensuous ebbs and flows of virgin sand. The sunset side is a two-mile chain of depressions filled with sand, gravel beds, or tiny hardpan of the finest white silt. On either side, the addictive rhythm of hills and swales may entice you to push on to the very southern tip of the dune's field, where it levels off into lazy surges of sand. And everywhere you go, you will almost certainly be alone. Cocooned by high mountains, divorced from the world by sheer distance, the southern dunes embody the closeness and privacy that make the desert so enormously seductive.

■

THE HIDDEN DUNES

When I think of the most isolated places I have visited in this desert, the Hidden Dunes often come to mind first. Besides their stunning beauty, what makes them so tantalizing is that they are hidden in a remote valley far away from any road. To see them up close you will have to take a long walk in Eureka Valley, and even then you will not get to set eyes on them until the last moment. Spread at the foot of a rugged mountain, overlooking an alien landscape of barren ranges, the Hidden Dunes offer stunning views, extreme solitude, and some of the highest and tallest mountains of sand in the park.

General Information
Jurisdiction: Death Valley National Park
Road status: Roadless; access from primitive road
First dune: 3.3 mi, 510 ft up, 10 ft down one way / easy
Highest dune: 5.3 mi, 1,690 ft up, 30 ft down one way / difficult
Main attractions: Valley hike to beautiful remote sand dunes
USGS 7.5′ topo maps: East of Joshua Flats*, Hanging Rock Canyon
Maps: pp. 95*, *61*

Location and Access

The Hidden Dunes are in the southwestern quadrant of Eureka Valley, just below the mouth of Marble Canyon. Tucked against the west side of a low ridge at the tip of the Saline Range, they are largely invisible from much of Eureka Valley, hence the name I gave them. There never was a road to these dunes, but you can get closer to them by driving to the dry well located on the valley floor northwest of the Eureka Dunes. The road to the dry well starts off the South Eureka Valley Road, on the west side, 3.4 miles south of the Big Pine Road (or 6.4 miles north of the Eureka Dunes). It is a little difficult to spot, so slow down and look carefully when you approach it. This primitive road heads west-northwest across the valley 2.35 miles and ends at the dry well. It is usually passable with a standard-clearance vehicle. At the well, another road heads approximately north. This old road is now closed to motorized traffic, so drive back the way you came.

The dry well is marked by a mound of sandy silt, the steel casings of two wells (one clogged with sand), a rusted boiler, and scattered odds and ends. The long spur that extends northward across the valley a few miles to the west is the northern tip of the Saline Range. In this ridge there is a pronounced gap. The sand hill that barely pokes through it is the Hidden Dunes.

Route Description

The approach. The hike to the Hidden Dunes is another pure desert extravaganza. You walk on and on across a level plain of sandy gravel dotted with creosote, aiming straight towards the gap, watching it getting closer painfully slowly. The walking *is* repetitious, but here again the desert has worked overtime to keep us distracted. In all directions the views are magnificent, encompassing most of Eureka Valley and its colorful rim of mountains. Up ahead, the low spur of the Saline Range beckons like a dark gem, a subtle blend of tans and blacks laced with pale veins of sand. Your attention will be drawn to animal tracks, to birds and zebra-tailed lizards dashing between bushes, and to the mosaic patterns of the desert pavement that liberally coats the fan. For me, the most effective distraction was the faceted rocks—a rare signature of the desert. These ventifacts are formed by the action of wind-blown particles on rocks resting on the fan. If the rock remains undisturbed long enough—a few thousand years will usually do—and if the wind direction is constant, the particles eventually etch a smooth facet on the rock. If the prevailing wind direction changes, or if the rock is displaced, perhaps by a careless coyote, a new facet is created. Eureka Valley meets these conditions flawlessly—lots of strong wind, very little rain, and a healthy supply of coyotes. Faceted rocks are exceptionally plentiful. Some specimens have only two facets, usually with a sharp and straight dividing edge. Others have so many that they look like oversized jewels.

The Hidden Dunes. At the far side of the gap, the scenery changes as abruptly as if you had stepped through Alice's mirror. The first dune literally leaps into view, a shining tower of white sand rearing up into the sky at a proud angle. Its narrow summit dominates a fantastic landscape. To the north, a sprawling apron of low sand descends gently to an almost enclosed valley. To the south, a long string of dunes connected by a sharp ridge unfolds in the distance. From end to end, the dune field stretches two and a half miles along the far side of the spur—far more sand than can be explored in a few days.

What makes the Hidden Dunes so special is their exceptional beauty. Long, sinuous, and exquisitely proportioned, they exude a combination of simplicity and elegance matched by few others. At lower elevations they are carpeted with sweeps of yellow grasses sprinkled with globemallow and saltbush. Higher up, the sand is

The Hidden Dunes looking north at Chocolate Mountain

naked and delicately rippled. In the late spring, every single globemallow sprouts dozens of blossoms, and acres of sand are dusted with a bright vermillion haze. Much of the charm of the Hidden Dunes comes also from their unusual setting, right up against a stark desert mountain. In contrast to the mountain, where every rock is dark and angular, the dunes' pale and smooth expanses seem oddly out of place. Herded by strong winds, the sand has migrated far up the mountain, spreading twisted tentacles that infiltrate canyons and overwhelm ridges. But what is perhaps most impressive is the seclusion. Whereas most dunes in the California Desert lie within sight of a road, here the only road is a short segment of the Big Pine Road, nearly 10 miles away and essentially invisible. The isolation is almost palpable. You feel stranded in a lost world, far away from everything.

The most exciting place to explore is the main dunes south of the gap. Past the first dune the land drops into a deep depression rimmed by plunging walls of sand. These smooth slides, free of obstacles, compel us to let loose and jump over the edge, to run down in effortless leaps until we stall at the distant bottom, then run back up the hill, breathless, to do it again, like children in a playground. Just past the depression, where the dunes abut the mountain, the sand drops precipitously into a long and straight corridor, bounded on one side by a wall of pure sand, on the other by hard rock. There, sheltered from the wind, the sand preserves a wealth of tracks, from lizards to rabbits, ravens, coyotes, insects, and even sidewinders. It is so quiet that you can hear the whisper of sand raining down over the crest 100 feet higher. When the wind stops, the only sound is the white noise of silence.

From here on south, the rest of this hike is one blissful discovery after another. The high backbone of the Hidden Dunes winds over to six more main dunes, all of similar elevation. All of it is a breathtaking vantage point overlooking the empty western quarters of Eureka Valley. Walking the thin edge of this long crest, taking in awesome views of denuded mountains and otherworldly peaks, inspires not only a feeling of freedom and exhilaration, but also a deep appreciation of the beauty and significance of this vast desert preserve.

At their south end the dunes curve sharply east and begin an interminable ascent of the steep mountainside. With one thousand feet of elevation gain from bottom to top, this is the tallest sand hill in the region. Its very top, near the crest of the mountain, is crowned by a beautiful dune that holds the distinction of being the region's highest. Reaching this remote landmark has to be the most strenuous workout in sand around Death Valley. For every two steps you climb you slide back down one, and every time you dare look up, the summit is precisely at the same place it was last time you looked. But this is one of the Hidden Dunes greatest and most unique visual rewards. All along the way the bird's-eye views of the surrounding valley and dunes are astounding. Rare are the visitors who venture this deep in the desert. But a few do: at the summit I found, neatly curled on the sand, the most perfect coyote dropping.

A few survival tips... Getting to the dunes is straightforward. So is returning to you car in daylight: the mound at the dry well protrudes

The Hidden Dunes

	Dist.(mi)	Elev.(ft)
Dry well (road)	0.0	2,974
Gap	3.1	3,340
First dune	3.3	3,485
North end of dune field	(0.9)	3,320
Sand depression	3.5	3,356
Highest dune	5.3	~4,570

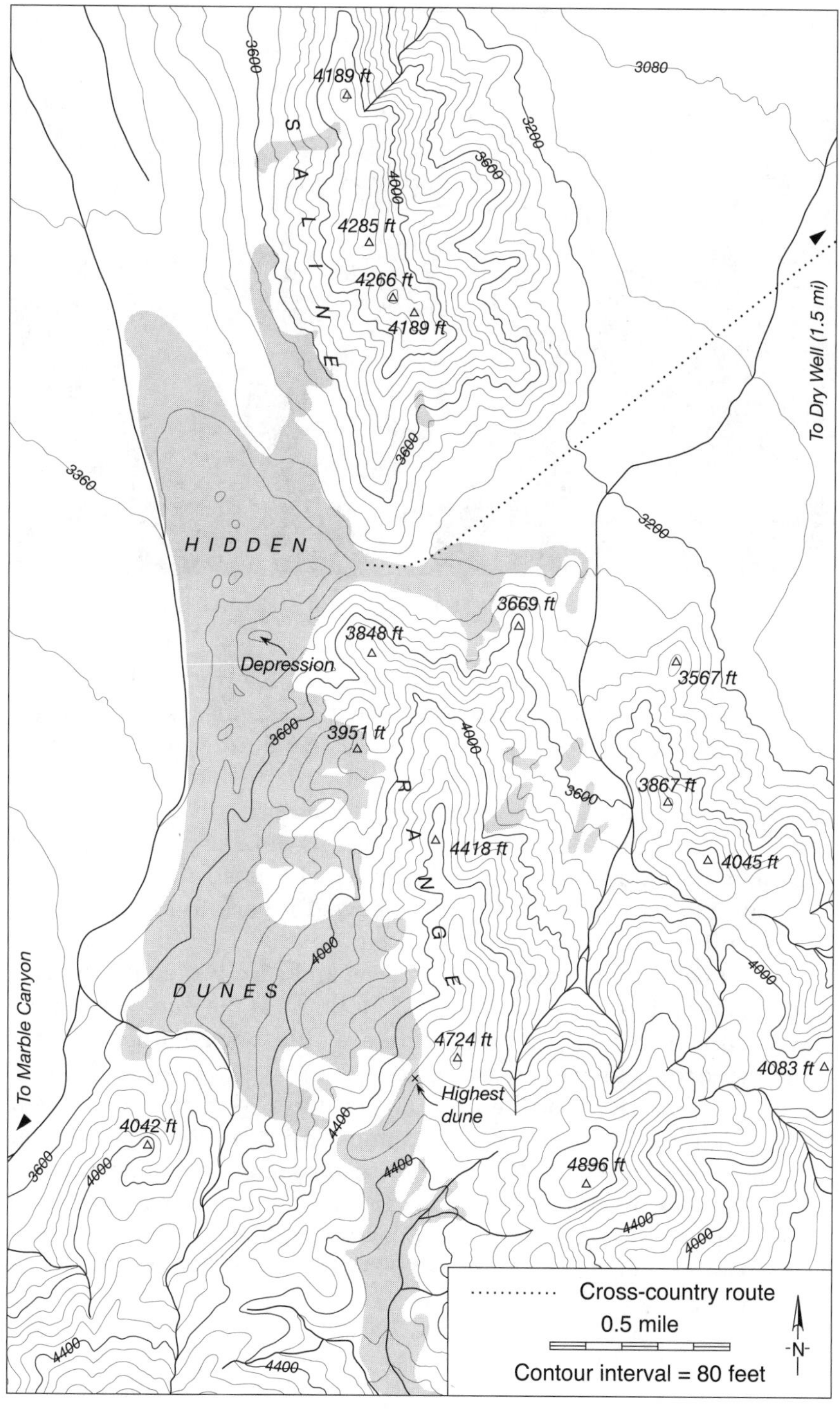

4189 ft
4285 ft
4266 ft
4189 ft
SALINE
RANGE
HIDDEN
DUNES
Depression
3848 ft
3669 ft
3567 ft
3951 ft
3867 ft
4418 ft
4045 ft
4724 ft
4083 ft
Highest dune
4042 ft
4896 ft
3080
3200
3360
3600
4000
4400
To Dry Well (1.5 mi)
To Marble Canyon
Cross-country route
0.5 mile
Contour interval = 80 feet
N

The Hidden Dunes, seen from the mouth of Marble Canyon

above the creosote cover just enough to be visible from as far back as the gap. To be safe, however, on your way to the dunes take your bearings with a compass or a peak in the Last Chance Range. If you do hike back at dark, deliberately aim slightly north, and you will intersect the old access road (the one closed to motorized traffic), which is much easier to find than the well. I put this old trick to the test one moonless night, and thankfully it worked: I missed the well by 800 feet, ran into the road instead, and followed it back to my car (and a long-overdue steak dinner under the stars).

The hike to the Hidden Dunes is level and easy, but it takes a good hour, longer if it is hot. Add three or four hours at the dunes, and your day is full. A two-day overnight hike would not be a bad idea; it would give more time to poke around.

There is no shade at the dunes or on the way there. Unless you have a high tolerance for heat, avoid mid-April to mid-October. If you find the dunes too hot and desperately need shade, seek shelter under one of the rock outcrops in the side canyons a few hundred yards east of the approximate center of the dunes. At midday, the best outcrops create barely enough shade for a whole human body, but this is far better than full sun.

■

THE PIPER ROAD

Whether you enjoy hiking solitary trails, searching for derelict mines, climbing peaks, scaling rock faces, or four-wheeling the Cambrian, you will find something to your liking along this long desert road through the wilderness of northern Eureka Valley.

General Information

Jurisdiction: Piper Mountain Wilderness
Road status: Hiking mostly on trails from primitive road (HC/4WD)
Tule Spring: 1.3 mi, 670 ft up, 10 ft down one way/easy
Sugarloaf Mountain Trail: 1.6 mi, 950 ft up, 0 ft down one way/easy
Piper Peak Trail: 3.0 mi, 1,560 ft up, 140 ft down one way/moderate
Main attractions: Long primitive road, trails, peak climbs, mines
USGS 7.5' topo maps: Soldier Pass, Chocolate Mountain
Maps: pp. 101*, *61*

Location and Access

The Piper Road transects northern Eureka Valley, climbing 14.3 miles from the Big Pine Road on the valley floor north to Gilbert Summit on Highway 168. To get to its south end, drive the Big Pine Road 6.3 miles west of the North Eureka Valley Road, or 1.4 miles east of the prominent bend at the west end of the valley. The Piper Road is the dirt road on the north side. To get to its north end, from Big Pine drive 32.3 miles east on Highway 168 to Gilbert Summit. It will take you over Westgard Pass, then into and out of Deep Springs Valley, a small and wonderfully isolated desert sink. It is best to drive the Piper Road downhill: the canyon is more impressive, and so are the views on the fan. With a standard-clearance vehicle, you can drive from the valley as far up as the Valley View Mine Trail (6.6 miles), or from Highway 168 as far down as the first wash crossing (3.7 miles). It will give you direct or close foot access to all the trails and the canyon. The mid-section requires high clearance, and perhaps four-wheel drive at a few soft wash crossings on the upper fan.

Route Description

The Piper Road. From Eureka Valley the Piper Road climbs the huge fan that floods the northern part of the valley, then slithers up through a hidden canyon to the valley's rim 3,000 feet higher. Roads like this are rare. The whole way it bisects the Piper Mountain

Wilderness, a lonesome and nearly virgin stretch of desert. You will see only a handful of man-made features, mostly forgotten prospect holes dug by hallucinating prospectors in search of illusory treasures. Their only legacy is the road, a crooked accretion of tracks bladed haphazardly over time. Being fairly recent, it is in decent shape and a pleasure to drive, with just enough small challenges to make it fun.

The Piper Road crosses a wide variety of terrains, and it is charged with scenery. Almost any point on the alluvial fan commands magnificent views of all of Eureka Valley, reaching as far south as Dedeckera Canyon. Up ahead, massive Chocolate Mountain rises abruptly, as brown as cocoa, so monolithic that it is hard to believe that the road goes through it. But it does, up a nameless canyon hidden in the mineral folds of the mountain. The canyon is nowhere narrow, but it is lined with impressive slopes. At its deepest you stare up at Piper Peak to the northwest, 2,500 feet higher and less than a mile away. The lower canyon slices through the thick upturned beds of vitreous quartzite and sandstone of the Harkless, Campito, and Saline Valley formations, from the Early Cambrian. They form the scenic low walls of near-vertical strata exposed off and on along the wash. The longest one is 0.6 mile into the canyon, on the east side (Harkless Formation). The strata have peeled off in sheets, exposing an alignment of cleaved surfaces so regular that it looks artificial. The blue-gray outcrops further on are Mule Spring Limestone. At higher elevation the wash tops the deep cleavage between Piper Peak and Sugarloaf Mountain. Swells of monzonite 175 million years old mold the landscape, dusted at their crests with scattered conifers. This is a great desert escapade. The isolation, the deep silence, the cobalt sky, and the pungent smells of desert shrubs compose an exhilarating feast for the senses.

Several remote side roads split off the Piper Road, five on the fan and six in the canyon. The only one open to driving is the Horse Thief Canyon Road. All others are in the Piper Mountain Wilderness and closed to vehicles. This section describes hikes on the most interesting side roads. Soldier Pass Canyon is covered in the next section.

Tule Spring. In Eureka Valley, springs are few and far between. Tule Spring is in fact one of only two on the west side, and you may not want to miss it. The trail to it starts 8.8 miles north of the Big Pine Road, at the third sharp right curve, where the road doubles back on itself. At the tip of the curve, an old road heads northwest to the Eureka Silver No. 4 prospect (its trenches, visible on the hillside to the north, have small exposures of light-brown jasperoid and hematite). Hike this road 200 yards to a faint spur on the left. Follow it 180 yards

Upturned quartzite formation in the nameless canyon along Piper Road

down to the wash of the wide canyon to the west, and continue up this canyon 0.8 mile until you see Tule Spring up on the south slope.

One of the delights of exploring nature is that you never know what you will find. When my cousin Jeff and I trudged up this bone-dry canyon one hot July afternoon, we started doubting the map. This was obviously no place for a spring. The cartographer must have been fantasizing. So when we finally spotted it, we feared a mirage. Yet there it was, an improbable circle of greenery pinned high against the rocky canyon slope. We climbed to it up a low ridge, retracing game tracks. Up there we found a few willows and a patch of cattail surrounded by tall vegetation. The ground was soaked with just enough water to wet my fingertips. A buried pipe delivered water from the spring 200 feet down to a metal tub in the wash. When Tule Spring is in the mood, the tub is full and the largest watering hole for miles around. While we were sitting under the willows, two bats repeatedly came flying as close as two feet from our faces. Moments later, just outside the spring heading back, we triggered the alarm system of a full-grown Mojave rattlesnake. It was coiled under a bush, rattles erect in front of its head. We had missed it by less than 10 feet.

Sugarloaf Mountain. If you drive the Piper Road northbound, Sugarloaf Mountain will be in plain view the whole way: it is the distinct conical peak just east of Piper Peak. From the road a short foot trail spirals 1.4 miles around it almost to its summit. Finding the trail is the only challenge. It starts 2.8 miles north of the road to Tule Spring, or 2.7 miles south of Gilbert Summit, on the east side. A small BLM wilderness boundary sign is posted across it. The trail is wide and easy to follow. It first heads up a gentle shallow wash, then angles right and screams up to a saddle looking over Eureka Valley. At the saddle, the left fork climbs to a small open cut. The short remaining distance to the summit is cross-country up an unstable sandy slope.

This trail wanders through a deep landscape of smooth monzonite hills dotted with big sagebrush, cliffrose, and prince's plume. It passes

The Piper Road

	Dist.(mi)	Elev.(ft)
The Piper Road (drive)		
Big Pine Road	0.0	3,415
Horse Thief Canyon Road	1.3	3,500
Soldier Pass Canyon Trail	5.3	4,145
Valley View Mine Trail	6.6	4,335
Tule Spring trailhead	8.8	4,665
Canyon mouth	~9.3	~4,785
Sugarloaf Mountain Trail	11.6	5,595
Piper Peak Trail	13.8	6,280
Gilbert Summit	14.3	6,374
Tule Spring (hike)		
Piper Road	0.0	4,665
Wash/end of road	0.2	4,730
Climb out of wash	0.95	5,020
Tule Spring	1.25	5,325
Piper Peak Trail (hike)		
Piper Road	0.0	6,280
Divide	1.7	~7,300
Junction with foot trail (right)	2.7	7,370
Piper Peak	3.0	7,703
Sugarloaf Mountain Trail (hike)		
Piper Road	0.0	5,595
First bend/Piper Prospect	0.55	5,845
Dugout	0.8	5,985
Saddle	1.2	~6,170
Sugarloaf Mtn Prosp./end of rd	1.35	6,285
Sugarloaf Mountain	1.6	~6,541

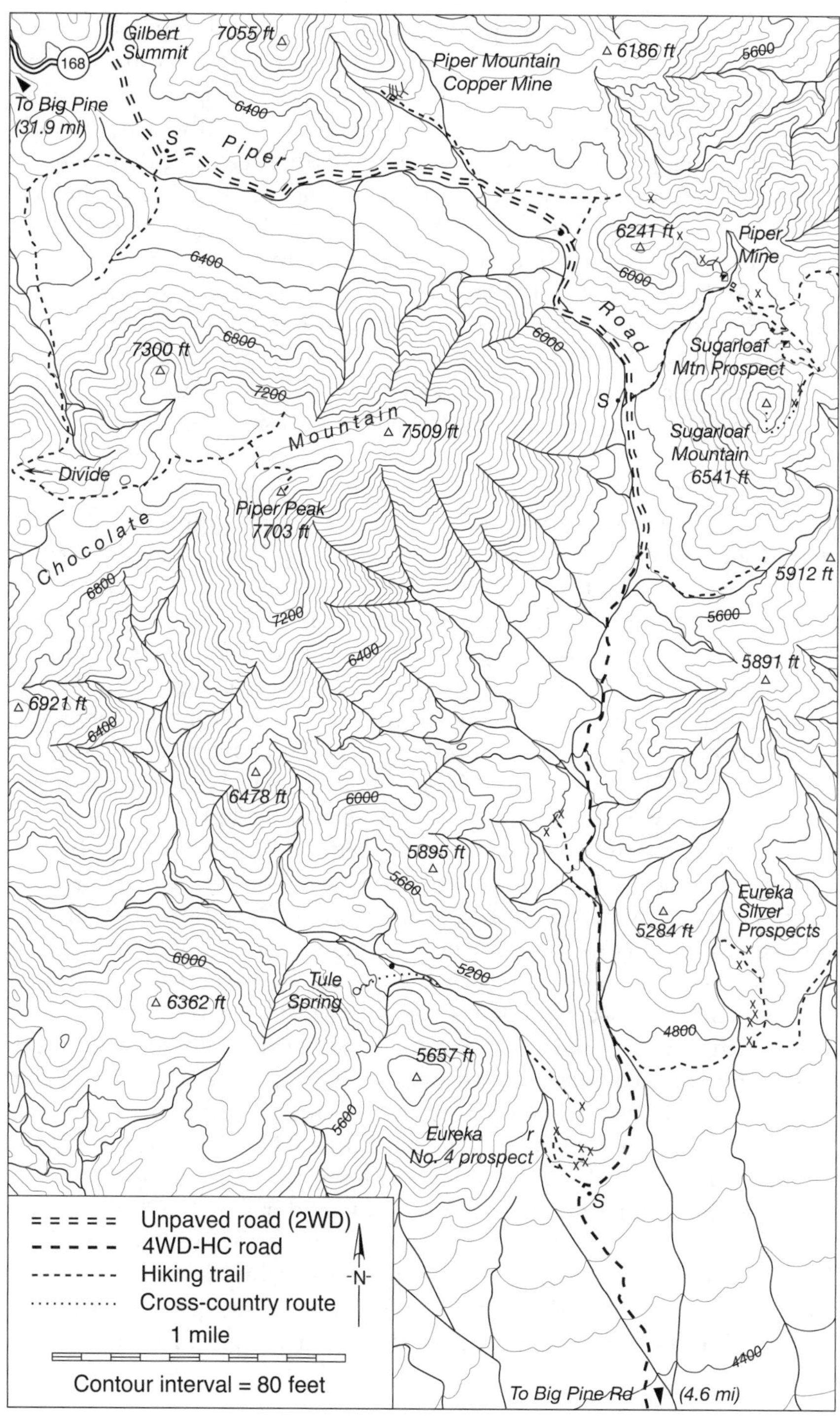
Gilbert Summit
168
To Big Pine (31.9 mi)
7055 ft
Piper Mountain Copper Mine
6186 ft
5600
6400
S
Piper
Road
6241 ft
Piper Mine
6000
Sugarloaf Mtn Prospect
Sugarloaf Mountain 6541 ft
7300 ft
6800
7200
Mountain
7509 ft
Divide
Chocolate
Piper Peak 7703 ft
6800
7200
6400
5912 ft
5600
5891 ft
6921 ft
6478 ft
6000
5895 ft
5600
5284 ft
Eureka Silver Prospects
6000
Tule Spring
5200
6362 ft
4800
5657 ft
5600
Eureka No. 4 prospect
S
Unpaved road (2WD)
4WD-HC road
Hiking trail
Cross-country route
N
1 mile
Contour interval = 80 feet
4400
To Big Pine Rd
(4.6 mi)

by the remains of two small gold and silver mines. The first one is the Piper Mine, in the vicinity of the bend. Its caved 230-foot tunnel and 100-foot shaft, still probed by a long wooden ladder, have been traced back to the early 1880s. The most interesting ruin is the little historic dugout further up the trail, finely constructed with a roughly hewn log beam, rafters, corrugated steel, and stone. The second mine, at the end of the trail, is the Sugarloaf Mountain Prospect. Its tailing contains nice chunks of vuggy quartz and light-blue copper minerals.

For only half the work, you will enjoy views almost as sumptuous as on the Piper Peak Trail. You do not even have to go all the way to the top: the saddle and the last stretch of road past it are almost as good, extending across all of Eureka Valley. The summit offers bonus vistas north to the White Mountains and Fish Lake Valley.

The Piper Peak Trail. The trail to this scenic summit starts off the Piper Road 0.45 mile from Gilbert Summit, on the right side. It is an abandoned mining road built in the 1950s by Huey Stewart, of Big Pine, to access his gold placer claims below Piper Peak. He would load his truck with gold-bearing gravel and take it to Deep Springs College to process it. The ore was so poor that it was not even worth taking it all the way to Big Pine! The trail crosses a typical North American upland steppe, steep rolling hills densely covered with big sagebrush, blackbrush, and ephedra. In summer, their dark foliage is heightened by the bright blossoms of mariposa, grizzly bear cactus, and Indian paintbrush. In winter, the upper trail can be snowed in.

Where the trail tops the spine of Chocolate Mountain, the barren ground is coated with the light-brown chunks of basalt that inspired its name. This divide offers the best views into Deep Springs Valley to the west, including the college and the emerald waters of its neat circular salt lake. The road ends soon after, past Stewart's claim markers. The final 330-foot ascent is on a single-track trail. The trailhead is faint: it is 0.2 mile before road's end, by a small cairn. A few switchbacks climb steeply past scattered juniper to the wind-swept summit. For such a modest peak, it commands an amazing panorama overlooking not one but three Great Basin valleys—Eureka, Deep Springs, and Fish Lake. To the south the view stretches down the full length of Eureka Valley to the Saline Range, Telescope Peak, and beyond. Mile after mile of the magnificent Sierra Nevada scarp claw at the western horizon. The summits furthest apart on the horizon—White Mountain east of Mammoth Lakes and Mount Charleston near Las Vegas—are separated by 170 miles and bookend all of the northern Mojave Desert.

■

SOLDIER PASS CANYON

Soldier Pass Canyon is a short drainage in the Piper Mountain Wilderness that traverses beautiful granitic formations. It provides easy hiking access to an impressive tight passage studded with falls, and to a field of fantastic boulders at the top of the Inyo Mountains, overlooking Deep Springs Valley. Nearby Wyler Canyon is equally scenic. It has crooked narrows, hoodoo rocks, good climbing areas, and the historic cabin and tunnels of a small lead-silver mine.

General Information

Jurisdiction: Piper Mountain Wilderness (BLM)
Road status: Roadless; access via primitive road
Wyler Spring cabin: 3.0 mi, 840 ft up, 10 ft down one way / easy
Deep Sprs. College overlook: 3.6 mi, 1,590 ft, 30 ft down one way / moder.
Main attractions: Scenic granitic canyons, panoramas, climbing, cabin
USGS 7.5' topo map: Soldier Pass
Maps: pp. 107*, *61*

Location and Access

Soldier Pass Canyon starts at a low pass called Soldier Pass on the rim of Deep Springs Valley and cuts eastward across the northern Inyo Mountains into Eureka Valley. All of it is in the Piper Mountain Wilderness. The starting point is the Soldier Pass Canyon Trail, a former mining road now closed to all vehicles. To get to it, drive the Piper Road 5.3 miles north from the Big Pine Road (or 9.0 miles south from Gilbert Summit, which requires high clearance; see *Piper Road*). The trailhead, on the west side, is marked by a small turnout and BLM wilderness signs. Soldier Pass Canyon is the wide opening about 1 mile to the west. The Piper Road is quite smooth up to this point, and a standard-clearance vehicle can usually make it. However, much of it has a crown of vegetation, and if you are concerned about scraping your car's delicate underbelly you may need a high-clearance vehicle.

Route Description

The lower and mid-canyon. The trail and the lower canyon are uneventful, but it takes little time getting to the more interesting mid-canyon. Walking is quite easy: the grade is low and the wash is coarse sand free of large rocks, with little vegetation. The first point of interest is the Eureka Copper Prospect, 0.25 mile past the side canyon from the north. It consists of a 20-foot-tall open cut in the north wall against the wash, reached by a short ramp of dump material. Minerals occur in dislocated quartz veins up to a foot wide. The cut is laced with veinlets of hematite—dark red, black, and metallic gray—chalcopyrite, and bright blue secondary copper ores. Exposures are limited but strikingly colorful against the white quartz.

From Eureka Valley to Deep Springs Valley, this 3-mile-wide spur of the Inyos is made of granitic rock, largely Quartz Monzonite of Beer Creek (150-163 million years old). Soldier Pass Canyon derives much of its scenic appeal (and all of its profusion of sand) from this beautiful intrusive rock, which nature loves fashioning into fanciful forms. Past the prospect, monzonite boulders of all sizes and shapes crowd the hills. The wash narrows gradually as it winds through this ever-changing erosional landscape, occasionally squeezing over low boulder jams. There are quite a few good areas for bouldering. Coyote and bighorn sheep inhabit this remote region, although you are more likely to sight a pair of chukars roosting among the rocks.

Soldier Pass. At an elevation of 5,145 feet, the canyon forks. The main canyon angles north abruptly, away from Soldier Pass, into pretty narrows (described below). The shortest route to the pass is up the steep, boulder-clogged ravine straight ahead (west). Hop the boulders until you have gained about 80 feet of elevation, and look for a tree south of the wash. You cannot miss it: it is the only one around. On the north side of the tree, a trail miraculously materializes. Narrow and faint, marked by a few cairns, it winds up the south side of the ravine to a low knoll of round boulders overlooking Soldier Pass to the south. From here it is a short cross-country walk down to the pass.

Soldier Pass is an unusual place. Defined by a short fault that slashes across the Inyos, it is a long and wide U-shaped saddle, like a glacial valley that never saw a glacier. Densely carpeted with big sagebrush, blackbrush, and ephedra, it dips gently westward into Deep Springs Valley. The lowest point (~5,500 ft) on the valley's rim, it is a mere 300 feet above Deep Springs College.

Deep Springs College overlook. For many hikers, the sprawling crest of the Inyos north of Soldier Pass will be the highlight of this hike. To get there from Soldier Pass, climb back north to the trail and follow it 0.25 mile west, up the side of a short ravine, to its end above a fall at the head of the ravine (see map). Continue cross-country 200 yards west across the crest. Here, on the abrupt edge of the range, you will get a bird's eye view of Deep Springs Valley, from the white shore

The narrows of Soldier Pass Canyon

of its blue lake (in winter/spring) to the high wall of the White Mountains. Down on the valley floor, the mosaic of green fields and scattered cabins of Deep Springs College seem to be just a stroll away.

North of the overlook the crest is a beautiful fairyland of boulders. Finish this hike in style by exploring it a little. Rounded, split, or exfoliated, seemingly cast from thousands of different molds, the boulders are arranged randomly across the subdued relief, like statues in a cluttered artist's den. One can wander for hours across this billowing landscape, on waves of sand decorated with the tall stalks of prince's plume. Cacti dot the scenery, some common, like silver cholla and calico cacti, others fairly rare, like mound and Mojave fishhook cacti. In the evening, the boulders' long shadows add a crisp depth to the land.

To return to Soldier Pass Canyon a different way, arrange for your ambling to take you to the ravine on the east side of the crest, 0.5 mile north of the trail's east end (see map). You can clamber down this very steep boulder-chocked ravine, then explore the narrows below the boulders (see next sub-section). Just remember that if you cannot down-climb the 10-foot fall, you will have to retrace your steps.

The narrows. The upper canyon, north from the fork below Soldier Pass, is the one section you will not want to miss. In seconds you are engulfed in a trench of vertical monzonite walls. The next few hundred yards display an impressive example of nature's artistry. A swath of smooth sand, only 10 feet wide at places, snakes beneath textured rock faces, slender spires, cleaved slabs, and boulders balanced 100 feet overhead. As you ascend through this steep passage, you will need to climb over piled chockstones, polished bedrock, and colossal slabs, which add satisfying small challenges to an otherwise easy hike. The only tricky climb, about halfway through, is a 10-foot fall capped by a spherical chockstone. The holds are huge and the climb may be only a Class 4, but it will stop hikers disinclined to climbing. If you are, try going as far as you can anyway, for the fun of it.

Wyler Canyon. The canyon just south of Soldier Pass Canyon is also well worth checking out. For convenience I refer to it as Wyler Canyon, after the historic name of its spring. To get to it, hike the Soldier Pass Canyon Trail about 1 mile, at which point it closely parallels the wide wash of Soldier Pass Canyon to the left. Look for a side

Soldier Pass Canyon

	Dist.(mi)	Elev.(ft)
Soldier Pass Canyon		
Piper Road / trailhead	0.0	4,145
End of Soldier Pass Cyn Trail	1.3	4,390
Eureka Copper Prospect	2.05	4,710
Fork below Soldier Pass	2.9	5,145
Soldier Pass	(0.35)	~5,500
Deep Sprs. College overlook	(0.7)	~5,720
Narrows (lower end)	2.95	5,200
Narrows (upper end)	3.35	5,575
Wyler Canyon		
Piper Road	0.0	4,145
Side road to Wyler Canyon	1.0	4,400
Canyon wash / end of road	1.3	4,380
Meanders (lower end)	2.0	4,610
Meanders (upper end)	2.4	4,790
Wyler Spring cabin	3.0	4,980
Lipp Prospect (shaft)	3.4	5,155

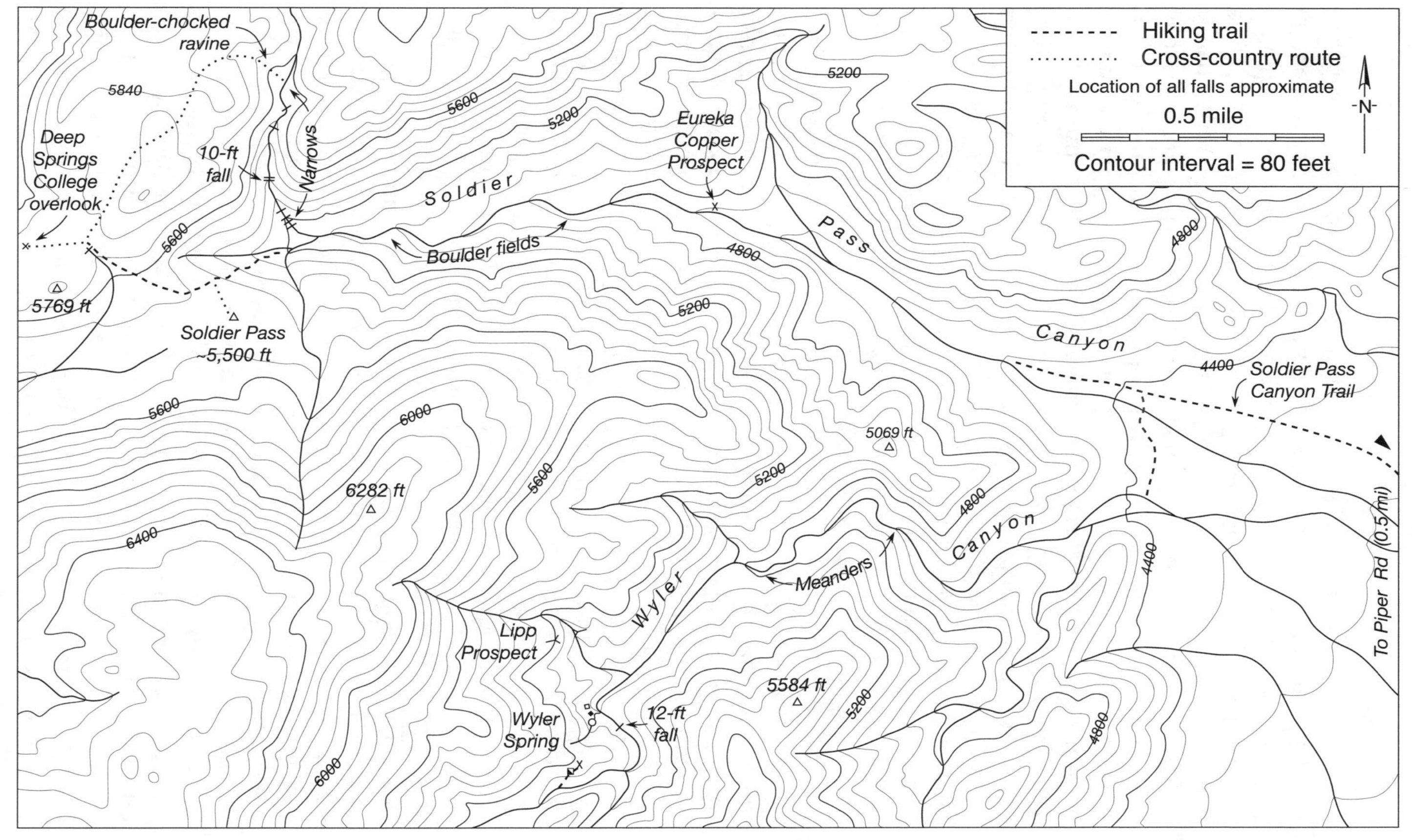
Boulder-chocked ravine
5840
Deep Springs College overlook
10-ft fall
Narrows
5600
5200
Soldier
Eureka Copper Prospect
Boulder fields
Pass
4800
5769 ft
Soldier Pass ~5,500 ft
Canyon
4400
Soldier Pass Canyon Trail
6000
5069 ft
6282 ft
6400
Canyon
Meanders
Wyler
Lipp Prospect
5584 ft
Wyler Spring
12-ft fall
To Piper Rd (0.5 mi)
Hiking trail
Cross-country route
Location of all falls approximate
0.5 mile
Contour interval = 80 feet
-N-

road cutting into the far bank of the wash. Follow it 0.3 mile across the bench between the two canyons to its end at the sandy wash of Wyler Canyon. The rest is cross-country up the canyon wash.

Here again, the lithology is pure intrusive rock, this time Monzonite of Joshua Flat, between 171 and 184 million years old. The main attraction is the hosts of nooks and crannies that erosion has carved into it, especially in the delightfully tight meanders 0.7 mile up canyon. It starts with a low gorge of stocky vertical walls and faceted slabs, continues with a grove of scenic goblins, turrets, and stacked boulders, then passes through two constrictions. This is a sculptor's paradise, and a good place for photography. Whether you want to scramble or climb hard, a whole spectrum of boulder problems and short face climbs is available, from friction slabs to cracks and overhangs—many of them with soft sand landings!

Prospecting in this canyon probably dates from the late nineteenth century. The largest remaining structure is a one-room cabin, on a narrow bench above the wash. Its architecture—low stone walls supporting a roof of lumber and corrugated metal—is typical of that era. Wyler Spring is right behind the cabin, a stone's throw up a steep, narrow ravine. It is so tiny that even if you were dying of thirst chances are you would walk right by it and miss it! It is betrayed only by slightly denser vegetation, hidden metal pipes, and the bleached limbs and trunks of trees that have died and fallen since the miner departed. The vegetation hides a two-foot hole in the ground that holds a few cubic inches of cold, limpid water.

The Lipp Prospect, which is the largest in the Piper Mountain Wilderness, was explored for silver, gold, and lead. In spite of its limited size, it was probably fairly rich: the tunnel dumps contain up to 7 ounces of silver and 2 ounces of gold per ton, and it is likely that some high-grade ore was produced. Pay dirt was locked in a highly fractured quartz vein exposed for nearly 1.5 miles along the north canyon slope. The vein was filled with massive hematite, silver-bearing galena, and a little malachite and gold. The workings are scattered at three widely spaced locations (see map). The side canyon below the cabin has a 15-foot tunnel at wash level, and a caved 45-foot incline high above the wash. The side canyon below it also has a few workings. Reaching the shallow inclined shaft up canyon requires climbing the easy 12-foot fall that blocks Wyler Canyon just past the cabin. In 0.3 mile there is a very faint trail on the right that climbs to the shaft. But all the workings are small and have little to show. Exploring the boulder-filled upper canyon is definitely a greater reward.

■

JOSHUA FLATS AND MOUNT NUNN

This off-beat peak climb through Joshua tree forests, cactus gardens, and pinyon-pine woodlands is a great way to experience the diversity of Eureka Valley's high country. The first part is up a trail across Joshua Flats to a small gold mine on the crest of the Inyo Mountains. The second part, harder, is cross-country along the forested, boulder-strewn crest, first to a spectacular overlook of Deep Springs Lake, then to 7,830-foot Mount Nunn. This remote summit commands superb views of Eureka Valley and the Sierra Nevada. Count on a long day—or better yet, camp overnight.

General Information

Jurisdiction: Piper Mountain Wilderness (BLM)
Road status: Cross-country hiking; paved access road
Rainbow Mine: 2.9 mi, 1,170 ft up, 140 ft down one way / easy
Deep Spr. Valley overlook: 5.0 mi, 2,120 ft up, 160 ft down one way / easy
Mount Nunn: 6.3 mi, 2,660 ft up, 880 ft down one way / difficult
Main attractions: Trail through Joshua tree forest, scenic peak climb
USGS 7.5' topo maps: Joshua Flats, Cowhorn Valley, Deep Springs Lake, Soldier Pass
Maps: pp. 113*, *61*

Location and Access

Mount Nunn is the summit in the northern Inyo Mountains that dominates the east side of Deep Springs Valley. The route described here is the easiest—although not exactly easy. It starts from Joshua Flats, where the primitive Rainbow Mine Road winds up to the crest of the range a few miles south of Mount Nunn. To get to this road from the west, take the scenic Big Pine Road over the crest, up through timberline then down to the shallow depression of Little Cowhorn Valley, then several miles down Joshua Flats. The Rainbow Mine Road branches off the Big Pine Road 8.1 miles east of the Saline Valley Road, on the north side. It is at the low end of Joshua Flats, just before a left bend, where the road starts climbing to the low pass out of the flats (if you go over this pass, you have gone 0.3 mile too far). A wooden post in the middle of this old mining road marks the boundary of the Piper Mountain Wilderness and prevents vehicle access. If you are coming from Eureka Valley, look for the Rainbow Mine Road 14.4 miles west of the North Eureka Valley Road. Park on the paved-road shoulder.

Route Description

Joshua Flats. Joshua Flats is, to say the least, a superb misnomer. It is indeed profusely covered with Joshua trees, but it is nowhere near flat. Imagine instead a narrow, strongly tilted valley flanked by steep alluvial fans. The first part of this walk goes right through this beautiful high-desert environment. From the pavement, the Rainbow Mine Road drops a short distance to the valley floor, then proceeds north down the valley. Up ahead, less than a mile away, Joshua Flats seems to dead-end right against a sheer escarpment, as if it were a sink with no outlet. It isn't. A narrow canyon does drain out of the flats, but it is hidden from view, and the illusion of heading into a sink is perfect until you get right up to it! To check this out, from the trailhead hike down the road 0.2 mile to the first fork on the right (see map), on a bench a few feet above the road, and follow this very faint road. In 0.65 mile it will take you to the head of Joshua Flats' natural drain, a twisted, fall-ridden canyon that cuts through bright ledges of Cambrian limestone and dolomite.

To hike to Mount Nunn, take the left fork instead, which is the main mining road. At the next junction, this one quite obvious, take the left fork, up the west-side fan. This is the best of Joshua Flats: it is furthest from the paved road, the Joshua trees are relatively dense, and it is home to one of the healthiest and most beautiful cactus gardens in Eureka Valley. The chollas are most impressive for their size and density. Some exceed 4 feet in height. As far as the eye can see, their dense crowns glow a surreal fluorescent yellow against the sunlight. Grizzly bear cacti are unusually large and numerous, their tussled manes of long flexible thorns as white as an old man's beard. Further on, above timberline, you may also spot the less common mound cactus. Some specimens gather over 250 heads, huddled tightly in rocky nests. In the late spring, it is quite a shock to come across one of them decorated with dozens of brilliant vermillion flowers.

If you leave the road for a closer look, move cautiously through this spiny jungle. The ochre dots on the beavertail cactus are clumps of tiny pricks that may stay in your skin for days. Chollas are particularly nasty. Their thorns, cleverly shaped like micro-drills, stick so well to clothes and skin that a segment of the plant comes off and clings to the intruder! Should you get stung, which is a little painful, do not touch the plant but pick it off with a stick or a comb. This is all part of the cholla's reproduction stratagem: hitching a ride from wandering mammals (and, lately, humans). If conditions are favorable, the segment you have dropped on the ground will sprout roots and become a new cholla. So do not feel so bad: you have helped the cholla reproduce.

Eureka Valley and the Last Chance Range from Mount Nunn

Deep Springs Valley Overlook. At the top of the fan the road reaches scattered conifers, enters a shallow canyon, then cuts a few switchbacks up and out of it to a fork on the Inyos' crest. The road on the left follows the crest 2.5 miles to end at the head of a canyon that drops precipitously into Deep Springs Valley. If you do not want to go all the way to Mount Nunn, this high road is a fine second best. The views of Deep Springs Valley are quite good, especially from the broad knoll just north of road's end.

The Rainbow Mine. The main road (right) ends shortly at the Rainbow Mine, a marginal gold property that probably predates the 1900s. Its only workings are a 40-foot shaft and a shallow prospect hole. This is the northwestern end of the same 175-million-year-old contact zone that holds the talc deposits on the west side of the valley (see *Eureka Valley's talc mines*). The shaft, now filled with collapsed lumber, was sunk on a gold-bearing quartz vein in a small skarn along this contact zone. Both workings are surrounded by bright blue-green copper minerals, and traces of galena, chalcopyrite, garnet, and epidote. The miner lived in a log cabin erected in a small cove of granitic boulders 150 yards before the shaft. The cabin has collapsed, but its imposing fireplace still attests to the rigor of local winters, as do the remains of a cast-iron stove.

The Deep Springs Lake overlook. To hike to Mount Nunn from the mine, the easiest way is not to follow the crest line but to skirt it slightly to the west (see map). Hike up the steep, boulder-filled ravine behind the shaft to a low pass. It overlooks a sagebrush flat to the north, the head of a canyon that drains west into Deep Springs Valley. The yellowish tailing of the Mejec Prospect is visible across the flat, 250 yards north. Hike down to the flat and cross it to the prospect (a shallow excavation rimmed with drusy milky quartz). The rest of the route follows the same pattern: over the next mile you will climb in and out of two more drainages separated by low passes. The descent into the third one is the most strenuous: 360 feet down a steep forested slope littered with rocks and fallen trees. The route then circles east of a low knoll and crosses over into the next drainage. Good orienteering skills are needed to navigate through this warped topography.

Up to this last drainage the views of Deep Springs Valley are deceptively limited, but this is about to change: the boulder-crowned hill to the west commands the most awesome views of this little-known valley. Climb to the top of the hill, then clamber down its west side to a level promontory about 180 feet below it. Beneath this airy overlook the land falls off in one unbroken sweep 2,000 feet into the glorious void of Deep Springs Valley. The slope is so steep that Deep Springs Lake, almost directly underfoot, is fully exposed, staring up like a bull's eye. In the winter and spring it is a sparkling jewel of turquoise water. Later in the year it metamorphoses into a shiny salt playa dotted with dark pools. Buckhorn Springs and Corral Springs, the fault-bound line of springs that feed the lake on its eastern shore, support a kaleidoscope of green shrubs, red algae, and black meander-

Joshua Flats and Mount Nunn

	Dist.(mi)	Elev.(ft)
Big Pine Rd/Rainbow Mine Rd	0.0	6,043
First junction (left)	0.2	5,973
Bottom of Joshua Flats	(0.65)	5,920
Second junction (left)	0.35	~5,985
Third junction at crest	2.4	~7,090
Deep Springs Val. overlook	(2.5)	~8,000
Rainbow Mine/end of road	2.9	~7,065
Side route to overlook	4.5	7,020
Deep Springs Lake overlook	(0.25)	~6,940
Mount Nunn	6.3	7,830

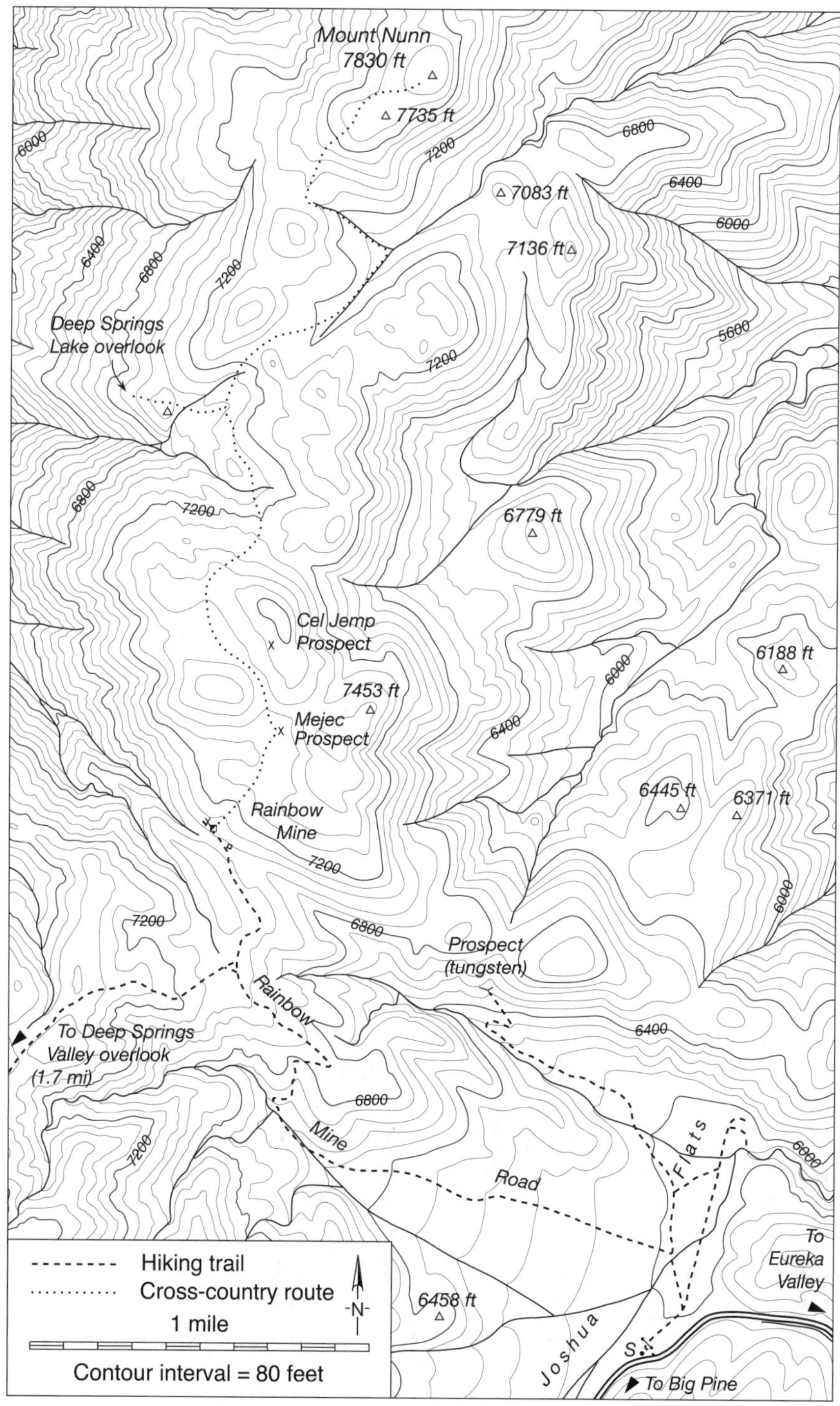
Mount Nunn
7830 ft
7735 ft
7200
6800
6400
6000
7083 ft
7136 ft
5600
Deep Springs
Lake overlook
6779 ft
Cel Jemp
Prospect
6188 ft
7453 ft
Mejec
Prospect
6445 ft
6371 ft
Rainbow
Mine
Prospect
(tungsten)
Rainbow
To Deep Springs
Valley overlook
(1.7 mi)
Mine
Road
Flats
Joshua
S.
To
Eureka
Valley
To Big Pine
6458 ft
Hiking trail
Cross-country route
N
1 mile
Contour interval = 80 feet

ing streams. Across the valley to the west soars the impressive rampart of the White Mountains. If on this hike you get tired early on, remember that it is well worth persevering to this majestic viewpoint.

The only sign of human life in this empty scape is the desultory thread of Highway 136 across the valley floor, and the toy buildings and green cultivated fields of Deep Springs College. The college was founded in 1917 by Lucien L. Nunn, after whom the nearby summit was named. A hydroelectric-power tycoon who worked alongside Tesla and Westinghouse, Nunn designed several major hydropower plants and pioneered the long-distance transportation of electricity via high-voltage power lines. He later invested his personal wealth to implement a new form of liberal education at this still-active college.

Mount Nunn. To get to Mount Nunn from the overlook, walk back up to the last drainage, climb northeast up the drainage to a pass at the crest, then drop down the far side along a narrow sandy wash. Half a mile down, another wash joins in from the left. Hike up this fork 0.4 mile, which will take you back to the crest at the saddle southwest of Mount Nunn. The final stretch is up the boulder-strewn crest line to the 7,830-foot summit.

The views from the summit are, pun intended, second to none. To the west, Deep Springs Valley is largely hidden by trees and boulders, but the serrated peaks of the high Sierras crown miles of skyline. To the east, Eureka Valley spreads wide open like a gaping hole in the Earth. In one breathtaking glance you can take in all of the valley, from Piper Peak down the layered walls of the Last Chance Range to the Eureka Dunes and Saline Peak, and beyond as far south as the Spring Mountains near Las Vegas.

Because of the large elevation gain, high elevation, and persistent obstacles, this hike is fairly demanding. Only a few hardy souls make it up here every year. Yet it is a delightful route, high in the cooler pine country where the light always seems a notch brighter. Its charm lies in the sharp contrast between the environments it embraces. You will travel through Joshua tree forests, woodlands of tall pinyon pines and scruffy juniper, fields of granite boulders, open meadows of big sagebrush, and understories of cliffrose and ephedra. Chances are you will spot chipmunks, rabbits, coyotes, solitary ravens flapping noisily overhead, and the heart-shaped prints of bighorn sheep, if not the real thing. You will get to rest on beds of pine needles and cones dappled with sun and shade. Except for certain human affairs, not wholly inconsistent with wilderness, life does not get much better than this.

■

LORETTO

A short drive or walk from the Big Pine Road will take you to Loretto, a historic copper mine that boomed twice, in 1907 and in the 1970s, but failed to produce both times. Remains include the deepest shaft in the region, an open pit lined with colorful ore, and a recent copper mill. This short visit can be extended by hiking the steep trail to the Nikolaus-Eureka Mine higher up the mountain, an interesting talc exploitation that boasts substantial remains.

General Information
Jurisdiction: Public lands and patented lands (BLM)
Road status: Short primitive road (4WD)
Loretto Mine: 1.0 mi, 580 ft up, 0 ft down one way / very easy
Nikolaus-Eureka Mine: 2.0 mi, 1,120 ft up, 320 ft down one way / moder.
Main attractions: Historic copper mine, copper minerals, talc mine
USGS 7.5' topo maps: Soldier Pass*, Joshua Flats
Maps: pp. 117*, *61*

Location and Access

The Loretto Mine is in the foothills of the Inyo Mountains west of central Eureka Valley. To drive to it, take the dirt road on the east side of the Big Pine Road 11.7 miles east of the Saline Valley Road (or 10.8 miles west of the North Eureka Valley Road). This road winds up into the mountain 0.75 mile to a junction at a wide bench, a short walking distance below the mine's open pit. Park here—this is essentially the end of the road. This road is fairly smooth but it has a few steep grades. If you are driving a lighter two-wheel-drive vehicle, you may have to quit after about a third of a mile in and walk. The other access road, 0.5 mile further west on the Big Pine Road, has major washouts.

History

The Loretto copper deposits were discovered in the late 19th century, probably before 1888. Originally developed by shallow tunnels, they were not extensively explored until 1907, when Charles Schwab took over the property and formed the Loretto Mining Company. Proclaimed at the time as one of the world's highest salaried and richest men, Schwab was a shrewd investor who became involved, among many other businesses, in some of the most famous mines in the Death Valley region. Around 1906 he was already controlling the richest mines in the Bullfrog and Greenwater districts, on the east side of Death Valley. Over the next few years, the Loretto Mining Company drilled a shaft down to a greater and greater depth, with the hope of intersecting a large body of rich sulfide copper ore. The area was then reached from Big Pine by a good wagon road known as the Loretto Mine Road, the precursor of today's Big Pine Road. By 1912 the shaft had reached 1,500 feet down to ore bodies that averaged 4 to 5 percent in copper and $3 per ton in gold. They looked promising enough that the company invested in the construction of a two-million-dollar smelter near the mine. Drilling continued, until by 1915 the shaft bottomed at 1,800 feet. At that depth a large deposit was discovered, but it was low-grade oxidized copper ore. Here as in Greenwater a decade earlier, Schwab had lost his gamble. After years of sustained development, operations were discontinued with little to show.

The Loretto Mine remained idle for some 60 years, until the Bristlecone Copper Company acquired mining rights to it in the mid-1970s. The company opened a pit above the historic shaft to mine an ore body containing probably only a few percent of oxidized copper. A small heap leach mill was also constructed across the Big Pine Road. However, the deposit died out quickly at depth. Only a small tonnage of ore was treated before the mine closed down in 1977.

Route Description

The Loretto Mine has four areas of interest: the historic shaft, the open pit, the smaller workings in the canyon to the north, and the Bristlecone Copper Company mill. The shaft is located on the bench at the top of the access road, where it loops back and begins to descend to the Big Pine Road. This gaping opening framed with heavy lumber is a staggering 1,800 feet deep, by far the deepest in western Death Valley. A stone dropped into it takes so long to hit bottom that the impact is inaudible! The shaft's heavy-duty hoisting equipment has collapsed into a heap of metal pipes. Its engine was removed, but the spool, cogwheels, hand brake, and battery are still anchored on the concrete platform near the shaft. Behind the shaft, a jail-grade steel door still guards what was once the mine's safe.

During the 1907-1915 copper mining period, the small town of Loretto thrived near the mine. Although it never acquired a post office, it had several large stone buildings and canvas tents. Browse and you will run into its old dwellings—tent platforms, crumbled walls, a dugout, and a couple of stone houses—as well as a giant stove, a rusted water tank, an ore chute, and compressors abandoned long ago. Treat them with respect; this is the only town Eureka Valley ever had.

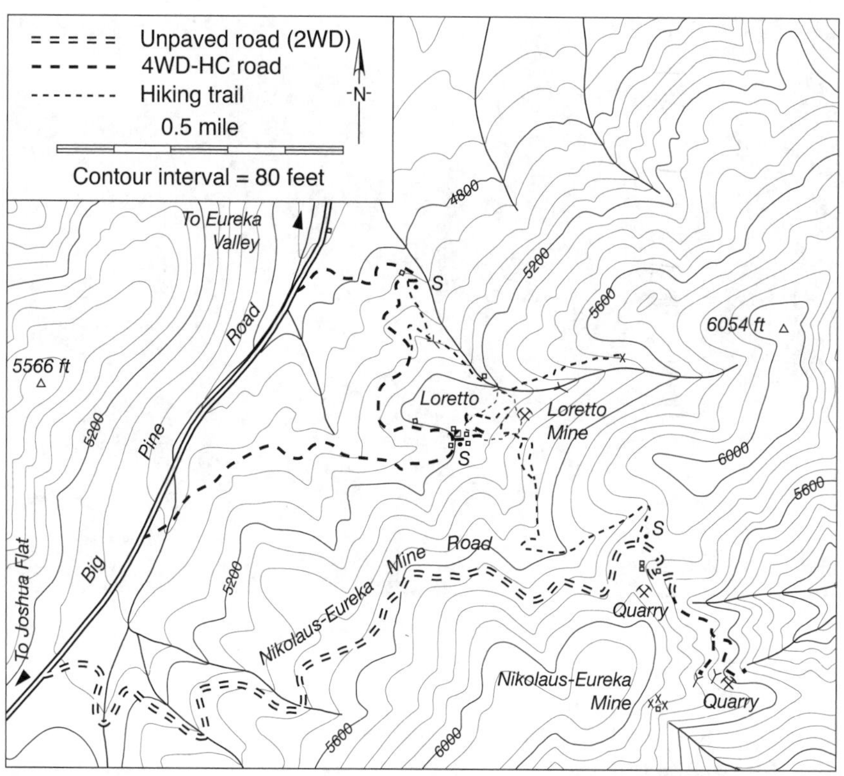

Loretto	Dist.(mi)	Elev.(ft)
Big Pine Road	0.0	4,757
The Loretto Mine (shaft)	0.75	5,230
Open pit	1.0	5,330
Top of ridge (junction)	1.6	5,880
Nikolaus-Eureka Mine (quarry)	2.0	5,560

From the shaft, a short walk east up the road leads to the open pit worked by the Bristlecone Copper Company in the 1970s, a staircase of eight shallow benches terraced into a hillside. Although this surface deposit was relatively marginal, more copper ore is exposed here than at most mines around Death Valley. The ore occurs in highly fractured veins of quartz and calcite in Monzonite of Joshua Flat. Most of it is malachite and azurite with a little chrysocolla, pyrite, chalcopyrite, and specular hematite, which coat the fracture surfaces. The minerals are particularly colorful, ranging from pale green to cobalt blue.

Hoisting machinery at the Loretto Mine

The third area of interest is the canyon north of the pit. It has several historic tunnels with abundant copper minerals. Start walking on the spur road along the Loretto access road, 0.35 mile from the Big Pine Road. At the end of it there is a constructed adit. The trail that starts above the adit (circle around it to avoid falling through its thin ceiling) leads up the canyon to the tunnels (0.4 mile to the third one).

The Bristlecone Copper Company mill is up the short road 0.4 mile down the Big Pine Road from the Loretto access road, on the west side. The dismantled complex sprawls on a broad bench surrounded by barren hills. It consists of metal tanks, concrete ponds once filled with blue-green copper-rich solutions, loading docks, and stockpiled crushed ore still waiting its turn to be treated. What is most interesting, as much as the mill itself and its size, is the sharp contrast between the new and old mining technologies.

This visit takes only a couple of hours, much less if you aren't into rocks. To turn it into a half-day outing, hike on to the interesting Nikolaus-Eureka Mine (see *Eureka Valley's Talc Mines*). Take the old road (blocked to vehicles part way up by enormous boulders) that starts at the top of the open pit. It heads south, then climbs very steeply east, to the Nikolaus-Eureka Mine Road on a high ridge. From there it is a short hike down to the road to the main workings.

■

EUREKA VALLEY'S TALC MINES

The Nikolaus-Eureka Mine and the Harlis and Broady Mine, Eureka Valley's main talc properties, are accessible by primitive roads, so you can get to them either the sissy way, sitting on your rear end in a gas-guzzling vehicle, or the noble way, on foot, which gives you more options. The access roads rank among the roughest, wildest, and most scenic in this valley. They will take you into a desolate range to spectacular overlooks, derelict camps, funky mining equipment, quarries and tunnels, and tons of colorful talc.

General Information

Jurisdiction: Public lands and patented lands (BLM)
Road status: Hiking on dirt roads; primitive access roads (HC/4WD)
Harlis and Broady Mine: 2.4 mi, 1,000 ft up, 650 ft down one way/easy
Nikolaus-Eureka Mine: 2.0 mi, 730 ft up, 320 ft down one way/easy
Main attractions: Historic talc mines, geology, panoramic views
USGS 7.5' topo maps: Soldier Pass, Joshua Flats
Maps: pp. 117*, 121*, *61*

Location and Access

These two talc mines are both on the spur of the Inyos that juts into the west side of Eureka Valley. To get to the Harlis and Broady Mine, drive the Big Pine Road 10.1 miles east of the Saline Valley Road to a dirt road on the right, just beyond a local pass. If you are coming from Eureka Valley, look for it 4.7 miles west of the pronounced left bend at the western edge of the valley. The Nikolaus-Eureka Mine Road starts 0.8 mile east on the Big Pine Road, also on the south side.

Route Description

The Harlis and Broady Mine. This primitive track crosses some really wild and scenic territory, and exploring it on foot or by car is an adventure. From its south end, it climbs east to the crest of a steep spur of the Inyos, then dips even more steeply on the far side into a canyon, only to climb again up its wash to a junction (2.2 miles). The straight fork ends 0.15 mile up canyon just below the Harlis and Broady Mine. This road is rough. A two-wheel drive can only make the first 0.3 mile to the first steep grade. The rest, especially the east mountainside, has steep pitches with large rocks. Appreciation of talc mines is not a prerequisite for a good time. Rugged rock walls, beautiful veined marble in roadcuts, wildflowers, stoic Joshua trees, panoramic views, and solitude are all par for the course.

Eureka Valley's talc deposits were formed about 175 million years ago, when quartz monzonite intruded Cambrian limestones and dolomites. Near their contact zone, which forms an 8-mile-long arcuate zone, metamorphism substituted large quantities of the carbonates' original calcium and carbon with magnesium and silicon (a process called silication), thus transforming the carbonate rock into talc.

The Harlis and Broady Mine is cramped on a steep slope, at the tight confluence of three narrow ravines. Its camp had a single cabin, erected on the only level real estate around. For years the cabin seemed to be held together solely by its spider webs, until it finally succumbed to gravity in the early 1990s. Today its fridge and sink stand awkwardly on the open floorboard, surrounded by lumber, twisted pipes, and zinc roofing. The mine was developed by a short tunnel across from the cabin and an adit with 280 feet of tunnels 65 feet up the slope. A 50-foot open cut gapes between the tunnels and the crest. The only recorded production is a meager 31 tons in 1957. The highlight here is the mining complex. A large ore bin supported by tall wooden posts collected the ore from both tunnels. The ore from the upper tunnel was delivered to the bin in an ore car that was winched down on a 320-foot inclined rail. This well-preserved unit, clamped to a 20% slope, may be

Eureka Valley's Talc Mines

	Dist.(mi)	Elev.(ft)
The Harlis and Broady Mine		
Big Pine Road	0.0	5,520
Crest	1.15	5,995
Junction	2.2	5,620
Harlis and Broady Mine	2.4	5,870
The Nikolaus-Eureka Mine		
Big Pine Road	0.0	5,150
Nikolaus-Eureka Mine camp	1.6	5,880
Lower loading structure	2.0	5,560

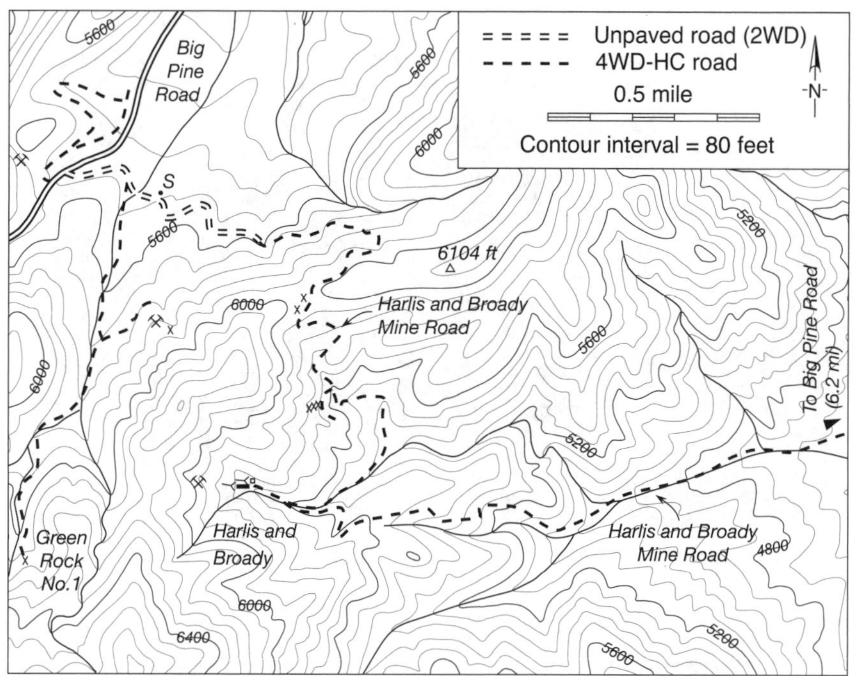

the only one of its kind remaining in the region. Both tunnels were blasted shut, presumably by the owners when they quit. A little talc and chlorite are exposed around the ore bin. Although nowhere numerous, several species of cactus live all around, including cotton-top, beavertail, calico, silver cholla, grizzly bear, and mound cacti.

The Nikolaus-Eureka Mine. By far the largest talc mine in Eureka Valley, this is also the most interesting. It is named after James Nikolaus, a man from Big Pine who owned the mine's two claims in the mid-1940s. The deposit contains both steatite and lower grade talc mixed with chlorite and alumina. Nikolaus mined his property actively for several years, producing 2,000 tons in 1945 and maintaining off and on a daily production of 20 to 25 tons with just a few miners on the job. Mining continued intermittently until 1970. The total production of 75,000 tons was used mostly in cosmetics and pharmaceuticals.

Located at the top of a sheer escarpment high above Eureka Valley, the Nikolaus-Eureka Mine is, above all, an impressive site. After winding 1.6 miles from the Big Pine Road, the Nikolaus-Eureka Mine Road tops a pass, and all of Eureka Valley literally bursts into view. In a single sweep you will take in its empty northern area, the distant Eureka Dunes and Last Chance Range, and the delicate dunes at the mouth of

Loading structure at the lower quarry of the Nikolaus-Eureka Mine

Marble Canyon. This spectacular panorama alone highly justifies walking the road if you do not have the right vehicle to drive it.

The mine's camp is at the pass, just south of the road. Of its original cluster of wooden cabins, only one dilapidated shack survived into this century. It has now collapsed onto its bedspring and antediluvian gas stoves. The mine's upper working is the tall open cut just behind the camp. It is littered with sparkling white boulders of dolomite that was crystallized by the intruding monzonite, and scattered chunks of hard, dark-gray talc.

From the summit the road winds down 0.3 mile to a fork. A four-wheel drive is definitely needed to make it down (and back up!) this steep, rocky grade. The right fork climbs 0.1 mile to a first tunnel, a quarry, and an interesting loading structure. The main road (left fork) continues 0.1 mile down to a second tunnel and the main quarry. This is quite a satisfying site, both for its large loading structure and spectacular setting, on the brink of a precipitous ravine that falls 2,200 feet to the valley floor. The loading structure is fairly complex and a pleasure to investigate. It housed the machinery that hauled the quarried talc into a huge ore bin. The mechanisms that controlled the ore bin's twin chutes, the cogwheels in the control room, and the ladders that gave access to various parts of the structure are still in place. The quarry's huge tailing contains large amounts of dark-green steatite and beautiful large rhombohedral crystals of orange-tinged calcite.

■

MARBLE CANYON

Marble Canyon's popular attraction is the historic cabins and mining rigs scattered along its wash. The remains of one of the largest gold placer mines in the northern Mojave Desert, they can be easily visited by driving the canyon road. Hikers seeking off-beat destinations can explore the long roadless lower canyon, which boasts miles of grand scenery, two scenic gorges, and virgin dunes below the canyon mouth.

General Information

Jurisdiction: Death Valley National Park
Road status: Primitive road in mid-canyon; lower canyon roadless
Upper gorge: 1.0 mi, 10 ft up, 270 ft down one way / very easy
Lower gorge: 4.0 mi, 20 ft up, 1,140 ft down one way / moderate
Hidden Dunes: 8.1 mi, 100 ft up, 2,080 ft down one way / difficult
Main attractions: Placer gold mines, remote canyon and sand dunes
USGS 7.5' topo maps: Waucoba Spring*, East of Waucoba Spring, East of Joshua Flats*
Maps: pp. 127*, *61*

Location and Access

Marble Canyon originates in the northern Inyo Mountains and drains east into west-central Eureka Valley, along the boundary between the Inyo Mountains and the Saline Range. The main access to it is the Saline Valley Road. Drive this road 6.4 miles south from the Big Pine Road, which will take you to the wash of Marble Canyon at the bottom of the Marble Canyon switchbacks. The Saline Valley Road continues down canyon, past the ruins of several placer mines and a small camp. After 1.4 miles it makes a sharp right bend to climb out of Marble Canyon into Opal Canyon. At the bend, look for the Jackass Flats Road on the left. Coming from Saline Valley, this junction is 20.0 miles north of Willow Creek Camp, at the bottom of the long grade down Opal Canyon. From this junction the Jackass Flats Road goes down the wash of Marble Canyon. After 1.25 miles it angles sharply right up into a narrow passage. Continue down canyon instead, on a smaller road that ends in 0.35 mile at a large cabin. Park here to hike into the roadless lower canyon. The Jackass Flats Road is rough and requires a high-clearance vehicle.

Geology: Gold Placers

Although gold is nowhere abundant in Marble Canyon, there is a little bit of it everywhere. It occurs in what is known as a placer: the gold particles are not locked in a hard rock but disseminated in consolidated alluvial material. Gold has been found along 9 miles of the canyon, from the bottom of its wash to the older gravels that form parts of its walls and cap its ridges. Placers are a minority in the desert. This is, in fact, one of the very few and most extensive placers in the northern Mojave Desert. There is good evidence that this gold may have been washed down by a pre-Tertiary river system that originated 30 miles north, in the White Mountains. The churning river forced the dense gold particles to settle toward the bottom of its thick gravel bed, where it now rests against hard bedrock.

Marble Canyon's placers were first mined around 1882, but extensive developments did not begin until 1934. The gravel was not rich—a cubic yard was typically worth a handful of dollars—but there was a prodigious amount of it. Over the years, the canyon wash was poked and probed by dozens of shafts on several independently operated claims. Each shaft was sunk through 70 to 150 feet of gravel down to bedrock, and from there more than 3,000 feet of horizontal drifts and crosscuts were burrowed into the pay zone. Production was largely unrecorded, but between 1936 and 1960 at least 330 ounces of gold and a little silver were recovered from 7,300 cubic yards of gravel—a tiny volume by today's strip-mining standards. Most of the gold was in the form of flour and grains the size of lead shots. The largest of the few good-size nuggets that were reported was as big as a golf ball.

Route Description

The canyon road. Most of the placer mines in Marble Canyon are in the upper canyon: nearly 30 shafts, all a short walk from the road, can be found along the 2-mile stretch of the Saline Valley Road and Jackass Flats Road. Because of their great depths, the shafts were steeply inclined rather than truly vertical to facilitate access and ore removal. They were all shored by a sturdy collar of thick boards to prevent the friable gravel walls from collapsing. The most interesting relics are the headframes—the clunky wooden towers that housed the machinery used to remove pay dirt from the shafts. Buckets loaded with gravel were hoisted with a cable guided by a pulley located at the top of the headframe. The gravel was stocked in an ore bin, usually attached to the structure, then screened and run over a dry washer (for lack of water) to recover the gold. Although similar in their function, the half a dozen remaining headframes vary greatly in size and design.

Cabins and headframe along Marble Canyon

The most complete one is 0.3 mile down the Jackass Flats Road. Be extremely careful while browsing. None of the shafts is marked or protected, and a fall would be fatal.

When mining was at its peak, cabins were clustered at several locations along the road. Some of them still remain. The camp just west of Opal Canyon was the largest. It still has a couple of empty wooden cabins, a large shed, and a few gutted cars. A lone chimney, a pile of scrap metal, a caved dugout, or an empty stone platform, is often the only sign left of the other camps. The cabin at the lower end of the road is the best preserved. It is still occasionally used by hikers as a winter shelter.

The roadless canyon. In a mountain range where almost every canyon is loaded with impassable obstacles, Marble Canyon stands out for its unobstructed course. No falls, no steep grades, no thorny thickets, yet more than enough delightful surprises to fill a day to the brim. The walking is so easy that for a change one can concentrate mostly on the scenery.

Marble Canyon is spacious. For many miles it descends gently through a serene setting of low, rolling hills, brushing by an unspoiled, slowly changing landscape that never seems to end. Most of the time the canyon bottom is an open wash of fine gravel snaking lazily between broad benches. This may be a little thin on excitement for some, but desert lovers will relish it. I enjoyed the openness, the heady sense of isolation, the deep-purple flowers of the indigo bush, and the elation of exploring an out-of-the-way place known to only a few.

The first treat is the upper gorge, a narrow and rocky passage that starts a little before the end of the road and continues well below it. Its tight meanders cut through a Jurassic granitic formation called Diorite of Marble Canyon, as well as shale, dolomite, and sandstone over 540 million years old. At places, especially at the gorge's lower end, these ancient strata have been warped into impressively tight synclines or tilted nearly vertically.

At one time most of Marble Canyon was covered by mining claims. Their boundaries are still marked by many mining monuments erected at wide intervals along the wash. The claims in the upper gorge were the Easy Pickings. They date back to the heyday of placer mining, and were relocated as late as the 1980s. The shaft of the Krater–Van Norman Prospect is on the edge of the south bench 450 yards below the upper gorge. Other historic remains dot the wash, from the carcass of a rusted model T (the door hinges still work!) to the trash of a small camp scattered around a caved-in shaft.

The lower gorge, starting 2.7 miles below the road, is Marble Canyon's most impressive section. This deep corridor winds in sharp curves through an erosion-resistant outcrop of diorite and sedimentary rocks. All of the region's Late to Middle Cambrian formations are represented, from the Harkless to the Bonanza King formations. At places, their stacks of shale, quartzite, limestone, and dolomite shoot skyward

Marble Canyon

	Dist.(mi)	Elev.(ft)
Road's end (cabin)	0.0	5,500
Shaft (Easy Pickings Mine)	0.3	5,410
Upper gorge (lower end)	1.0	~5,230
Shaft (Krater–Van Norman Pr.)	1.3	5,155
Lower gorge (upper end)	2.6	4,810
Twin side canyons	3.4	4,540
Lower gorge (lower end)	4.0	4,360
Main side canyon	4.45	4,260
Mouth	~6.5	~3,720
Hidden Dunes (ridge)	8.1	3,500
Road at dry well	12.1	2,974

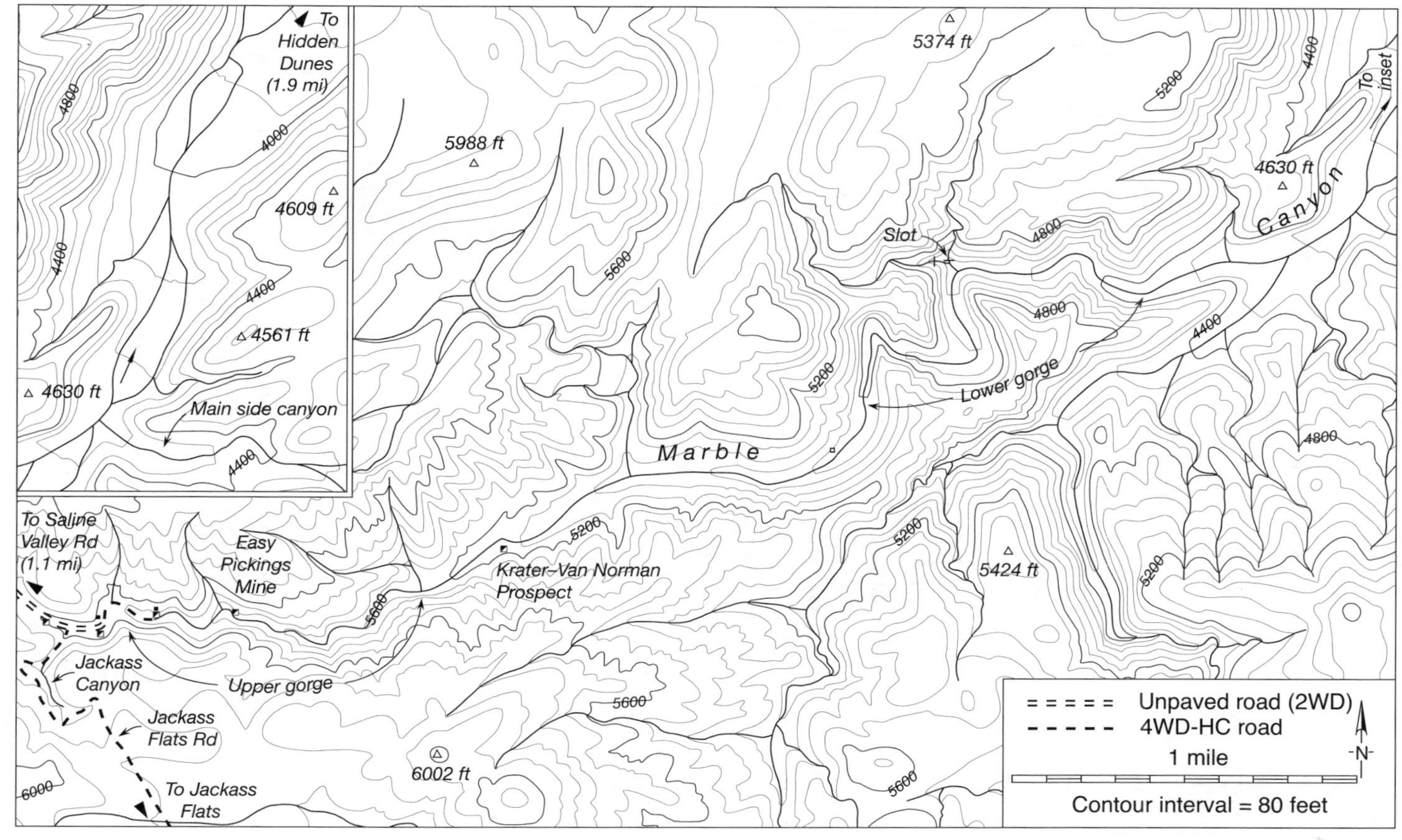
To Hidden Dunes (1.9 mi)
4609 ft
4561 ft
4630 ft
Main side canyon
5988 ft
5374 ft
Slot
4630 ft
Canyon
To inset
Lower gorge
Marble
To Saline Valley Rd (1.1 mi)
Easy Pickings Mine
Krater-Van Norman Prospect
5424 ft
Jackass Canyon
Upper gorge
Jackass Flats Rd
To Jackass Flats
6002 ft
Unpaved road (2WD)
4WD-HC road
1 mile
N
Contour interval = 80 feet

hundreds of vertical feet. Climbers will find good places to hone their 5.13 moves, starting with the large cubic monolith stranded in the wash at the head of the lower gorge. The twin side canyons in the second right bend down the gorge are the tightest in Marble Canyon. One of them is a short slot terminated by a fall (a dangerous place for stemming) that guards winding narrows above. In the summer, these side canyons offer the only serious shade for miles. If you do not want to go all the way to the dunes, this is a worthy final destination.

The Hidden Dunes. These isolated dunes are the crowing glory of Marble Canyon. To get to them, you will have to trudge another few miles along the very broad wash of lower Marble Canyon, amidst smooth auburn hills. At its very bottom the canyon opens up into a wonderfully secluded valley, a hidden arm of Eureka Valley tucked behind the long and narrow spur that forms the north end of the Saline Range. The final approach to the dunes, stretched a couple of miles away along the west side of the spur, is an unforgettable experience. The long, delicate string of dunes loosely stitched against the spur's rocky slopes composes an alien landscape that remains in full view the whole way, growing larger every step, until you reach the edge of the sand and become completely immersed in it. Refer to *The Hidden Dunes* for a description of this exceptional site.

Possible extensions. The hike down to the canyon mouth or to the dunes and back takes a very long day. Bring a flashlight, as you may well get back to your car after bedtime. A nice alternative, only marginally shorter but easier if you can talk someone into picking you up, is to continue hiking past the dunes across the low gap in the spur, then northeastward across Eureka Valley to either the dry well (3.1 miles from the gap) or to the South Eureka Valley Road (5.5 miles) (see *The Hidden Dunes* for directions to the dry well). This is a beautiful desert walk, clear across the pristine southwestern quadrant of Eureka Valley.

■

ANDREWS MOUNTAIN

This remote and seldom-visited mountain just shy of 10,000 feet can be climbed along two very different routes, cross-country up the north shoulder, or on the easier west shoulder via a rough mining road—or better still, on a loop combining both routes. Either way, you will pass through thick, shaded forests of ancient pinyon pine and mountain mahogany, puff up steep inclines, and ultimately enjoy expansive views of this wild corner of the Inyo Mountains.

General Information

Jurisdiction: National Forest Service
Road status: Hiking on dirt roads & cross-country; primitive access rd
Andrews Mtn (north): 2.2 mi, 2,110 ft up, 30 ft down one way / strenuous
Andrews Mtn (west): 2.4 mi, 1,750 ft up, 70 ft down one way / difficult
Main attractions: Seldom-climbed mountain, thick alpine forest, views
USGS 7.5' topo maps: Waucoba Mountain
Maps: pp. 131*, *61*

Location and Access

Andrews Mountain is at the north end of the Inyos' high central block, a few miles northwest of Waucoba Mountain. From Highway 168 2.3 miles east of Big Pine, drive the Big Pine Road 11.3 miles east to a primitive road on the right, in a left bend following a mile-long straight stretch. Follow this road 0.1 mile south to a fork, and turn right on 9S15. After climbing gently 1.4 miles south toward Andrews Mountain, visible up ahead, 9S15 makes a sharp right U turn. To ascend the mountain's north shoulder, park in the bend. A standard-clearance car is fine up to this point. To ascend the west shoulder, continue 1.6 miles (clearance is preferable but not essential) to a bulldozed parking spot on the right in a wooded area, and park. The road climbs on 1.6 miles to a saddle on the west shoulder, but it soon squeezes through a narrow passage with high bedrock steps and no place to turn around, and further on it is too steep for most vehicles.

Route Description

The west shoulder is the easiest route. From the car park the road is a convenient guide. After crossing the narrows, it forks at a clearing. The left fork climbs along the bottom of a narrow canyon thick with ancient pinyon pine. In 0.8 mile the road angles left out of the wash and climbs across the precipitous canyon slope to a narrow saddle on Andrews Mountain's west shoulder. Very steep, slippery with pebbles, this is the only part of the road that is a bit tedious. From the saddle the route continues east on the west shoulder, at first a broad forested ridge capped by a low summit (9,008'). The terrain then opens up onto a grassy meadow that curves gradually upward to the very steep talus girdling the summit. Made of unstable, foot-size slabs that clink underfoot like broken pottery, this is the only difficult segment on this route.

The northern route is wilder, more demanding, and, being mostly roadless, more liberating. An abandoned twin track does go partway up, but only in the lowest reaches where the walking is easy anyway. To get to it from the U bend, cut southwest 200 yards across a shallow ravine to a low north-south ridge, and you will run into it. For 0.7 mile it cuts a lazy path south up the gentle ridge, a broad spine of grasses and sagebrush sprinkled with the low crowns of juniper and pine. The track ends at the foot of the mountain's long steep brow. Beyond, cross-country climbing gradually worsens as the forest thickens and the slope increases. Most of the way up you weave between trees, clamber over fallen logs, and zigzag across rock-strewn taluses to minimize the grade. Three small saddles pace the ascent, one with a rocky outcrop, but they are too brief to catch your breath. Near the upper timberline, around 9,100 feet, the terrain morphs into the same unstable talus as on the west shoulder. To minimize the difficulty, angle right to the next ridge over, which is less cluttered and a little easier.

This is a strenuous climb. The average slope is 25%; on the steepest pitches, you gain a foot every step you take. But like every mountain

Andrews Mountain	Dist.(mi)	Elev.(ft)
Western route		
End of good road	0.0	7,780
Fork in road (left)	0.25	7,910
Saddle (leave road east)	1.6	8,930
Andrews Mountain	2.4	9,462
Northern route		
U bend in road	0.0	7,385
Old track	0.1	7,415
End of track	0.85	7,795
Andrews Mountain	2.2	9,462
Back via saddle and road	6.1	7,385

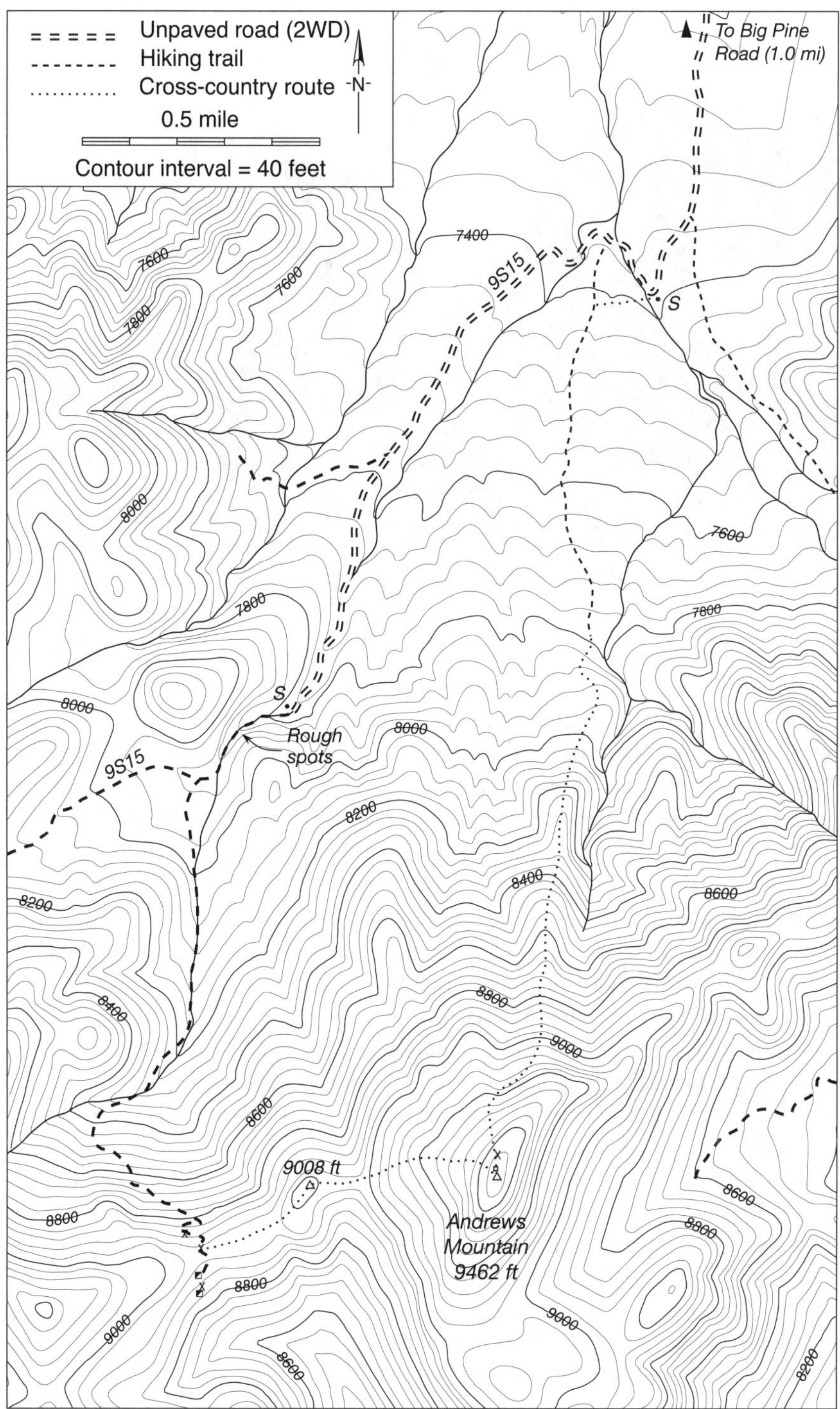

Unpaved road (2WD)
Hiking trail
Cross-country route
N
0.5 mile
Contour interval = 40 feet
To Big Pine Road (1.0 mi)
7400
7600
7800
8000
9S15
S
7600
7800
8000
Rough spots
8200
8400
8600
8800
9000
9008 ft
Andrews Mountain 9462 ft
8200

Half-dead, half-alive pinyon pine on north slope of Andrews Mountain

of generous proportions, Andrews is a universe in itself. The forest is magical. In the canyon, more sheltered from the sun and wind, and a natural conduit for rain and snow melt, mature pine dominate. They reach imposing dimensions, exceeding 25 feet in height and 1.5 feet in base diameter. They come right up to the road, their crowns touching and arching overhead. The air is cooler and fragrant with sap. Steller's jays argue in the foliage; deer and coyote lurk in the woods. On the north shoulder, many pine have sacrificed a part of themselves for the rest to survive. Their silvery, wind-sculpted skeletons are posed like works of art. The massive trunks of centennial pine that fell decades ago still lie on the ground, preserved by the dry air. The understory is a shaded mix of needles and cones, grizzly bear cactus, and ephedra. The most interesting of many plants is mountain mahogany, a rare species that locally thrives in small but nearly pure stands.

On Andrews Mountain, what draws attention most is not the imposing mass of White Mountain to the north or the sharp crest of the Sierras, but the gaping void of Squaw Flat to the southeast. The land drops 2,000 feet into this isolated high-desert valley, then on its far side rebounds in one giant wave up the deeply furrowed flanks of Squawk Peak and Waucoba Mountain. The sight of the hidden side of these wild mountains culminating more than two miles above sea level instantly wipes out the minor aches of the climb.

■

— 5 —

The Western Last Chance Range

The Last Chance Range is the long and narrow range separating Saline Valley and Eureka Valley from the northern arm of Death Valley to the east. It extends roughly north-south about 55 miles, from Hunter Mountain north to near the Nevada state line, at the very northern tip of the park. Part 5 focuses on hikes into the Last Chance Range originating from Saline Valley. It covers the west side of the southern portion of the range, which contains most of the range's highest peaks, including Dry Mountain (8,674'), Marble Peak (7,559'), and Hunter Mountain (7,454'). A few hikes into the northern portion of the range, originating from Eureka Valley, are described in Part 4. Drives and hikes on the Death Valley side, including in the Racetrack Valley area, are covered in *Hiking Death Valley*.

Access and Backcountry Roads

What makes the Last Chance Range so special for hiking is that it is generally difficult to access from Saline Valley. Only the south end of the range is crossed by a road, the Lippincott Road, which connects Saline Valley to Racetrack Valley. The rest of the range can only be viewed from a distance from either the Saline Valley Road or the four-wheel-drive road along the Steel Pass corridor. These three roads should be high on four-wheelers' lists. The Saline Valley Road is one of the longest unpaved desert roads in California. The other two are rough, rocky, and long. Ranking among the most challenging in the park, they take nothing short of a high-clearance four-wheel-drive vehicle to be tamed. A ride up the Lippincott Road makes for a great day outing from Saline Valley, culminating in a visit of the extensive

Suggested Backcountry Drives in the Western Last Chance Range					
Route/Destination	Dist. (mi)	Lowest elev.	Highest elev.	Road type	Pages
Lippincott Road	6.8	1,920'	3,850'	F	155
Saline Valley Road	78.1	1,080'	7,570'	G	174-177
Steel Pass Road	29.3	1,475'	5,091'	F	191-195
Key: G=Graded		F=Primitive (4WD)			

remains of the Lippincott Mine at the upper end of the road, and of the Racetrack and its mysterious moving rocks just beyond it (see *Hiking Death Valley*).

All three roads are about as far from civilization as it gets in California. The closest services, at Panamint Springs and Big Pine, are nearly 110 miles apart. Driving these roads is a lot of fun, but for inexperienced drivers it can quickly turn into a nightmare. Come prepared. Bring plenty of water and food, and a good book in case things do not go quite as planned.

Mining History

Although the Last Chance Range was never heavily mined, the Racetrack Valley area, at the south end of the range, witnessed nearly a century of mining. The first metal discovered here was copper, in July 1875. Not much happened until the mid-1890s when several of the properties that had been claimed in the intervening years became increasingly active. The mines were mostly located on the slopes of Ubehebe Peak, on the low range between Racetrack Valley and Hidden Valley, and in the Grapevine Canyon drainage—places like the Ulida Mine, the Copper Knife, and the Blue Boy claims. For many years, their only access was a rough track through Saline Valley. The journey was so long and difficult that only the best ore could be shipped with a profit, and the rest of it had to be stockpiled. In spite of this hardship, by 1902 there were 80 copper, gold, and silver claims in the area, all within a 6-mile radius. Production was probably minimal, although a few properties might have picked up after 1904, when the price of copper started to increase.

The era's most prominent figure was mining promoter Jack Salsberry, who controlled some of the largest and richest claims. To open the area, he first completed a road from Racetrack Valley up to the Montana Railway Station near Bonnie Claire, Nevada, via Tin Pass and Grapevine Canyon. In anticipation of a large production, he also negotiated with banking firms a 48-mile railroad extension from the Montana Station on the Las Vegas–Tonopah Railroad. The Ubehebe Mining District was created at the height of the copper boom, in the spring of 1907. The completion of the road that year provided improved access, sparked a new influx of miners, and allowed supplies to be teamed from Nevada. By fall, the area was so active that a coach service ran weekly between Montana Station and Ubehebe City, a mining camp near the south end of the Racetrack.

This heroic effort, as well as mining, continued feverishly until the middle of 1908, but Salsberry's dream never materialized. Soon after, perhaps as a result of the Panic of 1907, the investment banks interested in the area folded and the project died. In the following years, other railroad propositions were discussed in relation to the Ubehebe Mine, but they never came through.

Over the next 50 years or so, with slowly improving transportation, intermittent work at the best mines did produce a little copper—an estimated 120,000 pounds. Yet it was lead and gold, not copper, that kept the district busy. The Ubehebe Mine, at the north end of the Racetrack playa, began to show promising lead and silver veins in 1906, and it remained active, albeit sporadically, longer than any other mine in the district. Up until the 1960s, it produced about 1,300 tons of lead and 2,600 pounds of silver. The Lippincott Mine, at the south end of the valley, was active mostly between 1938 and 1952, and it became the third largest lead producer in Death Valley. The Lost Burro Mine, over in Hidden Valley, produced essentially all of the district's gold. All the district's other mines, mostly located on the Saline Valley side of the range, were much smaller and produced considerably less.

Geology

The vast majority of the Last Chance Range north of Ubehebe Peak is made of Paleozoic formations. Although most of this era is represented, the most common exposures are from the Ordovician, Cambrian, and Devonian. Broadly speaking, older formations (mostly Cambrian and Ordovician) dominate north of Marble Peak, and younger formations south of it. Although the stratigraphy is fairly complex, formations tend to get older towards the east side of the range. The southwestern tip of the range, where it juts into Saline Valley just east of the hot springs, has small exposures of quartz monzonite and Pliocene basalt. In contrast, from Ubehebe Peak south to Hunter Mountain the western Last Chance Range is composed largely of Jurassic quartz monzonite from the Hunter Mountain Pluton.

Suggested Hikes in the Western Last Chance Range					
Route/Destination	Dist. (mi)	Elev. gain	Mean elev.	Access road	Pages
Short hikes (under 5 miles round trip)					
Dedeckera Canyon narrows	0.9	380'	3,850'	P/6.0 mi	194-195
Grapevine Canyon spring	2.0	710'	3,670'	Graded	163-165
Hunter Mountain	1.0	400'	7,250'	F/18.5 mi	169-172
Inyo Copper Mine (shaft)	1.7	1350'	3,670'	F/6.8 mi	156
Little Dodd Spring	2.3	1,890'	4,340'	Graded	159-160
Ubehebe Trail loop	4.9	1,560'	3,340'	F/6.8 mi	162-164
Intermediate hikes (5-12 miles round trip)					
Big Dodd Spring	2.5	2,260'	4,320'	Graded	159-160
Blue Jay Mine base camp	4.1	840'	1,830'	Graded	145
Blue Jay Mine (road cut)	5.7	1,730'	2,040'	Graded	145-148
Grapevine Canyon					
loop	5.5	1,020'	3,600'	Graded	168
main side canyon spring	3.1	1,430'	3,660'	Graded	165-168
Lucky Rich Canyon					
Lucky Rich Prospect	3.0	2,230'	2,970'	H/4.0 mi	139-142
Tenth fall	3.3	2,350'	3,050'	H/4.0 mi	139-141
Long hikes (over 12 miles round trip)					
Copper Queen No. 2 Mine	6.1	2,340'	2,220'	P/28.8 mi	150-154
Copper Queen Trail					
to 130-ft shaft	6.5	2,690'	2,260'	P/28.8 mi	150-154
to Last Chance R. crest	7.6	3,600'	2,580'	P/28.8 mi	150-154
Ubehebe Peak	8.5	4,800'	2,860'	P/28.8 mi	150-154
Overnight hikes (2 days or more)					
Dodd Springs Trail					
to Lippincott Mine	6.5	4,400'	4,320'	Graded	159-162
Blue Jay Tr.–Copper Q. Trail					
Saline Valley to Racetrack	9.4	4,810'	2,890'	P/28.8 mi	149-154
Steel Pass Road					
Palm Spring to dunes	26.9	3,260'	3,840'	Graded	191-195
Ubehebe Trail					
Racetrack Val. to Lee Flat	13.8	7,570'	4,140'	F/6.8 mi	155-158

Key: P=Primitive (2WD) H=Primitive (HC) F=Primitive (4WD)
Distances: one way for out-and-back hikes, round-trip for loops
Elev. gain: sum of all elevation gains on round-trip or loop hike

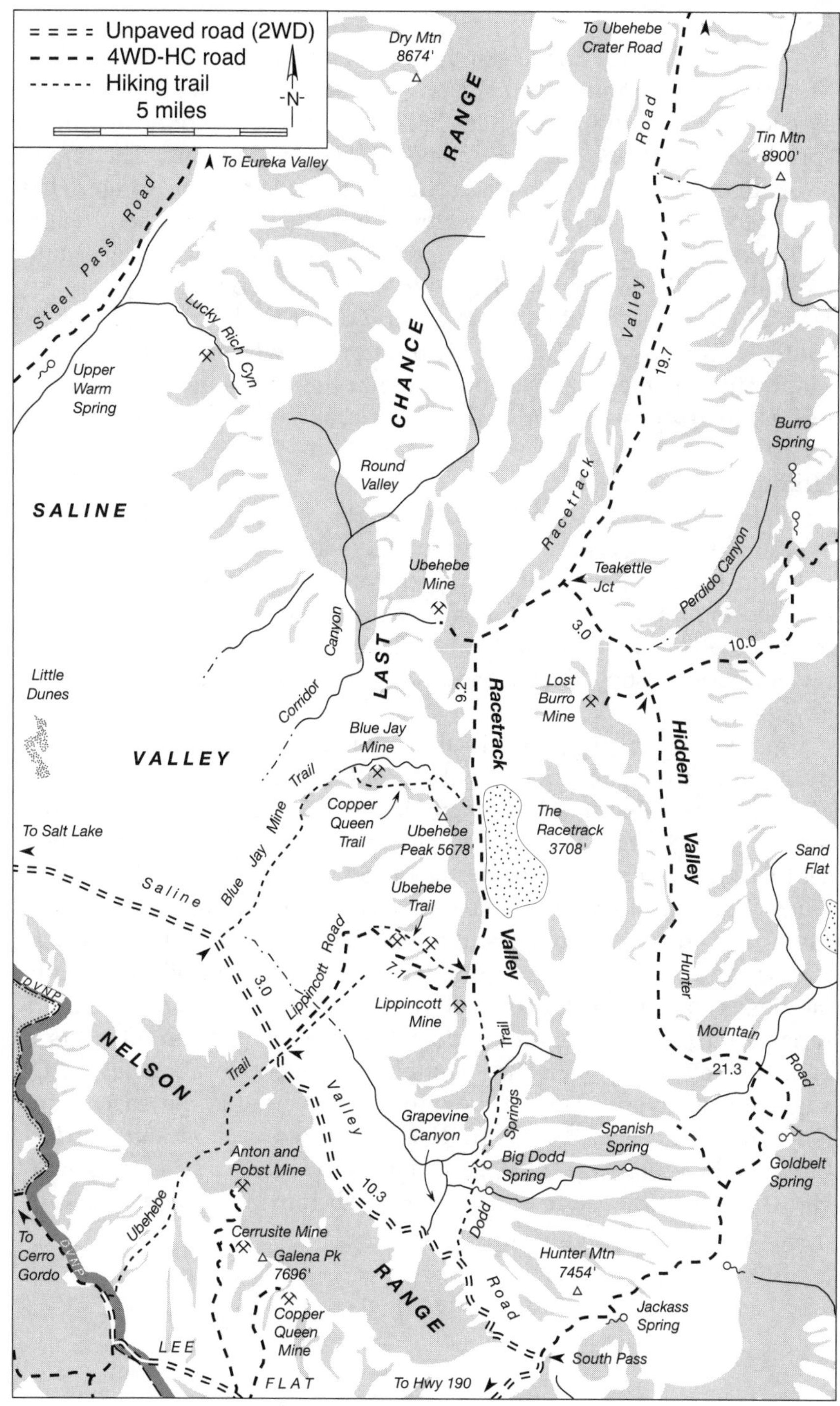
Unpaved road (2WD)
4WD-HC road
Hiking trail
5 miles
N
Dry Mtn
8674'
To Ubehebe
Crater Road
To Eureka Valley
Steel Pass Road
Tin Mtn
8900'
LAST CHANCE RANGE
Lucky Rich Cyn
Upper
Warm
Spring
Round
Valley
Racetrack Valley Road
19.7
Burro
Spring
SALINE VALLEY
Ubehebe
Mine
Teakettle
Jct
Perdido Canyon
Corridor Canyon
3.0
10.0
Little
Dunes
Lost
Burro
Mine
9.2
Racetrack Valley
Hidden Valley
Blue Jay
Mine
Copper
Queen
Trail
Ubehebe
Peak 5678'
The
Racetrack
3708'
To Salt Lake
Saline
Blue Jay Mine Trail
Sand
Flat
Ubehebe
Trail
Lippincott Road
7.1
3.0
Lippincott
Mine
Hunter Mountain Road
NELSON RANGE
Trail
21.3
Valley
Grapevine
Canyon
Springs Trail
Spanish
Spring
Big Dodd
Spring
Goldbelt
Spring
Anton and
Pobst Mine
10.3
Ubehebe
Cerrusite Mine
Galena Pk
7696'
To
Cerro
Gordo
DVNP
Dodd Road
Hunter Mtn
7454'
Copper
Queen
Mine
Jackass
Spring
LEE FLAT
South Pass
To Hwy 190

Springs

The Last Chance Range stands in the rain shadow of the high Inyo Mountains to the west, and it is generally fairly dry. Springs are exceedingly rare. In the southern half of the range, the only significant springs are found on the west slope of Hunter Mountain. The largest ones are in Grapevine Canyon, at the southern end of the range. They support several lush riparian systems and small year-round streams. The next largest springs are not nearly as wet: Jackass Spring usually has only a little flow, while Big Dodd and Little Dodd springs are dry most of the time. In spite of this general dryness, the high crest of the southern range can receive a bit of snow in winter, especially Dry Mountain. The mountain supports one of the park's healthiest conifer forests, and extensive stands of small Joshua trees at lower elevations.

Hiking

Hiking in the western Last Chance Range is, above all, a solitary experience. It takes so long to get to this place, and access roads are so few and rough, that hikers are even fewer than elsewhere. Yet this parched mountain range offers a wide range of wonderful hikes, both for the well-seasoned desert rat and for the novice, perhaps a little uneasy about testing their route-finding skills in such an unforgiving environment.

The selection suggested in the following pages includes a long peak climb from the floor of Saline Valley (Ubehebe Peak), an easy climb (Hunter Mountain), three moderate to difficult hikes on historic mining trails that have not seen regular use since the early twentieth century (the Ubehebe Trail, the Dodd Springs Trail, and the Copper Queen Trail), a valley-floor hike to a historic copper mine (the Blue Jay Mine), and three canyon hikes to remote narrows (Lucky Rich Canyon, Grapevine Canyon, and the Blue Jay Mine). The trail hikes all go by old mines and prospects. The high routes offer spectacular views of the range's wrinkled topography, the Racetrack, and different parts of Saline Valley. There is also fun climbing at several locations along the suggested canyons. The Grapevine Canyon hike is the easiest and most straightforward. If you are looking for more, check out Corridor Canyon, the Lippincott Mine, and some of the other destinations out of Hidden Valley and Racetrack Valley described in *Hiking Death Valley*.

▪

LUCKY RICH CANYON

In the heart of the Last Chance Range there is an impressive little gorge with towering walls of massive limestone, filled with falls, boulders, and chockstones, where a man by the name of Lucky Rich once claimed he had a rich lead mine. Remote, rough, and rarely visited, this is a place for nature lovers and geology nuts, for adrenaline junkies and fitness freaks, and for the hopeless romantics whose minds reel at the sight of rocks 400 million years old. Come on in. It is well worth a day of your life.

General Information
Jurisdiction: Death Valley National Park
Road status: Roadless; primitive access road (HC)
Lucky Rich Prospect: 3.0 mi, 2,180 ft up, 50 ft down one way / moderate
Upper narrows: 3.3 mi, 2,330 ft up, 20 ft down one way / difficult
Main attractions: Scenic hike along a canyon gorge, falls, geology
USGS 7.5' topo map: West of Teakettle Junction
Maps: pp. 141*, *137*

Location and Access

Lucky Rich Canyon is in the Last Chance Range northeast of Saline Valley's warm springs. The starting point of this hike is about 1.6 miles north from Upper Warm Spring on the Steel Pass Road (see *The Warm Springs* for directions and road conditions). When you get close, look for a low dark-brown hill of basalt a couple of miles to the east, where the fan meets the range. The mouth of Lucky Rich Canyon is right against the hill's south side. Park so that your vehicle is not hidden from the east by the tall gravel bank that lines the road. Homing in on it on your way back will be all that much easier.

Route Description

Directions are simple: just hike cross-country up the fan, aiming for the wash on the south side of the dark basaltic hill. To find your vehicle more easily on your way back, identify early on a peak on the western horizon that you can use as a beacon. The surface of the fan is rough and gets worse along the way. Hiking is a little faster if you follow washes rather than benches, especially near the top of the fan.

No matter how well prepared you are, there is always a strong element of surprise when you enter a canyon for the first time. This one turned out to be a complete surprise: all of it is a narrow gorge trapped between angular walls that soar hundreds of feet to craggy summits. Its geology is also particularly entertaining. As you hike through Lucky Rich Canyon you will time-travel back to the Paleozoic, with a short time warp in and out of the Jurassic along the way. You start in the early Ordovician at the canyon mouth and move through successively younger formations, to eventually end 140 million years later, in the late Devonian. The stately walls looming just inside the mouth are limestone of the Pogonip Group. Further on, they are replaced by orangy quartz monzonite (Hunter Mountain), the Jurassic formation that litters the wash. Wander deeper along the sinuous wash and you will cross snow-white quartzite boulders (Eureka Quartzite), then a tall gateway and straight narrows of striated dolomite (Ely Springs Dolomite), and finally solid walls of limestone and dolomite (Hidden Valley Dolomite and Lost Burro Formation). The most spectacular formation is tucked at the very end—a 60-foot-high pile of monumental conglomerate chockstones stuffed with boulder-size inclusions!

In spite of all this beauty, the single feature that overwhelms the mood of this canyon is its raw character. The Last Chance Range has risen so fast that erosion has not kept up with it, and Lucky Rich Canyon is one insanely steep place. In all of it, there may not be a single square yard of smooth level gravel. Every step you take the ground tilts more strongly, as if you were walking up inside a giant parabola. The cobbles underfoot give way to boulders. The boulders get bigger. In the end it gets completely out of hand and the inevitable happens: in one grand finale, the ground turns vertical.

It is both an unsettling and curiously lush sensation to walk in a world where the concept of horizontality has been abolished. It is also, as it turns out, rather strenuous. Expect physical challenges, hard work, and sweat, as you puff, hop, scramble, and climb. It is hardly

Lucky Rich Canyon

	Dist.(mi)	Elev.(ft)
Steel Pass Road	0.0	2,150
Mouth	2.0	3,040
First fall	2.4	3,460
Lucky Rich Prospect	(0.6)	4,310
Side canyon	1.60	3,680
Fourth fall	2.55	3,610
Tenth fall	3.3	4,480

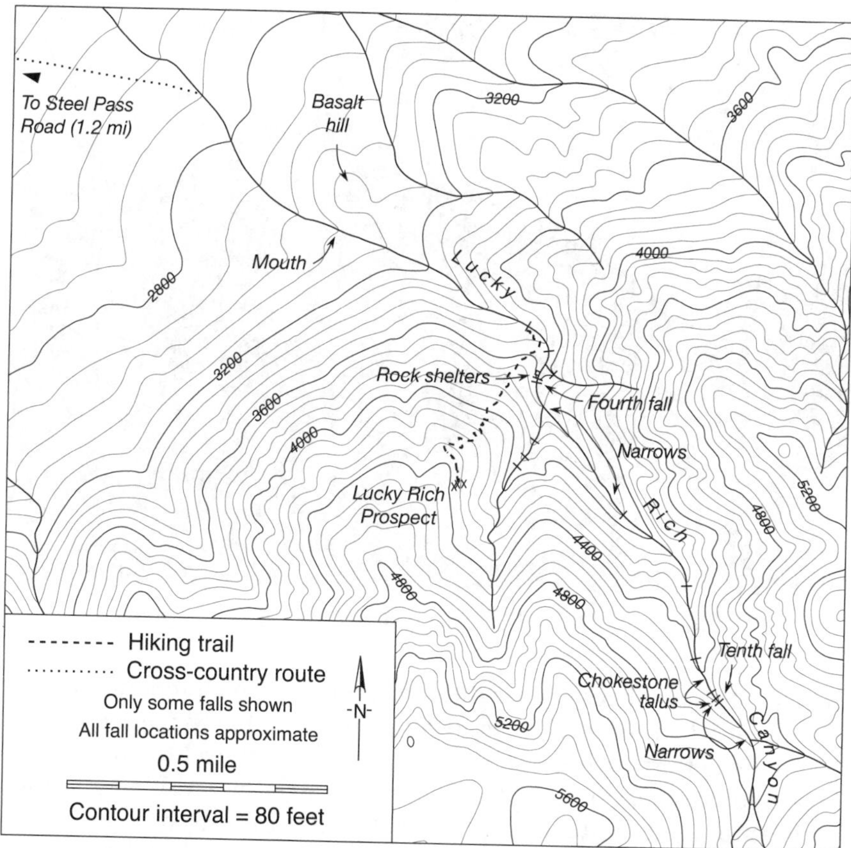

surprising that a place this steep has ten falls. What is surprising is that most of them are easy to climb. The first exception is the fourth fall, which requires technical climbing. Most hikers will shy away from scaling its 16-foot chute, but the short slot against the chockstone on its south side is manageable. One approach is to wedge your body into the slot sideways—back against the wall, feet against the chockstone—and to wiggle up, a few inches at a time (remember that climbing back down is scarier and harder). The second exception is the tenth fall. Wedged at the entrance to the second narrows, enclosed by unscalable walls, it very effectively blocks access to the last half-mile of canyon. It is about 12 feet high at its shortest, and the climb is probably a 5.10 or easier, but the rock is too loose for comfort. Unless you are an excellent climber or have a thing for pain, this will be your turning point.

This canyon's namesake is Lucky Rich Baldwin, a long-time camp host at Saline Valley's hot springs who enjoyed dabbling in prospecting (see *Lead Canyon*). Baldwin had a prospect in this canyon. The two

Towering scarps at the entrance to Lucky Rich Canyon

rock shelters at the foot of the third fall and the mining monument and bits of bleached lumber in the lower canyon are likely the remains of his mining efforts. His prospect is perched 650 feet up the side canyon on the south side. Climbing the falls up through this steep and narrow gully is fun, but the half-mile trail that Lucky Rich used to get to his diggings is easier. It starts on the right just before the base of the first fall. The lower segment is hard to locate and discontinuous, but follow the rocky spine to the ridge that parallels the side canyon (see map), then it is easy to trace. There it switchbacks up the ridge to a knoll. Lucky Rich Prospect is 120 yards to the south-southeast, 30 feet below the knoll. It does not amount to much: half a dozen shallow pits dug in whitish skarns speckled with garnet, silver, zinc, and copper ores. Its lack of commercial value may explain the story I was told by an old timer: Lucky Rich used to show melted battery lead to government officials as evidence of the annual assessment work the law required him to perform on his claim! Lucky Rich may not have been so lucky with mines, but he had it made: a secluded hangout in the desert hills, and warm springs practically all to himself. The search for his hidden trail, which only a handful of people have walked since he last did, is a gem in itself. The trail commands grand perspectives of the canyon's giant stratified walls, and of the Saline Range's furrowed volcanic hills.

■

THE BLUE JAY MINE

The appeal of this small historic copper mine lies not so much in its tunnels as in the scenic trail that leads up to it, across the beautiful southern reaches of Saline Valley. The mine's small camp, its unusual geology and bright-blue ore, and the impressive canyon in which it is located, all conspire to make this pleasant hike a wonderfully diverse desert experience.

General Information

Jurisdiction: Death Valley National Park
Road status: Easy hiking access from primitive road
Blue Jay Mine base camp: 4.1 mi, 830 ft up, 10 ft down one way / easy
Blue Jay Mine: 5.7 mi, 1,710 ft up, 20 ft down one way / moderate
Main attractions: Historic copper mine, long valley-floor hike
USGS 7.5' topo maps: West of Ubehebe Peak, Ubehebe Peak
Maps: pp. 147*, 153, *137*

Location and Access

The Blue Jay Mine is tucked in the lower end of a nameless canyon of the southern Last Chance Range, almost due east of Salt Lake. It is accessed by an old mining road (now a foot trail) that starts off the Saline Valley Road 2.95 miles north of the Lippincott Road turnoff (or 8.1 miles east of the Salt Tramway Junction). Keep good track of your mileage, as this road is easy to miss. Look for a level, open area on the east side of the road. The Blue Jay Mine Trail starts about 20 yards to the east, past a field of rocks scattered by the NPS to discourage four-wheelers from driving this road. The area up ahead is a wilderness, and the Blue Jay Mine Trail is closed to motor vehicles and bikes.

Geology: Metasomatism

Most mines in the southern Last Chance Range are found near metamorphic rocks known as skarns. When magma comes in contact with limestone, elements like silicon, magnesium, and iron diffuse from the magma into the limestone and react with it to produce a skarn. This is called metasomatism—the addition and/or subtraction of material through migrating fluids. A skarn is often rich in silicate minerals and heavy-metal sulfides. The garnet skarn at the Blue Jay Mine was formed in the Late Jurassic or Early Cretaceous, when the quartz monzonite pluton that now makes up the bulk of Ubehebe Peak

Limestone spur above the Blue Jay Mine

pushed its way through Lost Burro Formation limestone. The host rock was extensively crystallized and locally metamorphosed into tactite. The minerals contained in and around the skarn include chalcopyrite and bornite (copper), magnetite and hematite (iron), and molybdenite.

History

The Blue Jay Mine is an old property that had already been claimed by 1902 and became an active component of the Ubehebe Mining District. Its owner, a man from Independence named Arlie Mairs, worked it episodically for at least three decades, to the tune of the copper market. Around 1914, Mairs took advantage of the salt mining operations down by Salt Lake. He transported his ore 13 miles across the valley to the salt tramway, which trammed it over the Inyo Mountains to Owens Valley (see *The Salt Tramway*). The Blue Jay Mine's only recorded production is 20 tons of high-grade ore in 1915, which yielded 4,000 pounds of copper and nearly 1,200 ounces of silver. The mine remained idle for decades. It was briefly active again as the Jarosite Mine in 1971, when M. S. & W. Resources drilled holes along the mineralized zone, down to 540 feet, to assess the property value. The drill cores turned out to average only about 1% copper and 0.1% molybdenum, and the mine has been left alone ever since. Mairs probably exhausted the Blue Jay's few high-grade pockets.

Route Description

The Blue Jay Mine Trail. If you love the desert, you will enjoy this unique trail. The longest in the valley, it offers a rare opportunity to take a leisurely hike across the valley floor and admire the spectacular surrounding ranges. Although at places it is slowly being reclaimed by nature, it is mostly in good shape. The grades are gentle, the ground is well-compacted sandy silt, and the walking is easy. The scenery is beautiful, embracing Saline Valley and the Saline Range to the north, and the deeply furrowed Last Chance Range up ahead. Although the Blue Jay Mine is hidden from view, you can see its approximate location the whole way: it is at the southern base of the sheer whitish spur straight ahead. The most incredible event here, if the winter has been wet, is the spring flower show. On one of my visits, golden and brown-eyed evening primrose grew knee high as far as the eye could see, merging in the distance into a fluorescent dusting of gold. The cover was so dense that in minutes my shoes were coated with yellow pollen. Many other plants contributed to the display—gravel ghost, turtleback, locoweed, desert gold poppy, and Mojave desert star. The wash beyond the end of the trail hosts the highest concentration of Death Valley Mohavea I have seen anywhere.

The base camp. After 3.5 miles the road makes a pronounced left, levels off, and disappears on the edge of a wide rocky wash. From here on to the mine, only segments of road remain. Walk 0.6 mile on the south side of the wash until you run into another road segment heading up the wash. It leads shortly to shallow terraces bulldozed on the hillside to the south. This area was a base camp for miners prospecting in the nearby hills. The terraces are littered with odds and ends—a cold box, a rusted bedspring, scattered lumber and pipes, a small corral, and the collapsed shell of a trailer. The smooth, inch-diameter cylinders at the trailer are the drill cores of colorful quartz monzonite and marble taken from the Blue Jay Mine in the 1970s.

The Blue Jay Mine. The Blue Jay Mine is not up this wash but in the next canyon north, which is well hidden in the wrinkles of the range's foothills. To find it, from the base camp hike up the wash 400 yards to a segment of road on the left, invaded by creosote. Follow it north-northeast up over a low swell 0.3 mile to the ill-defined wash of the next canyon north. At that point the road ends. Ignore the faint prospecting roads to the north and hike up the wash to the mouth of the canyon, less than 100 yards away.

The historic camp of the Blue Jay Mine is on the south bank 0.4 mile into the canyon, shortly after the first right bend. Its small wind shelter and curious home-made stove shaped like a headless dog are hidden from the wash, but its prominent stone house will draw your attention to it. Erected at the opposite ends of a large quartz-monzonite boulder shaped like a faceted crystal, the two roofless rooms are just large enough for a single person to curl up and sleep.

Historic camp of the Blue Jay Mine

What is most striking about the Blue Jay Mine is not its workings but its location. As you proceed up canyon the scenery is gradually dominated by the whitish spur you have been aiming for all along, an imposing monolith that rises smoothly more than 400 precipitous feet and looms over the entire area. Like all exposures on the north side of the canyon, it is made of limestone of the Lost Burro Formation. The quartz monzonite that intruded it is exposed south of the wash. The skarn zone that developed at their boundary is located in between, on either side of the wash. The workings of the Blue Jay Mine coincide with the portion of the skarn zone that was most strongly mineralized, which extends for 600 feet in the vicinity of the limestone wall.

The Blue Jay Mine		
	Dist.(mi)	Elev.(ft)
Saline Valley Road	0.0	1,425
Blue Jay Mine Trail washed out	3.6	2,010
Base camp	4.1	2,240
Canyon mouth	4.7	2,480
Historic camp (stone house)	5.0	2,660
Blue Jay Mine (lowest working)	5.3	2,810
Blue Jay Mine (roadcut)	5.7	3,110

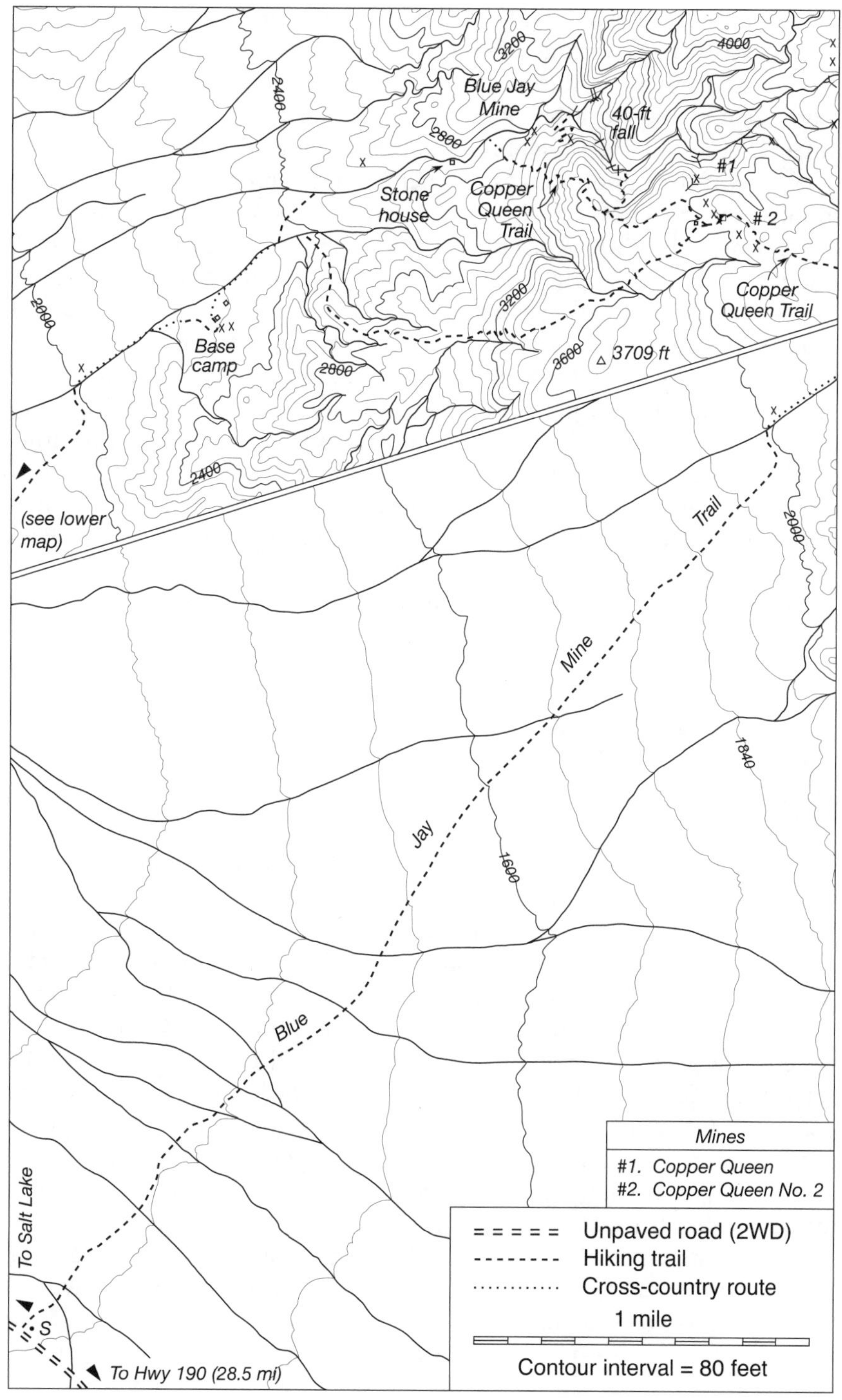
3200
4000
2400
Blue Jay
Mine
40-ft
fall
2800
#1
Stone
house
Copper
Queen
Trail
2
3200
Copper
Queen Trail
2000
Base
camp
2800
3600
3709 ft
2400
(see lower
map)
Trail
2000
Mine
1840
Jay
1600
Blue
Mines
#1. Copper Queen
#2. Copper Queen No. 2
Unpaved road (2WD)
Hiking trail
Cross-country route
1 mile
Contour interval = 80 feet
To Salt Lake
S
To Hwy 190 (28.5 mi)

One of the pleasures of exploring this area is to search for the many scattered workings of the Blue Jay Mine. The lowest ones are two short tunnels on the south side of the wash. Little ore is exposed here. One of the workings was converted into a storage and sleeping area. There is another one at the mouth of the third side canyon on the left. One of the mine's longest tunnels, it has been partly backfilled by floods. The rock face all around its entrance is sprinkled with green copper ore. There are other tunnels in the steep side canyons, some of them reached by hanging segments of road. The most interesting area is the 100-foot roadcut at the very end of the old road. This last bit of road starts on the south side, across from the third side canyon. It zigzags steeply up to the roadcut, offering good views of the wall and the canyon. There is no tunnel here; the roadcut was the mine. This heavily mineralized area is a wonderful outdoor geology museum. The roadway is covered with beautiful porphyritic samples sparkling with pink calcite, quartz, epidote, garnet, and chalcopyrite. The copper ore scattered here and in the wash below is mostly malachite and chalcocite. It bears the deepest shades of blue I have seen in the region, an unusual color that may well have inspired the mine's name.

Possible extensions. Make sure to save time to explore deeper in the canyon. The next stretch is a narrow granitic gorge filled with boulders, slickrock slants, and falls, and it would be a shame to come this far and not get to see it. If you manage to climb the exposed 40-foot fall (refer to *Ubehebe Peak* before trying it), you can loop back by continuing up canyon past two falls to the pronounced left bend. On the south side of the wash, a vague, overgrown foot trail climbs steeply south, then west, 0.25 mile to a saddle (3,670') on the canyon rim, where it joins the Copper Queen Trail (see map). From there you have two options to return. You can go down the Copper Queen Trail 0.65 mile to the canyon wash (2,735') between the Blue Jay Mine and its historic camp. Or you can take the trail the other way, 0.5 mile up to another mining camp (see *Ubehebe Peak*). The right fork (southwest) at the camp drops 1,620 feet in 1.7 miles to the base of the mountains, where it ends at the wash 0.4 mile above the base camp.

■

UBEHEBE PEAK

Been there? Done that? What about trying again from Saline Valley? Longer and more strenuous than the trail hike from the Racetrack, this seldom-used route will take you on a mining trail across the valley to the Last Chance Range, then up either a ridge trail or a deep canyon to the divide with Racetrack Valley, and finally up a rough trail to 5,678-foot Ubehebe Peak. Look forward to spectacular vistas of Saline Valley and the Racetrack, and a chance to explore several remote historic copper mines.

General Information

Jurisdiction: Death Valley National Park
Road status: Roadless; graded access road
Copper Queen Mine: 6.5 mi, 2,650 ft up, 40 ft down one way / difficult
Ubehebe Peak: 8.5 mi, 4,530 ft up, 270 ft down one way / strenuous
Main attractions: A spectacular peak climb, old trails, copper mines
USGS 7.5′ topo maps: West of Ubehebe Peak, Ubehebe Peak
Maps: pp. 147*, 153*, *137*

Location and Access

Ubehebe Peak is the highest summit in the southern Last Chance Range, almost due east of Salt Lake. The shortest route to it, described in *Hiking Death Valley*, is from the Racetrack via the Ubehebe Peak Trail. The longer route described here starts from the Saline Valley Road, proceeds to the foot of the range along the Blue Jay Mine Trail, then climbs along either a canyon or the Copper Queen Trail to join the Ubehebe Peak Trail at the crest. The rest of the climb is on this trail to the summit. The Blue Jay Mine Trail starts on the Saline Valley Road 2.95 miles north of the Lippincott Road (or 8.1 miles east of the Salt Tramway Junction). Refer to *The Blue Jay Mine* for details.

Route Description

The Blue Jay Mine Trail. The first part of this hike, northeast across Saline Valley on the Blue Jay Mine Trail, is described under *The Blue Jay Mine*. When you reach the mine area in the canyon, you will have a choice of two routes to the crest, both about 2.4 miles long. The first one continues up the canyon to the Ubehebe Peak Trail at the crest. The second route is on the Copper Queen Trail, which was used historically to access the extensive Copper Queen claims from

Racetrack Valley, and after which I named it. This trail ascends the canyon's south rim and ends at the same point on the crest.

The canyon route. Beyond the Blue Jay Mine the canyon narrows abruptly as it veers west and cuts straight into a hard shelf of quartz monzonite. As you enter the dark, chaotic narrows, you wonder how it will manage to go through. In fact, it doesn't. Past a series of short falls, slants, and boulders, a huge, nearly vertical fall, over 40 feet high, blocks the way. Unless you are an excellent climber, do not attempt scaling it. It is an easy climb up to the middle, perhaps only a Class 4, but the rest is technical (low 5s). The holds are good, but the route is exposed. In the next 100 yards above this fall there are two lower falls, easy to climb. The second one, just past the narrows, is made of white crystallized tactite bisected by a band of apple-green copper ore. If you are not certain you can climb the 40-foot fall safely, turn around and use the Copper Queen Trail, which circumvents the narrows.

The next stretch of canyon is open and straight. At the first fork, head right into the side canyon. Shortly into it you will reach the Copper Queen Mine. A faint trail leads up a steep talus to its tunnel high above the wash on the south side. About 0.15 mile further, on the same side, are the 60-foot shaft, short tunnel, and trenches of the Copper Queen No. 2 Mine. The yellowish ore-bearing rock is tactite heavily stained with iron. Both properties were probably part of the claims controlled around 1905-1908 by Jack Salsberry, a promoter who generated a lot of the original interest in the Ubehebe Mining District. Past the Copper Queen Mine, the canyon becomes gradually shallower. After 0.35 mile, take the right fork again. With a little cross-country travel near the end (see map), it will take you in 0.4 mile to the Copper Queen Trail on a ridge (~4,450'), with only 0.5 mile left to the crest.

The Copper Queen Trail. This route is less demanding than the canyon, but two difficulties must be overcome. The first one is finding the trail, and the second one is staying on it. To find the trail, 0.3 mile in the canyon look for the stone house on the south bench (see *The Blue Jay Mine*). Go 300 yards further, past a sharp left bend and in the middle of a right bend, to a broad, shallow ravine coming down on the right. This is where the Copper Queen Trail used to end, but its lower end is washed out. Leave the wash and head southeast towards the west end of the conspicuous exposure of gray limestone in the sheer canyon wall. You should run into the Copper Queen Trail in 50 yards.

From here the trail zigzags 0.65 mile up to a saddle (3,670') at the canyon rim, and it forks. If you are bypassing the falls and want to

Wrinkled hills and Saline Valley from the Copper Queen Trail

return to the canyon, take the left fork, which descends steeply to the wash just above the upper fall. Otherwise take the right fork, which is the Copper Queen Trail. From here to the crest, it climbs five steep, rocky slopes separated by level terraces of various lengths. The trail is fairly well defined on the terraces, but on the three upper slopes its switchbacks are so faint you will have to believe it is there to see it. Expect to lose it for brief periods. Try to spot the trail ahead of you as often as possible, and look for the small historic cairns that mark the way. If you loose it, follow the ridge and you will never be far from it. If you cross a wash or a canyon, you are not at the right place.

If you hike the trail downhill, it is generally easier to stay on it, but there are still two tricky areas where the trail is faint and easy to miss. The first one is 0.15 mile west of the crest, where the trail makes a sharp right. Look for the next visible section of trail at the whitish serrated outcrop 50 yards to the west. The second spot is at the fork at the mining camp (4,030'). The better defined trail goes straight, passing to the left of the camp: this is the trail to the base camp trail (it is visible to the southwest, across a wash 400 feet below). The Copper Queen Trail is actually the faint right fork, just before (east of) the camp, where it heads northwest and begins its descent to the saddle.

There is a danger to this hike: it is easy to let the constant search for the trail consume your attention. The scenery is spectacular, so try not to let these technicalities spoil it. The whole way you will be on an exposed ridge overlooking Saline Valley. The views are superb, extending from Salt Lake to the dunes, Willow Creek Camp, and beyond. You are constantly immersed in this aerial landscape, dominated to the north by the deeply chiseled shoulder of Dry Mountain, and to the east by the dark, soaring crags of Ubehebe Peak. Desert lovers will revel in this wasteland wilderness, where vegetation is scarce and the land is carved out of naked quartz monzonite. The bedrock is part of the Hunter Mountain batholith, which intruded this area around 170 million years ago and is now exposed over most of the southern Last Chance Range. At the halfway point it forms a scenic field of weathered boulders, crowned by an oddly tilted pinnacle.

In the middle of this supreme desolation there is a little mine, up against a low hill, not shown on any maps. It is 0.55 mile past the saddle, on a broad ridge 0.1 mile after the trail angles 90° to the right The ruins of a camp lie 10–20 yards to the right of the trail, the main structure a crude stone wall erected against a low quartz-monzonite outcrop. Long ago a lonesome miner came to this far-flung place, dug a few exploratory trenches and, liking what he unearthed, proceeded to heroically sink a 130-foot shaft. The low, primitive headframe that caps the shaft and its hand winch attest to its antiquity. A rickety wooden

Ubehebe Peak

	Dist.(mi)	Elev.(ft)
Saline Valley Road	0.0	1,425
Blue Jay Mine Trail washed out	3.6	2,010
Canyon mouth	4.7	2,480
Historic camp (stone house)	5.0	2,660
Wash below Copper Queen Tr.	5.1	2,740
Copper Queen Mine via cyn	(0.8)	3,580
Copper Queen No. 2	(1.0)	3,730
Join Copper Queen Trail	(1.8)	~4,450
Crest/Ubehebe Peak Trail	(2.3)	4,920
Saddle (trail junction)	5.75	3,670
Mining camp (trail junction)	6.3	4,030
Copper Queen's 130-ft shaft	6.35	4,040
Crest/Ubehebe Peak Trail	7.5	4,920
Racetrack Valley Road	(1.7)	3,710
Saddle	8.1	5,220
Ubehebe Peak	8.5	5,678

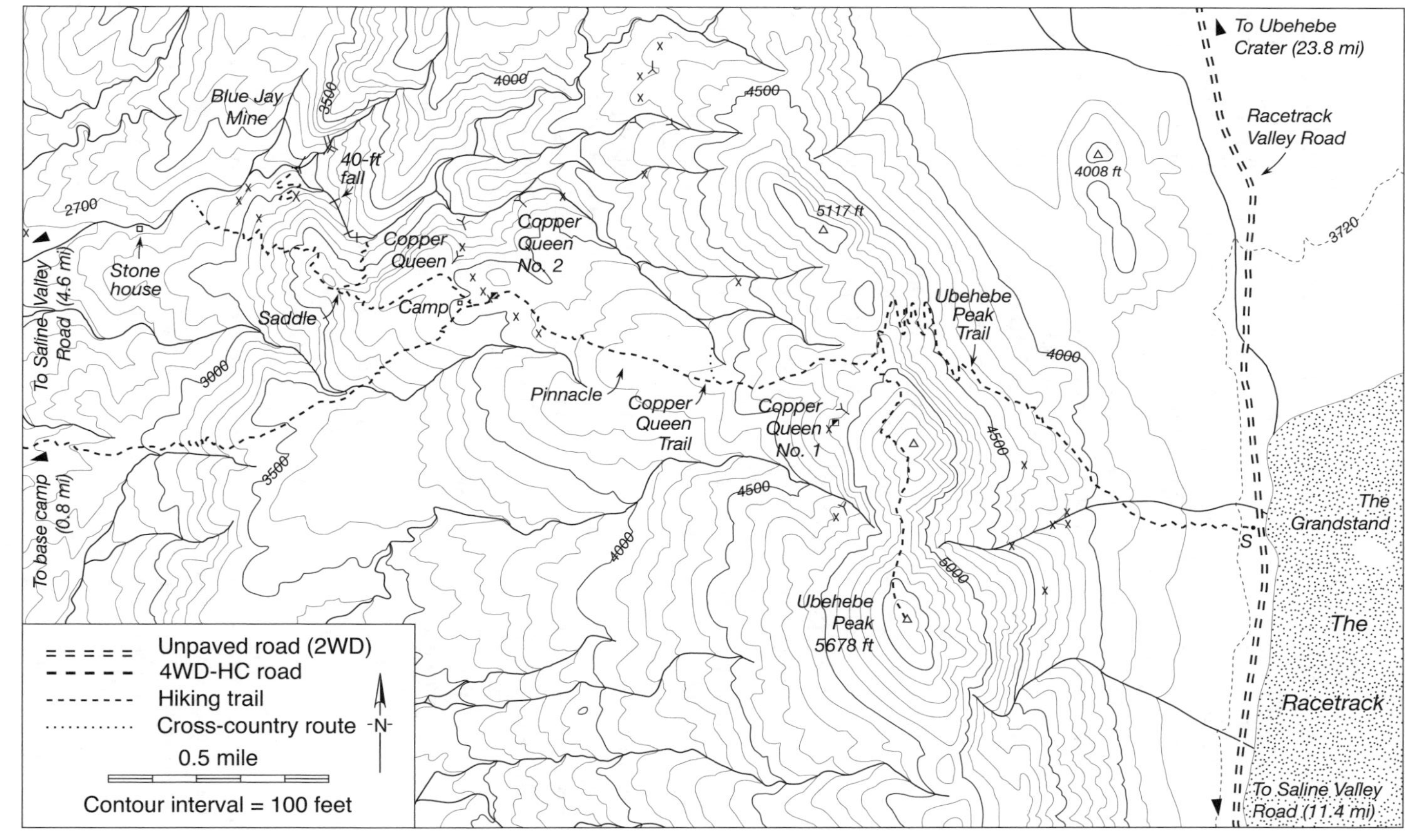
Blue Jay Mine
3500
4000
4500
To Ubehebe Crater (23.8 mi)
Racetrack Valley Road
40-ft fall
4008 ft
2700
5117 ft
3720
Copper Queen
Copper Queen No. 2
Stone house
To Saline Valley Road (4.6 mi)
Saddle
Camp
Ubehebe Peak Trail
3000
4000
Pinnacle
Copper Queen Trail
Copper Queen No. 1
To base camp (0.8 mi)
3500
4500
4500
4000
The Grandstand
S
5000
Ubehebe Peak 5678 ft
The Racetrack
Unpaved road (2WD)
4WD-HC road
Hiking trail
Cross-country route
N
0.5 mile
Contour interval = 100 feet
To Saline Valley Road (11.4 mi)

ladder drops out of sight into the shaft. Chunks of copper ore shine a supernatural blue in the harsh sunlight. This mine was likely part of the Copper Queen claims. Up and down the ridge stone monuments and engraved boulders mark its now meaningless boundaries.

Just east of the camp the trail splits. The trail that heads southwest descends to the foot of the mountain near the base camp of the Blue Jay Mine (see *The Blue Jay Mine*)—an adventurous alternative return route. The trail on the left is the Copper Queen Trail. It climbs 1 mile to the ultimate terrace, angles sharply left, and continues north 0.15 mile to the crest overlooking the Racetrack. There it meets with the Ubehebe Peak Trail coming up from the Racetrack Valley Road.

From the crest to the peak. To get to the peak (1 mile), follow this trail south up along the ridge. It circumvents a high point near the nameless peak north of Ubehebe Peak (a hiker with a sense of humor baptized it "Ubeshebe" in the summit log). In spite of a few switchbacks and stairs, this stretch is steep and rough. The trail then drops to the saddle between the two peaks. The rest of it, harder to find, stays close to the ridge line. This is strenuous hiking, over a slope approaching 45% and covered with large rocks—not all of them rock steady. But as usual the rewards make it all well worth it. At several points along the way, you will be staring down the razor-sharp edge of Ubehebe Peak and enjoy breathtaking views of Racetrack Valley. The vistas from the narrow summit of Ubehebe Peak are unsurpassed. To the east, you look straight down at the pristine Racetrack playa and its tiny island of dark rounded rocks, with the high Cottonwood Mountains sprawling in the background. Turn around and you are peering into the silent immensity of Saline Valley, half a mile deeper.

Suggested Hikes and Hiking Times

If you can arrange to be picked up, the point-to-point hike from Saline Valley to the Racetrack, which takes a moderately long day, is the best. The second best hike is the round trip to Ubehebe Peak. Try hiking the canyon on the way up and returning on the trail to better appreciate the panoramic views. Also, at midday the canyon offers a little shade, whereas the trail has none. Both routes are steep, averaging about 1,000 feet per mile in the mountain. The round-trip takes a very long day. Some hikers will prefer to make it an overnight hike, although to visit all the mines three days would be more comfortable. The main problem then, of course, is that there is not a single free molecule of water the whole way. Bring your own, and plenty of it.

■

THE UBEHEBE TRAIL

The Ubehebe Trail is a long track used by miners and their pack trains around the turn of the previous century to commute between Owens Valley and Racetrack Valley. The short segment that crosses the southern Last Chance Range commands spacious vistas of Saline Valley and gives access to a steep-walled canyon and what was once the most promising copper mine in the district. More ambitious hikers can take a couple of days to push on, across the southern tip of Saline Valley, over the Nelson Range, and down into Lee Flat's open forest Joshua trees, to retrace the rest of this largely forgotten historic route.

General Information

Jurisdiction: Death Valley National Park
Road status: Roadless; primitive access road (4WD/HC)
Inyo Copper Mine: 1.7 mi, 280 ft up, 1,070 ft down one way/easy
Ubehebe Trail–Lippincott Road: 4.9 mi, 1,560 ft up loop/easy–moderate
Racetrack V.–Lee Flat: 13.8 mi, 4,840 ft up, 2,730 ft down one way/stren.
Main attractions: Long historic trail, views, copper mines, Joshua trees
USGS 7.5' topo maps: Ubehebe Pk*, West of Ubehebe Pk, Nelson Range
Maps: pp. 157*, *137*

Location and Access

The segment of the Ubehebe Trail that crosses the Last Chance Range parallels the Lippincott Road. To get to the trail, drive the Saline Valley Road 10.3 miles north from South Pass (or 11.0 miles south from the Salt Tramway Junction) to the Lippincott Road, marked by a 4-foot cairn. Drive this high-clearance road 4.1 miles northeast to a side road on the left, below the Bonanza Prospect. The west end of the Ubehebe Trail is at the top of the quarry (it is hard to find). Since the views are better when hiking this trail westbound, you can drive another 2.7 miles to the loop at the top of the Lippincott Road, where the east end of the trail is located, and hike from there. However, this road is rocky and requires four-wheel drive at a few hairy places. To spare you the drive, park at the prospect, walk up the road, and return on the trail.

Route Description

The east end of the Ubehebe Trail starts 0.1 mile east of the loop at the top of the Lippincott Road, on the north side. It climbs west then northwest to the divide between Racetrack Valley and Saline Valley (0.4 mile) and soon reaches its high point (0.2 mile). It then begins its slow descent into Saline Valley, along a narrow ridge at the rim of a twisted canyon to the north. The greatest payoff of this hike is the views. From almost anywhere they encompass all of the valley and its magnificent ring of mountains. Wildlife, though scarce, can be an unexpected attraction. Even in a desert range almost destitute of springs, life finds hospitable niches. I scared a jackrabbit near the summit. A little further, a dozen quails returned the favor and made me jump out of my skin. In the morning the trail was stitched with fresh bighorn tracks neatly overlapping my own from the previous day.

In the early 1900s, the steep-walled monzonite canyon below the trail was the site of a large property owned by the Inyo Copper Mines and Smelter Company. With 19 claims covering some 400 acres, it was then the district's most developed mine. Ore containing as much as 40% copper was exposed, but subsequent drilling revealed little ore at depth, and the claims were never exploited. Searching for a way down into the canyon to the mine is a lot of fun. There is a decent route 0.6 mile from the high point, where a faint trail on the right leads to a level area on the abrupt canyon rim. This was the mine's camp, which had a large cabin. From there a very steep but passable dirt talus drops to the canyon wash. There is a crooked 90-foot tunnel at wash level 500 feet down canyon, and a shaft with pale-green ore specked with chalcopyrite on the ridge to the north. A second shaft, bordered by a colorful apron of copper oxides, is 0.3 mile down canyon. Passage is interrupted by two falls, the first one 11 feet high and easy, the second one 35 feet, only a 5.6 but quite exposed and dangerous. It can fortunately be bypassed down the steep talus on its north side. The workings are not exactly earth-shattering, but do not rule out serendipitous encounters. Mine was with a wooden door hanging 40 feet up a cliff, a scene right out of the twilight zone. It opened onto a tiny dugout, the lair of a forgotten hermit with a craving for canned lobster and evaporated milk.

West from the camp, the Ubehebe Trail is intermittent, and a trail only in the loosest sense. Where it is gone, just follow the ridge. After 0.5 mile, it leaves the ridge, drops southwest in a few switchbacks, circles the foot of a short cliff, and reaches the top of the Bonanza Prospect quarry. This copper property was first assessed around 1880, during the early days of the Ubehebe Mining District. Then known as the Hessen Clipper, it consisted of a 65-foot tunnel and a 30-foot shaft. It became the Bonanza Prospect in 1951 when it was acquired by George Lippincott, Jr., whose father owned the nearby silver-lead mine. Subsequent surface mining obliterated the older workings and

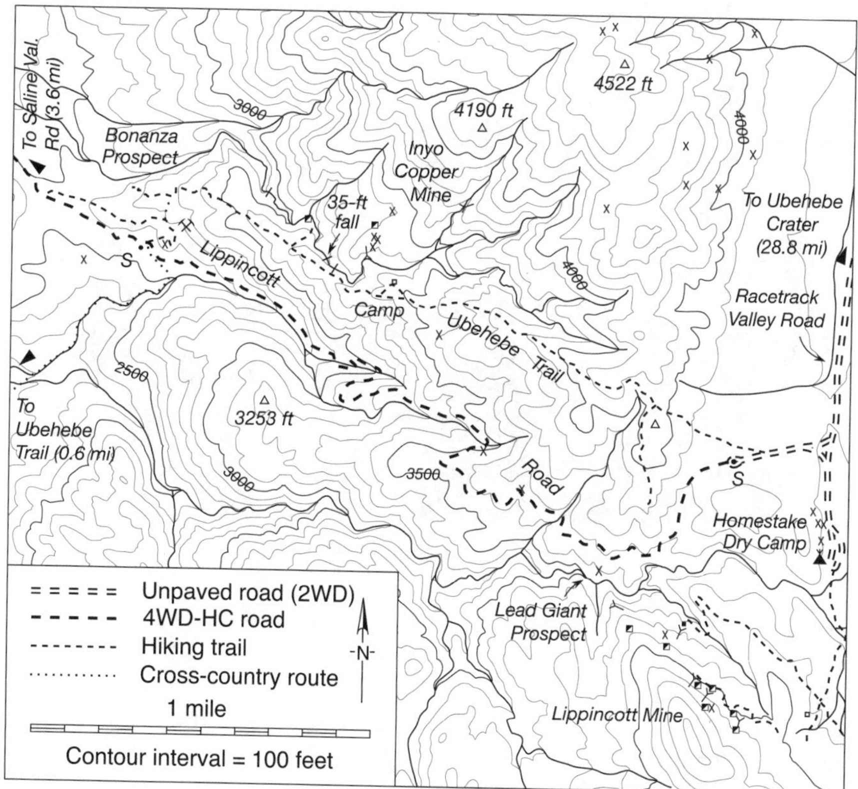

The Ubehebe Trail

	Dist.(mi)	Elev.(ft)
Lippincott Road (east end)	0.0	3,830
Divide (fork in trail)	0.35	4,020
High point on trail	0.55	4,100
Inyo Copper Mine (camp)	1.15	3,440
Inyo Copper Mine (shaft)	(0.5)	3,040
Bonanza Prospect	2.0	2,660
Trail resumes past sandy flat	3.4	2,070
Saline Valley Road crossing	5.4	2,280
Mouth of nameless canyon	6.15	2,640
Fork (left)	7.0	3,140
Gully 250 feet past right bend	7.45	3,590
Trail resumes at rim	7.6	3,910
Crest of Nelson Range	10.6	6,600
San Lucas Canyon Road	13.8	5,960

Rolling hills below the Ubehebe Trail

produced the 50-foot wide quarry that now dominates the site. The numerous minerals exposed here will put your rock-identification skills to the test. The host rocks are marble, tactite, and skarn. Malachite, chrysocolla, and a little azurite still stain the steep quarry walls. Other minerals include silver, garnet, zoisite, wollastonite, and epidotes, and traces of gold, tungsten, and uranium.

There is much more to this perduring trail. From the Bonanza Prospect it follows a short canyon southwest to the valley, then closely parallels the Lippincott Road on its south side, crosses the Saline Valley Road, and continues in the same direction to the Nelson Range. There it sneaks into a nameless canyon, veers left at the first fork, and exits the canyon up its south slope. The best part comes next—the long crossing of the Nelson Range, up a series of aerial switchbacks on a prominent ridge. The final leg is an easy descent on the west flank of the range, in a shallow canyon then across Lee Flat, to the San Lucas Canyon Road, where the Ubehebe Trail ends. This is wild and scenic hiking. The mountain is studded with Joshua trees, and the crest with pine. The trail is gone at a few places only—below the prospect, in the canyon wash and where it climbed out of the canyon, and west of the crest. Losing and finding it over and over again where it is extant will keep your adrenaline going. That a historic track 120 years old would still be preserved well enough to give us the opportunity to follow privately in the footsteps of miners long-gone is simply amazing.

■

THE DODD SPRINGS TRAIL

This elusive mining trail at the southern end of the Last Chance Range traverses wild and spectacular mountain country dotted with springs and a dozen small historic copper and silver mines. Sample it with the short hike to the lush groves of Little Dodd or Big Dodd springs, or take the longer day or overnight hike to the Lippincott Mine at the edge of Racetrack Valley.

General Information

Jurisdiction: Death Valley National Park
Road status: Graded road; hiking on old mining trail and cross-country
Big Dodd Spring: 2.5 mi, 880 ft up, 1,380 ft down, one way / moderate
Lippincott Mine: 6.5 mi, 1,930 ft up, 2,470 ft down, one way / strenuous
Main attractions: Springs, historic trail and copper mines, wildflowers
USGS 7.5' topo maps: Jackass Canyon*, Ubehebe Peak
Maps: pp. 161*, 167, *137*

Location and Access

The Dodd Springs Trail was used by miners starting around the 1900s to travel between Racetrack Valley and Grapevine Canyon and to access several mines and Big Dodd Spring, one of the few watering holes in the area. To hike this trail from Grapevine Canyon, drive the Saline Valley Road 3.6 miles north from South Pass (or 6.7 miles south of the Lippincott Road). This will put you on a straight section of road, midway between two stretches of spring vegetation. Look for the trail climbing the steep hillside across the wash north of the road. The other option is to start from the northern trailhead, at the Lippincott Mine (see map or refer to *Hiking Death Valley*).

Route Description

From the trailhead, hike up the trail to the top of the first ridge. This part of the trail is used by cattle and well defined—this area has one of the park's few grazing easements. The rest of the trail, however, is not nearly this good. Past the first ridge it is completely washed out, and you will have to go some distance down the shallow canyon on the far side to find it again, on the right side, a little before the first wash crossing. There is a small spring there, usually dry, with dense thickets of willow and wildrose. The trail resumes near the upper end of the spring, heading north up to the next saddle.

The rest of the way follows the same up-and-down rhythm. Little Dodd Spring is in the ravine beyond the third ridge. Trapped in a narrow canyon just up from the trail crossing, it has very thick vegetation. To visit it you will need to scramble along the slopes on either side of the spring, as it is for the most part impenetrable.

On the next ridge, a short distance west of the trail, look for the Shirley Ann Mine. Last located in 1940, it was undoubtedly mined at earlier times under other names, probably starting as the Eureka claim in 1902 or earlier. It produced primarily copper (mostly malachite, and some covellite), in limited quantity given its remoteness. The deposits, all in quartz veins, also contain lead (galena and cerussite), iron (hematite and limonite), silver, and traces of gold, tungsten, and molybdenum. This is the largest of the many mines and prospects scattered along the Dodd Springs Trail, most of which were discovered around the 1900s. It has eight tunnels 10 to 100 feet long, a 35-foot shaft, and quite a few prospects, with colorful copper-stained walls.

Big Dodd Spring, in the next drainage north, is impressively large and lush. Being in a more open canyon than its little brother, it is easier to visit. Follow the trail until it descends to the north end of the spring, then walk up along its north side. Most of it is a giant grove of willow festooned with looping grapevine, home to quite a diverse flora. If there is any surface water here, as the spring's historic significance suggests, it is well hidden under its dense vegetation.

Like a giant roller coaster, from Big Dodd Spring the trail goes over four more main ridges before finally reaching Racetrack Valley. After each ridge it drops into a minor west-draining canyon, usually with a dry spring in it. Although the trail is not continuous, it is often present where it is most needed, on the steeper slopes. Elsewhere, it is faster to follow its approximate route than to search for it. Along the last segment, down into Racetrack Valley to the Lippincott Mine, the trail was washed out long ago; the wide wash is a fine enough guide.

The Dodd Springs Trail

	Dist.(mi)	Elev.(ft)
Saline Valley Road	0.0	4,410
Little Dodd Spring (wash)	2.0	3,910
Big Dodd Spring	2.5	3,915
Pass into Racetrack Valley	4.7	4,660
Lippincott Mine (water truck)	6.5	3,870
Homestake Dry Camp	6.9	3,780

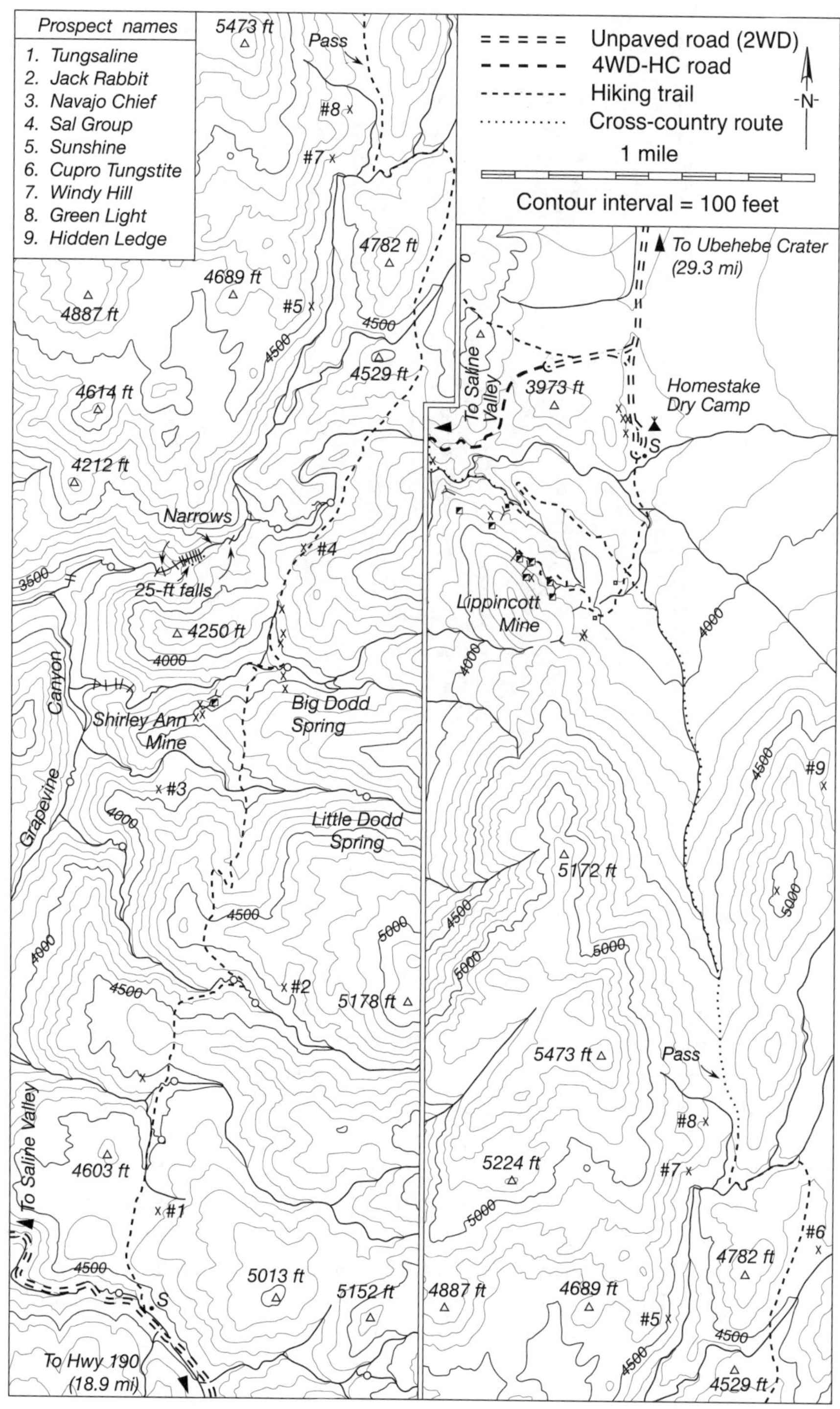
Prospect names
1. Tungsaline
2. Jack Rabbit
3. Navajo Chief
4. Sal Group
5. Sunshine
6. Cupro Tungstite
7. Windy Hill
8. Green Light
9. Hidden Ledge
Unpaved road (2WD)
4WD-HC road
Hiking trail
Cross-country route
1 mile
Contour interval = 100 feet
N
To Ubehebe Crater (29.3 mi)
Homestake Dry Camp
To Saline Valley
Lippincott Mine
Pass
Narrows
25-ft falls
Grapevine Canyon
Shirley Ann Mine
Big Dodd Spring
Little Dodd Spring
To Hwy 190 (18.9 mi)
5473 ft
4782 ft
4689 ft
4887 ft
4614 ft
4529 ft
4212 ft
4250 ft
3973 ft
5172 ft
5178 ft
5224 ft
4603 ft
5013 ft
5152 ft

Big Dodd Spring

Between Big Dodd Spring and the Lippincott Mine the trail skirts four small copper and silver prospects (see map). The largest ones are the Cupro Tungstite Prospect, rich in malachite, azurite, and cuprotungstite exposed in a 20-foot long slot, and the Green Light Prospect, about 0.1 mile west of the trail south of the pass into Racetrack Valley. It has a 30-foot tunnel in marble with traces of silver.

This is a great hike, faithful to the desert spirit, spiced by the constant search for the almost imaginary trail. Much of the landscape is dominated by the hard outcrops and exfoliating boulders of Hunter Mountain quartz monzonite. The views are wild and the isolation exhilarating, yet what got me was the wildflowers. In the spring of a particularly wet year, I saw more plants in bloom here than anywhere else around Death Valley, including less common species like mariposa and Parish larkspur. Dozens of species, in exuberant profusion, painted flamboyant canvasses all over the desert hills.

■

GRAPEVINE CANYON

This is one of the best short hikes in the Last Chance Range. An easy stroll down a sandy wash will take you to the spectacular lower gorge of Grapevine Canyon, a deep defile where a perennial stream gurgles along tree-lined banks beneath towering cliffs. On a hot day, this serene shelter of shade, greenery, and running water provides welcome relief from the relentless sun. Hikers with a taste for climbing will enjoy exploring the side canyons, which are stocked with an unusual number of slots, narrows, falls, slickrock, and boulders, as well as springs and abandoned copper prospects.

General Information

Jurisdiction: Death Valley National Park
Road status: Roadless; easy access from graded road
Grapevine Canyon loop: 5.5 mi, 1,020 ft up loop / easy–moderate
Main side canyon spring: 3.1 mi, 690 ft up, 740 ft down one way / moder.
Main attractions: A sheer-walled granite gorge, springs, and creeks
USGS 7.5' topo map: Jackass Canyon
Maps: pp. 161, 167*, *137*

Location and Access

Grapevine Canyon is the steep drainage that the Saline Valley Road follows as it drops from South Pass into Saline Valley. The portion of it described here is the roadless lower canyon. To get there, drive the Saline Valley Road north 4.6 miles from South Pass. At this point the road crosses the wash one last time, makes a sharp right and begins to climb out of the wash, while the canyon wash veers north. Drive 100 yards past the wash crossing to the next bend, which angles left, and park in the small turnout on the right. Alternatively, continue 0.5 mile to a side road on the right, on a broad swell. Drive this side road 0.15 mile downhill, north toward a hill of granitic boulders, and park on the level open area on the right. Coming from Saline Valley, this side road is 5.2 miles past the Lippincott Road.

Route Description

The canyon. If you start from the turnout, walk down the short slope below the road to the canyon wash, then follow the narrow trench along the bottom of the canyon. A little water usually flows in it, marred by the cattle that graze in this area. If you start from the side road, follow any of the cattle tracks 0.2 mile up the broad gully to the east-northeast to a low pass into Grapevine Canyon. You can then either clamber down the boulder-choked ravine straight ahead, or hike down the foot trail just south of it that winds down to the canyon wash. From both starting points it is about 0.7 mile to the gorge.

Grapevine Canyon is, above all, a rare wonderland of rocks. As you progress down its sandy wash, you become quickly entrenched in a deepening gorge framed first by broken bluffs of jointed boulders, then by veritable walls. The highlight is the bulging cliff of sheer granite more than 500 feet high that lines the canyon's west side. Over half a mile long, this soaring monolith is a tantalizing world of precipitous couloirs, hanging alcoves, and towering knolls, reminiscent of the sandstone splendors of southern Utah. We owe this imposing gorge to 170-million-year-old Quartz Monzonite of Hunter Mountain, a formation that varies greatly in composition and appearance, from monzonite to quartz monzonite, granite, and diorite, sometimes brightened by pink feldspar, green apatite, and other eye-catching minerals. The wash and nearby slopes sparkle with colorful combinations of porphyritic crystals of all sizes. Rock climbers will find here a small mecca, virtually unknown, rich in boulder problems, mind-bending traverses, and walls of all heights and difficulties.

A good part of Grapevine Canyon's magic comes from its spring and charming perennial creek. A large grove of willow loosely stitched with threads of grapevine, the spring starts just before the cliff and fills in most of the next 0.7 mile of canyon. A tiny creek cloaked with jade-tinged algae and watercress flows along it, dwarfed by the looming granite cliff. The spring is thick enough that it occasionally takes a little bushwhacking to get through. At one place the water is funneled through a slanted cleft between two chockstones and breaks into an 8-foot water slide. Further down the vegetation meanders between a sprinkling of tall boulders. What impressed me here is the serenity, the haunting piles of rocks peering down from great heights like a thousand faces, the rich contrast between the green trees and the golden walls, and the way the patina of desert varnish deepens to brilliant reds in the evening light. In the warmer months, the deep shade of the wall and higher humidity combine to form an idyllic island in the desert. The murmur of running water is a unifying thread that weaves peacefully through this surreal jumble of rocks.

At its lower end the canyon veers left and opens up into a broad wash of pure sand, a place filled with light and sculpted turrets, domes, and pinnacles. The creek usually withers and dies here, soaked up by the thirsty sand. On wet years it survives heroically as far as the chockstone jam just above the canyon mouth, where it pours over one last lip of rock into a shallow pool.

This drainage is graced with wildflowers much of the year. Although they are most impressive in the spring, even in late December I have seen primrose, desert bear poppy, Mojave aster, and Indian paintbrush in bloom poking through patches of snow!

The Grapevine Canyon creek is small and fragile. Bypass the head of the spring on the west bench, where cattle tracks wander through thick mats of grapevine. The rest of the way, avoid stepping on wet or muddy portions of the creek bed, which spreads the water and dries the creek. Instead, walk on rocks and higher benches.

The side canyons. If this hike is a little too short for your liking, turn to the side canyons. All five of them are fairly narrow, deep, and windy, and as they burrow west into Hunter Mountain they offer a surprising variety of scenery. The first side canyon inside the gorge has

Slot in main side canyon of Grapevine Canyon

a small spring, often dry, a short distance into it. The second one, Little Dodd Canyon, is irrigated by a short creek at least part of the year. Progress is challenged by a high boulder jam, then by the thick vegetation of Little Dodd Spring. Its next neighbor north, Big Dodd Canyon, is deeper and interrupted by a series of falls. The only one that is not trivial to climb is a giant pile of chockstones. It does take one technical move, easy (low 5s) but 15 feet off the ground. If you are not comfortable with it, try the steep miner's trail just below it on the south side, which circumvents the highest falls. This side canyon leads to Big Dodd Spring, an impressive grove rich in mining history.

The last side canyon is the most action-packed, and because it cuts mostly through Paleozoic limestone and dolomite, it is different from all others. In the first mile it packs in several small cascades, slots, slickrock slants, two large boulder jams, narrows occluded by four chockstones, and two 25-foot falls. The climbing is generally easy, except for the first 25-foot fall, at the center of the narrows, which requires an exposed and dangerous climb. It can be bypassed instead, up the steep ravine to the right of it, then down a boulder-strewn slope. You can then walk back down into the narrows to the top of the 25-foot fall, though one of the chockstones is slick and requires a technical climb to make it back up. The second 25-foot fall, not far past the narrows, also requires a technical climb (low 5s), with good holds.

Like a rite of passage, conquering these obstacles unlocks seldom-visited territory. In the right fork past the 25-foot fall, the canyon erupts into greenery at two small springs. The second one is just large

Grapevine Canyon		
	Dist.(mi)	Elev.(ft)
Saline Valley Road turnoff	0.0	4,025
Spring (head)	1.3	3,545
Little Dodd Canyon (mouth)	1.4	3,510
Dodd Springs Trail	(0.6)	3,910
Big Dodd Canyon (mouth)	1.7	3,450
Big Dodd Spring/trail	(0.7)	3,830
Main side canyon (mouth)	2.1	3,290
Top of narrows (25-ft fall)	(0.7)	3,810
Spring	(1.05)	3,980
Grapevine Canyon mouth	2.8	3,060
Return along base of range	5.5	4,025

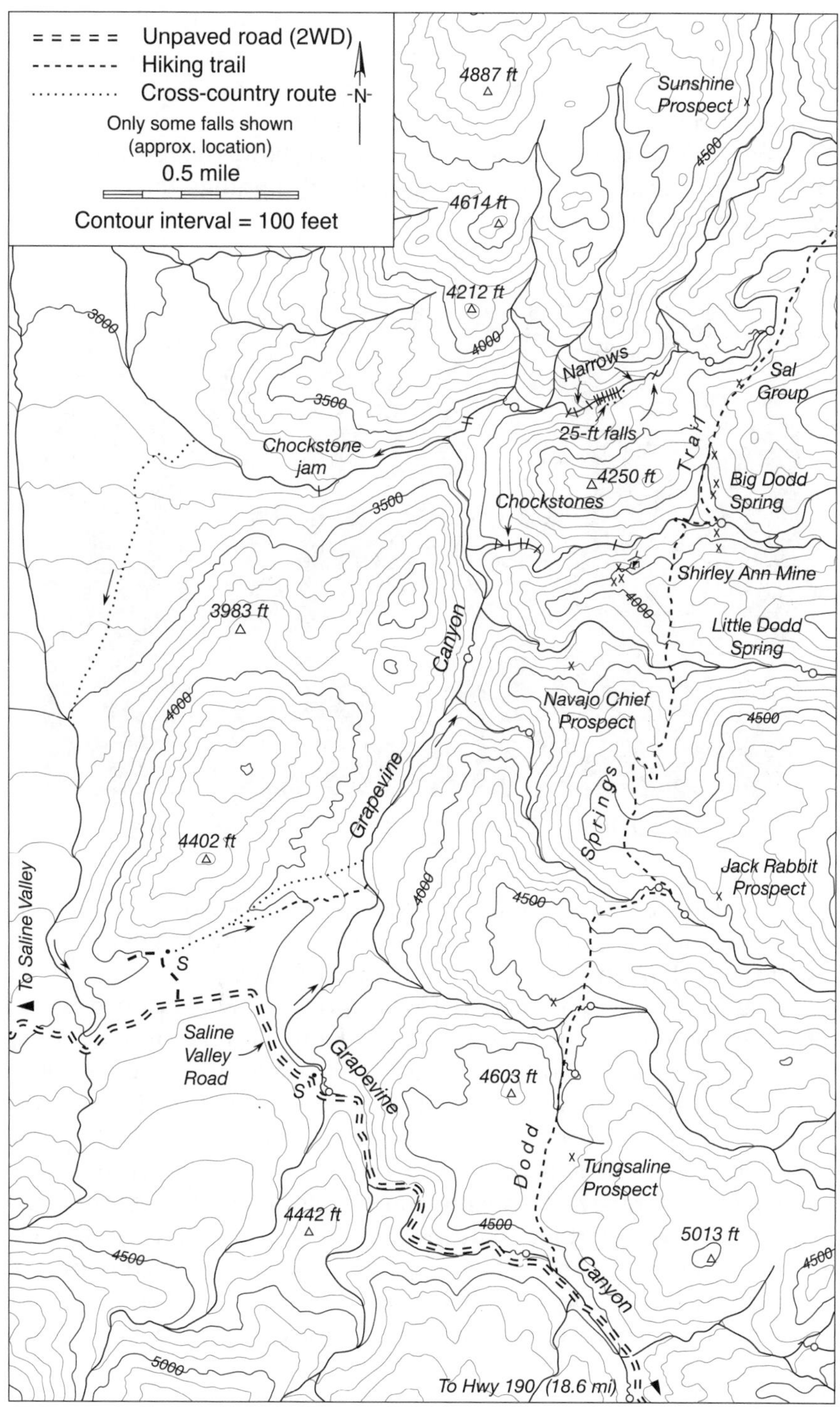

= = = = = Unpaved road (2WD)
- - - - - - - - Hiking trail
. . . . Cross-country route
N
Only some falls shown
(approx. location)
0.5 mile
Contour interval = 100 feet
4887 ft
Sunshine Prospect
4500
4614 ft
4212 ft
3000
4000
Narrows
Sal Group
3500
25-ft falls
Trail
Chockstone jam
4250 ft
Big Dodd Spring
3500
Chockstones
Shirley Ann Mine
3983 ft
4000
Little Dodd Spring
Canyon
4000
Navajo Chief Prospect
4500
Springs
Grapevine
4402 ft
Jack Rabbit Prospect
To Saline Valley
4000
4500
S
Saline Valley Road
Grapevine
S
4603 ft
Dodd
Tungsaline Prospect
4442 ft
4500
5013 ft
4500
Canyon
4500
5000
To Hwy 190 (18.6 mi)

enough to provide shade and cooler air. The left fork has three silver-lead prospects, high on the western wall (see map). While hiking through this canyon system, it is not uncommon to spot bright green chunks of copper ore washed down from these and other mineral-rich outcrops. The prospects do not have much to show. The reward is simply the gratification of discovering isolated diggings that were last worked many decades ago.

Lone tree at one of the springs along lower Grapevine Canyon

Possible extensions. From the mouth of Grapevine Canyon, you can make a loop hike (counterclockwise) by returning to your starting point south along the foot of the Last Chance Range.

Another option is to use the Dodd Springs Trail, described in the previous section, to create any number of loop hikes. The trail parallels lower Grapevine Canyon and is less than a mile up any of the side canyons. You can hike up one side canyon to the trail (if it is not washed out in this particular area, which it often is), follow the trail either direction to the next side canyon, then return down this side canyon to the Grapevine Canyon. You can also make a longer loop by returning to your starting point south on the Dodd Springs Trail, then northwest on the Saline Valley Road. Keep in mind that this trail is remarkably easy to lose, and that some side canyons may not go through. Allow ample time in case you are forced to backtrack.

■

HUNTER MOUNTAIN

This is a short and uncommonly easy climb through a pleasant conifer forest peppered with aromatic plants and monzonite boulders. The summit's scenic repository of granitic outcrops, reached by an easy scramble, commands an exceptional view of Saline Valley's awesome sink and its majestic ring of mountains.

General Information
Jurisdiction: Death Valley National Park
Road status: Roadless; access by long primitive road (HC)
Hunter Mountain: 1.0 mi, 360 ft up, 40 ft down one way / very easy
Main attractions: Forested summit, views of Saline Valley
USGS 7.5' topo map: Jackass Canyon
Maps: pp. 171*, *179*

Location and Access

Hunter Mountain is a sprawling mountainous mass at the confluence of the Nelson Range to the west, the Last Chance Range to the north, and the Cottonwood Mountains to the east. Its high point, Jackass Peak, is but a short distance from the Hunter Mountain Road, which crosses the mountain. To get to this road, work your way to the signed Saline Valley Road, which is 13.7 miles west of Panamint Springs on Highway 190, on the north side. Head north on the Saline Valley Road 8.2 miles, crossing the Santa Rosa Hills, to the Y junction at Lee Flat. Take the right fork, into the rubbly volcanic foothills of Hunter Mountain. The scenery changes rapidly as the sparse desert vegetation morphs into a healthy conifer forest. South Pass, the junction with the Hunter Mountain Road, is 7.4 miles from the Y junction.

At South Pass, turn right on the Hunter Mountain Road, and drive northeast 2.7 miles, up through an increasingly dense forest, then along Jackass Canyon and its spring-fed groves of willows, to a sharp right U-shaped bend at the head of the canyon. The climb starts 0.1 mile further, at the low point in the road just after the next left bend. However, there is not much room to park without damaging roadside vegetation. Park 0.15 mile further, where there is a bare spot up on the left side. Jackass Peak is hidden behind the top of the forested slope less than a mile to the west.

Up to Lee Flat, the Saline Valley Road is partly paved, partly (and mostly) dirt. In dry weather, a standard-clearance vehicle can normally

Saline Valley from the summit of Hunter Mountain

push on to South Pass. The Hunter Mountain Road is steep and locally rocky, and both high clearance and good power are required.

Route Description

Hunter Mountain is named after William Lyle Hunter, an adventurer who moved to the Inyo Mountains–Saline Valley area in the late 1860s, when he was in his mid-twenties, and spent his life dabbling in all kinds of trades. He was for a time a mule skinner for the booming Cerro Gordo mines. He discovered valuable copper deposits on Ulida Flat in 1875, then rich silver outcrops near Cerro Gordo and gold in the Inyo Mountains in 1877. He worked his gold and copper ledges off and on for 16 years. He also had a ranch and a picturesque log cabin on the forested heights of what is now Hunter Mountain. In recognition of his pioneering contributions, his name was given to a record number of local features—a spring, two canyons, a formation, a peak, a road, a cabin, and a whole mountain.

From the car park, backtrack 250 yards to just before the next right bend in the road. A narrow trail, plowed by the cattle that roam this area, takes off on the right. It wanders off into a broad hollow that climbs gently to the west. At this altitude the vegetation is remarkably

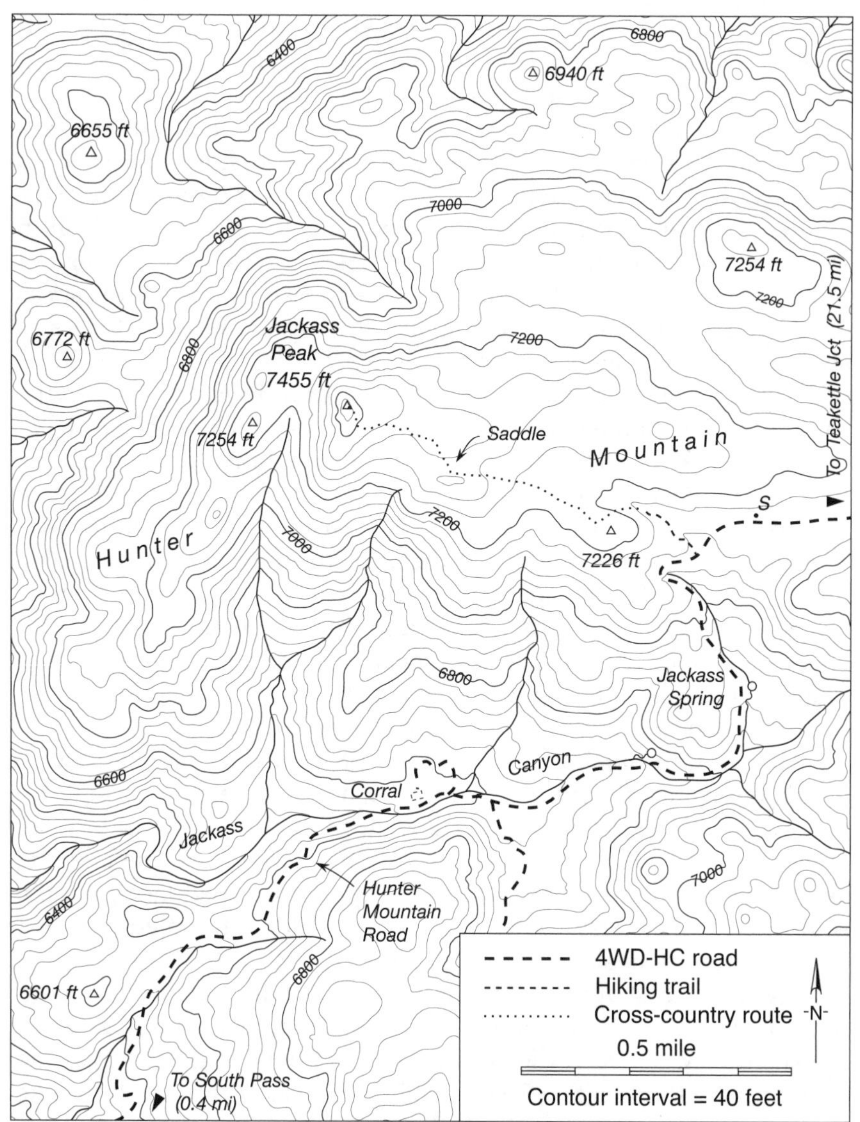

Hunter Mountain		
	Dist.(mi)	Elev.(ft)
Hunter Mountain Road	0.0	~7,140
Leave road at wash/trail	0.15	7,100
Pass	0.7	7,310
Hunter Mountain	1.0	7,455

exuberant, a thigh-high carpeting of big sagebrush, bitterbrush, saltbush, and ephedra, as well as several uncommon species, including silver lupine. The low ridges on both sides are lined with scenic boulders and conifers. The trail meanders between bushes, then soon peters out. The slope of least resistance leads west-northwest to an open saddle. Selected unnaturally by generations of domesticated herbivores, grasses have gone humorously berserk. Refreshingly lush in the springtime, they overcompensate in the dry season by putting out countless needle-shaped seeds with an obsessive appetite for socks and shoe linings, making walking an itchy misery. Weeks later I was still plucking the little pricks off my shoes.

At the saddle the tree cover thickens abruptly. From there to the summit, visible to the northwest as a mound of chubby outcrops barely rising above the forest, there is hardly a straight path, and it takes a little bushwhacking to get around the pinyon pine, cliffrose, large shrubs, and fallen trunks. In pre-settler times, the Panamint and Timbisha Indians traveled great distances to hunt and harvest pine nuts and plants on this mountain. It is easy to see why. Apart from its abundance of springs and natural resources, and cooler weather, it exudes a serenity that infiltrates your mind and makes you want to linger. If you do, you might run across the descendants of the mule deer and bighorn sheep that fed them—or escaped their arrows.

The summit block is a tall mound of hard plutonic boulders—quartz monzonite of Hunter Mountain again. Relatively poor in ferromagnesian minerals like biotite and hornblende, the boulders are unusually pale and contrast sharply with the dark-green pine growing among them. The east side has only steep and exposed faces, but the south side has an easy route, over lower boulders huddled together, and only one 6-foot slant requiring hands.

This is the best approach for another reason: it gives no clue about how incredible the view is until the very last moment, when you reach the shallow V between the summit's twin knobs and peer over the edge into the shiny heart of Saline Valley. Hunter Mountain drops like a grand staircase into the valley's deep basin, its dune fields, salt lake, marshes, and hot springs dwarfed by the towering Inyo Mountains. Desert rats will recognize many of the classic summits that surround this stunning tectonic sink—Waucoba and Cerro Gordo, Saline and Dry and the twin chocolate cones of Ubehebe, and lonesome Galena. Together with the Salt Tramway Trail, this unassuming peak commands one of the most spectacular views of one of the most spectacular desert valleys in California.

■

— 6 —

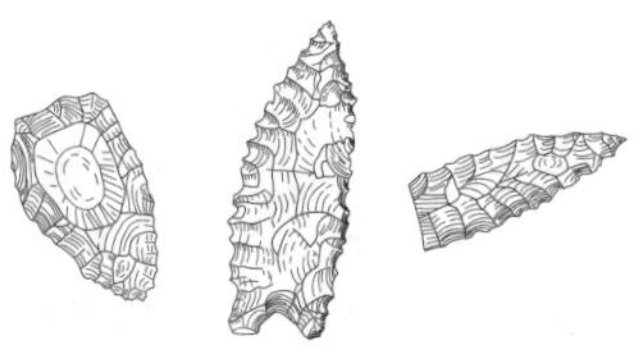

SALINE VALLEY

SALINE VALLEY IS a rare and special place. It is one of the largest essentially uninhabited valleys in the California desert. Framed between tremendous mountain ranges, hard to reach and cut off from the rest of the world, it is nothing short of a lost paradise. It is in many ways a scaled-down replica of Death Valley, made of the same building blocks, only strangely rearranged. A Death Valley of years ago, with no paved roads, no towns, next to no road signs, and few visitors. From almost anywhere you will not see a single light at night.

Saline Valley is not a true valley but a graben, a narrow, northwest-southeast-trending tectonic sink defined by fault-block mountains. About 27 miles in length, it is bounded by the Saline Range to the north, the Last Chance Range to the east, the Inyo Mountains to the west, and the Nelson Range to the south. All of this hydrologic basin belongs to Death Valley National Park, except for the Inyo Mountains, which are protected as a wilderness area administered by the Bureau of Land Management and the National Forest Service. The closest permanent centers of human activity are Darwin and the small resort of Panamint Springs in Panamint Valley. The only other settlements are isolated private properties on the valley floor. Panamint Springs is also the closest place that offers services—food, lodging, camping, showers, and gas. The closest towns (Big Pine, Lone Pine, and Olancha) are at least a two-and-a-half-hour drive from the center of the valley. There is no drinking water in Saline Valley—at least not the kind that comes out of a tap. You have to bring everything you need to survive for the duration of your stay.

Access and Backcountry Roads

Saline Valley can be reached by car via the mostly graded Saline Valley Road, which connects Highway 190 to the south to the Big Pine Road to the north. The only two other access roads are the Lippincott Road from Racetrack Valley to the east (see *Hiking Death Valley*), and the Steel Pass Road from Eureka Valley to the northeast (see *The Steel Pass Road*). These two routes are considerably rougher and require sturdy, high-clearance four-wheel-drive vehicles.

The Saline Valley Road. This is one of the most scenic and varied roads in the California desert. Starting from Highway 190 just west of Death Valley National Park's boundary, it wanders north across the colorful rolling terrain of Santa Rosa Flat, then crosses the low Santa Rosa Hills. On the other side of the hills is Lee Flat, a narrow high desert valley hosting one of the largest Joshua tree forests in the park, and one of the most impressive in the northern Mojave Desert. Some of the trees reach over 25 feet and have exceptionally dense crowns. Past Lee Flat, the Saline Valley Road ascends the southwestern slope of Hunter Mountain. Over just a few miles the scenery changes rapidly as the sparse desert vegetation is replaced by one of the thickest pine forests in the park. The junction with the Hunter Mountain Road is known as South Pass (~6,200'), at the southern rim of Saline Valley. Stop just before it to enjoy the magnificent views of Panamint Valley down steep-walled Mill Canyon, especially the pale Panamint Valley Dunes resting on the sweeping fan several thousand feet below. From here the road winds down along spring-dotted Grapevine Canyon into

Suggested Backcountry Drives in Saline Valley

Route/Destination	Dist. (mi)	Lowest elev.	Highest elev.	Road type	Pages
Artesian Well Road	3.5	1,071'	1,142'	H	203
Big Silver Mine Road	1.1	1,094'	1,520'	P	281
Lippincott Road	6.8	1,920'	3,850'	F	155
Saline Valley Road	78.1	1,080'	7,570'	G	174-177
Snow Flake Mine Road	3.6	1,146'	3,300'	F	200
Steel Pass Road	29.3	1,475'	5,091'	F	191-195
Trio Mill Site	1.5	1,142'	1,770'	H	259
Warm Springs Road	9.9	1,135'	1,860'	G	181-184

Key: G=Graded; H=Primitive (HC); P=Primitive (2WD); F=Primitive (4WD)

Saline Valley Road		
	Dist.(mi)	Elev.(ft)
Highway 190	0.0	4,860
Lee Mine Road	6.0	5,300
Y junction/Lee Flat Road	8.2	5,249
South Pass/Hunter Mtn Rd	15.6	~6,200
Lippincott Road	26.0	2,245
Salt Tramway Jct/Road	37.1	1,094
Saline Valley Marsh jct	38.6	1,115
Hunter Canyon Road	39.0	1,115
Conn and Trudo Borax Works	39.6	1,106
Artesian Well Rd (south end)	39.7	1,107
Beveridge Canyon Road	41.5	1,142
Keynot Canyon Road	42.3	1,146
Dunes road (south end)	42.9	1,148
Dunes road (north end)	44.1	1,178
McElvoy Canyon Road	44.7	1,225
Warm Springs Road	45.7	1,300
Pat Keyes Canyon Road	46.0	1,340
Willow Creek Camp jct	50.3	~2,260
Lead Canyon Road	55.8	3,580
North Pass	66.0	~7,300
Marble Cyn/Jackass Flats Rd	70.3	5,900
Big Pine Road	78.1	7,570

Saline Valley. It then drops more gradually down a long, widening alluvial fan to the southern valley floor and veers west towards the Inyo Mountains and Salt Lake, at the valley's lowest point. For many miles, the Saline Valley Road closely follows the foot of the Inyo Mountains northward, before climbing up steeply through Whippoorwill Canyon to forested North Pass (~7,300'), the divide with Eureka Valley to the north. The last stretch is down into Marble Canyon, then up and out of this canyon on tight switchbacks, and finally across more open high-desert country to the pavement at the Big Pine Road (7,570') 15.4 miles east of Big Pine.

The Saline Valley Road is mostly graded but it is long—78 miles from asphalt to asphalt. Driving it should not be undertaken lightly. The closest services are far away. The long, rattling stretches of washboards may trigger a mechanical breakdown, especially in summer.

Salt Lake and the Saline Range (left) from the Saline Valley Road

Getting a flat tire is also a common problem. I have heard of unfortunate travelers getting *two* flat tires on the same day, the second one while driving out to get the first one repaired. A robust, preferably high-clearance, vehicle will reduce the chances of running into trouble, as will a second spare tire. This is not meant to discourage anyone from coming here without an SUV, however. Every year in the dry season many standard-clearance vehicles make it to the warm springs. In fact, I have used mostly compact cars to get to Saline Valley. Even in the early spring of 1998, after the most powerful El Niño in over 500 years, the road was passable with regular clearance. But no matter what you are driving, always come prepared for an emergency.

In the winter, North Pass and South Pass, especially the former, are often closed due to snow, sometimes for a few weeks. At South Pass the spot where snow lingers the longest is just below the pass, where the road drops into Grapevine Canyon. If there is snow or ice on the road, do not go further without chains. You may not need them to get down but you probably will to come back up, *even with a four-wheel-drive vehicle*. I have seen beefy SUVs get stuck here on icy snow. Chains will also come in handy if it snows on the passes while you are down in the valley. Check current road conditions at a ranger station.

Another good reason for contacting a ranger station just before your trip is that the Saline Valley Road may be closed for extended periods of time. A "road closed" sign is often posted across the road at its south end on Highway 190 and at its north end on the Big Pine Road. Sometimes a "road closed" sign is posted as far back as the Big Pine Road in Owens Valley. At times these signs are justified, for example on the rare occasions when North Pass or South Pass are snowed in. But often they are just there because the county is concerned about liability. I have often been forced by this road closure sign to drive all the way around and to enter Saline Valley via the Lippincott Road, which is almost always open, only to find that there was nothing unusual along the entire Saline Valley Road to justify its closure. If you have to drive a long way to visit Saline Valley, call Death Valley National Park ahead of time to avoid an unpleasant surprise. The Park Service knows when the Saline Valley Road is truly closed.

Safety Tips

Saline Valley is one of the most remote places in California. To get to the heart of it takes a few hours of driving on a bumpy unpaved road. Isolation is certainly a strong ingredient of its charm. I hope you will not encounter too many people while you are there, since exploring it on your own makes this experience even more special. But the downside of isolation is danger. When you are in the middle of Saline Valley, you are far from help. A vehicle breakdown or a physical injury a few miles from the main road could leave you stranded for hours, if not longer, without human contact.

Be prepared to handle such emergencies. Make sure you are driving a vehicle with a full-size spare tire. Top off your tank at the last town. Most SUVs are such guzzlers that they have little autonomy. By the time you reach Saline Valley, you may well have just enough gas left to make it back out. If you try to drive out over Steel Pass and find out that you cannot make it and turn around, your fuel gauge will likely be too low to reach the nearest gas station. Bring extra gas, plenty of water and food, enough for a few days longer than your intended stay, and a first aid kit. This is also true for winter, in the event a snow storm cuts you off from a highway overnight. Bring tire chains, even if the forecast is favorable. Take warm clothes and sleeping gear with you, even if you are not planning to stay overnight.

Saline Valley has a few residents. Respect their privacy, and contact them only in an emergency. If possible, check Saline Valley's Lower Warm Springs first. The camp host has a park radio, basic tools, and a tire repair kit.

If you run out of water, your best option for a refill is to contact the camp host at Warm Springs or the warden at Willow Creek Camp.

Suggested Hikes in Saline Valley					
Route/Destination	Dist. (mi)	Elev. gain	Mean elev.	Access road	Pages
Short hikes (under 5 miles round trip)					
Artesian Well grove	0.7	10'	1,080'	P/2.1 mi	205-208
Big Silver Mine	0.8	1,360'	2,070'	P/1.5 mi	219-222
Black Mountain Loop Trail	4.8	1,540'	1,680'	Graded	189-190
Conn & Trudo Borax Works	0.4	10'	1,195'	Graded	213-214
Dedeckera Canyon narrows	0.9	380'	3,850'	P/6.0 mi	194-195
Joy and Vega Mine loop	3.2	890'	1,700'	P/0.5 mi	216-218
Little Dunes	3.6	~210'	1,100'	Graded	208
Little Hunter Cyn Spr. loop	1.7	540'	1,510'	P/0.5 mi	215-216
Palm Spring	0.7	100'	1,430'	Graded	182-184
Red Cinder Cone	2.0	640'	1,500'	Graded	187-189
Saline Valley Marsh	0.6	10'	1,070'	Graded	210-211
Salt Tramway Road	1.6	630'	1,460'	Graded	285
Seven Sisters Springs loop	3.8	100'	1,230'	Graded	185-187
Shoreline Trail	1.1	10'	1,065'	Graded	211-213
Shoreline Trail loop	3.9	110'	1,080'	Graded	211-213
White Cliffs (narrows)	2.4	1,420'	3,770'	F/9.3 mi	196
White Cliffs Prospect	1.5	700'	3,510'	F/9.3 mi	196
White Eagle Mine	2.0	1,160'	2,870'	Graded	198-199
Intermediate hikes (5-12 miles round trip)					
Blue Jay Mine (road cut)	5.7	1,730'	2,040'	Graded	145-148
Saline Valley Sand Dunes	3.0	190'	1,120'	P/2.1 mi	204-205
Snow Flake Mine (west)	2.5	1,970'	2,540'	P/1.1 mi	199-202
Warm Springs Rd (springs)	3.1	490'	1,610'	Graded	181-184
Long hikes (over 12 miles round trip)					
Steel Pass Road				Graded	
Palm Spring to Steel Pass	15.4	3,620'	2,950'		191-193
Palm Spring to dunes	26.9	3,260'	5,091'		191-195

Key: P=Primitive (2WD) H=Primitive (HC) F=Primitive (4WD)
Distances: one way for out-and-back hikes, round-trip for loops
Elev. gain: sum of all elevation gains on round-trip or loop hike

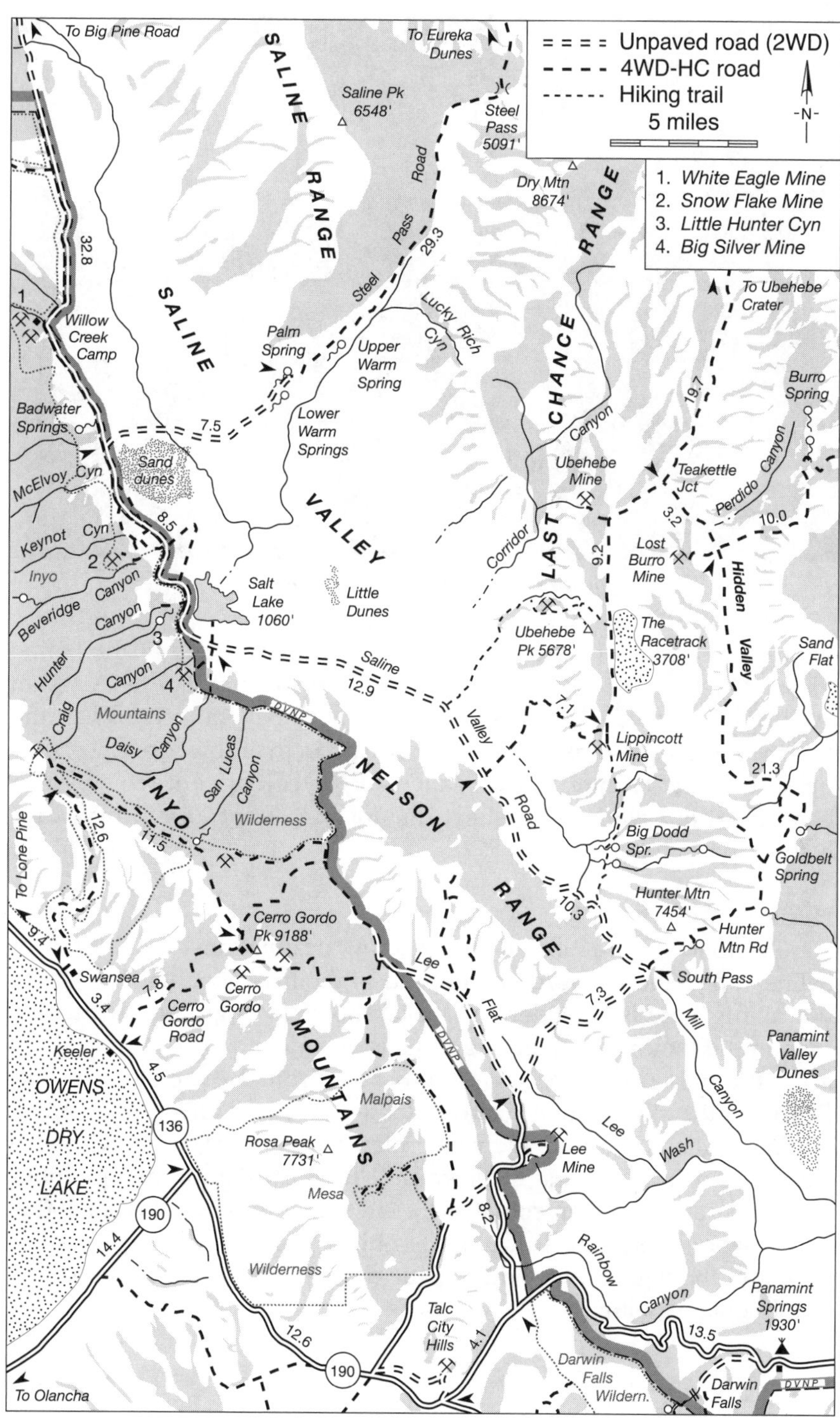

Unpaved road (2WD)
4WD-HC road
Hiking trail
5 miles
N
1. White Eagle Mine
2. Snow Flake Mine
3. Little Hunter Cyn
4. Big Silver Mine
To Big Pine Road
To Eureka Dunes
SALINE RANGE
Saline Pk 6548'
Steel Pass 5091'
Steel Pass Road
Dry Mtn 8674'
LAST CHANCE RANGE
SALINE VALLEY
Willow Creek Camp
Palm Spring
Upper Warm Spring
Lower Warm Springs
Lucky Rich Cyn
Badwater Springs
Sand dunes
McElvoy Cyn
Keynot Cyn
Inyo
Beveridge Canyon
Hunter Canyon
Craig Canyon
Salt Lake 1060'
Little Dunes
Ubehebe Mine
Corridor Canyon
To Ubehebe Crater
Teakettle Jct
Burro Spring
Perdido Canyon
Lost Burro Mine
Hidden Valley
Ubehebe Pk 5678'
The Racetrack 3708'
Sand Flat
Saline Valley Road
Lippincott Mine
Mountains
Daisy Canyon
San Lucas Canyon
INYO Wilderness
DVNP
NELSON RANGE
Big Dodd Spr.
Goldbelt Spring
Hunter Mtn 7454'
Hunter Mtn Rd
South Pass
To Lone Pine
Cerro Gordo Pk 9188'
Cerro Gordo
Cerro Gordo Road
Swansea
Keeler
Lee Flat
Mill Canyon
Panamint Valley Dunes
OWENS DRY LAKE
INYO MOUNTAINS
Malpais Mesa Wilderness
Rosa Peak 7731'
Lee Mine
Lee Wash
Rainbow Canyon
Panamint Springs 1930'
Talc City Hills
Darwin Falls Wildern.
Darwin Falls
To Olancha
136
190
32.8
29.3
19.7
7.5
8.5
3.2
10.0
9.2
12.9
7.1
21.3
12.6
11.5
10.3
9.4
7.8
3.4
7.3
4.5
14.4
8.2
12.6
4.1
13.5

Inyo Mountains from the Saline Valley Sand Dunes

There is also almost always water in the concrete basin at the Saline Valley Marsh (see *Salt Lake*), and at the two wells along the Artesian Well Road (see *The Saline Valley Sand Dunes*). Several canyons in the Inyo Mountains also have a running stream in their lower reaches, particularly Little Hunter Canyon and Pat Keyes Canyon, which has a beautiful high waterfall a short distance in. Treat all spring water before drinking it.

Hiking

The following sections describe a few destinations on the floor of Saline Valley and in the lower foothills of the Inyo Mountains. Most of the hiking here is considerably easier, both in length and difficulty, than in the mountains. Although this is generally a year-round hiking area, the best times are spring and fall. From November through February the sky is often overcast (courtesy of the Inyo Mountains). The mean temperature in the valley may be around 50°F, and closer to freezing during cold snaps. From mid-June through mid-September the temperature is often above 90°F, and sometimes in excess of 100°F. Some people may find it too hot for hiking. At such times, consider hiking in the high country during the day, and returning to the valley in the cooler evening.

■

THE WARM SPRINGS

One could hardly write a book about Saline Valley without celebrating its three wonderful hot springs. Set on open benches overlooking Saline Valley, they are the most popular destination in the valley. You will find great places to camp, to relax in refreshing palm groves, to enjoy a hot bath or a walk, or to just savor the vivid contrast between a lush oasis and its harsh desert host.

General Information

Jurisdiction: Death Valley National Park
Road status: Hiking on dirt road; primitive access road
Palm Spring: 0.7 mi, 100 ft up, 0 ft down one way / very easy
Upper Warm Spring: 3.1 mi, 460 ft up, 30 ft down one way / easy
Main attractions: Hot springs spa and camping in remote settings
USGS 7.5' topo maps: Lower Warm Springs, West of Teakettle Junction
Maps: pp. 183*, *179*

Location and Access

Saline Valley's three main warm springs are reached by a primitive road known as the Warm Springs Road or Painted Rock Road. It starts off the Saline Valley Road just north of the dunes. With a standard-clearance vehicle, this road is often passable up to Palm Spring (there may be loose sand at times), a distance of 7.5 miles.

Route Description

Lower Warm Springs. This is the largest and most developed of Saline Valley's warm springs, and the most popular campground. First altered for recreation purposes in the 1920s, it has been used regularly ever since, in particular by a small hippie community in the 1960s and 1970s. At its heart is Crystal Pool, a shaded, rock-rimmed basin on the edge of a small lawn screened from the desert by a tall hedge of arrowweed and fan palms. It is fed by highly mineralized natural spring water, usually around 110°F. The camp hosts who take turns living here keep this place shipshape and clean. Visitors congregate in this serene setting to enjoy a hot bath, to read or eat at a picnic table, rest on the lawn, or warm up by a roaring fire on cold evenings. The surroundings are sprinkled with unlikely treasures—an outdoor shower and a tub, a lizard mosaic, a goldfish pond, a cluster of large quartz crystals, a plaque honoring former camp host Lucky Rich Baldwin, a

Pool at Lower Warm Springs

small library, and many others. Nearby is Sunrise Pool, a smaller hot tub out in the open. Next to it is the largest undisturbed natural pool, off limits to bathing—a deep hole filled with limpid hot water the color of emerald. It is a local tradition, and a memento of the hippie days, to hang around naked. So do not be surprised to find a woman with bare breasts sharing the pool with you, or a man suntanning in the buff on the lawn. If this is going to offend you, do not come here.

The campsites, all designated, are distributed among the mesquite trees surrounding the spring, facing out to the desert. Camping is not allowed at Upper Warm Spring. People travel from far just to see this place. It is indeed an idyllic spot, but it is small and easily spoiled by too many people during the peak seasons. Avoid it during rush hour. Come here on week days instead, when it is still a peaceful oasis.

Palm Spring. Past Lower Warm Springs the road continues 0.7 mile to Palm Spring. The creamy white rock exposed along the way and at the three springs is travertine, a form of calcite deposited by the springs when they had considerably heavier flows. Developed around the 1970s, Palm Spring is smaller and less crowded. Unlike Lower Warm Springs, its charm is not seclusion but surreal openness.

The Warm Springs Road

	Dist.(mi)	Elev.(ft)
Saline Valley Road	0.0	1,300
Lower Warm Springs	6.8	~1,380
Palm Spring	7.5	1,475
Rough steps (HC/hike)	9.35	~1,790
Upper Warm Spring	9.9	1,835

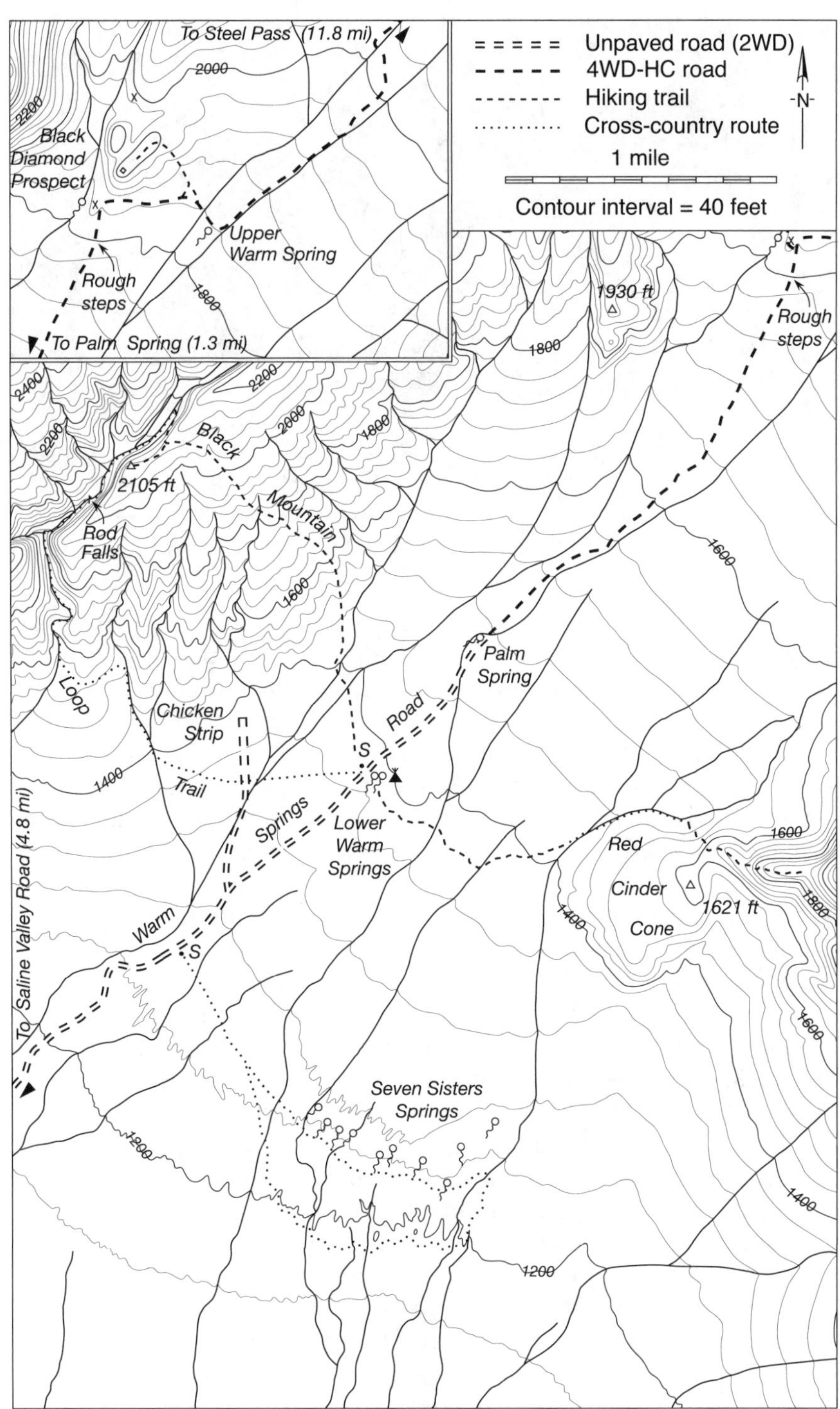
Unpaved road (2WD)
4WD-HC road
Hiking trail
Cross-country route
N
1 mile
Contour interval = 40 feet
To Steel Pass (11.8 mi)
Black Diamond Prospect
Upper Warm Spring
Rough steps
To Palm Spring (1.3 mi)
1930 ft
Rough steps
Black Mountain
2105 ft
Rod Falls
Palm Spring
Loop
Chicken Strip Trail
Road
Springs
Warm
Lower Warm Springs
Red Cinder Cone
1621 ft
To Saline Valley Road (4.8 mi)
Seven Sisters Springs

Lower Warm Springs from Black Mountain Loop Trail

Imagine two pools, each partly shaded by a few slender palm trees, set on a wide swell of barren rock. The large hexagonal pool just south of the road is called Wizard, after the man who built it, a camp host at the springs for over 40 years. The smaller raised pool on the north side is known as either Volcano or Barnacle. Both pools, as well as the outdoor shower behind Wizard Pool, command great views of Saline Valley. Taking a warm shower in this awesome setting, especially after roughing it for a few days, is an unforgettable treat.

Upper Warm Spring. Past Palm Spring the road is narrower and much rougher. Good clearance is needed to drive the 2.4 miles to Upper Warm Spring, and four-wheel drive helps to climb over the sharp bedrock steps along the way (1.85 miles). If you cannot drive it, hike it; in cooler weather it is an easy walk. At the sharp right bend in the road past the bedrock steps, there is a series of small pits and a drill hole on the left side of the road. This is the Black Diamond Prospect. Explored prior to 1950, this small deposit in reddish black travertine contained up to 30% of manganese (pyrolusite).

Upper Warm Spring is the smallest and least disturbed of the main springs. It has been fenced off for years for protection against burros, which abound throughout the springs area. Inside the enclosure there is a deep pool of lukewarm azure water surrounded by cattail, arrowweed, and grasses, in full view of the Saline Range.

■

HIKES AROUND THE WARM SPRINGS

If you get tired of hanging around the warm springs, or if lethargy sets in from an overdose of hot tub, you may want to go on one of these classic local hikes. They will take you to a red cinder cone stamped with a giant peace sign, to a series of green springs haunted by wild burros known as the Seven Sisters, and to the Martian scape of the nearby Saline Range. No driving required: just throw on some clothes and start walking.

General Information

Jurisdiction: Death Valley National Park
Road status: Access from primitive road
Red Cinder Cone: 2.0 mi, 590 ft up, 50 ft down one way/easy
Seven Sisters Springs: 3.8 mi, 100 ft up loop/easy
Black Mountain Loop Trail: 4.8 mi, 1,540 ft loop/moderate
Main attractions: Warm springs, cinder cone, volcanic canyon trail
USGS 7.5' topo maps: Lower Warm Springs, West of Teakettle Junction
Maps: pp. 183*, *179*

Location and Access

The three hikes described here start from the vicinity of either Lower Warm Springs or Palm Spring. Refer to the previous section for road access to these two springs.

Route Description

Seven Sisters Springs. This series of small springs is reached by a short hike from the Warm Springs Road. Start about 1 mile below Lower Warm Springs, or 5.8 miles from the Saline Valley Road. The first part of this hike is southeast across the fan, essentially following a contour line. After 15 minutes you will spot the trees of the closest spring scattered on a low white terrace ahead. Near the foot of the terrace, look for one of several parallel burro trails climbing onto it. Any of them will take you to the first spring. All the other springs are connected by a network of trails. Please help preserve these fragile water sources and the crumbly crust of the terrace by staying on these trails.

This is a delightful hike, across bright open spaces, and a great opportunity to sample the many microcosms intertwined in the desert fabric. The fan itself is a good example. Like most fans, it is filled with unexpected gems, from small patches of desert pavement to bubble-

Salt and basalt cobbles at Seven Sisters Springs

filled basalt cobbles and fluorescent chollas poised like dynamic statues. Ventifacts—rocks shaped by erosion—are common. Some of them are covered with crisscrossing rills (the combined action of rain and wind), etched like rough sandpaper, or carved into distorted sculptures (the work of wind-blown particles). Near the terrace the salt that saturates the fan has helped create another kind of ventifact—whole rocks neatly sliced like a loaf of bread. The terrace is yet another world. Covering nearly one square mile, it is composed of travertine, a calcareous rock formed in the Quaternary by evaporation of the carbonate-rich spring water. The travertine is covered with powdery salt, as blinding as sun-drenched snow. Basalt cobbles brought all the way here from the mountains by flashfloods are stranded on the terrace, their dark spheroidal shapes in odd contrast with the pale ground.

The Seven Sisters Springs do comprise seven main springs, almost aligned along a common fault. Each one has thickets of arrowweed and a few to two dozen mesquite trees strung along the narrow parallel gullies that drain the terrace. The trees add unexpected colors to this chemical wasteland—light green foliage in the summer and reddish bare limbs in the winter. A few of the springs are livened, at least part of the year, by a tiny creek of briny water. Their flows, though meager—pushing one gallon per hour—support colorful algae and carpets of green grass.

Both honey and screwbean mesquites, the two species found in the Mojave Desert, grow at the springs. An unmistakable difference between them is their pod. One looks like a string bean (honey mesquite) and the other like a fat, inch-long spring (screwbean). Year-round, pods are plentiful under the trees—and in the dung of coyotes and burros, who often come here to feast on the sweet pods.

The seventh spring is at the east end of the travertine terrace. From there you can make a loop back along the southern foot of the terrace (see map), and enjoy different views of the springs.

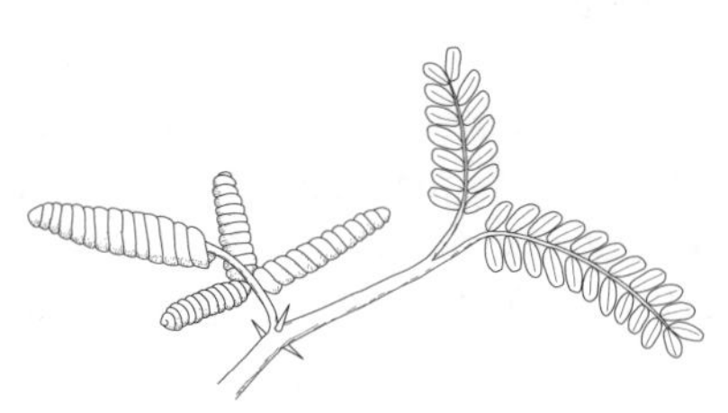

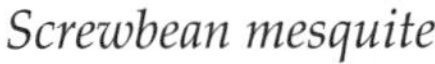

Screwbean mesquite

Honey mesquite

Red Cinder Cone. The goal of this classic Saline Valley hike is the distinct red cinder cone at the foot of the Last Chance Range east of Lower Warm Springs, and the huge peace sign etched across it. Back in the 1960s, when the Vietnam War was raging and the Korean War was still fresh on everyone's mind, the springs community liberally surrounded its desert holdout with peace signs to ward off the war spirit, a bit like Rumanians strategically placing garlic bulbs around their house to keep Count Dracula at bay. There is a peace sign on the foothill north of Palm Spring, another one in a wash northwest of the main springs, and several others. The cinder-cone sign, most prominent of all, is visible from miles away (and more intrusive than most of the local mines that the peace-sign artists loved to despise).

If you get them to talk, the warm-springs locals (this plural is often rather singular) might tell you, depending on their degree of confidence, either that there is a trail from Lower Warm Springs to the cinder cone, or that there was one but that it was wiped out by El Niño in 1998. There is in fact a trail, most of the way, although it is a little faint at places. Start at the outhouse at the east end of the campground. Follow the obvious abandoned road southeast 150 yards to the end of the mesquite grove on your right. There the old roadbed veers east and follows the base of a low travertine bench 250 yards to the edge of a wash. Cross the wash east-southeast and on its far side you should see a narrow foot trail cutting in the same general direction across the fan. After 0.2 mile the trail angles north-northeast and ends in 0.2 mile at the edge of a wide wash at the base of Red Cinder Cone. Follow this sandy wash uphill 0.5 mile to the conspicuous trail that winds up the narrow western shoulder of Red Cinder Cone. If you miss the trail on the fan, just cut a beeline to the cone trail, which is visible from as far back as the springs. Much of this hike crosses a wide-open, gently sloping fan. The terrain is a mixture of desert pavement and alluvia, both an entertaining collection of volcanic and sedimentary rocks. Other than wispy creosotes, there is virtually no shade, so pick the right season or time to come here.

Red Cinder Cone is a beautiful hill of blood-red cinder formed in the late Tertiary, as sensuously curvaceous as dunes. Desert holly is the only perennial plant hardy enough to grow on it. The pale bushes against the dark volcanic ground produce a strikingly contrasted land-

Hikes Around The Warm Springs

	Dist.(mi)	Elev.(ft)
Seven Sisters Springs		
Warm Springs Road	0.0	1,260
First spring	0.8	1,235
Seventh spring	1.6	1,230
Return along base of terrace	3.8	1,260
Red Cinder Cone		
Lower Warm Springs	0.0	~1,380
Base of Red Cinder Cone/trail	1.35	1,475
Peace sign	1.7	1,770
Red Cinder Cone summit	(0.15)	1,621
Upper end of trail	1.95	1,920
Black Mountain Loop Trail		
Lower Warm Springs (road)	0.0	~1,380
Trail junction at crest	1.7	2,085
2,105-ft summit/viewpoint	(0.1)	2,105
Wash	1.8	1,965
Rod Falls	2.2	1,840
Canyon mouth	3.1	1,545
Lower Warm Springs	4.6	~1,380

scape, almost too manicured to be natural. The peace sign was created by selectively removing the surface cinder, thereby exposing the much paler hard-packed soil underneath it. At close range, it is an impressive giant figure 70 feet across, on a slope so steep that standing on it is a challenge. The trail is slippery, but please stay on it. If you walk on the rocks next to it instead, they will roll under your feet, which will widen the trail and make it even more visible from afar. Above the peace sign, the trail passes by a low windbreak shaped like a heart. About 250 yards past it the trail ends at a geological curiosity: the cinder stops abruptly at a fault, against a vast exposure of quartz monzonite. The time gap between these formations exceeds 140 million years, yet the transition between them covers a fraction of an inch.

The views from the Cinder Cone are magnificent. There may be no better place to appreciate the true proportions of Saline Valley's long eastern arm. From miles away near Steel Pass, it flows like a great sinuous river of gravel between the auburn swell of the Saline Range and the great wall of the Last Chance Range, skirting the foot of the cone on its way down to the valley floor. To the south, the perspective of Saline Valley is so unusual from this angle that it could be a different place. Allow a little time to savor this viewpoint—if the wind lets you. One time it was so strong that if it weren't for my heavy pack I might have become airborne!

Black Mountain Loop Trail. This scenic loop hike explores the open volcanic foothills northwest of Lower Warm Springs, which form the southern tip of the Saline Range. It will take you up the range to the rim of a major canyon, down into and along this canyon back to the valley floor, then along the valley back to the springs. The loop takes about two and a half hours. There is a trail up the range. You can catch it from Palm Spring (see map), but it is easier to find it from Lower Warm Springs: look roughly north and you should see it snaking up the slope. The trailhead is across the road at the north end of the open area known as the "baseball field." The trail is lined with rocks at first, then grows a little vague as it cuts north up the fan to the foot of the range, but once it begins its ascent it is hard to lose it.

This is one of those hikes where the ratio of payoff to physical effort is a bargain. For the price of a modest workout, you will be constantly treated to spectacular views of Saline Valley, of the colorful Last Chance Range, and of the phenomenal scarp of the Inyo Mountains. Yet what makes this hike so special is the local scenery, which is one grand volcanic desolation. This part of the Saline Range is a bulging dome of late Tertiary basalt and andesite. Plants have trouble making a living on these inert silicates. Vast tracks of the dark-brown ground are utterly barren, raw and unadorned. The cobbles littering it are coated with extremely thick desert varnish, as black as space, created by centuries of southern exposure to the ferocious sun. Like meteors, their surfaces are gauged with prominent "thumb prints." If it were not for the occasional desert holly, it would be easy to imagine yourself on another planet. This sensation is particularly strong around the top of the trail. The similarities to the Pathfinder images of the Martian ground are striking—the hues of the land, the mean size and distribution of the rocks, even the oddly close horizon. This has to be one of the best places on Earth to see Mars.

At the crest, you are standing on the abrupt rim of a nameless canyon, a long trench 100 to 200 feet deep, unusually homogeneous. The trail drops down its very steep and rocky wall to the bottom of the canyon. There is no trail in the canyon; you just hike down its smooth wash of crushed volcanic gravel. The only obstacle is a 14-foot wall of solid basalt known as Rod Falls, bypassed by a short trail. Here too, the landscape screams of desolation. The wash is as scarcely vegetated as if it were plagued. Everything around, from the boulders in the wash to the sheer walls of broken basalt and even the wash itself, is a dark shade of brown, gray, or red—the colors of the underworld.

At the wide canyon mouth, head southeast (left) and follow the base of the range. Here also there is no trail, only disconnected trail segments. After half a mile you will round a low hill and see Lower Warm Springs about a mile to the east. This stretch offers good opportunities for low-angle photography of Saline Valley, especially of the hot springs stranded in the middle of the desert. Cross the landing strip with care; this is not exactly O'Hare, but it would be a bummer to get hit by a plane in Saline Valley.

Other local destinations. Looking for more? Try the two undeveloped springs at the foot of the Saline Range west of the Black Diamond Prospect (1.3 miles round-trip). Or hike to the Coffee Stop Prospect, the only mercury mine in Saline Valley. Walk the road 1.3 miles past Upper Warm Spring, then cut north across a raised fan, a wide wash, and another raised fan 0.45 mile. The mine consists of half a dozen shallow pits coated with reddish cinnabar. A straight road cuts 0.1 mile west to scattered remains at the edge of a wash. Aside from the ruins of a wooden cabin, the site's most interesting contraption is the primitive oven made of local rocks and pipes once used to roast the mercury out of the ore (see *The Up and Down Mine*).

■

THE STEEL PASS ROAD

Nearly 30 miles long, the Steel Pass Road is one of the wildest, longest, most difficult, and most fun driving routes in all of Death Valley National Park. It connects the warm springs in Saline Valley to the sand dunes in Eureka Valley over Steel Pass, an isolated divide trapped between the Last Chance and Saline ranges. Driving it is slow, difficult at places, and it requires perseverance. For some people, these attributes are all the more reason for coming here. Besides the challenge of the drive, this itinerary offers plenty of opportunities to explore on foot some of the most isolated canyons and mountains in the California desert.

General Information

Jurisdiction: Death Valley National Park
Road status: Primitive road (4WD / HC)
Dedeckera Cyn narrows: 0.9 mi, 380 ft up, 0 ft down one way / very easy
White Cliffs narrows: 2.4 mi, 1,340 ft up, 80 ft down one way / easy–mod.
Main attractions: Long and rough 4WD road, narrows, scenery, mine
USGS 7.5' topo maps: Lower Warm Springs*, W. of Teakettle Junction*, Saline Peak*, Last Chance Range SW*, Last Chance Range SE
Maps: pp. 89*, 193, 195*, *61*, 179*

Location and Access

From its south end at Upper Warm Spring, the Steel Pass Road climbs north through the eastern arm of Saline Valley to Steel Pass (5,091'), then drops along Dedeckera Canyon to the Eureka Dunes at the south end of Eureka Valley. To find these two end points, refer to *The Warm Springs* and *The Eureka Dunes*. The Steel Pass Road is rough, unmaintained, remote, and infrequently used. Count on at least two days to complete the circuit from asphalt to asphalt without rushing. Except for long weekends and holidays, you will likely not see a soul. It is good news for your desert experience, bad news if you run into trouble. Load up on food, water, and gas. It would be madness to attempt driving it with an urban SUV, let alone with a sedan. What is needed is a robust, narrow-wheel-base, four-wheel-drive vehicle with *a lot* of clearance. If you do not happen to have one of those handy, try driving it from the Eureka Dunes. That end of the road is a little sandy, but it can be driven to the entrance to Dedeckera Canyon (described further on) and the canyon's mile-long narrows explored on foot. You may also consider a multiple-day backpacking outing along the Steel Pass Road (29.3 miles, with 3,880 feet of elevation gain and 2,480 feet of elevation loss). This section describes the northbound itinerary, starting from Saline Valley.

Petroglyphs, Saline Range

Route Description

The Steel Pass Road. Over its 30-mile course, the Steel Pass Road traverses what may be the most lonesome region in the park. We are talking *wild*. Built illegally before the creation of the park, it bisects what would otherwise be the largest roadless area in the country outside of Alaska. Just to get to the road, you have to drive more than 50 miles of uninhabited desert, all of it on primitive roads.

The Steel Pass Road is heavily altered, usually towards greater entropy, by every flashflood that scours the drainages it follows. I would not even venture a guess about what its condition will be when you go there. There are, however, a few persistent problem areas. The first one is north of Upper Warm Spring. For over 10 miles the road follows a wide wash up the northeastern arm of Saline Valley. Although the road is relatively smooth, long segments of it are washed out and barely distinguishable from their surroundings. This is as close as it gets to an off-road driving experience in a national park. Keeping track of the road's whereabouts can be tedious. To avoid creating new tracks, look ahead for signs of where the road is going. Also, heed the rock alignments that block closed-off side roads and channels that look like roads but aren't. The next problem area starts shortly after the road leaves the main wash and angles east towards Steel Pass. There is some deep gravel, then a couple of rocky spots that require careful maneuvering around small boulders. The Steel Pass area is usually OK, except for a short but steep down-grade about 0.4 mile north of it, which might be tricky coming up the other way when it is muddy.

For over 3 miles north from the pass the land unfolds into a broad, nearly level corridor that curves up westward to the Saline Range and

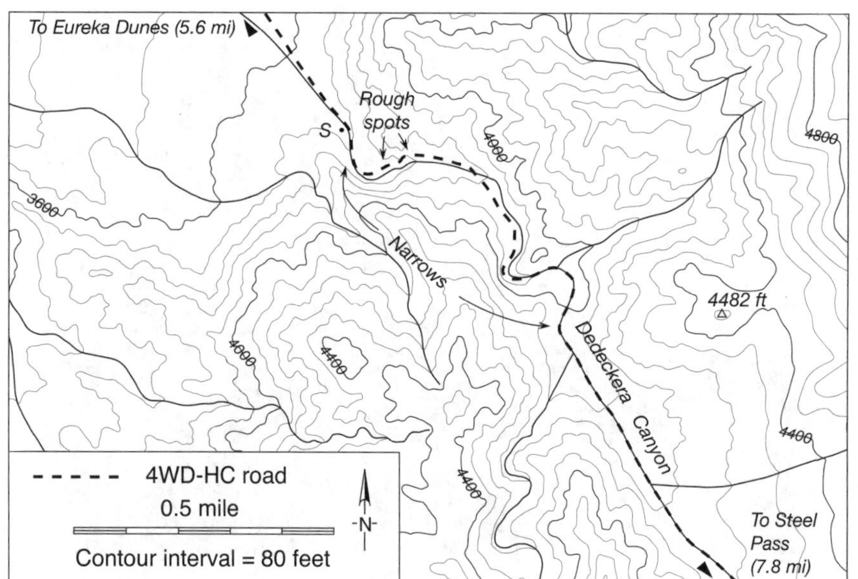

The Steel Pass Road		
	Dist.(mi)	Elev.(ft)
Palm Spring	0.0	1,475
Rough steps in road	1.8	~1,790
Upper Warm Spring	2.4	1,835
Road leaves wash	13.2	3,980
Rough spot	14.3	~4,510
Steel Pass	15.4	5,091
Dedeckera Canyon (head)	18.5	~5,080
Narrows (upper end)	22.4	4,040
High step in road	23.1	3,760
Dedeckera Canyon mouth	23.3	3,660
Eureka Dunes (campground)	29.3	2,871

to the Last Chance Range. This is high desert country, densely covered with sagebrush, cliffrose, and ephedra. Gnarled Joshua trees sprout out of the nearby foothills. It is a stark place, beautiful in its own way, suffused with the remoteness, mystery, and timelessness that embody the very essence of the desert. It also has a generous reserve of cross-country hikes in the many canyons that drain into it. Some of them may not have been visited much since the mining days, and perhaps not since prehistoric times.

Summer storm over Steel Pass Road

At its north end, the Steel Pass Road descends through Dedeckera Canyon, a scenic gem named in honor of distinguished desert botanist Mary DeDecker. What makes it special is that it occurs at the boundary between two strikingly different rocks. On its west side it skirts a vast field of nearly black basalt, formed in the Tertiary by flowing lava, while its east side is flanked by a soaring wall of Paleozoic formations, banded in striking shades of gray, ochre, and rust. Over one mile long and 1,500 feet high, this wall forms the backdrop of much of upper Dedeckera Canyon, looming larger as you lose elevation. At one place the road comes within feet of the basalt field. Two of the three main types of lava coexist—aa lava and pahoehoe lava. They have essentially the same composition, but aa lava is more viscous and breaks up into pieces as it flows. Pahoehoe lava, hotter and more gaseous, flows smoothly and forms dense basalt. Both types are exposed in the windy side canyon to the west just above the narrows—a dark and gloomy place that does not encourage loitering.

In its lower reaches, Dedeckera Canyon squeezes through impressive convoluted narrows. For nearly a mile the road snakes beneath polished walls of dark-gray dolomite, then bluish limestone (Bonanza King and Carrara formations). The greatest driving challenges are usually the four closely spaced rough spots near the bottom of the narrows. The first one is a two-foot fall in bedrock; the next three are jagged outcrops, one of them tightly trapped between the canyon

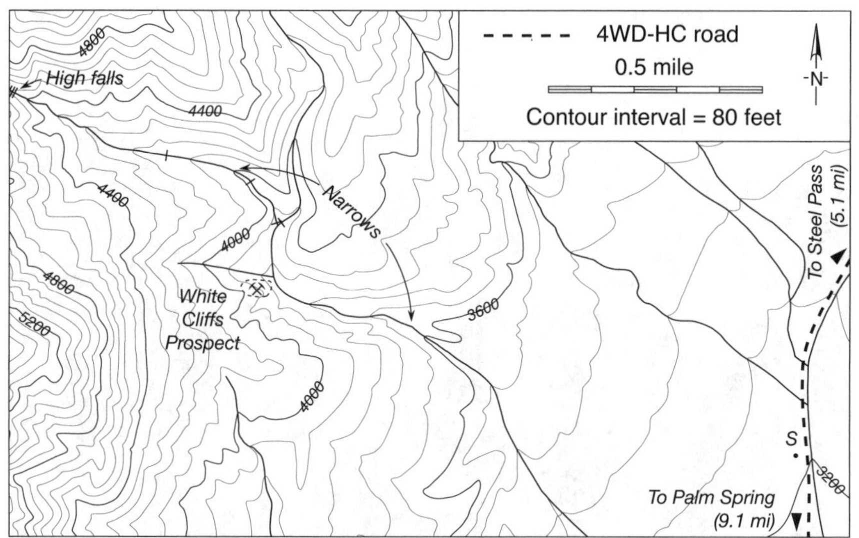

The White Cliffs Prospect	Dist.(mi)	Elev.(ft)
Steel Pass Road	0.0	3,200
Canyon mouth	0.9	3,560
Side canyon	1.4	3,820
White Cliffs Prospect	(0.1)	~3,900
End of pozzolan exposure	~2.0	4,160
High falls	2.3	4,460

walls. The fall is the most difficult. Whether you can make it will depend on your experience and your vehicle's clearance. Once, I drove through here with a brand-new Mountaineer, a low-slung 4WD vehicle designed with little concern for off-asphalt performance. I would have had better luck with an 18-wheeler, and better mileage. Without an hour's worth of road work and help from another driver, the truck might still be there. If your vehicle does not have a narrow base and at least 18 inches of clearance, you may have to turn around at this point. The rest of the road to the South Eureka Valley Road is easier, although it is locally sandy. Look for displays of ancient sea ripples, in particular just below the first tight spot in the narrows. These ripples are vestiges of an ocean that covered this area more than 500 million years ago. At the bottom of the narrows, the canyon rounds a final bend and opens up abruptly onto a spectacular viewpoint of the Eureka Dunes.

Eureka Dunes from the mouth of Dedeckera Canyon

White Cliffs Prospect. This place is hard to miss: it is so glaringly white that it is visible from as far back as the crest of the Inyo Mountains! Count 6.9 miles from Upper Warm Spring, and look for a large chalk-like exposure at the foot of the Saline Range to the west. Park and hike up the fan to the small canyon 0.9 mile to the west-northwest, marked by a small white outcrop to the right of its mouth. Thick flows of olivine basalt are exposed just inside the canyon, soon replaced by the white rock that drew you here. It is called pozzolan, a leucitic tuff named after the town of Pozzuoli in Italy where it was quarried on a large scale. This deposit also contains zeolites and traces of mercury. It resulted from extensive ash falls 10.5 to 11.5 million years ago. Pozzolan is used in the manufacture of hydraulic cement, and zeolites for water softening. Some years ago a few miners tried to cash in on this uncommon resource. Their exploitation, alternatively named the Cerro-Albino and the White Cliffs Prospect, never took off. The numerous egg-shaped cavities that pockmark the eerie south wall of the canyon are the only signs of their activity. Pozzolan is exposed for another half a mile up canyon. Erosion sculpted into it an unusual landscape of smooth, winding, white narrows interrupted by sensual falls and basalt boulders.

■

SALINE VALLEY'S TALC MINES

These selected hikes, neither rough mountain climbs nor trivial valley walks, explore two of Saline Valley's historic talc mines, the White Eagle Mine and the Snow Flake Mine, both accessed on foot by old roads. The highlights include a glimpse at the area's history, interesting minerals, geology, and mining equipment, and panoramic views of the valley. These mines are privately owned and still periodically active. Please obtain permission from the caretaker at Willow Creek Camp before coming here.

General Information
Jurisdiction: Private claims on BLM land
Road status: Hiking on old roads; access from primitive or graded road
White Eagle Mine: 2.0 mi, 1,160 ft up, 0 ft down one way / easy–moder.
Snow Flake Mine: 2.5 mi, 1,800 ft up, 170 ft down one way / moderate
Main attractions: Historic talc mines, valley views, trail hiking
USGS 7.5' topo maps: Pat Keyes Cyn, Craig Cyn, New York Butte
Maps: pp. 201*, *179*

Location and Access

The White Eagle Mine and the Snow Flake Mine are located in the lower foothills of the Inyo Mountains, between Willow Creek Camp and Beveridge Canyon. Directions are provided below.

History

The Snow Flake Mine is the oldest of Saline Valley's talc mines. Formerly known as the Hilderman Mine, it has been worked intermittently since its discovery in the 1890s. In 1984, Pfizer Inc. acquired an interest in the property and extended its existing developments. No production record is available, although it is estimated that over the years it extracted around 5,000 tons of talc.

The White Eagle Mine and the Grey Eagle Mine were located in 1941 and 1942, respectively, and exploited intermittently until about 1985. By 1979 they had produced jointly around 50,000 tons of talc, most of which came from the White Eagle Mine. In modern times they were operated by the Okuniewicz Mining Company. In 1985 the company switched its operations entirely to the White Eagle Mine, extracting 2,000 to 4,000 tons of steatite annually for ceramic tile and cosmetic manufacturers.

Gilbert Price "G. P." Rogers was a prominent figure in the history of these mines. In the 1920s he gave up his real-estate career to exploit Saline Valley's talc deposits. His mines have been in the family ever since. A Timbisha Shoshone named Johnny Hunter—a name probably inspired by William Hunter—helped him develop the Grey Eagle Mine. Its ore chute, which was still in use in the 2000s, was constructed with recycled parts from the Salt Tramway. G. P. Rogers' grandson David Rogers worked here with his wife as early as the 1970s, "a time," he recalls, "when one would not see a single visitor in a whole month." Until recently, Rogers periodically hauled out a few tons of talc under the label of International Talc and Steatite. The ore, free of asbestos and of unusually high quality, is very different in tone from mine to mine, as is reflected in the mines' names. Some of the talc is shipped in large blocks, in particular to the Inuits, who use it to carve statues.

Route Description

The access roads to the White Eagle Mine and the Snow Flake Mine are on private land. The owners keep them open to hikers who want to visit the mines or access the high Inyos. This situation may change in the future. The roads may become public, or they may be closed if trouble develops. Before coming here, please get the latest information and *obtain permission* from the caretaker at Willow Creek Camp, which is part of the Rogers' property. If you are allowed in, *respect the owners' privacy, obey all posted signs, and do not disturb anything*.

The White Eagle Mine. For this one, start from Willow Creek Camp, which is on the Saline Valley Road 4.6 miles north of the Warm Springs Road. Nestled on the edge of the parched valley floor, the camp is a miraculously verdant oasis. Half a dozen cabins and a few trailers, used by miners during periods of activity, are scattered on an expansive green lawn, among healthy trees irrigated with the abundant water from nearby Willow Creek. The road to the White Eagle Mine starts to the left of the camp's entrance gate. The two steep and windy miles to the mine offer grand views of the Inyo Mountains' buttressed foothills, and of the pale, deeply gouged bluffs that frame Willow Creek below.

Near its upper end the road splits into three levels. A derelict trailer and caterpillar were for years marooned on the lower level, just before the mine's loading structure. This tall metallic contraption sorted the ore through a giant sieve called a grizzly, which dumped the finer material into a tipple, from which the ore was loaded into trucks

Ore loading area at the White Eagle Mine

via a short conveyor belt. The intermediate road circles up the top of the loading structure. The upper terminal of the cableway is visible at the top of the cliff above it. This cableway was used in the early days of mining to lower the ore from higher tunnels. In half a mile it dropped 900 feet to the lone ore bin on the fan south of the access road. The upper terminal was once accessed by the upper road, but it has been completely wiped out by landslides. The terrain is so steep that it would be suicidal to attempt crossing it without at least carving a trail with a shovel, so that the upper area is essentially inaccessible. Of the mine's five original tunnels, only one is still open, on the intermediate level about 50 yards before the loading structure. Its timbered adit gives access to more than 1,700 feet of workings, a phantasmal maze of wide, high-ceilinged galleries cloaked with talc powder.

The local talc deposit occurs within a faulted section of Badger Flat Limestone (Ordovician) in close proximity to quartz monzonite (Jurassic Pat Keyes Pluton). The talc bodies, most likely formed by hydrothermal alteration of the country rocks, are highly irregular but quite extensive. The tailings contain good-size chunks of white to greenish talc, and large crystals of light-gray, translucent calcite.

The Snow Flake Mine. Drive the Saline Valley Road 5.2 miles north of the Salt Tramway Junction (3.4 miles south of the Warm

Springs Road) to the Keynot Canyon Road. Follow this road west 1.15 miles (bear right, then left, and right again, at the three junctions) to a junction on a low rise at the foot of the range (there is a metal chute by the road). The Keynot Canyon Road is often passable with a passenger car, but not always. The Snow Flake Mine Road is the grade that climbs left up the mountain slope. From the foot of the range its sharp switchbacks ascend nearly 1,400 feet in 1.8 miles to the mine's large wooden ore bin, right by the side of the road. The slope is so precipitous that at places this aerial road seems to barely hang on to it. The roadway is locally soft, littered with rocks, and deeply rutted. Good clearance, power, and off-road tires will improve your chances of making it through, if it is passable at all. Otherwise it does provide a welcome foot path up the insanely steep mountain. The views into Saline Valley are breathtaking. At its upper end you will also get impressive glimpses into the abyss of Beveridge Canyon to the south, and even hear the distant sound of its waterfalls. Keep an eye open for turtleback, for colorful species of eriogonum, and a peculiar mushroom called desert puffball

The Snow Flake Mine is striking for its seemingly precarious location, high on a narrow ridge surrounded on three sides by sheer slopes. It has two groups of workings. The ore bin marks the beginning of the east group. The spur road just above it on the left leads to a collapsed 100-foot adit with a small ore chute and an open cut. Just a little further up the main road, a spur on the right ends shortly at a

Saline Valley's Talc Mines

	Dist.(mi)	Elev.(ft)
White Eagle Mine		
Willow Creek Camp	0.0	2,280
White Eagle Mine (tipple)	2.0	3,440
Snow Flake Mine		
Saline Valley Road	0.0	1,142
Snow Flake Mine Road	1.15	1,635
Ore bin (east group)	3.0	3,020
Fork in road	3.1	3,040
360-foot tunnel	(0.05)	3,040
Open cut	(0.05)	~3,120
Road junction	3.45	3,300
Tunnel (west group)	3.55	3,260

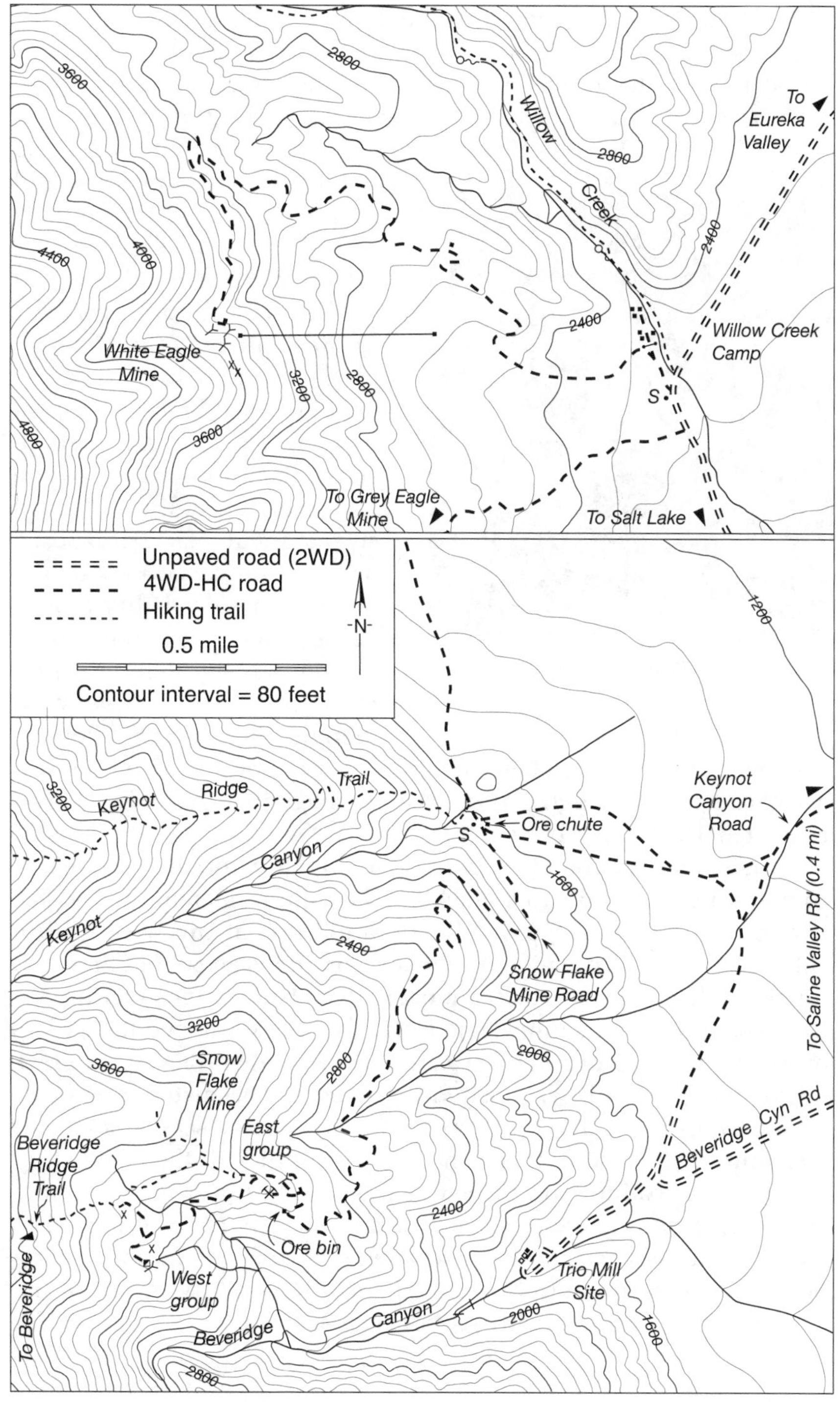
To Eureka Valley
Willow Creek
White Eagle Mine
Willow Creek Camp
To Grey Eagle Mine
To Salt Lake
Unpaved road (2WD)
4WD-HC road
Hiking trail
0.5 mile
N
Contour interval = 80 feet
Keynot Ridge Trail
Keynot Canyon
Ore chute
Keynot Canyon Road
To Saline Valley Rd (0.4 mi)
Snow Flake Mine Road
Snow Flake Mine
East group
Beveridge Ridge Trail
Ore bin
West group
Beveridge Canyon
Beveridge Cyn Rd
Trio Mill Site
To Beveridge

collared adit. This 360-foot tunnel, the mine's longest, cuts under the main road clear to the open cut, but it has collapsed. The small open cut just above this tunnel exposes one of the mine's four talc lenses. They were formed in the early Mesozoic, when Diorite of New York Butte, the rock exposed along the access road, intruded and thermally altered the country rock (Hidden Valley Dolomite) into talc. Steatite, also called "soft talc" by miners, is the highest purity talc. When it contains impurities that prevent its use as high-grade commercial talc, it is called soapstone. Beautiful steatite, white to green, translucent, and streaked with black, is exposed near the tunnel. It may be the ore that inspired this mine's name. Away from the tunnel the talc visibly degrades into tremolite, a harder product of thermal alteration of dolomite. Commercial talc that contains a high percentage of tremolite is known as "hard talc." Although exposures are limited, this area still holds an estimated 340,000 tons of tremolitic talc!

Ore car at talc tunnel

The main road continues 0.1 mile to a high point, then drops and climbs a little 0.25 mile to a junction. The right fork ends shortly. The left fork descends steeply 0.1 mile and ends at the west group, entrenched in a deep ravine. The main working is an 80-foot timbered tunnel with three short drifts, inhabited by bats. A meandering rail track comes out of the tunnel and forks. One track dumped the useless overburden on a tailing in the wash below. The other track took the ore to the road, where it was loaded into trucks. The rusted, open-bottomed scoop across the ravine is called a slusher or a scraper loader. It was dug into the soft talc of an open cut until full, then pulled by cables to the loading point where it was dragged over a ramp into a truck. The nearby piece of cogged machinery may have been used to haul the slusher back and forth between the open cut and the loading point. In the spring, bright red globemallow grow right out of the baby powder that abundantly covers the road.

■

THE SALINE VALLEY SAND DUNES

Saline Valley has two lovely sets of sand dunes, one in a spectacular setting against the 10,000-foot wall of the Inyo Mountains, the other lost in the middle of the valley floor. Pristine and rarely visited, these sensuous expanses of pure sand are delightful playgrounds to experience the beauty and vastness of this isolated valley.

General Information
Jurisdiction: Death Valley National Park
Road status: Roadless; hiking access from graded or primitive road
Saline Valley Sand Dunes: 3.0 mi, 130 ft up, 60 ft down one way/easy
Little Dunes: 3.6 mi, ~80 ft up, ~130 ft down one way/easy
Main attractions: Sand dunes, botany, easy valley-floor walks
USGS 7.5' topo maps: Lower Warm Springs*, West of Ubehebe Peak*, Craig Canyon
Maps: pp. 205*, 207*, *179*

Location and Access

Saline Valley's main dunes are located in the west central valley, a couple of miles north of Salt Lake. The usual starting point for exploring them is the short road that bypasses the Saline Valley Road southwest of the dunes. The south end of this cutoff is 3.9 miles north of the Hunter Canyon Road. Its north end is 1.2 miles further north (1.5 miles south of the Warm Springs Road). From this cutoff two short roads head to the foot of the dunes. These roads are closed to all vehicles. Park on the bypass road and walk from there.

Another starting point is the Artesian Well Road. This road makes a 3.5-mile loop from and back to the Saline Valley Road. Its south end is 0.75 mile north of the Hunter Canyon Road, on the east side. From there it cuts north-northeast 2.1 miles to a cattle guard at the apex of the road, where it makes a sharp left U-turn and returns in 1.4 miles to the Saline Valley Road. The dunes are less than a mile northwest of the cattle guard. This road crosses rutted, hard-packed clay (which turns to slick mud in wet weather). High clearance is preferable.

Saline Valley's second set of dunes is farther south, approximately 4 miles east of Salt Lake. To hike to them, start from the Saline Valley Road 4.5 miles east of the Salt Tramway Junction (or 6.5 miles north from the Lippincott Road), where the road makes a pronounced, gradual bend. The Little Dunes are approximately 2 miles due north.

Saline Valley's main dunes. Saline Valley's sand dunes are not very extensive: they cover only about 2.2 square miles. Nor are they exactly imposing: the highest dune is not much more than 20 feet tall. But they have all the magical attributes of dunes, plus one: they are virgin. On all of my visits I did not see a single human footprint; it was even a little painful to leave tracks on such immaculate terrain. These dunes draw much of their beauty from their spectacular setting against the formidable escarpment of the Inyo Mountains. Their uniqueness lies in this stunning juxtaposition of sand and stone: light against dark, smoothness against ruggedness, ripples against towering heights.

For a short exploration, start at the cutoff road on the west side and take a stroll east to one of the highest dunes. You can then follow the whaleback dunes northeast to the far end of the sand apron (a little over 1 mile). A good portion of these dunes is whaleback dunes, half-cylinders of sand that often form extensive, parallel waves. Whalebacks are almost always at an angle to the prevailing wind, which here comes from the south. If you follow the path of least resistance, you will find yourself funneled northeastward by the long, smooth corridors of sand between them. If you walk north instead, you will have to scramble up and down numerous whalebacks.

Each of California's many desert dune systems supports a specific association of perennial plants. Some plants here, like creosote and cattle spinach, are common in other dunes. Conversely, others do not normally occur in sand dunes, for instance bursage, desert holly, inkweed, and arrowweed (which thrives all around the Saline Valley dunes). You may also spot Thurber sandpaper plant, uncommon in northern Mojave Desert dunes. Its green leaves and stems are covered with microscopic hard spines that do feel like sandpaper.

Occasionally, I have encountered here an uncommon beetle—a quarter inch in size, almost round, black with a delicate gold trim around its head. Although they are immobile most of the time, they

The Saline Valley Sand Dunes

	Dist.(mi)	Elev.(ft)
Artesian Well Rd (cattle guard)	0.0	1,081
Artesian Well	0.1	~1,081
End of mesquite grove	0.65	1,090
Southeast end of dunes	1.0	1,115
Highest dune	2.7	1,165
Cutoff road	3.0	1,146

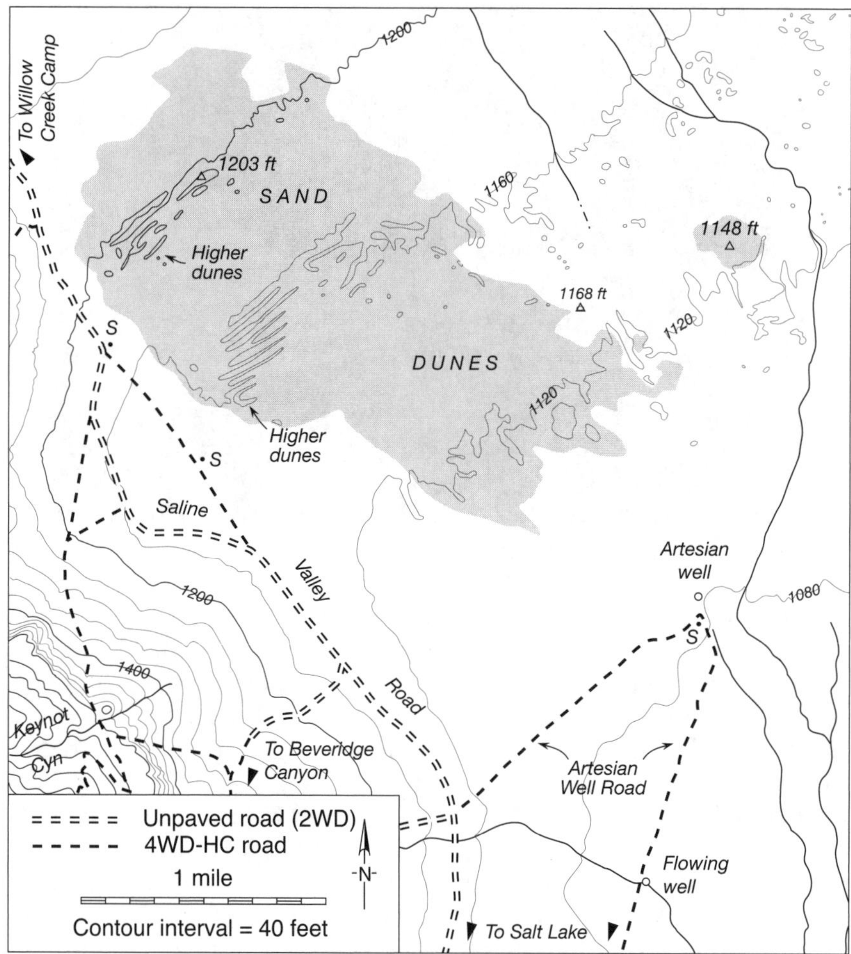

will suddenly scurry madly across the sand as if their life depended on it, only to stop seconds later and fall again into an apparent coma. Be careful where you walk: this species may be endangered.

Hike from the Artesian Well Road. This longer approach will enable you to sample not only sand, but also western Saline Valley's extensive mesquite belt. Start from the cattle guard. The fenced area just north of it protects six acres of dense mesquite grove, including one of the valley's artesian wells, against the ravenous appetite of feral burros. The well is 50 yards past the cattle guard, in the deep shade of a tall willow. In an artesian well, water is forced out of the ground by the sheer hydrostatic pressure of the aquifer. Here it is pushed through

Saline Valley Sand Dunes and Inyo Mountains in early morning light

a vertical pipe and gushes two feet above ground! The well flows year-round, about a liter per minute, enough to support a stand of cattail.

From the cattle guard, a burro trail runs clockwise (west) along the fence. Follow it 250 yards to the third bend in the fence, then head northwest away from the fence. The dunes are just visible less than a mile away. The area on the way to them is vegetated with mesquites, arrowweed, and saltbush. Burros have blazed miles of trails through this maze of low mesquite groves. Use them to plot your own course to the western edge of the forest, where the dunes will be in full view. This is a fun hike, level and partly shaded. Burros often hang around in small groups. Chances are that they will see you first and surprise you with a throaty warning. If you get too close they will gallop away, kicking up dust, then turn around and stare at you, as curious as cats.

This hike will take you to the more desolate eastern dunes, a mixture of exquisitely expansive sand playas and low sand knolls. The far eastern fringe is covered with mesquite trees. They hold back the sand so well that some dunes have nearly vertical slopes! From this general area it is a short walk west across the sand to the slightly higher dunes near the Saline Valley Road. From there, return along the southern edge of the dunes for a slight change of scenery.

Getting to the dunes is easy, but pinpointing your car in this sea of trees when you decide to return may well seem frighteningly hopeless. The saving grace is the willow at the artesian well: being the tallest tree, it sticks out above the canopy and is easy to spot from the dunes.

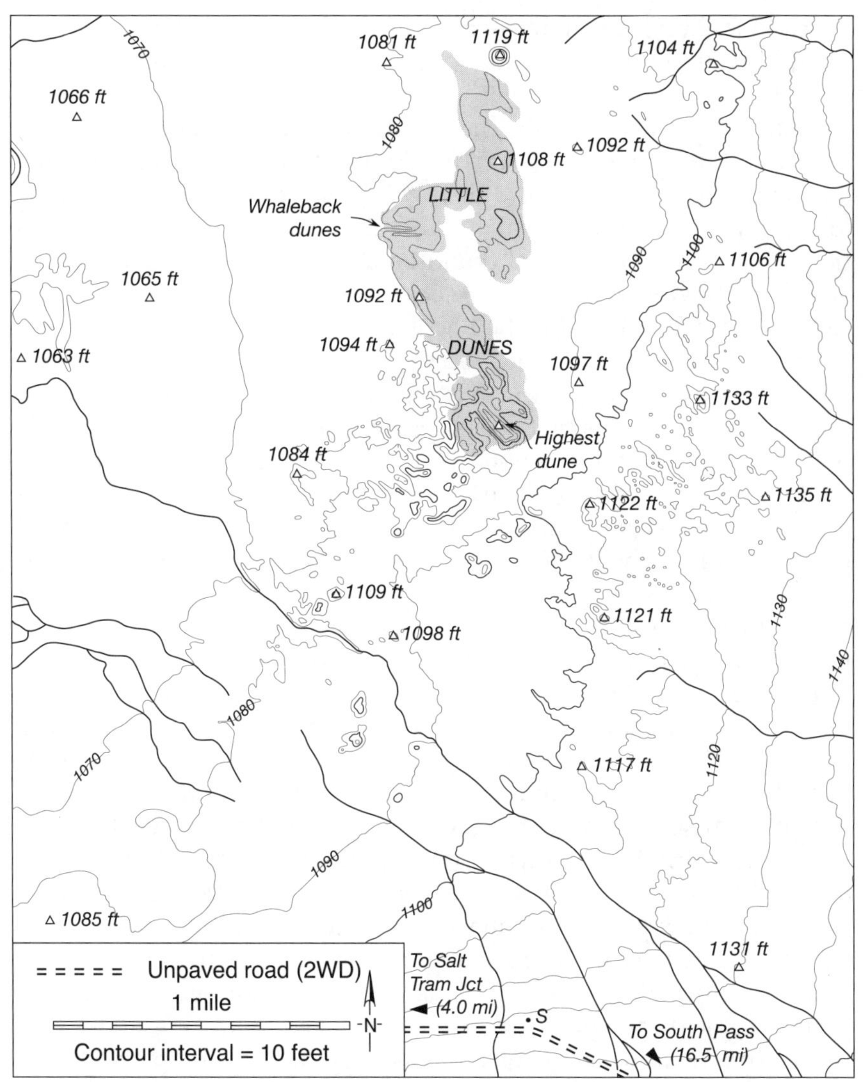

The Little Dunes		
	Dist.(mi)	Elev.(ft)
Saline Valley Road	0.0	1,133
Southern end of dunes	2.0	~1,090
Highest dune	2.1	1,127
Whaleback dunes	2.9	1,085
Northern end of dunes	3.6	~1,085

Learn to identify its umbrella-shaped crown when you first head out. It works well—except at night! Make sure to hike back before dark.

The Little Dunes. Of the thousands of people who drive by these beautiful dunes every year, very few know of their existence, and only a handful visits them. Yet it is an easy hike, far more pleasant than the long jostling ride to Saline Valley. From the bend in the road (see directions), aim for the highest of the Little Dunes visible sticking out just above the low vegetation cover about 2 miles due north. If you lose sight of them, aim towards the Red Cinder Cone, visible 8 miles north at the foot of the Last Chance Range. This is a quintessential desert hike. You wander across a vast desert floor, embracing 360° views of the pristine mountains that enclose Saline Valley. This is, by and large, the desert's rendition of a flood plain. When a serious rainstorm hits the Last Chance Range to the east, canyons send sheets of water pouring down the valley floor. Areas the size of football fields get flooded under mud-laden water. Over time the sandy soil has become coated with thick layers of desiccated mud that have cracked into striking geometric patterns or peeled into paper-thin shavings. On your way to the dunes you will cross many such areas. Flood waters also bring in salt leached from the mountains rocks. The ground has enough of it to repel all but the most salt-tolerant plants. From the road to the dunes only two kinds of shrub manage to grow: creosote and four-wing saltbush, their bases buried under wind-blown drifts of sand.

The Little Dunes cover a narrow north-south band about 1.2 miles long by less than 0.5 mile wide. What distinguishes them from neighboring dune fields is their cover of mesquites. Even the highest dune, rising painstakingly 35 feet above its surroundings, is crowned with this shrub's disheveled limbs, madly clawing at the sky. They lend the dunes an unusually green and ragged look and profoundly alter their shapes. Some dunes are so effectively stabilized by the mesquites that their slopes have angles of repose much too steep to climb. Understandably, wildlife relishes the rare shade. Raven and wren, rabbits and burros, all leave their marks in the sand.

North-northwest from the highest dune the terrain changes dramatically. Low swells of sand waver into the distance to a series of whaleback dunes. This is the one area where the Little Dunes look like dunes—reduced to essentials, naked and curvaceous, wrinkled by the wind. Further north the dune field breaks into wide sheets of sand. This whole area offers unusual views up into the largely unexplored canyons that slash the central Last Chance Range.

■

SALT LAKE

The small alkaline lake that lingers at the bottom of Saline Valley is one of the desert's rarest treats. The trail hike along its scenic shore passes by curious salt formations, historic salt evaporators, expansive mud flats, artesian wells, and one of the park's largest mesquite forests. Hike back a different way and you will get to see the remains of the region's earliest borax refinery. This is a peaceful area, livened by burros and birds, and a haven for photographers.

General Information

Jurisdiction: Death Valley National Park
Road status: Hiking on old trails; graded access road
Saline Valley Marsh: 0.6 mi, 10 ft up, 10 ft down one way / very easy
Shoreline Trail: 3.9 mi, 110 ft up loop / easy
Main attractions: Salt lake, salt and borax mines, history, photography
USGS 7.5' topo map: Craig Canyon
Maps: pp. 213*, 214, *179*

Location and Access

Salt Lake is the shallow body of alkaline water at the bottom of Saline Valley, at an elevation of 1,060 feet. This section describes three areas of interest on the west side of the lake: the Saline Valley Marsh, the Shoreline Trail, and the Conn and Trudo Borax Works. A fourth point of interest is described under *The Salt Tramway*. These sites are easily reached by car from the Saline Valley Road. The key landmark is the Salt Tramway Junction, 21.5 miles north of South Pass (or 8.6 miles south of the Warm Springs Road), where the tramway towers to the north are perfectly aligned. Refer to individual sections for directions.

History: Earliest Borax Mining in the Mojave Desert

Although early borax mining is often associated with Death Valley, the first discovery of borax in the region was actually made in Saline Valley in 1874, on the playa surrounding Salt Lake. The following year, Frederick Conn and Edward Trudo started a borax mining and refining operation at the lake's northwest corner. They both came from Candelaria, Nevada, where borax was discovered in 1871, and they knew just what to do. They took control of about 700 acres of playa, partly crusted with up to 2 feet of tincal (sodium tetraborate), and erected a small refinery with a capacity to concentrate 40 tons per month. To supply it with fresh water, they diverted water from two small ponds below Hunter Canyon via a mile-long iron pipeline. Their business was thriving: by 1889 they had 30 men on the job, and they earned the distinction of being the largest single borax producer in the country. They mined continuously until 1895. By then, much larger borax mines had come to life, driving the price of borax down from 10 cents per pound in 1874 to a record low of 5 cents, and operations became more sporadic. The last shipments were made in 1907.

Route Description

Saline Valley Marsh. The extensive marsh on the west side of Salt Lake is a remarkably lush oasis visible from miles away. Most of it is fenced in to keep feral burros out, but there is a short road that lets you drive right into it. This road is 1.5 miles north of the Salt Tramway Junction, on the east side. If you are coming from the north, look for it 0.4 mile south of the start of the fence. The road goes over a cattle guard and through mesquite thickets to a barren expanse of salt-laden clay that stretches out to the lakeshore. Park on the edge of the open area and explore this fragile wetland on foot.

Take a short walk around (only a few acres are accessible), preferably quietly, as one of the perks here is wildlife. Many denizens of the desert take advantage of this rare abundance of water, including coyotes, foxes, bobcats, rabbits, and 120 species of birds. Start along the west side of the marsh, heading north from the access road. This area is densely vegetated with thorny mesquites and sticky stands of arrowweed. The water that feeds Salt Lake and the marsh originates from the canyons of the Inyo Mountains. The largest point of discharge is Wopschau Spring, which puts out hundreds of gallons per minute. Poke around a little and you will come across one of its outlets, the pipe of an artesian well that constantly spews out a gushing stream. At dusk you might get to meet the native red-spotted toad that lives in the spring's concrete basin.

To the south the lakeshore is crowded with fields of grasses and cattail, rippling in the breeze like wheat in the Midwest. It is hard to get near it; bring binoculars to observe it from a distance. Its shallow waters are home to bullfrogs, chub, and other introduced fish. To the east, the shore is fringed with salt grass and pickleweed. Over time I spotted sandpipers and stilts—birds more at home on seashores than in the desert. For a different kind of experience, come here after dark, preferably on a moonless night. I don't know what it is—the damp-

Salt Lake from the Lonesome Miner Trail in the Inyo Mountains

ness, the gloomy calls of frogs, the skeletal mesquites, or the faint smell of rot—but it may well make you an instant believer in evil spirits.

The Shoreline Trail. This scenic trail is the best way to discover Salt Lake. It is also about as level and easy as trails come in the desert. It is most enjoyable on warm evenings, when the lake is shaded by the mountains. Drive the Saline Valley Road 1.9 miles north of the Salt Tramway Junction to the Hunter Canyon Road. Make a right (east) along the fence and park after 0.3 mile at the turnout. The faded road that cuts north between tall arrowweed is the Shoreline Trail. It is in a designated wilderness area and off-limits to motor vehicles.

For the first 0.7 mile, the trail closely follows the shore. In the summer, Salt Lake can dry out completely, but in the spring it typically covers 1 to 1.5 square miles, depending on how wet the winter has been. In Minnesota it would barely pass for a pond, but by desert standards it is huge. The odds of so much water in such a sunbaked place are very low. This is one of the desert's rarest environments. For a closer look, hike the burro trail that hugs the water's edge. Many of the unique features of desert lakes are on display: dark pools crusted with salt, wood debris shredded by saline water, paper-thin salt plates, cubic salt crystals, and salt flats partitioned into giant polygonal figures. Carpets of salt grass, saltbush, and sacaton grass thrive right up to the waterline. Here and there, fresh water fringed with black algae oozes out along the shore. This is the terminus of Hunter Canyon's creek, which has traveled a mile under the fan before resurging here, at the valley's lowest point. At sunset, reflections of the sky and mountains torch the shaded lake with flaming amber and deep purples.

After 0.45 mile, the trail crosses the ruins of an old evaporite mine, perhaps part of Conn and Trudo's operation. The hardened ramp of dark clay that juts into the lake to the east gave access to the lake bed. The large salt mound shored with wooden boards just west of the trail was used to load the ore into wagons. Off in the distance, the stunted poles of abandoned evaporators often poke out of the lake.

The lake ends soon after, and the scenery changes abruptly. The trail enters the lake's vast flood plain, thousands of sterile acres of crunchy mud-and-salt blisters without a single blade of grass. Not even the burros venture across this lifeless moonscape. Such are the vagaries of nature that just a stone's throw to the west, this wasteland borders one of the park's largest low-desert forests—the long belt of mesquite trees that covers Saline Valley from the lake to the dunes.

After 1 mile the Shoreline Trail ends at a large tree stump, out in the middle of nowhere. To continue, walk 100 yards west to the mesquite belt, then northwest on one of the many burro trails that parallel the boundary between the mesquite belt and the mud flat. Make your own itinerary, either just inside the mesquite belt, just outside on the mud flat, or a bit of both. The sharp contrast between these adjacent terrains is one of the hallmarks of this hike.

After ten minutes you will see a larger grove to the northwest, on the edge of the mud flat. The burro trails converge to it and Artesian Well Road, which passes right behind the grove. In the deep shade of the grove's screwbean mesquites lies a shallow pool with clumps of cattail. This is the first and southernmost of the two artesian wells that inspired the road's name. The well's tall metal casing, plugged years

The Shoreline Trail

	Dist.(mi)	Elev.(ft)
Trailhead	0.0	1,068
Evaporative mine ruins	0.45	1,062
End of trail	1.1	1,061
Artesian Well Road (first well)	1.8	1,071
Conn and Trudo Borax Works	2.9	1,110
Back via Saline Valley Road	3.9	1,068

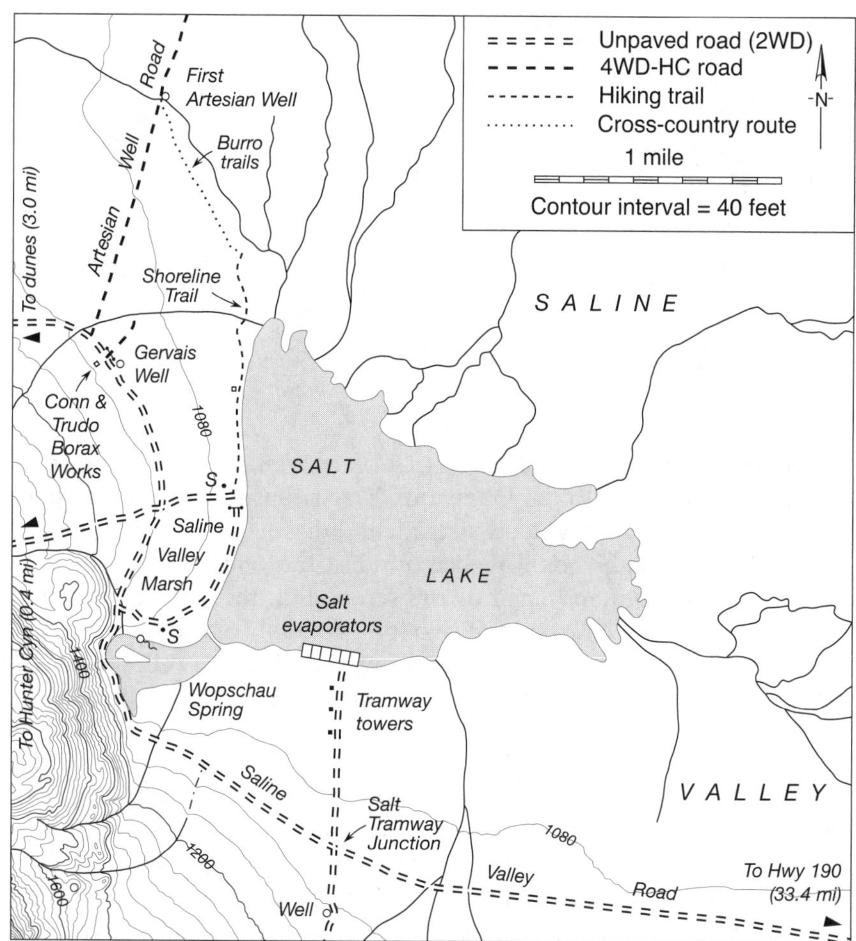

ago, is still erect by the pool. The tepid spring water now bubbles out of the ground just beneath the surface of the pond. Here and all along this hike, chances of seeing wildlife are quite good. Coyotes and burros are regulars at happy hour. Ravens, red-shafted flickers, and many other birds hang out in the trees. The only critters to fear are gnats: if they are around, which is often, wear long pants!

From here you can return the way you came. Better yet, hike the Artesian Well Road 1 mile south to the Saline Valley Road (see map) and loop back to your car along this road (another 1.1 miles), visiting the Conn and Trudo Borax Works along the way.

Conn and Trudo Borax Works. The remains of this significant early borax millsite are located 0.65 mile north of the Hunter Canyon

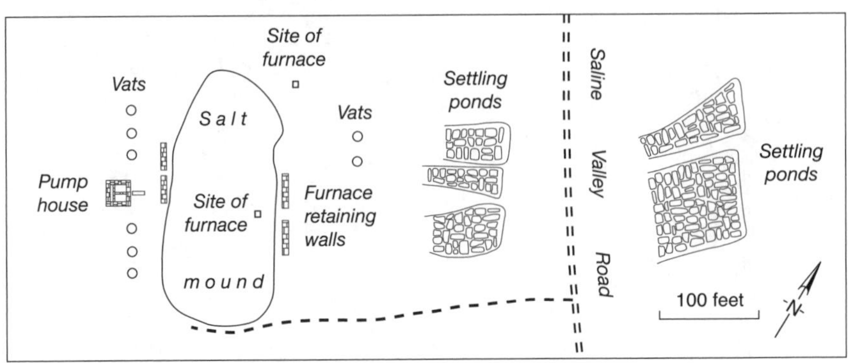

Conn and Trudo Borax Works

Road, just past the water tower at Gervais Well. A rutted side road leads 100 yards west to the main ruin. This site is historic and fragile. Park on the Saline Valley Road instead, and discover it on foot.

The 10-foot-high rock-walled mound at the center of the site was the heart of the refinery. The raw ore scraped off the salt pan was dissolved in hot water contained in two long boilers. To heat them up, the mesquite grove by the lake was cut down and burnt, until eventually other sources of wood had to be used. Insoluble salts precipitated in the boilers, and the borax solution was emptied into crystallization vats. As the water cooled the borate minerals crystallized first, while the more soluble salts like halite remained dissolved. The liquid was then drawn off, and the purified borax dried, packed, and shipped.

The two retaining walls of finely stacked cobbles flanking the mound's east side supported the workhorse of the refinery—two huge cylindrical boilers and their furnaces. They lay in the two long trenches behind the walls. The hoops that clamped the boilers still line the trenches. The boilers are gone, although one of them did not go very far: its torn-up steel carcass rests in the weeds fifty yards to the west. The outline of the six large crystallization vats can still be seen west of the mound, together with the vats' hoops. The 6-foot-high stone ruin between the vats, filled with rubble and pipes, was the pump house that piped hot water from the boilers into the vats.

The three large rectangular ponds between the mound and the road are the best preserved ruins. Enclosed on three sides by low dirt walls, they are finely tiled with colorful flat rocks of all kinds. (There are three similar ponds on the east side of the road, but that land is private property.) The ponds may have been used to dry the processed borax before shipping.

■

LITTLE HUNTER CANYON

Two easy loop hikes, mostly on trails, explore the luxuriant spring and small silver-gold mine in Little Hunter Canyon. With its unlikely perennial creek and profuse vegetation, the spring will transport you into a humid jungle strikingly different from the surrounding desert. The mine has minimal remains, but it is fun to browse through it, and it offers good views of Saline Valley.

General Information

Jurisdiction: Inyo Mountains Wilderness (BLM)
Road status: Roadless, easy access from primitive road
Little Hunter Spring: 1.7 mi, 540 ft up loop/easy
Joy and Vega Mine: 3.2 mi, 890 ft up loop/easy
Main attractions: Lush, well-watered spring, silver and gold mine
USGS 7.5' topo map: Craig Canyon
Maps: pp. 217*, 273, *179*

Location and Access

Little Hunter Canyon is a short drainage in the eastern Inyo Mountains, just south of Hunter Canyon. The Hunter Canyon Road used to go all the way to Little Hunter Canyon, but the spring in the canyon has reclaimed the upper part of the road, which is no longer drivable. Drive the Hunter Canyon Road about half a mile and park. The road is a little rough, but standard clearance is usually sufficient.

Route Description

The spring loop. From your parking spot, walk up the road about a third of a mile, where the vegetation gets too thick to continue. Then walk the remaining 0.3 mile along the northern edge of the road, to the cleared area at what used to be the end of the road. Little Hunter Canyon is the wide opening to the southeast, just beyond the spring. Because of its abundant runoff and shade, this spring was used by generations of miners. During the salt mining days the creek was tapped for water. Later on a camp was erected here, first for the Gold Standard Mine up in the Inyos (see *The Bighorn Mine*), then for the nearby Vega Mine. Prior to that, the area was occupied by Native Americans, and signs of both cultures overlap. The camp consisted of a few decrepit cabins and trailers under the trees south of the road; it was dismantled at the request of the BLM in early 1999. If you browse through the greenery, you will still find scattered litter, a cattle pond dug by the miners, imprints of the old houses, and a raised flume that may date back to pre-settlers time.

The lush, well-watered spring in Little Hunter Canyon is one of the largest and most interesting springs in Saline Valley. To get to it, from the cleared area walk south to the edge of the spring, and look for a faint trail on the right. It climbs 250 feet to the low rim of Little Hunter Canyon, where you will get a bird's eye view of the sprawling vegetation that fills the canyon below. After 0.2 mile the trail drops to the canyon wash and disappears. Walk down the wide wash towards the spring. The trail resumes on the south side of the wash, where it winds through a stand of tall arrowweed before entering the spring. In just a few steps the desert is completely eclipsed by a dense oasis. The narrow trail wanders under a green canopy of willow, mesquite, and grapevine. A little creek runs through it, gurgling in the deep shade, forking several times. Watercress and orchids thrive in these tiny waterways, while alyssum and other wildflowers dot the soggy banks. Where the creek floods the ground, you will need to balance yourself on shaky boards and stepping stones to stay dry. In the summer the high evaporation rate creates a tiny microclimate of steamy tropical jungle. The luxuriant plants, the heady smells of wet earth, and the sound of the creek and birds, all conspire to fool your senses. The re-entry into the desert is equally sudden: in a few steps you exit this miniature jungle and find yourself on the searing edge of the desert, back to the cleared area.

The Joy and Vega Mine–spring loop. The start of this loop is the same as the spring loop. Where the rim trail reaches the wash of Little Hunter Canyon above the spring, instead of turning left down the wash toward the spring, turn right and walk up canyon 0.15 mile to a fork at short white narrows. Take the left fork (a side canyon), and hike southeast up its narrow wash, past a small spring, to a short trail that zigzags up to the low canyon rim. The area you are entering is a massive landslide that stretches for about 1 mile south from the spring and 1 mile east to the Saline Valley Road. It occurred in the Quaternary, when a chunk of land the size of a small town sheared off the mountainside and crashed down onto the valley floor. The steep hill that the Saline Valley Road closely follows southwest of Salt Lake is the base of this monster slide. Continue generally southeast to a tiny dry lake at the approximate center of the slide, then cut east across the gently rolling, open terrain a quarter of a mile to the upper end of the road at the Joy and Vega Mine.

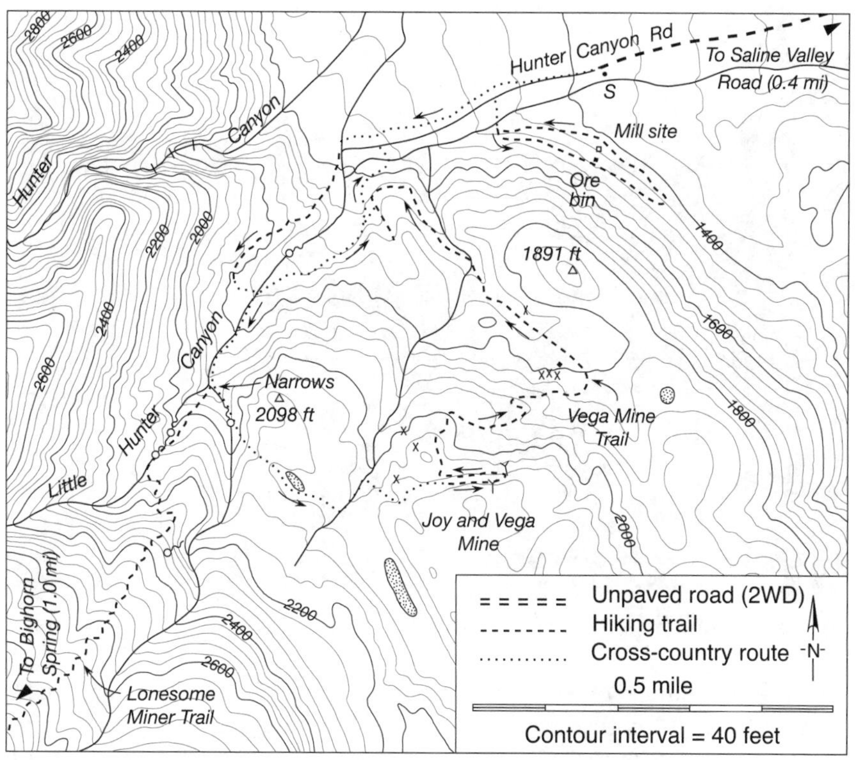

Little Hunter Canyon	Dist.(mi)	Elev.(ft)
The spring loop		
Hunter Canyon Road	0.0	1,290
Old end of road / trail	0.65	1,580
Rim trail	0.7	1,585
Little Hunter Canyon wash	0.95	1,780
Spring (upper end)	1.0	1,720
Back to starting point	1.7	1,290
The Joy and Vega Mine loop		
Hunter Canyon Road	0.0	1,290
Little Hunter Canyon wash	0.95	1,780
Side canyon (go left)	1.1	1,900
Upper tunnels (road)	1.55	~2,080
Joy claims	2.5	1,640
Back to starting point	3.2	1,290

Looking down the lower reaches of Little Hunter Canyon and Saline Valley

The two superposed tunnels along this road were the mine's main workings. The longest of the two is 50 feet deep. They tapped thin, poorly exposed veins of quartz and calcite in this slump block of quartz monzonite. Assessment work was carried out here until the late 1980s by southern California owner W. Means, who named the claim after his wife Joy. The veins contain malachite, chalcopyrite, pyrite, and a little silver (1.4 ounces per ton) and gold (0.2 ounce per ton). Several trenches, pits, and mining monuments are located west of the tunnels. The tailings are marginally interesting, but the low-angle views of the valley make up for it. Continue down the road as it winds down 300 steep feet toward the valley. At the bottom of the grade, it reaches the shallow dozer cuts of the Joy No. 1 claim, on the left. A winch on wheels, a shredded camper, and a funky ore chute made of two truck beds, are the only physical remains. After exploring the mine, continue down the road to the edge of the spring, and find a way through it back to the old Hunter Canyon Road (see map).

To complete the visit of this mine, check out its mill site. It is located just south of the end of the drivable portion of the road. Hike through the screen of vegetation to the loop road that serviced the mill. The upper fork leads to a one-of-a-kind metal ore bin and chute, and the lower fork to the mill's concrete foundations.

■

THE BIG SILVER MINE

This short hike up the steep flank of the Inyos follows the abandoned trail of the historic Big Silver Mine, the largest producer of silver in Saline Valley, and its neighbor the Morning Sun Prospect. The tunnels are impressive, and the three cableways offer an interesting comparison between several generations of mining technology. The views of Salt Lake and Saline Valley alone are well worth the hike.

General Information

Jurisdiction: Inyo Mountains Wilderness (BLM)
Road status: Hiking on old mining trail; access on short primitive road
Big Silver Mine: 0.8 mi, 1,300 ft up, 60 ft down one way/moderate
Main attractions: Historic silver mine, wireline tramways, valley views
USGS 7.5' topo map: Craig Canyon
Maps: pp. 221*, 283, *179*

Location and Access

The Big Silver Mine is in the lower foothills of the Inyo Mountains, southwest of Salt Lake. The starting point is the same as for Craig Canyon; refer to that section for directions and road conditions.

Route Description

The Big Silver Mine is an old property probably discovered in the early 1900s. It originally consisted of two groups of five silver claims each, known as Essex and Hudson, covering 200 acres. In its early years it was owned by the Big Silver Mining Company. One of the company's officers was W. W. Watterson, a prominent mining investor involved a few years earlier in the first copper and lead mines in the Ubehebe Mining District. The Big Silver was exploited mostly in the 1920s, although development work continued intermittently under various lessees until at least the 1940s. The company sunk a tunnel on each of the property's five quartz veins. Silver was found in all of them, largely in the form of argentite with sprinklings of native silver. What made the Big Silver special was its relative accessibility, and the high value of its ore. Assays from different veins averaged 30 ounces of silver per ton and 9% in lead, one of the highest silver contents in the eastern Inyos. The ore was hand sorted, often up to 200 ounces per ton, and lowered to the valley floor via two wireline tramways. In its historic years the Big Silver produced at least 7,600 ounces of silver.

The area still holds an estimated 40 tons of silver. This buried treasure was coveted by many. Although the Big Silver remained mostly idle for decades, between 1968 and 1981 some 35 claims were located here, including at its neighbor the Morning Sun Prospect.

The Big Silver Mine. The leveled area at the end of the road once supported a small mining camp, marked by two small stone dugouts and a few relics, including a gargantuan cooking stove. The well-built lower dugout still has its door frame, and had until recently some of its original mesquite-log roof. In front of it, the old mining road makes a left U-bend and passes by the second, more dilapidated dugout. It continues under the mine's first cableway before ending shortly at the first tunnel, which has a small bench and wood cabinet near its entrance. About 400 feet long, it may have been dug to intercept a higher vein.

Just past this tunnel the road turns into a faint foot trail that ascends the precipitous mountain slope in tight switchbacks. Narrow by design, smoothed by years of erosion, it manages the rare feat of providing footing without scarring the land. It is a pleasure to follow this twisted and overgrown path, and experience an intimacy with the land usually reserved for cross-country hiking. From almost anywhere the views of Salt Lake and Saline Valley are superb.

The Big Silver quartz veins occur at the contact between dolomitic limestone (Keeler Canyon Formation) and Mesozoic quartz monzonite and diorite. From the end of the road the veins run in an approximate line southwest up the mountainside, separating the igneous rocks west of the road from the limestone generally south of the tunnels. In addition to silver, the quartz contained galena (lead), sphalerite (zinc), malachite (copper), as well as pyrite (iron). The tunnels, reached by very short side trails, are all quite different. The first five tunnels belonged to the Big Silver Mine. Although their walls are relatively solid, they have hidden shafts and crumbling stopes. Stay out of them.

Although physical remains are minimal, there is a little something to discover everywhere—a pipeline, air duct, rock platforms, remnants of ore chutes, forgotten scaffoldings wedged high in narrow stopes, and rickety ladders dropping into sepulchral shafts. The most interesting remains are the cableways. There are three of them, each one a single-span cable that lowered the ore to the foot of the mountain in one fell swoop. Being from different eras, their designs are quite distinct. The first one, at the second tunnel, is the oldest. The descent of the ore bucket along the cable was controlled by a primitive hand winch. The winch used to be at the top of the metallic ore chute above the tunnel, but erosion washed it down to near the tunnel entrance.

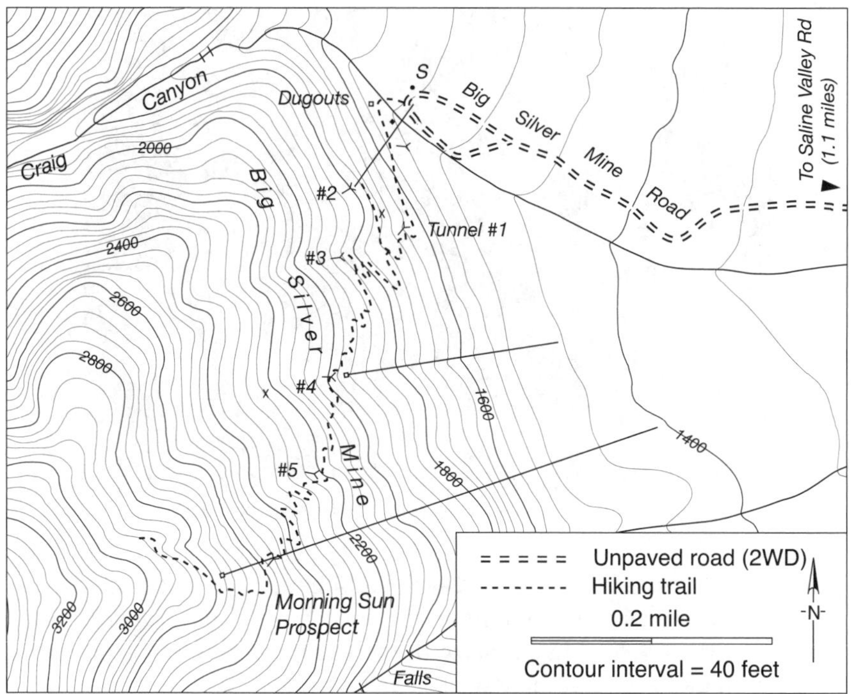

The Big Silver Mine		
	Dist.(mi)	Elev.(ft)
Big Silver Mine Road (end)	0.0	1,520
First tunnel	0.1	1,640
Side trail	0.25	1,720
First tramway and tunnel #2	(0.05)	~1,790
Second tramway	0.4	1,960
Morning Sun Prospect tunnel	0.65	2,520
Third tramway	0.8	2,760

The second cableway is at the fourth tunnel. More recent, it is better preserved and more elaborate. Its upper terminal is mounted on a wooden platform just below the level area fronting the tunnel. The ore was dropped in a wooden ore chute, now collapsed, to a second, lower platform, where it was loaded into buckets. This is known as a jig-back tramway. The buckets were suspended on the two large cables that drop to the valley floor. Each bucket was attached to a thinner cable that went around one of the two horizontal steel wheels on the upper

Cableway upper terminal at the Big Silver Mine

terminal. The speed of the descending buckets was controlled by a hand brake with a design similar to those found on San Francisco's cable cars: the brake slowed down the wheel by simply pressing a ring of wooden pads against the wheel's rim.

The Morning Sun Prospect. The last and longest cableway is at the sixth tunnel, which belonged to the Morning Sun Prospect. It is easy to recognize: the mine's name is painted by its entrance, and a bright-orange wheelbarrow is wedged up in the steep gully to the right of it. The quartz vein it tapped is exposed up and down this gully. An extension of the Big Silver deposit, it also had high assays, up to 22 ounces of silver per ton.

From here the trail continues up to the top of the third cableway. This segment is steeper, rocky, and a little slippery. You may have to use your hands to hang on to rocky outcrops. At places it offers thrilling views down the abrupt, fall-ridden ravines it crosses. The cableway is anchored high on a rock spur. Its cable is as impressive as the views. In two thirds of a mile its single span drops 1,400 feet to the valley, riding high above the ground. Remains at this site, located in 1970 and 1974, illustrate the major improvements brought by technology to small mining operations such as this one. Wood was replaced by steel, and equipment became more compact. The tramway winch, equipped with a drum brake, was powered by a small four-cycle gasoline engine, and a portable generator provided electricity to the site.

■

— 7 —

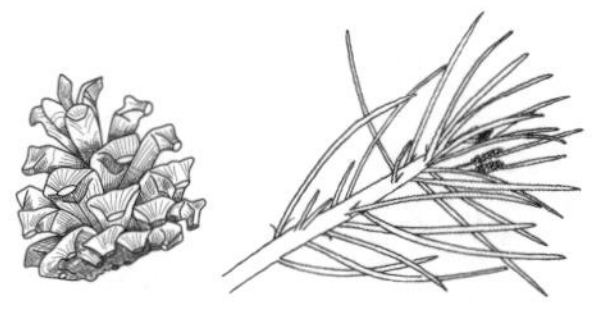

THE INYO MOUNTAINS

PRESERVED AS A 205,000-ACRE WILDERNESS adjacent to Death Valley National Park, the Inyo Mountains rank among the most formidable desert ranges in California. Forming the western backdrop of Saline Valley, they rise in just a few miles from a little over 1,000 feet at the valley floor to above 11,000 feet. Very few places in the desert are this steep over such distances. From Saline Valley, this abrupt wall appears to be impassable—and it is nearly that. Few roads make ingress into this sheer wilderness of stone. The deeply incised canyons that slice through the Inyos' precipitous flank offer some of the most tremendous hiking anywhere in the desert. The northern third of the Inyo Mountains Wilderness is administered by the National Forest Service, and the southern two thirds by the Bureau of Land Management.

Weather

Because of their great height and their location farther north and west, the Inyos enjoy a weather pattern quite different from the rest of the Death Valley region. With about 60 miles of crest between 8,000 and over 11,000 feet, they capture a fair amount of moisture from the Pacific Ocean and often create their own weather. In the winter and spring, they often disappear under thick clouds that cool down the air significantly. Every winter the high summits are covered with snow, and snowfalls down to 5,000 feet as late as May are not unheard of. As in the nearby Sierra Nevada, hikers should be prepared to handle sudden changes in weather. Getting caught in a snow storm without proper gear can easily create a life-threatening situation. In the summer, daytime temperatures are high in the mid-range and comfortable near

Suggested Backcountry Drives in the Inyo Mountains					
Route/Destination	Dist. (mi)	Lowest elev.	Highest elev.	Road type	Pages
Andrews Mountain (saddle)	4.6	7,040'	8,940'	F	129-130
Cerro Gordo–Lee Flat Road	16.8	5,249'	~8,220'	F	291-292
Cerro Gordo Road	7.7	3,640'	8,145'	H	291
Lead Canyon Road	3.5	3,580'	5,380'	P	241-243
Loretto	0.8	4,757'	5,230'	H	115-116
Marble Canyon	1.6	5,500'	5,900'	H	123-125
Nikolaus-Eureka Mine Road	2.0	5,150'	5,880'	F	119, 121
Santa Rosa Mine	10.8	4,930'	6,610'	F	305
Snow Flake Mine Road	3.6	1,146'	3,350'	F	200
Swansea–Cerro Gordo Road	23.9	3,645'	9,310'	F	299-302
Viking Mine camp	1.8	4,830'	4,950'	H	309-310
Talc City Mine	2.7	4,880'	5,190'	G	309-312
Trio Mill Site	1.5	1,142'	1,770'	H	259
White Swan Mine	1.9	4,730'	4,935'	H	309-312
Key: P=Primitive (2WD) H=Primitive (HC) F=Primitive (4WD)					

the crest; it can even get a little cold at night. At such times they offer a welcome escape from the heat of the surrounding desert valleys.

Access and Backcountry Roads

The eastern Inyo Mountains have never been conquered by roads. You can drive close to them on the Saline Valley Road, which hugs the foot of the range, but you cannot drive into them very far. The few tracks that do approach the Inyos from Saline Valley quickly peter out, as if repelled by the sheer volume of rocks. These roads, and the mining sites they lead to, are described in the following sections. Cerro Gordo was also included, even though it is on the west side of the Inyos, because of its large influence on the region in historic times, and because its unique Bed and Breakfast makes a perfect headquarter while visiting the area. The three access roads to Cerro Gordo are the longest and most adventurous in this range, and the only ones that give access to the high Inyos.

Geology

The eastern Inyo Mountains are a patchwork of pre-Mesozoic marine sedimentary and granitic rocks altered by a complex history of faulting. To get a general idea of its origin, one must go back to the end of the Paleozoic, when the region was composed only of Precambrian and Paleozoic sedimentary strata. In the ensuing Mesozoic, these strata were shattered and folded by numerous fault movements. One of the most traumatic events was caused by the Last Chance Thrust Fault, which displaced a county-size slab of pre-Mesozoic rocks eastward over more than 20 miles. Later on, in the Jurassic, the area was repeatedly intruded by small batholiths, mostly quartz monzonite and diorite, which bowed the Precambrian and Cambrian strata and altered them through contact metamorphism.

The Inyo Mountains began to take their present shape much later, in the late Pliocene, when the area was subjected to the same tectonic events that created the Basin and Range province. Along major fault lines the land broke into blocks that were either uplifted, sunk, or uplifted on one side and sunk on the other, resulting in the alternation of valleys and ranges we know today. The Inyo Mountains are what is called a horst. They were uplifted on both the Saline Valley and Owens Valley sides. The precipitous slope facing Saline Valley is the fault scarp along which their east side was exhumed. It developed along the weakened contact zone between Paleozoic rocks and the Jurassic plutons. The pluton was uplifted, while the Paleozoic rocks against its east side collapsed and slowly became buried under Saline Valley. The irregular patches of Paleozoic rocks covering the eastern Inyos are leftovers clinging to the surface of the plutons. The fault on the Saline Valley side, called the Hunter Mountain Fault Zone, can be easily traced almost continuously from Daisy Canyon to Willow Creek, along the sharp base of the mountains. The Inyos are so young and they have risen so fast that erosion has barely made a dent in them. A few million years after their birth, they rank among the most impressively high and steep in the western Basin and Range. And they are still rising.

Springs and wildlife

The eastern Inyos being the wettest area in the Death Valley region, most major canyons are blessed with dozens of springs that support a stream and enchanted oases. Cove Spring, Bighorn Spring, and the springs in upper McElvoy Canyon have the heaviest flows. The upper drainages of Pat Keyes Canyon and Craig Canyon also have well-watered springs. This is fortunate for hikers, since covering any distance in this range can take days. Starting around 2010, however, lower average precipitation resulting from climate change has seriously reduced the size of most springs. The silver lining is that the brush is not nearly as thick, and canyon hiking is somewhat easier.

Inyo Mountains at sunrise from Lee Flat

This relative abundance of water supports more large wildlife than any other range around Death Valley. Several herds of bighorn sheep thrive throughout the higher elevations, as well as deer, coyotes, badgers, and a few mountain lions. Birds are plentiful, both in population and number of species. Most of the well-watered drainages between Lead Canyon and Hunter Canyon are home to the Inyo Mountains salamander, a rare nocturnal amphibian endemic to this range.

History: The Beveridge Mining District

In spite of their extreme isolation, the eastern Inyo Mountains witnessed more than a century of mining activity. The main commodity was gold, which outcropped a little bit everywhere, but talc was also exploited near the foot of the mountains, as well as a little lead, silver, and zinc. The earliest mining goes back to around 1865, when gold was discovered near Cerro Gordo Peak, on the southern crest of the range. Following Cerro Gordo's quick rise to stardom, a few rugged prospectors began surveying the range's unchartered eastern slopes. Although the first claims were located in 1866, near Beveridge, it was not until William Hunter's discovery of the rich gold seams at the Bighorn Mine in 1877 that mining began in earnest. The Beveridge Mining District was organized in December that year. Named after John Beveridge, a friend of Hunter and Justice of the Peace in Inyo County, it covered much of the eastern slopes, from San Lucas Canyon up to Cougar Canyon. Over the next few years numerous mines sprouted all over the range's intricate maze of canyons and ridges.

Most of the district's gold mining was carried out between 1878 and 1906. Isolation precluded transporting heavy equipment and large quantities of ore. The ore was sorted by hand to isolate the richest free-milling ore (at least 6 ounces per ton), treated at primitive burro-powered arrastres located near springs, and transported by burro to Owens Valley. Later on, a few small steam-powered stamp mills and amalgamation plants were brought in. In the 1880s and 1890s, camps grew around these mills along all main drainages. Early mills wasted about 50% of the gold, and operations could only be lucrative by mining the near-surface high-grade pockets. When these were cleaned out, mining simply stopped. The large low-grade veins were left unexploited.

Production figures are difficult to assess because detailed records were not kept, and some of the gold was traded for supplies and services. The Keynot Mine was the district's richest. Discovered in 1878, it was operated continuously for five years, then intermittently until 1906, and produced about $420,000. The Gavalan and Bighorn mines, second and third richest, came up together to only about 20% of this figure. The silver mines produced very little. The district's gold production of $2 million reported in 1903 was likely vastly inflated. Although its return in dollars was lower, talc mining was also fairly lucrative, largely because of the large size and relative accessibility of the deposits. Between 1890 and present, the string of talc mines in the eastern foothills produced over 50,000 tons.

Yet the Beveridge Mining District was rich. It contained—and still does—an estimated 1.1 million ounces of gold and 5.2 million ounces of silver, worth over two billion dollars at current prices. Over the next 80 years, many attempts were made to cash in on this buried treasure. Between 1906 and 1930, small cyanide mills were erected at a few locations to extract gold from finely crushed ore, but they failed due to the high cost of milling small quantities. In 1934 the price of gold jumped to $35 per ounce, and again improved mills were installed, but the next few years produced less than $4,000. For two decades starting in 1940, mainly assessment work was carried out, until the gold market highs of the 1970s stimulated renewed interest. In the 1980s, heavy milling equipment was flown in by helicopter to treat ore from the tailings of the largest historic mines. But without roads to transport large volumes of ore, operations were unprofitable and short-lived. Thanks to its ruggedness and remoteness, the land was spared from extensive mining development and preserved as the Inyo Mountains Wilderness—a far greater treasure that everyone can enjoy.

Hiking

The canyons. The eastern Inyo Mountains are dissected by about 20 named main canyons and several unnamed canyons. Because the canyons have alluvial fans that are quite short, foot access to most of them from the Saline Valley Road is quick and easy. North from Willow Creek Camp, the mountains are less abrupt and the canyons comparatively easy to negotiate in their lower reaches. But this is as far as the easy stuff goes. All canyons south of Willow Creek Camp are very steep and strewn with massive taluses, boulder jams, and high falls. In the many canyons that have perennial streams, water can be a problem, this time because there is too much of it, and because of the thick brush. Technical climbing is often needed to get through—some canyons can in fact be traversed only downhill, by rappelling down high fall after high fall. This unusual coalition of challenges makes for some of the roughest canyoneering in the North American deserts. To make any kind of progress here and have fun doing it, you need to be physically fit and well prepared for this kind of activity.

The trails. In spite of their ruggedness, the eastern Inyos are crisscrossed by more than 100 miles of foot trails. They were built from the 1860s through the late 1930s by miners working the gold and silver deposits around the range's mid-elevations. This rare legacy of primitive access routes is undoubtedly one of the greatest assets of the Inyo Mountains Wilderness. What is even more appealing is that these historic trails have seen extremely limited use for decades, first because they have remained largely unknown, and second because they are strenuous. Since the district was abandoned in the 1940s, long sections of trails have been wiped out by vegetation, landslides, or other forms of erosion, so these trails have also become hard to follow. Most of them have never appeared on USGS maps. The implications are phenomenal: we have access to a network of unsigned, unmapped, and challenging trails leading to historic mining sites and natural treasures that very few people have the stamina to access. For adventurous hikers, the recreational potential is unprecedented.

A total of 16 trails are known to exist. Many of them are short east-west trails that climb from the edge of Saline Valley to a mine at mid-elevations. One such trail is the Keynot Ridge Trail, which starts at the mouth of Keynot Canyon and ascends the Keynot Ridge to the Sweitzer Mine (elev. ~7280'). The Beveridge Ridge Trail starts from the same vicinity and follows the north rim of Beveridge Canyon to Beveridge, one of the most extensive and isolated ghost towns in the American deserts. Still further south the trail to the Big Silver Mine

Suggested Hikes in the Inyo Mountains					
Route/Destination	Dist. (mi)	Elev. gain	Mean elev.	Access road	Pages
Short hikes (under 5 miles round trip)					
Andrews Mtn (north route)	2.2	2,140'	8,200'	P/1.5 mi	130
Andrews Mtn (west route)	2.4	1,820'	8,500'	P/1.5 mi	129
Beveridge Cyn wet narrows	0.8	810'	2,140'	P/1.5 mi	259-262
Bunker Hill (camp)	0.7	520'	4,980'	P/2.4 mi	237-238
Bunker Hill Mine	1.4	1,490'	5,300'	P/2.4 mi	237-240
Cerro Gordo loop	~0.5	~200'	8,250'	H/7.7 mi	294-298
Cerro Gordo Peak	1.2	1,080'	8,630'	H/7.7 mi	298
Craig Canyon narrows	2.3	2,130'	2,590'	P/1.5 mi	281-284
Harlis and Broady Mine	2.4	1,650'	5,670'	Paved	119-121
Hunter Canyon (50-ft fall)	1.9	1,550'	1,900'	P/0.5 mi	271-274
Lead Cyn Springs Canyon	1.3	1,260'	5910'	H/3.5 mi	244
Loretto Mine (quarry)	1.0	580'	5,060'	Paved	116-117
McElvoy Cyn first waterfall	1.1	960'	2,010'	H/1.0 mi	255-256
McElvoy Canyon third fall	1.7	1,560'	2,310'	H/1.0 mi	255-257
Nebula Mill Site	0.9	680'	5,720'	H/3.5 mi	241-244
New York Butte	1.1	970'	10,220'	F/14.1 mi	303-304
Nikolaus-Eureka Mine	2.0	1,050'	5,560'	Paved	121-122
Obsidian Spring	1.2	380'	5,850'	Graded	234
Salt Tram upper control sta.	2.3	3,030'	7,310'	F/7.1 mi	300
Santa Rosa Mine	0.7	350'	6,780'	F/10.8 mi	305-306
Silver Ridge No. 2 Mine	1.2	1,830'	4,300'	F/3.4 mi	264-265
Trapier Mine Trail	0.8	270'	9,080'	F/17.5 mi	301
Intermediate hikes (5-12 miles round trip)					
Addie Canyon Springs	2.7	2,390'	5,810'	P/2.4 mi	240
Andrews Mountain loop	6.1	2,230'	8,160'	P/1.5 mi	129-132
Baxter Mine cableway	4.7	2,390'	4,550'	P/1.7 mi	248
Beveridge from Saline Valley				F/3.4 mi	
Beveridge Mine's mill	4.8	5,730'	5,700'		264-270
Laskey's mill	4.3	5,370'	5,730'		264-266
Blue Monster Mine	3.0	1,620'	4,300'	P/1.7 mi	245-246
Goat Springs	3.3	2,420'	10,030'	F/14.1 mi	302-304
Paiute Canyon narrows	3.0	770'	2,730'	Graded	249-250

Key: P=Primitive (2WD) H=Primitive (HC) F=Primitive (4WD)
Distances: one way for out-and-back hikes, round-trip for loops
Elev. gain: sum of all elevation gains on round-trip or loop hike

Suggested Hikes in the Inyo Mountains (Cont'd)					
Route/Destination	Dist. (mi)	Elev. gain	Mean elev.	Access road	Pages
Intermediate hikes (5-12 miles round trip) (Cont'd)					
Gold Standard Mine	3.2	2,950'	2,540'	P/0.5 mi	276-278
Lucky Boy Mine	3.9	2,020'	4,420'	P/1.7 mi	246-247
Piper Peak Trail	3.2	1,700'	6,970'	P/0.5 mi	102
Rosa Peak	2.7	1,250'	7,310'	F/10.8 mi	305-308
Salt Tramway (No. 5 tower)	3.9	2,610'	2,190'	P/0.4 mi	287-288
Salt Tramway (No. 9 tower)	5.4	3,900'	2,830'	P/0.4 mi	287-290
Snow Flake Mine (west)	2.5	1,970'	2,540'	P/1.1 mi	199-202
Soldier Pass Cyn narrows	3.4	1,450'	4,670'	P/5.3 mi	106
Waucoba Cyn (Pine Springs)	4.8	1,970'	6,580'	Graded	233-236
Waucoba Cyn (Twin Sprs.)	2.8	1,030'	6,150'	Graded	233-234
Wyler Spring cabin	3.0	850'	4,520'	P/5.3 mi	106-108
Long hikes (over 12 miles round trip)					
Beveridge from Inyos' crest	7.0	6,290'	8,700'	F/14.1 mi	302-304
Bighorn Mine/Cabin	7.8	7,830'	4,230'	P/0.5 mi	276-280
Bighorn Spr./Hunter's mill	6.3	6,080'	3,890'	P/0.5 mi	276-280
Cerro Gordo to Salt Tram	7.1	3,620'	8,530'	H/7.7 mi	299-300
Harlis & Broady Mine loop	13.7	3,070'	4,440'	Paved	62
Hunter Canyon (125-ft fall)	8.7	8,450'	3,980'	P/0.5 mi	276-280
Paiute Canyon waterfall	6.5	1,980'	3,300'	Graded	249-254
Mount Nunn	6.3	3,540'	6,950'	Paved	109-114
Salt Tramway: crest to valley	9.2	8,500'	4,530'	F/7.1 mi	287-290
Key: P=Primitive (2WD) H=Primitive (HC) F=Primitive (4WD) Distances: one way for out-and-back hikes, round-trip for loops Elev. gain: sum of all elevation gains on round-trip or loop hike					

may have once continued up to the American Flag Mine (elev. ~6,560'). The southernmost main trail out of Saline Valley is the Salt Tramway Trail, which follows the Salt Tramway about half way up to the crest.

A few trails go the other way—down from the Inyos' crest. The Beveridge Trail descends several thousand feet to Beveridge. The Bighorn Trail cuts a path down Craig Canyon and Hunter Canyon to Hunter's old mill at Bighorn Spring. An abandoned maintenance trail starts north of Cerro Gordo and follows the upper portion of the tramway. There may also have been a trail further north down to the Trapier Mine, but its remains are too vague to tell.

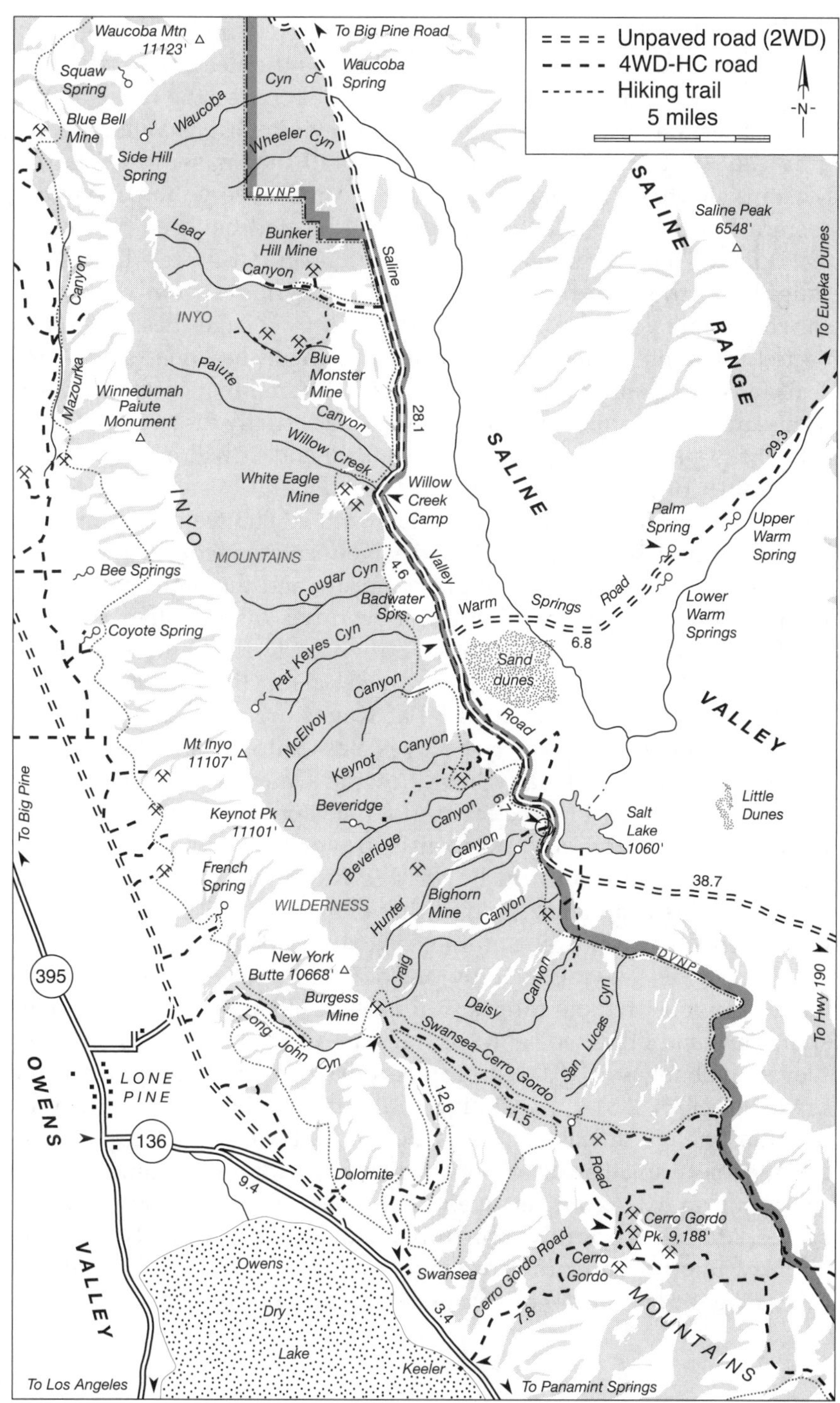

Unpaved road (2WD)
4WD-HC road
Hiking trail
5 miles
N
Waucoba Mtn 11123'
To Big Pine Road
Waucoba Spring
Squaw Spring
Waucoba Cyn
Blue Bell Mine
Side Hill Spring
Wheeler Cyn
DVNP
Lead Canyon
Bunker Hill Mine
Saline
SALINE RANGE
Saline Peak 6548'
To Eureka Dunes
Mazourka Canyon
INYO
Blue Monster Mine
Paiute Canyon
Winnedumah Paiute Monument
28.1
Willow Creek
White Eagle Mine
Willow Creek Camp
SALINE
29.3
INYO MOUNTAINS
Bee Springs
Cougar Cyn
4.6
Valley
Palm Spring
Upper Warm Spring
Badwater Sprs.
Warm Springs Road
Lower Warm Springs
Coyote Spring
6.8
Pat Keyes Cyn
Sand dunes
McElvoy Canyon
Road
VALLEY
Mt Inyo 11107'
Keynot Canyon
To Big Pine
Beveridge
Keynot Pk 11101'
6.7
Salt Lake 1060'
Little Dunes
Beveridge Canyon
Canyon
French Spring
38.7
Hunter Canyon
Bighorn Mine
WILDERNESS
395
New York Butte 10668'
Craig
Daisy
Canyon
San Lucas Cyn
To Hwy 190
Burgess Mine
Long John Cyn
Swansea–Cerro Gordo Road
OWENS
LONE PINE
12.6
11.5
136
Dolomite
9.4
Cerro Gordo Pk. 9,188'
Owens Dry Lake
Swansea
Cerro Gordo Road
Cerro Gordo
VALLEY
3.4
7.8
MOUNTAINS
Keeler
To Los Angeles
To Panamint Springs

The eastern Inyos are so rough that only a few trails ever connected Saline Valley to the crest. One of them is the Lead Canyon Trail. Funneled by relatively gentle Lead Canyon, it crosses the range at one of its easiest passes, and continues west down to Owens Valley. Today only the western segment, from the 9,440-foot pass down to the Mazourka Canyon Road, is well defined. Almost every drainage in the eastern Inyos had one or more mills, all located between 5,100 and 8,400 feet. These valuable facilities were—and still are—linked by roughly north-south trails that hopped over ridges from canyon to canyon. Some years ago, the BLM decided to collage these interconnected trails into a single one and rename them the Lonesome Miner Trail (a convenient move, although it is a shame that historic names hard-earned by heroic trail builders were so casually discarded). If you hike the Lonesome Miner Trail from end to end, it will take you from the mouth of Hunter Canyon all the way to Owens Valley near Reward, a distance of about 40 miles, with 17,000 feet of ascent and 21,000 feet of descent. The trail successively crosses six ridges and five drainages—up and down to Bighorn Spring and the Bighorn Mine in Hunter Canyon, over the divide to Beveridge, over another ridge to the Keynot Mine in Keynot Canyon, then on to the Taylor–McElvoy Mill in McElvoy Canyon, up to and west along the rim of McElvoy Canyon before dropping to the Pat Keyes arrastres in Pat Keyes Canyon, and finally over Pat Keyes Pass into Owens Valley. All canyons but Keynot usually have flowing water at or near the trail crossings, and a few historic cabins dot the way—Bighorn Cabin at the Bighorn Mine, Frenchy's Cabin in Beveridge Canyon, and the Beveridge Ridge Cabin on Beveridge Ridge (all three have been restored). This is an amazing trail that only a handful of people have hiked from end to end—the ultimate in extreme desert trekking.

These trails provide the only practical access to what is still today one of the most remote ranges in the West. Hiking them is generally strenuous, and often worse. Most trails are worn out and easy to lose. Elevation changes of 10,000 feet in less than 15 miles are typical, and grades often exceed 20%. Getting to the top of the Inyos is likely to take most people at least two days. Before venturing into these isolated areas, explore small areas to become familiar with trail alignments and the topography. Avoid hot weather—at lower elevations, shade is scarce. Most importantly, remember that this is extremely isolated country. Should you run into trouble and become immobilized, no other hiker or other form of assistance will be available.

■

WAUCOBA CANYON

From its headwaters at 10,500 feet down to Saline Valley, Waucoba Canyon carves a major swath through the Inyo Mountains, then continues as a meandering wash many miles across the valley to end at Salt Lake—a descent of nearly two vertical miles. In spite of these impressive metrics, most of it is comparatively well behaved. It gives us a rare chance to indulge in relatively easy canyoneering and explore both the many creek-fed springs that dot its windy wash and the stately pine forest that thrives on its high-riding slopes.

General Information

Jurisdiction: DVNP (NPS), Inyo Mountains Wilderness (NFS)
Road status: Roadless; access from primitive road (2WD)
Obsidian Spring: 1.2 mi, 350 ft up, 30 ft down one way / very easy
Pine Springs: 4.8 mi, 1,940 ft up, 30 ft down one way / moderate
Main attractions: Lush springs and creek, deep canyon, pine forest
USGS 7.5' topo maps: Waucoba Canyon*, Waucoba Spring
Maps: pp. 235*, *61*, *231*

Location and Access

Waucoba Canyon empties into Saline Valley at its very northern tip, where the Saline Valley Road emerges from Whippoorwill Canyon and enters the valley. To get to it, from the Big Pine Road drive the Saline Valley Road 15.8 miles south, past the tremendous east wall of Cowhorn Valley, down the tight switchbacks into Marble Canyon, then up through the dense forest around North Pass, and finally down through Whippoorwill Canyon to the bottom of a deep dip in the road. The wash that crosses the road at the dip is Waucoba Wash. This is approximately the mouth of Waucoba Canyon. Drive 0.15 mile further to the flat at the top of the dip, and park on the cleared space on the left. This spot is 16.5 miles north of the Warm Springs Road turnoff.

Route Description

The more scenic way to enter Waucoba Canyon is to walk back 0.15 mile to the bottom of the dip, then hike up the canyon wash. Much of the lower canyon is like this: a narrow detrital wash of mixed gravel and small boulders walled in by sheer 40-foot banks of fan-glomerate; a narrow bench above one or both banks; and steep, bulky hills over 1,000 feet tall beyond on both sides. At first the canyon is a bone-dry shambles of rabbitbrush and baked stone that does not bode well for water. Yet signs of frequent and forceful floods are plentiful. The tight, V-shaped channel, as much as 5 feet deep, cut into the wash was dug by floods. The rocks underfoot are abnormally loose and pale; regularly churned by rushing water, they never stay put long enough to settle or develop varnish. Pine cones and pine logs two feet in diameter are strewn across the wash, their closest source a mile up canyon.

The first water is at Obsidian Spring, past a few lazy bends. The wash is suddenly overwhelmed by a riot of water-loving plants—rush, horsetail, cattail, willow shoots, and bunch grass—hemmed in on both sides by masses of willow, cliffrose, and wildrose. It is a peaceful place, unexpectedly green, decorated with prince's plume and Indian paintbrush. Even in late fall, water survives in small muddy pools, the final stages of the lively little creek that flows through it at wetter times.

There are eight more springs over the next 3.6 miles. Some of them are broken into isolated pockets, although there is more dry wash than springs. Each one is different in its setting, plant assortment, and abundance of water. The third spring and the last one—Pine Springs—are fairly long. Twin Springs, although the thickest, is the easiest of the large ones to cross, along a relatively clear wash sandwiched between facing springs. Some springs are enlivened by stands of mountain mahogany, others by the apple-green crowns of cottonwood and hollyleaf redberry. The horsetail is the most puzzling resident: this thirsty plant happiest in wet spots in coastal redwood forests grows in thick ranks everywhere. Sometimes water will surface abruptly as a foot-wide creek, break up into a tiny cascade, linger at a pool, or fizzle along a gooey channel of rusty-orange algae. It is tempting to bypass the springs on the benches, but climbing onto them and finding a way back down takes more energy than traversing the springs. The bighorn know it; where the willows get too thick they have trampled narrow paths that help. You find yourself suspended on dreadlocks of live plants combed down by their passage. Your skin and clothes still

Waucoba Canyon		
	Dist.(mi)	Elev.(ft)
Saline Valley Road	0.0	5,720
Canyon mouth	0.15	5,710
Obsidian Spring (head)	1.2	6,040
Twin Springs (head)	2.75	6,690
Pine Springs (head)	4.8	7,640

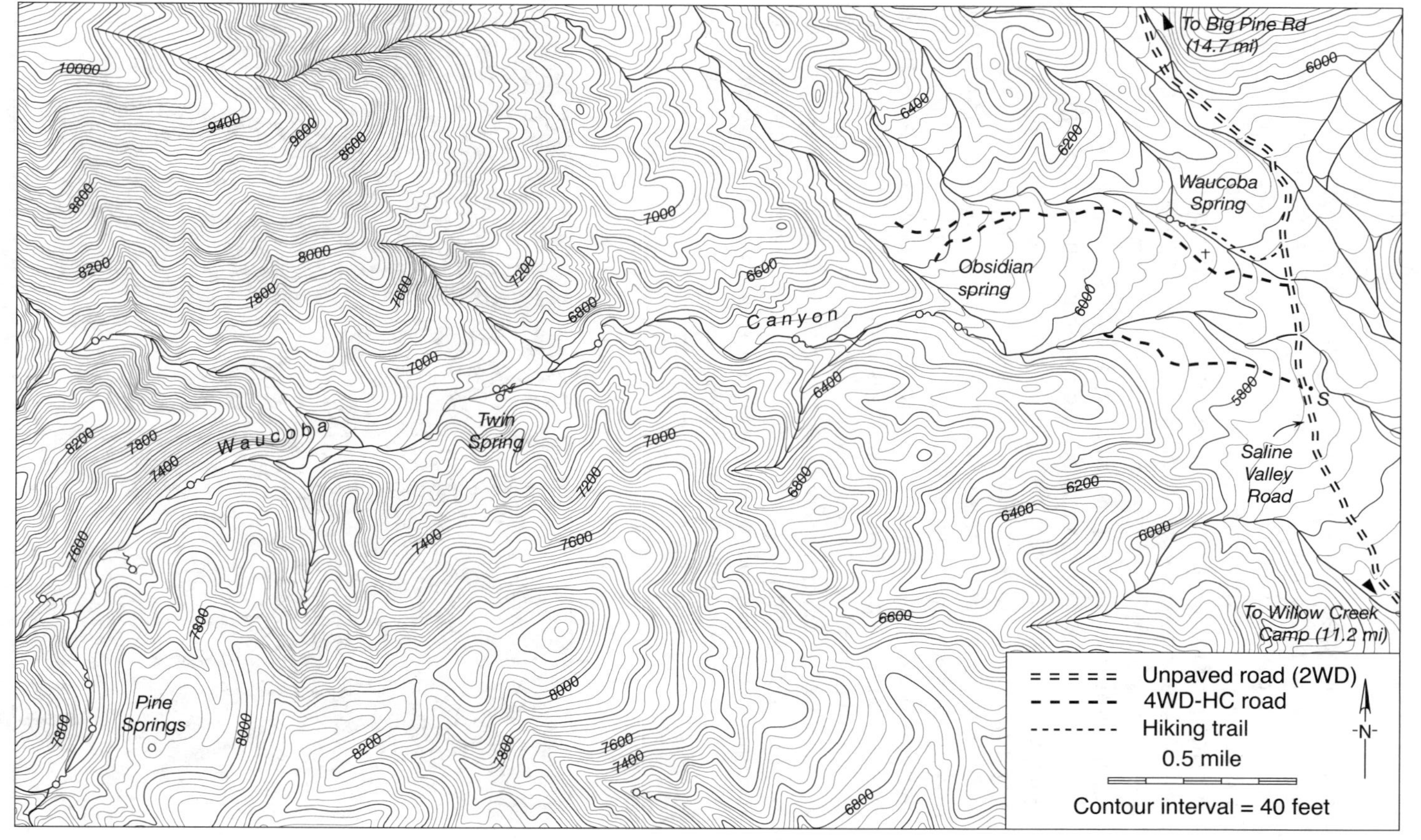
To Big Pine Rd (14.7 mi)
Waucoba Spring
Obsidian spring
Canyon
Twin Spring
Waucoba
S
Saline Valley Road
To Willow Creek Camp (11.2 mi)
Pine Springs
Unpaved road (2WD)
4WD-HC road
Hiking trail
0.5 mile
Contour interval = 40 feet
N

Fourth spring in Waucoba Canyon

become dusted with pollen, ants, bits of twigs, and shredded leaves. In the heat of summer, the air is as steamy as in a Louisiana bayou.

Waucoba Canyon's year-round water, however limited, has attracted wildlife and humans for a very long time. Dragonflies and tarantula hawks dodge over the water, lizards dash into hiding, chukars scatter noisily. Native Americans used the lower springs as seasonal hunting and harvesting camps. Bighorn sheep were then, and still are, relatively numerous. They eat the bark off fallen trees, and leave droppings and heart-shaped prints all over. On the benches where they like to hang out, they have crushed crude paths through the thick cover of big sagebrush and ephedra. The oases in Waucoba Canyon are all this—time capsules forgotten by time itself and priceless havens of endemic species, all locked in the tiniest of microclimates.

As the wash creeps above timberline, the pinyon pine on the slopes grow closer, bigger, denser, as stately as on temperate mountains. The higher springs merge with the conifers. Pine Springs, several miles up canyon at the rugged heart of the Inyos, is a rare hybrid of riparian vegetation and sub-alpine forest. The canyon in this area is magnificent, fragrant with evergreens, dwarfed by escarpments that seem to rise forever. The transformation is astonishing, from a hot arid wash to a cool shaded forest, thanks to the timeless medicine of water.

■

BUNKER HILL CANYON

Centered on the extensive remains of the 1930s Bunker Hill Mine, this hike is packed. You will get to visit the many buildings of the ghost camp; climb steep switchbacks to the mine's lead-silver tunnels; survey Saline Valley from the top of the well-preserved 1,500-foot aerial tramway; and follow an elusive trail up a forested canyon to the well-watered springs that once supported the camp.

General Information

Jurisdiction: Inyo Mountains Wilderness (NFS)
Road status: Hiking on trails and cross-country; 2WD access road
Bunker Hill Mine: 1.4 mi, 1,350 ft up, 140 ft down one way / moderate
Addie Canyon Spr.: 2.7 mi, 2,300 ft up, 90 ft down one way / mod.–diff.
Main attractions: Mining camp, lead mine, aerial tramway, springs
USGS 7.5' topo maps: Waucoba Canyon
Maps: pp. 239*, *231*

Location and Access

Bunker Hill Canyon is a side canyon of Lead Canyon, in the central section of the eastern Inyo Mountains. To get to it, drive the Lead Canyon Road (see *Lead Canyon* for directions) 2.35 miles west to a fork just before Lead Canyon. Turn right and park after 0.2 mile at a locked gate. With a standard-clearance vehicle you can drive to the fork. The last stretch, steep and overgrown, is just as easy to walk.

Route Description

From the gate, the mining road winds about half a mile up Bunker Hill Canyon, a tortuous passage just wide enough for the road, before reaching Bunker Hill. The mining camp has several comparatively recent corrugated-iron buildings. A long shed and a large, two-room house crown a low knoll to the left of the road. Behind the house, in the shade of large cottonwoods, the hefty flow of the camp's pipeline once replenished a pool of clear water. After the pipeline broke in the 2010s, the pool dried up and the trees died and fell. Across the road there is a furnished cabin that hikers occasionally use as a shelter. Several interesting mining structures are scattered around the camp. The largest one is the lower terminal of the mine's aerial tramway, its huge ore bin gradually falling to pieces. The tin shack next to it still houses a large gasoline engine. The short adit across the way was once used as a troglodytic house—it is cool year-round. The large rusted gear behind the house is a steam-powered hoist. The tramway cable hanging down the mountain points to the upper terminal, teetering on the edge of a cliff 600 feet higher.

This impressive little mine was never accessed by anything more sophisticated than a foot trail, and to reach it you will have to labor up the same switchbacks as the miners did decades ago. The 0.4-mile trail starts in the steep gully to the right of the cable. It climbs, mostly up the gully, to the saddle on the ridge to the northeast. The lower trail has been severely damaged by landslides. Climb 120 feet up the gully instead, where the trail is in better shape. At the saddle it angles north along the ridge, then cuts a few more switchbacks to the mine at the top of the cliff. The Bunker Hill Mine exploited veins of massive black argentiferous galena, with some cerussite and hematite, which filled fractures in Cambrian limestone. The rich ore shipped in the late 1920s and 1930s contained 30% to 60% of lead, 33 ounces of silver per ton, and a touch of gold. Tunnel 1000, at the top of the trail, is 200 feet long and one of the mine's longest. A dozen tunnels and several small pits are clustered on the very steep hillside above it. A faint foot trail loops by most of them. Some of the tunnels branch off over and over into veritable mazes. If for no other reason, hike up to this high vantage point for the expansive views of Saline Valley.

The large upper terminal just below Tunnel 1000 is characteristic of the mining technology of the 1930s. It collected ore from several of the tunnels. The short rail track precariously balanced on a trestle bridge, the cableway, and the metallic ore chute that stand nearby are prime examples of the typical equipment used to haul ore from such hard-to-reach tunnels. The 100-foot wooden trestle is a rare occurrence in the Death Valley region. The short cableway above it still supports a

Bunker Hill Canyon

	Dist.(mi)	Elev.(ft)
Bunker Hill Canyon Road	0.0	4,723
Locked gate	0.2	4,870
Bunker Hill (camp)	0.7	5,240
Bunker Hill Mine (Tunnel 1000)	(0.4)	5,830
Loop back to Tunnel 1000	(0.7)	5,830
End of road/start of trail	1.4	5,930
Divide	1.6	6,180
Addie Canyon Springs	2.7	6,930

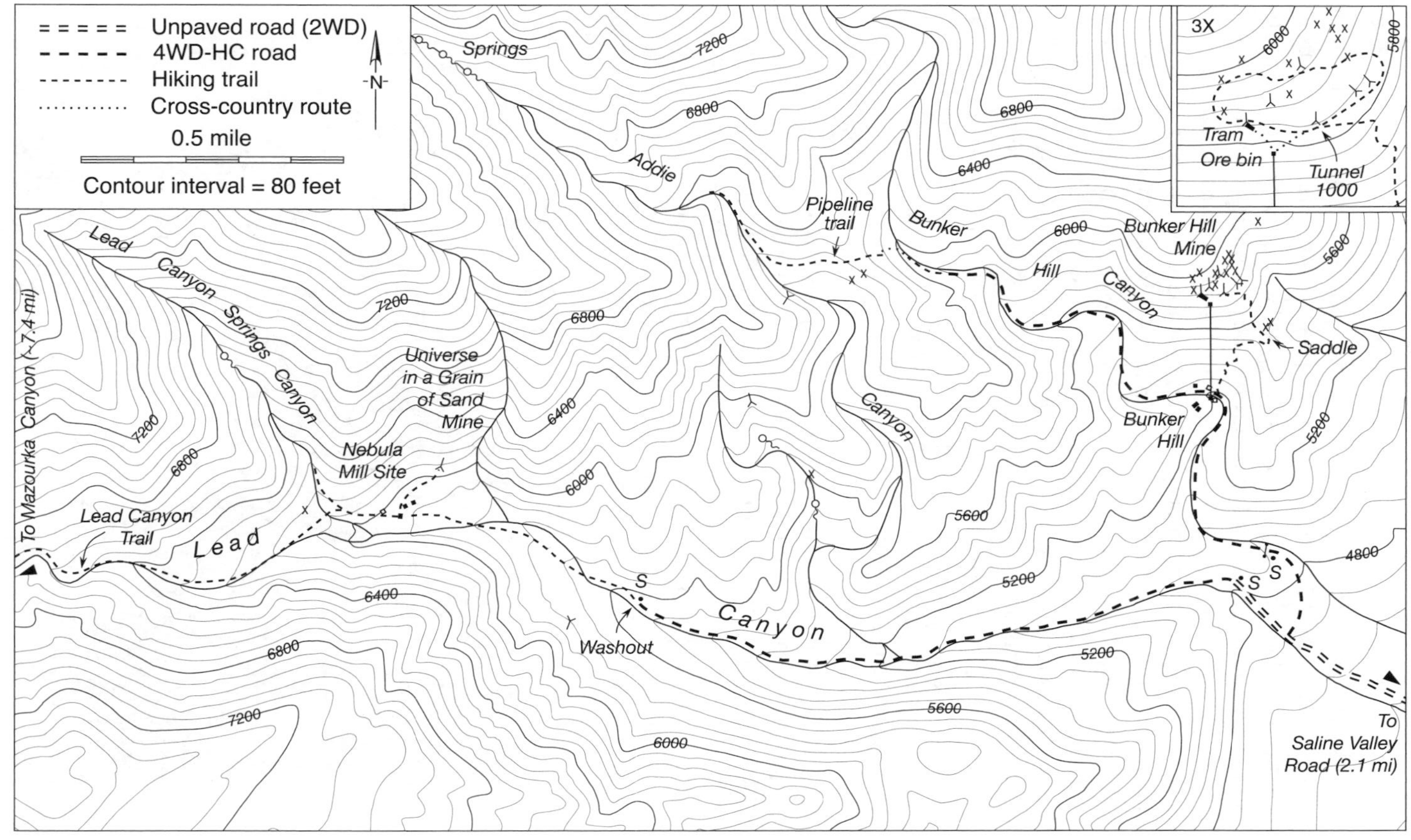
Unpaved road (2WD)
4WD-HC road
Hiking trail
Cross-country route
N
0.5 mile
Contour interval = 80 feet
Springs
Addie
Pipeline trail
Bunker Hill Canyon
Bunker Hill Mine
Saddle
Bunker Hill
3X
Tram
Ore bin
Tunnel 1000
Lead Canyon Springs Canyon
Universe in a Grain of Sand Mine
Nebula Mill Site
Canyon
To Mazourka Canyon (~7.4 mi)
Lead Canyon Trail
Lead Canyon
S
Washout
S
S
To Saline Valley Road (2.1 mi)
7200
6800
6400
6000
5600
5200
4800
5800

Trestle bridge at the Bunker Hill Mine

makeshift ore bucket, frozen since its last delivery. These contraptions dumped the ore into the upper terminal ore bin, where it was loaded in buckets and trammed down to Bunker Hill. The system of pulleys, cables, and handbrakes that lowered the buckets is still extant. As interesting as this structure is, the trail to it is gone, and reaching it requires scrambling down a slippery talus at the very edge of the cliff...

The 2-mile pipeline that delivered water to the camp tapped springs high in Addie Canyon, Lead Canyon's next side canyon to the west. The hike to the springs crosses a diversity of terrain and is quite pleasant. From the camp the overgrown road climbs along the tortuous bottom of Bunker Hill Canyon. It follows not one but three parallel pipelines—the modern black plastic pipe and two 3-inch metal pipelines, both a century old. After 0.7 mile the wash squeezes through a shallow passage and the road pinches out to a foot trail. Soon after, the pipeline angles west up the canyon slope. The next segment of trail is missing. Go 50 yards past the pipeline to a ravine, up the ravine to a small pine grove, and cut south across the grove back to the pipeline. There the trail resumes, follows the pipeline up to the low divide with Addie Canyon, then ramps gently down into Addie Canyon. The wash leads through a healthy forest to the spring, a long river of greenery funneled in a narrow canyon. This is a magical spot, steeped in the fragrance of pinyon and juniper, far from everything, with fresh water, a little wildlife, and cozy spots to indulge in a night under the stars.

■

LEAD CANYON

Located on the edge of the high desert, Lead Canyon is a perfect hiking destination in the warmer months. An old road, washed out part way up, climbs along this wide drainage to the scenic Nebula Mill Site, a fairly recent mining camp just below timberline, and the sparkling tunnels of its quartz mine. A short trail continues up canyon, along the pipeline that once delivered water to the camp, to an enchanting spring of willows bordered by orchids and columbine.

General Information
Jurisdiction: Inyo Mountains Wilderness (NFS)
Road status: Hiking on trails; HC access road in lower canyon
Nebula Mill Site: 0.9 mi, 680 ft up, 0 ft down one way / very easy
Lead Canyon Sprgs. Cyn: 1.3 mi, 1,240 ft up, 20 ft down one way / easy
Main attractions: Mining camp, quartz mine, well-watered spring
USGS 7.5' topo maps: Waucoba Canyon*, Mazourka Peak
Maps: pp. 239*, *231*

Location and Access

Lead Canyon drains the Inyo Mountains near the north end of Saline Valley. To get to it, drive the Saline Valley Road 5.6 miles north of Willow Creek Camp (or 10.2 miles south of North Pass) to the Lead Canyon Road, on the west side. As it crosses Lead Canyon's bulging fan, this bouncy road dips in and out of several small washes. At the junction after 1.65 miles, the road on the left is closed to all motor vehicles. Continue right, along the rim of Lead Canyon's wash, 0.7 mile to a second junction just below the canyon mouth. Lead Canyon is straight ahead. Up to this point the road is crowned with vegetation, but manageable with a standard-clearance vehicle. With high clearance, you can drive another 1.1 miles up canyon to the boundary of the Inyo Mountains Wilderness at an elevation of 5,380 feet.

Route Description

Lead Canyon is quite different from other canyons in the eastern Inyos: except for short narrows just inside the canyon, the first few miles are uncharacteristically wide. There are no monumental rock walls either, but the canyon is deep and its south slope impressive: it is a long talus that arches up more and more steeply to a rocky crest. Light-colored rock slides that have tumbled down from the high crest drape the dark slopes with giant fan-shaped stringers. The road cavorts along the open canyon bottom, tracing the edge of its entrenched wash. The area is thickly vegetated with a mix of low-desert and high-desert plants. Timberline is never far: even from the lower canyon trees are visible just a few hundred feet higher. This prime real estate is home to hummingbirds, flycatchers, falcons, gold finch, and chukars, whose loud calls enliven the entire canyon.

After a wet winter, Lead Canyon boasts beautiful flower gardens. One late May, the road and entire hillsides were inundated with the Indian paintbrush, desert mat, and globemallow. Large bouquets of lupine grew on the lower slopes, and the canyon floor was carpeted with random arrangements of phacelia, chia, indigo bush, penstemon, and Mojave aster. One of the most flashy plants was a variety of globe-mallow called *rosacea*—its flowers are not vermillion but pastel shades of purple. In the summer other flowers take over, including prince's plume, mariposa, and locoweed.

A third of a mile into the wilderness, look for the yellow truck crashed upside-down in the wash 20 feet below the road—if it is still there. While most desert car wrecks are boringly anonymous, this one has a funny story—or is it a legend? High up in nearby Paiute Canyon there is a gold mine called Baxter. The two brothers who owned it, both fighter pilots, died on a mission in the Korean War around 1951, and the mine was up for grabs. Soon after, two Saline Valley regulars became interested in it. One was Rogers, who operated the valley's talc mines. The other was his friend Lucky "Banjo" Baldwin, also known as Lucky Rich, who owned a lead claim in the Last Chance Range (see *Lucky Rich Canyon*). Rather than splitting the Baxter Mine, the two friends gambled it: the first one to reach it from Willow Creek Camp would be the new owner. Lucky Rich tried his luck up Lead Canyon, but at a steep roadcut his truck overturned and crashed. The mangled wreck in the canyon wash is Lucky Rich's old truck. He did not get the

Lead Canyon

	Dist.(mi)	Elev.(ft)
Wilderness boundary	0.0	5,380
Wash crossing / road degrades	0.3	5,620
Nebula Mill Site (camp)	0.8	5,970
Univ. in a Grain of Sand Mine	(0.15)	6,050
Lead Canyon Springs Canyon	1.0	6,180
Spring (upper end)	1.4	6,620

The Nebula Mill Site in Lead Canyon

Baxter Mine, but more importantly he survived the crash and lived to be an old man—he passed away in 1998 at his Petaluma home.

A hundred yards past the truck wreckage, in sight of the camp, the road deteriorates noticeably. Just beyond, at a steep-sided wash, the road turns into a beat-up trail. The cluster of cabins half a mile up the trail is the Nebula Mill Site, a scenic camp nestled in a small valley just below timberline. The main structure is a long wooden cabin, painted barn red and artistically framed by two stately cottonwoods. It has three rooms, partly furnished, that once had water and electricity. The long terrace fronting the cabin offers a game of horseshoe, a funky stone fireplace for summer cookouts, and a shady bench to admire the canyon below. A footpath leads to the decaying wooden deck of a home-made jacuzzi and a second cabin. This is a peaceful place, reminiscent of the lonesome homesteads that once dotted the byways of the American West.

This site was used from 1972 until the 2000s by owner David Howell, who also owns the nearby mine he named—with both philosophical and poetical inspiration—Universe in a Grain of Sand. Howell came here every year to mine a little and repair the relentless damage of time. He mined his minerals by hand, "as much to save ecological impact," he said, "as to protect the specimen values." Some workings are high above the camp to the northeast and a little hard to get to, across rough, steep terrain. The lower tunnel is easier to reach,

Old mining equipment near the Nebula Mill Site

via the trail that starts at the main cabin. Its path is lined with interesting machinery, and fine specimens of mound cactus.

A note pinned to a wall in the main cabin, hand-written by David Howell, invited visitors to use it as an overnight shelter. Hikers occasionally took him up on his generous offer. The glowing messages they inscribed on the cabin's logbook spoke highly of the charms of this camp, and the cabin's cozy warmth on snowy nights. Remember that this is private property. Take good care of it. Keep windows and doors locked or closed to keep out rodents and bad weather.

What made life possible here is a good water supply that originates in Lead Canyon Springs Canyon, the side canyon past the camp. In the winter the pipeline's valves were shut off to avoid frost damage and the camp had no water—but the side canyon never dries up. It is well worth taking the short hike to it. The trail starts just behind the main cabin. It passes by the ruin of an old stone house, then follows the pipeline to a fork just below the side canyon. The left fork once continued about 8 miles over the Inyos to Mazourka Canyon on the Owens Valley side; from here to the crest most of the trail is now very faint. The right fork climbs into the side canyon to the lower end of the spring-fed creek, where it is tapped at two 55-gallon drums. The trail disappears soon after, but you can continue up the steep and narrow wash, where willows mingle with healthy pinyon pine and Utah juniper. This is a restful spring, shaded and refreshing on a hot day. The creek supports a wealth of plants that are hard to reconcile with the desert—patches of green grass and miner's lettuce, tufts of horsetail and thistle, and miniature gardens of orchid and columbine.

■

THE BLUE MONSTER MINE

> *This relatively easy hike on an abandoned road will take you several miles up through one of the very few well-behaved canyons in the Inyo Mountains, a pretty passage sprinkled with interesting mines, including the silver mill and tramway of the Blue Monster Mine, and the funky tunnels of the Lucky Boy Mine. The road eventually ends at the top of a scenic ridge overlooking Saline Valley, where an impressive cableway spans more than a mile of spectacular canyon.*

General Information

Jurisdiction: Inyo Mountains Wilderness (NFS)
Road status: Hiking on trails; 2WD access road
Blue Monster Mine: 3.0 mi, 1,100 ft up, 520 ft down one way / easy–mod.
Lucky Boy Mine: 3.9 mi, 1,500 ft up, 520 ft down one way / moderate
Baxter Mine cableway: 4.7 mi, 1,870 ft up, 520 ft down one way / difficult
Main attractions: Primitive road to silver mill, tunnels, cableway, views
USGS 7.5′ topo map: Waucoba Canyon
Maps: pp. 247*, *231*

Location and Access

The Blue Monster Mine is in a nameless canyon south of Lead Canyon. To get to it, take the Lead Canyon Road, off the Saline Valley Road (see *Lead Canyon*). Drive this road 1.65 miles west to a sharp right bend, where the faint side road to the Blue Monster Mine takes off on the left. One can usually drive this far with a standard-clearance vehicle. The Blue Monster Mine Road is in a wilderness area and closed to all motor vehicles. Driving it is punishable by Federal law. Please respect this act of Congress, park by the junction, and start walking.

Route Description

The Blue Monster Mine. Overgrown with large creosotes and often rocky, the old road to the Blue Monster Mine has aged quite a bit since its heyday. It still provides a nice path to explore this neglected canyon, which it reaches fairly quickly. The most scenic area is the 0.3-mile stretch of narrows just inside the canyon. The pointed, knotted walls that line this passage are Cambrian shale from the Deep Spring Formation. This rock sequence contains fossils of some of the planet's earliest life forms. Baked to a nearly black finish by metamorphism, the walls lend the narrows a stern mood, almost forbidding.

The ruins in the narrows are the primitive mill of the Blue Monster Mine. This mine was known for decades as the Monster Mine, perhaps in acknowledgment of the unusual size of its original lode: a vein of solid galena over 3 feet wide and 40 feet long worth $100 per ton! Quartz veins also contained a little pyrite, cerussite, tetrahedrite, chrysocolla, linarite, and caledonite. From the mine high up the canyon wall, the ore was trammed down to the mill, processed, then packed over the Inyos to Mazourka Canyon, and teamed to the railroad in Owens Valley. Most of the galena had been removed by 1911, just four years after its discovery. A new tunnel was driven below the original one, but it turned out to be largely barren. Since 1912, except for short-lived exploitations, the property has been idle. The only recorded production was in 1935, when 50 tons were shipped to a smelter in Utah. It was around then that "Blue" was appended to the mine's name, perhaps following the discovery of copper.

The main structure at the aging mill is the wooden ore bin that collected the ore from the jig-back tramway. Unfortunately it has partly collapsed. The foundations of the machinery are still in place, as well as the crude containers where the milled ore was stocked. The minimal tailings suggest that the mill did not produce much; it may have been installed after the main ore body played out. Check out the cables' tensioning devices. They are curious precursors of a modern turnbuckle.

Part of the fun of hiking this canyon is hunting for the many beat-up trails and the derelict workings they access. The Blue Monster Mine is a good place to start. About 0.1 mile past the mill, a steep side canyon opens up on the right. The gravel ramp that curves up into it is the washed-out road to the mine. Walk it 500 feet until it narrows to a foot trail. In the next 250 yards it forks twice (see map). The left trail climbs to two tunnels, perhaps the ones exploited in 1935. The right trail dead-ends at an overlook of the tramway towers. The middle trail climbs on to the main 150-foot tunnel. This area has several interesting remains, including a compressor from the 1930s, two large sifters, a rail spur, the tramway's sturdy upper terminal, two large open cuts, and a shady tunnel where bats hang out, usually upside down.

The Lucky Boy Mine. The ruins of the Lucky Boy Mine start about a mile past the Blue Monster Mill, and they are more spread out. The road passes by a dusty dugout, the floor of a collapsed cabin where visitors once camped, then two short tunnels side by side, but here again the best lies beyond the road. A tenth of a mile past the two tunnels, look for the mouth of a side canyon coming down from the north. Four of the Lucky Boy tunnels are a quarter of a mile up this side

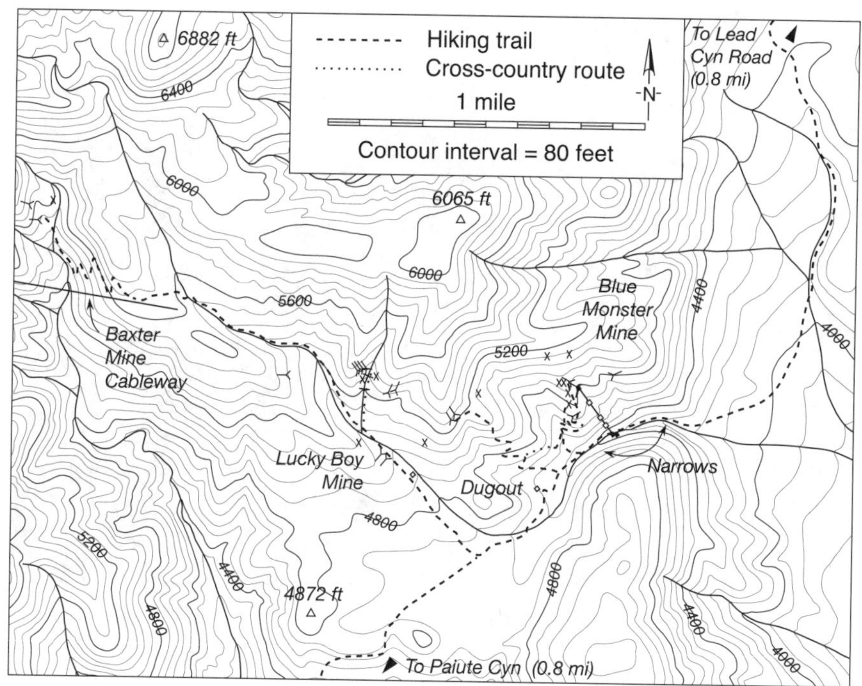

The Blue Monster Mine		
	Dist.(mi)	Elev.(ft)
Lead Canyon Road	0.0	4,325
Blue Monster Mine mill	2.5	4,360
Blue Monster Mine	(0.4)	4,870
Lucky Boy Mine lower tunnels	3.6	~4,960
Lucky Boy upper tunnels	(0.25)	~5,340
End of road / cableway	4.7	5,670

canyon. The trail to them, on the side canyon's west ridge, is hard to locate. The wash is faster, even though two falls are in the way. The first fall is a knobby aggregate of Cambrian dolomite close to 25 feet high (careful!), the second one a 6-foot wall that the miners ironically climbed with a ladder. The four tunnels were assessed until as recently as 1992, yet given their lousy access they likely did not produce much. Clustered in the face of a cliff, they resemble troglodytic dwellings. The lower tunnel was called the Dungeon. The one above it has a 15-foot shaft with a primitive hand winch. The next one up is a shallow slot speckled with deep-blue and green copper minerals.

View of Saline Valley from the Blue Monster Mine

The Baxter Mine cableway. The climax is about a mile further, where the road shoots up a rutted grade and ends on a high ridge in the middle of a grand setting. To the west and south the land falls off into a deep, convoluted arm of Paiute Canyon. Behind it the forested high Inyos tower thousands of feet up, while Saline Valley shines brightly to the east. Yet what is most impressive is the incredible cableway of the Baxter Mine that spans the canyon's gaping precipice. From the end of the road it boldly leaps across the void, stretching so far out that one loses sight of it long before it reaches the opposite rim. With binoculars one can just make out the mine's slender tailing. The mine was accessed by the Lead Canyon Trail, a route so impractical that the mine owners salvaged a cable from the Salt Tramway and erected it here to haul their ore down through this canyon instead. This mile-long cable levitating across thin air is a vision to behold as one of the wonders of desert mining. The mind recoils when attempting to gauge the Herculean task of deploying this five-ton behemoth across such unforgiving terrain.

This exceptional spot alone makes this hike. Pitch a tent and stay overnight, surrounded by the smell of big sagebrush, to enjoy the pleasure of being out here alone, and of gazing over desert land untrammeled as far as the eye can see.

■

PAIUTE CANYON

Paiute Canyon offers a unique chance to explore two very different desert environments. In the lower canyon a smooth river of gravel wanders through a colorful granitic gorge, eventually reaching a small oasis and shaded narrows irrigated by a small mountain stream. In contrast, the upper canyon is a lush and beautiful jungle of willow, largely impenetrable. With its perennial creek, impassable thickets, and difficult bypasses, it is a challenging place, reminiscent of some of the more rugged canyons of southern Utah.

General Information

Jurisdiction: Inyo Mountains Wilderness (BLM)
Road status: Roadless; easy access from the Saline Valley Road
Paiute Canyon narrows: 3.0 mi, 770 ft up, 0 ft down one way / easy
Paiute Cyn waterfall: 6.5 mi, 1,940 ft up, 40 ft down one way / strenuous
Main attractions: Scenic canyon with narrows, creek, and lush springs
USGS 7.5' topo maps: Pat Keyes Canyon*, Waucoba Canyon
Maps: pp. 253*, 231

Location and Access

Paiute Canyon is the main canyon south of Lead Canyon. To get to it, drive the Saline Valley Road 0.8 mile north of Willow Creek Camp (or 15.0 miles south of North Pass). At this point the road dips in and out of the sandy wash of Paiute Canyon. Park either before or after the dip and hike up the wash from here.

Route Description

The lower canyon. Access to Paiute Canyon from the road is very easy, along a smooth wash entrenched between vertical fanglomerate banks. In just 0.4 mile you will reach the canyon mouth and enter right away the scenic, open gorge that makes up the lower canyon. It is a beautiful place, dominated by impressive, rugged walls rising hundreds of feet. Almost all of this canyon cuts through a Jurassic formation called Quartz Monzonite of Paiute Monument. This granite-like rock is responsible for the canyon's striking land forms, from the large isolated boulders in the wash to the short cliffs that occasionally rise on either side. The wash is a peculiar river of fine gravel. With the exception of wildflowers in the spring, it is almost devoid of vegetation. The likely reason is that Paiute Canyon is regularly scoured by serious flashfloods. Perennial plants, which grow slowly, may never get a chance to develop before being wiped out. Signs of flashfloods are ubiquitous. One of them is the deeply cut wash below the canyon mouth. Another one is the large piles of sun-bleached driftwood stranded in outer bends and in the middle of the wash.

Less than a mile into the canyon you will pass under a long and colorful painted bluff on the north side (there is one also on the opposite side; look back to see it). The quartz monzonite is capped by thick layers of volcanic flows and sedimentary rocks, alternately cream-colored, pink, and dark brown. Out of these softer formations, erosion has carved multicolored badlands of buttresses, pinnacles, domes, and huge balanced rocks, pinned high above the wash. It is a pleasure to amble beneath this ever-changing rock palette, along a wash so gentle that it did not seem to belong to the Inyo Mountains.

Paiute Canyon has a little creek, and it is a delightful surprise to come across it in the middle of this empty wash. The element of surprise lies in the creek's unpredictability. After a winter flood you may find it near the road, while in the summer you may have to go as far as the springs to see it. One year in early March I even saw it recede 300 yards in a few hours! The first place to expect flowing water is generally the lower end of the first spring, 1.8 miles into the canyon. Here a small oasis of honey mesquite, large willows, and arrowweed crowds the sandy banks at a tightening in the canyon. Shaded and beautifully situated beneath looming canyon walls, it is a restful place for a break.

The narrows. A few more canyon bends and the walls come together to form Paiute Canyon's deep narrows. At their lower end I paused in admiration at a beach of coarse sand that stretched from wall to wall, smooth and barren. In the middle of it flowed a foot-wide, inch-deep stream. Water and sand had struck this miraculous relationship, for the only purpose, it seemed, of producing this improbable scene. The short, cathedral-like narrows just beyond are refreshingly dark and cool. The stream flows in and out of shallow pools, echoing as it glides along the base of high polished walls.

The springs. Past the narrows the character of the canyon changes rapidly. For a while the wash is entrenched, and to avoid getting wet you hop back and forth over the rust-colored creek. The head of the first spring, at the next bend in the canyon, is marked by a thick grove of screwbean mesquite. Bypassing it is not difficult, but the beginning of trouble is in sight: the dense growth of trees that fills the wash ahead, which is the lower end of the second spring. From here on up,

Creek at Paiute Canyon's first spring

the springs form a nearly continuous string of trees and brush, most of it impossible to cross. The rest of Paiute Canyon is as difficult to hike as the lower canyon is easy.

The second spring is a good preview. Right away it is too thick to enter. Before reaching it, look on the north side for a short trail that climbs the narrow fin on the inside of the sharp U-shaped bend. Take it up to the top of the fin, then down the far side to the edge of the vegetation. Here the only option is to bushwhack across the thick jungle of willows to the south side, then continue on that side along the vegetation. About half way through this spring the tree cover opens up a little, and one can proceed along one of the creek's multiple arms. You will be able to savor the rare chance to walk through a desert forest, not just a few isolated trees but a genuine grove of willows with ample space between trees to wander. I enjoyed the serenity of this lush oasis, its sun-dappled shade and tropical mood, and the occasional wildflowers poking through the decaying leaves. I was reminded of hiking through some of the brushy side canyons of southern Utah's Escalante River—especially after sinking ankle-deep in a pool of quicksand!

The third spring is similar. Its lower third is relatively easy. The creek flows beneath high banks of fanglomerate, its course punctuated with cobbles of pink granite and musical cascades. You will have to cross it numerous times, hopping on muddy banks. Near elev. 3,680 ft,

Miner's lettuce

where the willows start to grow taller, look for a trail on the south bench. Though vague at places, it bypasses the rest of the spring, which is essentially impenetrable. In the late spring the bench is decorated with the large magenta flowers of beavertail cacti. High vantage points offer good views of the green ribbon of foliage threading through the windy canyon below. At the head of the spring the vegetation ends abruptly, and so does the creek. Above it, the wash is as open and bare as it was hopelessly obstructed moments ago.

The most difficult part is yet to come: the fourth spring, which starts shortly, just past the next side canyon. Most of it is a forest so dense that it will make what you have gone through so far look like a walk in the park. Because it is crammed at the bottom of a narrow, steep-walled canyon, there is almost no space along its edges to find a passage. There is no trail. Even burros shun this place. I remained on the north side the whole way; not once did I even consider crossing this mad tangle of trees. I teetered up and down countless taluses, scrambled along unstable rock slides, and trudged through water where the walls forced me into the thorny spring. I sloshed through rippling mats of grass and cattail combed back by recent floods. Hikers in search of new challenges will find here a place to probe their boundaries and push their personal limits.

Paiute Canyon

	Dist.(mi)	Elev.(ft)
Saline Valley Road	0.0	2,350
Mouth	0.4	2,480
Painted bluff (lower end)	1.35	2,710
Oasis	2.3	2,940
Narrows (lower end)	2.7	3,065
Narrows (upper end)	3.0	3,115
First spring (head)	3.2	3,180
Second spring (head)	4.3	3,505
Third spring (head)	5.2	3,805
Waterfall/Fork	6.5	4,255
Fourth spring (side canyon)	7.2	4,630

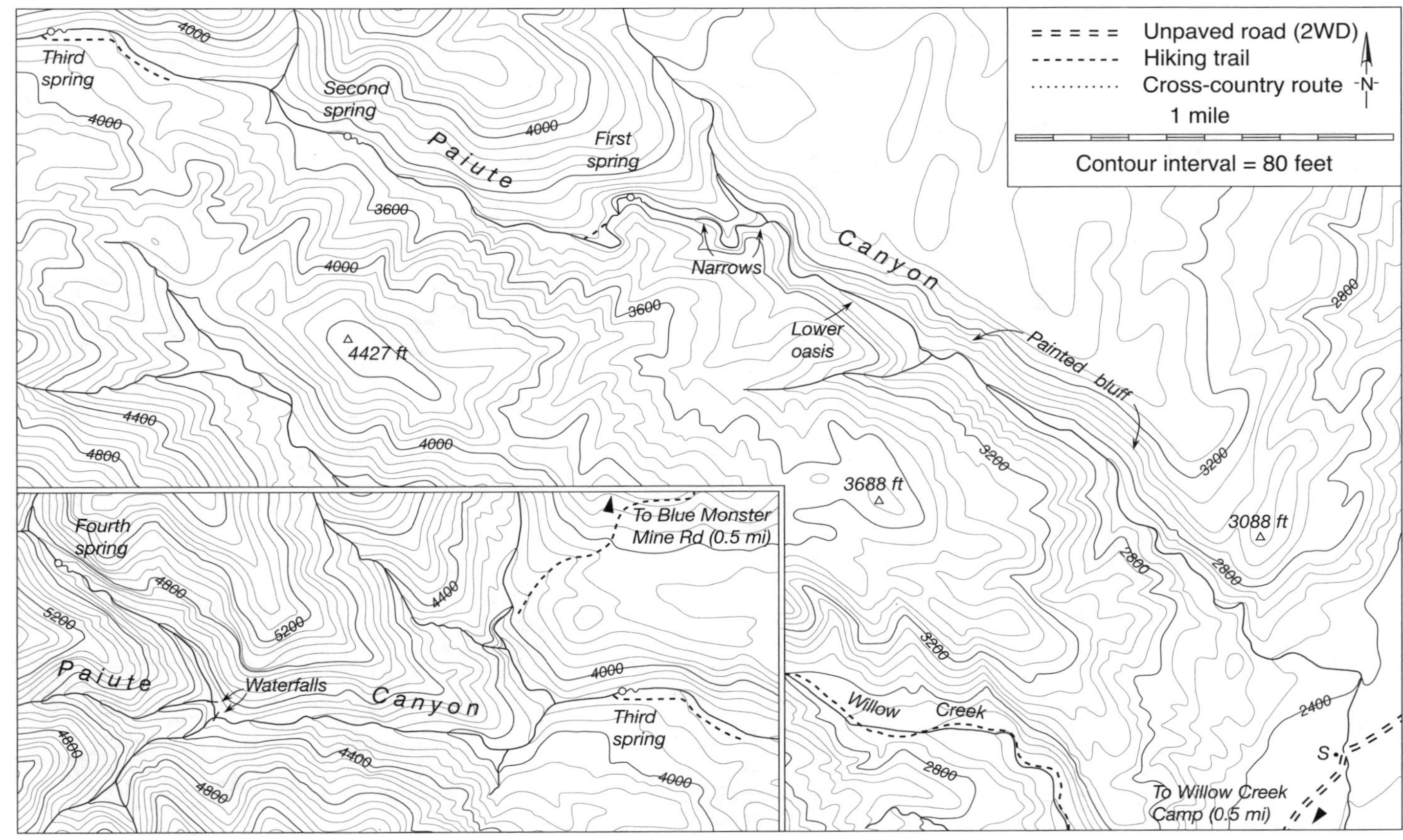
Unpaved road (2WD)
Hiking trail
Cross-country route
N
1 mile
Contour interval = 80 feet
Third spring
Second spring
Paiute Canyon
First spring
Narrows
Lower oasis
Painted bluff
4427 ft
3688 ft
3088 ft
Fourth spring
To Blue Monster Mine Rd (0.5 mi)
Paiute Canyon
Waterfalls
Third spring
Willow Creek
S
To Willow Creek Camp (0.5 mi)
4000
3600
4400
4800
5200
3200
2800
2400

Creek in the narrows of Paiute Canyon

But the rewards are matched to the labor. In the midst of the spring I came across creek banks flushed with orchids in bloom. Underneath a huge boulder wedged across the wash, a small waterfall arched gracefully into a ferny pool. All around, the Inyo Mountains rose thousands of feet, studded with conifers and patches of snow.

Just beyond, the canyon forks one last time before entering the high Inyos. The main canyon continues to the left. With its small waterfall and bubbling mountain stream, the right fork is more inviting. The grade steepens markedly and the difficulty increases one more notch, but you may want to explore its unchartered gorge to the head of the fourth spring—or beyond.

Caution. In case I did not make it clear, the upper canyon is a savage place. By the time I had gone through it and back, my shirt and hat were history, my legs looked like they had been dragged through miles of brush—which they had—and my shoes never quite looked the same. Wear long pants and clothes ready for sacrifice. Count on a long day to the head of the fourth spring and back.

■

McELVOY CANYON

If you want to see a desert spring and waterfalls without having to climb hairy falls, try McElvoy Canyon. A short walk along its deep gorge and lively creek will take you to two high waterfalls that tumble across sweeping walls of fern and orchids. Climbing the second waterfall requires technical skills. It will appeal, like the rest of this remarkable canyon filled with high falls, history, and surprises, to experienced climbers with a taste for adventure.

General Information

Jurisdiction: Inyo Mountains Wilderness (BLM)
Road status: Roadless; road access from the Saline Valley Road
Second waterfall: 1.1 mi, 950 ft up, 10 ft down one way / easy
Third fall: 1.7 mi, 1,550 ft up, 10 ft down one way / moder. (climbing)
Main attractions: Waterfalls, gorge, lush spring, and perennial creek
USGS 7.5' topo maps: Pat Keyes Canyon*, New York Butte
Maps: pp. 257*, *231*

Location and Access

McElvoy Canyon drains the extremely steep eastern slope of Mount Inyo, just west of Saline Valley's main sand dunes. To get to it, drive the Saline Valley Road 7.6 miles north of the Salt Tramway Junction (or 1 mile south of the Warm Springs Road) to a road on the west side. This rocky, high-clearance road climbs the fan just south of McElvoy Canyon. Drive it just under a mile to a very short spur road on the right. The main road continues straight, but getting into McElvoy Canyon from further up is difficult. Instead, park on the spur.

Route Description

From the spur road, hike northwest across the fan about 250 yards to a trail along the abrupt canyon rim. Follow the trail up canyon along the rim a short distance to a wide break in the rim where it is easy to descend into the wash. In a few minutes the trail will take you to the first willows and mesquite at the mouth of the canyon, and sometimes a little running water. This is McElvoy Creek, the perennial stream that threads through most of this canyon.

As the impressive views of McElvoy Canyon from the fan foreshadow, the canyon starts right away as a deep and narrow gorge, a geometric slot sculpted into the base of the Inyos. Much deeper than it

The first fall in McElvoy Canyon

is wide, it is hemmed in by sheer walls of hard granite that crystallized over 160 million years ago. Your eyes are constantly drawn skyward, like in an outdoor cathedral. The slightest sound stirs haunting echoes. You begin to expect miracles. And you are about to witness a few.

Just 0.3 mile into the gorge is the first waterfall, a unique and wonderful gem. Unlike most waterfalls, it does not flow down the wash but over the canyon rim. Sixty feet overhead, water leaps over a ledge, free-falls in a widening spray, and explodes in a spatter of thick drops into a shallow pool. On the overhanging wall behind the waterfall hangs a 20-foot tapestry of maidenhair fern. In the spring, dozens of stream orchis in bloom and flaming-red columbine poke out of the fern cover. Everything tricks you into feeling you have been transported to the tropics. It is a great place to cool off, and perhaps accept the waterfall's tempting invitation for a brisk shower.

The trail perseveres up the steep wash. It ducks under willows, wanders up and down rocky landslides, and flirts every chance it gets with the moss-covered creek. It passes by a second fern-coated wall with a seasonal waterfall, and snakes around two tight hairpin bends deep beneath pale granite cliffs. The creek pours over a small cascade, floods a swamp of brackish water, then fields of 4-foot thistle. The trees and high walls create plenty of shade; even on a hot summer day this is a relatively cool place to experience the magic of a desert spring.

About 0.7 mile, past a dry bouldery stretch, the trail vanishes near the base of the beautiful first fall. Gushing from the mouth of tight

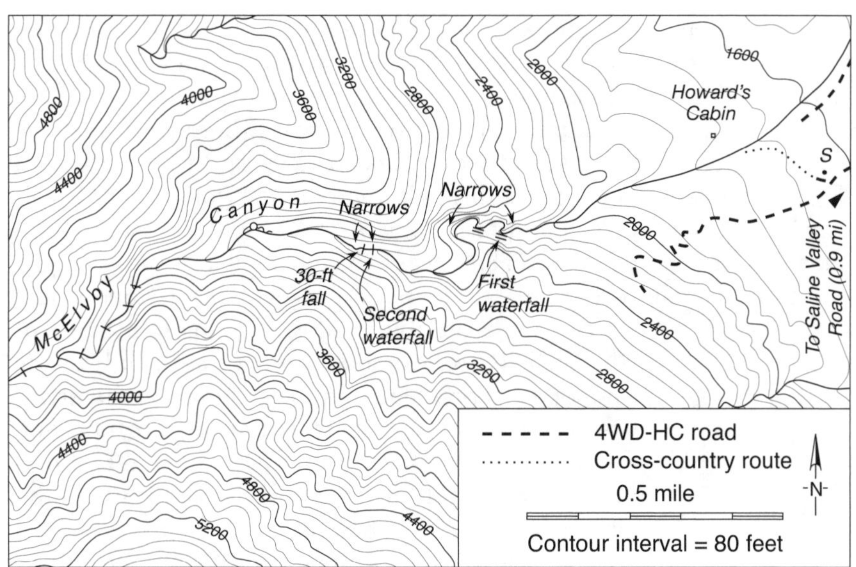

McElvoy Canyon		
	Dist.(mi)	Elev.(ft)
End of spur road	0.0	~1,650
Mouth	~0.5	~1,900
First waterfall	0.7	2,160
Second waterfall/50-ft fall	1.1	2,570
Spring	1.4	2,790
Third fall	1.7	3,190

narrows 50 feet up, McElvoy Creek feathers down a hanging garden of moss and fern. This is a hauntingly beautiful spot, framed by towering walls and graced by healthy willows, cattails, and orchids.

Hiking further up McElvoy Canyon should be undertaken only by adept rock climbers. The easiest route is up the smooth vertical wall to the right of the waterfall. It is about a 5.4 climb, and it is protected by two bolts and a piton. If you are a climber, come here with a partner, two harnesses, a 50-meter rope, and a few carabiners. If you do not have climbing equipment and experience, this is the wrong place to improvise. If a rope is hanging down the wall, do not trust your life to it, as it may be too weak to hold you, and a fall could be deadly.

The narrows at the top of the waterfall, about 25 yards long, are flooded and crowded with trees and more stream orchis than I have seen anywhere. They end at the second fall. It is only a 30-foot climb but it is difficult when it is dry, worse when water pours over it. The wire that was recently installed, if still there, definitely helps.

Above the second fall, the canyon is very different. In historic times, it was a green river of well-irrigated trees up to timberline. In 2012, a 100-year flood ripped through McElvoy Canyon, rolling truck-size boulders, uprooting and ferrying trees, burying the wash under a slurry of gravel and rocks. The loss of this enchanted oasis is tragic. Now, only small groves dot the denuded gravel. The next one is just up canyon, a clump of willow clinging to the base of the wall. There is a silver lining: the thick brush is no longer a problem, and the canyon's grand architecture takes center stage. Unfortunately, not long enough. The next fall is not far away, the first of a giant staircase of six vertical discontinuities, the last one a 150-foot behemoth.

McElvoy Canyon has a ghost. In the upper canyon there once lived a hermit by the name of Marion Howard. After serving in the Army during World War II and bouncing from job to job, he moved to the Lone Pine area, where he lived for a time in a mine tunnel. Around 1965 he discovered McElvoy Canyon, a perfect refuge for his bohemian lifestyle, remote, inaccessible, flushed with fresh water. There he built a cabin, lugged in a potbelly stove to ward off the bite of winter, and made it his residence until around 1980. About once a week he took the arduous cross-country hike over a 10,000-foot pass to pick up supplies in town, which he carried on his back up to the age of 70. He had a passion for beekeeping. All along his route—at his cabin, at rock shelters, and at the abandoned McElvoy Mine up canyon—he stashed helmets, netting, beehive boxes, and jars of honey collected from local bees. He built a second home at the canyon mouth, a stone and wood cabin with a shingle roof on artful rafters of twisted driftwood. To hike down to Saline Valley he rigged up on every fall a ladder of wooden rungs held by heavy wire. It made traveling quicker and safer, although he admitted to a few blood-curdling close calls. It was a hard way to live, in his mind a fair price to be a free spirit.

Hiking in the footsteps of the Beekeeper of McElvoy Canyon gives us a chance to pay homage to this unsung pioneer who survived 15 winters in the harsh high desert, and to his resilience and ingenuity. If you persevere you may be rewarded with the sight of one of his rickety ladders still hanging down a fall.

■

BEVERIDGE CANYON

Beveridge Canyon is a powerful place. In the middle of one of the driest deserts on Earth, this deep gorge manages the impossible feat of combining a bubbling creek, graceful waterfalls, and luxuriant vegetation, in a spectacular setting of monumental walls and awesome narrows. This is a rare and magical experience, heightened by the challenge of the wet terrain and high waterfalls. It may well be the most exceptional hike out of Saline Valley.

General Information

Jurisdiction: Inyo Mountains Wilderness (BLM)
Road status: Roadless; hiking from end of short primitive road
Ultimate Fall: 0.8 mi, 790 ft up, 20 ft down one way/difficult (climbing)
Main attractions: Lush narrows with creek & waterfalls, rock climbing
USGS 7.5' topo maps: Craig Canyon*, New York Butte
Maps: pp. 261*, 231

Location and Access

Beveridge Canyon is the Inyo Mountains' first main canyon north of Salt Lake. The lower gorge is reached via the Beveridge Canyon Road, which starts 2.5 miles north of the Hunter Canyon Road (4.1 miles south of the Warm Springs Road). It climbs the fan 1.2 miles to a junction at the mouth of Beveridge Canyon. Continue up the canyon, past a vintage dump truck, 0.3 mile to the small camp at the end of the road, and park. The lower road is a little rocky, but it does not require high clearance. High clearance is needed in the canyon. The camp is an interesting place to browse through. Known as the Trio Mill Site, it was used in historic times to support operations at talc claims near Willow Creek and lode claims near Cerro Gordo. It still has a fairly large furnished cabin, a plywood shed, a cistern, another dump truck, and a rusted swing where children once played.

Route Description

A short distance beyond the camp, the massive canyon walls converge into a dark passage soon livened by a narrow bubbly stream. This is the lower end of Beveridge Creek, which runs through most of this canyon. The first obstacle is within earshot: a small waterfall that cascades in multiple strands over granitic stairs. It is usually climbed on the dry slant to the right. Just past it there is a second waterfall, a single span of water arching delicately over a slick rock face. In hot weather the misty, rock-rimmed pool into which it crashes is a delightful spot to cool off. To go on, climb the steep rock talus to the right, up to a ledge that circumvents the waterfall. Beyond, the canyon opens up onto a long, deep, and impressive gorge squeezed between rugged walls that shoot hundreds of feet up. The rock is Diorite of the New York Butte, a stark granite from the dawn of the dinosaurs. A trail of sorts meanders along this spectacular passage, swinging back and forth across the creek, skillfully minimizing bushwhacking. You will pass beneath towering pink-colored cliffs, and gaze up at impossibly tall taluses and side drainages too sheer to climb.

At the end of this stretch the canyon walls close in again to create some of the most outstanding narrows in the Inyo Mountains. Carved out of dazzling white marble, they are a masterpiece of natural archi-

Beveridge Canyon's white marble narrows above Fern Fall

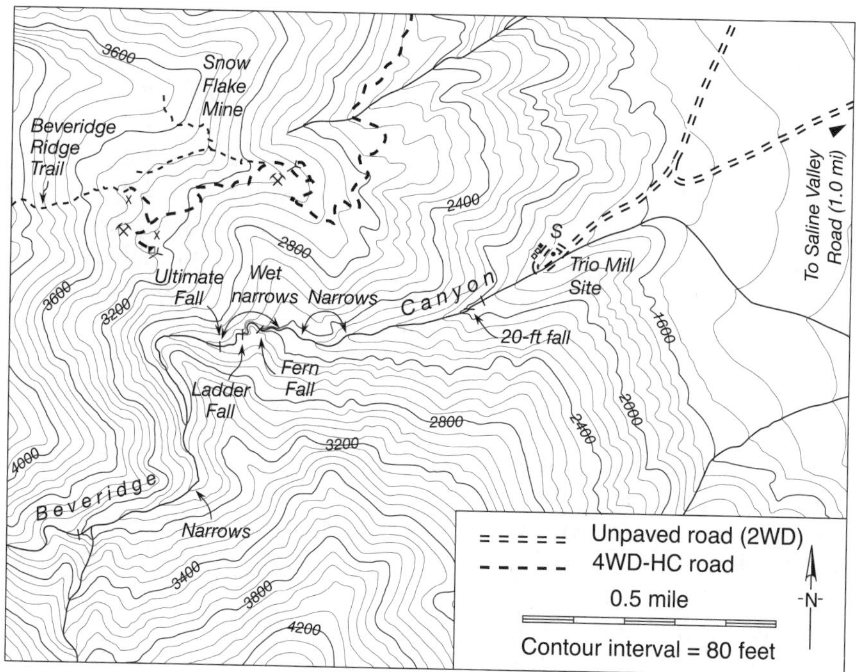

Beveridge Canyon		
	Dist.(mi)	Elev.(ft)
Trio Mill Site (cabin)	0.0	1,770
20-foot waterfall	0.2	1,970
Fern Fall	0.7	2,400
Ladder Fall	0.75	2,480
Ultimate Fall	0.8	2,540

tecture. Grand vertical sweeps of water-worn stone wave in every direction to enclose a secret world of tight bends, suspended alcoves, and sensuous overhangs. Tall tapestries of black stains drape the walls, emphasizing their great height. It is a strangely primordial experience to wander through this timeless corridor of naked stone, cold to the touch, trapped in perpetual darkness, haunted by the constant murmur of running water. Thick wall-to-wall mats of maidenhair fern cloak the stream, under the shelter of thick willows. In the summer, orchids bloom right out of the water, poised in surreal defiance.

There is a price for all this beauty. To get through it you will need to negotiate three waterfalls, which John Hart, in his visionary 1981 book *Hiking the Great Basin*, named Fern, Ladder, and Ultimate. Fern Fall is a short distance into the narrows. Two ribbons of water glide 14 feet down on either side of a plush wall of fern. To its left, shallow natural notches in the wall offer enough purchase to climb to the top of the fall, with a wide ledge half way up to rest. It is not a difficult climb (low 5s), but do not attempt it unless you are certain you can make it. Beyond it, much of the narrows is wet, and it is no longer possible to keep your feet dry. At one place you will need to walk through a flooded corridor, then wade thigh deep through a pool to reach and scramble over a short cascade. In the winter and spring the water is snow melt and ice cold.

The crux of this hike is Ladder Fall, a wide curtain of water plunging 14 vertical feet into a dark pool. Its namesake was a wooden ladder that helped hikers climb it for years. The ladder split long ago into two useless, rungless posts. The climb is not difficult either, but it starts in the thigh-deep pool, you will be soaked by the waterfall in seconds, and the holds are mossy and flushed by running water. Think twice before climbing it.

If you must turn around here, do not feel bad. The winding narrows above Ladder Fall are soon interrupted by Ultimate Fall, which stops most hikers. The stream pours around and under a huge chockstone wedged between the high walls at the top of the fall. Climbing the surrounding 60-foot walls requires a very difficult and exposed technical climb only the world's best climbers might scale safely.

Reaching beyond Ultimate Fall to learn the end of the story is enormously attractive—there are more falls and narrows, and the vegetation gets increasingly luxuriant. There are ways to get there—there is almost always a way—though not from here, or not without great effort. Half of the pleasure is finding the passage.

Beveridge Canyon's mood, and much of its magic, fluctuate in unison with the flow of its creek, which is at the mercy of climate change. Over the last decade the spring vegetation has slowly receded up canyon, then it started coming back down a little. There is no telling what you will find. To maximize the chance of experiencing Beveridge Canyon in its full glory, come here in late winter to early spring, when the creek is swollen with winter rain and snow melt. Because of the wet terrain, all the climbs are dangerous. Remain safety-conscious at all times. Unless you are an experienced rock climber, do not climb here alone. Do not rely on ropes left behind (especially at Ultimate Fall). They have been weakened by prolonged exposure to sunlight and moisture. To spare the fragile vegetation, follow existing paths.

■

BEVERIDGE

Lost in one of the region's most inaccessible canyons, Beveridge is the most remote ghost town in the California desert. It is reached by a very strenuous overnight hike on a precipitous miners' trail. Beautifully situated along a lush oasis coursed by a mountain stream, this rare historic site still holds cabins, tramways, mills, and obsolete equipment that date back to the 1870s. As you bushwhack through the creek-side vegetation in search of ruins, you will be overwhelmed by the sense that time has been suspended. When you return, you will feel as if you have gone to another world and back.

General Information
Jurisdiction: Inyo Mountains Wilderness (BLM)
Road status: Roadless; hiking from primitive road (HC-4WD)
Laskey's mill: 4.3 mi, 3,790 ft up, 1,580 ft down one way / strenuous
Huntington mills: 4.8 mi, 3,830 ft up, 1,900 ft down one way / strenuous
Main attractions: Strenuous overnight hike, isolated ghost town, history
USGS 7.5' topo maps: Craig Canyon, New York Butte*
Maps: pp. 267*, 269*, 303*, *231*

Location and Access

Beveridge is in the mid-section of Beveridge Canyon. The shortest route to it out of Saline Valley is the Beveridge Ridge Trail, which starts at the top of the Snow Flake Mine and traces the canyon's north ridge. To get to the trailhead, follow directions to the Snow Flake Mine Road (see *Saline Valley's Talc Mines*). Drive this road 1.8 miles to the sharp right bend at the mine's ore bin, then 0.45 mile to a junction. Turn right and go 100 yards to the wilderness sign on the south side. The narrow path at the sign is the Beveridge Ridge Trail. This is a rough road. Drive as far as you can and walk from there.

Beveridge can also be reached a little more easily from the crest of the Inyos by hiking down from the Burgess Mine on the Beveridge Trail. Refer to *The Swansea-Cerro Gordo Road* for a trail description.

History

The town of Beveridge was settled in 1878, shortly after the Beveridge Mining District was organized. Both were named after John Beveridge, a prominent pioneer who was among the first to discover gold in the area. Over the next twenty-some years, around 35 mines were intermittently operated in the district. Most of them had some silver, and a few of them a little lead, but the main commodity was gold. However, of the dozens of mine workings developed in Beveridge Canyon, few produced more than an occasional sack of ore. The three richest mines—the Beveridge, the Horseshoe, and the Beveridge Canyon No. 12—had an estimated production of only a few hundred ounces of gold each. All other figures were under, and typically well under, 50 ounces. Altogether, no more than 1,000 ounces of gold came out of this canyon, less than 4% of the Keynot Mine's production in the next canyon north. But Beveridge had plenty of another precious commodity—clean flowing water—that was heavily used to mill the ore of the more fortunate mines. One of Beveridge's earliest mills was Cove Spring arrastre. Built in the 1870s, this primitive 10-foot-diameter structure could crush up to about one ton of ore in a day. In 1880, a man named Laskey erected a more advanced mill down the creek, with five stamps, a steam engine, and 10 times the arrastre's output. Until it closed down in 1907, it treated about 4,100 tons of hand-sorted ore from the Keynot Mine and recovered 24,000 ounces of gold. As the main community in an empty range, Beveridge served as the local social center. It remained occupied until the late 1900s. By then the high-grade pockets had been exhausted and most mines had closed down. A few remained sporadically active until the 1930s, with little to show. Beveridge's greatest wealth was, after all, not gold but water.

Route Description

The Beveridge Ridge Trail. Prepare yourself for a memorable workout. To get to Beveridge, you will have to gain 3,700 feet of elevation in 3.2 miles, then drop 1,500 feet in a little over a mile. This is the same elevation change as Yosemite's notorious grind to Half Dome, except here the distance is less than one third and the trail, abandoned since the 1910s, is slippery and elusive. Along the first mile the slope averages 30%. It is hard to believe we come here for fun. There is ample consolation in the scenery. The trail commands dramatic views of Saline Valley, from the salt-crusted lake to the volcanic dregs of the Saline Range, and across the dunes to the Last Chance Range. The clouds' crisp shadows slowly drifting across trace the valley's soft undulations, adding scale and perspective to this raw landscape.

The first relief is where the trail crests the narrow ridge that divides Beveridge and Keynot canyons. The next 1.3 miles are up along this ridge and not quite as steep. On both sides the land plummets into the two canyons' majestic gorges, and the valley opens up as if you were flying over it. The Silver Ridge No. 2 Mine provides a welcome excuse for a break. Chunks of galena, tetrahedrite, and argentite still adorn its 45-foot adit—as well as a six-cylinder Rolls-Royce radial engine. Another mile or so and 1,600 feet up, and the trail finally reaches close to its highest point at a small pine-shaded campsite.

The Beveridge Ridge Trail angles southwest off the ridge and cuts a roughly level path across the canyon's north slope. In 0.25 mile it veers west at a ridge and splits near shallow prospects. The left fork ends in 100 yards at a tilted stone platform. From there it is possible to drop to the east end of Beveridge (see map), but it is a grueling 1,400-foot drop. The main benefit is that it avoids bushwhacking through Beveridge twice. The trail is almost leisurely in comparison. It picks up just west of the junction—look for it carefully. It contours west-southwest, skirts the No. 49 Mine, then the No. 50 Mine, identifiable by its stone ruin and tall tailings spilling below it. In 0.7 mile the trail angles briefly south down a broad ridge, wiggles southwest into a side canyon, crosses it, and climbs a little to the No. 12 Mine. It is then only 0.6 mile to Laskey's mill. Either way, the descent into Beveridge is an intense experience. You struggle across an immense gorge, catching glimpses of the canyon's emerald spring way down below, acutely aware that you are approaching the rarest of the rare—a lost world.

Beveridge Canyon No. 12 Mine. This is the first major mining operation you will come across before reaching the creek. Its tramway is one of Beveridge's most conspicuous structures. At the two uppermost tunnels, the 5-foot stone masonry once supported a water tank, now betrayed by scattered hoops, pipes, tensioning devices, and water valves. The ore bin below it is the tramway's upper terminal. With its ore buckets and large steel wheel, more than enough of it is left to work out which cable was stationary and which one moved, and how the buckets were clamped onto it. The four tunnels, the longest 180 feet, are spread over a 150-yard bench. The ore vein, crystal-bearing quartz up to three feet thick stained with malachite, chalcopyrite, and gold, is still widely exposed at some adits. From the highest tunnel the trail switchbacks down 0.6 mile to the creek, swinging by the four tramway towers, frail contraptions anchored on crude stone platforms.

Laskey's mill. Better than any other site, Laskey's mill captures the essence of Beveridge—the place that time forgot. This valuable facility was probably the town's greatest pride, and today it remains its greatest treasure. The original five stamps are still in place, as are the imposing wheel, cams, and rods that transmitted power to them from the single-piston engine lying in the weeds. The cast-iron boiler and its

Laskey's mill

wood-burning furnace have changed little since they were last fired up. The steel vessel where steam pressure was built up seems to be waiting for the next run. It is a rare treat to visualize the mill in full swing—steam whistling, vapor clouds, the deafening clatter of metal crushing rocks. It boggles the mind to think of how this heavy machinery was brought all the way here on anything wider than a mule trail!

Two wooden cabins with rusted roofs are decaying in the creek below. The inviting open camp above the mill has a picnic table and a panoply of recent utensils. The outhouse just down canyon is a riot. Accessed by a narrow board, it was erected *over* a drop-off. This gut-wrenching location must have facilitated the evacuation of human wastes in more ways than one.

Beveridge. The old town does not give out its secrets easily. Spread along a one-mile stretch of narrow, hopelessly overgrown wash from which the historic trail has been largely erased, it can only be visited by painful bushwhacking from site to site through the jungle. What makes progress particularly tedious is the ubiquitous thickets of thorny wildrose. You get poked by branches, scratched by grasses, and showered by clouds of seeds from disturbed cattails. You constantly struggle for balance on the springy mats of decaying plants that cover the creek, occasionally sinking calf deep into muddy swamps. Covering half a mile in an hour would be heroic.

The payoffs for this hard work are phenomenal. This riparian corridor is a restful oasis livened by the mumbles of Beveridge Creek. I saw many more orchids here than in Costa Rica. Prince's plume, columbine, and watercress crowd the understory. The sweet fragrance of crushed mint drifts through the air. Steller's jays, Clark's nutcrackers, doves, and wrens share this slice of eden. At dusk, bats come out to perform their aerial ballets. You may see a fat frog lumbering

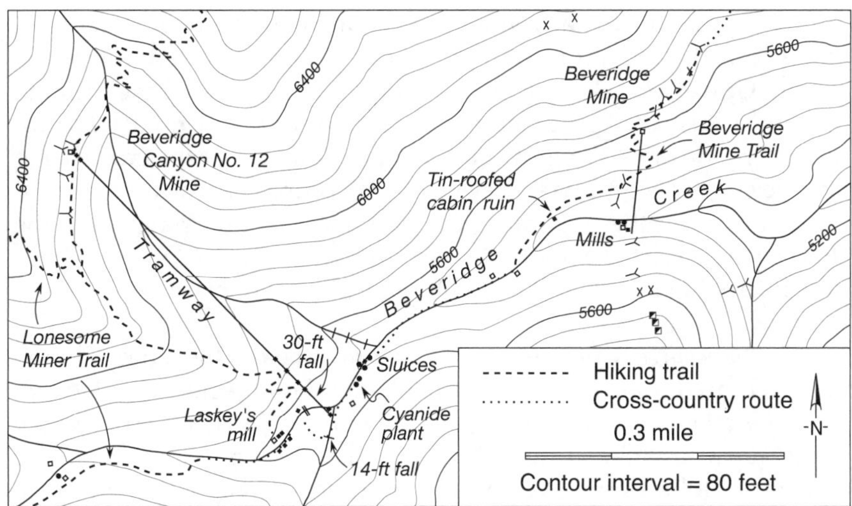

through the shadows, unaware that such large creatures as humans existed. The willows growing in the creek were seedlings when the town was booming. Now they are stately elders 20 inches across, their roots entangled with the ruins, their foliage guarding from the outside world the dreams of men who toiled here over a century ago.

The canyon starts with a bang: just below Laskey's mill the creek tumbles over a 30-foot waterfall. The easiest bypass is via the side canyon on the south side. Clamber up the steep gully southeast of the mill, over a low ridge and down the far side into the side canyon. This will put you at the head of a 14-foot fall that can be down-climbed fairly easily. The canyon is a short distance down.

The first site you will come across is the lower tramway terminal and mill of the No. 12 Mine, at the mouth of the side canyon. The large one-of-a-kind terminal is wedged in a recess against a low granite cliff. Hauling lumber to Beveridge was so costly that the terminal was constructed mostly with raw pine. It is a rickety assemblage of split platforms, ladders, and wheels that still supports the four cables and a couple of buckets. The ore was crushed in the equally unique one-stamp mill just below the terminal—its grinder lies nearby in the shrubs.

The next main ruins are the two huge wooden vats of a cyanide plant, set right in the creek. The vats were filled with a cyanide solution and crushed ore, and long stirring rods mixed them together to extract the gold. The vats still contain the last batch of ore they processed. Enough remains—stirrers, pinion-and-rack gear, belts, pipes, and valves—to reconstruct how the plant functioned.

Fifty yards down canyon are the remains of an elaborate sluicing operation. It used three slanted wooden sluices raised above the stream. Gravel was shoveled into a sluice, and water running through the sluice flushed the lighter gravel while the denser gold was captured behind riffles along the bottom. The flow rate of the creek being insufficient, a clever recycling system was set up. Water was piped into the sluices from the two tanks just up the creek. The water from the sluices was collected into a third tank below them and pumped back into the uphill tanks. Most of the plumbing is still in place.

The Beveridge Mine. A quarter of a mile below the sluices, in the vicinity of two stone ruins, a providential trail on the north bank offers welcome relief from the thorns and fallen trees. This is the Beveridge Mine Trail you will end up on if you dropped cross-country from the junction. It follows the edge of the spring to a stone cabin, once protected by a sparkling tin-roof. Used from 1975 to 1992 by miners carrying out assessment work, it was a touching museum until it burned around 2015. Fifty yards down canyon, at a graveyard of rusted parts, beat a path across the creek to the Beveridge Mine's mill. It gathers a few generations of equipment and ranks among Beveridge's most interesting. The main structures are the cableway's ore bin and two Huntington Mills. Never widely used, these ingenious mills are now nearly extinct. Each mill is a vertical cylinder four feet across with three mullers hanging inside it. When rotated, the mullers were pressed outward and crushed the ore caught between them and the cylinder's wall. The ore bin's sophisticated power feeder, which was

Beveridge

	Dist.(mi)	Elev.(ft)
Trailhead (Snow Flake M. Rd)	0.0	3,180
Beveridge Ridge	1.0	5,010
Silver Ridge No. 2 Mine	1.15	5,200
Trail leaves ridge	2.3	~6,770
Fork	2.55	~6,730
Cabin ruin (cross-country)	(0.8)	5,330
Bev. Cyn No. 12 Mine Tramway	3.8	6,190
Laskey's mill	4.3	5,600
Cabin ruin	4.7	5,330
Beveridge Mine mill	4.8	5,310

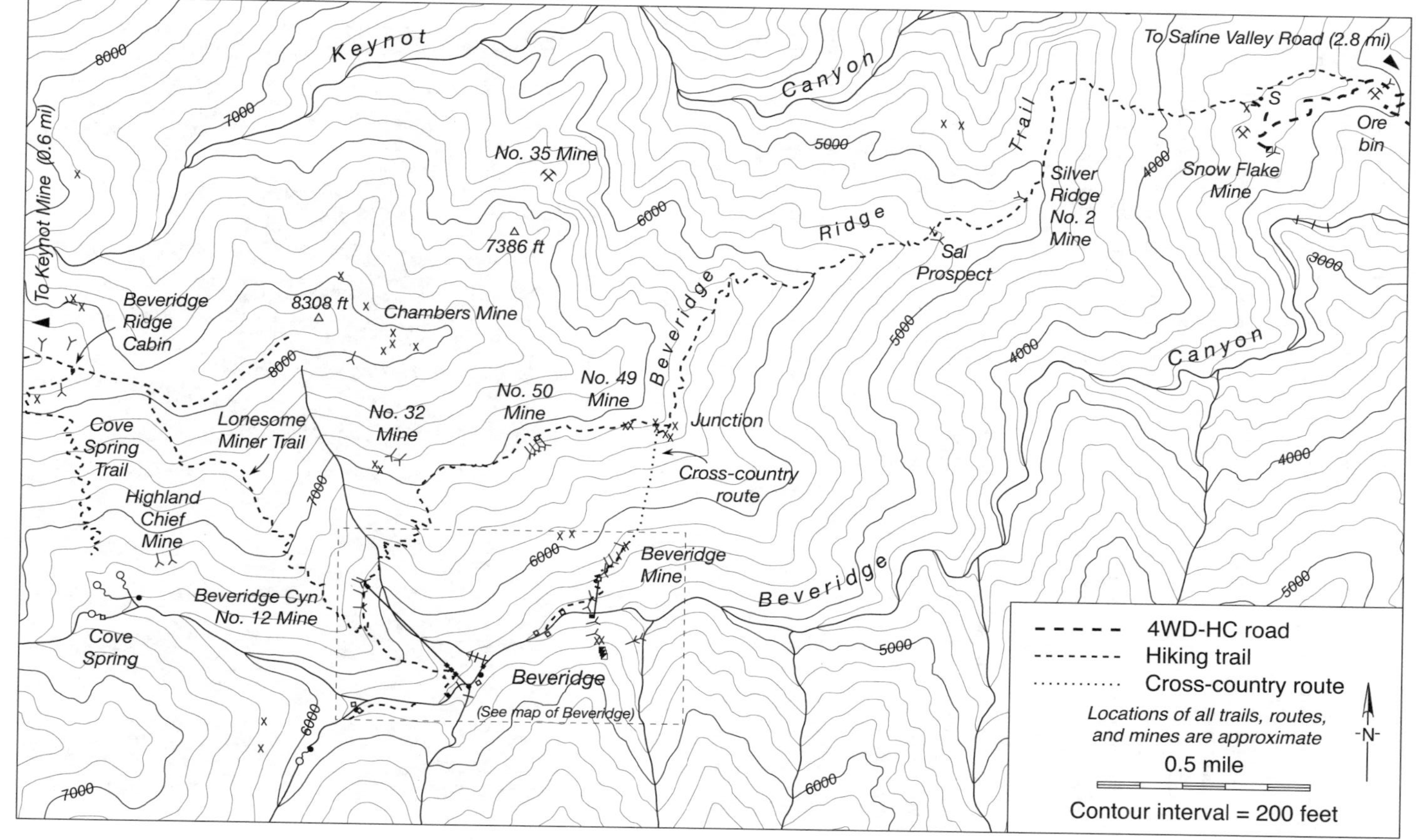

Keynot Canyon
To Saline Valley Road (2.8 mi)
To Keynot Mine (0.6 mi)
No. 35 Mine
7386 ft
Ridge
Trail
Silver Ridge No. 2 Mine
Snow Flake Mine
Ore bin
S
Sal Prospect
Beveridge Ridge Cabin
8308 ft
Chambers Mine
Beveridge
Canyon
No. 49 Mine
No. 50 Mine
No. 32 Mine
Junction
Lonesome Miner Trail
Cove Spring Trail
Cross-country route
Highland Chief Mine
Beveridge Mine
Beveridge Cyn No. 12 Mine
Beveridge
Cove Spring
Beveridge
(See map of Beveridge)
8000
7000
6000
5000
4000
3000
4WD-HC road
Hiking trail
Cross-country route
Locations of all trails, routes, and mines are approximate
-N-
0.5 mile
Contour interval = 200 feet

Huntington Mills at the Beveridge Mine

used to regulate the mill's ore intake, is a mechanical gem. Below are the entrenched stone walls of an earlier mill and large cyanide vats.

From the burned cabin, the trail climbs northeast 0.3 mile, past the mine's downed cableway, to the Beveridge Mine. An ore car is parked outside the first tunnel. Above it, a level rail grade connects three tunnels to a loading chute. Together with the gaping tunnel by the creek and workings on the opposite slope, they produced the most gold (300 ounces) and silver (1,000 ounces) in this canyon. In some galleries the quartz veins are exceptionally thick and as white as driven snow. Entire walls are covered with sparkling crystal facets, flushed with blue-green malachite, golden iron ore, and gray specks of silver ore.

Logistics

Beveridge can be reached in one long day, but making it in two days is more reasonable, especially if you cannot drive to the Snow Flake Mine. Beveridge Creek is *probably* perennial, but it is safest to carry enough water to make it back alive should you find the creek dry. Several mills along the creek still contain cyanide, so the creek is possibly poisoned. Since filters do not take out cyanide, try to pump water only upstream from the highest cyanide mill. Keep water in your car. Bring a trekking pole for the steep downhills. Long pants and sleeves also come in handy to negotiate the ferocious roses.

■

HUNTER CANYON

Hunter Canyon is a rugged gorge filled with waterfalls and lush riparian vegetation. Spiced with many climbing challenges and difficult hiking, it offers some of the best canyoneering in the Inyo Mountains. This a perfect place for well-trained hikers and seasoned rock climbers with a taste for treasure hunts à la Indiana Jones.

General Information

Jurisdiction: Inyo Mountains Wilderness (BLM)
Road status: Roadless; access via short primitive road
50-ft waterfall: 1.9 mi, 1,530 ft up, 20 ft down one way / diff. (climbing)
125-ft fall via upper cyn: 8.7 mi, 4,940 ft up, 3,510 ft down one way / diff.
Main attractions: Spectacular narrow canyon, waterfalls, rock climbing
USGS 7.5' topo maps: Craig Canyon*, New York Butte
Maps: pp. 273*, 217, 231

Location and Access

Hunter Canyon drains the eastern Inyo Mountains roughly west of Saline Valley's Salt Lake. The directions are the same as for Little Hunter Canyon.

Route Description

Considering that Hunter Canyon and Craig Canyon are only a couple of miles apart, the difference between them is amazing. They are equally deep and narrow, but in its lower reaches Hunter Canyon has flowing water, and plenty of it. The rocky wash becomes a musical creek, bone-dry falls are transformed into misty waterfalls, and sparse bushes are supplanted by green spring vegetation. This rare union of water and desert, flirting in the confines of an awesome gorge, has created one of the mightiest places in a mighty range. Most of the time you will be walking near water, splashing through flooded mats of maidenhair fern, following banks blanketed with willows, mesquite trees, honeysweet, Mojave thistle, and a mind-boggling profusion of stream orchis. The rocky canyon walls that rise vertically above this luxuriant microcosm constantly force your eyes upward.

Hunter Canyon starts right away as an impressively tight gorge. Just inside there is a primitive trail, and walking is easy for a while. But in spaces so steep and wet, such luxury is short-lived. The real problem is not bushwhacking or crossing the creek—although there is some of that too—but the waterfalls a short distance in. They may well stop you altogether. The first one is bypassed by the trail, but the second one, about 40 feet high, is more trouble. The only way to stay dry is to climb up the natural steps in the diorite wall to the right of it. It is an easy climb (low 5s), but it is also 18 feet high and some hikers will find it too risky. The third waterfall is much worse. I once went around it along the lopsided cornice that swings high up the vertical wall on the south side. It is also an easy technical climb (about 5.4), but it crests 60 feet above the creek and definitely gets a high mark on the scare meter! I would not have attempted it without climbing shoes. Fortunately, there is an easier route, just to the right of the waterfall, where the rotted skeleton of a useless ladder points the way. You will need to hoist yourself up to the narrow dirt bench to the right of it, then climb *in* the waterfall, using the holes in the wall as steps.

This hike is slow, wet, muddy, and rich in adrenaline, yet I cannot over-emphasize how wonderful it is. The creek, the high walls, the lush oases, and the waterfalls compose a magical and ever-changing scenery unexpected in the desert. The first waterfall glides through a gently sloped garden of tall bunch grass. The imposing walls that loom all around it display colorful patchworks of cream-colored limestone and dark-gray diorite. The second waterfall tumbles vertically against a bare rock face and splatters into a shallow pool. The third one disperses itself through thick draperies of maidenhair fern. There are narrows just above it, a tightly convoluted corridor of stone filled with algae, fern, and watercress. The creek gurgles through it along shallow troughs scooped in naked bedrock, breaks into small cascades, and gathers in dark pools of perpetually cool water.

Hunter Canyon	Dist.(mi)	Elev.(ft)
Hunter Canyon Road	0.0	1,290
Mouth of Hunter Canyon	0.7	1,600
30-ft waterfall (#1)	0.85	1,780
40-ft waterfall (#3)	0.95	1,920
50-ft waterfall (#5)	1.8	~2,810
50-ft waterfall (#6)	1.85	~2,880
35-ft waterfall (#7)	1.95	~3,020
125-ft waterfall (#8)	2.1	~3,200
Roble Canyon	4.15	4,880
Bighorn Spring (Hunter's mill)	4.5	5,090

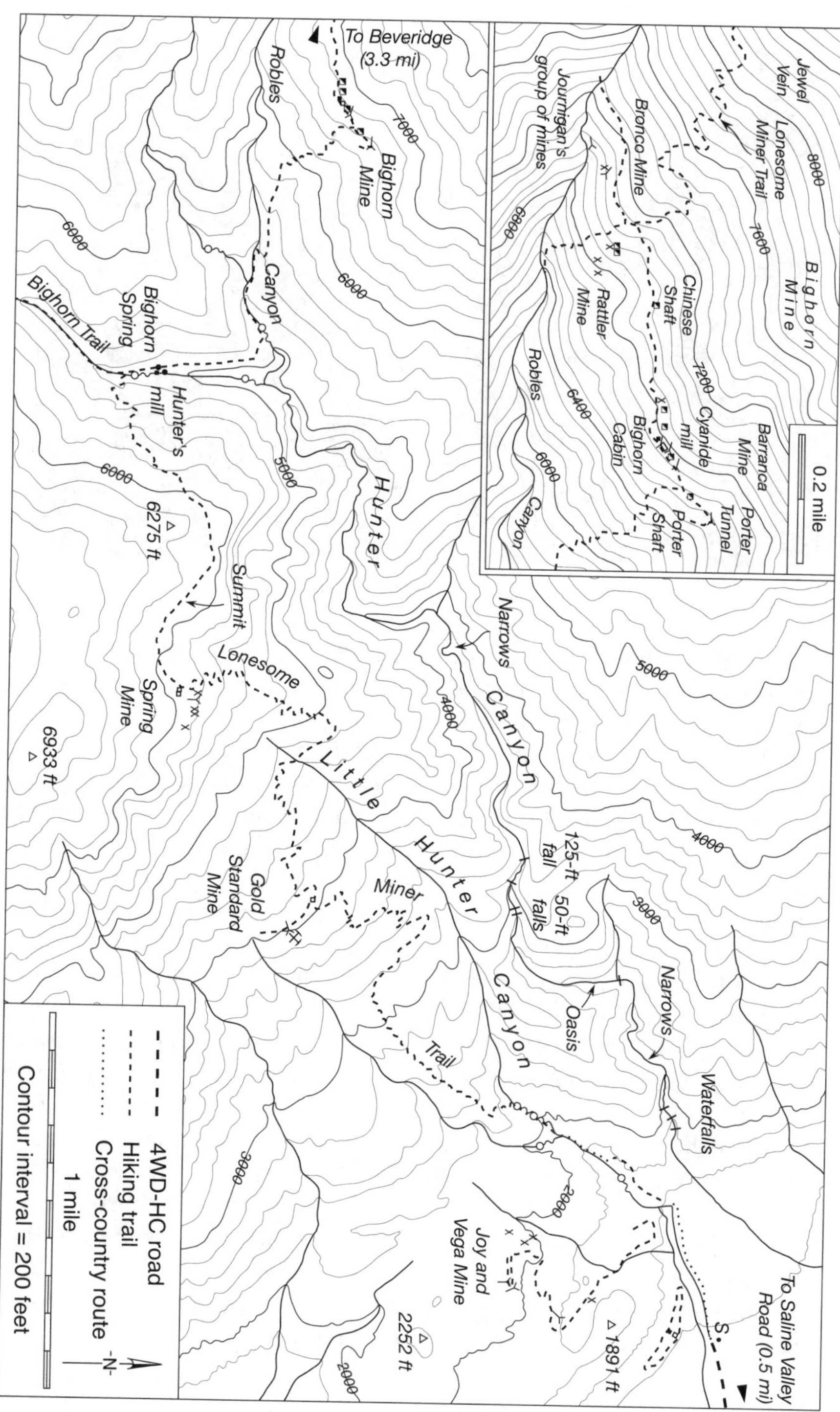
To Beveridge (3.3 mi)
Robles
Bighorn Mine
7000
Canyon
6000
Bighorn Spring
Bighorn Trail
Hunter's mill
5000
Hunter
6275 ft
Summit
Lonesome
Spring Mine
6933 ft
Narrows
Canyon
4000
Little Hunter Canyon
125-ft fall
50-ft falls
Gold Standard Mine
Miner
Trail
3000
Oasis
Narrows
Waterfalls
2000
Joy and Vega Mine
2252 ft
1891 ft
To Saline Valley Road (0.5 mi)
S.
Jewel Vein
Lonesome Miner Trail
8000
7600
Bighorn Mine
Journigan's group of mines
Bronco Mine
6800
Chinese Shaft
Rattler Mine
7200
Cyanide mill
Barranca Mine
Porter Tunnel
Porter Shaft
Bighorn Cabin
6400
Robles
6000
Canyon
0.2 mile
4WD-HC road
Hiking trail
Cross-country route
1 mile
N
Contour interval = 200 feet

Hunter Canyon above Bighorn Spring

Further on the canyon opens up a little. You will pass by two solitary cottonwoods, then climb another fall at the first side canyon to reach a long oasis of willows. Here walking gets tricky again. You will need to cross the creek, to bushwhack through thickets of wildrose and willow shoots, and to clamber over taluses so enormous that they fill up most of the canyon floor and crowd the stream. A few feet away, dark dikes of diorite run up and down the sheer walls. At the crisp edges of the dikes, the walls' original limestone has been metamorphosed into white marble. The true treasure here is to be immersed in these two opposed yet closely intertwined landscapes, one a lush wash animated by a stream, the other a waterless desert. In a short walk you can absorb the essence of both of them.

The next two waterfalls are back-to-back and about 50 feet high each. Going around the first one is not too difficult, but the second is the hard limit. Not far above it there are two more high falls that require technical climbing, the last one a 125-foot waterfall! The only way to see the upper canyon is to start from the top. You will likely need to take three days to first work your way up to Bighorn Spring (see *The Bighorn Mine*), then hike down canyon, and either return the same way—or rappel down the falls. It is an adventure, along a continuous ribbon of irrigated vegetation cascading down a tortuous gorge, and spiced by beautiful narrows trapped between polished walls.

■

THE BIGHORN MINE

The Lonesome Miner Trail, an assemblage of old mining tracks that traverses the eastern Inyos from the edge of Saline Valley to the crest of the mountains, is one of the steepest and most spectacular trails in the entire California desert. Sample it either a short distance for magnificent views of the valley, to its mid-point to visit well-watered Bighorn Spring in upper Hunter Canyon, or try to meet the physical challenge of climbing all the way to the remains of the historic Bighorn Mine. From Saline Valley it is 7.8 miles and 7,800 feet of total elevation change. It would be comparable to hiking the South Kaibab Trail and back in a day, if the trail had not been used in a century and if the Grand Canyon was 50% deeper. Most likely, you will have this formidable place to yourself.

General Information
Jurisdiction: Inyo Mountains Wilderness (BLM)
Road status: Roadless; primitive road to trailhead
Gold Standard Mine: 3.2 mi, 2,830 ft up, 120 ft down one way / difficult
Hunter's mill: 6.3 mi, 4,900 ft up, 1,180 ft down one way / strenuous
Bighorn Mine: 7.8 mi, 6,620 ft up, 1,210 ft down one way / grueling
The attractions: Spectacular trails, gold mine, springs, high country
USGS 7.5' topo maps: Craig Canyon*, New York Butte
Maps: pp. 273*, 231

Location and Access

The Bighorn Mine is in the upper drainage of Hunter Canyon, around an elevation of 6,700 feet. It can be reached from Saline Valley on the Lonesome Miner Trail. From Saline Valley this trail climbs to the rim of upper Hunter Canyon, drops into this canyon to Bighorn Spring, then climbs to the Bighorn Mine. To get to the trailhead, refer to *Little Hunter Canyon* and follow directions to the canyon mouth.

History: The Fortunes of William Lyle Hunter

The gold deposits of the Bighorn Mine, high on the eastern slopes of the Inyo Mountains, were discovered by William Lyle Hunter in 1877. Hunter was a miner and explorer, and a great achiever. Born in Virginia in 1842, he came to the Saline Valley region in the late 1860s. In the heyday of Cerro Gordo, he made a small fortune driving pack mules for the town, before gaining fame by making strike after strike.

In July 1875 he and a friend, John Porter, were first to enter the Ubehebe region and discover valuable copper deposits. Two years later, he and John Beveridge discovered the rich silver outcrops east of Cerro Gordo that became the Belmont Mine. Soon after the discovery of the Bighorn lode, he was instrumental in the creation of the Beveridge Mining District, for which he acted as chairman. In 1885 and 1886 he served as clerk, recorder, and auditor for Inyo County. In his fifties he was still working the Ulida Mine, up in the Ubehebe district. In recognition of his pioneering contributions to the region, a whole mountain was named after him—Hunter Mountain, at the south end of the Last Chance Range, where he built a log cabin and kept a small ranch for his stock while he was out mining. Hunter's name survives today on many other geographical features, more than any other old timer—including rugged Hunter Canyon, where his mine was located.

The Bighorn Mine quickly turned out to be one of the district's richest. Late in 1877, Hunter erected three arrastres at nearby Bighorn Spring to grind and amalgamate his ore. The gold was packed by burro up canyon on the Bighorn Trail to the crest, then down the west side of the Inyos on the trail in Long John Canyon, before it was trucked to Owenyo and shipped to smelters in Salt Lake City. Hunter worked his mine until 1893, reportedly recovering $8,000 to $10,000 in gold. By 1900 he was living with his family at George's Creek, south of Independence, where he died in 1902.

After Hunter's era, the property was exploited episodically by small crews under various owners until at least the 1930s. Over the years, its three quartz veins were probed by two dozen tunnels, shafts, and bench cuts. All told, they produced around 4,000 tons of ore containing an estimated 1,600 ounces of gold and 9,600 ounces of silver, worth about $40,000. The deposit was not depleted, but what was left was not rich enough for viable mining in such a remote setting.

Route Description

The Lonesome Miner Trail. From the mouth of Little Hunter Canyon, the Lonesome Miner Trail ascends the ridge on the canyon's south rim 4.6 miles to a high point, then drops a mile to Bighorn Spring in Hunter Canyon. Besides the steepness of the terrain, the main problem is the high probability of losing the trail very early on. In Little Hunter Canyon the trail first bypasses the spring on the right. It vanishes briefly in the canyon wash, up to short, shallow narrows. At this point (elev. 1,900') the canyon forks. Little Hunter Canyon goes straight, while the trail veers south into a side canyon, crosses its wash, and forks. This is the first tricky part. The better-defined trail that

Hunter Canyon's central gorge from the Lonesome Miner Trail

continues along the wash goes to the Joy and Vega Mine. The trail you want is the one on the right, which is very easy to miss. Look for it climbing the steep, dusty hillside in the left canyon bend, 10 yards past the end of the narrows. After a few minutes the trail drops back into Little Hunter Canyon, squeezes between a short wall and a mesquite thicket, then disappears in the rocky wash. Continue 50 yards to a second mesquite thicket. The second tricky part is here: the trail resumes just past it, in a steep breach in the south wall.

Although mostly rocky and not exactly in its prime, from here almost all the way to the summit the trail is easier to follow. Occasional cairns and BLM posts help. But it is steep—a 4,000-feet ascent in 4 miles—and slow-going. The switchbacks are so numerous they will make your head swim, and the slope so steep that at the few places where the grade eases up you will think you are going downhill.

The rewards certainly match the hard work. The views from the trail, centered on the chemical sink of Salt Lake, are Saline Valley's replica of Dante's View. As you gain elevation the lake slowly expands, revealing its eastern shore, twisted like a fractal, fringed with shades of pink, until it eventually clears the foot of the range and begins to shrink with distance. At the summit you will be standing on the brink of a phenomenal sink, almost a mile above a pristine valley cocooned between cinnamon ranges. Few views in the desert are as riveting.

The Gold Standard Mine. About halfway to the summit the trail goes right through the ruins of this mine's tiny camp, three wooden tent platforms on a narrow stone wall. Three bedsprings and a stove, dark with rust, still rest incongruously on the warped floor boards. Nearby there is a small metal box securely shut by tight clasps, a Pandora's box fun to root through—in spite of its "explosives" label!

From the camp a trail heads left (south) 150 yards to the Gold Standard Mine. The workings, dominated by a deep open cut, are reached by a short scramble below the trail. They include 500 feet of tunnels, two benches, and several small pits and open cuts. The tunnels intercept a small vein system of drusy quartz dusted with limonite, pyrite, galena, and tetrahedrite. The Gold Standard Mine did produce some gold, at least 600 ounces. In spite of its name, it turned out to be one of the district's largest producers of silver (upward of 12,000 ounces), and just about the only one that produced copper, though only a shy 4,000 pounds.

Bighorn Spring. From the camp, the Lonesome Miner Trail wiggles up 2.2 miles to its highest point. A little before this summit it passes by the ruins of two stone shelters, east of the trail on a wide sloping meadow. They were likely associated with the nearby Spring Mine, a small operation that produced a mere 100 ounces of gold. Past the ruins the trail is fainter, but it continues, west and up, along the rim of Hunter Canyon. The summit is marked by a stone cairn and another Pandora's box. Beyond it, the trail is still vague. Just head northwest, down about 100 feet into a broad ravine coming down from the left. The trail resumes on its far side, climbs to a slightly lower high point, then drops into Hunter Canyon. The descent is awe-inspiring. In 0.6

The Bighorn Mine

	Dist.(mi)	Elev.(ft)
Hunter Canyon Road	0.0	1,290
Little Hunter Canyon (mouth)	0.7	1,580
Gold Standard Mine camp	3.1	4,060
Gold Standard Mine	(0.1)	~4,000
Spring Mine camp	4.9	5,960
Highest point	5.3	6,100
Bighorn Spring/Hunter's mill	6.3	5,070
Robles Canyon (leave wash)	7.0	5,360
Bighorn Mine (Bighorn Cabin)	7.8	~6,680

Hunter's mill at Bighorn Spring

mile the trail dives 930 feet into a gorge so narrow and abrupt that the bottom remains concealed much of the way. Across the gorge, the opposite canyon wall rises like a colossal fortress. Down canyon, the gorge sinks into hidden depths; up canyon it squeezes through two facing prongs of massive monzonite. Beyond, through the tight V of the canyon walls, soars the hulking mass of New York Butte, its sheer face scintillating with virgin snow in the colder months. This extreme setting strains our understanding, as if it was the brainchild not of nature but of some exalted illustrator who brushed aside the laws of gravity to create this improbable landscape.

The trail bottoms out at the wash of Hunter Canyon, at the head of Bighorn Spring—a thick belt of healthy trees strung along the wash, hiding in its womb a singing brook of cold bubbling water. Hunter's

1877 mill, betrayed from some distance up the trail by its looming smokestack, is just across the wash. Its venerable age is a moving tribute to a great man. Its furnace and steam engine are ancient mastodons of rusted steel, branded with defunct labels, hooked to cogged shafts that have been silent for a century. The engine powered three arrastres, the nearby circular pits rimmed with polished stones. As much as 12 feet in diameter, they could grind five tons of ore in a single day. Invaded by brambles, partly dismantled, these primitive mills are still embossed with the grooves gouged by the drag stones as they moved around and around, squeezing gold from stone.

The Bighorn Mine. From the mill the Lonesome Miner Trail heads down Hunter Canyon along a road cut in the west slope. It soon veers left into Robles Canyon, descends into it, and disappears in its wash at the head of a spring. Except for short segments, the rest of the trail to the mine is very faint to not existent. Hike up the wash 0.3 mile, then scramble up to the top of the bench on the north side (0.1 mile). Then follow the steepening bench west 0.3 mile to the approximate location of the old trail to the Bighorn Mine. At this point the mine is betrayed by three tall pale tailings spilling down the slopes 50 feet up. The last 0.3-mile stretch, up the extremely steep and rubbly canyon slope, is by far the most strenuous on this trek.

The main workings are clustered at the top of the central tailing. They consist of three collared shafts and three tunnels, some of them connected underground. The tailings and tunnels are stained with the colorful ores that drew miners this far into the wilderness—copper, pyrite, hematite, and silver-bearing galena. A ruined trail wanders across the slope past the remains of a pipeline, a dismantled cyanide mill, and the Bighorn Cabin. Stabilized by BLM volunteers, the 1930s cabin is furnished with a cast-iron stove and a couple of bedsprings. From this central area the trail descends 200 steep feet east past the Porter Shaft to the Porter Tunnel, which were part of the Barranca Mine. Going the other way, the Lonesome Miner Trail, fainter still where it has not been obliterated by rock slides, climbs west to smaller mines, and then continues north to the ghost town of Beveridge.

When pressed by the fierce solitude of this rugged wilderness, one can only feel admiration for William Hunter, who over 100 years ago was able to pinpoint a mineral deposit of value in this implacable land, to build a trail to it, and exploit it, all in one lifetime. The remote mine he left us, lost at the thin edge of timberline on terrain so steep that it seems to hang onto thin air, will stay in your memory for a long time.

■

CRAIG CANYON

Blessed with a plethora of awe-inspiring scenery, pretty falls, impressive high walls, and exceptionally deep and tight narrows, Craig Canyon is one of the most awesome canyons in the Inyo Mountains. For a change the lower canyon has no running water or bramble to make hiking a nuisance, most of the falls are easy to climb, and the two that are not can be bypassed. Seemingly lost on the far edge of reality, it epitomizes on an epic scale everything that is secret and hauntingly beautiful about this extraordinary range.

General Information

Jurisdiction: Inyo Mountains Wilderness (BLM)
Road status: Roadless; access via short primitive road
First fall: 1.2 mi, 1,210 ft up, 0 ft down one way / easy–moderate
Third fall: 2.3 mi, 2,110 ft up, 20 ft down one way / moderate (climbing)
Main attractions: Spectacular canyon, falls, rock climbing, narrows
USGS 7.5′ topo maps: Craig Canyon
Maps: pp. 283*, 221, *231*

Location and Access

To get to Craig Canyon, drive the Saline Valley Road to the Salt Tramway Road, just south of Salt Lake where the tramway towers to the north are perfectly aligned. Drive it south 0.4 mile to a faint junction. Keep right on the Big Silver Mine Road. Park 1.1 miles further, at the wide turnout just below the dugout of the Big Silver Mine. This road is a little rocky but not steep. With care, a standard-clearance vehicle can make it without scraping off vital organs. The mouth of Craig Canyon is 0.1 mile up the steep rocky wash to the northwest.

Route Description

The lower gorge. Steep, deep, and fall-ridden are the best qualifiers for lower Craig Canyon. Almost right away, and for several miles, it is a stupendous gorge deeply entrenched between very steep rock walls up to 2,000 feet high. On a clear November day, I spent a whole day here and only saw the sun twice. I felt dwarfed by immense sweeps of stone that never seemed to end.

For a welcome change, this is one of the few canyons in the Inyo Mountains that is dry in its lower portion. It has not been dry for very long: some falls are still festooned with shreds of travertine leftover from recent waterfalls. But for the time being, hiking is not impeded by rushing water and obnoxious thickets. This is still not exactly a walk in the park, mostly because of the slope, which averages a healthy 23%, and the inordinate number of obstructions. To get to the narrows 2 miles in, you will have to go over nine falls and many boulder jams, and in between, the wash is often one huge boulder field. At places, you gain 20, 50, 100 feet of elevation at a crack. Only two of the falls are impassable. The first one, about 45 feet high, is a pretty polished chimney in black shale. A two-ton boulder is precariously balanced part way up its deep recess. The second one is a dark vertical slot tucked at the end of a narrow passageway, crowned 40 feet up by a huge overhanging chockstone. The first fall is bypassed by a trail on the south side. To get around the second one, you will need to climb a steep rock talus on the south side to a level cornice 35 feet above the wash, then follow it past the fall. The cornice is wide, except for one

The second impassable fall in lower Craig Canyon

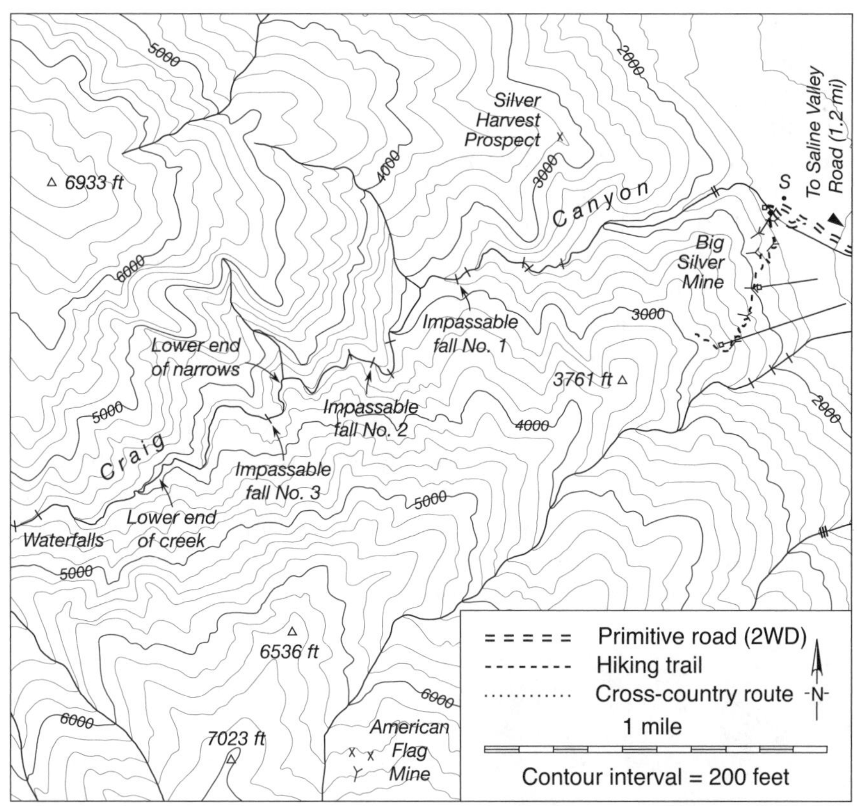

Craig Canyon		
	Dist.(mi)	Elev.(ft)
Big Silver Mine Road (end)	0.0	1,520
Mouth	0.15	1,620
First impassable fall	1.2	2,730
Second impassable fall	1.7	3,200
Central narrows (start)	2.1	3,510
Third impassable fall	2.25	3,610

short, narrow tightening on the brink of a sheer drop that leaves little room for error. The other falls are climbable, with varying degrees of difficulty. Fortunately, the harder falls can also be bypassed with a little scrambling, so non-climbers can have a go at it too.

The scenery is exceptional. The lower canyon is a phenomenal outdoor geology exhibit featuring a wealth of kaleidoscopic formations.

Naked canyon slopes hundreds of feet tall display giant panels of brightly colored Paleozoic rocks, neatly stratified or bizarrely contorted, highlighted by white veins and faults. Fluid taluses of loose rocks tumble down from the far-away rims, so steep that they seem suspended in mid-air. Twisted narrows alternate with bright open areas, polished walls of charcoal slate with shiny white-marble chutes, limestone slickrock with chaotic fields of granitic boulders, darkness with light. High between the canyon rims, swifts swim endless aerial ballets, piercing the silence with their joyous calls. This is a perfect desert experience, both visual and physical, hard-edged and soft, endlessly changing yet never repeated.

The narrows. At the end of all of this is the central narrows, a corridor that ranks among the deepest, tightest, and windiest in the Inyo Mountains. Water has sculpted the rocks in every direction, forward and upward, creating an underworld of slots, hanging alcoves, dark undercuts, and sharp buttresses, much of it polished to a slick finish. The diaphanous light that filters down from the narrow wedge of sky overhead is a silent intimation to respect. As you wander in awe along this subterranean gallery, you brush by cold curves of limestone, bulges of beaded conglomerate, and colorful mosaics, not knowing what lies 50 feet ahead.

Craig Canyon's central narrows

The magic is interrupted all too soon by the third impassable fall, a deep, 45-foot grotto piled high with chockstones. A more formidable challenge, it marks the end of the trail for most hikers. A bypass might be possible on the south side just below the largest undercut, but it would take a lot of exposed scrambling. Above, the narrows continue for three breathtaking miles of twisted, claustrophobic spaces, most of it packed with spring vegetation and flooded by a perennial creek. Like the handful of diehards who have ever laid eyes on it, to see it you will likely have to hike down from the crest and rappel down, fall after waterfall.

■

THE SALT TRAMWAY

Saline Valley's Salt Tramway is one of the wonders of California mining history. Built in 1912–1913 to deliver salt to Owens Valley, it climbs 7,700 feet in 13.5 miles clear across the Inyo Mountains. To discover the well-preserved towers of this breathtaking monument, hike the spectacular Salt Tramway Trail either up from the valley floor or down from the crest. Few trails in the desert are so compelling. This one will entice you to go on, constantly lured by the next tower in sight and superb views of Saline Valley.

General Information

Jurisdiction: DVNP (NPS), Inyo Mountains Wilderness (BLM)
Road status: Hiking on old miner's trail; primitive access road (2WD)
Lower control tower: 3.9 mi, 2,590 ft up, 20 ft down one way / difficult
Tower No. 9: 5.4 mi, 3,810 ft up, 90 ft down one way / strenuous
Upper control tower: 2.3 mi, 200 ft up, 2,830 ft down one way / strenuous
Main attractions: Mountain trail along a monumental historic tramway
USGS 7.5' topo maps: Craig Canyon, Cerro Gordo Peak
Maps: pp. 289*, 231

Location and Access

To reach the Salt Tramway, drive the Saline Valley Road to just south of Salt Lake. About a mile east of the Inyo Mountains, look for the tramway towers on the valley floor north of the road. The road you will be crossing when the towers are perfectly aligned is the Salt Tramway Road. It parallels the valley portion of the tramway from the lakeshore north of the road to the foot of the Inyo Mountains south of the road. To inspect the small lakeshore towers, drive or walk the Salt Tramway Road north 0.6 mile. To get to the Salt Tramway Trail, drive it south instead 0.4 mile to a junction with a faint road on the left, which is the Salt Tramway Road. This road is in a wilderness area and closed to motor vehicles. Park at this junction and hike from there.

History: Smith's Grand Dream

Of the entire Death Valley region, Saline Valley witnessed what was one of the grandest and most unusual mining ventures. Unlike most, it was not concerned with precious metals but with a dirt-cheap commodity known as halite—table salt. The main driving force behind it was White Smith, an attorney who first came to Saline Valley to work as a teamster for the borax mines. Smith became fascinated by the vast halite deposits surrounding the lake. Discovered as early as 1864, they were worked superficially in 1903 and 1904, but full-blown exploitation did not start until around 1911, when Smith organized the Saline Valley Salt Company. Although a rough road already connected the valley to Big Pine, the company decided to contract for the construction of a 13.5-mile aerial tramway across the Inyos. It would climb 7,700 feet to a control station at the 8,740-foot crest, then drop 5,100 feet to a railroad terminal in Owens Valley. Crossing one of the highest, steepest, and roughest ranges in the California desert, the tramway was a tremendous engineering challenge. Powered by electric motors, it called for 21 rail structures and about 100 towers, including four control towers and 12 anchorage-tension stations. The project consumed 1.3 million board-feet of lumber, 650 tons of nuts and bolts, and 54 miles of cable. When completed in 1913, it was the steepest tramway in the country, and it still is one of the largest of its kind today.

In July 1913 the first salt was delivered at Tramway, the discharge terminal by Owens Lake. The salt was mined using a system of dikes to flood selected areas of the salt playa with local fresh water. Upon evaporation, the salt was loaded into special half-ton capacity buggies with foot-wide steel wheels that were winched back to shore, where wooden cars transported the ore to the terminal. The salt was loaded into one of 286 buckets, which were hauled at a rate of about one bucket per minute. By the end of 1913, 5,000 tons of salt had been delivered.

For two years, however, the grips that clamped the buckets onto the cable slipped when the buckets were more than two thirds full, and the tramway had to be operated at partial capacity. In spite of a steady delivery of salt, the company ran into financial trouble. It was forced to lease its salt claims and tramway to the Owens Valley Salt Company, and split its profits evenly. By 1916, the grip problem was fixed and the tramway was running at full capacity. Mining employed 40 men, the mill at Tramway was handling 25 to 30 tons a day, and for a few years a steady stream of salt came out of Saline Valley. The resale value of salt being what it is, profits were still insufficient to reimburse the enormous cost of the tramway. In 1920 the company that had erected the tramway repossessed it, and the two salt companies went under.

Smith did not give up. While salt mining stood idle, he convinced the county to construct a road to Owens Valley via San Lucas Canyon. The road took two years to complete. In May 1926 the salt fields, then owned by Smith and a partner, George Russell, were reactivated under the newly formed Sierra Salt Company. Trucks hauled 10-ton loads of salt over the new road to the railroad at Tramway. Smith died in 1927

The first control tower of the Salt Tramway, looking down into Saline Valley

and never saw his tramway come back to life. But it did the following year, when Sierra Salt acquired it and revamped it. By December 1928, it was delivering 60 to 100 tons every day. It did so until prices plummeted in the Depression and production stopped around 1933. Against all odds, Smith's dream had come true: in its 12 years of operation, his tramway successfully hauled 30,000 tons of salt out of Saline Valley.

Route Description

The lower tramway. Even if you are not up to tackling the Salt Tramway Trail, try the easy valley portion of the Salt Tramway Road. It passes by 10 towers, concrete foundations, and power poles, in various states of disrepair. The last one, at the end of the road, is the largest on the valley floor. Although it collapsed into a tangle of lumber and steel, its sheer bulk gives a good idea of the tramway's proportion.

At the end of the road you are standing on the edge of the wide wash of Daisy Canyon. The tramway's next five towers are clearly visible, perched hundreds of feet up the steep flank of the mountains to the south. To get to them, walk 100 feet south of the last tower, where a short trail drops into the wash. Cut across the rocky wash towards the small ravine just east of Daisy Canyon's mouth. You will cross the six downed tramway cables, then the wires of the power line that parallels the tramway. Buckets are scattered around. At the ravine's entrance, look for a narrow trail climbing its east slope. Yes, this vague, foot-wide, dusty track is the Salt Tramway Trail, the sole access used to build, operate, and maintain this colossal masterpiece.

I cannot possibly overemphasize how exceptional this trail is. As it wanders from tower to tower, it draws a giant stitchery across the face of the mountain, conquering 3,100 feet in less than 4 miles. The views of Saline Valley are magnificent, growing more dramatic with elevation. It is hard work, and it begins right here.

The trail first switchbacks 700 feet to a low saddle, across a narrow plateau, then up Daisy Canyon's rim to the first tower. Misshapen and partly collapsed, this anchorage-tension station resembles a giant crystal poised on the edge of a precipice. The next two structures are small towers identical to those by Salt Lake. The fourth tower is also an anchorage-tension station, in far better shape. The buckets passed through two side-by-side rectangular openings that run the length of the tower. There were not one but two tramway lines, one going up and one going down. The two fat cables above each opening, one for each direction, were stationary. The buckets were suspended on them with twin pulleys and attached to the smaller cables, which moved them up or down the tramway. The main role of this station was to modify the cables' pitch, which at this point steepens sharply.

The next structure is the lower control tower, by far the most impressive. About 270 feet long by 25–30 feet tall and wide, it is an immense wooden trestle. Anchored on a steep ledge 1,800 feet above the valley, it is a stunning piece of architecture for both its fluid design and impossible setting. It was designed to change the direction of the cables along the gradual bend in its middle section. Thanks to its enormous foundations, it is still in excellent shape. It is fun to decipher its enigmatic arrangements of pulleys, wheels, cables, chains, and buckets. There is a small room underneath it, the ruins of a small camp nearby, and the transformers that converted the power-line voltage.

The trail resumes on the uphill side of the control station. It climbs south in short switchbacks to a mid-sized tower, then to the seventh tower, impressively balanced on the narrow rim of a deep side canyon of Daisy Canyon. While some towers are anchored to the ground with thick cables as protection against the strong wind, this one is weighed down by wooden boxes six feet on the side loaded with rocks and secured to the tower ceiling with chains four inches across.

Along the next 1.5 air miles, the tramway crosses Daisy Canyon's gorge in four vertiginous spans. The terrain and the scenery change drastically. Your attention is constantly drawn to this awesome trench, so deep that most of its bottom is hidden from view. The trail perseveres across the first span. It climbs south in a straight line to the side

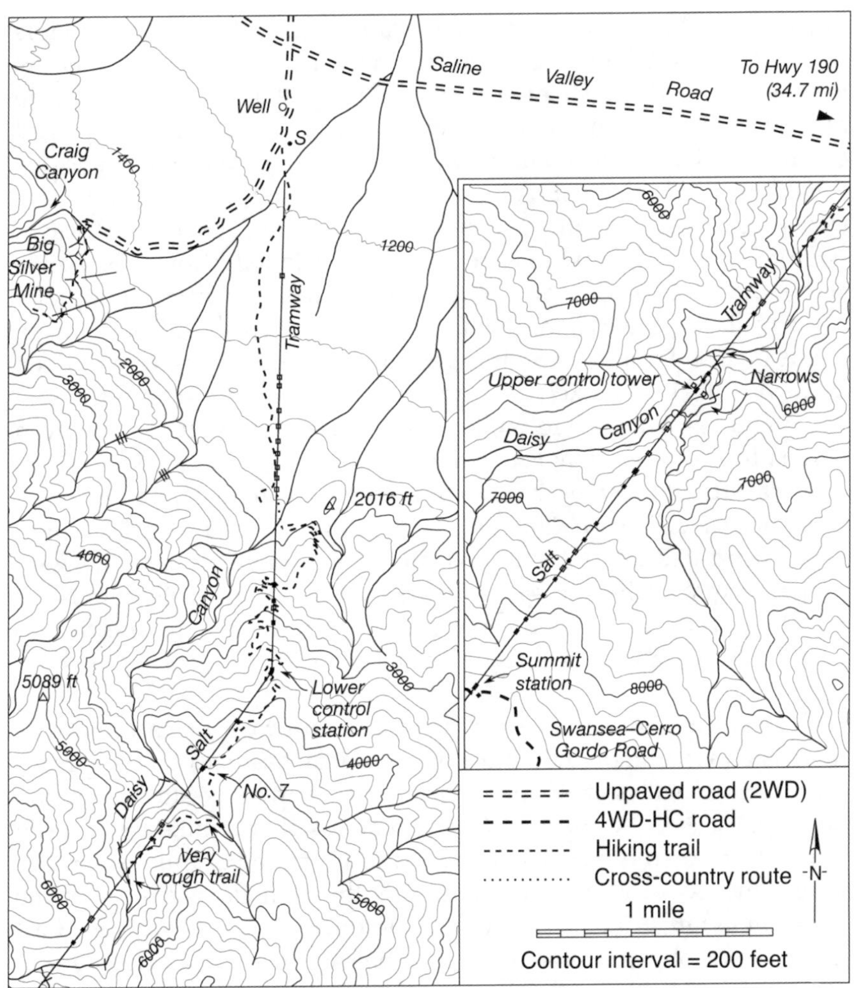

The Salt Tramway		
	Dist.(mi)	Elev.(ft)
Salt Tramway Road (junction)	0.0	1,147
Salt Tramway Trail	1.85	1,900
Tower No. 1	2.7	2,640
Lower control station (No. 5)	3.9	3,720
Tower No. 7	4.7	4,610
End of trail in Daisy Canyon	5.7	4,810
Upper control station (No. 15)	6.9	6,100
Summit station (road on crest)	9.2	8,720

canyon, vanishes at the wash, then resumes on the far side, where it is betrayed by a retaining wall. The next stretch is quite a bit rougher. As it circles around the sheer edge of the ridge that separates the side canyon from the main canyon, it winds down, then up between jagged outcrops and across steep narrow ravines. In 0.3 mile it passes above a small tower hidden behind an outcrop. The ninth tower is 0.1 mile further, precariously hanging on the canyon's edge. Timberline is near—large pinyon pine grow just up the slope. The tenth tower is visible across the next span, balanced hundreds of feet higher at the top of a sheer wall. The cables hang 450 feet down to the wash, still supporting a lone bucket. From here on it is very rough terrain going uphill. Even hard-core hikers will likely turn around at the ninth tower, or sooner.

If you still want to go on, it is best to stay on the trail, now even fainter, to avoid two major falls in the canyon. Go 200 yards, up then down a little, to a steep rocky couloir, and switchback down to the wash of Daisy Canyon. Up canyon there are a few falls up to a tight left U bend (0.7 mile), then exquisitely claustrophobic narrows with perpendicular walls and several slick slides, not all easily climbable traveling up canyon. If you can make it, the reward is the spectacular upper control station at the top of the narrows (0.4 mile).

The upper tramway. To see the upper tramway, you can continue: there is only one more fall. But it is an ordeal, best tackled by spreading it over two days. It is much easier to drive up to the summit station on the crest (see *The Swansea-Cerro Gordo Road*), and hike down from there. Aim for the next tramway station visible 0.3 mile down the rolling meadow to the east. The trail is the path cleared through the dense pine forest for the tramway. The downed cables are your best guide as you slip and slide on steep rubble of dusty slabs. There are 13 towers down to the rim of Daisy Canyon, including four imposing anchorage-tension stations. At the last tower, drop left into the canyon wash. In 300 feet there is a wide 25-foot fall overlooking a small willow spring, then 600 feet further, up on the west slope, the huge upper control station. It is an amazing tunnel of lumber filled with hanging rails and pulleys, giant cogs, rusted tools, valves and flywheels. A salt bucket is still suspended on the cable. It also has its own camp and bank of transformers. The camp's discarded household items—cast-ion stoves, pans and enamel pots—recount the daily life of the man who lived in this harsh environment to operate this remote section of the tramway. Together with the narrows just below it, it makes for an exciting destination for a rough outing in the high Inyo Mountains.

■

CERRO GORDO

Perched at the top of the Inyo Mountains and reached by spectacular mountain roads, Cerro Gordo was California's leading silver-lead producer for about a decade following the Civil War. Today, the privately owned ghost town offers a rare opportunity to experience an authentic mining town of the Far West, and perhaps to stay overnight in one of its restored historic buildings "re-used" as a bed and breakfast inn. With the owners' permission, explore the local mining structures, tramways, and smelters, or climb one of the surrounding peaks for breathtaking views of Owens Valley.

General Information
Jurisdiction: Private property ((760) 876-5030)
Road status: Hiking on roads; long primitive road (4WD when wet)
Cerro Gordo walkabout: ~0.5 mi, ~200 ft up loop/very easy
Cerro Gordo Peak: 1.2 mi, 1,060 ft up, 20 ft down/easy
Main attractions: Rich silver mines, high country, grand panoramas
USGS 7.5' topo map: Cerro Gordo Peak
Maps: pp. 297*, 231

Location and Access

Cerro Gordo is near the crest of the southern Inyo Mountains, at an elevation of ~8,140 feet. The easiest access is from Owens Valley. Drive Highway 136 to Keeler, 12.6 miles southeast of Lone Pine. The Cerro Gordo Road is signed at the historical marker 0.35 mile east of town. Built in 1868 and known for years as the Yellow Grade, it is one of the most spectacular roads in the region. In 7.7 miles it ascends 4,500 feet to Cerro Gordo, on a course so crooked that miners used to say one had to be drunk to drive it. It first squeezes through a scenic canyon with rust-stained walls, twisted narrows, and knob-covered slopes. Higher up, it swings across steep slopes sprinkled with Joshua trees, with sweeping vistas of Owens Lake and the Sierras. This road is graded. It has long grades, but I once saw a little old lady with a tiny poodle in her lap make it all the way to the top in a compact car.

Cerro Gordo can also be accessed from the Saline Valley Road. From Highway 190, drive this road 8.2 miles to the Y junction at Lee Flat. Make a left on the Lee Flat Road. Continue 7.0 miles to a junction at a sharp right bend. Stay right with the main road and go 4.6 miles down San Lucas Canyon, then angles sharply left out of the wash. The remaining 4.9 miles wind up a forested canyon to the crest and down a little to Cerro Gordo. This road traverses untrammeled country and is much wilder. It requires a four-wheel-drive, high-clearance vehicle.

The third route is the Swansea-Cerro Gordo Road. Refer to *The Swansea-Cerro Gordo Road* for details. From November through May, all access roads may be impassable due to snow.

History

In a land of illusions that lured and disappointed generations of miners, Cerro Gordo is one of the very few mines that were rich, and of these it was by far the richest. The original silver-lead discovery at Cerro Gordo—"fat hill" in Spanish—was made in 1865 by Pablo Flores and his Mexican companions. In these post-Civil War years, mineral exploration was high on the national agenda. The rave reports from the prospectors quickly attracted investors. Such was the magnitude of the strike that in spite of its remoteness, the site was fully productive by 1869. A year later, large shipments of silver were made regularly, and the town of Cerro Gordo was thriving. When the Cerro Gordo Mining District was formed in 1872, it already had 11 active mines.

The richest ore was silver-bearing galena and uncommon lead minerals like caledonite, linarite, and leadhillite. Gold was also an important by-product. Most deposits were near-surface high-grade pockets that were worked from open pits and tunnels. Three of the original claimed areas quickly turned out to be the richest. The Union Mine was the most important one. It was owned by Mortimer W. Belshaw, a mining engineer from San Francisco, and French Canadian Victor Beaudry, who became key figures in the history of Cerro Gordo. The two other main mines were the Santa Maria and the San Felipe, controlled by the Owens Lake Silver Mining and Smelting Company.

Concentration of the ore by on-site smelting, essential to turn a profit, was a major part of Cerro Gordo's activities. The Owens Lake company had its smelter at Swansea, on the lakeshore. The Union Mine initially roasted its hand-sorted ore in primitive on-site furnaces that wasted much of the silver. By 1871, the situation had been greatly improved with the installation of two efficient on-site refineries, the Belshaw-Judson and the Beaudry smelters. The large quantities of charcoal that they required were prepared from local pine.

The silver-lead bullion from the smelters was cast into 80- to 90-pound ingots and freighted to markets by mule teams. Renowned freighter Remi Nadeau landed the first contract in 1868. For three years his wagons hauled Cerro Gordo's huge production on the Bullion Trail, down Owens Valley and across southern California to San Pedro.

From there the ore was steamed up the coast to the Selby smelter on the San Francisco Bay. Everything was going well until the contract was up for renewal in December 1871. Nadeau refused to reduce his rates, and a new freighter was hired. James Brady, superintendent of the Swansea smelter, built and launched two steamers, the *Bessie Brady* and the *Molly Stevens*, to ferry the bars across Owens Lake to Cartago. Although it saved three days on the trail, the new freighter was unable to keep up. By May 1873, 30,000 silver bars had been stockpiled at Swansea and Cartago, which employees used to erect temporary shelters! In June, Beaudry and Belshaw contacted Nadeau and promptly accepted his terms. They joined him in forming a new freighting company and put up $150,000 to buy new mules and wagons and build stations along the Bullion Trail. By October, Nadeau's fleet had grown to 80 teams of 14 to 22 mules that pulled three huge high-sided wagons. In the summer of 1874, they had caught up with the surplus and were keeping pace with production, which had doubled to 400 bars a day. In the following years, as the railroad was gradually extended to Bakersfield, then Mojave, the Bullion Trail kept getting shorter.

Cerro Gordo's boom attracted many other businesses. To meet the town's growing need for timber and fuel, a sawmill and a flume were built in nearby Cottonwood Canyon. Cerro Gordo also suffered from a severe water shortage. Early on, 100 burros were used to haul 6,000 gallons of water from Keeler every day, which was barely sufficient. In 1874, a new company took up the challenge and erected an 11.5-mile pipeline from Miller Spring, which supplied 90,000 gallons per day.

In spite of hash conditions, until 1876 Cerro Gordo enjoyed seven years of prosperity, producing nearly $7 million. At its peak, it boasted around 4,700 souls—it was then larger than Los Angeles. For a time, Cerro Gordo accounted for about 15% of all trade out of LA, and it was the main supplier of the important Selby smelter. This financial influx contributed to much of the two towns' original growth.

The mines peaked in 1874. By then most of the ore bodies were showing signs of depletion. Production continued through 1876, but it kept on dropping. That year, after more than three years of encroachment litigation opposing the Union Mine and the Owens Lake companies, the two parties merged. A new shaft called Belshaw was sunk 900 feet to serve as main access to the existing tunnels and to see whether the rich Union vein continued downward. But it didn't. Another blow was the destruction of the Union Mine hoist by fire in August 1877. It spelled the shutdown of the Union furnaces in February 1878. The Beaudry smelter closed down shortly after. Production continued into the early 1880s, but the golden years were over.

Cerro Gordo, 1914-1915 (Courtesy of Eastern California Museum)

For the next 32 years, Cerro Gordo witnessed sporadic activity in the hands of small companies. Then it came back to life, twice. The first revival occurred in 1911, when Louis Gordon and associates began exploiting rich zinc deposits. In 1915 they installed a 5.5-mile Leschen tramway down to Keeler. Until 1919 Cerro Gordo was a major source of the highest grade zinc carbonate ore in the country. Cerro Gordo's third boom occurred in 1925 following an important ore body discovery. The Estelle Mines Corporation worked it from 1929 to 1933, extracting 265,000 ounces of silver and 860 ounces of gold.

This was Cerro Gordo's last significant historic activity. By then it had produced 4,840,000 ounces of silver, 37,000 tons of lead, and 12,000 tons of zinc. It was worth an estimated $17 million, more than ten times the production of Death Valley's richest historic mine.

Route Description

Cerro Gordo. Everything, it seems, has conspired to make Cerro Gordo the most unique ghost town in the California desert. What will get you first is its breathtaking setting. Nestled in a shallow bowl rimmed by towering peaks, it overlooks Owens Valley and its huge lake from nearly a mile up. Cerro Gordo's remoteness has protected it effectively against vandalism, and today it is still an extensive site. In 1984, when it was in shambles after close to a century of neglect, former actress Jody Stewart and Michael Patterson acquired the property

Cerro Gordo, overlooking Owens Lake and the Sierra Nevada (2001)

and pursued their vision of giving Cerro Gordo a second lease on life. They created a special place where you can touch and feel the old and the forgotten, in a peaceful and uncrowded setting. In spite of limited resources, with the help of a few dedicated volunteers they restored several of the main historic buildings. The heart of town was then the American Hotel, a two-story house with a spacious dining room and a fully functional kitchen with stoves, utensils, and appliances from a distant era. Upon your arrival you would have been welcomed then by Jody or Michael themselves, who were congenial hosts and great story tellers. After a long fight against cancer, Jody passed away in December 2001. Under a new ownership, for years the property continued to be tended by caretakers. In 2018, Cerro Gordo was purchased by Brent Underwood, a young entrepreneur from Austin, Texas, and his business partner Jon Bier. The new owners have plans to revive the town again and open it to tourism.

Cerro Gordo suffered a major loss on June 15, 2020, when the American Hotel went up in flames—it was its 149th birthday. It was one of the oldest hotels in California. The other buildings were fortunately spared. The building above the hotel site is the Gordon House. The one past it is the 1868 Belshaw House, the oldest house in town. The large tin building across the street is the restored hardware store, now a museum. The long building further out is the 1904 bunkhouse. The town is surrounded by more than a dozen buildings and mining structures, including an assay office, two-storied Hunter's cabin, and Lola Travis' House of Pleasure. The brick furnace and its tall chimney below the town are the ruins of the Beaudry smelter. The Belshaw–Judson smelter is just north of the pass above town. The historic cemetery is on the steep barren slope north of town. The graves, said to number around 500, are betrayed only by mounds, some of which contain the victims of Cerro Gordo's lawless days.

Staying overnight, if and when it is offered again, is the ultimate Cerro Gordo experience. A night in one of the bunkhouse's six bedrooms is the quietest experience—unless you sleep in the ghost room, that is. Each room is tastefully decorated with old-fashioned wallpaper, cozy quilts, oil lamps, curtains, paintings, and artifacts from the past that create a quaint atmosphere. In the Belshaw House you can warm up by a roaring fireplace (even in summer!), sleep in a heated four-poster bed, or cook dinner on a gas stove that was stylish when your great-great grandma was dating.

All of Cerro Gordo, including the mines, roads, and land, is private property. Whether you want to drive or hike on the property, *do not wander off anywhere without asking the caretaker for permission*. He may not grant it to you, but he can provide directions and road information. Guided tours may be offered again. It will likely include a visit of the museum, which overflows with Chinese vessels, blue bottles, minerals, tools, ore cars, historic photographs, and a mind-bending map of the 37 miles of tunnels that worm underneath the town.

The Belshaw Shaft. This major historic shaft stands on top of the huge tailing that overlooks the town. Walk up the main road (east) and take the last road on the right before the pass. It is impossible to miss it: the enormous tin building that covers the shaft is by far the largest historic building in the Death Valley region. Over 30 feet tall and 100 feet long, it houses three enormous pieces of equipment: the shaft ele-

Cerro Gordo		
	Dist.(mi)	Elev.(ft)
Cerro Gordo	0.0	8,145
to Buena Vista Peak	1.4	9,140
to Cerro Gordo Peak (hike)	1.2	9,188
to Keeler	7.7	3,640
to Saline Valley Rd at Lee Flat	16.5	5,249
to Salt Tramway	7.1	8,720

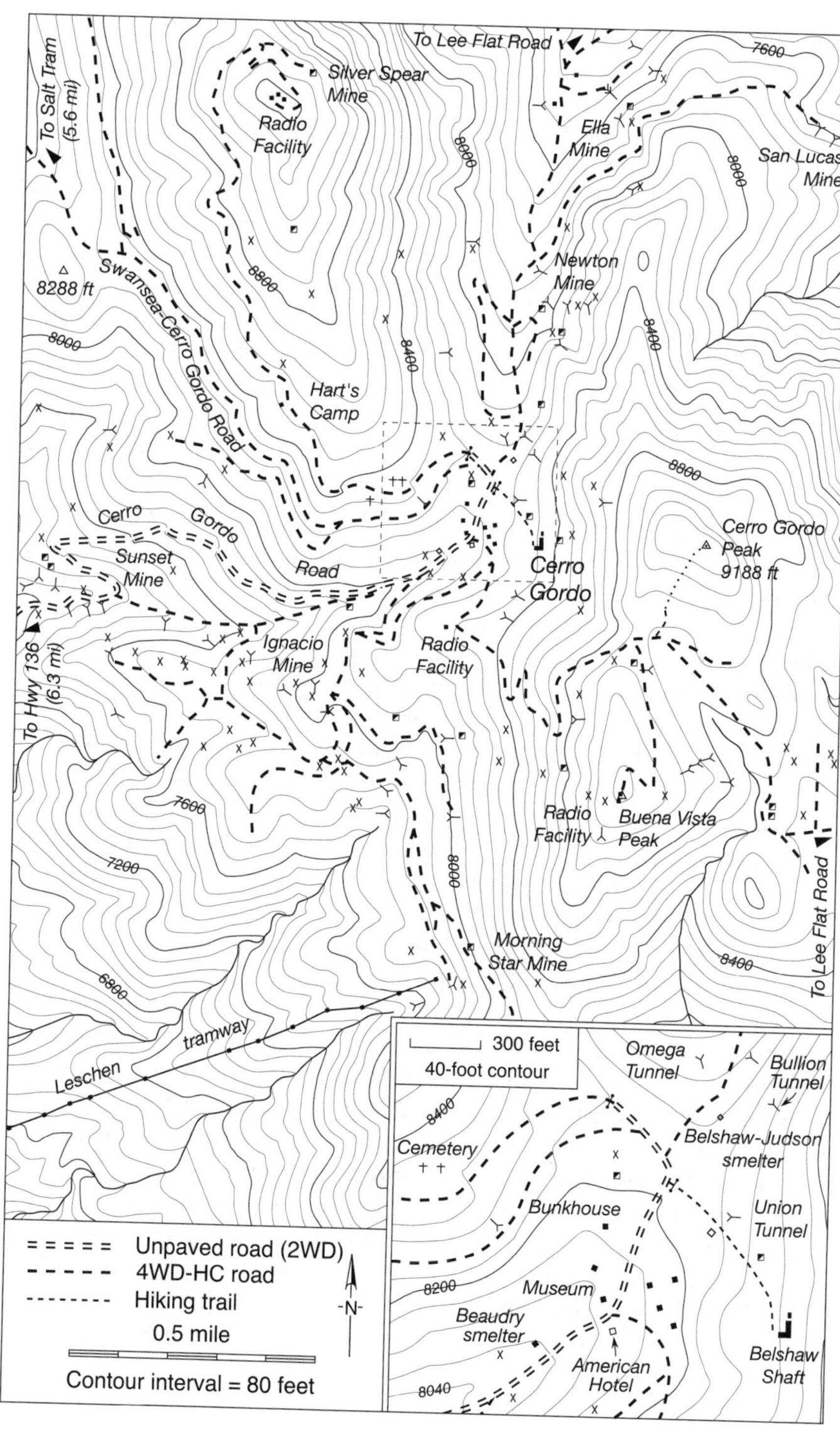
To Lee Flat Road
Silver Spear Mine
Radio Facility
To Salt Tram (5.6 mi)
Ella Mine
San Lucas Mine
8288 ft
Swansea-Cerro Gordo Road
Newton Mine
Hart's Camp
Cerro Gordo Road
Sunset Mine
Cerro Gordo
Cerro Gordo Peak 9188 ft
Ignacio Mine
Radio Facility
To Hwy 136 (6.3 mi)
Radio Facility
Buena Vista Peak
To Lee Flat Road
Morning Star Mine
Leschen tramway
300 feet
40-foot contour
Omega Tunnel
Bullion Tunnel
Cemetery
Belshaw-Judson smelter
Bunkhouse
Union Tunnel
Museum
Beaudry smelter
American Hotel
Belshaw Shaft
Unpaved road (2WD)
4WD-HC road
Hiking trail
0.5 mile
Contour interval = 80 feet
N

vator machinery, a monstrosity of a furnace, and the compressor that pumped air into the shaft. They all date from the 1870s and are remarkably well-preserved. The shaft is on the north side of the building, covered by the elevator cabin. It gave access to eight levels of tunnels and several sublevels, down to a depth of 900 feet. The adit on the building' east wall is the historic Zero Tunnel. In 1997, the owners installed a cistern at the shaft's 700-foot level to collect underground water—about 10 gallons per hour—for use in town. The elevator is still used for maintenance. The original electric motor that powered it, over 2 feet in diameter, was replaced by a modern hydraulic motor that still drives the outlandish original gear but is no bigger than a shoebox!

Cerro Gordo Peak. The massive summit laced with silvery limestone that broods over town is Cerro Gordo Peak. The one south of it is Buena Vista Peak. There is no trail to Cerro Gordo Peak, but if you can drive to the saddle between them, the rest of the way is easy.

From Cerro Gordo, make a right at the first fork above the American Hotel, and go 1 mile up to the saddle between the two peaks. Driving this dizzying bit of roadway is a thrill. Carved right into the precipitous face of Cerro Gordo Peak, it commands awesome views of Owens Valley. The steep grade—up to 25%—is negotiated with switchbacks so tight that larger vehicles have to resort to three-point turns! High clearance and four-wheel drive are a must. At the saddle the road on the right climbs south 0.4 mile to a radio facility at the top of Buena Vista Peak. The views are more limited but well worth checking out. To climb Cerro Gordo Peak, from the saddle walk 50 yards east down the other road to a track on the left. It climbs 125 yards north towards the peak and ends. The rest of the way is cross-country, 0.25 mile for a 240-foot elevation gain. If you can, follow the ridgeline, which seems to float right over Cerro Gordo.

The views from Cerro Gordo Peak left me absolutely stunned. As I crested the round summit, the vast tract of desert I had been exploring for several years to write this book jumped at me, from Sylvania Peak down to the Slate Range, and Waucoba Mountain to the Panamint Range. All three basins—Eureka, Saline, and Panamint—sprawled under the hot October sun, thousands of square miles of primeval land, mysterious even when fully exposed. If you are familiar with this region, the views will send your mind racing. Can you spot the Seven Sisters Springs? The White Cliffs Mine? The Racetrack beckoning from behind Ubehebe Peak? Turn around and you will be staring at the edge of the desert—the long serrated skyline of the Sierra Nevada.

■

THE SWANSEA–CERRO GORDO ROAD

If you like your four-wheel-drive roads uncompromisingly rough, this long one from Owens Valley to the 10,000-foot crest of the Inyo Mountains and the ghost town of Cerro Gordo is a must. The crest offers unequaled views of Owens Valley and the Range of Light, interesting historic sites, and secluded spots for summer camping in high-desert forests. The surrounding wilderness offers spectacular hikes to springs and little-known peaks. This road also gives access to the legendary trail to the remote ghost town of Beveridge.

General Information

Jurisdiction: Inyo Mountains Wilderness (BLM)
Road status: Long primitive road (4WD-HC)
Trapier Mine Trail: 0.8 mi, 130 ft up, 140 ft down one way / very easy
New York Butte: 1.1 mi, 890 ft up, 80 ft down one way / easy
Goat Springs: 3.3 mi, 1,010 ft up, 1,410 ft down one way / moder.–diff.
Beveridge: 7.0 mi, 1,010 ft up, 5,280 ft down, one way / strenuous
Main attractions: 4WD road, panoramic views, high country, mines
USGS 7.5' topo maps: Keeler, Cerro Gordo Peak*, Dolomite, Craig Canyon*, New York Butte*
Maps: pp. 297*, 303*, *231*

Location and Access

The Swansea-Cerro Gordo Road starts at the west end of Swansea, a one-block homestead marked by a few trees on Highway 136 9.6 miles east of Highway 395. It climbs to the top of the Inyos, then follows the crest southeast to Cerro Gordo, a distance of 24 miles. From there the Cerro Gordo Road drops 7.7 miles back to Highway 136 at Keeler, 3 miles southeast of Swansea. This loop requires a sturdy 4WD vehicle with very good clearance. Driving it clockwise, up from Swansea, is most challenging: many 4WD vehicles do not have enough power. Driving this loop the other way is still tough, but easier.

Route Description

The Swansea-Cerro Gordo Road. This road has character. Not far out of Cerro Gordo, it plunges 850 feet down the precipitous flank of the Inyos, then shoots straight 1,500 feet back up to the crest. Both grades are steep, rutted, and deeply scooped out by churning wheels. If your vehicle cannot make it up the grade, and you turn around and cannot drive back up the grade you just came down, you will be stranded at the low point... Knowing your vehicle's limitations and your own can save the day. There are also a few white-knuckle stretches where the narrow road cants dangerously toward the precipice.

At the top of this roller coaster, the road follows the more gentle crest and adrenaline drops back to reasonable levels. It passes by many side roads, then scoots under the cables of the Salt Tramway. At the junction 4.2 miles past the tramway, the road straight ahead goes to the Burgess Mine before ending at a great sheltered campsite (1.5 miles). The road on the left drops to Swansea. If you found the driving challenging so far, this descent will seem like a nightmare. In 12.7 miles the road loses 5,600 feet of elevation, first down a long forested ridge to a windy canyon, then along two drainages, and finally down a broad canyon. On the ridge, it is so steep and slippery with loose rocks that heavy vehicles will slip down even with the brakes on! The crossings between drainages are the worst, with gauged bedrocks, narrow passages, and steep grades right by unprotected drop-offs.

The payoffs are as exciting as the ride is wild. The Inyos' crest is a scenic woodland of pine and mountain mahogany. The views are spectacular, alternating between Owens Valley and the sharp peaks of the Sierra Nevada on one side, and the deep sink of Saline Valley on the other. The Swansea grade traverses dense pine forests, deep canyons, narrows, and scenic badlands near the bottom. There are excellent pine-shaded campsites down the ridge, and great vistas of Owens Lake at lower elevations. Several abandoned roads and trails along the grade, between 7,160 feet and ~6,100 feet, give foot access to several large,well-preserved, and seldom-visited towers of the Salt Tramway.

Except for the road to the Burgess Mine, *all of the twenty-some side roads between Cerro Gordo and Swansea are in the Inyo Mountains Wilderness and closed to motor vehicles*. The BLM posted a closure sign across each of them. The absence of signs does not mean that it is open.

The Salt Tramway. The most popular stop along the Swansea-Cerro Gordo Road is the Salt Tramway, which crosses the road 7.1 miles north of Cerro Gordo. The long arching structure east of the road is the summit station. The high point of this formidable 13.5-mile aerial tramway, it was designed to control the cables on both sides of the mountain. The station's massive beams, floors, and cable guides attest to the size of the operation. The large, six-room house across the road is the Tender Cabin, the refurbished residence of the station operator, which boasts an observation deck with a breathtaking view. Refer to *The Salt Tramway* for the incredible history of this enduring monument.

Salt Tramway's summit station from Swansea-Cerro Gordo Road

The Trapier Mine Trail. Historical maps show a foot trail dropping from the crest of the Inyos along a ridge south of Craig Canyon all the way down to Saline Valley. It was likely no more than a cross-country route to the very isolated Trapier Mine and American Flag Mine. The only portion of it still extant is its short upper end, and it is so scenic that it would be a shame to miss it. To get to it, from the Salt Tramway drive 2.7 miles north to a side road on the right, in a left bend (or 1.5 miles south of the junction to Swansea), and park.

The trail first heads down a shallow ravine, veers left up another ravine to the rim of Craig Canyon, then follows the rim to end at a wide overlook (0.8 mile). This is easy hiking: the ravines are seriously overgrown, but the rest of the road is clear and nearly level. The views down into Craig Canyon are awesome, encompassing its monumental upper valley and the imposing walls of its central gorge, and the lacy shores of Salt Lake, more than 8,000 feet below.

The Burgess Mine. This sprawling mine was a latecomer that somehow managed to hold out, with mixed fortunes, into the 1940s. It was a gold mine, with a side of silver, lead, zinc, and manganese. Unfortunately, this wealth was disseminated in swarms of dislocated quartz veins, and it took an army of workings to dig them up. In the 1910s, the Burgess Mine consisted of two shallow inclined tunnels. By

1920, they had been supplemented by a 160-foot shaft, a 700-foot cross-cut tunnel, and 2,000 feet of galleries. Today, the mine's 1.5 square miles are pockmarked with more than 100 workings. In its heyday, the property was reached by a wagon road from Swansea, and supplies were brought in by pack train over the Long John Canyon Trail. The ore, hand-sorted and milled in a small arrastre, assayed $20 to $40 per ton. Production figures are too scarce to tell whether it ever paid off.

Today, the mine's sole survivors are a narrow cabin and the crumbled rock walls of three shacks, propped on an airy saddle above timberline. The cabin is a curious mix of corrugated metal and pine boards, a stovepipe its only ornament. Visitors sometimes use it as a shelter, or to warm up by its smoky stove. Most of the workings are eminently uninteresting, but an ore bin, fun minerals, and a few other nuggets remain. The views alone certainly make the search worth it.

The Beveridge Trail. Built in the 1870s to access Beveridge and the gold mines in Beveridge Canyon, this trail was for years a major route between Saline and Owens valleys. To get to the trailhead, drive 0.8 mile past the Burgess Mine cabin and park below the saddle at road's end. Walk back down the road 150 yards and take the faint spur road on the right. In 200 yards it fades behind two large pines. The trail starts a few yards to the west. From there on you are in the Inyo

The Swansea-Cerro Gordo Road

	Dist.(mi)	Elev.(ft)
Swansea-Cerro Gordo Road		
Cerro Gordo	0.0	8,145
Salt Tramway crossing	7.1	8,720
Trapier Mine Trail	9.8	9,140
Junction to Swansea	11.3	9,220
Burgess Mine (cabin)	(0.75)	9,625
End of road	(1.5)	9,860
Swansea	23.9	3,645
Beveridge Trail (hike)		
End of road at saddle	0.0	9,860
New York Butte	1.1	10,668
Goat Springs	3.3	9,460
Frenchy's Cabin	5.9	6,360
Beveridge (Laskey's Mill)	7.0	5,590

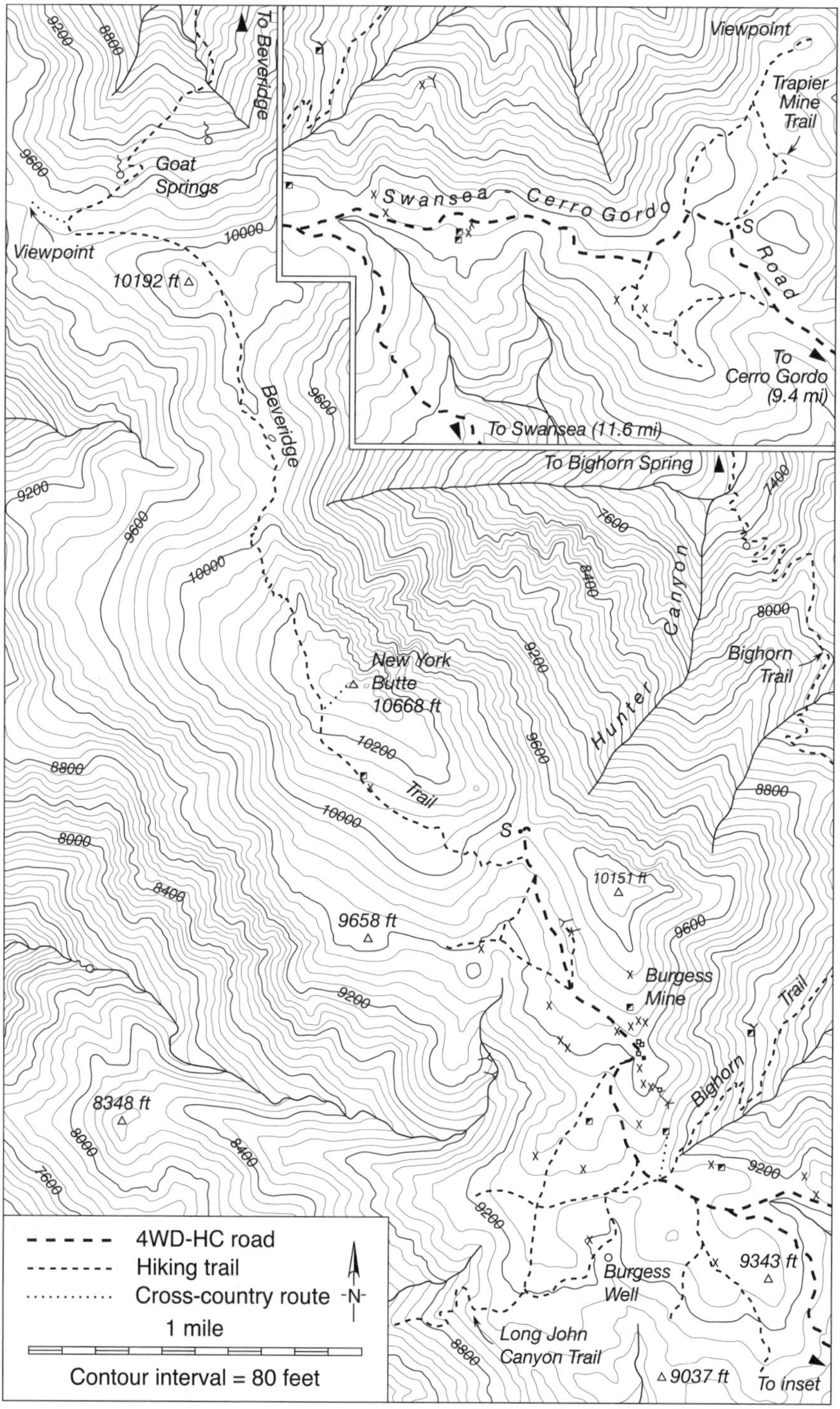

To Beveridge
Goat Springs
Viewpoint
10192 ft
Beveridge
Swansea - Cerro Gordo Road
S
Viewpoint
Trapier Mine Trail
To Cerro Gordo (9.4 mi)
To Swansea (11.6 mi)
To Bighorn Spring
Hunter Canyon
Bighorn Trail
New York Butte 10668 ft
Trail
S
10151 ft
9658 ft
Burgess Mine
Bighorn Trail
8348 ft
Burgess Well
9343 ft
Long John Canyon Trail
9037 ft
To inset
9200
8800
9600
10000
7600
8400
8000
10200
4WD-HC road
Hiking trail
Cross-country route
N
1 mile
Contour interval = 80 feet

Mountains Wilderness; do not expect a well-groomed park-grade trail, with neat signs, storm culverts, and strategically located outhouses. Time has taken its toll on the abandoned trail. A trained eye and a map are essential not to lose it and enjoy yourself.

The trail first winds up to a level area surrounded by granite boulders, then climbs more steadily to a pass on the shoulder of New York Butte. This stretch is highly scenic, overlooking various portions of Owens Valley and the Sierras. The trail bypasses New York Butte, so the final ascent to this summit is cross-country. Leave the trail about 500 feet before the pass and cut northeast toward the trees that cap the summit. The views are impressive. To the east, New York Butte plunges between sharp spires into the gaping void of Hunter Canyon. Saline Valley shimmers beyond, against the chocolate swells of the Last Chance Range. All of Owens Lake and the Coso Range are sprawled to the south, and 60 miles of the Sierras crest to the west.

The trail wanders on, close to the crest, steeply down to a first saddle, then up around a local peak, and finally down to just below the saddle at the head of Beveridge Canyon. This stretch is increasingly overgrown and easy to lose, especially on the uphills. This whole area is beautiful brush-covered meadows and rolling hills sprinkled with boulders, mahogany groves, and artfully gnarled bristlecone pines.

Goat Springs, the highest flowing spring in the Inyo Mountains, is just minutes down into upper Beveridge Canyon. Cool water bubbles out of a crack in a boulder and nurtures a green patch of bunch grass, tule, and columbine. It is a great spot to snack and rest while gazing down into the stately upper valley of Beveridge Canyon. If you are quiet, in due time chukars, Clark's nutcrackers, and hummingbirds might come flying by, survey the scene for predators, and dart into the spring for a quick sip.

For the long trip beyond Goat Springs to Beveridge (3.7 miles and 3,870 feet down), backpacking gear is a must. It is a true mountain experience, the trail reduced to a steep track barely distinguishable from natural gaps through the dense brush cover. It tumbles down a deep valley bursting with juniper and pinyon pine to the thick, brushy spring at the headwaters of Beveridge Creek. The first structure you will encounter is the two-room Frenchy's Cabin, just below the spring. Its rusted corrugated roof and chimney are still supported by sturdy walls of interlocked stones. Laskey's mill, the heart of Beveridge, is 1.1 miles down canyon, past a series of stone ruins. It is one of the hardest places to reach in the Mojave Desert, but if you are fit and prepared, you cannot afford to miss it (see *Beveridge*).

■

MALPAIS MESA

No matter how exciting you anticipate a desert climb will be, the desert will surprise you. A serene volcanic plateau sprinkled with Joshua trees, Malpais Mesa and its high point Rosa Peak deliver grand views of the Range of Light and the northern Mojave Desert, from Mount Inyo across Panamint Valley to Manly Peak and from Olancha Peak to Nevada. The most exciting sight is Owens Lake sprawling 4,000 feet below, its once-toxic chemical playa revived by recent conservation efforts into a vast desert wetland.

General Information
Jurisdiction: Malpais Mesa Wilderness (BLM)
Road status: Hiking on trail and cross-country; primitive access road
Santa Rosa Mine: ~0.7 mi, ~350 ft up loop / easy-moderate
Rosa Peak: 2.7 mi, 1,190 ft up, 60 ft down one way / easy-moderate
Main attractions: Easy climb of a volcanic plateau, views, Joshua trees
USGS 7.5′ topo map: Santa Rosa Flat
Maps: pp. 307*, *179*

Location and Access

The summit of Malpais Mesa is easiest to reach from the Santa Rosa Mine on the east side of the Inyo Mountains, as the road to the mine climbs to just below the mesa. From Highway 136 at the eastern edge of Owens Lake, drive Highway 190 10 miles east to a wide dirt road on the left. When coming from the east, this is 20.7 miles from Panamint Springs. This road splits right away. The historic Santa Rosa Mine Road is the road roughly perpendicular to the highway, and incorrectly signed Saline Valley Road. Follow this partly paved road north-northeast 5.8 miles, up to a pass and a fork shortly after it. Angle left and go 2.5 miles to the base of the Inyo Mountains, then 2.5 miles up a crooked canyon to the Santa Rosa Mine. These roads are mostly smooth, with small rocks locally embedded in them. They are passable with a standard-clearance car to about 0.5 mile of the mine. The rest requires high clearance, and power at the very steep last pitch.

Route Description

Although little of it is left today, the Santa Rosa Mine was in its day one of the most productive lead properties in California. Between 1911 and 1950, 12 million pounds of lead and 427,000 ounces of silver valued at around $1,000,000 were pulled out of 4,000 feet of galleries. It was then a vibrant hub, with a few houses and offices on the flats at the end of the road, and a massive system of timbered tramways and inclined rails that dropped the ore several hundred feet to the road.

The mine's main workings—four shafts and inclined tunnels—hang high on the steep rocky slope above the apron. To reach them, the first option is to scramble up to the right of the deep ravine that cuts into the mountain. Segments of mining trails help (the main one is shown on the map). The second option is to walk the upper end of the mining road, which starts on the north side of the apron. Partly obstructed by boulders to prevent cars and motorcycles from driving into the wilderness, it switchbacks up to the top of the mine. From there the two upper shafts are an easy scramble down the slope. There are scores of other workings and tailings, with a surfeit of lead, zinc, copper, and gangue minerals. The challenging access, geologic diversity (fossiliferous limestone intruded by syenodiorite dikes and later smothered under tuff, basalt, and andesite), Joshua trees, and the views make for a scenic and satisfying exploration.

To climb Rosa Peak, take the upper mining road 0.4 mile to the top of a broad ridge, where the road begins to descend. On the right, a foot trail perpendicular to the road climbs west toward an obvious opening in the mesa's rim. Follow it 0.1 mile until it fades, then continue climbing mostly cross-country (there are bits of use trail) toward the opening. In 0.1 mile another use trail climbs the rest of the way to the rim.

As soon as you reach the rim, the Sierra Nevada's spectacular silvery scarp bursts into view, and you know you are in for a lasting treat. From there to the summit, it fills much of your field of vision. If the steep first part of the climb is a bit tedious, slippery with loose dirt and ball-bearing rocks, most of the second part is as easy as a valley walk. Malpais Mesa is a gently sloped, unobstructed plateau of grasses and small, far-apart bushes. Invitingly airy, it is haunted by mid-size Joshua trees, dozens per acre, that add an alien spirit to this far-flung meadow suspended between heaven and Earth. The summit remains out of sight the whole time, but it is easy to find. Circle southwest to north around the head of a canyon, then follow the mesa's broad spine just west of north. After a mile the land dips into a shallow vale. On its far side, a grassy ramp climbs easily to the base of the peak, where a little climbing over an eroded volcanic field completes the ascent.

Perhaps what Malpais Mesa epitomizes best is the diversity and wildness of eastern California. Located at the crossroads between the Sierras and the desert, the gnarled summit of coarse black lava overlooks two very different worlds. On one side rises a 90-mile stretch of

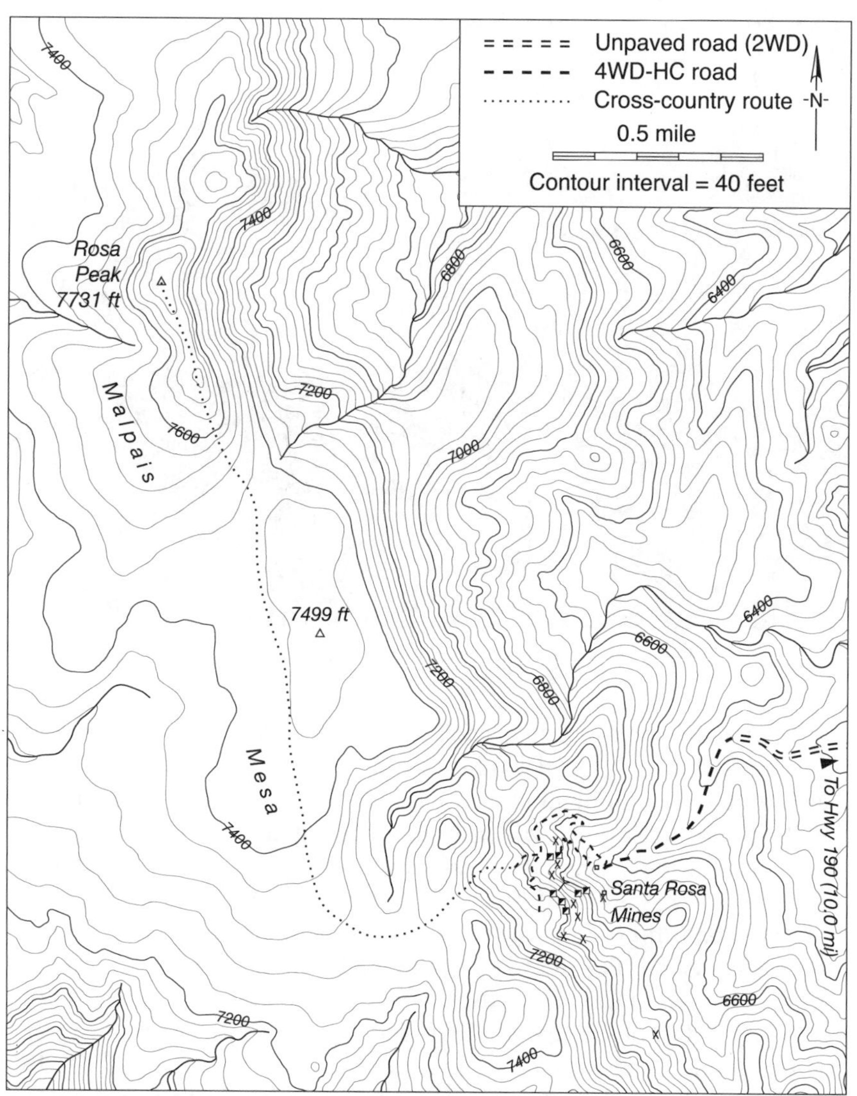

Malpais Mesa		
	Dist.(mi)	Elev.(ft)
Santa Rosa Mine	0.0	6,610
High point on dirt track	0.4	6,950
Crest of Malpais Mesa	0.75	7,320
Low point in meadow	2.0	7,415
Rosa Peak	2.7	7,731

Owens Lake and the eastern Sierras from Malpais Mesa near Rosa Peak

the Sierra Nevada's serrated crest, over two miles high and crowned by Mount Whitney. On the other the desert unfolds in rows of vivid earth-tone ranges filing all the way into Nevada. The vision of this vast territory, most of it preserved, is both inspiring and elating.

Malpais Mesa's biggest surprise is Owens Lake, once a 120-square-mile high-desert jewel of blue salt water. After the Owens River, its main water intake, was diverted to Los Angeles in 1913, the lake quickly vanished. For decades, the fierce local winds regularly kicked up huge clouds of dust from the dry lake playa, resulting in one of the worst air pollutions in the country and a high rate of respiratory ailments among local residents. Since 2001, thanks to a court order the Los Angeles Department of Water and Power has been restoring the lake with flooding, gravel, ditches, and salt grass. Bacteria, algae, then brine flies, returned in astronomical numbers, then tens of thousands of shorebirds and waders. Owens Lake has been transformed from a dust bowl into a critical stop-over for migratory birds. All along Malpais Mesa, the lake's giant mosaic of flooded parcels fringed with white shorelines draws constant attention. The lake is once again in symbiosis with the sky, cerulean on clear days, ashen gray in stormy weather, and big enough to reflect a fractured image of the Sierras.

■

TALC CITY HILLS

At their very southern tip, the Inyo Mountains break up into a scatter of hills protruding from their own alluvia like icebergs on the sea. Exploited for their high-quality talc deposits in the first half of the 20th century, they are now a vast repository of mining relics. There are houses, water tanks, ore bins, ore chutes, hoists, narrow-gauge rails, and a unique collection of shafts and headframes. The mines being spread over some 10 square miles, a visit here takes on a different rhythm. You drive as close to a mine as you can, explore it on foot, drive to the next mine, and repeat.

General Information

Jurisdiction: Public lands (BLM)
Road status: Hiking on old roads; graded access roads
The mines: 0.7–3.6 mi, 190–500 ft up one way / very easy–easy
Main attractions: Talc mines, ghost town, mining relics, geology
USGS 7.5' topo map: Talc City Hills
Maps: pp. 311*, *179, 457*

Location and Access

To get to the Talc City Hills, follow the directions to the Santa Rosa Mine Road off Highway 190 (see *Malpais Mesa*). The Talc City Hills are the colorful hills that rise a couple of miles to the north and east. This road splits right away. The road on the right, signed Talc City Road, goes east to the Talc City Mine (2.65 miles). The road heading north, incorrectly signed Saline Valley Road, is the Santa Rosa Mine Road. To get to the Viking Mine, drive this partly paved road north-northeast 0.6 mile to a road at 11 o'clock. Follow this road 0.15 mile to SE 9 (see map), then take SE 9 0.5 mile to a road on the left. This last road climbs 0.5 mile to the Viking Mine's camp. For other destinations, refer to the map. Most local roads are suitable for a standard-clearance vehicle.

Route Description

The Talc City Hills look and are very old, stooping low and blunted by erosion, their steepness the last hint of a grander past. Their antiquity is written in the broad vertical strata stamped across their flanks, the cream limestones, rosy quartzites, and bluish dolomites from the remote Paleozoic, now upended by tectonic forces. In this landscape that reads like an open book, prospectors found not gold or

Miner's cabin at the Viking Mine

silver but talc, a prized commodity during the budding industrialism of the 1910s. Of the many mines that sprouted all over the hills then, the Talc City Mine was the uncontested queen, and the hills inherited its name. Until the 1940s it provided nearly all of the high-grade talc in the country. By 1948 it had put out 220,000 tons. The hills are dotted with the white tailings of these abandoned properties. On this sparse canvas of scant Joshua trees, barbed cottontop cactus, and low shrubs permanently half-dead, these bright touches are points of focus, forgotten time capsules waiting to be rediscovered.

Considering their easy access, the Talc City Hills still hold a surprising number of well-preserved mining ruins. Although it never was large enough to qualify as a town, the camp at the Viking Mine is one of the region's largest. Built on a broad shelf below a steep hill with far-reaching views, its three large bunkhouses and dugout are a priceless memento from the past. The mine is tucked away in a narrow canyon just up the road. It still has a headframe and the long chute that funneled the white talc from the main shaft down to the road.

Talc City Hills

	Dist.(mi)	Elev.(ft)
SE 9 rd to Viking Mine	0.7	5,050
SE 9 rd to Hard Scramble Mine	1.0	5,300
SE 9 rd to White Swan Mine	1.9	4,935
Talc City Rd to Talc City Mine	2.9	5,220
Talc City Rd to Alliance Talc M	3.6	5,370

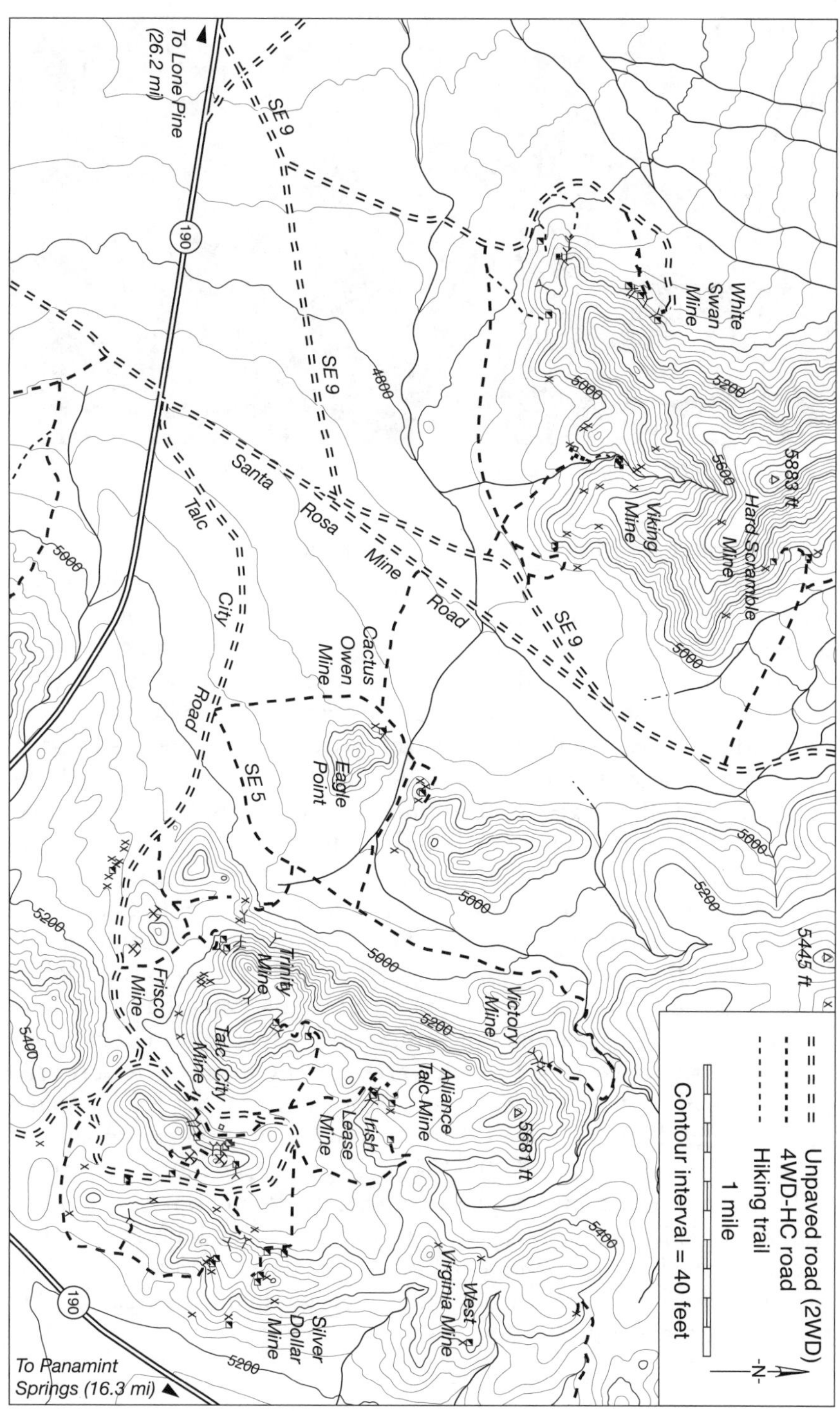

To Lone Pine (26.2 mi)
190
SE 9
SE 9
SE 9
SE 5
Santa Rosa Mine Road
Talc City Road
White Swan Mine
5883 ft
Hard Scramble Mine
Viking Mine
Cactus Owen Mine
Eagle Point
5445 ft
Victory Mine
Trinity Mine
Frisco Mine
Talc City Mine
Alliance Talc Mine
Irish Lease Mine
5681 ft
West Virginia Mine
Silver Dollar Mine
To Panamint Springs (16.3 mi)
190
4800
5000
5200
5400
5600
Unpaved road (2WD)
4WD-HC road
Hiking trail
1 mile
Contour interval = 40 feet
N

Hoist machinery and shed ruin at the Talc City Mine

The Talc City Mine outshines all other local mines. Exploited on multiple levels across 800 feet of hillside, it is now an impressive cascade of overlapping tailings. When it was active, a set of tracks and a dozen buildings stood on and below the tailings. A few still remain by the road. Higher up, a headframe incorporating a hoisting shack looms over a collared shaft. The most complex ruin is the main hoist, surrounded by the splayed walls of its collapsed housing, and a short rail resting on a ramp above it. The 100-ft shaft it serviced explored the west ore body, the largest of the mine's four deposits. If you scramble to the crest and follow it north 200 yards, you will get to the two imposing glory holes of the Evening Star, the northernmost ore body.

All other sites produced only a few hundred tons of talc each, but they all have something to show. There is a metallic ore chute at the Irish Lease Mine, and an ore bin in good condition at the Silver Dollar Mine and the Victory Mine. The Hard Scramble Mine has a slender headframe with a steel-lined ore chute. The Alliance Mine has more ruins than any other site. The talc varies greatly in color, from nearly pure white at the Irish Lease Mine to mottled gray at the Alliance, and pale green at the White Swan. The Frisco Mine has amesite, an apple-green ore resembling talc. At the Viking and Talc City mines the half-a-billion-year rock is an exquisite aggregate of inch-size carbonate chunks eroded to a razor-sharp finish. To end on a high note, drive the circuitous road to the White Swan Mine. Its tall two-chute ore bin is a rare construction of amber wood still connected to the tailing behind it by a bridge that supports the tracks to the tunnel.

■

— 8 —

The Western Panamint Range

For 60 miles the Panamint Mountains and the southern Cottonwood Mountains loom over the east side of Panamint Valley, their crest nearly two miles above the valley floor. Part of the Panamint Range, they are one of the most phenomenal pieces of geological engineering in the Mojave. With the exception of the Inyos, one must travel far to find a desert range this high, this abrupt, this rough, and this imposing. Given such statistics, it is not surprising that it holds some of the finest backcountry. The steep terrain has spawned monumental canyons, many of them irrigated by a year-round stream. Mesozoic plutonic activity sprinkled valuable precious metals throughout the range. Miners have left behind hundreds of tunnels, colorful camps, elaborate mills, and miles of canyon roads for us to explore all of this. Add luxuriant springs, a diverse flora, spectacular vistas, cliff-hugging trails, and an assortment of backcountry cabins to spend the night, and you will get a good picture of what is in store. Whether you are looking for an earthshaking ride up a long rocky road or an eventful hike into a roadless canyon, you will find plenty of opportunities.

Access and Backcountry Roads

The only paved roads in the western Panamint Range are the Emigrant Canyon Road, the Wildrose Canyon Road, and Highway 190, the only paved road that crosses it. The main unpaved access roads from Panamint Valley are the Big Four Mine Road at the north end of the valley, the Indian Ranch Road in the central valley, and the Wingate Road in the south. These last two roads are graded, and suitable for all vehicles in dry weather. The Wingate Road enters the China

Lake Naval Weapons Center 5 miles south of Goler Canyon (this section is briefly washed out after a couple of miles) and is closed to the public beyond. From the Indian Ranch Road and the Wingate Road, rough tracks provide ingress into several major canyons in the western Panamint Mountains south of Wildrose Canyon. The roads in Pleasant, South Park, and Goler canyons are the only ones that go up to the crest. Of these, only the Goler Canyon Road crosses over to Death Valley, via isolated Butte Valley and Warm Spring Canyon. All other roads just tease the edge of the range. All roads require sturdy vehicles in the canyons and offer some of the best four-wheeling in the region. The most popular drives are the Pleasant Canyon–South Park Canyon loop, and the Goler Canyon–Butte Valley–Warm Spring Canyon circuit. Long and locally challenging, both drives give access to a great variety of scenery, historic sites, and abandoned mines.

Geology

The Panamint Range is one of the largest fault blocks in the western Basin and Range. It was uplifted over the last few million years along the Hunter Mountain Fault Zone, which extends along the east side of Panamint Valley. The whole block was tilted eastward around a general axis located at the alluvial fan level in Death Valley. The por-

Suggested Backcountry Drives in the Western Panamint Range

Route/Destination	Dist. (mi)	Lowest elev.	Highest elev.	Road type	Pages
Barker Ranch	6.6	1,130'	3,255'	H	412-414
Big Four Mine Road	7.2	1,556'	2,210'	F	321
Gold Spur Mine camp	3.4	1,070'	2,400'	H	402-403
Goler Cyn Rd (Mengel Pass)	9.2	1,120'	~4,315'	F	407-414
Happy Canyon Road	2.5	1,060'	1,965'	H	373
Jail Canyon Road	5.5	1,100'	3,520'	F	339
Keystone Mine Road	6.3	1,120'	3,855'	H	410-411
Mahogany Flat Road	8.7	4,020'	8,140'	H	333
Pleasant–Sth Park Cyn loop	28.3	1,042'	7,360'	F	379, 395
Porter Mine	10.9	1,075'	7,530'	F	386
Ratcliff Mine	9.4	1,075'	6,520'	F	384
Rogers Pass	11.5	1,075'	7,165'	F	388, 400
South Park Canyon Road	12.8	1,050'	7,360'	F	395-400
Surprise Canyon Road	4.0	1,080'	2,620'	H	351

Key: P=Primitive (2WD) H=Primitive (HC) F=Primitive (4WD)

tion of the block east of this axis was sunk into Death Valley, while the west side was uplifted to its present lofty position. As a consequence, the steepest escarpments occur on the thrust side, in Panamint Valley. The most abrupt canyons are found along this western scarp—they often climb 1,000 feet per mile for many miles. The physiography of the alluvial fans that spill out of these canyons onto the valley reflects this general eastward tilting. They are miles long and massive in Death Valley, but short and low almost everywhere in Panamint Valley.

One of the least appreciated treasures of the Panamint Range is its geological diversity. The fault block was originally a stack of marine strata many miles thick deposited over several hundred million years. As it was pushed out of the ground, older formations became exposed along the fault in Panamint Valley. At the same time, the younger layers at the top of the block rose higher and were stripped off by erosion. Eventually, the whole stack was exhumed, as well as some of the underlying crystalline basement. Today, the western Panamints are a kaleidoscope of the Proterozoic formations—Johnnie, Noonday, Kingston Peak, Beck Spring, and Crystal Spring—that once rested beneath the stack. The record goes to the basal gneiss and schist that outcrop at the base of the mountains, especially around South Park Canyon. Between 1.35 and 1.82 billion years old, they rank among the oldest rocks in the northern Mojave. The exception is Pinto Peak, in the northern Panamints. Made of a fanglomerate formed in a valley about five million years ago, it is just about the youngest rock in the range.

Although part of the same range, the Cottonwood Mountains were not thrust nearly as far up. They only display the Paleozoic sedimentary formations that make up the mid-section of the Panamint fault block. It includes the colorful formations that are missing in the western Panamint Mountains, from the Pogonip Group to the Perdido Formation. The lower, older formations are still deep underground.

In the Jurassic and lower Tertiary, small granitic plutons intruded the country rock. They now outcrop at Manly Peak, around South Park Canyon, in Hall Canyon, and in the southwestern Cottonwood Mountains. In the latter, the granitic exposures are quartz monzonite, part of the larger Hunter Mountain Pluton.

Springs

The name "Panamint" first appeared in 1861, in a report of the Nevada Boundary Commission. Probably coined by the Darwin French party a year earlier, it is believed to be derived from southern Paiute *pa* (water) and *nïwïntsi* (person). Like the Inyos, by desert standards the Panamints are indeed comparatively wet. Their lofty peaks

Clair Camp and Ratcliff Mine mill, ca. 1920
(Courtesy of Eastern California Museum, County of Inyo)

capture a fair amount of rain and snow, which is stored underground and resurfaces in the form of springs and creeks. Most of the major west-side canyons have a perennial stream. Many other canyons have at least a wet spring. These modest waterways turn rocky washes into streams, dry falls into waterfalls, scrawny desert cover into lush oases. The higher moisture also supports an extensive woodland belt in the high Panamints. One of the healthiest in the Mojave, this green ecological island perched high above the sweltering desert is accessible by car in Wildrose, Pleasant, and South Park canyons. In comparison, the southwestern Cottonwood Mountains are substantially lower. They receive far less precipitation, and are essentially devoid of springs.

History: From Antimony to Briggs' Folly

In addition to these natural wonders, the Panamints boast one of the region's richest mining history. Mining here holds the local longevity record, having been active for 150 years—and still counting. This range was the site of Death Valley's very first mining venture, after antimony was discovered in Wildrose Canyon in 1861. The first major strike occurred in 1872, when a major silver lode was found high in Surprise Canyon. In just two years, in spite of extreme conditions, hundreds of claims were filed, dozens of tunnels sunk, and the town of

Suggested Hikes in the Western Panamint Range					
Route/Destination	Dist. (mi)	Elev. gain	Mean elev.	Access road	Pages
Short hikes (under 5 miles round trip)					
Big Four Mine (east group)	1.8	1,220'	2,080'	P/5.8 mi	321-324
Big Four Mine (west group)	1.4	850'	1,940'	P/5.8 mi	321-322
Clair Camp	0.6	~60'	4,520'	H/6.1 mi	381-383
Goler Canyon narrows	0.9	420'	1,790'	P/1.5 mi	407-408
Happy Canyon narrows	1.2	750'	2,310'	F/2.4 mi	373-374
Limekiln Spring	2.0	1,450'	3,300'	H/4.0 mi	352-354
Mormon Peak	1.2	1,250'	7,640'	F/11.5 mi	391-392
Ratcliff Mine tramway	2.2	1,860'	6,020'	H/6.1 mi	384-386
South Park Canyon narrows	1.3	940'	3,120'	H/2.7 mi	395-396
Suitcase Mine viewpoint	0.9	810'	3,950'	H/4.0 mi	396
Surprise Canyon narrows	0.9	640'	2,910'	H/4.0 mi	352-354
Thorndike Mine upper trail	0.9	610'	5,600'	F/6.1 mi	397-400
World Beater Mine	0.8	540'	5,460'	H/7.1 mi	383-384
Intermediate hikes (5-12 miles round trip)					
Bennett Peak	3.0	2,060'	9,100'	P/1.6 mi	338
Big Four Mine viewpoint	2.9	1,750'	2,450'	P/5.8 mi	321-324
Burro Mine (west tunnel)	3.6	2,060'	3,130'	F/3.0 mi	344
Corona Mine tramway	2.9	1,840'	2,960'	F/3.0 mi	342
Coyote Canyon gorge	4.2	2,190'	2,510'	P/14.9 mi	401-404
Dolomite Canyon narrows	5.6	2,660'	2,640'	P/2.2 mi	329-330
Dolomite Cyn side canyon	5.9	2,880'	2,730'	P/2.2 mi	329-330
Gold Spur Mine	2.5	1,660'	2,110'	P/14.9 mi	402-403
Goler Canyon mouth to				P/1.5 mi	
Barker Ranch	5.1	1,670'	2,500'		412-414
Keystone Mine camp	3.2	1,190'	2,210'		410
Keystone Mine tunnels	5.0	2,840'	2,460'		410-411
Hall Canyon (Rim Trail)	5.8	4,030'	4,680'	F/2.1 mi	346-348
Hall Cyn (Rowland Cabin)	4.7	3,470'	4,720'	F/2.1 mi	346
Hall Canyon Trail	5.8	5,460'	3,100'	Graded	350
Happy Cyn (camp and mill)	2.6	1,820'	2,800'	P/2.4 mi	376
Happy Cyn (sixth spring)	5.9	4,170'	3,940'	P/2.4 mi	378
Jail Canyon (Gem Mine mill)	2.7	1,500'	2,880'	F/3.0 mi	342-344

Key: P=Primitive (2WD) H=Primitive (HC) F=Primitive (4WD)
Distances: one way for out-and-back hikes, round-trip for loops
Elev. gain: sum of all elevation gains on round-trip or loop hike

Suggested Hikes in the Western Panamint Range (Cont'd)					
Route/Destination	Dist. (mi)	Elev. gain	Mean elev.	Access road	Pages
Intermediate hikes (5-12 miles round trip) (Cont'd)					
Lestro Mountain Mine trails	2.8	1,730'	2,150'	P/1.5 mi	408-409
Panamint Canyon mullion	2.7	1,270'	2,090'	P/3.1 mi	325-326
Panamint Canyon 100-ft fall	3.6	2,490'	2,380'	P/3.1 mi	325-328
Panamint City	5.5	3,780'	4,520'	H/4.0 mi	357-368
Pleasant Canyon spring	2.9	1,560'	2,380'	P/0.9 mi	381
Porter Peak	3.4	2,920'	8,030'	F/11.5 mi	391-394
Slims Peak	2.8	2,600'	6,300'	H/7.1 mi	389-390
Sth Park Cyn narrows loop	5.5	1,700'	1,890'	Graded	395-396
Surprise Cyn (Brewery Spr.)	3.2	2,310'	3,710'	H/4.0 mi	356
Wildrose Peak Trail	4.2	2,580'	7,800'	Graded	336
Long hikes (over 12 miles round trip)					
Coyote–Goler canyon loop	13.2	2,870'	2,630'	P/14.9 mi	401-406
Dolomite Cyn wonderland	7.1	3,990'	3,100'	P/2.2 mi	329-332
South Park (camp)	6.7	4,080'	4,520'	H/2.7 mi	400
Telescope Peak Trail	6.4	3,480'	9,590'	P/1.6 mi	338
Overnight hikes (2 days or more)					
Hall Cyn to Telescope Peak	11.1	10,100'	6,510'	F/3.0 mi	350
Hall Canyon Trail (loop)	16.6	5,600'	3,140'	Graded	350
Happy Cyn (7,770-ft peak)	7.0	6,190'	4,560'	P/2.4 mi	373-378
Manly Peak	8.8	6,130'	4,080'	P/14.9 mi	406
Panamint City area				H/4.0 mi	
Blue Jay Mine	7.0	4,790'	5,000'		364
Hemlock Mine (via road)	6.3	5,340'	4,880'		366-368
Hudson River Mine	7.5	6,100'	5,430'		368
Panamint Pass	7.5	5,550'	5,220'		369-370
Stewart's Wonder Mine	5.9	3,990'	4,650'		364-365
Thompson Camp	6.0	4,010'	4,810'		363
Wyoming Mine	6.9	5,100'	5,000'		365-366
Pleasant Cyn to Rogers Pass	10.6	5,570'	4,400'	P/0.9 mi	379-388
Sentinel Peak	8.5	7,080'	5,650'	H/4.0 mi	369-372
Surprise–Happy cyn loop	22.0	7,700'	4,800'	P/0.8 mi	368, 378

Key: P=Primitive (2WD) H=Primitive (HC) F=Primitive (4WD)
Distances: one way for out-and-back hikes, round-trip for loops
Elev. gain: sum of all elevation gains on round-trip or loop hike

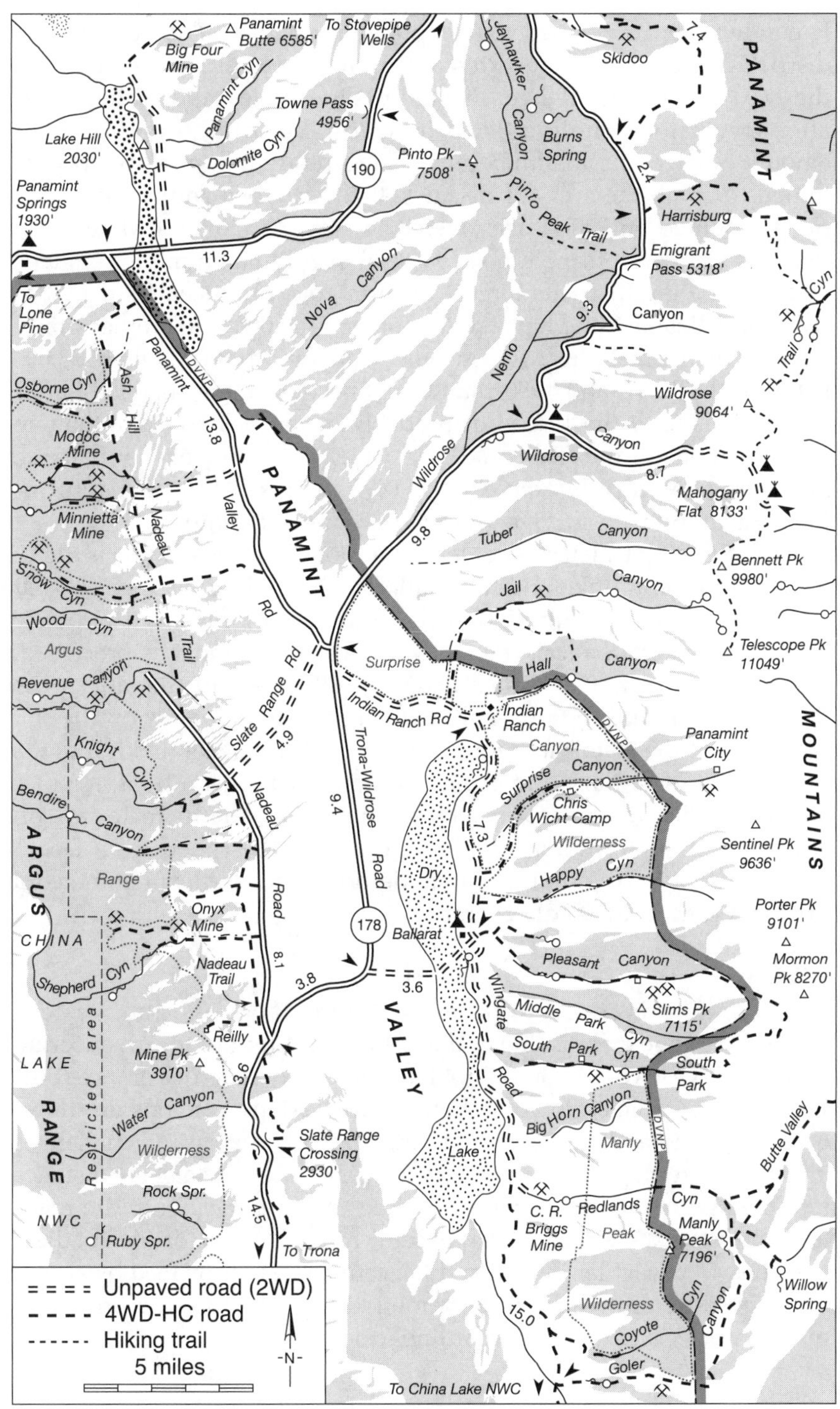
Panamint Butte 6585'
To Stovepipe Wells
Big Four Mine
Panamint Cyn
Towne Pass 4956'
Lake Hill 2030'
Dolomite Cyn
Panamint Springs 1930'
190
Pinto Pk 7508'
Jayhawker Canyon
Burns Spring
Skidoo
PANAMINT
Pinto Peak Trail
Harrisburg
Emigrant Pass 5318'
11.3
To Lone Pine
Nova Canyon
Nemo
Canyon
Panamint
DVNP
Osborne Cyn
Ash Hill
13.8
Wildrose 9064'
Wildrose
Canyon
Modoc Mine
PANAMINT
Valley
Nadeau
Minnietta Mine
Mahogany Flat 8133'
Tuber
Canyon
Bennett Pk 9980'
Snow Cyn
Jail
Canyon
Wood Cyn
Rd
Trail
Argus
Telescope Pk 11049'
Surprise
Hall
Canyon
Revenue Canyon
Slate Range Rd
Indian Ranch Rd
Indian Ranch
Knight Cyn
Trona-Wildrose Road
Canyon
Panamint City
Surprise Canyon
MOUNTAINS
Bendire Canyon
Nadeau
9.4
Chris Wicht Camp
Wilderness
Sentinel Pk 9636'
ARGUS
Range
Happy Cyn
Dry
Road
Porter Pk 9101'
Onyx Mine
178
Ballarat
CHINA
Pleasant Canyon
Mormon Pk 8270'
Nadeau Trail
8.1
3.8
3.6
Shepherd Cyn
VALLEY
Wingate
Middle Park
Slims Pk 7115'
Reilly
South Park Cyn
South Park
LAKE
Mine Pk 3910'
Road
Restricted area
Water Canyon
Big Horn Canyon
RANGE
Wilderness
Manly
Butte Valley
Slate Range Crossing 2930'
Lake
Rock Spr.
C. R. Briggs Mine
Redlands
Cyn
NWC
Peak
Manly Peak 7196'
Ruby Spr.
14.5
To Trona
Willow Spring
Wilderness
15.0
Coyote
Canyon
Goler
To China Lake NWC
Unpaved road (2WD)
4WD-HC road
Hiking trail
5 miles
N

Panamint City burgeoned to a population of 2,000. The new mining district, named Panamint, extended from Wildrose Canyon south all the way to the Slate Range. Panamint City made national headlines after speculators wildly inflated its worth, but it did produce a fair amount of silver. Its wealth became so legendary that prospectors continued to comb the area for decades. Over canyons and ridges many mines boomed and died. Discovered in 1896, the Ratcliff Mine up in Pleasant Canyon returned in seven years nearly half a million dollars, and became the district's largest historic gold producer. Its neighbor the World Beater Mine harvested another $180,000. Most other mines were failures. The Lotus Mine in Goler Canyon produced all of $32,000 between the 1930s and 1950s. Jail Canyon's gold mine changed hands many times until the 1950s but probably never yielded more than an occasional bag of ore. The Gold Bug Mine, on a ridge east of Ballarat, has been sporadically active since 1893 in spite of meager returns. Even Panamint City survived into the twenty-first century.

The Panamints, latest—not least, but hopefully last—mine is the C. R. Briggs, several miles south of Ballarat. Opened in the mid-1990s, it exploits an extensive but extremely dilute gold deposit—0.02 ounce per ton. To be economical, colossal volumes of rock must be processed. Almost every day, 10,000 tons of rock are blasted off the face of the Panamints, ground to flour, and leached in cyanide ponds on the salt flats. One of the state's top gold producers, it has generated hundreds of millions of dollars. But it has desecrated thousands of acres of Native Americans' ancestral lands, obliterated the historic canyon where argonauts William Manly and his party escaped from Death Valley in 1850, disfigured a unique desert range, and contaminated a pristine valley with deadly chemicals.

Hiking

Thanks to its exceptional height and steepness, the western Panamint Range offers some of the wildest and roughest canyoneering in the Mojave. Even if you do not have access to a high-clearance four-wheel-drive vehicle, do come here on foot. Many canyons are infrequently visited and offer a bewildering array of scenery and challenges in a remote setting. Most canyon roads penetrate only a short distance into the mountains, so that most middle and upper canyons are roadless and perfectly suitable for peaceful hiking. A few of the roadless stretches, in particular in Hall and Jail canyons, are traversed by a rambunctious stream, which adds tremendous difficulty—the only genuine canyoneering there is, according to some.

■

THE BIG FOUR MINE

The main attraction of this short hike up a colorful canyon is the Big Four Mine, a small historic lead-zinc mine with several tunnels and interesting ore chutes and other remains. A short hike past the mine leads to a sweeping vista point of northern Panamint Valley.

General Information

Jurisdiction: Death Valley National Park
Road status: Primitive road to below canyon; roadless canyon
Big Four Mine east group: 1.8 mi, 1,220 ft up, 0 ft down one way / easy
Viewpoint: 2.9 mi, 1,680 ft up, 70 ft down one way / easy–moderate
Main attractions: Lead mine, panoramic views of Panamint Valley
USGS 7.5' topo map: The Dunes
Maps: pp. 323*, *319*

Location and Access

The Big Four Mine is located just inside an unnamed canyon in the southwestern Cottonwood Mountains. It is reached via the Big Four Mine Road, which starts on Highway 190 1.95 miles east of the Panamint Valley Road. Follow the Big Four Mine Road 5.8 miles north to a pronounced right bend. The road up to this point is usually passable with an ordinary vehicle. However, past the bend it ascends the steep canyon fan and quickly worsens. Over the remaining 1.6 miles to the mine, the road is locally hard to tell apart from the rocky fan, and the last 0.2 mile is washed out. Park at the bend and walk from there.

Route Description

The Big Four Mine exploited a small lead-zinc deposit speckled with silver. First located in 1907, it witnessed limited activity until it was relocated in 1940 by William Reid, owner of the small resort at Panamint Springs, and work started in 1942. Most of the production came from rich pockets, but there were so few of them that they ran through the patience of several lessees. Between 1944 and 1945, Elmer Perry produced 370 tons of ore. In 1946, then in 1947, a couple of miners tried their luck, but they shipped less than 60 tons. The property was leased again in May 1949, this time to Lee Foreman and William Skinner, who were exploiting the Defense Mine across the valley. When the Big Four Mine closed down in August 1952, it had generated only 70 tons of lead, 50 tons of zinc, and 1,200 ounces of silver.

The Big Four Mine has two groups of workings. The west group is visible from quite a distance, 250 feet up the wall north of the canyon mouth. The foot trail to it starts 40 yards past the bend in the road, at the canyon mouth (elev. 2,120'). Its middle section is faint, so it takes a little scrambling. Up there you will find the two 30-foot tunnels that yielded the 1947 production, which contained galena (lead sulfide) and sphalerite (zinc sulfide). It occurred in brecciated limestone of the Keeler Canyon Formation. Both tunnels are still collared, and the easternmost one has a small wooden structure outside its adit.

The trace of the old road ends 0.5 mile in the canyon on the south side of the wash, at the ruins of the mining camp, now reduced to the outline of a house and water tank. It is littered with railroad ties, pipes, and rusted cans. The mine's main area, known as the east group, is across the wash, starting at the lower wooden ore chute visible up the rocky slope. It was worked on three levels. The lower tunnel is about 50 yards up canyon and 50 feet above the wash. This 540-foot crosscut, which failed to intercept valuable ore, is now difficult to reach. To climb to the upper and intermediate levels, which are perched 200 feet up the north canyon wall, from the camp locate the haulage road on the north bench, just down the wash from the lower chute, and follow it to its end at the foot of the lower chute. Scramble up the slope along the chute to its mid-point, and look for a faint trail on its north side. This trail ascends in 150 yards to the upper level's 100-foot tunnel. The make-shift ore bucket at the camp was used to lower ore from this tunnel via the cableway that hangs down the canyon wall.

To reach the intermediate level, from the top of the lower chute climb up to the rail grade 40 yards to a short tunnel at the base of the upper ore chute. The intermediate tunnel is at the top of this chute. You will need to scramble up its tall, very steep, and highly unstable

The Big Four Mine

	Dist.(mi)	Elev.(ft)
Right bend in graded road	0.0	1,580
Canyon mouth/Trail to mine	1.05	2,120
Big Four Mine's west group	(0.3)	2,410
Camp/side road to east group	1.6	2,530
Big Four Mine's east group	(0.2)	~2,790
Fork at white fin	2.2	3,020
Top of knoll	2.7	3,260
Viewpoint	2.9	3,230

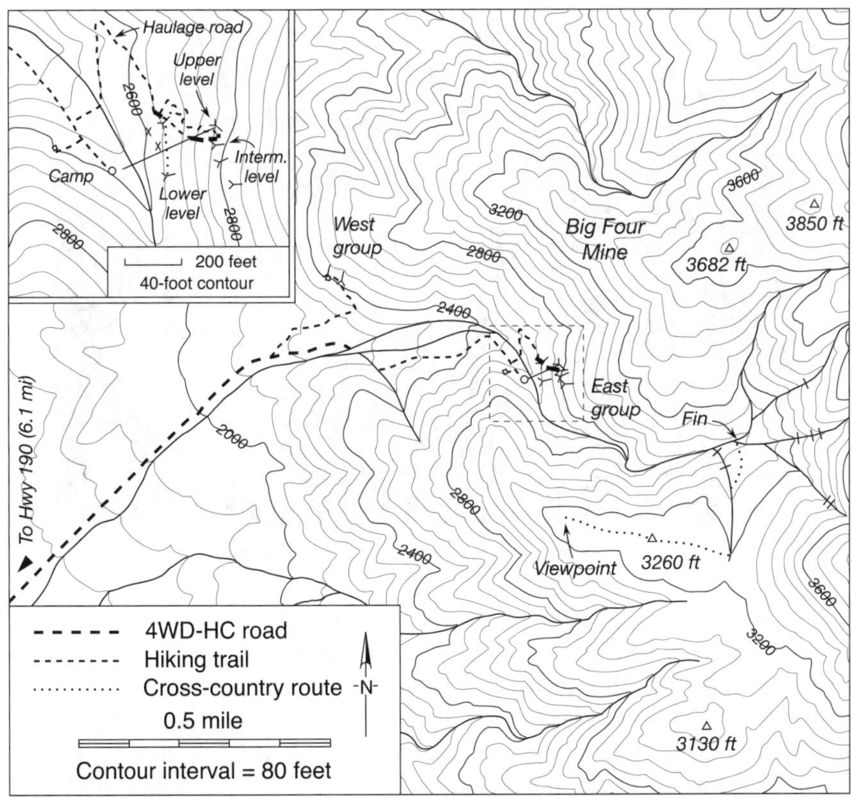

tailing along the chute. About 110 feet long, the intermediate tunnel produced most of the ore. A narrow-gauge rail courses its curvy path, past several short drifts and stopes. The ore was mostly cerussite (lead carbonate), hemimorphite, specularite, and hematite. It occurred in narrow seams in dolomitic marble of the Pogonip Group. This pretty rock makes up most of the tailing; it sparkles with white, translucent crystals. The sorted ore was tossed down the upper chute to the rail track, hauled on the track in a mine car to the lower chute, then dropped down that chute to the haulage road. Although the upper chute broke up into two pieces, the two chutes are exceptionally long.

Beyond the mine the canyon is nowhere narrow, yet its steep, 1,000-foot slopes provide a strong sense of confinement. The sheer canyon wall across from the mine, made of a succession of wide, protruding, vertical strata of Pennsylvanian marble and limestone, resembles a giant fossilized rib cage. Further up, bright, cream-colored limestone sequences are draped with long taluses of gray gravel and giant coulees of nearly black basalt and andesite.

Canyon view from above the Big Four Mine

Half a mile above the camp the canyon forks at a prominent, 20-foot high white fin topped with claim monuments. The main canyon (the left fork) rapidly becomes shallower and steeper until progress is essentially impossible after half a mile. The fork area has several side canyons worth exploring. The one straight ahead has short narrows with falls, the second fall difficult to climb, the third one about 40 feet high and impassable. The side canyon just south of it starts as a narrow gully, and it can be followed quite high to good viewpoints before it also becomes too steep to continue.

The best deal yet may be climbing to the canyon's south rim for great views of Panamint Valley. The obvious best route is via the side canyon that heads south from a little below the fork. However, its lower end has high falls. To bypass them, climb on the bench south of the fin, then cut south and west across a few gullies to the upper part of the side canyon. From there it is a short walk south up to the rim, then west along the rim to the top of the knoll. This desolate summit and the ridge dropping west of it command spectacular vistas of northern Panamint Valley. The rocky spurs of Lake Hill stand eerily against the barren dry lake, more alien-looking than the pictures the Mars rovers sent back from the Red Planet. Off in the distance, the sand dunes glow pale against the high rampart of Hunter Mountain. If you end up hiking back late, you will be rewarded by ghostly images of the dunes slowly turning to amber between the canyon walls.

■

PANAMINT CANYON

Rough and difficult, devoid of springs and mines, Panamint Canyon never had a road in it, and it is as virgin as it was hundreds of thousands of years ago. I included it here for the benefit of the free-spirited, rock-loving and sun-crazed desert rat, who will appreciate its silence and remoteness, and perhaps find a route, over hard crags and shifting taluses, to its beautiful and hard-to-reach inner narrows.

General Information

Jurisdiction: Death Valley National Park
Road status: Roadless; hiking from graded road
Mullion: 2.7 mi, 1,230 ft up, 40 feet down one way / moderate
100-ft drop-off: 3.6 mi, 2,430 ft up, 60 ft down one way / strenuous
Main attractions: A hard canyon, fossils, falls, narrows, climbing
USGS 7.5' topo maps: The Dunes, Panamint Butte*
Maps: pp. 327*, *319, 419*

Location and Access

Panamint Canyon drains the southwestern Cottonwood Mountains into Panamint Valley east of Lake Hill. Hike to this roadless canyon from the Big Four Mine Road (see *The Big Four Mine*) 3.1 miles from Highway 190, or about 0.7 mile past the southern tip of Lake Hill. Panamint Canyon is about 2 miles up the steep fan to the east.

Route Description

The Panamint Canyon fan is geologically one of the most interesting in Panamint Valley. Erosion has worked overtime here to collect a fabulous diversity of rocks. A friend and I ooohed and aaahed the whole way at colorful chunks of thinly banded limestone, dolomite cobbles delicately veined with calcite, stones faceted by the wind, and other artfully crafted ventifacts. The upper fan also has a number of fossils shed by Panamint Canyon's Paleozoic formations, including the broken stems of crinoids, extinct sea animals from the Devonian or earlier. Other fossils include favosites (a coral) and gastropods. It is a good hour's walk to the mouth of the canyon, but it would take skill to get bored. Just remember that rock hounding is prohibited.

A steep and deeply dissected wash winds along lower Panamint Canyon. Even in mid-winter you will develop a sweat trudging up its

15% slope. Attractions are sparse—even the spring flower show is modest—but the scenery is grand. As in a cathedral, everything here points up. The high walls, strongly faulted and brecciated, are partly buried in impossibly tall taluses that hang down like celestial drapes. In the left bend 120 yards past the first side canyon, a large slickenside on the south canyon wall bears witness to the tremendous forces that created this canyon. This 30-foot high, nearly vertical flat surface marks the plane of a strike-slip fault—a fault where the predominant movement is horizontal, which in this region is less common than vertical motion. The horizontal white scratch marks across its dark surface are called a mullion structure.

A mile into Panamint Canyon you will reach the lower end of the narrows, soon plugged by a towering drop-off of cleaved dolomite that rises 80 vertical feet from the wash like a fortress. Nested at the end of a deep alcove, it is flanked on one side by a mud-coated wall, and on the other by a cascade of small grottoes. From top to bottom a tall chute was gouged into it by a long-gone waterfall. Even if you decide to turn here, this hidden treasure is well worth the hike.

The spectacular, almost inaccessible narrows above the 80-foot drop-off are the climax of Panamint Canyon, and the place you will want to see—if it lets you in. The only way—besides an airlift or a genuinely life-threatening free climb—is up the very steep, long, and crumbly talus that tumbles down on the north side just before the drop-off. Climbing it is hard work. Where it became too unstable I clambered onto the rocky ridge that separates it from the narrows' rim and got bird's eye views of the chasm I was bypassing. I stared down at a tight passage stitched with high falls, one of them formed by two mammoth chockstones jammed between the walls. I continued up the ledge, hanging onto dolomite fins pitted by erosion, as rough as a file. The route eventually reaches a shallow saddle, then drops on its far side into the canyon wash. A short distance up the winding narrows

Panamint Canyon		
	Dist.(mi)	Elev.(ft)
Fig Four Mine Road	0.0	1,554
Mouth	2.2	2,400
Mullion/slickenside	2.7	2,740
80-foot drop-off (narrows)	3.1	~3,240
End of bypass	3.4	~3,660
100-foot drop-off	3.6	~3,920

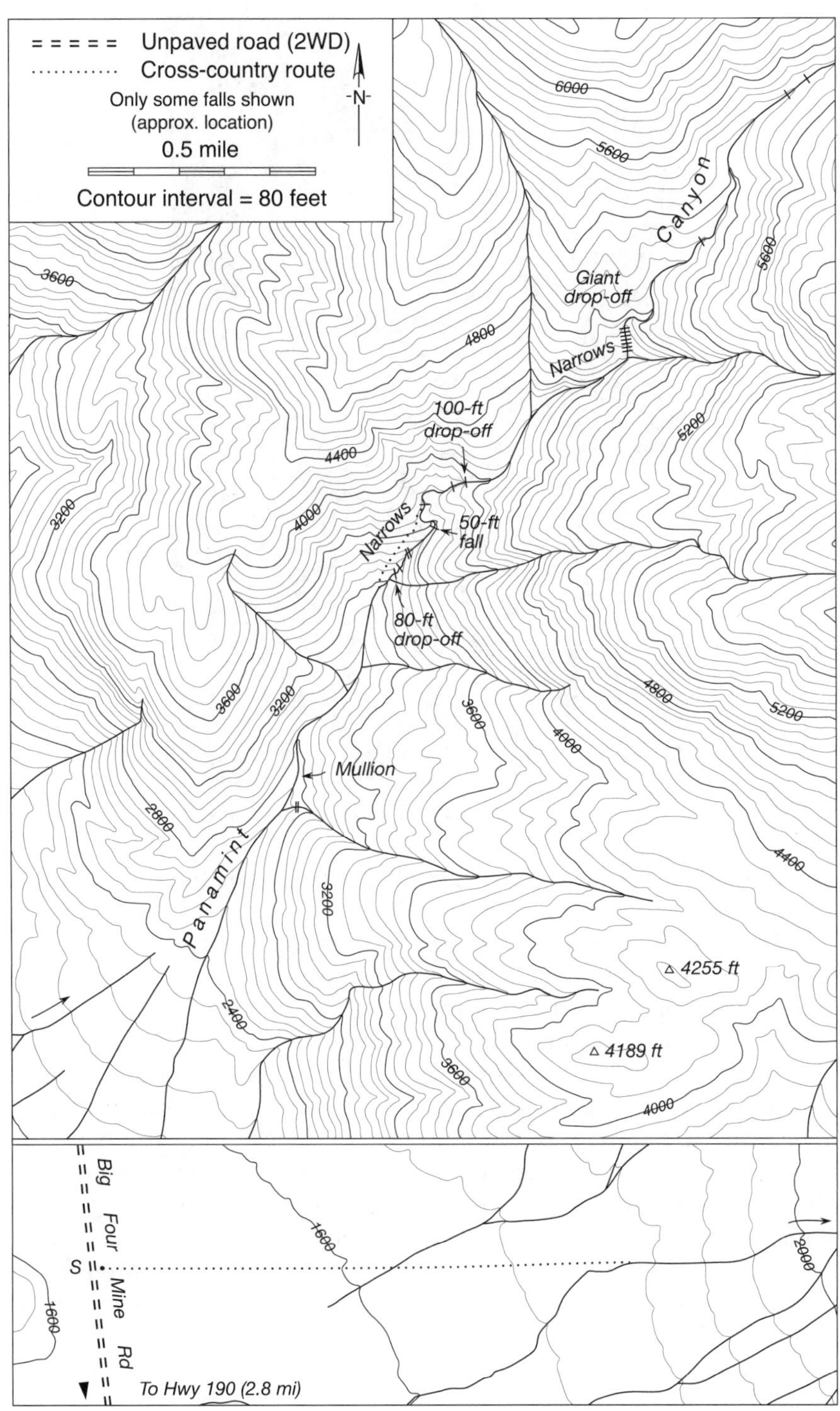

= = = = = Unpaved road (2WD)
Cross-country route
Only some falls shown (approx. location)
0.5 mile
Contour interval = 80 feet
N
6000
5600
Canyon
5600
Giant drop-off
4800
Narrows
3600
100-ft drop-off
5200
4400
3200
4000
Narrows
50-ft fall
80-ft drop-off
3600
3200
3600
4800
5200
4000
Mullion
2800
Panamint
4400
3200
4255 ft
2400
4189 ft
3600
4000
Big Four Mine Rd
1600
2000
S
1600
To Hwy 190 (2.8 mi)

The lower, 80-foot drop-off in Panamint Canyon

comes the second check, two high falls back to back, the second one a titanic drop-off well over 100 feet high.

There is more beyond, more falls reaching up into more narrows interspaced with stretches of unobstructed wash. It is a raw and persistently overproportioned landscape, entrenched in slopes that shoot up a very long way at an imposing 45° angle, interrupted by phenomenal drop-offs, dwarfed by awesome walls of multicolored strata straight out of the Paleozoic. To see it, you will need to apply trial and error repeatedly to find bypasses around major obstacles. This is a place for die-hards who thrive on strenuous and dangerous terrains. Visitors are few. But at the lip of one of the falls I came upon a crumbling piece of webbing looped around a boulder, a carabiner still hooked onto it, that a climber rigged up years ago to rappel down fall after fall through the narrows. If you know what you are doing, this may be the only way to become intimate with this well-guarded canyon.

■

DOLOMITE CANYON

This exciting canyon provides an unusually easy hiking route deep into the Cottonwood Mountains. You will enjoy searching this vast multifaceted passage for narrows, wild flowers, fossils, signs of bighorn sheep, and a scenic wonderland of rocks. Since many of these highlights are located in the remote upper canyon, count on a long day. You may even find that one visit is just not enough.

General Information

Jurisdiction: Death Valley National Park
Road status: Roadless; hiking from graded road
Dolomite Cyn narrows: 5.6 mi, 2,630 ft up, 30 ft down one way/moder.
Side-canyon narrows: 5.9 mi, 2,850 ft, 30 ft down one way/moderate
Dolomite wonderland: 7.1 mi, 3,960 ft up, 30 ft down one way/difficult
Main attractions: A remote canyon, narrows, scenic rock formations
USGS 7.5' topo maps: The Dunes, Panamint Butte*, Nemo Canyon
Maps: pp. 331*, *319*, *419*

Location and Access

Dolomite Canyon is located in the extreme southwestern Cottonwood Mountains. To hike to this roadless canyon, start from the Big Four Mine Road 2.2 miles from Highway 190 (see *The Big Four Mine*). A good landmark is the two car bodies rusting away on the west side of the road. Dolomite Canyon is up the wide fan to the east.

Route Description

The fan and lower canyon. It is a fairly long hike up the fan to Dolomite Canyon, but the walking is easy and desert lovers will find much to keep them entertained. On the fan as in the canyon, wildflowers are quite diverse. Over the course of the year they vary from desertgold and evening primrose to Death Valley mohavea, phacelia, stingbush, and less common species like turtleback and Mojave desert star. Cacti are fairly abundant, especially cottontop cactus, which grows in very large clusters. You will cross vast expanses of desert pavement and fields of heavily varnished basalt cobbles washed down from the volcanic flows that cap the distant canyon rim.

Dolomite Canyon was aptly named. From the Nopah Formation at its mouth to the Owens Valley Formation near its head, it cuts through 11 formations largely composed of dolomite and limestone. Generally younger toward higher elevations, they cover 235 million years of Paleozoic sedimentation. The vagaries of tectonics are such that a single formation—the Pogonip Group—is exposed along most of the lower two thirds of the canyon. All younger formations are squeezed along its upper third. This assemblage provides a colorful backdrop all along the broad lower canyon, including strikingly banded high walls. Most formations contain fossils, in particular gastropods and receptaculites in the upper Pogonip Group—try the side canyons.

Dolomite Canyon stands out for its gentle, unobstructed, and well-compacted wash. Walking is unusually easy. About 1.4 miles in, you will reach a more open area where several side canyons converge. The main wash makes a long, gradual left bend, passing by a smooth, vertical bank of fanglomerate. Its fine layers of gravel recount the long history of episodic flooding of the wash. Just a little further, a narrow gateway marks the entrance to the more scenic upper canyon.

The upper canyon. Over the remaining 3 miles, the canyon gradually deepens and changes character several times, often abruptly. In the long bend past the gateway, high-rising ochre walls are draped in very high and steep taluses of beige gravel almost as fine as sand. Soon after there is a short stretch of narrows, which ends at the first Y junction. The side canyon to the right has the best narrows. For 0.6 mile the wash winds beneath vertical 80-foot walls as little as 12 feet apart. Higher up, contorted rock faces are pockmarked with hollows, caves, and fine slickensides—smoothly striated surfaces formed when they ground past each other along a fault. There is a large one on the north wall 15 feet above the wash, facing up canyon. The friction involved was so enormous that it melted the rock, leaving behind the reddish glaze that coats the slickenside. The striations are vertical—here as in many regional faults, motion is predominantly up and down.

Dolomite Canyon

	Dist.(mi)	Elev.(ft)
Fig Four Mine Road	0.0	1,556
Mouth	2.7	2,360
Gateway to upper canyon	4.5	~3,550
First Y-junction/start narrows	5.3	4,015
Top of narrows	5.6	4,170
Second Y-junction	6.9	5,210
Dolomite wonderland (30-ft fall)	7.1	5,490

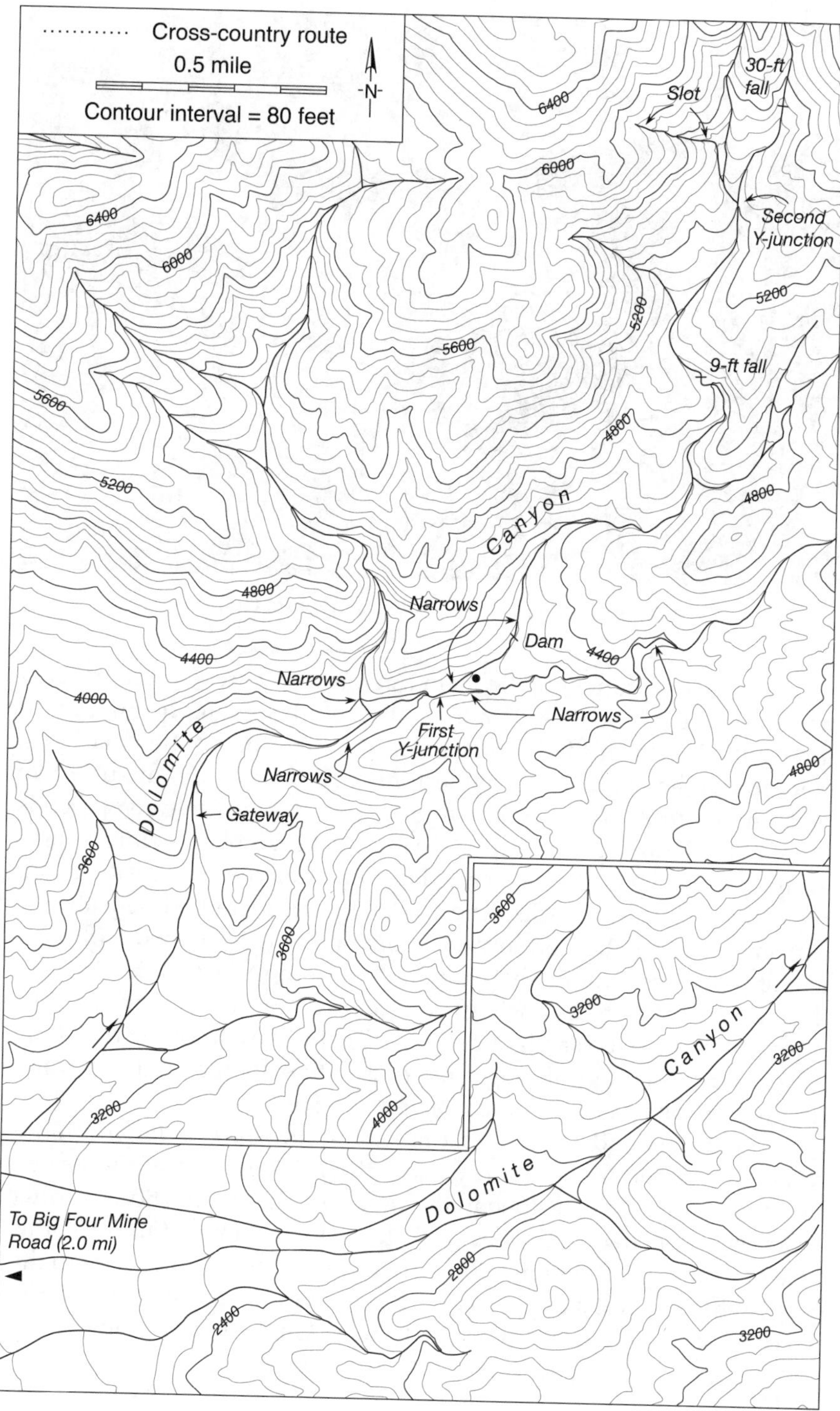

Cross-country route
0.5 mile
Contour interval = 80 feet
N
Slot
30-ft fall
6400
6000
Second Y-junction
5200
5600
9-ft fall
4800
Canyon
Narrows
Dam
4400
Narrows
First Y-junction
Narrows
4000
Dolomite
Narrows
Gateway
3600
3200
Canyon
To Big Four Mine Road (2.0 mi)
Dolomite
2800
2400

Wonderland of rocks in upper Dolomite Canyon

Back to the Y junction, the main canyon soon enters a second set of narrows, with a little rock dam that once supplied water to a tank resting on the bench in the Y. Further on there are other short narrows, smooth overhangs of bluish limestone, and a little fall, about 9 feet high and naturally bypassed by a fork in the wash. The canyon bends twice in the looming shadow of two sculpted high walls before it forks again. Here, at its farthest reaches, Dolomite Canyon has created a fantastic wonderland of rocks. The colorful slopes, cradled beneath the cinnamon crest of the Cottonwood Mountains, are festooned with clusters of pinnacles and misshapen outcrops. Both forks wander through this intricate playground, where you can explore side canyons for narrows or scramble in search of the most fanciful formations. Everything here is permeated by a strong sense of isolation, by the exciting awareness that no one has been here in a very long time.

Both forks lead shortly to the first serious obstacles in a long canyon—a boulder-choked ravine in the left fork and a 30-foot fall topped by a huge chockstone in the right fork. In all directions, further progress is impeded by increasingly steep slopes. Some of us relish this type of challenge. If you do, you may want to find a ridge route to the crest, which is not far, to Towne Pass beyond—or perhaps to the wreckage of the military aircraft that crashed in the upper drainage.

■

WILDROSE CANYON

A broad high-desert valley framed by forested peaks, Wildrose Canyon is an ideal place to escape from the summer heat and explore or camp in the high country. The graded canyon road provides easy access to the famous charcoal kilns, one of Death Valley's earliest mining wonders. Hikers can puff up the Wildrose Peak Trail, or drive to Mahogany Flat at the canyon rim and tackle the longer trail to Telescope Peak. As the park's highest summit, it commands awesome views of Death Valley, from over two miles above its eerie salt pan.

General Information

Jurisdiction: Death Valley National Park
Road status: Hiking on trails from graded or primitive road
Wildrose Peak: 4.2 mi, 2,390 ft up, 190 ft down one way/difficult
Telescope Peak: 6.4 mi, 3,200 ft up, 280 ft down one way/strenuous
Main attractions: Charcoal kilns, forested trails to spectacular peaks
USGS 7.5' topo maps: Wildrose Peak*, Telescope Peak*
Maps: pp. 335*, 337*, *319*

Location and Access

Wildrose Canyon is the largest canyon in the western Panamint Mountains. A road runs though it, from Panamint Valley to Mahogany Flat at the crest of the range. To get to it, drive the Trona-Wildrose Road 9.8 miles east of the Panamint Valley Road to Wildrose Junction. The road heading straight is the Mahogany Flat Road. In the next 0.3 mile it passes by the Wildrose Campground. Wildrose Canyon's charcoal kilns are 6.8 miles further. This road is partly paved, partly graded, and suitable for passenger cars. The Wildrose Peak Trail is posted just behind the westernmost kiln. For Telescope Peak, drive 1.6 miles further to Mahogany Flat. This is a little rough and steep at places, but in dry weather it is usually manageable with standard clearance.

Route Description

The charcoal kilns. Wildrose Canyon's impressive kilns, high in the thickly forested upper canyon, are a wonder of early desert mining. They are connected to the rich silver strike that took place in 1875 at the Modoc Mine, in the Argus Range (see *Lookout and the Modoc Mine*). Charcoal was needed to operate two smelters near the mines, and wood was needed to produce charcoal. The closest wood supply

Wildrose Canyon's charcoal kilns in snow

was the forest up in Wildrose Canyon, nearly 25 miles away, but this did not stop the enterprising mine managers. By the spring of 1877 the ten huge furnaces had been erected and were ready to produce. They were loaded with 4-foot conifer logs, which were left to burn for several days until the wood had turned to charcoal. The operation probably employed a small crew to cut the wood and stack, fire, and tend the kilns. It looked so promising that for a while a railway was envisioned to haul the charcoal across Panamint Valley, to replace Remi Nadeau's mule teams (see *The Nadeau Trail*). The Modoc Mine remained active until the early 1890s. However, perhaps because it temporarily ran out of good ore, or perhaps because cheaper smelting was identified elsewhere, the kilns were last fired up in 1879, never to be reactivated.

The kilns are made of limestone blocks quarried locally and mortared with sand, lime, and gravel. Like other charcoal-burning ovens of that era, they were designed like an opera house, to reflect as much heat as possible. Walk into a kiln: the faintest sound is audibly reflected by the curved walls. The portholes in the back served to stack the logs. When the kilns were fired, the arched entranceways were closed with sheet-metal doors. The stone ruin behind the fourth kiln is a lime kiln. It was loaded with wood, topped with limestone, and fired. The heat cooked the limestone into lime, which fell through a grate into a draw hole. The lime was likely used to make the kilns' mortar, and perhaps also for ore milling and cyaniding at the mines.

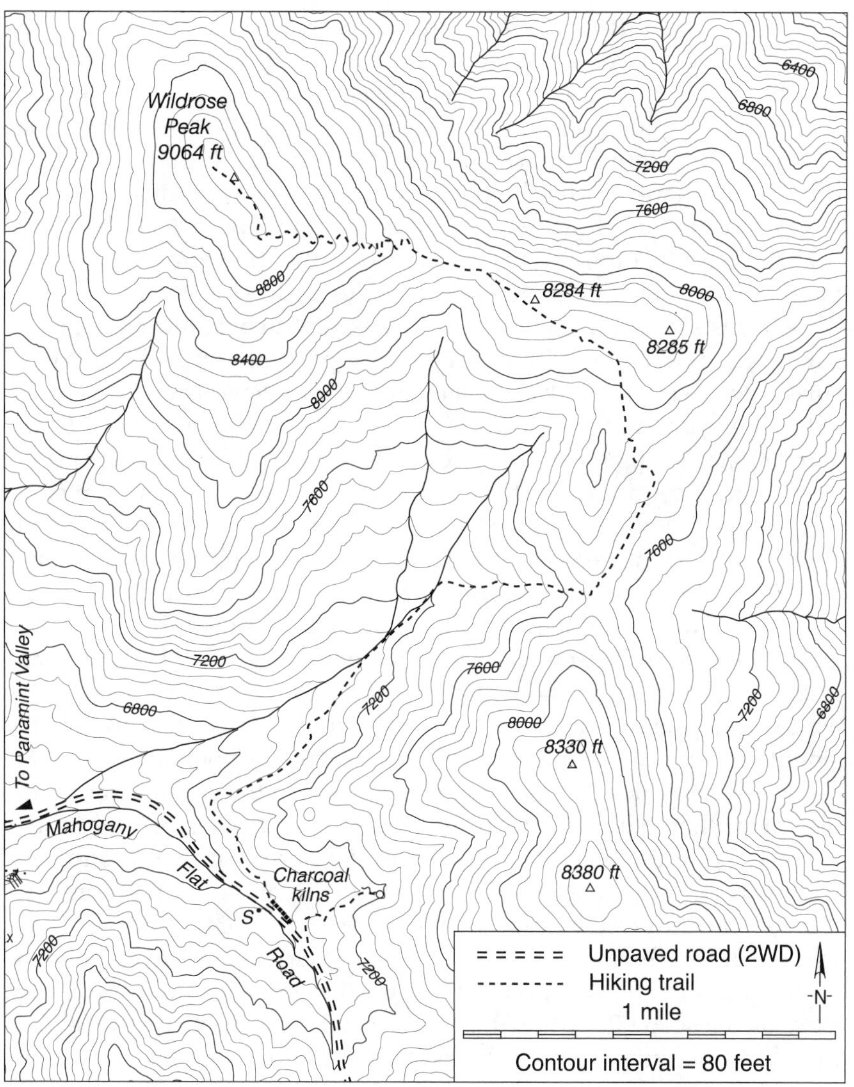

Wildrose Peak Trail		
	Dist.(mi)	Elev.(ft)
Trailhead	0.0	6,870
Crest	1.75	7,740
False summit	2.95	8,280
Saddle	3.15	8,220
Wildrose Peak	4.2	9,064

The Wildrose Peak Trail. From the charcoal kilns the trail climbs steadily along an open drainage, then more steeply through a thickening forest. The vegetation is largely mixed stands of pinyon pine and Utah juniper, many laden with mistletoe. Stumps 130 years old from the kilns' logging operations still survive along the trail. Many plants thrive here thanks to the higher elevations—big sagebrush, cliffrose, wild cabbage, tansybush, Panamint eriogonum, and grizzly bear cactus. Purple sage, lupine, and other less common flowering species also bloom in summer. Surrounded on all sides by low desert, at that time of year this sky island is a rare treat blessed with a comfortable mix of sun and shade. After 1.7 miles the trail tops the crest, and the bright, sun-beaten expanse of Death Valley bursts into view. The scenery only gets better from here on up, but if your time or energy is limited, this is a great place to enjoy the magnificent scenery before turning around.

The trail continues north near the crest, then reaches a false summit and a shallow saddle just beyond it. The steep last mile, most of it switchbacks, is the most strenuous. Closer to the summit, the greening process reverses itself. Discouraged by the nasty weather that prevails several months a year, the trees thin out, then disappear. The summit is a long plateau of broken shale with a scant cover of Mormon tea and grizzly bear cactus. In the winter it can be a bone-chilling place, covered with icy snow and swept by fierce winds. The scenery then looks singularly alpine, with muffled sounds and trees festooned with snow.

Wildrose Peak overlooks a huge territory. To the east the land tumbles more than 9,000 feet to Death Valley's alkali flats, backed by the fierce scarp of the Black Mountains. To the northeast rises the rugged wall of Trail Canyon, emblazoned with tilted parallel strata representing several hundred million years of Paleozoic sedimentation. The white band in the middle of it is Eureka Quartzite, a convenient geological marker that pinpoints the Middle Ordovician. The hulking mass of Telescope Peak fills the southern horizon. To the west, beyond the bleak volcanic expanse of the Darwin Plateau, the long sawtooth crest of the Sierra Nevada shines brightly more than 60 miles away.

Telescope Peak Trail

	Dist.(mi)	Elev.(ft)
Trailhead at Mahogany Flat	0.0	8,140
Arcane Meadows	2.5	~9,610
Bennett Peak	(0.5)	9,980
Telescope Peak	6.4	11,049

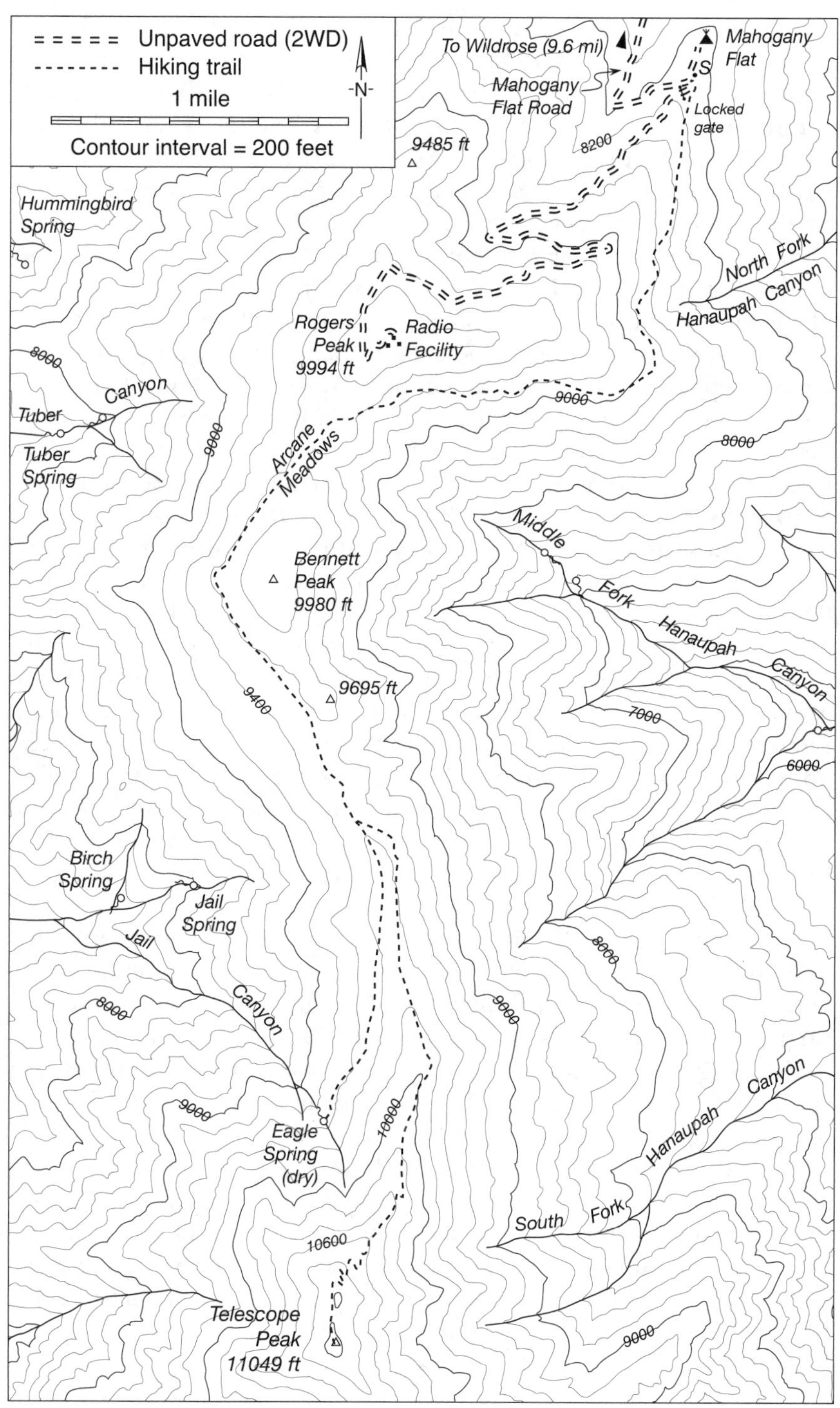

= = = = = Unpaved road (2WD)
-------- Hiking trail
1 mile
Contour interval = 200 feet
N
To Wildrose (9.6 mi)
Mahogany Flat
Mahogany Flat Road
S
Locked gate
9485 ft
8200
Hummingbird Spring
North Fork
Hanaupah Canyon
Rogers Peak 9994 ft
Radio Facility
8000
Canyon
Tuber
Tuber Spring
9000
Arcane Meadows
Middle
Fork
Hanaupah
Canyon
Bennett Peak 9980 ft
9695 ft
9400
7000
6000
Birch Spring
Jail Spring
Jail
Canyon
Eagle Spring (dry)
10000
Hanaupah
Canyon
South
Fork
10600
Telescope Peak 11049 ft

The Telescope Peak Trail. Telescope Peak is one of the highest mountains in the California desert. The maintained foot trail from Mahogany Flat to this lofty summit is one of Death Valley's classics, and it is tackled every year by many visitors. The first part of the trail circles the east side of Rogers Peak, under a thick canopy of trees—mostly pinyon pines, with some junipers and scattered mahogany. The small colorful slabs covering the ground are slate from the Johnnie Formation, a Proterozoic formation brought all the way up here by the same forces that pried Death Valley apart. In the summer, flowering plants grow right between the slabs, in essentially humus-free ground. This somewhat steep stretch ends at Arcane Meadows, a barren, often wind-swept pass offering the first glimpse west to the Argus Range.

If you cannot make it to Telescope Peak, try to push on to Bennett Peak, the summit south of Arcane Meadows. The route is straightforward, south up the narrow ridge. Just shy of 10,000 feet, Bennett Peak commands great views of Death Valley for half the effort.

The next few miles essentially follow the high spine of the Panamints and are fairly level. As the trail swings back and forth over the crest, you will be alternatively rewarded with awe-inspiring vistas of Death Valley, Panamint Valley, and several deep canyons—the three forks of Hanaupah Canyon on the east side, and Tuber and Jail canyons on the west side. The tree cover gradually thins to a scarce forest of limber pines and grizzled bristlecone pines. If you were transported to the same elevation in the Sierra Nevada, only 100 air miles away, you would be in the deep shade of a temperate forest, dwarfed by trees more than a hundred feet high. But as the Sierra robs most of the moisture from the Pacific Ocean, precipitation here is too scant, even this far up, to support such a luxuriant forest.

The last segment of this hike is up tight switchbacks cut into the steep north face of Telescope Peak. Oxygen is a scarce commodity up here. If you are not used to this elevation you will grope for air and progress very slowly. Pause often to quiet your heart and smell the roses. Some of the park's largest trees are found along here, impressive specimens several feet across at their base and tens of feet tall. Even late in the spring high snow drifts may linger along the trail.

The ultimate rewards of this climb are the stunning views from Telescope Peak, which encompass much of the surrounding desert, from the hazy valley of Las Vegas to the distant Sierra Nevada. From the rocky summit it is more than two vertical miles down to the eerie swirls of Death Valley's salt pan—to get higher above ground in the lower 48 states, you will have to fly.

■

JAIL CANYON

Deep in Jail Canyon, at the end of a bouncy road, lies the camp and ruins of the old Gem Mine. Shaded by cliffs and tall cottonwoods, cooled by a melodious creek, it is a refreshing oasis and a perfect place for a base camp. On day one, explore nearby mining relics and Jail Canyon's fabulous gold mill, one of the region's largest and best preserved. On day two, trudge up canyon through the well-watered spring to the Burro Mine and beyond. On day three, hike the spectacular high trail to Hall Canyon. Or stay at the camp the whole time, barbecue all day, and listen to your arteries clog up.

General Information
Jurisdiction: BLM, Death Valley National Park
Road status: Cross-country hiking; 2WD dirt road to lower canyon
Gem Mine mill: 2.7 mi, 1,470 ft up, ~30 ft down one way / easy–moder.
Burro Mine: 3.6 mi, 2,020 ft up, 40 ft down one way / moderate
Corona Mine: 2.9 mi, 1,790 ft up, 50 ft down one way / moderate
Main attractions: Gold mine and camp, perennial creek, narrows
USGS 7.5' topo maps: Jail Canyon*, Telescope Peak
Maps: pp. 343*, *319*

Location and Access

Jail Canyon is the second major canyon south of Wildrose Canyon, in the central Panamint Mountains. The Jail Canyon Road starts on the north side of the Indian Ranch Road 4.1 miles east of the Trona-Wildrose Road (or 0.55 mile west of the Indian Ranch junction). It heads north up the fan for 3.0 miles to a ramp that drops gently into the wash of Jail Canyon. This is a beautiful desert road. As it bounces up a sloping creosote desert, it skirts the mountains' looming escarpments, a grand sweep of deeply incised hills banded in pastel shades of white, cream, and brown. A few odd mining mementos lie by the roadside; burros often amble across the fan. Up to the ramp the road requires high clearance. In the canyon, a major flood wiped out entire road sections in July 2021. For most people, until the road is repaired the only option is to park above the ramp and hike the 2.5 miles to the spring at the end of the road.

As of this writing, the portion of the road in the park and the canyon are closed to driving and hiking, until chemical contamination of the creek by illegal activities has been corrected. Check the latest update with the park service.

Gem Mine mill, Jail Canyon

History

The little gold mine at the heart of Jail Canyon probably never had much to show, but there was something about it—maybe its idyllic location—that kept attracting miners to it, and it came to life and died no less than three times. Gold was first discovered here in 1899 by Jack Curran, a miner involved earlier on in Panamint City. With the financial backing of Ballarat merchant Charles Weaver, he opened the Gem Mine and installed a three-stamp mill, which he powered with Jail Canyon's hefty creek. Curran produced a little gold for a while, until a flood wiped out his mill in 1901. In the following years, other lode claims were explored at the Burro Mine, a quarter of a mile up canyon. A 116-foot shaft and a few tunnels were sunk into a series of gold-bearing quartz veins up to 10 feet wide, which yielded a small quantity of ore worth up to $25 per ton. These claims were later consolidated as the Protection Group of Mines, but by 1920 they were abandoned.

The Gem Mine was resuscitated a first time around 1930, when it was relocated as the New Discovery and Gem Mines. The property only had a short shaft and tunnel, but the ore looked good enough that around 1932, the mine operators hedged their bet and erected an imposing 25-ton mill. The mill incorporated all the bells and whistles—a jaw crusher, an elevator bin, a ball mill, a rake classifier, a flotation unit, a concentrating table, and a 50-horsepower diesel engine to drive it all. Mining employed a few men, who worked almost exclusively on the shaft. By 1938 its depth had nearly doubled, to 260 feet, and three levels of crosscuts had been driven into ore shoots. Desert mining usually suffers from lack of water, but ironically here there was too much of it. The shaft being right next to the creek, infiltration water poured into it and had to be constantly pumped out, to the tune of 3,500 gallons a day! In spite of all this work, returns were deceiving. The mill processed only a few hundred tons of rock, hardly enough to justify its high cost, and operations ceased after a few years.

The aging mine was fired up a third time in the 1940s by a miner named A. F. Troster, who relocated the claims. He opened a stope in the tunnel and shipped a few tons of ore. He sank a 42-foot shaft across the creek from the older shaft, but all he ran into was barren quartz and caved crosscuts from the shaft. His efforts paid back only a few hundred dollars now and then, so in 1949 he sold his claims to the Trona-based Corona Mining Company,. In February 1950 the company de-watered and re-timbered the main shaft down to 95 feet. On the Corona No. 2 claim, a tunnel was sunk on an 8-foot vein assaying $10 in gold per ton. But the pickings were even slimmer than in the past. The company quit, and Troster moved back in. In the late 1950s he was still living at the mining camp. By then he had lost all hope of striking it rich, but life in his little canyon was just too pleasant to leave.

Route Description

The Gem Mine camp. Its headwaters being right below Telescope Peak, the park's highest point, Jail Canyon is subject to destructive flashfloods more often than most. For millennia, the steep canyon slopes have also been shedding formidable volumes of rock—and it is starting to show. The wash is a chaotic river of stones swept clean of vegetation. Graphic remnants of cataclysmic events stud the way. One of them is a 25-foot tall, 200-ton granodiorite monolith that recently sheered off the north wall and crashed into the wash. A little further, a grove of honey mesquites on the south bank has been all but uprooted. Still further, a mangled wheel protruding awkwardly from the gravel is all that is visible of a good-size trailer buried under flood debris.

The scenery changes dramatically 2.4 miles in: the canyon narrows and suddenly fills up with trees. This is the lower end of Jail Canyon Creek, one of the longest streams around Death Valley. The Gem Mine's camp is cradled there, in a small, scenic amphitheater encircled by vertical stone walls. A tar-shingle cabin in decent shape and a smaller concrete cabin filled with odds and ends line the road, against a screen of majestic 50-foot cottonwoods. In sharp contrast to the barren lower canyon, this is a refreshing oasis, green and inviting, lulled by the creek and the breeze rustling through the trees. There are plenty of level spots for tents, and clear, crisp water in the creek. You will be entertained during the day by hummingbirds, swifts, and song birds, lullabied at night by crickets, toads, and wild burros tiptoeing through your camp on their way to water. In the summer the canyon walls provide deep shade in the morning and evening, and the trees take over during the day. In the winter the cabin's cast-iron stove provides welcome warmth. Wood collecting is prohibited, so bring your own.

In the summer a curious phenomenon takes place at the camp: every evening the creek vanishes! Touching the water will point to the explanation. During the day the water warms up, the evaporation rate soars, and the lower end of the creek gradually recedes up canyon. At night the creek cools down and its gurgles fill the camp again.

Mining buffs will enjoy the camp, which boasts a few generations of relics. The concrete and stone platforms across the cabins date back to the earliest mining days. They may have supported the cableway terminal of the Corona Mine. An antediluvian furnace crowned with a curious ampoule stands vigil below the camp, next to a yellow water truck and a graveyard of rusting parts. In the side canyon behind it, there is a collapsed cabin, and an International pickup that has probably not turned over since Eisenhower was in the White House.

The Corona Mine. Hike up the roadless side canyon 0.2 mile, and you will run into the rock-lined trail to this mine on the right. The trail's good switchbacks, supported by sturdy retaining walls, offer bird's eye views of the impressive gulch it bypasses, clogged by two massive falls. In 0.25 mile the trail forks. The left fork ends at the short tunnel of the Corona Mine's No. 2 claim, which tapped a vein of auriferous milky quartz. The right fork skirts the ridge to the collapsed frame and pulley of the cableway that dropped the ore to the camp.

The Gem Mine gold mill. From the camp a narrow trail heads up into Jail Canyon. Right away it enters a short constriction, where it vies for space with the stream and a dense grove of spindly trees. After a few minutes it reaches a wooden ore bin, then climbs onto the north bank to one of the mining wonders of the Panamints—the Gem Mine gold mill. To make the most of this cramped location, its designers custom-built it to fit right into a vertical recess in the rock wall. Weathered into rippled sweeps of cinnamon and chocolate, it is one of the most elaborate and best preserved mills from that era, a mind-bending concoction of timber and metal, giant wheels and cogs, pulleys, cables, pipes, ladders, tipples, and tanks. The main structure supported the

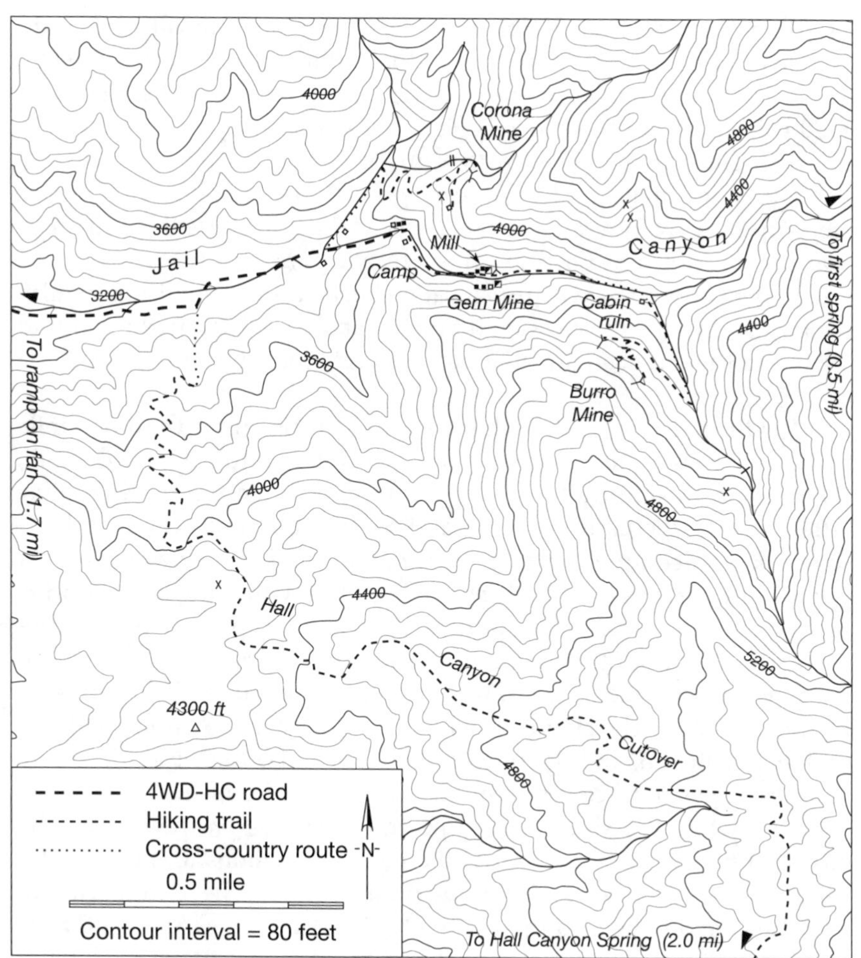

Jail Canyon

	Dist.(mi)	Elev.(ft)
Ramp below canyon mouth	0.0	2,180
Side canyon	2.4	3,430
Corona Mine (tramway)	(0.5)	3,910
Gem Mine's Camp/end of road	2.5	3,520
Gem Mine mill	2.7	3,620
Side canyon/cabin ruin	3.1	3,840
Trail to Burro Mine	(0.2)	4,060
Burro Mine (west tunnel)	(0.45)	4,160
First spring (head)	4.4	5,340

grinding machinery, dismantled long ago. The lanky tower to its right is a headframe: it hoisted ore out of the 260-foot shaft located directly under it, now flooded. The headframe's cable and spool lie nearby in the bushes, next to the concrete slab that supported its engine. Half a dozen engines are scattered further up the bank.

The other main gold producer, the 370-foot tunnel, is just a few steps up canyon. The rail track that serviced it still skirts the mill on its way to the ore bin. On the opposite bank, across the entrenched streambed, there are two tin storage shacks and a small blacksmith shop. Just up canyon is a second flooded shaft, sunk by Troster around 1950, and the diesel engine that powered its spooled cable.

The Burro Mine. Although the Burro Mine is only a third of a mile away as the crow flies, it takes a little work to get to it. From the mill, take the north-side trail as it waves up and down the narrow talus. After 0.2 mile the talus runs out, and so does the trail. Now you have to sneak between the rocky canyon wall and the thick vegetation. At two or three places trees hug the wall so closely that the only resort is to step over the creek or slosh through inundated patches of scouring rush. Progress is a little slow, but the scenery is first class. The stream is fringed with algae, grasses, watercress, and an outlandish profusion of stream orchis. The stands of willow, mesquite, and cottonwood, the melodious stream, and the blue dragonflies and butterflies drifting by compose a pastoral scene seemingly out-of-place in this harsh land.

Just before the side canyon the trail resumes on the north side, crowded by shrubs, then crosses the creek and climbs to the ruin of a cabin on the south bench. Continue on the old road beyond it, up into the side canyon, then up the wash after the road ends. About 0.2 mile from the cabin, a dusty foot trail climbs steeply onto the west slope. It ascends gently northwest to an overlook of Jail Canyon (0.2 mile), then splits. The right fork ends in 150 yards at the Burro Mine's wiggly west tunnel, which exposes a slanted vein of milky quartz stained with blue-green copper ore. The left fork climbs 250 yards to the middle tunnel. About 40 yards before reaching it, a side trail on the left climbs 130 yards to the east tunnel. The mining trails are overlapped by swarms of recent burro trails, which adds a little challenge to locating the tunnels. The tunnels are not overly exciting. The main reason for coming here is to get exposed to this rarest of desert environments—a narrow canyon bottom crowded with riparian vegetation—first intimately by bushwhacking through it, then by taking a peak at it from above, an impossibly lush oasis snaking between bone-dry rock walls.

■

HALL CANYON

Imagine a lonesome trail crossing the rugged scarp of the Panamint Mountains, floating a mile above the valley floor...reaching a remote canyon inaccessible from below, where a perennial mountain stream wanders through a luxuriant oasis...a little cabin on the edge of the greenery, the starting point of narrow trails wandering up and down the canyon...to an awesome gorge of sheer granite walls and waterfalls...and forgotten cabins lost at timberline. Of all the trails in Panamint Valley, this may well be the most magnificent.

General Information

Jurisdiction: Death Valley National Park
Road status: Hiking on old roads and trails; 4WD access road
Goosenecks Overlook: 5.1 mi, 2,430 ft up, 1,250 ft down one way / difficult
Hall Canyon Trail: 5.8 mi, 4,410 ft up, 1,050 ft down one way / strenuous
Rim Trail: 5.8 mi, 2,760 ft up, 1,270 ft down one way / difficult
Main attractions: Spectacular trails, spring, creek, waterfalls, gorge
USGS 7.5' topo maps: Jail Canyon*, Telescope Peak
Maps: pp. 343*, 349*, *319*

Location and Access

Hall Canyon drains the central Panamints Mountains west of Telescope Peak. It was named after Ed Hall, who operated a blacksmith shop at Wildrose in the late 1870s when the charcoal kilns were running. The lower half mile of Hall Canyon and the road that leads to it are part of privately owned Indian Ranch. To hike in this way *you must first obtain permission at Indian Ranch.* The creek in Hall Canyon is piped to the ranch for domestic use, and the residents are understandably leery about letting anyone clamber all over their water supply. If permission is granted, walk up the canyon to the Hall Canyon Trail (1,750'), and hike up the trail described below.

When it is open, the most practical route to Hall Canyon is the cutover road from Jail Canyon, the next canyon north. From the Indian Ranch Road, drive the Jail Canyon Road 3.0 miles to the ramp below the mouth of Jail Canyon (see *Jail Canyon*), then 2.1 miles up canyon to a sharp 90° left bend toward the wash. The Hall Canyon Cutover, a primitive road now closed to motor vehicles, used to branch off to the right. Its lower end is now washed out. Hike up the side canyon to the south 300 yards, and you will see the road up on the right.

Route Description

The Hall Canyon Cutover. From Jail Canyon the wide road winds up to a ridge, slithers far up along this ridge, and angles south to a first pass. It then loses and gains a little elevation to a second, slightly lower pass. Shortly past it, at a first junction, the left fork climbs a short distance to a viewpoint of Hall Canyon. At the second junction, which is at the bottom of the first steep down-grade, the main road on the left drops steeply in a few wide curves to the wash of Hall Canyon.

Wash to wash, the distance is 4.7 miles, with an elevation gain of 2,350 feet and a loss of 1,120 feet. It is fairly demanding, and there is almost no shade, but it is spectacular. The road rides on high ridges in full view of Panamint Valley, the Argus Range, the Inyo Mountains, and the Sierra Nevada brooding beyond. At places you look straight down at Warm Sulfur Springs and Indian Ranch, tucked near the foot of the range. You might run into heavy burro commuter traffic, honking obnoxiously to demand the right-of-way. This area, especially the first mile of road, is home to a rare sub-species of *Enceliopsis argophylla* known as Panamint daisy. It is hard to miss: it looks like an open artichoke with large pale-green leaves. In the late spring its tall stalks bear a lemon-yellow sunflower, the largest in the Mojave Desert.

The Rowland Cabin. Where the road meets the wash of Hall Canyon you are standing at the top of the Hall Canyon Pluton, a hard plug of 80-million-year-old granodiorite exposed over several square miles in the lower Panamint Mountains. Water surfaces right here and gives rise to the Hall Canyon Creek. To the east, Hall Canyon is a broad, dry valley framed by lofty peaks; to the west it is a precipitous water-worn gorge filled with riparian vegetation and waterfalls. The transition between these two worlds, just below the road, is amazingly abrupt. In mere feet, drab rabbitbrush is supplanted by a lush oasis.

At the head of the spring, there is a small shack shaded under 30-foot cottonwoods, named Rowland Cabin after its former owner. A flat-roofed shell of disjointed plywood with tattered plastic sheets for window panes, it was rustic in its prime, which was decades ago. It is furnished with a shaky table, a mildewed cot, and a recent stove. Parched magazines lie on dusty shelves next to food cans, water bottles, firewood, ropes, and decks of cards. It would make a decent shelter if it weren't for the layers of rodent droppings that litter it. The grove right outside is a peaceful place to rest after the tiring crossing.

The Rim Trail. For 2 miles below the cabin, Hall Canyon's gorge forms a spellbinding slice of Earth coursed by a spirited stream that

The Goosenecks near the top of the lush spring in Hall Canyon

links a long chain of cascades and waterfalls, several over 100 feet high. There is no easy way through this treacherous passage. Only climbers have ever traversed this gorge, and only *downhill*, by rappelling down the 15 waterfalls and bushwhacking through the willow groves between them. Rare are the people who have the motivation, skills, and stamina for such an odyssey. On this ever-shrinking planet of ours, this is as close as it gets to *terra incognita*.

Fortunately, discovering this awesome place need not be so rich in adrenaline. The fearless burros, determined to boldly go anywhere they choose to, gave us humans a trail that provides exquisite details of the gorge's inner sanctum. Ten yards up canyon from the cabin a track crosses the shrub-invaded open wash to the south side, where two interconnected trails head down canyon. The lower one follows the edge of the wash to a crude fence of wooden posts. Below it is one of the few easy access points to the creek. Its limpid water flows by earthy banks covered with maidenhair fern, scouring rush, watercress, and willow shoots, a refreshing spot livened by dragonflies.

The second trail, about 30 feet up the slope, is the Rim Trail. It soon goes through an opening in a long, 5-foot stone wall parallel to the slope, one of several corrals rumored to have been used as sheep pasture by Indian Ranch residents in the 1950s. It then climbs on to the Gooseneck Overlook, a sharp ridge hanging over the gorge. Down below, the creek has carved into the pluton a tightly winding trench, a mating dance of narrow rock fins and rounded alcoves. The strained walls have split into stacks of imbalanced boulders seemingly ready to topple. At the base of the gooseneck, 140 feet down, the canyon bottom is a wall-to-wall ribbon of luxuriant vegetation. The creek is hidden beneath it, betrayed only by white cascades, the roar of turbulent water, and the gorge's uppermost waterfall, which free-falls 30 feet into a pool of dark water. Above this lush tableau, the slopes are bone-dry and studded with barrel cactus.

The trail continues as faint switchbacks up the ridge line, gaining 120 feet in 100 yards, to a more level trail on the right heading down canyon. This dusty path is a masterpiece of burro engineering. Dismissing vertigo, it clings to the abrupt margin where the pluton carries the mountain on its shoulders. Several hundred feet beneath it, the twisted chasm holds in its grip the green snake of Hall Canyon's spring. From this far up the logic of the stream searching for a path through solid rock becomes crystal clear. It curves beneath scalloped cliffs, angles sharply where it runs headlong into rock faces, slithers through slim cracks, and splinters around fallen boulders the size of cabins. The creek sounds like a lunatic, mumbling incoherently to itself. The trail reveals the creek's struggles one piece at a time, a turbulent story you stitch together from one dizzying viewpoint to the next. Where the edge is too close and sheer, gravity tugs at your stomach. A mile out, where the trail fades at a sharp ridge, Panamint Valley bursts into view, its long basin a patchwork of hard pans, salt flats, and dunes cupped in a mayhem of wrinkled ranges. Up canyon, several miles to the east, metamorphic ridges jet upward until there is only sky—Telescope Peak, the headwaters of this impossible stream.

Hall Canyon

	Dist.(mi)	Elev.(ft)
Hall Canyon Cutover (Jail Cyn)	0.0	3,260
First pass	2.45	5,450
Second pass	3.1	5,420
Hall Cyn Spr./Rowland Cabin	4.7	4,490
to Gooseneck Overlook	(0.4)	4,440
to Rim Trail (end)	(1.0)	4,740
to Indian R. via Hall Cyn Tr.	(5.8)	1,140
to Mine (cabin)	(2.1)	6,485
to Telescope Peak	(6.5)	11,049

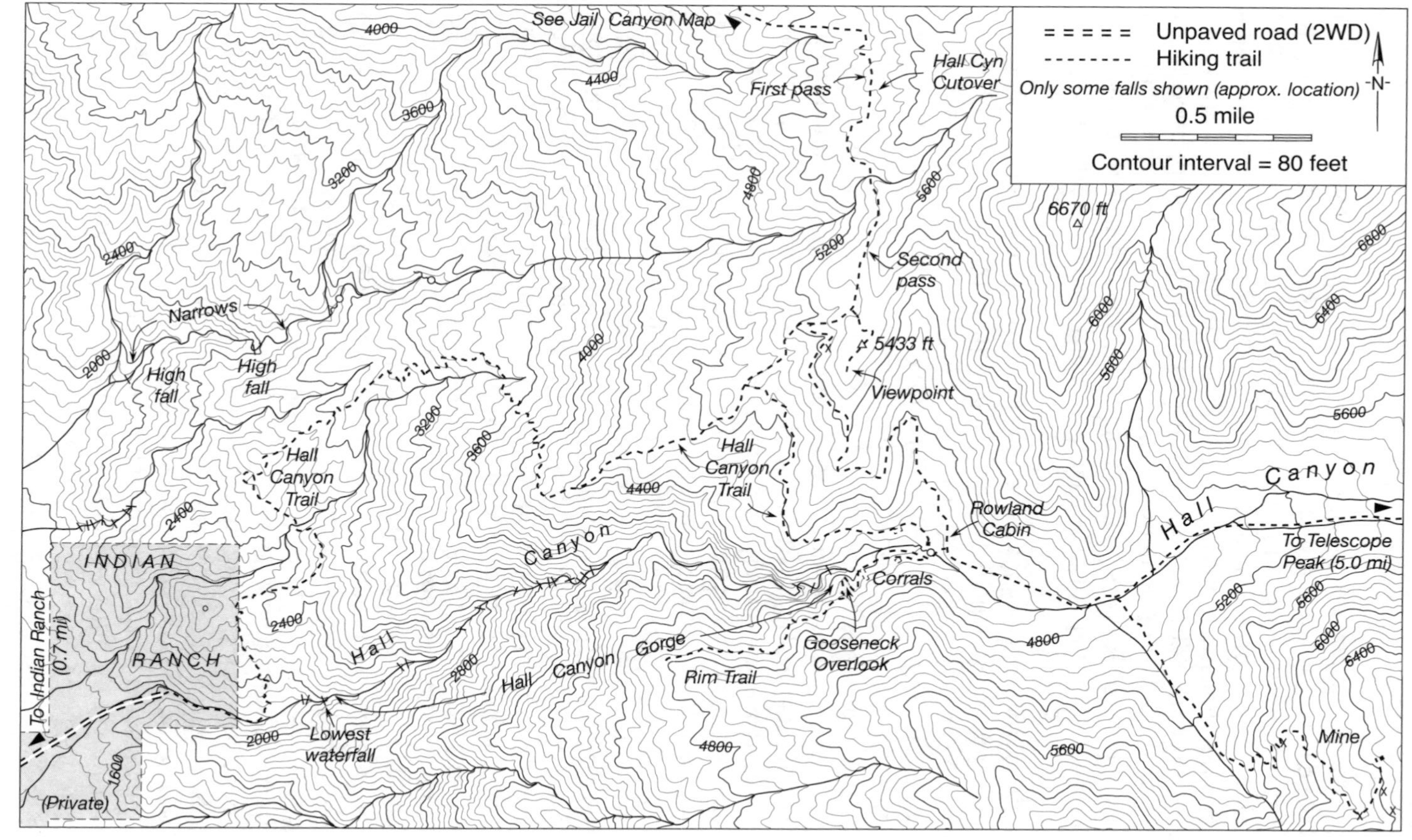
See Jail Canyon Map
Unpaved road (2WD)
Hiking trail
Only some falls shown (approx. location)
N
0.5 mile
Contour interval = 80 feet
Hall Cyn Cutover
First pass
Second pass
6670 ft
5433 ft
Viewpoint
Narrows
High fall
High fall
Hall Canyon Trail
Hall Canyon Trail
Rowland Cabin
Hall Canyon
To Telescope Peak (5.0 mi)
INDIAN RANCH
To Indian Ranch (0.7 mi)
(Private)
Hall Canyon
Corrals
Hall Canyon Gorge
Rim Trail
Gooseneck Overlook
Lowest waterfall
Mine

The Hall Canyon Trail. To get in and out of Hall Canyon there is another, little-known route—the original trail on the gorge's north side. It starts behind the cabin and skirts the northern edge of the spring. It passes by the long stone wall of another corral, then ascends the north slope to a ridge. It contours the ridge, weaves northwest across steep rubbly slopes, and after 1 mile reaches a second ridge. There it meets a faint road dropping from the right. If this is as far as you want to venture, turn right on this road, which joins the Hall Canyon Cutover in 0.3 mile. This section of the trail offers good glimpses into the gorge first, then into Panamint Valley, especially the Wildrose graben, a steep-sided depression pried open by earthquakes.

At the road junction, the Hall Canyon Trail angles left down the ridge, as a road first, then a trail. At 4,230′, it curves north off the ridge. From there to the creek, a distance of 2.6 miles, it twists and turns northwest down across the broad head of a drainage to a major ridge, then wiggles west-southwest down this ridge. At 2,740′ it leaves the ridge and dips south across this same drainage before dropping to the Hall Canyon Creek 0.4 mile above the canyon mouth. Desert erosion is slow. Most of this trail, abandoned long ago, is still extant. Some guess work is needed at a few places, notably around 3,600′, between the middle ridge and the final switchbacks to the creek, and wherever the burro tracks get too numerous. This is wild hiking. The scenery switches from hard outcrops to finely rilled badlands and serpentine canyons. Short spurs drop to springs or narrows that dead-end at dry falls. Panamint Valley is a constant presence, inundated with light.

This route is not for everyone. It requires excellent navigation skills, physical fitness, and an acquired eagerness to meddle with rough terrain. The main canyon north of the trail is not an option to avoid the Indian Ranch (again, do ask permission first): it has at least two high falls. That said, while the Jail Canyon Road is closed, this trail provides the easiest foot access to Hall Canyon. It is well worth asking.

Upper Hall Canyon. There is much more to Hall Canyon—the nameless mine and its decaying cabin reached by a beat-up track high up the south canyon wall; the large corrugated-metal cabin at the Hornspoon Mine (~7,700'), a gold property owned by Chris Wicht in the 1930s, and one of the park's most remote; and a grueling route to Telescope Peak. For most people, these destinations are much too far and hard for a day hike from Jail Canyon. But if you camp in the canyon, water and time are no longer issues. You may become in a few days one of the very few experts on this outstanding canyon.

■

SURPRISE CANYON

Surprise Canyon is one of those places you just cannot afford to miss. For nearly two miles beyond the end of the canyon road, you walk through a lush oasis of cottonwood and willows irrigated by a vivacious creek. Part of it squeezes through striking white-marble narrows where the creek erupts into sparkling waterfalls. Hardy hikers can continue further up canyon, usually with a backpack, to the fascinating ghost town of Panamint City.

General Information

Jurisdiction: Surprise Canyon Wilderness (BLM), DVNP (NPS)
Road status: Roadless; primitive road to mid-canyon (HC)
Surprise Canyon narrows: 0.9 mi, 620 ft up, 20 ft down one way/easy
Brewery Spring: 3.2 mi, 2,270 ft up, 40 ft down one way/moderate
Panamint City: 5.5 mi, 3,740 ft up, 40 ft down one way/difficult
Main attractions: Lush narrows, creeks, waterfalls, Panamint City
USGS 7.5′ topo maps: Ballarat*, Panamint
Maps: pp. 355*, 367, *319*

Location and Access

Surprise Canyon drains the central western Panamints, just west of Telescope Peak. The canyon road starts from the graded Indian Ranch Road. A small sign points to it 1.9 miles north of the general store in Ballarat (or 5.3 miles south of the Indian Ranch junction). The Surprise Canyon Road first climbs 2.3 miles to the mouth of Surprise Canyon, then 1.7 miles in the canyon to its end at the site of Chris Wicht Camp. The lower canyon is pure Panamints vintage. What is most impressive is the height of the walls and their unusually colorful exposures. Taluses over 500 feet tall drape the north slopes, as smooth as sand yet tilted at a crazy 45° angle. The narrow wash, sunk beneath low gravel banks, is lost in this immensity of rock. So is the road. Often forced into the wash by hard-rock outcrops, it barely manages to squeeze by. The road is a little steep, but if it has been recently bladed by the county, it should be passable with a passenger car.

Route Description

Chris Wicht Camp. Once set on a high bank under ancient cottonwoods, this precious oasis was in use off and on for some 130 years, starting as far back as the 1870s. Chris Wicht, superintendent of the

Campbird Mine at Panamint City in the mid-1920s, lived here for many years. In the early 1980s, Rocky Novak and his father George took over the camp for about 20 years, until their cabin and the lush spring went up in flame while they were burning brush in September 2006. Both were small-time miners at heart, the last of a dying breed. They had mined at Panamint City and at the Golden Eagle Mine across the valley, and prospected for the C. R. Briggs Mine. Rocky still occasionally drove to his gold mine in the southern Panamints, popped a few sticks of dynamite, and hauled the ore up here for processing. His mill was an assemblage of recycled prehistoric contraptions slowly yielding to rust: jaw and impact crushers, a ball mill, and a concentration table. Instead of cyanide, Novak used benign chemicals and electrolysis. "It is cheaper, more efficient, and it does not pollute the stream," he said. His ore was not the richest. But he could harvest a couple of ounces of gold in a day. This was about the income of a Silicon Valley manager—if Novak was working five days a week, which he was much too smart to do. Unless he was out shopping for dynamite, he was usually at his camp, and always eager to chat. Rocky went on to be caretaker at Ballarat. So you can still get to meet him and enjoy his encyclopedic knowledge of the local history—and his vitriolic views on government agencies.

The charred remains of Novak's camp were cleaned up in 2007 and 2008. If you want to hike up canyon, park at the small parking area below the ruins of the camp.

The narrows. From Chris Wicht Camp up to the head of Limekiln Spring, a distance of nearly 2 miles, Surprise Canyon is an idyllic oasis coursed by a spirited stream. This stretch holds some of the most beautiful scenery out of Panamint Valley. You walk by the tree-shaded stream, crossing it over and over. At first you meticulously avoid getting your shoes wet, but you soon abandon all hope of staying dry. On a warm day, this is quite pleasant—splashing through cold water, wetting your clothes, enjoying the higher humidity. By the time you reach the narrows, half a mile up canyon, you are walking *in* the creek.

Few places in the California desert offer as striking a combination of rock, running water, and lush vegetation as the narrows of Surprise Canyon. The vertical walls are solid white aplite nearly one billion years old, as dazzling as virgin snow. At one place, a dark-brown dike of diabase shoots straight up to the canyon rim—the one stain in an immaculate landscape. Every streamside rock surface has been polished into curvaceous shapes or gleaming slickrock. The tight banks are bordered by green willows, grass, rush, and slender orchids. The

Waterfall in the narrows of Surprise Canyon

narrows gradually tighten up, until there are no more banks, no more vegetation, and all that is left is the creek. This is the most exciting part: over a distance of 400 yards the stream is graced with seven waterfalls and multiple cascades. Water sluices down grooved chutes, gushes over bedrock lips, foams from pothole to pothole. The falls are all gently sloped and only 4 to 15 feet high. Except during spring high water, they are easy to negotiate, by stepping from pool to pool, balancing yourself on slippery boulders, or wiggling up dry slickrock. This is as much water fun as one can get in this overwhelmingly dry land.

Driving through the narrows was once permitted. In the past, Novak recalled, up to dozens of jeeps a day would parade past his camp on their way to Panamint City, churning his water supply into pools of oil and mud. One day he got so angry that he stalled the traffic by smearing Crisco over strategically located rocks. As hard to believe as it may be, this harmless prank cost him two months in jail (although he later sued the government for a legal technicality and was compensated). Novak did not manage to keep Surprise Canyon car-free, but nature almost did. In 1984, a violent storm scoured the narrows, wiping out the road and resuscitating dormant waterfalls. The hefty equipment stranded at the top of the narrows—a mine car, metal duct, and an overturned truck—are testimony to the awesome power of floods: they were all flushed miles down the canyon. With the road gone, car traffic plummeted. Novak was happy. But die-hards continued to drive through, now drawn by the challenge of winching their one-ton vehicles up the waterfalls." It took them nine hours getting to Panamint City," Novak said," and a little less coming back, just to say they made it." That jeeps could be winched up this chaos of stone, à la Hayduke, *is* amazing; that they made it down, sometimes without a winch, is incredible. What finally closed the BLM portion of the road (above Chris Wicht Camp) to vehicle access is a court ruling to protect its riparian habitats. The Surprise Canyon Creek was recently designated by the US Congress as a Wild and Scenic River. The road is permanently closed in the upper canyon, which is on NPS land.

The mid-canyon. Past the narrows, the water fun continues for a little over a mile to the head of Limekiln Spring. Since the road closure, about two thirds of this stretch have been taken over by four patches of thick spring vegetation, and the road is mostly gone. Bushwhacking is now par for the course, which makes hiking more painstaking and slower. The stream flows intermittently, here in full sun, there in the shade of willows or along hedges of grapevine. Butterflies, dragonflies (and unfortunately horse flies in summer) are common sights. You may also see little green frogs parked by the stream. The main water intake of Limekiln Spring is marked by an impressively large mass of grapevine that spills down the north canyon slope. Most of the stream comes gushing out from under it, at the rate of hundreds of gallons per minute. The second outlet is in the wash just around the bend, hidden under willows and salt cedars at the head of the spring. Above it, the tree cover ends and the canyon is dry.

Surprise Canyon

	Dist.(mi)	Elev.(ft)
Chris Wicht Camp (ruins)	0.0	2,620
Narrows (lower end)	0.5	2,950
Narrows (upper end)	0.85	3,220
Limekiln Spring (upper)	1.95	3,985
Brewery Spring (head)	3.15	4,850
Hemlock Mine Road	4.5	5,755
Sourdough Canyon Road	5.2	6,135
Panamint City (road junction)	5.5	6,315

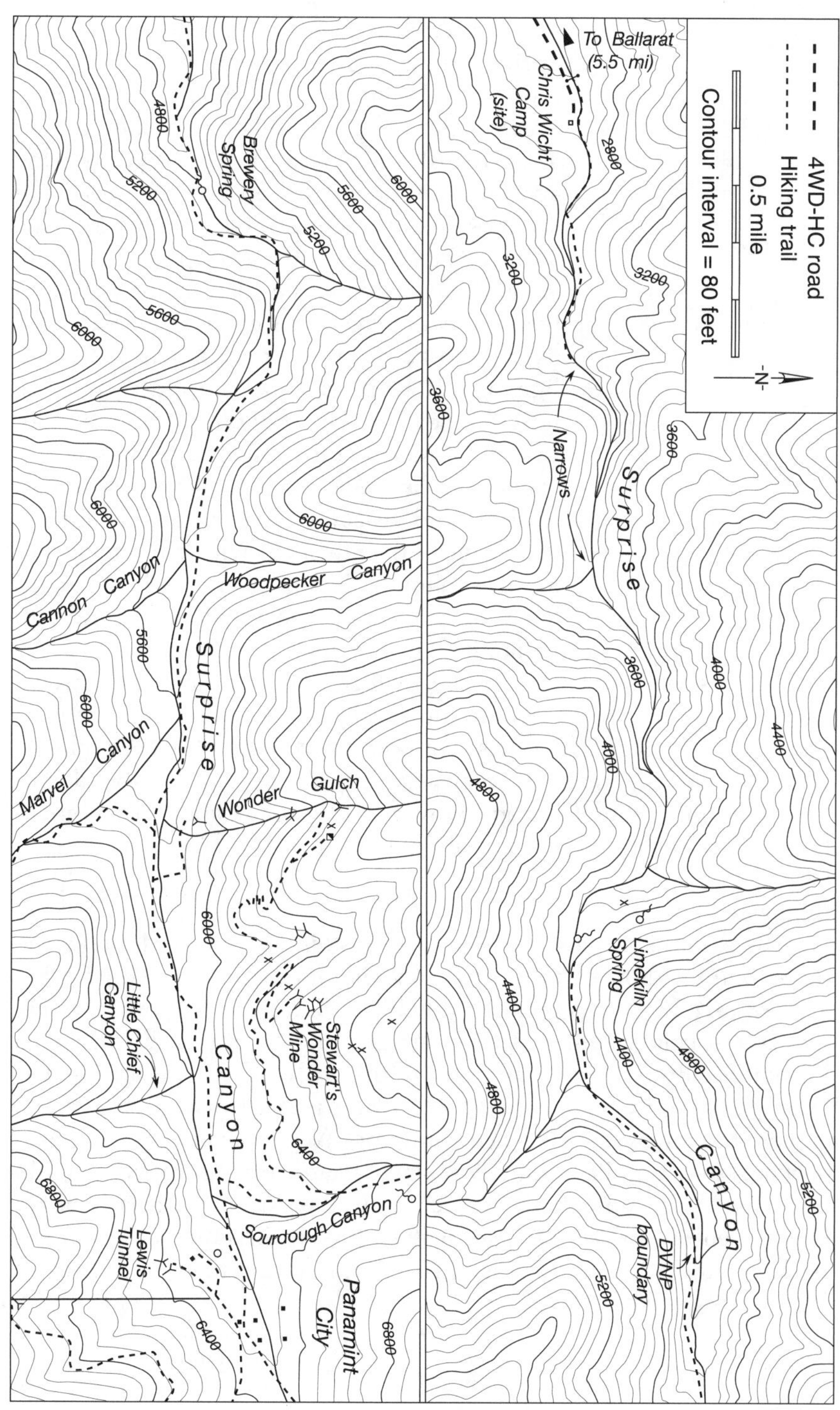
4WD-HC road
Hiking trail
0.5 mile
Contour interval = 80 feet
N
To Ballarat (5.5 mi)
Chris Wicht Camp (site)
Narrows
Surprise Canyon
Limekiln Spring
DVNP boundary
Brewery Spring
Woodpecker Canyon
Cannon Canyon
Marvel Canyon
Wonder Gulch
Surprise Canyon
Little Chief Canyon
Stewart's Wonder Mine
Sourdough Canyon
Lewis Tunnel
Panamint City

Stream Orchis

The road resumes at the head of Limekiln Spring, and is essentially continuous the rest of the way to Panamint City. The next water is at Brewery Spring, a half-mile-long ribbon of willows that fills the wash. The road bypasses the spring's lower half, then scoots under the spring's shady tree canopy to the head of the spring. This area is both pretty and refreshing. A swift creek floods the road, irrigating sidewalks of watercress and nettle. The trees arch over the road, forming cool tunnels of filtered light and violet penumbra. The stream surfaces near the head of the spring, right by the road. In the warmer months, this is a good place to cool off in the shade while the breeze sprinkles mist around. Together with Limekiln Spring, this is one of the few areas where you may spot a rare Panamint alligator lizard. It is also your last chance to fill up: the remaining 2.3 miles to Panamint City are dry.

The first signs of Panamint City will be stone ruins along the wash, starting just past Marvel Canyon: not isolated ruins but dozens of them, the ghosts of the homes that once lined Main Street. Up ahead, between the canyon walls, looms the improbably tall smokestack of Panamint City's smelter. You know instantly that something momentous took place here. The fun is about to begin.

Suggested Hikes

The easy hike up the narrows is a must: it is a gem, and it takes no more than two hours round-trip. Limekiln Spring and Brewery Spring are also excellent goals for short day hikes. Since you will probably get wet, avoid cold weather. A fit hiker carrying a light pack can get to Panamint City in three hours and return in two hours, which leaves enough daylight for a quick tour of the ghost town. However, to explore the towns' extensive surroundings (see *Panamint City*) requires backpacking in and staying a few days. Water is plentiful; you should not have to carry more than three quarts at any time (this is burro Grand Central, so do purify all water). It is a still a demanding backpacking outing. Count on four to six hours to get there and three to four hours to hike back.

■

PANAMINT CITY

For its many well-preserved structures, historic significance, and beautiful setting in high forested mountains, Panamint City is one of the most exceptional mining sites in the California desert. The best way to explore it is to backpack in, camp or stay in a cabin at the ghost town, and take day hikes around. Miles of roads zigzag up into the mountains to dozens of sites—cabins, mills, tunnels, mining equipment, and colorful silver ore. You will see lots of birds and wildflowers in the warm season, run into burros every day, soak in cool springs, and walk through forests scented with sagebrush and sap. Everywhere you go the isolation, both geographic and temporal, is almost palpable. A trip to Panamint City is a bit of all this: you get caught in a spellbinding space-time capsule.

General Information
Jurisdiction: Surprise Canyon Wilderness (BLM), DVNP
Road status: Roadless; access on foot from primitive road
Blue Jay Mine: 7.0 mi, 4,750 ft up, 40 ft down one way / strenuous
Hemlock Mine: 6.3 mi, 5,280 ft up, 60 ft down one way / strenuous
Stewart's Wonder Mine: 5.9 mi, 3,950 ft up, 40 ft down one way / stren.
Wyoming Mine: 6.9 mi, 5,060 ft up, 40 ft down one way / strenuous
Main attractions: Remote historic ghost town, silver mines, pine forest
USGS 7.5' topo maps: Panamint*, Telescope Peak
Maps: pp. 355, 367*, *319*

Location and Access

Panamint City is located deep in the upper reaches of Surprise Canyon. The easiest route, described in the previous section, is up Surprise Canyon. The second easiest route is from Death Valley up Johnson Canyon to Panamint Pass, then down Frenchman's Canyon to Panamint City (7.5 miles, 4,200 feet up and 1,780 feet down; see *Hiking Death Valley*). The hardest route is up Happy Canyon, the next canyon south (see *Happy Canyon*). None of these hikes are easy, although all three canyons have flowing water, which will lighten your pack.

The Panamint City area holds miles of roads and trails, several camps, and over a dozen mines, spread out over square miles of steep terrain. If you hike up Surprise Canyon, the round-trip can be done in one day, but you will not have time to see much more than the ghost town. To visit this site properly, plan on staying a few days.

History

The story of Panamint City began late in the fall of 1872, when Richard Jacobs and his partner Robert Stewart trudged up a nameless canyon in the western Panamints, hoping to locate the source of silver float Jacobs had spotted earlier in the lower canyon. Back then, this was rough, unchartered wilderness. Neither Ballarat, Lookout, nor Skidoo were yet on the map. Only a handful of emigrants had set foot in Panamint Valley. But both men had a keen eye for minerals: Jacobs had spent much of his life prospecting in California and Mexico, and Stewart had prospected up and down Panamint Valley for a decade. Deep in the mountain, the canyon flared into a valley so unexpectedly green that they called it Surprise Canyon. It was there, on the pine-dotted slopes, that they discovered the silver-bearing quartz veins they had been looking for. After returning to civilization and finding that their samples assayed hundreds of dollars per ton, they returned in April 1873 to claim their finds. Jacobs optimistically named his the Wonder of the World, and Stewart located the Stewart's Wonder.

The discovery occurred in the wake of rich silver strikes at Cerro Gordo and Nevada's Comstock, and it sparked wild speculations. Throngs of prospectors and miners rushed to Surprise Canyon. By the end of 1873 every square foot of ground that showed the slightest promise had been claimed, and the Panamint Mining District was in place. Jacobs was first to develop his property. In association with a few friends, he incorporated the Panamint Mining Company in November and hired no fewer than three dozen miners to sink exploratory shafts. The following summer he hauled a second-hand mill to his mine, hoping to reduce his ore to a hefty $1,000 per ton.

Mining did not start in earnest, however, until Nevada senators John Jones and William Stewart stepped in. Both men had just made a fortune at the Comstock Mine, Jones as a superintendent and Stewart as a lawyer. In the summer of 1874, they and a lawyer partner, Trenor Park, purchased almost every claim in sight, as well as Jacobs' mill, for about $250,000. This high-stake acquisition triggered a second, even wilder rush, one of the biggest the Death Valley region ever witnessed.

Although at first sight silver was plentiful, a lot of it was surficial ore, and most exploratory tunnels failed to turn up much silver at depth. But it did not stop the astute senators. They would play on the credulity of investors and raise from them far more than the half a million dollars worth of mineable silver. Investing nearly $100,000 of their personal fortune, they formed nine companies, about one for each group of claims, and offered $50 million in public stock. In September, they organized the Surprise Valley Mill and Water Company, which

Main Street, Panamint City, ca. 1875 (Courtesy of Eastern Calif. Museum)

was to mill the ore from all nine companies and collect a cozy percentage of the profits. "The Company," as it soon became known, brought in several hundred men to build offices, boarding houses, and trails, and to work the tunnels. Before long, it owned most of the town.

In retrospect, financing Panamint City was foolish: the deposits were modest and poorly accessible, and the three principals had shaky reputations. Three years earlier, Jones had deceived investors while in a position of trust, and Stewart and Park had masterminded a clever swindle at the Emma Mine in Utah. Expectedly, their exorbitant capitalization offer was met with suspicion. In the winter of 1874, they sensed trouble and began extensive developments. They erected a tramway to the more promising Wyoming tunnels, a pipeline and reservoir, and a 20-stamp mill and roasting furnace. They even merged their nine companies into two to increase investors' return. It all looked so good that when the companies went public in early 1875, their $300,000 worth of shares sold in two weeks. Playing their role to the hilt, they incorporated another company to build a railroad from Santa Monica to Panamint Valley. There was enough ore, they claimed, to generate $50 million annually! Major negotiations were initiated with prominent railroad tycoons, but no railroad ever came out of it.

Panamint City was located in 1873 in the valley below the mines. By year's end its mixed citizenry of miners, prospectors, and merchants topped the 100 mark. A year later it was 2,000 strong and by far the largest community for 100 miles around. Had you then been strolling down Main Street, the town's mile long and only artery, you would have found fresh bread and cakes, oysters, meat, boots, garments, medication, and jewelry. You could have consulted a doctor, indulged in a cut and a shave, boarded a stagecoach to Los Angeles, picked up a copy of the *Panamint News*, sipped foreign wines at a French restaurant, gambled away your earnings, or quenched your thirst at one of the saloons, which outnumbered all other businesses. In the back streets, behind this veneer of civilization, less fortunate citizens lived in improvised dugouts and huts. Spirits often ran high. So did the murder rate, which became one of the country's highest.

By the spring of 1875, adventurers had moved on and the population settled back to around 600. But the mines were still going strong. Jacobs' mine had a new five-stamp mill and was generating up to $900 a day. The Company completed its own monumental mill in June. It was soon running full time, churning out an impressive $1,300 of nearly pure silver bullion every day. To protect this tempting treasure from robbers, of which Panamint City had an ample supply, Stewart had the silver cast into 400-pound ingots, much too heavy to be lifted. His trick was so effective that over the next few months the Company shipped around $300,000 of silver by 20-mule team without a single robbery.

Just when everything was going so well, Stewart's and Park's pasts came back to haunt them. In May 1876, Congress denounced their earlier activities at the Emma Mine as fraudulent, and what little credibility they still had evaporated. So did their hope to pocket millions by selling the rest of their stock. Two days later, the Company announced that the tunnels had played out and shut down the mill.

Panamint City's early fame continued to inflame imaginations for over a century. Until 1882, a few dozen workers remained and the mill was fired up off and on, producing a few bars of bullion. Through the 1890s, old claims were revived and abandoned. In June 1925, the Panamint Mining Company revamped the tramway and worked the Wyoming tunnels, only to quit a year later. In 1926, two miners produced ore worth $10 to $15 per ton at the Campbird Mine. In 1947-1948 the American Silver Corporation fixed the canyon road, built a few facilities at Panamint City, and mined the Marvel, Hemlock, and Wyoming mines, although no production was recorded. Sporadic mining continued as late as the 1980s. All in all, in the 1870s Panamint City returned about $500,000 in silver and $300,000 in stock, for an investment approaching $1,000,000. When the Company shut down in 1876, the tunnels had already given out their best. All subsequent mining produced about $100,000. Panamint City was as much a spectacular

Smelter smokestack at Panamint City (May 2001)

loss as it was a ludicrous frenzy. But it was Panamint Valley's greatest adventures, and it spawned some of its most enduring memories.

Route Description

Panamint City is beautifully situated in a narrow valley enclosed by 3,000-foot mountains. To the east looms the final ridge of the Panamints; on the other side is Death Valley. The area is sparsely to densely forested with pinyon pine and juniper. Spring to early fall, profuse gardens of lupine, penstemon, globemallow, and Indian paintbrush brighten the landscape. Summer days are warm to hot but hardly ever overbearing. Almost everywhere trees provide pleasant shade. But in winter, be prepared for very cold weather and snow.

Water is available at Panamint City's main cabin and workshop (tap water, no less!) and at the largest cabin on the north side. When the plumbing gives out, you will still find water at Slaughterhouse Spring, in Water Canyon, and at the spring (and sometimes cabin) in Sourdough Canyon. Given the large burro population, treat all spring and tap water. Good campsites are plentiful. Some visitors stay in the cabins. If you do, be aware of possible exposure to hantavirus.

Panamint City. What makes this site so special is its large number of well-preserved structures spanning well over 150 years. Several buildings are clustered at the crossroad on the valley floor—a two-room plywood cabin, a large workshop, and a quarried-stone quadrangle. The cabin's glass windows and working tap have earned it the nickname of Panamint City Hilton. A row of four wooden cabins on the north side and the colorful buildings of a recent mill on the south side overlook the valley. One of the cabins has a tin roof, a cast-iron stove, and its original glass windows. A tiny spring surfaces right behind it. A hose redirects its flow into a stone tub in the front yard.

The towering smokestack of the historic smelter is the town's crowning jewel. Built of half a million bricks, it is a magnificent 45-foot tower tapering from a massive square base to a finely ornate crown. In all of the California desert, there is not another structure like it. Erected in 1875 at a cost of $210,000, it was for one short year the silver-churning heart of the Panamint mines, their lifeline and pride, and it survives today as their finest symbol.

The mill and valley-floor buildings were in use in the 1970s and 1980s when a few mines, including the Wyoming, were active. The town was then powered by the ingenious water wheel housed in the easternmost cabin: water piped from Water Canyon spun an antique Pelton wheel, which drove a generator. The mill is the best example of a modern mill in the park. The ore was screened at the top ore bin, pulverized in the jaw crusher beneath it, then transported on a conveyor belt to the cylindrical metal bin. From there it dropped into the mill's two-story building, where it was cycled repeatedly through two enormous tumblers and a rake classifier before being treated in a cyanide tank. The mill was powered by the large diesel generator down in the workshop. Operations were probably discontinued after the road was washed out in 1984. The historic tunnel behind the mill may well be the park's straightest. Called Lewis Tunnel, it was driven 750 perfectly straight yards in a failed attempt to intercept the rich Wyoming vein, 1000 feet up the slope. At the end of it, almost directly under the Wyoming shaft, the tunnel entrance appears smaller than a cherry pit held at arm's length, yet it casts shadows as clearly as the full moon.

Panamint City's oldest remains are the stone ruins of the 1870s houses and businesses that line the wash for 1.5 miles down-canyon from the smelter. There are dozens of rooms, walls, dugouts, and canvas-tent platforms. The large stone terraces at the mouth of Little Chief Canyon was the red-light district, the undisputed turf of the Oriental Saloon. The old town is filled with moving tidbits: flights of stairs climbing nowhere, pieces of China, embossed cans, or black shards of Champagne bottles. Beds of ornamental irises, originally planted to brighten the streets, took a liking to the high desert and have been blooming over and over for more than a hundred springs.

Sunrise in Panamint City (May 2001)

Water Canyon. If it is hot and you are looking for a refreshing short hike, try this scenic canyon at the very end of Surprise Canyon. It is aptly named: year-round, a little creek flows along its willow-shaded wash. From Panamint City, walk up the road, past the water wheel and the tank at Slaughterhouse Spring, until it angles left into Water Canyon. The scenery is dominated by the canyon's spectacular eastern wall, a 3,000-foot high, mile-long tableau of giant granite fins tinged with pink. Panamint City owes its mineral wealth to the intrusion of this formation, called Little Chief Porphyry, in the Cretaceous.

The creek flow usually starts just inside Water Canyon. Not far beyond is Thompson Camp, named after the couple who mined here in the 1930s. The main cabin, now decrepit, looks out to Sentinel Peak from under large cottonwoods festooned with vine. There is a collapsed cabin behind it, a shed, an outhouse, the foundations of a crude mill across the road, and a 1957 Chevrolet proving that sedans once made it this far up canyon. Behind the camp, the creek floods shallow swamps of watercress, rush, and bright-yellow monkey flower. Do not miss the camp's water tank, hidden among willows where the road crosses the creek 130 yards above the camp. It is a pleasure to sit on its low rim and relax to the sound of the overflow cascading below, while soaking your feet in the cold, creek-fed water.

Water Canyon has two very different mines. From the camp you can see the foot trail to the Curran Mine cut in the dirt hillside to the west. Work your way to it, follow it up to a road, then hike 0.5 mile up to the mine's four inclined tunnels at the end of the road. The remains of a rickety tramway are posed in front of the main tunnel like esoteric modern art. Two tree trunks propped up with cables served as the upper tower. The steel wheel nailed to it was its pulley, and the box of rusted cogs its winch and hand brake. Another tower lies by the road 200 feet below. This mine produced ore with $13 to $17 of gold per ton. The vein is well mineralized with pyrrhotite, pyrite, and marcasite.

To reach the Blue Jay Mine, from the camp continue up the main road. It parallels the creek under shady willows, then winds up the west slope to the mine's five tunnels (1 mile). The main tunnel has a huge timbered adit and a rail track. A forest of timber beams supports its sagging roof. The main tunnels are steeply inclined, littered with fallen rocks, and poorly mineralized—but the views are great.

Sourdough Canyon. The highlight here is not the canyon—a steep, forested, open valley—but its eclectic mill and camp. From the smelter, walk down Surprise Canyon 0.3 mile, turn right on the Sourdough Canyon Road, and in 0.2 mile you are there. Over a few hundred feet, the road is lined with 1950s and 1960s trucks, trailers, and sheds. The high point is the picturesque wood-and-stone cabin up the side road to the right. The front yard is landscaped with pines and terraced flower beds. The cabin is dark, but when downtown is all booked visitors enjoy staying here overnight. It is partly furnished, and stocked with cooking utensils and emergency food. It even has water—when the pipe from the spring up canyon has been recently repaired.

The mill is across the road. In the 1960s, it treated ore from tunnels higher up the road. Still in good condition, it is an interesting piece of machinery. Start from the pile of blue-green quartz at the top of the mill and work your way down to the backhoe used to load the ore into the tipple, to the chute, the tumbler, the inevitable generator, and the empty pond at the bottom. Check out the tumbler—its principle is different from most. Like at most mines, it is snow-white quartz coated with intensely blue and green copper minerals (mainly malachite and azurite) and dark-gray silver minerals (mainly tetrahedrite).

The Stewart's Wonder Mine. This is one of the area's oldest mines, and the third largest producer. It is accessed by an easy trail that starts in Sourdough Canyon, a few steps below the mill's pond. Old trails this well engineered are rare. From here to the lower tunnel, a distance of 0.65 mile, it is almost perfectly level, supported by sturdy retaining walls and paved with flat rocks—all for the benefit of pack animals. Where it hugs the steep wall of Surprise Canyon, it had to be blasted into the rock, and there is not much more than thin air between you and the wash 250 feet below. The views into the canyon are excellent, especially of the smokestack, the huge vertical ribs of white dolomite across the facing wall, and the ruins of the red light district.

After 0.5 mile the trail angles into Wonder Gulch, then splits. The lower trail ends in 100 yards at a major wash-out, 10 yards short of the 200-foot lower tunnel. The upper trail ends shortly up the slope. The 230-foot middle tunnel is a short scramble up the rocky slope. The upper tunnel above it is a monstrous vertical crack held open by tree trunks harvested over 150 years ago. The Stewart's Wonder Mine was, indeed, a bit of a wonder: its best ore assayed $900 per ton, mostly in silver, some of it in gold. The ore is exposed in colorful quartz veins.

The Wyoming Mine. Located 1,100 feet up the mountain south of Panamint City, this mine was the second largest historic producer. The Wyoming Mine Road starts just south of the workshop. At the fork 0.35 mile out, stay right with the main road. It winds steeply through pinyon pines and offers good views of Panamint City. The lower tunnel is two thirds of the way up, in a sharp left turn. The plywood workshop next to it dates from the 1970s. It still houses the electric blower that circulated fresh air into the tunnel. Heavy timber frames support the tunnel's high roof, and a dusty air duct courses its 1,000-foot length. The cool breeze in the tunnel comes from a fissure at its very end. The 1875 Wyoming Mine tramway is hidden in the trees 50 feet to the west. Its stocky towers of roughly hewn timber are simply designed but they have survived to this day.

Wyoming Mine tramway

The area at the end of the road has an interesting mix of modern and historic remains. The 350-foot tunnel was known as Tramway. A rail track links it to a trestle bridge, where the ore was dumped into the tramway terminal (now collapsed) below it and lowered 1,100 feet to the 20-stamp mill. Two ore cars are still parked inside the tunnel. The wide quartz vein wavering along the tunnel walls is speckled with silver, but do not go in: there is a deep unprotected shaft part way in.

Most of the Wyoming ore came from a stope at the end of the 250-foot Kennedy Tunnel, and a stope part way in the Limestone Tunnel. The Kennedy Tunnel is about 250 feet higher up the slope, near the top of the ridge to the south. To reach the Limestone Tunnel, take the level constructed trail past the road and level with it. It circles around the ridge and ends in 0.2 mile at a wide tailing. The next stretch is a little complicated. Scramble 80 feet up the slope to a second level trail (which actually starts at the Tramway Tunnel), and follow it south a short distance to its end. Scramble again 80 feet up to a third, level trail (upper trail). The Limestone Tunnel was located in this vicinity. It is now obscured by later mining, but the area is rich in colorful tailings.

The Hemlock Mine. This was the district's largest producer, and it is also the most impressive. It can be reached two ways. The longer but foolproof route is the Hemlock Mine Road, 0.95 mile down-canyon from the smelter on the south side, then up this road. It zigzags steeply 1.3 miles along Marvel Canyon, then angles sharply right straight up a steep ravine. In 0.25 mile, the ravine forks. The road ends shortly up the right fork. Take the roadless left fork instead, towards the two tall tailings of the Hemlock Mine. The main tunnel is at the top of the lower tailing, and the deep trench is at the top of the upper tailing. Both tailings are made of fine material and quite steep, and climbing them is tedious... Go up along the tailing's eastern edge instead, hanging on to the cable lying on the ground for better traction.

The second route is the level connector trail used in historic days to haul the Hemlock Mine ore to the Wyoming tramway for easier access to the mill (see map). It avoids the tailings, but it is less obvious. From the end of the Wyoming Mine Road, work your way to the upper trail (see previous section). Follow it 0.6 mile to a sharp right

Panamint City

	Dist.(mi)	Elev.(ft)
Panamint City (main cabin)	0.0	6,290
to Blue Jay Mine	1.5	~7,320
to Curran Mine	0.9	~6,920
to Happy Canyon (wash)	7.5	4,720
to Hemlock Mine (via road)	2.7	~7,840
to Hemlock Mine (via Wyom.)	2.6	~7,840
to Hudson River Mine	7.5	~8,360
to Lewis Tunnel and mill	0.15	6,360
to Sourdough Canyon cabin	0.6	~6,370
to Stewart's Wonder Mine	1.2	~6,520
to Thompson Camp	0.5	6,540
to Wyoming Mine (tramway)	1.4	7,360

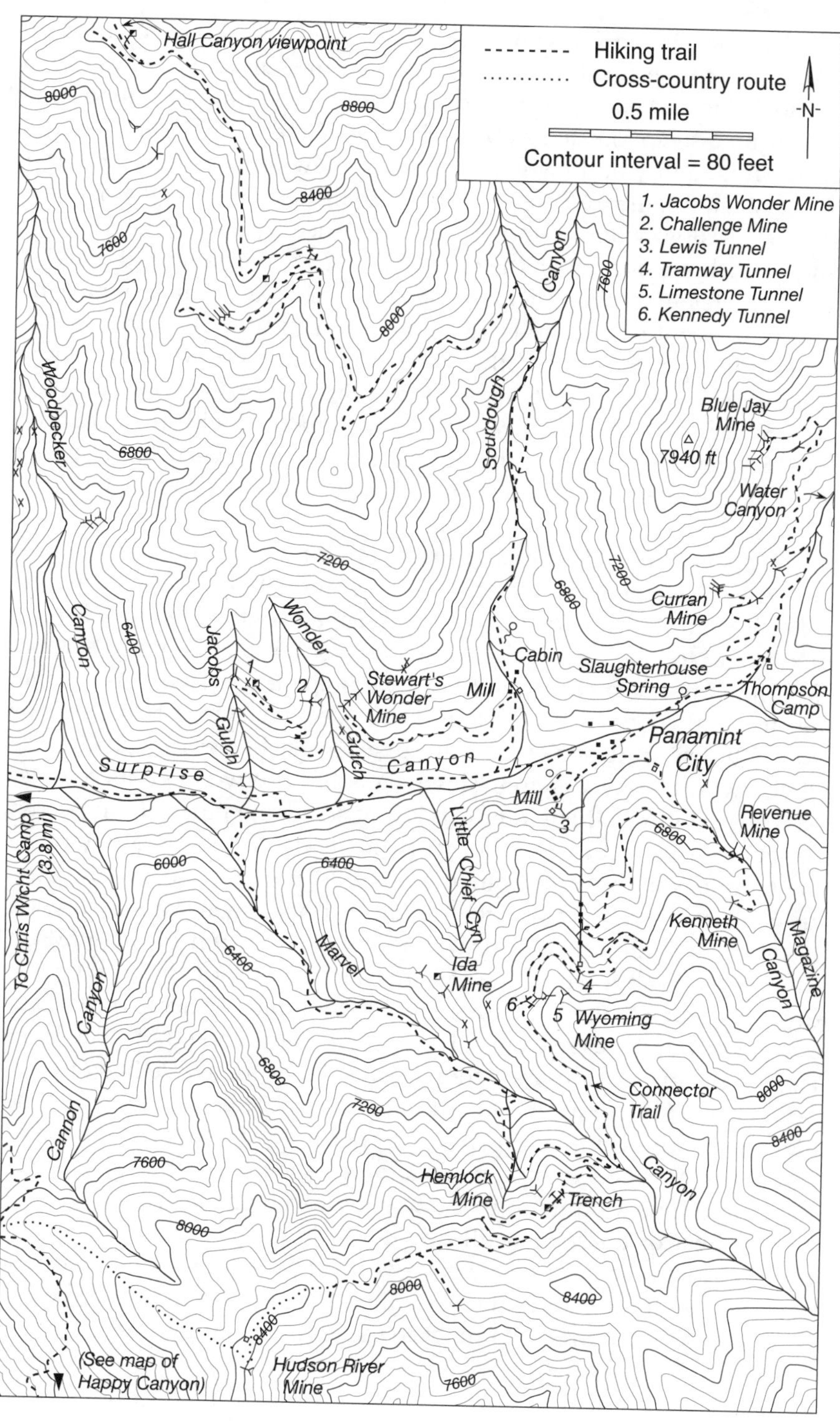
Hiking trail
Cross-country route
0.5 mile
N
Contour interval = 80 feet
1. Jacobs Wonder Mine
2. Challenge Mine
3. Lewis Tunnel
4. Tramway Tunnel
5. Limestone Tunnel
6. Kennedy Tunnel
Hall Canyon viewpoint
Woodpecker Canyon
Sourdough Canyon
Blue Jay Mine
7940 ft
Water Canyon
Curran Mine
Jacobs Gulch
Wonder Gulch
Stewart's Wonder Mine
Mill
Cabin
Slaughterhouse Spring
Thompson Camp
Panamint City
Surprise Canyon
Mill
Revenue Mine
Little Chief Cyn
Kenneth Mine
Magazine Canyon
To Chris Wicht Camp (3.8 mi)
Marvel Canyon
Ida Mine
Wyoming Mine
Connector Trail
Cannon Canyon
Hemlock Mine
Trench
(See map of Happy Canyon)
Hudson River Mine
8800
8400
8000
7600
7200
6800
6400
6000

bend at the Marvel Canyon wash crossing. Across the wash, the trail forks. The connector (lower) trail circles 0.3 mile around the ridge on a contour line and ends part way down the lower tailing. The upper trail winds up a steep forested slope to the trench at the top of the Hemlock Mine. It is faint; you may end up trying a few dead-ends. At the top, be very careful: the trail comes right up to the sharp rim of the trench.

What is particularly impressive is the sheer height of the two tailings, which are one above the other. Combined, they engulf the ravine over an elevation drop of over 350 feet! The main tunnel is nothing short of exceptional. It follows a smooth vertical fault plane on one side, solid quartz on the other. The walls are covered with cryptic glyphs, as in an ancient temple. Deeper in, it opens up onto a cathedral-like chamber, its high vaulted ceiling streaked with reds and yellows. Water drops echo in the darkness. But think twice before going in: ceilings have collapsed, and there is a hidden 15-foot vertical drop.

Hudson River Mine and Happy Canyon. Unbeknownst even to repeat visitors, there is a way to cross over into Happy Canyon, almost all of it is on trails. Start from the trail just above the Hemlock Mine's trench and follow it generally southwest up the steep mountain slope. To call it a trail is an exaggeration; a vague path concealed under pine needles and cones is more like it. Don't stop believing in the trail, or you will lose it! It hooks two sharp switchbacks before cresting the divide with Happy Canyon. This area is heavily wooded; its remoteness spared it from Panamint City's loggers. Some pines are imposing specimens two feet across and over 800 years old. At the divide, take the right fork in the trail, along the ridge's southern edge. Where it fizzles out, continue up along the divide. You will soon walk by a wide stone circle, and 50 yards further by the sunken ruin of the Hudson River Mine's cabin. The mine's yellowish tailing is less than 100 yards down the slope to the southeast. The 100-foot tunnel does show copper and silver, but it was marginal. It may have been worked by a latecomer, pushed this far from the action because everything else had already been claimed. Here as all along the divide, the greatest reward is the view half a vertical mile down into upper Happy Canyon. It stretches from Searles Lake to northern Panamint Valley and across the Argus Range and Inyo Mountains to the saw-toothed high Sierras.

The rest of the way is all downhill. From the mine, hike cross-country down the crest of the east–west ridge. After 0.8 mile you will reach a road at the saddle above Cannon Canyon. The track on the left is a good road that drops 2.7 miles to the wash of Happy Canyon.

■

SENTINEL PEAK

Sentinel Peak puts up a great fight. Just to get to the mountain itself you will have to cross a lush oasis, climb through polished narrows flushed by a vivacious creek, and trudge up a deep canyon to the ruins of legendary Panamint City. It is then a hard climb through a forested canyon and up a sheer crest of liquid taluses to the barren summit where a relic grove of bristlecone pine survives. Few are the climbs that offer such thrilling diversity.

General Information

Jurisdiction: Surprise Canyon Wilderness, Death Valley National Park
Road status: Abandoned road in canyon; primitive access road (HC)
Sentinel Peak: 8.5 mi, 7,040 ft up, 40 ft down one way/grueling
Main attractions: Creek, narrows, ghost town, forest, a long hard climb
USGS 7.5' topo maps: Ballarat, Panamint
Maps: pp. 371*, *319*

Location and Access

Sentinel Peak is on the high crest of the central Panamints, 5 air miles south of Telescope Peak. The rare people who tackle this challenging summit typically climb it from Panamint Valley via Surprise Canyon and Panamint City, starting at old Chris Wicht Camp at the end of the canyon road (see *Surprise Canyon* for driving directions).

Route Description

The traditional route to Sentinel Peak is southeast up Frenchman's Canyon to Panamint Pass, then south along the crest. From Panamint City, the main road goes 0.25 mile to the water tank at Slaughterhouse Spring. The wide forested opening 0.1 mile further on the right is Frenchman's Canyon. In historic times a road bounced along its tumbled wash to Panamint Pass. From there a trail switchbacked down to Swiss Ranch in Johnson Canyon, which provided fresh vegetables to the rough-and-ready citizens of Panamint City. Much of the road has now been washed out, buried by slides, and reclaimed by pinyon pine. What little remains still helps climb the steep canyon. The wash is sprinkled with well-rounded granitic boulders, fragrant big sagebrush, Indian paintbrush, and other wildflowers after late spring.

Panamint Pass is a wooded saddle offering a tantalizing preview of panoramas to come. To the west it overlooks Surprise Canyon's

Bristlecone Pine

lofty rim, and to the east Death Valley's blinding abyss. To the north the crest is straddled by a stunning band of reddish fins and cliffs, the Cretaceous formation known as Little Chief Porphyry that delivered the Panamint City silver.

At this point you have covered nearly 90% of the distance but a fraction of the difficulty. From the pass the route is west-southwest up a ridge that shoots straight up through a forest sprinkled with outcrops. Obstacles must often be circumvented awkwardly, sideways across steep unstable slopes. The worst spot is a talus of loose rocks that careens hundreds of feet down at the angle of repose. At the junction with the main ridge coming up from Surprise Canyon, around 8,600 feet, the pinyon pine reach their limit and give up. Above, it is almost all bare rock, the product of a high desert too cold in winter, too hot in summer, and windy too often. The crest narrows to a precarious wedge, too precipitous to stand on the east side, steep and unstable on the west side. A series of rocky summits must be climbed or circumvented just to get to see Sentinel Peak, and a few more after them to reach it. This is a wild landscape, stressed and emaciated, where frigid

Sentinel Peak		
	Dist.(mi)	Elev.(ft)
Chris Wicht Camp	0.0	2,630
End of narrows	0.8	3,295
Limekiln Spring	1.8	3,945
Brewery Spring	3.1	4,810
Panamint City (road junction)	5.45	~6,290
Frenchman's Canyon	~5.8	~6,480
Panamint Pass	7.4	8,070
Junction with ridge	7.75	8,680
Sentinel Peak	8.5	9,634

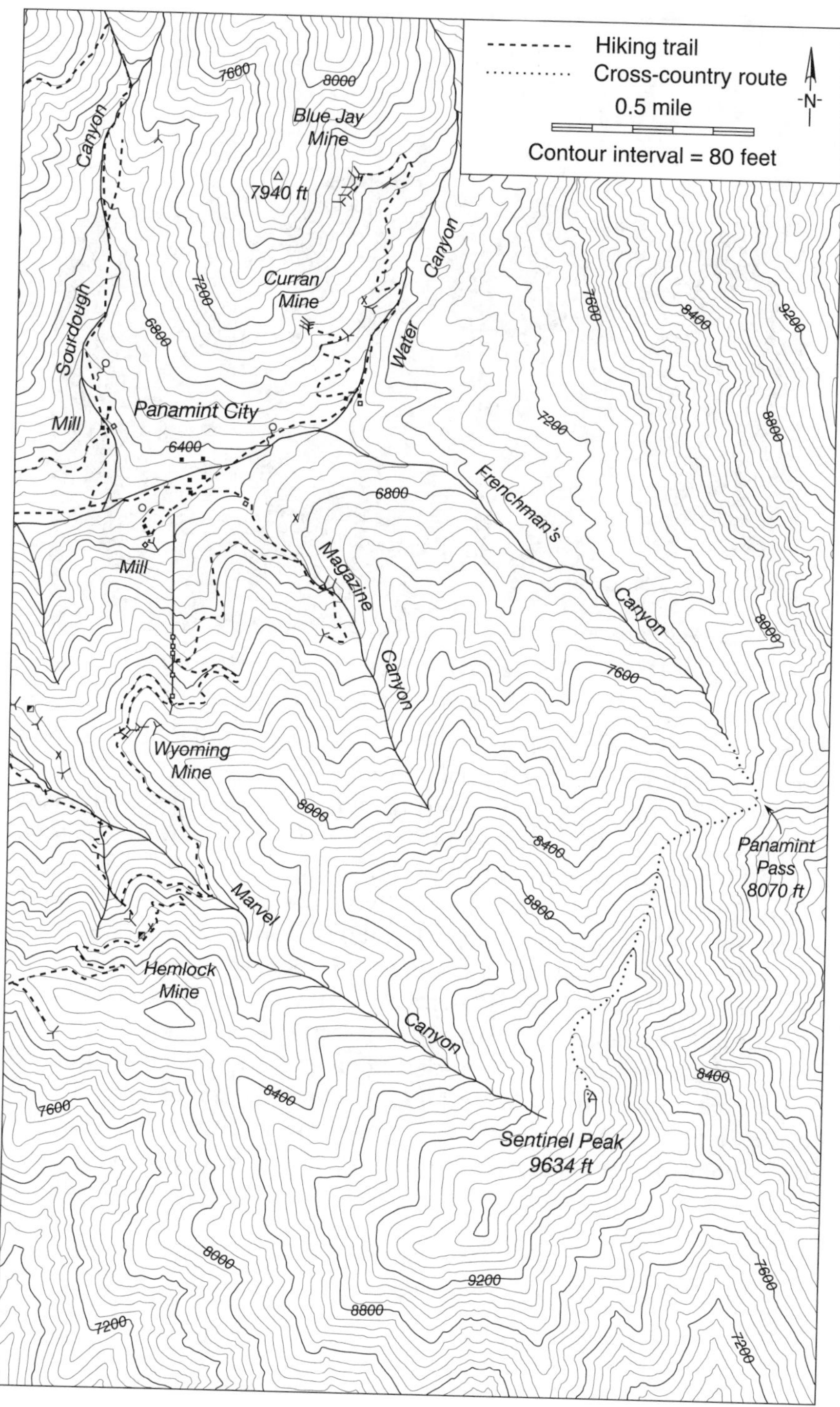

Hiking trail
Cross-country route
0.5 mile
Contour interval = 80 feet
N
Blue Jay Mine
7940 ft
Curran Mine
Canyon
Sourdough
Water
Canyon
Mill
Panamint City
Mill
Frenchman's
Canyon
Magazine
Canyon
Wyoming Mine
Panamint Pass
8070 ft
Marvel
Canyon
Hemlock Mine
Sentinel Peak
9634 ft
7600
8000
7200
6800
6400
8400
9200
8800

Surprise Canyon from below the slope northwest of Sentinel Peak

lichen, scrawny ephedra, and the twisted, erect trunks of dead pine accentuate more than hide the nakedness.

From the summit as from the ridge the views are superb, and constant excuses for a break. The land falls into Death Valley like a stone, in tight battalions of sharp outcrops, too abrupt to hold but a scatter of valiant bristlecone pine. From nearly two miles up, the valley is daunting in its depth and immensity. Mountains ripple in every direction. The satisfaction of having conquered this persistently gnarly bit of ground is exhilarating. Years later, you may well remember this climb as your most extraordinary trip in the desert wilds.

For this strenuous ascent bordering on epic, most people will need to set up a base camp in Panamint City. Given the remoteness, it pays to throw in an extra day or two to explore the ghost town and the many interesting ruins in the surrounding mountains.

■

HAPPY CANYON

Happy Canyon has been largely taken over by spring vegetation. It is an easy enough walk through the narrows in the lower canyon, a walled-in corridor livened by a running creek, cascades, and a 16-foot waterfall. But the rest of the way is a tedious obstacle course where you splash through muddy swamps and bushwhack through thick undergrowth. Plan on a long day or an overnight trip for this small ordeal, eventually redeemed by a small gold-mining camp and mill, the serene setting of the deep upper canyon, or great views of Surprise Canyon from the canyon rim. For diehards only.

General Information

Jurisdiction: Surprise Canyon Wilderness (BLM), DVNP (NPS)
Road status: Roadless; access via primitive road
The narrows: 1.2 mi, 750 ft up, 0 ft down one way / easy
Mining camp and mill: 2.6 mi, 1,790 ft up, 30 ft down one way / difficult
Sixth spring: 5.9 mi, 4,060 ft up, 110 ft down one way / strenuous
Main attractions: Lush spring and creek, narrows, gold mines
USGS 7.5′ topo maps: Ballarat*, Panamint
Maps: pp. 377*, 319

Location and Access

Happy Canyon is in the central Panamints, just south of Surprise Canyon. To get to it, from the Ballarat store drive the Indian Ranch Road 1.15 miles north to the first primitive road on the right, which is the Happy Canyon Road. Coming from the other direction, look for it 6.1 miles south of the Indian Ranch junction. Drive this road 2.1 miles to just inside the canyon, where it drops into the wash along a short steep ramp, then 0.35 mile up the wash to a fence at the wilderness boundary. From there on up, Happy Canyon is part of the Surprise Canyon Wilderness, then Death Valley National Park, and closed to vehicles. Park at the fence. The road is decent up to the ramp, but high clearance and possibly four-wheel drive are needed in the wash.

Route Description

The narrows. Happy Canyon stands out, above all, for its miraculous abundance of water: it is blessed with no fewer than six springs. They give rise to Happy Canyon Creek, a lively desert stream that flows, mostly above ground, along more than two canyon miles. The creek's lower end is usually just up the wash from the wilderness boundary. By the time you reach the narrows, 0.45 mile in, you will be following a genuine stream of clear, fast-moving water.

Like many wet desert canyons, Happy Canyon is a surprisingly dynamic environment. When I hiked through the narrows in March 2000, I found a corridor of sheer rock walls delightfully shaded by a tree canopy and echoing with the cheerful gurgles of the creek. A verdant oasis of willow, screwbean mesquite, tamarisk, grasses, and many other water-loving plants thrived along fertile banks. Small cascades glided musically over polished bedrock coated with colorful algae. At the head of the narrows, where the canyon opens up onto a deeper gorge, the vegetation thickened abruptly, and the rest of the first spring was wildly overgrown. When I returned two and a half years later, a raging flashflood had annihilated this paradisiacal setting. All the trees—hundreds of them—had been uprooted and flushed out of the canyon, and the banks and wash scoured clean down to bedrock. All that was left was the creek flowing over barren gravel. I could have sworn I had never been here before. Such was the force of the flood that the small waterfalls I had casually hopped over in 2000 had been excavated into high waterfalls, one of them a 16-foot plunge that now has to be climbed with care. Twenty years later, this part of the wash has still been only partly revegetated.

As improbable as it seems, a road once made its way through this canyon. It required drastic alteration of the wash, including re-channeling the creek, and constant repair of water damage. When the park was created, the road was closed to protect this rare and delicate riparian system. Four-wheelers should not feel too bad: the first waterfall now makes it impossible to drive through, and very few people would be willing to winch their two-ton hunk of steel up this vertical drop.

The lower springs. There are three more springs in the lower canyon. Except for a short open stretch between the head of a spring and the tail of the next spring, they form a continuous grove. For more than a mile, the canyon is a meandering thread of luxuriant greenery irrigated by the singing creek, snaking at the foot of soaring walls. The downside of all this water is that much of the wash is plugged with dense thickets and offers little room for walking. There are virtually no open taluses along the canyon walls to bypass this persistent obstacle. The only approach is bushwhacking, which makes progress sloppy, difficult, and slow. The best route through the second spring is along the old roadway, which is crowded with shrubbery and flooded under an inch or two of running water. The third spring is by far the tough-

Waterfall in Happy Canyon narrows

est. Much of the road there has become a wet and overgrown creek bed. You will need perseverance to fight off tangle after tangle of spiny plants and vine, to crouch where they grow too low, and even go on all fours at the clogged upper end of the spring. The fourth spring is a little easier, only because two short trails bypass bits of it on the north side. By the time you are through with the springs, however, you will be dusted with shredded plants, your limbs crisscrossed with bloody lacerations, and your shoes unrecognizable lumps of mud. It helps to wear long pants and sleeves, and glasses for eye protection.

This is tedious hiking, but if you can put aside your frustration you will find that this long oasis is beautiful. At places the road bores a luminous tunnel through the jungle. Sunlight diffusing through the high canopy bounces off the creek and reveals a paradoxical tropical selva, complete with mugginess and mosquitoes. As you slosh across miniature swamps of watercress and orchids, you half expect pythons writhing underfoot and monkeys howling down at you. Yet just a stone's throw away, all that manages to grow on the bone-dry canyon slopes are barrel cactus and scrawny shrubs. This juxtaposition of extremes is one of Happy Canyon's true treasures.

You will likely see wildlife in Happy Canyon, all of it probably in happier spirit than you. Coyotes and burros often wander in for a drink. Birds, butterflies, and dragonflies drift among the trees. Crickets fill the air with their insistent songs. The most unusual dwellers are the frogs. Miraculous survivors of wetter times, they have been stranded on this slender ecological island so long that they may now be endemic to this canyon. They croak in concert at dusk, so loudly that you expect fat ugly frogs, when in fact they are inch-long cuties.

The milling camp and mine. If you get tired of bushwhacking, the mill in the second spring makes a fine turning point. Active until the 1950s, this site consists of the mill itself, on the south side of the creek, and a small camp on a broad bench across the creek. The camp's plywood shack is particularly unattractive, although it was at one time quite functional. The mill operator took advantage of the ample water supply and built, attached to the cabin, what may be the largest shower in the Death Valley backcountry. It would have been pleasant, after a hard day's work, to relax on the flagstone terrace overlooking the trees and cook on the outdoor stone fireplace. The mill includes a metallic hopper, a storage tank, and a large corrugated structure, now collapsed, that housed the mill machinery. It treated ore from a small gold mine located in the canyon 0.15 mile past the fourth spring. The mine's cableway still spans the canyon wash and supports a funky bucket assembled from a 55-gallon drum. The workings are clustered 640 feet up the sheer south wall, and reached by a precarious trail.

Happy Canyon

	Dist.(mi)	Elev.(ft)
Happy Canyon Rd (upper end)	0.0	1,965
Narrows (lower end)	0.45	2,210
Narrows (upper end)	1.2	2,710
First spring (head)	2.0	3,300
Camp and mill	~2.6	~3,700
Second spring (head)	2.85	3,860
Third spring (head)	3.3	4,220
Fourth spring (head)	3.55	4,390
Cableway	3.7	4,480
Fork in road	4.0	4,720
Tunnels	(2.2)	~6,900
Surprise Canyon divide	(2.7)	7,590
7,770-foot peak	(3.0)	7,770
Fifth spring	5.35	5,530
Sixth spring (head)	5.9	5,915
Upper mine	7.6	7,770

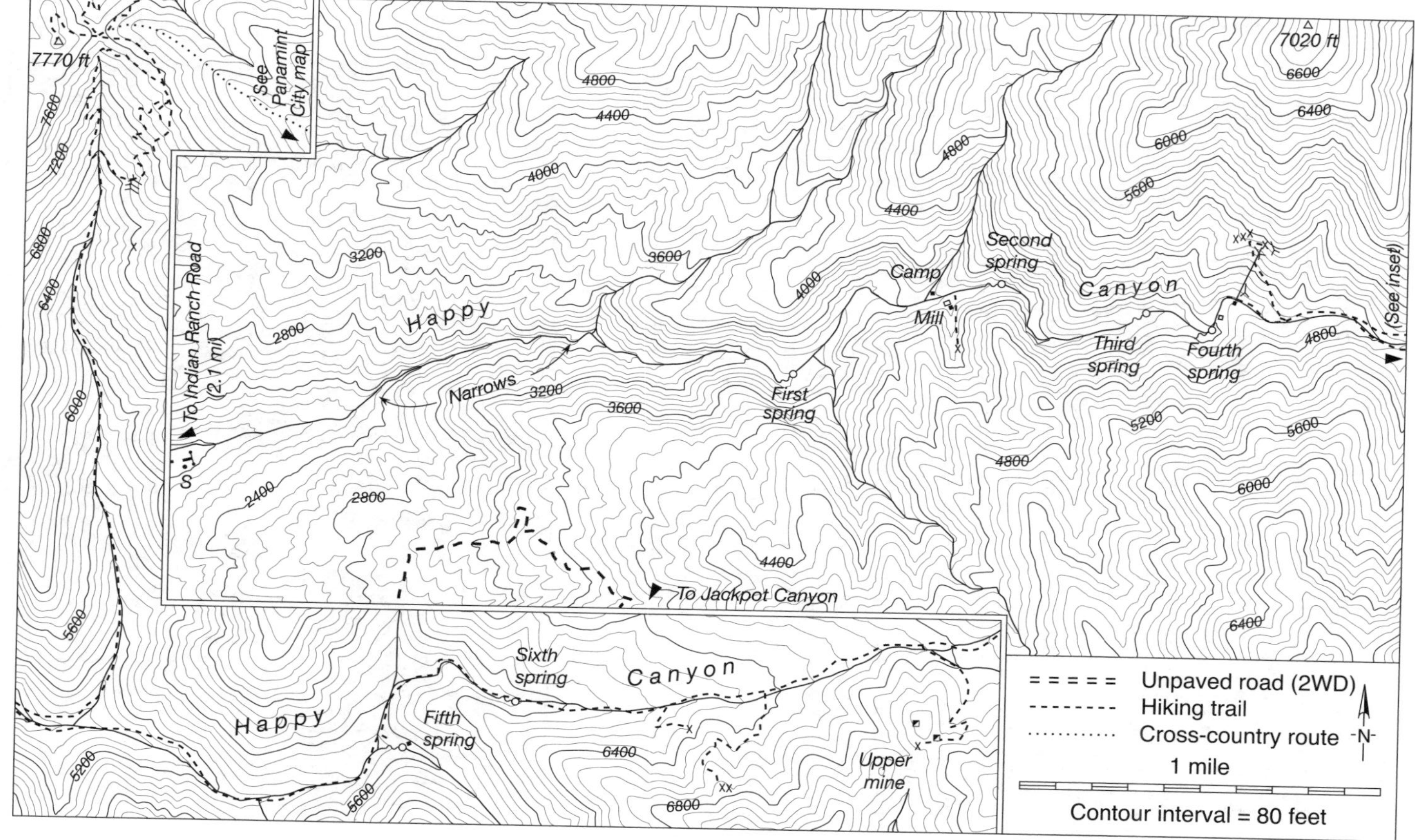
7770 ft
See
Panamint
City map
To Indian Ranch Road
(2.1 mi)
Happy
Narrows
First
spring
Camp
Mill
Second
spring
Canyon
Third
spring
Fourth
spring
7020 ft
(See inset)
To Jackpot Canyon
Sixth
spring
Canyon
Happy
Fifth
spring
Upper
mine
Unpaved road (2WD)
Hiking trail
Cross-country route
N
1 mile
Contour interval = 80 feet

Mining camp and mill at the second spring in Happy Canyon

The upper canyon. A third of a mile above the cableway the road forks. The fork that follows the wash is almost gone in this area. Although badly eroded at places, it wanders up through an upper canyon typical of the Panamint Mountains—broad, deep, rocky, and steep. Before ending at the foot of Sentinel Peak, it passes by two small springs (fifth and sixth) and three marginal mines reached by short side roads on the south side. A devastating wildfire swept through this area on July 22, 2000. The second largest fire in the history of the park, it consumed 5,500 acres of forest between about 5,000 and 8,000 feet of elevation before it was contained by firefighters. The burnt scars that deface the canyon slopes will remain visible for many years.

The left fork in the road, better defined although also locally erased, ascends the narrow wash of a main side canyon to the divide with Surprise Canyon to the north, gaining 2,800 feet of elevation in 2.8 miles. About two thirds of the way there, the road forks. The east fork goes right by a group of silver tunnels. Both forks meet again not far from the divide. At the road junction at the divide, climb the quarter-mile westbound trail to the unnamed twin peak around the 7,770-foot benchmark for memorable views of Panamint Valley and Surprise Canyon. From the divide, a cross-country hike up the ridge to the southeast connects to a trail that drops to Panamint City (see *Panamint City*), a seldom-used route to this historic silver-mining center.

■

PLEASANT CANYON

The long four-wheel-drive road that winds through Pleasant Canyon provides an extraordinary sampling of the historic wealth and scenic splendor of the Panamint Mountains. It leads through a lush, creek-fed spring to century-old Clair Camp, one of the region's greatest ghost towns, and to the Ratcliff and World Beater mines, which rank among the Panamints' richest historic gold producers. The road continues many miles past other mines, camps, and backcountry cabins, all the way to timberline and spectacular Rogers Pass. Combined with the return drive via nearby South Park Canyon, this is one of the most exciting loop drives in the park.

General Information

Jurisdiction: BLM (lower canyon), DVNP (upper canyon)
Road status: Primitive road (4WD/HC)
Pleasant Canyon Spring: 2.9 mi, 1,560 ft up, 0 ft down one way/moder.
Clair Camp: 0.6 mi, 60 ft up loop/very easy
World Beater Mine: 0.8 mi, 520 ft up, 20 ft down one way/easy
Ratcliff Mine: 2.2 mi, 1,380 ft up, 480 ft down one way/moderate
Main attractions: Ghost town, mines, lush spring and creek, 4WD road
USGS 7.5' topo maps: Ballarat, Panamint
Maps: pp. 387*, *319*

Location and Access

Pleasant Canyon is one of the major canyons that gouge the abrupt western front of the central Panamint Mountains—10.6 miles and 5,600 feet up to Rogers Pass at the crest. The Pleasant Canyon Road, which follows the entire canyon, starts at Ballarat. It is the road that heads northeast from the signed four-way junction 50 yards south of the general store. At the two forks 0.5 mile out, bear right. With a standard-clearance vehicle you will probably be able to drive only another 0.5 mile, to just inside the canyon. The Ratcliff Mine in the mid-canyon was re-opened by a small outfit in the early 2010s. Although the miners improved the road up to Clair Camp (4.1 miles), high clearance is still needed. Four-wheel drive is mandatory at a few spots beyond.

History: The Ratcliff and World Beater Mines

The gold rush that put Ballarat on the map and opened the western Panamints to its second wave of mining started in Pleasant

Canyon, 16 years after the silver boom at Panamint City had died out. One of the first gold strikes was made in 1893 by Charles Anthony (see *Reilly*), a 60-year old prospector who discovered a rich gold outcrop above Ballarat, which he claimed as the Mineral Ranch (today's Gold Bug Mine). Over the next few years, while the ranch enjoyed limited success due to poor management, other prospectors followed in his footsteps and combed the canyon for gold. The discovery of the Ratcliff Mine, which was to become the area's main player, is credited to Henry Ratcliff, a pioneer from Kentucky. In May 1896, Ratcliff located the Never Give Up claims 2 miles further up canyon. Four months later, brothers George and Bob Montgomery, who had been struggling with other mines around Death Valley, discovered the World Beater just a few hundred yards away. The South Park Mining District was organized that same month, and three towns sprang up overnight: Ballarat and Post Office Spring, on the edge of the salt flats below the canyon mouth, and Pleasant City up near the mines.

In March 1897, the Montgomery brothers relocated their 10-stamp mill from the Confidence Mine at the south end of Death Valley to the lower spring in Pleasant Canyon, where it would process the World Beater's ore. By the fall of 1898 they had milled $50,000 worth of gold, and 16,000 tons of reserves were in sight. The remaining ore, however, turned out to be too resilient to mill efficiently. Being astute miners, they did what was best for them—they sold their property. In the spring of 1899 the mine was purchased by Los Angeles investors. The mill tailings, which still contained a third of the original gold, were sold to a second party, who set up a small cyanide plant near the mine and promptly recovered $20,000 in gold. The mine's new owners upgraded the mill and moved it a second time, to its present location just below the World Beater Mine. It was fired up again in July 1899 and operated into the new century, but it could also handle only so much of the tough ore and produced only a few thousand dollars before shutting down again. In 1903, George Montgomery and another brother, Frank, returned to the World Beater and discovered a high-grade pocket everyone had missed. George relocated the property and cranked up his old mill again. By the time the vein ran out in the summer of 1905, he had squeezed out another $107,000.

In the meantime, Ratcliff kept busy exposing enough of his rich lode to sell it for $30,000 in September 1898. The new owners, brothers Albert and William Godsmark, formed the Ratcliff Consolidated Gold Mines. They installed a 10-stamp mill on the canyon floor, a long tramway from mine to mill, and a 2-mile pipeline to supply water to the mill. The plant became operational in February 1899, but only briefly, as the mill proved to be inefficient and the tramway fraught with problems. Undeterred, the company erected a new tramway, upgraded its mill to 20 stamps, and installed a cyanide plant. Perseverance was rewarded. The new facility began churning out gold bullion in January 1900, at a hefty rate of $15,000 a month. By the summer of 1903, when the ore became too rebellious to continue, the Ratcliff Mine had produced $450,000 and had become the district's largest gold producer.

The Ratcliff Mine remained idle for nearly 30 years, until around 1930 when W. D. Clair realized that the historic tailings were still worth $4 a ton, and he moved in on the abandoned site. He installed a large ore processing plant in the old mill and began reworking the tailings. Clair had been searching for lead at Sylvania unsuccessfully for 20 years, but his efforts finally paid off. Over the next few years he cleaned out some $80,000 in gold—a small fortune at the time.

Suggested Drives and Hikes

A popular day-long excursion among four-wheelers is the long drive up Pleasant Canyon to Rogers Pass, with a possible return via South Park Canyon. There are plenty of options for short hikes along the way at Clair Camp, the Ratcliff Mine, and the World Beater Mine. Allow at least three days if you want to include the Cooper and Porter mines. If you are driving a standard-clearance vehicle, drive as far as you can, then hike to the spring and back, which takes two or three hours. If you have a whole day, hike on to the camp and mines. The ultimate is the overnight hike up to Rogers Pass; allow at least three days (round-trip). You will enjoy the rare luxury of water at two evenly spaced locations, as well as cabins to spend the night.

Route Description

The lower spring. Irrigated by a perennial stream, the lush lower springs are one of the highlights of Pleasant Canyon. What you will see first is the stream itself, which flows over the barren gravel wash for quite some distance below the springs. On a hot summer day, its very presence in this parched environment is a magical encounter. A little further on you will be treated to the first sight of mesquite and baccharis, then thick stands of willow festooned with grapevine. For the next 2 miles trees completely obstruct the wash. The road brushes by this luxuriant oasis, crossing its narrow creek half a dozen times.

Clair Camp. For its imposing ore-processing plant, large number of buildings, and historic significance, Clair Camp is one of the

The gold mill at Clair Camp (2016)

greatest ghost towns in the Death Valley region. Located deep in the canyon, at the base of steep, high-rising slopes, it is also a delightfully isolated and scenic site.

Clair Camp's most elaborate structure is the mill. The partitioned ore bin above it is the lower terminal of the historic tramway. Its cables point to the distant tailings of the Ratcliff Mine, 1,800 feet up the mountain. This advanced mill consisted of various types of crushers installed on several stories. Each crusher ground the ore to finer material than the one above it. The main machinery that remains today is the crusher. Its long cylinder, five feet in diameter, was filled with ore and short sections of rail, and as it was spun around the rails ground the ore into powder. It was powered by a steam engine via the enormous cogwheels installed next to it. The engine was hauled away, but the steam power plant's large boilers still stand just outside the building.

The open site below the mill was the cyanide plant. The milled ore was stirred in a cyanide solution in the large metallic tank. The shack abutting it still houses the gasoline engine that powered the stirring rod. The mixture was then allowed to stand in the nearby 12-foot high tanks until the gold bonded to the cyanide. The yellowish sand drifts down the wash are the leftovers—the mill tailings.

Many interesting mining relics lie dormant in the weeds. The steel grid bolted to a wooden platform west of the mill is a crusher. The shallow, circular metallic structure with fine-mesh walls next to it used centrifugal force to separate gold particles. The three converted gasoline engines parked on the north side of the road are also a treat. The Fairbanks and Morse engine and the one next to it were water pumps. The third one, which looks like a lunar vehicle from a science-fiction B movie, was an air compressor on wheels.

The ghost town itself is a fascinating site. Its sturdy stone dugouts are among the oldest structures. One of them is behind the corral at the east end of town. Two others are tucked behind larger cabins in the middle of town. Because they are built partly underground, they remain cool in the summer and may have been used for food storage. Most of the cabins were built in the 1930s and remodeled through the 1950s. In the 2010s a few cabins were granted a second lease on life by the miners. Their pale plywood walls stamped with bar codes from Home Depot are oddly out of place in this suntanned ghost town. Expect company, and respect all signs.

Clair Camp is a vivid reminder of times gone by. Dismantled space heaters and refrigerators recount forgotten struggles against the cold of winter and the merciless heat of summer. Washing machine wringers recall obsolete domestic chores. The two imprints of a child's hand in the foundation of a fireplace tell us that youngsters, and therefore women, lived here as late as the mid-1950s. The burros have recolonized the haunts of their forefathers, and they often hang around town and along the spring.

The World Beater Mine. A mile up canyon from Clair Camp the side road to the World Beater Mine branches out on the right. It leads shortly to a rustic wooden cabin that visitors use as a base camp. After 0.5 mile the road makes a sharp left U-bend at the bottom of the World Beater Mine, next to the stone ruins of its 10-stamp mill, boiler, and ore bin. The mill was a five-story construction erected into the steep mountainside. The large steel boiler resting on its cradle of stone is a fine example of a steam power plant. The fire box underneath it was loaded with pinyon pine logs and fired up. Water from the vertical tank standing next to it passed through the boiler's array of pipes and was turned into steam, which powered the mill's machinery. The mill was destroyed by an accidental fire sometime after 1968. The nearby concrete foundations, giant axles, and wheels bear witness to the former size of the mill. The beige tailings and scattered remains about 120 yards down the slope mark the site of the cyanide plant.

The World Beater Mine's half a dozen tunnels are strewn along the steep ravine above the mill. The main tunnel is at the top of the cableway connected to the ore bin. It can be reached by a side road that starts about 100 yards up the road from the mill. In the last left bend in this side road, an overgrown foot trail cuts west across the slope to the main tunnel. A small ore bin, bleached by decades of sunlight, was erected just outside the main tunnel to collect ore from a higher tunnel.

The World Beater's tunnels rank high on the spelunking meter. They branch out both horizontally and vertically, forming veritable three-dimensional mazes. At the most unexpected places, ladders climb tens of feet up through dark winzes to higher tunnels. So many drifts and crosscuts have been burrowed in seemingly random directions that it feels like drifting through a giant chunk of Swiss cheese! The bad news is that most of the tunnels are crumbly. Roofs are threatening to collapse. Low ceilings and deep shafts are begging for a careless human being to stumble in. If you decide to go in, which I hereby officially discourage you to do, be extremely cautious. In the summer, however, don't pass up on the one safe use of these tunnels—as natural air conditioning units. Just sit a few feet *outside* of a tunnel and enjoy the cool air wafting out of it.

Steam engine boiler, World Beater Mine

The Ratcliff Mine. To reach the Ratcliff Mine, continue on the road past the World Beater Mine, either driving or on foot. This scenic byway first climbs steeply 1.3 miles to a high crest above timberline, flirting with disaster along the plunging canyon walls. It then descends 450 yards on the far side to end on the edge of the Ratcliff Mine. Along this final stretch you will pass by a first side road climbing on the right, then a second one on the left that twists down to more recent prospects. If you are driving, park at this second junction, which is the last convenient place to turn around.

The Ratcliff Mine's workings, which aggregate 2,500 feet of gallery, are located just beyond and below the end of the road. The richest quartz vein occurs at or near the steep contact between schist and gneiss over 1.3 billion years old. The main minerals were gold, pyrrhotite, pyrite, and chalcopyrite. Most of the historic production came from a glory hole, the open cut at the top of the mine and east of

Top of tramway at level No. 5 tunnel, Ratcliff Mine

the end of the lower road, where the vein outcrops. The short tunnel on its south wall was known as level No. 1. The other tunnels (levels No. 2 through 5) are approximately aligned across the steep slope below. From the glory hole, windy and eroded trails drop down to all four tunnels. Level No. 2 is a crosscut to the vein. The lower three tunnels explored a smaller vein of sulfide ore.

The Ratcliff Mine had two tramways, and today they are the most interesting remains. The collapsed wooden structure just below the glory hole was the upper terminal of the older tramway. It serviced all four lower tunnels, to which it was connected by short cableways and rails. Below level No. 4, a small wooden cabin stands right along a rail track. The track cuts west to the level No. 5 tunnel. The winch, cable, and slanted rail that connected it to the tramway are still in place outside the awesome, cave-like tunnel entrance. The large collapsed structure about 80 feet below to the northwest was the control tower where the tramway angled sharply before shooting straight down to the mill.

The second tramway's upper terminal is at the opposite end of the rail track, just east of the cabin. Securely anchored on an exposed rocky outcrop, it still has its lumber frame, cables, brakes, and machinery. Operated at a later date, it delivered the ore from levels No. 2 and No.

4 to the canyon road above Clair Camp. If you like mechanical equipment, you will enjoy studying the terminal's large engine and complex drive gear. If you don't, the stunning views of Panamint Valley sprawling a mile below will more than make up for it.

Upper Pleasant Canyon. Beyond the mines Pleasant Canyon gradually opens onto a valley. The low-desert vegetation is replaced by sagebrush, ephedra, cliffrose, and eventually pinyon pine, growing into a healthier forest with increasing elevation. One of the pleasures of this canyon is that it provides an unbroken path to experience this progressive, and in the end dramatic, evolution of the desert ecology.

The upper canyon offers several points of interest. The first one is 1.2 miles past the World Beater Mine Road. Water piped from a nearby spring collects into a small tub. The strong overflow—a few gallons per minute—nourishes a tiny swamp of grasses and watercress that attracts dragonflies and butterflies. In the warm season, this is a delightful spot to get wet and cool off. Burros are fond of it. Do not take water from the tub but from the pipe, and purify it.

A tenth of a mile further, a side road on the left climbs 2.4 scenic miles to the Porter Mine. Its owner, a former coal miner named Henry "Harry" Porter, discovered gold here in 1908 and lived by his mine for over 40 years. Stranded high up Happy Canyon in ancient pinyon forest, the mine still has numerous workings and half a dozen buildings.

Pleasant Canyon

	Dist.(mi)	Elev.(ft)
Ballarat	0.0	1,075
Canyon mouth	0.9	1,600
Spring (head)	3.8	3,155
Clair Camp	6.1	~4,520
World Beater Mine Road	7.1	5,160
World Beater Mine (mill)	(0.5)	5,520
End of road (Ratcliff Mine)	(2.3)	6,350
Stone Corral/Porter Mine Rd	8.5	5,910
Porter Mine (camp)	(2.4)	7,530
Cooper Mine Road	8.6	5,940
Cooper Mine (upper tunnels)	(1.8)	7,520
Pine Tree Cabin	10.2	6,420
Rogers Pass	11.5	7,165
Wingate Rd via Sth Park Cyn	24.4	1,050

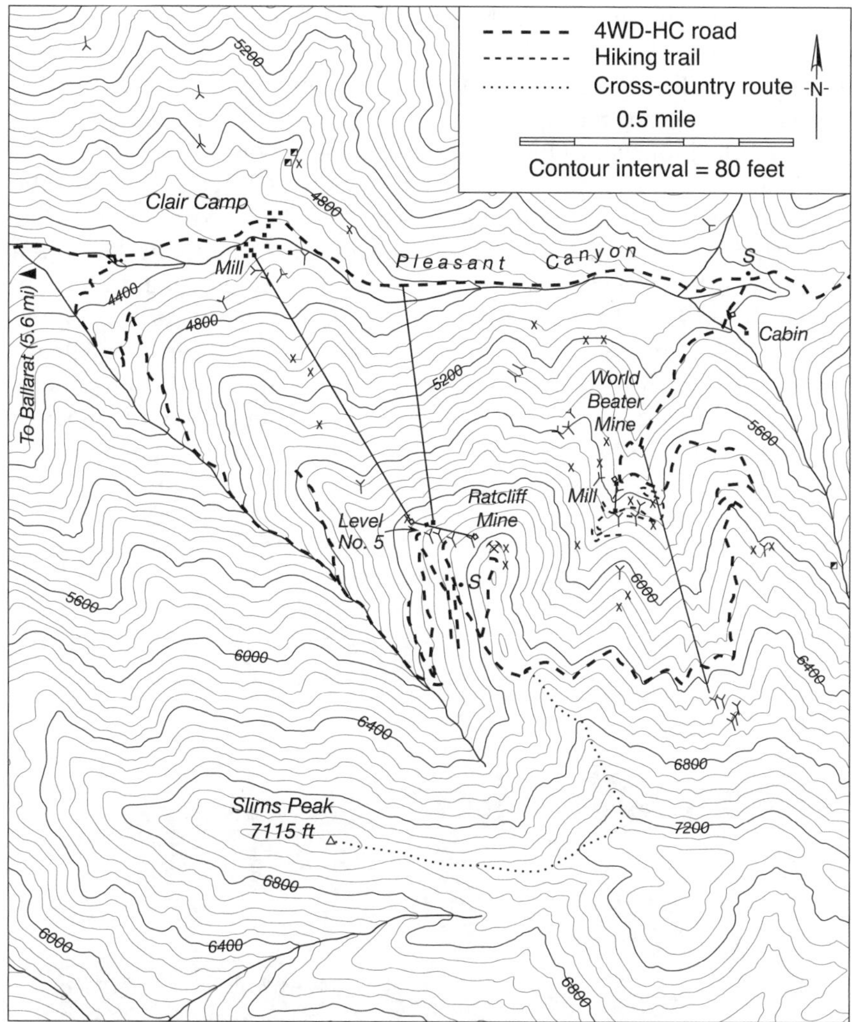

The thick, decaying stone walls across from the Porter Mine Road are the ruins of Stone Corral. It was once the property of Shoshone Panamint Tom, who became famous for the raids he made, sometimes as far as Los Angeles, to steal horses from settlers. Stone Corral may have been one of the places where the horses were corralled.

About 0.1 mile further, another road splits off on the left to the Cooper Mine (1.8 miles). The mine's shaft and half a dozen tunnels were first exploited for gold in 1896 by veteran miner James Cooper. The small roadside ruins and boiler just before the road junction are the remains of the mill he erected around 1897.

The small homestead at the four-road junction 1.7 miles further is known as the Pine Tree Cabin. It was built in 1971 by the Bearcroft family, who lived here while mining nearby claims. Located in the midst of a fragrant forest, the furnished cabin and the adjacent picnic area are ideal for a short break or to camp for the night.

The canyon road ends 1.4 miles further at Rogers Pass, on the brink of Death Valley's hydrologic basin. It is believed to be over this pass that on February 14, 1850, pioneers John Rogers and William Manly led the Bennett-Arcane party out of Death Valley and to safety in San Fernando. Upon leaving the scene of their heroic ordeal, one of the party members uttered the famous words "Good bye, Death Valley!" The high road that follows the crest south from here connects to Middle Park and South Park canyons. It commands superb views of desolate Butte Valley, southern Death Valley, and row upon row of stark desert ranges marching to the horizon.

■

Panamint Valley's salt flats and Argus Range from ridge below Slims Peak

SLIMS PEAK

From the ghost town of Clair Camp in Pleasant Canyon, this thrilling climb ascends the steep canyon wall, first on a twisted mining road, then cross country, to the high canyon rim and Slims Peak. There are plenty of opportunities to check out ruins of early-twentieth-century gold mining, the upper canyon is pleasantly forested, and the view into Panamint Valley is a befitting climax.

General Information
Jurisdiction: Public lands (BLM)
Road status: Roadless; primitive access road (HC-4WD)
Slims Peak: 2.8 mi, 2,280 ft up, 320 ft down one way / difficult
Main attractions: Ghost town, mines, burros, springs and creek, views
USGS 7.5' topo maps: Ballarat*, Panamint*
Maps: pp. 387*, *319*

Location and Access

Slims Peak was named in honor of Charles Ferge, a prospector who came to Ballarat in the mid-1910s and lived there until his death in 1968. Tall and lean, prone to seclusion and grumpiness, he was known to all as Seldom Seen Slim. Ballarat had flourished between around 1890 and the early 1910s as a lively supply and entertainment center for miners working in the Panamint Mountains, and it was already declining when Slim arrived. Slim continued to make a living prospecting, mining, and selling rocks and minerals. He outlived all of the colorful characters who fueled the local mining history—Pete Aguereberry, Harry Porter, Carl Mengel, Chris Wicht, Shorty Harris—ultimately becoming Ballarat's sole resident and the last single-blanket jackass prospector.

Slims Peak		
	Dist.(mi)	Elev.(ft)
Foot of World Beater Mine Rd	0.0	5,160
World Beater Mine (mill)	0.5	5,520
Road crosses ridge (leave road)	1.8	6,520
Divide	2.2	7,280
Slims Peak	2.8	7,115

You will first need to get to Clair Camp (see *Pleasant Canyon*). One mile past Clair Camp, a road on the right climbs to the World Beater and the Ratcliff mines. With a high-clearance, four-wheel-drive vehicle, it can get you much closer to Slims Peak. But it is a rough and hairy drive, and you may prefer to park and climb from this junction.

Route Description

From the main canyon road, hike up the World Beater Mine Road half a mile to the World Beater Mine and its many ruins (see *Pleasant Canyon*). Past this mine the road switchbacks up onto a broad ridge to timberline, then climbs straight up. About 800 feet above the mill it veers west and levels off as it cuts in and out of several sheer ravines, flirting with disaster along the plunging canyon wall. Across the deep gash of Pleasant Canyon, the opposite wall looks huge. After 1.3 miles the road crests as it crosses a northwest-southeast ridge, just before angling right and down toward the Ratcliff Mine. Slims Peak is the highest of the two adjacent bumps 600 feet up to the southwest, on the divide with Middle Park Canyon, the next canyon south. The best route is up the ridge. The mountain is an open woodland of pinyon pine, some with forked trunks over 30 feet tall. The valley plants have given way to ephedra, big sagebrush, and fuzzy spreads of grizzly bear cactus. The ascent is short but quite steep (40%!) and slippery, over unconsolidated dirt mixed with small angular slabs. It would help to be, as Slim claimed he was, half coyote and half wild burro... Once the divide is gained it is a breeze to follow it west, a little down then up, to Slims Peak.

The divide is impressive, a straight catwalk that plummets a long way on both sides. The views from it and the peak are pure Panamint Mountains—deep, complex, and dramatic. On almost all sides you are surrounded by lofty peaks and tumbled ridges. The centerpiece is Panamint Valley, compelling in its graceful sweep. Way down below it stretches for miles, from its slender salt playa to its dry lake and far-off star dunes pinned against Hunter Mountain. Across the valley rises the long wall of the Argus Range. Maturango Peak, its high point, is just across the way. Its east face is cleaved by the deep gash of Bendire Canyon, which spills into the valley in a tremendous fan several miles long. If you go just a little further, you will get even better views west, and catch a glimpse of Ballarat's scattered buildings, Slim's home for more than 50 years and his final resting place, slowly dissolving into the landscape.

■

PORTER PEAK

This one takes determination. It is a long hard drive through remote, spring-fed Pleasant Canyon just to get to the start at historic Rogers Pass. The forested crest that winds up to Mormon Peak, then Porter Peak, is a steep roller coaster packed with trees and rock slides. The panorama is breathtaking, and the geology will break a rockhound's heart. The view changes constantly, from isolated Butte Valley to Middle Park and from Death Valley's vast alkali flats to the central Panamint Mountains' loftiest summits.

General Information

Jurisdiction: Death Valley National Park
Road status: Roadless; primitive access road (HC-4WD)
Mormon Peak: 1.2 mi, 1,180 ft up, 70 ft down one way / moderate
Porter Peak: 3.4 mi, 2,430 ft up, 490 ft down one way / difficult
Main attractions: A forested ridge with deep views, geology, wildlife
USGS 7.5' topo map: Panamint
Maps: pp. 393*, *319*

Location and Access

Porter Peak (9,101') is on the crest of the southern Panamints north of Rogers Pass, at the head of Pleasant Canyon. Drive to Clair Camp (see *Pleasant Canyon*), then continue up through the increasingly forested canyon. You will pass by the World Beater Mine Road on the right (1 mile), the Porter Mine Road (2.3 miles), the Cooper Mine Road (2.35 miles), and the Mormon Gulch Road (3.85 miles), all on the left, and the junction to the Pine Tree Cabin on the right (4.0 miles). Porter Peak is first visible around the Cooper Mine Road, soaring to the northeast. Mormon Peak is just south of it. Park at Rogers Pass on the crest, 5.4 miles from Clair Camp. In the early 2010s miners at the Ratcliff Mine graded the Pleasant Canyon Road up to Clair Camp, so this stretch is not too rough. The rest of the road is rocky and very slow going. Past the Pine Tree Cabin deep wavering trenches eroded in the center of the road make perfect traps for lighter vehicles. A four-wheel-drive vehicle with excess power and clearance is mandatory.

Route Description

Rogers Pass holds a special place in Death Valley's human history. It is here that on February 14, 1850, John Rogers and William Manly famously led the Bennett-Arcane party out of Death Valley. The party waited and starved for nearly a month at what is now Bennetts Well in the valley while the two men scouted a route to San Fernando and brought back supplies. Upon leaving the scene of their ordeal, one of the members uttered the famous words "Good bye, Death Valley!" that gave the valley its name. From the pass, the sight of rows of desert ranges was a befitting farewell to the country they had crossed—and perhaps a disheartening vision of the country that still lay ahead.

From Rogers Pass it is 1.2 miles north along the crest to Mormon Peak. There is a beat-up road at first, closed to vehicles, up and down a low hill, then up again until it fades in 0.6 mile. The rest is a steep cross-country ascent split into two types of terrain, open taluses of large angular rocks and smoother ground covered with trees. Much of the time you have to pick your battle. The ridge commands singular views into Butte Valley, not much different from what the 49ers must have seen. With as many as 200 trees per acre, the woodland is quite forest-like, mostly pinyon pine, some with trunks two feet across, and scattered mountain mahogany. Cliffrose, exalted by the altitude, grow stout branches and shredding bark, with the dignity of a tree. Wildlife enjoys the four-season weather. We saw falcon, tens of quails, Steller's jays bickering in the trees, collared lizards, hyperactive ground squirrels and rabbits, and a bighorn so furtive it might have been a ghost.

The crest leads directly to Mormon Peak, a broad plateau too densely wooded for a panorama. Not that you would want to hang around, being as it is a stone's throw from a massive microwave repeater, installed in the 1980s to service Death Valley. But the outcrop west of the summit is a good wide-open spot to soak in the scenery, especially if this is your turning point. It overlooks Middle Park's curious suspended valley, Pleasant Canyon's crazy green slopes, and the long crest of the Panamint Mountains winding up to Porter Peak.

To continue to Porter Peak, first cross the summit plateau northeast about 0.2 mile, then stay on the crest as it veers northwest and hops down over rocky ledges. At the bottom, a long and slender land bridge braced by sheer slopes links Mormon Peak to the lower slopes of Porter Peak. On one side it plunges into forested Pleasant Canyon, on the other into Six Spring Canyon, dried bare by Death Valley's fiery breath. The fierce winds have sculpted the pine into stunted works of art. Badwater Basin's alkali sink sprawls a long way down, blinding against the Black Mountains' stark 50-mile escarpment. From the north end of the land bridge, the final pitch to Porter Peak is a similar mix of unstable taluses and mad woodland, except steeper—nearly 1,000 feet in only 0.6 mile—with even more rarefied oxygen.

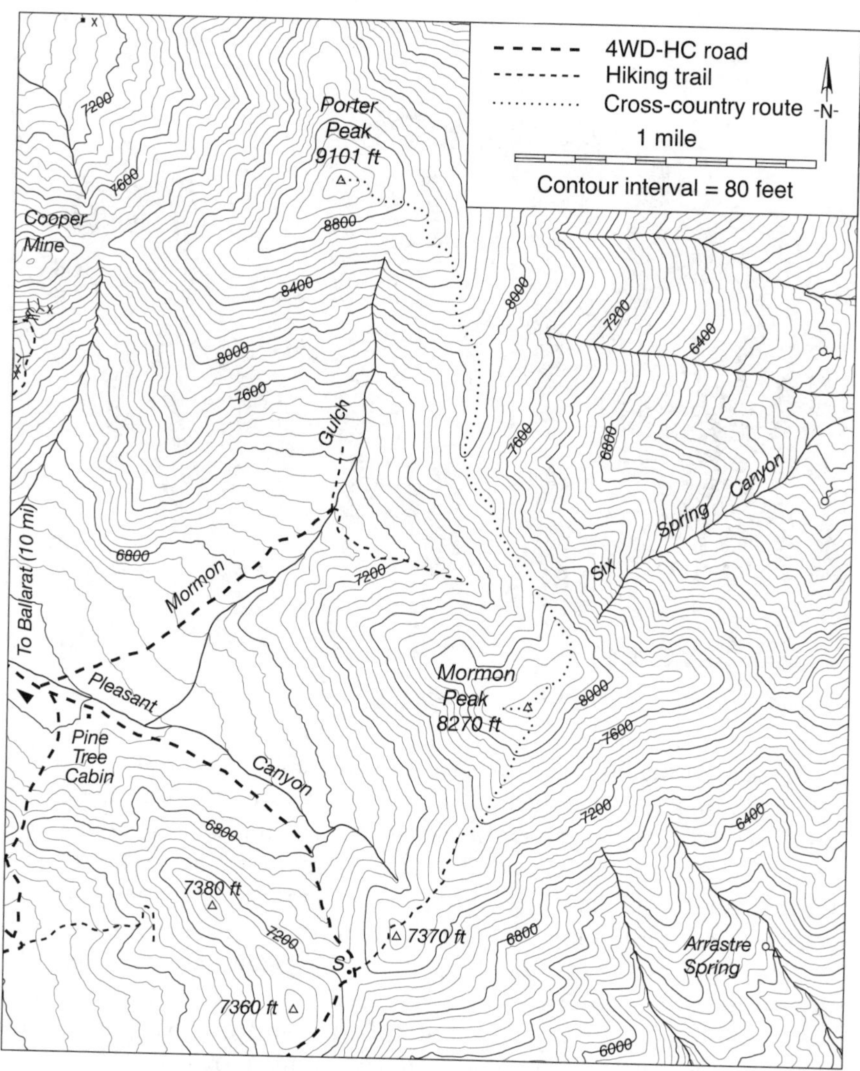

Porter Peak		
	Dist.(mi)	Elev.(ft)
Rogers Pass	0.0	7,165
Hilltop	0.2	7,370
Saddle	0.35	7,300
Mormon Peak	1.2	8,270
Middle of land bridge	1.8	7,860
Porter Peak	3.4	9,101

Porter Peak from just east of Mormon Peak

What got me on this climb was the unusually diverse and atypical geology, almost all of it metamorphic. The lower taluses are all angular quartzite, whitish streaked with red stains. The middle section is dark-gray slate, its surface exfoliated in closed patterns as rhythmic as a written language. The ledges down to the land bridge are ancient sand beds hardened into pink sandstone and graywacke. The land bridge is the most impressive, a litter of small ink-black slate shingles peppered with tiny gold- and silver-colored flakes. The area is unexpectedly luminous, the isolated clumps of ephedra and grizzly bear cactus seemingly shining from within against the somber ground.

Porter Peak offers on a grander scale all of the views collected along the climb, plus a seldom-seen perspective of Sentinel Peak and Telescope Peak. To the south, Middle Park takes center stage, backed by creased ridges marching out to the Slate Range and Searles Lake's enormous salt playa beyond. Early morning in the wintertime, when the sun knifes in from Nevada, you might be lucky and witness a rare sight—the Amargosa River, resuscitated by rainstorms, shining in the sunlight on its age-old journey into Death Valley.

■

SOUTH PARK CANYON

Although most visitors to South Park Canyon are four-wheelers drawn to the challenge of its rough road, I recommend this canyon to hikers and backpackers as well. The scenic narrows are a short walk from the lower canyon road, Briggs Camp just beyond is a wonderful oasis to spend the night, and nearby Thorndike Mine is an interesting site to visit on foot. The crowning glory is South Park, a lovely high-elevation basin rimmed with forested hills.

General Information

Jurisdiction: BLM (lower canyon), DVNP (upper canyon)
Road status: Primitive road through canyon (4WD/HC)
South Park Canyon narrows: 1.3 mi, 940 ft up, 0 ft down one way/easy
Suitcase Mine viewpoint: 0.9 mi, 850 ft up, 70 ft down one way/easy
Thorndike Mine: 0.9 mi, 610 ft up, 0 ft down one way/easy
Main attractions: Narrows, mines, camp, springs, rough 4WD road
USGS 7.5' topo maps: Manly Fall*, Manly Peak
Maps: pp. 399*, *319*

Location and Access

The South Park Canyon Road starts off the Wingate Road 3.85 miles south of Ballarat. To bypass the fall-ridden lower canyon, it winds up an impressively steep ridge that commands sensational views of Panamint Valley, crests at an overlook, then drops into the canyon wash after 2.7 miles. I once made it to the overlook with a Ford Grand Am, but it clearly did not care for the ride. To drive on through the canyon, you will definitely need a four-wheel-drive vehicle with serious clearance, and nerves of steel. If this is not your idea of fun, drive it downhill from Pleasant Canyon, which is easier—or hike it.

Route Description

The narrows. One of the treasures of South Park Canyon is its narrows, which start where the road first reaches the canyon wash. For 1.3 miles they twist and turn under low vertical walls speckled with barrel cactus. From the valley, this part of the canyon looks like a wiggly fissure unable to host a whole road. At places it comes awfully close. The narrows' tormented rocks are quartz-feldspar gneiss, part of the ancient crystalline basement that underlies much of the region. At 1.8 billion years old, they are among the oldest rocks in the region.

The wash along the narrows is interrupted by half a dozen bedrock outcrops. If you are walking you will not even notice them, but cars being more finicky than human legs, if you are driving you will. It is thrilling, but it also tends to divert the driver's (and passengers) attention away from the scenery. Stop occasionally and poke around. Better yet, park at the lower end of the narrows and take the short hike through them. I did not appreciate the wealth of geologic wonders—or even the wildflowers and the burros parked on the hillsides—until I did just that. Down canyon from the road, the narrows are full of falls and boulders and fun to scramble through. Being roadless, this part of the canyon is rarely visited. It is best to hike it up from the Wingate Road. The hike will be shorter if you get stopped early by a fall, and if you can make all 16 falls you will get to enjoy an easy return down the road, and the views (5.5-mile loop).

The Suitcase Mine. The side road to this small historic gold mine starts right at the upper end of the narrows, on the north side. It winds up and over 0.5 mile into a parallel canyon and forks. The narrow right fork switchbacks up to a small quarry and an overlook. The left fork ends shortly at the mine's only tunnel, a shored gallery with a narrow rail reminiscent of the World Beater Mine's convoluted galleries. This mine's best feature, however, is its wide-open views of Panamint Valley, a melting landscape of blinding salt flats and auburn ranges spreading 3,000 feet below.

Briggs Camp. This camp, 0.7 mile past the narrows, has two of the loveliest and best furnished backcountry cabins on this side of Cerro Gordo, thanks to a nonprofit organization called Friends of Briggs Camp, which maintains them periodically. The refurbished upper cabin is squeaky clean and has six beds, a gas stove, a table and chairs, a shower stall, cooking utensils, and even running water! Much of its charm lies in the delightful yard. Its well-kept lawn, vines, and cactus garden are surrounded by healthy trees. You can rest on the sofa and chairs on the small patio, in the shade of beautiful fig trees, while contemplating the high canyon walls. The lower cabin is an unusual building of stone, wood, and corrugated steel. It is more rustic but offers similar facilities, minus the garden. Visitors are welcome to stay at Briggs Camp on a first-come, first-serve basis. The long house between the cabins shelters a small mill and a car-repair shop, probably associated with the small shaft 350 yards to the east. The mill still has its ore bin, belt drive, and engine. The milled ore was treated in the concrete vat and pond at the small cyanide plant below the cabin.

The improbable road in the narrows of South Park Canyon

The bridge. Shortly past Briggs Camp the road climbs up onto the south canyon wall to bypass a constriction in the canyon. For about 300 yards it squeezes down to a single lane blasted into the rock wall 150 feet above the wash, too narrow to turn around. This may well be the hairiest spot in all of the Panamints. To make matters worse, the road is not exactly in its prime. Chicken wire was anchored across portions of it to improve traction, and a narrow log bridge was erected over a serious washout. In 1998, the maximum weight it could safely support was rated at 3 tons. This figure will drop in the future as the structure ages. In November 2002, a long section of the cliff-hugging road just above the bridge collapsed, leaving only 3 to 4 feet of roadway and making the road undrivable. The bridge was rebuilt, but it may happen again. Obey posted signs and use the bridge at your own risk. If you have passengers, let them out before each rough spot.

The Thorndike Mine. This small lead-silver-zinc mine 0.9 mile past Briggs Camp was discovered in 1886 and first known as the Gibraltar Mine. In the 1920s Ballarat resident John Thorndike leased the property, and later purchased it. The mine was split into the lower area (the Honolulu, Carbonate, and Iron claims) and the Big Horn workings, 1,100 feet higher. Early operations produced ore that assayed up to 30% lead and 20 ounces of silver per ton. Mule trains hauled out the ore until 1924, when Thorndike built the road up South Park Canyon and trucks replaced the mules. An aerial tramway was then erected between the Big Horn workings and the road at the Honolulu Camp. The mine was intermittently active until 1944 and produced at least 460 tons of lead/zinc and 5,000 ounces of silver. John Thorndike and his wife had other ambitions besides mining. In the 1930s they opened a few tourist cabins below Mahogany Flat. The cabins were later torn down and replaced by a campground, which still bears their name.

The lower workings are accessed by a side road on the right, 0.1 mile past where the canyon road returns to the wash. In 0.2 mile this side road forks. The left fork leads to the site of the Honolulu Camp and the tramway. The right fork ends shortly at a tin shack and the historic lower tunnels. The shack houses the air compressor that powered the mine's pneumatic drills. Behind the shack is the 250-foot Honolulu Tunnel, guarded by a wooden door. Its winze and small stopes yielded rich zinc sulfide. From the shack a trail leads down canyon 250 feet to the Iron Tunnel. It contained small pockets of lead carbonate. A trail climbs along the eastern edge of the tall tailing behind the shack to the Carbonate Tunnel. A fantastic maze of split tunnels, winzes, shafts, and gaping stopes supported by giant timber, it produced mostly zinc.

South Park Canyon

	Dist.(mi)	Elev.(ft)
Wingate Road	0.0	1,050
Canyon wash/narrows	2.7	2,650
Suitcase Mine Road	4.0	3,590
Suitcase Mine	(0.5)	4,010
Viewpoint above mine	(0.9)	4,370
Briggs Camp (mill)	4.7	4,100
Bridge	~5.4	~4,430
Thorndike Mine Road	5.6	4,630
Thorndike Mine (lower)	(0.25)	~4,820
Thorndike Mine upper trail	6.1	5,300
Thorndike Mine (upper)	(0.9)	~5,910
Colter Spring	6.5	5,570
South Park (western edge)	7.6	6,230
South Park (camp)	9.4	~6,270
Pass into Middle Park Cyn	9.9	6,400
Middle Park (center)	~10.7	~6,270
Crest	12.3	7,020
Rogers Pass	12.8	7,165

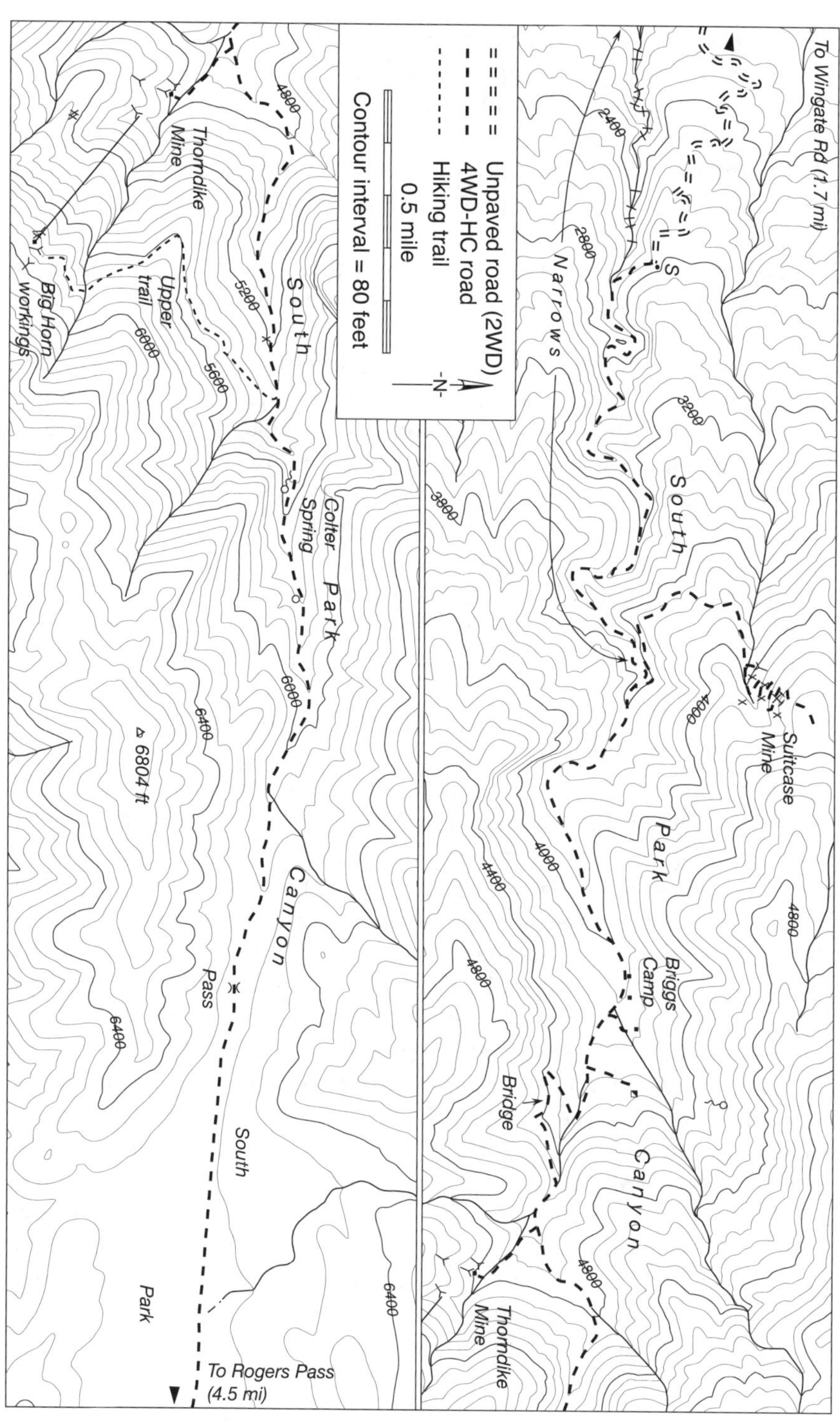
To Wingate Rd (1.7 mi)
Unpaved road (2WD)
4WD-HC road
Hiking trail
0.5 mile
Contour interval = 80 feet
N
Narrows
South Park Canyon
Suitcase Mine
Briggs Camp
Bridge
Thorndike Mine
South Park Canyon
Colter Spring
Upper trail
Big Horn workings
Thorndike Mine
6804 ft
Pass
South Park
To Rogers Pass (4.5 mi)
2400
2800
3200
3800
4000
4400
4800
5200
5600
6000
6400

The best part is the Big Horn workings. The road to them starts 0.5 mile further up the main canyon road, just before Colter Spring. It is now washed out and you will have to hike its steep grade, across a sweeping wilderness of Noonday Dolomite, to the Big Horn's historic shaft, tunnels, and tramway terminal. The ore was mostly cerussite and galena. This area offers great views of South Park Canyon.

Colter Spring. The rocks in much of the upper canyon belong to the Kingston Peak Formation. It contains limestone, sandstone, and a coarse conglomerate deposited during a glaciation period around one billion years ago—all intensely deformed by Mesozoic metamorphism (see *Coyote Canyon*). Spectacular exposures of limestone as convoluted as intestines and diamictites flattened like pancakes occur right along the road, and short walks will uncover many more.

Well-watered Colter Spring supports a thick stand of willows that plugs the steep, narrow wash. For up to half a mile, the creek floods the road and turns it into a slick, muddy mess. At the creek's upper end there is a small water hole, surrounded by a dense cover of big sagebrush and cliffrose. This area is graced in the summer by exceptionally large and colorful bushes of desert mountain penstemon.

South Park. The namesake of this canyon, South Park is one of the high points of this bone-jarring journey. It is a shallow sink, densely covered with low, light-green plants, and surrounded by pine-studded hills. Together with its twin Middle Park to the north, it stands apart from anything else in this desert. When I first saw it, I immediately thought of the Serengeti. Coincidentally, what I spotted next was a group of eight large mammals grazing in the middle distance. The illusion was nearly complete, even though they weren't wildebeest but wild burros—which, ironically, originally came from Africa. This is a scenic, serene valley, restful to the eye compared to the rough canyon that leads to it, and an excellent spot for summer camping.

In the northeast corner of South Park a road heads north, past two old mining camps, then crosses Middle Park and climbs to Rogers Pass, where it connects with the Pleasant Canyon Road. As scenic as this route is, if you are in for a truly exhilarating ride, take the high road instead. From South Park, drive the road that climbs east to the head of the canyon. From there a rough track bounces up and down the forested crest of the Panamints to Rogers Pass. This breathtaking road commands unforgettable views of Butte Valley and the rugged southern Death Valley mountains beyond.

▪

COYOTE CANYON

Most of Coyote Canyon is an impressive gorge filled with ancient formations, enigmatic cacti, and awesome scenery. The short road in the lower canyon ends at the camp and massive tramway of the Gold Spur Mine. Two short steep trails zigzag up to the aerial mining complex, which ranks among the region's most complete and interesting. Hikers can amble several miles up the roadless canyon through scenic galleries of sculpted granite walls and boulders, and either return via neighboring Goler Canyon or ascend Manly Peak for rare views of Butte Valley and the southern Panamints.

General Information

Jurisdiction: Manly Peak Wilderness (BLM), DVNP
Road status: Hiking on roads, trails, & cross-country; 2WD access road
Gold Spur Mine: 2.5 mi, 1,610 ft up, 50 ft down one way / moderate
Coyote Canyon gorge: 4.2 mi, 2,170 ft up, 20 ft down one way / moderate
Manly Peak: 8.8 mi, 5,950 ft up, 180 ft down one way / strenuous
Coyote–Goler canyon loop: 13.2 mi, 2,870 ft up loop / strenuous
Main attractions: Gorges, gold mine, geology, canyon loop hike
USGS 7.5' topo maps: Manly Fall, Copper Queen Cyn*, Manly Peak*
Maps: pp. 405*, *319*

Location and Access

Coyote Canyon is the first canyon north of Goler Canyon, in the southern Panamints. To get to it, drive the Wingate Road 13.3 miles south from Ballarat. The road on the left is the Coyote Canyon Road. It climbs 1.35 miles to a sharp left bend at the mouth of the canyon. Park 0.15 mile further, at a faint road on the right that climbs to the low canyon bank. This battered cutoff road, closed to motor vehicles, cuts south across the open fan 1.1 miles to just below the mouth of Goler Canyon. If you decide to hike the Coyote Canyon–Goler Canyon loop, this shortcut is the road you will take to return from Goler Canyon.

With a standard-clearance vehicle it is easy to drive this far. In the canyon the road is rough, locally rocky or washed out. The 1.9 miles to the mining camp at the end of the road require high clearance.

Route Description

The lower canyon. Coyote Canyon starts right away as a deep and narrow gorge, hemmed in hard on both sides by soaring rock walls and steeply sloped taluses. Its imposing character is intensified by the presence of an eerie dweller—the barrel cactus, a locally common plant that thrives on the steepest, driest, and rockiest bits of real estate. One of the largest cacti in the Mojave Desert, it has a thick cylindrical trunk up to 6 feet in height and one foot in diameter, shielded by a tight mesh of steel-hard spines. Because their seeds germinate only after rare high rainfalls, in a given area all specimens have the same age and roughly the same size. In the slanting sunrays of early morning, they burn like flames sprouting right out of the rock.

The geology of Coyote Canyon is particularly varied and interesting. For the first 0.8 mile, the gorge winds through Triassic granodiorite, then late Precambrian dolomite and quartzite. Past the pronounced left U-bend, where the wash broadens, and for about 0.3 mile, the road crosses the Kingston Peak Formation, a complex melange from the Proterozoic era that has gained fame for the compelling story it tells. It is hard to miss: a gray rock filled with distinctive inclusions, pale, inch-size, oblong and roughly parallel, that justify its name of stretched-pebble conglomerate. First cobbles, then boulders, and ultimately entire walls of it are exposed here. What makes this formation special is that it records an ice age that occurred 680 million years ago. Over time, the glaciers that smothered the land dumped thousands of vertical feet of debris—anything from sand to blimp-size boulders—into the ocean that covered this region. This enormous pile of sediment was later cemented into a conglomerate. In the Mesozoic, metamorphism squashed the whole formation, pebbles and all, creating this striking lattice of parallel "stretched" pebbles. The next formation, exposed from the next narrowing in the canyon up to the mine, is quartz-feldspar gneiss, the region's ancient basement. Somewhere between 1.35 and 1.82 billion years old, it holds the respectable distinction of being the oldest rock around.

The Gold Spur Mine. The small camp of the Gold Spur Mine at the end of the road is a delightful surprise. Its cramped wooden cabin, tank trailer, camper shell, and obligatory outhouse are huddled on the shadier south side of the wash, across from the hulking lower terminal of the mine's jig-back tramway. Anchored to a rock face with 4-inch chains, the tramway is an interesting one-of-a-kind structure. A catwalk skirts the top of its three-chute ore bin to the 12-foot steel wheel that guided the thick tramway cable. Its engine was gravity: the descending ore-filled bucket simply pulled the empty bucket back up.

The Gold Spur Mine, out of sight high on the south slope, is well worth puffing up the steep climb to it. It consists of the upper terminal, a tunnel, and a long rail that connected them via an ore bin, all of it hanging on a precipitous slope several hundred feet above the wash. The upper terminal and the tunnel are accessed by two different foot trails. The terminal trail starts behind the tank trailer. In 0.35 mile it climbs 460 feet, approximately following the tramway's suspended cables and two pipelines. The trail's lower third is interrupted by rocky outcrops and easy to lose. The middle third, in better shape, passes by a sturdy intermediate tower, which still has its wheels. The upper third is gone, and you will have to scramble over slippery rocks and dirt to reach the upper terminal. The trail to the mine starts 50 yards up canyon from the lower tramway, on the right. It parallels the wash for 50 yards, switchbacks 570 steep feet to a high point, then descends a little to the ore bin. It is a little longer (0.6 mile) but better preserved.

The well-preserved upper terminal is a fascinating contraption of sun-cured lumber and rust-coated steel. The bulk of it is a wooden ore bin, moored with hefty cables. Underneath it there is a replica of the lower terminal's 12-foot wheel, mounted on a five-inch shaft, and its brake mechanism, including the brake's wheel, handle, and wooden pads. The Nissan engine propped next to the bin is a recent addition, hardly touched by rust. It was probably used by the present owner to give the stiff, aging tramway a boost.

To negotiate the rough terrain between them, the tunnel and the tramway were connected by a long split-level rail. From the upper terminal, the lower level, partly supported by a trestle bridge, winds through two gaps blasted in the rock to the single-chute ore bin. The upper level connects the top of the bin to the tunnel. The rails are partly gone, but they still make fine walking paths. The 125-foot tunnel, which exploited gold-bearing smoky quartz, is still coursed by a rail—and partly blocked by a large ore car! With its pipelines, cars, suspended tram buckets, and other paraphernalia, this elaborate mining complex can easily keep a mining buff entertained for a few hours.

The mid-canyon gorge. Beyond the camp, Coyote Canyon is roadless and part of the Manly Peak Wilderness. The rock changes abruptly to quartz monzonite, and for the next hour you will wander along a beautiful gorge slithering through a paradise of granite. The walking is generally easy, often on gravel lined with boulders of all sizes. Keep an eye open for barrel cacti, prickle poppy, sacred datura, chia, rock spiraea hiding in shaded cracks, and the creeping vines of coyote melon.

The monzonite is part of a small pluton that covers about 15 square miles centered on Manly Peak. By measuring its relative content in potassium and argon isotopes, geologists were able to pinpoint with devilish precision that it intruded this area 137 million years ago. The monzonite has been locally dissected, sliced, polished, and domed by erosion into a scenic wonderland. At its heart, the gorge squeezes through short narrows guarded by a 10-foot boulder jam. The walls quickly flare into a deep, neatly polished amphitheater. This is Coyote Canyon's most beautiful area. Enclosed by vertical walls, this tighter passage ends at a sheer, 15-foot chockstone fall, easily bypassed up a graceful sweep of pale slickrock.

Over the next 1.3 miles the wash wiggles through a few lazy bends, then the canyon forks. This is the one possibly confusing area. Straight ahead, the obvious way to go, is actually a side canyon. The main canyon, to the right, is accessed by a short scramble out of the entrenched wash. The gorge ends in half a mile, at the next fork.

Coyote Canyon was aptly named: for reasons of their own, coyotes love it here. Their tracks and droppings are commonplace. If you camp here you might catch a glimpse of a coyote at dawn, trotting through the brush as it hunts down one last living tidbit.

The connecting route to Goler Canyon. For a change there is an easy way to make a canyon loop hike, and you may not want to pass it up. At the top of the gorge, take the side canyon on the right and continue 0.75 mile to a saddle at the divide with Goler Canyon. Before getting there, this side canyon forks three times, and making the wrong turn is easy. To minimize trial and error, of the few saddles on the

Coyote Canyon

	Dist.(mi)	Elev.(ft)
Coyote Canyon Road at cutoff	0.0	1,340
Mining camp/road's end	1.9	2,400
Gold Spur Mine (tunnel)	(0.6)	2,990
Narrows (chockstone fall)	2.85	2,920
Upper end of gorge/fork	4.2	3,580
Divide with Goler Canyon	(0.75)	4,120
Return via Goler Canyon	(8.0)	1,340
Leave wash	6.5	4,680
Saddle on southeast shoulder	6.75	5,065
Manly Peak	8.8	7,196

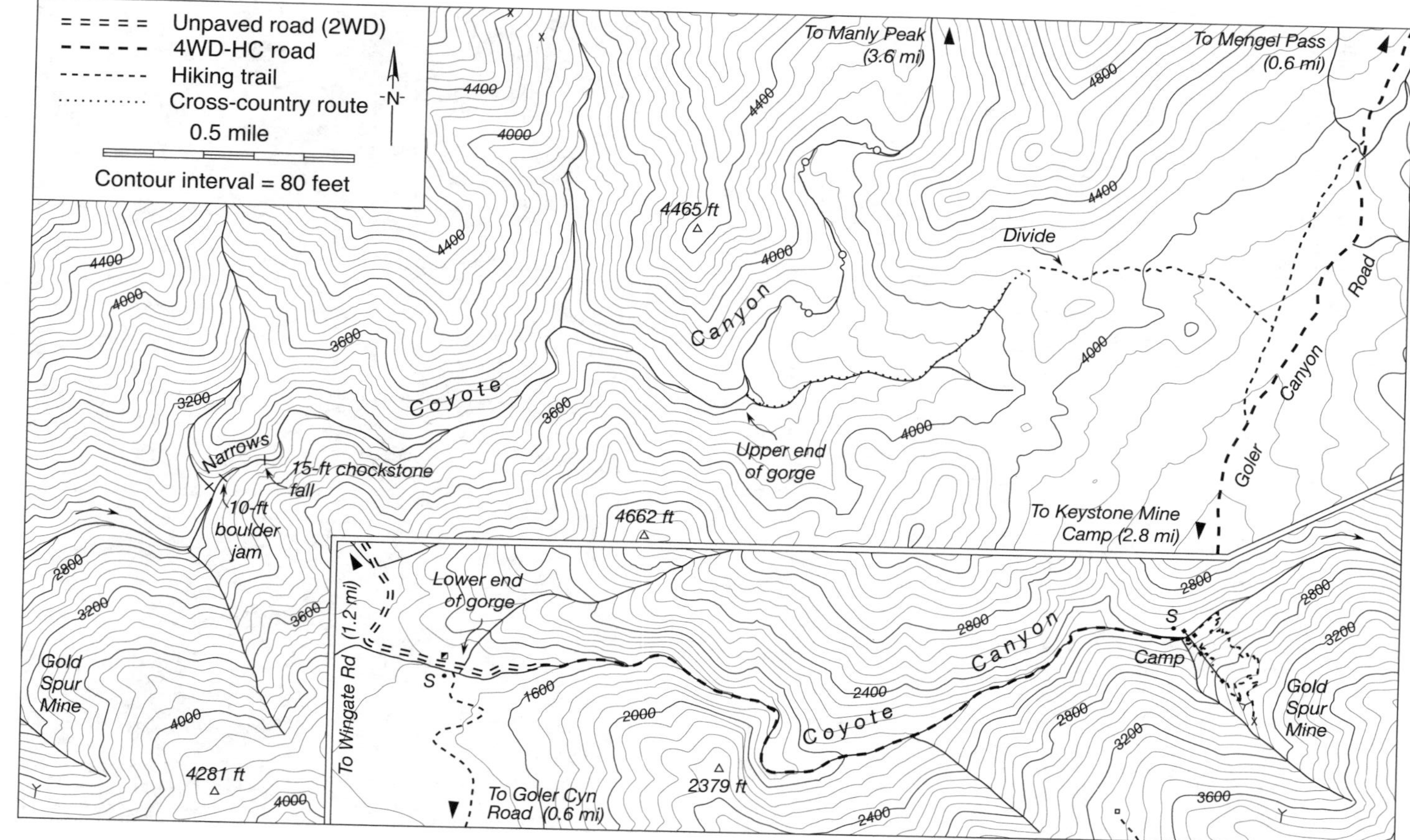

Unpaved road (2WD)
4WD-HC road
Hiking trail
Cross-country route
N
0.5 mile
Contour interval = 80 feet
To Manly Peak (3.6 mi)
To Mengel Pass (0.6 mi)
4465 ft
Divide
Canyon
Coyote
Road
Goler Canyon Road
Narrows
15-ft chockstone fall
10-ft boulder jam
Upper end of gorge
4662 ft
To Keystone Mine Camp (2.8 mi)
To Wingate Rd (1.2 mi)
Lower end of gorge
Coyote Canyon
Camp
Gold Spur Mine
4281 ft
2379 ft
To Goler Cyn Road (0.6 mi)
S

Narrows in the mid-section of Coyote Canyon

western horizon aim for the one closest to the high ridge to the north, which means taking the left fork, then the right fork, and finally the left fork. Consult your map. Just before the saddle, you will pick up the end of a beat-up road that drops 0.75 mile to the Goler Canyon Road. It is then 6.3 miles to the mouth of Goler Canyon (see *Goler Canyon*), 0.2 mile down the road to the side trail (on the north side), and 1.1 miles on this trail back to the mouth of Coyote Canyon.

Upper Coyote Canyon to Manly Peak. Above the last fork the main canyon is more open, though still deep and deepening with increasing elevation. A great extension of this hike is to climb Manly Peak, the towering summit at the head of Coyote Canyon. After passing by a string of small springs, leave the wash (4,920') and scramble northeast to the obvious saddle (~5,070'). Then follow the peak's long and steep southeastern shoulder, barren at first, then lightly forested, and finally sprinkled with boulders, to the peak (7,196'). The summit block is capped by a Class-5 plug of smooth sloped granite, not difficult but exposed; a rope comes in handy. This ascent offers deep views into Butte Valley on one side, and southern Panamint Valley on the other. Allow a couple of days for this vigorous trek.

■

GOLER CANYON

Being the only primitive road connecting Panamint Valley to Death Valley across the Panamint Mountains, and a rough one at that, the Goler Canyon Road is highly prized among four-wheelers. The ride from valley to valley is indeed one of the longest and most eventful in the region. Goler Canyon has springs, cool desert creeks, cactus-studded narrows, ancient rocks, gold mines big and small, and the former lair of serial killer Charles Manson. If you do not have the right vehicle, drive to the canyon mouth and hike in. The grades are modest, and no matter where you go your day will be packed.

General Information

Jurisdiction: Bureau of Land Management, Death Valley National Park
Road status: Hiking on roads; primitive canyon road (4WD/HC)
Goler Canyon narrows: 0.9 mi, 420 ft up, 0 ft down one way/very easy
Lestro Mtn Mine trails: 2.8 mi, 1,660 ft up, 70 ft down one way/moder.
Keystone Mine: 6.5 mi, 2,480 ft up, 360 ft down one way/difficult
Barker Ranch: 5.1 mi, 1,670 ft up, 0 ft down one way/moderate-difficult
Main attractions: Narrows, mines, springs, 4WD road to Death Valley
USGS 7.5′ topo maps: Copper Queen Cyn*, Sourdough Spr.*, Manly Pk
Maps: pp. 413*, *319*

Location and Access

Goler Canyon is the southernmost named major canyon in the southern Panamint Mountains. The road that runs through it climbs from Panamint Valley to Mengel Pass at the crest of the mountains. It then descends into Butte Valley and connects with the Warm Spring Canyon Road, which drops to the West Side Road in Death Valley. This section focuses on the Goler Canyon portion, up to Mengel Pass. From Ballarat, drive the Wingate Road 15.0 miles south and turn left on the Goler Canyon Road. After 1.5 miles you will reach the mouth of Goler Canyon. If you are driving a standard-clearance vehicle, park here: this is as far as you can go without redesigning the underside of your car. High clearance is imperative in the canyon, as well as four-wheel drive and serious experience on either side of Mengel Pass.

If you are four-wheeling, remember that it takes time to see Goler Canyon's many points of interest. Count on a full day to explore this canyon. If you hike in from the mouth, it takes a short day to visit the Keystone Mine, and a long day for Barker Ranch or Mengel Pass.

Route Description

The lower gorge. The most impressive part of Goler Canyon is the deep gorge that makes up the entire lower canyon, up to the Keystone Mine. And of this, the best part is the narrows. For 0.9 mile starting right at its entrance, the canyon folds upon itself in tight goosenecks, no more than 14 feet wide at places. The lower walls rise vertically to steep higher slopes, dotted with jagged rocks jade-black with desert varnish. Year-round a little water surfaces here and there. The largest flow, usually a couple of gallons per minute, gushes out of the ground as a musical foot-high, foot-wide cascade hidden under thickets. The creek it spawns flows down the twin ruts of the road, sometimes as far as a thousand feet, irrigating a few mesquite groves along the way.

Past the narrows the gorge opens up gradually and deepens markedly. The upper walls are peppered with barrel cacti, their yellow tips fluorescent against the dark rocks. The geologic formations are much the same as in neighboring Coyote Canyon. Just before the second pronounced left bend past the narrows (1.2 miles in) look for a wall of Kingston Peak Formation conglomerate on the south side. Its inclusions are made of a granitic rock that obviously predates the conglomerate itself, and may top the billion-year mark. Quartz-feldspar gneiss, even older, is exposed all along the upper half of the gorge.

The Lestro Mountain Mine. The first mining structure in the canyon is a well-preserved ore bin just south of the road. It is still connected to a cableway that drops from a tunnel perched 540 feet up the sheer north canyon wall. This is part of a sprawling gold mine that spans the ridge between here and Coyote Canyon to the north. It was first operated in the 1910s as the Gold Spur Mine by two Ballarat owners, who produced ore worth a measly $9 a ton. In the 1930s it was recorded as the Lestro Mountain Mine and owned by Angelinos James Lester and John Rogers. Several of the mine's 16 claims, including the Soft Spot and the Caliente, were developed and did produce a little, including $12,000 in 1940. From the 1960s to the 1980s Riverside owners David and Hallett Newman regularly assessed the mine, although apparently more for fun than for lucrative purposes.

Two short but steep trails climb to the mine workings—places that likely see no more than a visitor every decade. The first one starts 0.15 mile up canyon from the ore bin, on the left side, across from a stone ruin. It screams up 440 feet in 0.3 mile to the interesting ruins of the cableway's upper installations. For the second trail, continue up canyon 0.25 mile to the mine's second cableway, then 0.15 mile to a small alcove on the north side, in a right bend. It takes no effort at all

The Goler Canyon Road in the narrows along the lower canyon

to miss this trail. Its low retaining stone wall is the best clue. Look back frequently—the trail climbs westward and is easier to spot from up canyon. Its steep switchbacks wind 0.3 mile to the top of the cableway. The trail is mostly well preserved, except for a short stretch near the top where I had to hang on to a wall. There are several prospects and a short tunnel just before and past the cableway. The trail then descends a little to the largest tunnel, a tight, sinuous corridor that intersects poor gold-bearing quartz veins.

If this is out of your league, consider instead the next mining trail, just behind the third cableway, 0.1 mile up canyon on the south side. This site has an ore bin, as well as the foundations of a small mill and what may have been a cyanide tank. The trail climbs 750 feet in 0.5 mile (steep!) to a shaft near the crest line—all of it commands plunging views into the canyon gorge.

Just up canyon there is a second spring, on a high bank in the wash. A small cabin, historically associated with the Lestro Mountain Mine, is hidden in a grove of mesquite. Its frayed wood has been burnished by sunlight into delightful blends of orange and brown. Sometimes visitors use the cabin, especially on cold nights. They enjoy the decadent comfort of a table and chairs, just enough floor space for a sleeping bag or two, and the half-inch-deep flow of the nearby creek.

The Keystone Mine. At the upper end of the gorge the canyon opens up and the road reaches the Keystone Mine area. Carl Mengel, a well-educated mining engineer who had filed claims all over the Mojave Desert, purchased this gold property in 1912, when it was known as the Monte Cristo Mines. Mengel worked it off and on for many years while living in a rustic cabin over the pass at Greater View Spring. He did not make much money on it, and ended up selling it in 1935 to the Lotus Mine. Development was stepped up. Two aerials tramways and a half-mile inclined-rail tramway were erected to lower the ore from the tunnels, up near the canyon's south rim, to the canyon road. But by the early 1950s the mine had still produced only about $32,000. In more recent years, it was operated as the Keystone Mine. Mining was scaled up again, the derelict tramways were replaced by trucks and dynamite sticks by heavy equipment, but production was relatively small and operations were suspended in 1993.

From the main canyon road, a four-wheel-drive road on the south side winds up the steep mountainside to the mine. The Keystone Mine Road passes first by the mining camp, made of a stone house, a concrete shed, and a few trailers. Like most abandoned enclaves of civilization accessible to four-wheelers—a minority of whom display a staggering paucity of respect—in just a few years this once shipshape camp was ruined by vandals. It still has interesting ruins, notably the cabins and the large terminal of one of the tramways.

Past the camp the road climbs in long hairpins to the Keystone Mine, perched high on the ridge separating Goler Canyon and the next canyon south. It follows the tramway cable, several pipelines, and a long grade of railroad ties marching up the ravine to the west. This is the ruin of the mine's inclined-rail tramway, one of the longest in the region. After almost a mile the road forks. The short side road on the right goes by two tunnels and some hefty equipment, including a dump truck and a compressor the size of a boxcar, and ends at a dilapidated wooden maintenance shed on a high ridge. Having been in operation until 1993, these tunnels are a good illustration of the gradual increase in mining scale over the decades. Whereas most older tunnels are too small to stand, these are large enough to accommodate a whole truck.

Back at the fork, the main road makes two more switchbacks to the divide with the next canyon south. This stretch is almost blocked by a huge boulder that leaves just enough room for a narrow vehicle to clear the sheer, crumbly edge of the road by about a foot. Further on the road is also partly blocked by rockslides. Walking from the boulder the short remaining distance is not a bad alternative. On the far side of

Old cottonwood at Sourdough Spring

the divide, the road drops 0.25 mile to the foot of the historic workings. This is the most interesting mining area in Goler Canyon. Half a dozen tunnels and several prospects are scattered up and down the slope. The lower tunnel is heavily timbered and about 420 feet long. The next one up, about half as long, was serviced by a 100-foot inclined rail. Both have dusty stopes, rail tracks, and an interesting mechanical shovel. The higher tunnels are harder to reach but worth the effort. The ore, mostly gold with a little silver, occurs in quartz veins and seams in fractured quartzite. Check out also the trucks and giant stirrers by the roadside. This mine is still privately owned. Treat it with respect, and leave everything as you find it.

The mid-canyon narrows. Past the Keystone Mine the road continues up what appears to be Goler Canyon but is in fact a side canyon. Goler Canyon actually goes up the wide opening north of the Keystone Mine Road. The reason for this road diversion is a short set of narrows 0.7 mile up this roadless stretch of Goler Canyon, too tight for a road. If you hike it, you will find a boulder-filled canyon that gradually deepens and tapers down to a pristine sandy wash. An impressive vertical wall, as flat as a crystal facet, marks the entrance to the narrows. This defile is barely 4 feet wide and has two 7-foot stairway-like jams of polished boulders. It emerges into a widening gorge lined with walls of angular monzonite blocks. You can make a loop walk by continuing 0.8 mile up canyon to the road, then following it back to the Keystone Mine Camp.

Barker Ranch. Past the Keystone Mine the road skirts an unusual formation, a towering, 500-yard wide plug of rhyolite that cuts a cheerful pink streak across the northern canyon wall. As naked as when it flowed out of the earth in the Tertiary, it has been sculpted by rain and wind into a phantasmagoria of knolls, hollows, and fins. A little further, a square stone cistern marks the lower end of another spring. A vague foot trail wanders past the cistern into a tight, shaded trench where a small intermittent creek tumbles through the brush. The pipelines that litter the road once supplied water to the Lotus Mine.

At the road fork shortly past this spring, turn right to go to Barker Ranch (or continue straight to Mengel Pass). Sourdough Spring, a stone's throw away, is small and usually waterless, yet it is the most scenic spring in this canyon. Trapped in a shallow constriction, its healthy grove of 30-foot willows arches gracefully over the road. Tall vehicles may even have trouble clearing the massive low branch of the aging cottonwood at the head of the spring!

In October 1969, Barker Ranch and what was then known as Goler Wash made national headlines when Charles Manson and 25 members

Goler Canyon Road

	Dist.(mi)	Elev.(ft)
Wingate Road	0.0	1,130
Goler Canyon mouth/narrows	1.5	1,580
Upper end of narrows	2.35	1,995
Ore bin	3.1	2,200
1st trail to Lestro Mtn Mine	3.25	2,290
Lestro Mountain Mine (hike)	(0.35)	2,740
2nd trail to Lestro Mtn Mine	3.65	2,420
Lestro Mountain Mine (hike)	(0.3)	2,730
Spring and cabin	3.9	~2,510
Keystone Mine Road	4.6	2,720
Keystone Mine (road's end)	(1.7)	3,500
Barker Ranch Road	5.95	3,120
Sourdough Spring	(~0.1)	~3,130
Barker Ranch	(0.65)	3,255
Mengel Pass	9.2	~4,315

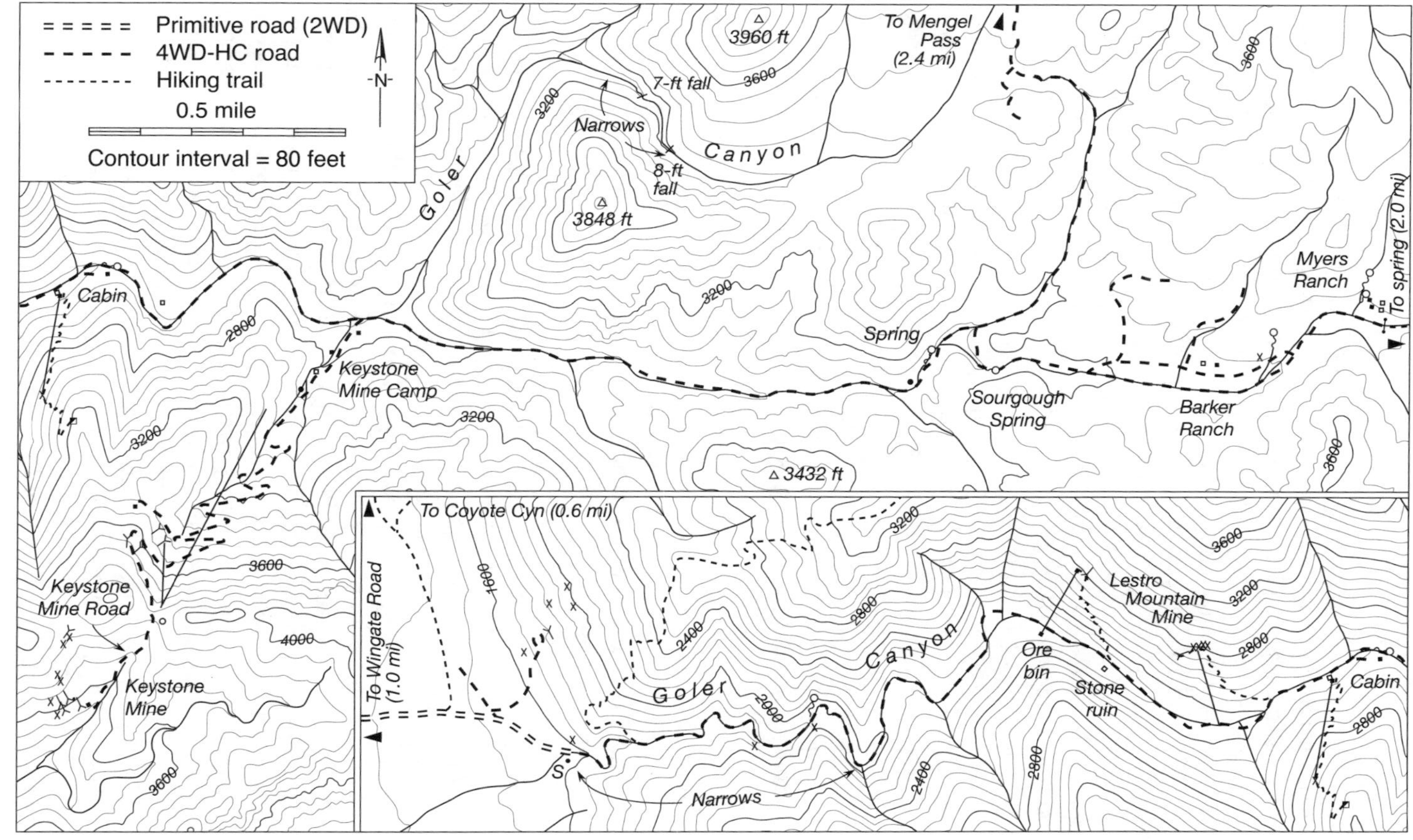
Primitive road (2WD)
4WD-HC road
Hiking trail
0.5 mile
Contour interval = 80 feet
N
3960 ft
To Mengel Pass (2.4 mi)
7-ft fall
Narrows
8-ft fall
Goler
Canyon
3848 ft
Cabin
Keystone Mine Camp
Spring
Sourgough Spring
Barker Ranch
Myers Ranch
To spring (2.0 mi)
3432 ft
Keystone Mine Road
Keystone Mine
To Coyote Cyn (0.6 mi)
To Wingate Road (1.0 mi)
Lestro Mountain Mine
Ore bin
Stone ruin
Narrows
S
1600
2000
2400
2800
3200
3600
4000

of his "family" were arrested here. This group of young misfits hooped up on drugs, many of them teenage girls, were held under the spell of Manson's bizarre cult. Manson, then 34, was a mentally troubled ex-convict with a record of theft, forgery, and armed robbery so long that he had already spent half of his life in jail. His cult hinged on his prediction of Helter Skelter, an imminent apocalypse during which African Americans would wipe out the Caucasian race. He and his followers had come to the Death Valley region searching for what he claimed was a large cave where they would hide, multiply, and eventually emerge to overthrow black supremacy. Ironically, the Barker Ranch arrests were prompted by suspicion of arson, not murder. It took investigators several months to link the Manson Family to the gruesome Tate-LaBianca slayings of August 1969 in Los Angeles, where seven innocent people were brutally slaughtered. Several members received the death penalty, although their sentences were later changed to life imprisonment. Manson was still serving his sentence when he died in 2017.

Set against a background of golden rolling hills, Barker Ranch has a large verandaed stone house and a log cabin, surrounded by tall cottonwoods, fallow gardens, and irrigated iris beds. In spite of its peacefulness, the ghosts of the Manson Family make it a creepy place. Myers Ranch, just up the road, is inhabited and closed to the public.

Mengel Pass. For the last few miles the Goler Canyon Road circles widely around the foot of Manly Peak to the north. The canyon is wide open, bordered to the east by eroded hills of reddish volcanic flows, tuffs, and andesite plugs (one of them, a 30-foot beehive, is right by the road). For people with a fondness for driving where motor vehicles aren't really designed to go, this stretch is good news: it is one of the best bad roads around Death Valley. For a mile it is reduced to two deep ruts swerving through liquid sand, and you will be wishing for a few rocks. Then it is all rocks, jagged and lopsided, and you will be wishing you were back in the sand. The road goes over a series of rocky outcrops canted sideways and bedrock cascades nicknamed, for self-explanatory reasons, "Hubcap Rock" and "Oilpan Rock." If you are not experienced with this kind of road, chances of getting into some sort of trouble are impressively high. Stop while you are ahead, and either walk on or head back. The round cairn at the pass is Mengel Monument, where the ashes and wooden leg of Carl Mengel were buried in 1944. Anvil Spring Junction in Butte Valley is 2 miles down the road—another perfectly rough ride.

■

— 9 —

PANAMINT VALLEY

PANAMINT VALLEY HAS LONG BEEN touted as Death Valley's twin. The similarities between them are indeed remarkable. Both valleys are divided into two main hydrological basins; the northern one has dunes and a dry mud playa, while the deeper, much larger southern basin is wetter and partly covered by an extensive salt pan. Both valleys are bounded by long mountain ranges of similar elevations; one drops gently to the valley, the other one falls off like a wall. Coincidentally, the resemblance is not limited to geophysical features. Like Death Valley, Panamint Valley has a small community in its northwestern corner (Panamint Springs) and another one on the southeast side (Ballarat). However, there is one overwhelming difference: Panamint Valley is far less visited. Most of the minimal traffic it witnesses is on its way to or from Death Valley. Only a minute fraction of visitors actually comes to Panamint Valley for the sake of Panamint Valley. A definite blessing for those who do take the time to stop, look around, and realize the wealth of places they can have all to themselves.

Access and Backcountry Roads

The main paved roads in Panamint Valley are Highway 190, the Trona-Wildrose Road, the Panamint Valley Road, and the Nadeau Road. Highway 190 cuts east-west across the northern half of the valley and connects Owens Valley to the west to Death Valley to the east. The Trona-Wildrose Road comes in from Searles Valley, enters Panamint Valley at its southwestern corner, and cuts north across the mid-valley to Wildrose Canyon. The Panamint Valley Road provides a north-south link between these two roads. The Nadeau Road heads

Suggested Backcountry Drives in Panamint Valley					
Route/Destination	Dist. (mi)	Lowest elev.	Highest elev.	Road type	Pages
Big Four Mine Road	7.2	1,556'	2,210'	F	321
Indian Ranch Road	11.9	1,045'	1,268'	P	416
Nadeau Trail to Hwy 190	28.9	1,560'	~2,930'	F	431-434
Nadeau Tr. to Modoc Mine	26.0	1,668'	3,970'	F	497-498
Onyx Mine Road	2.8	1,976'	2,850'	H	527-528
Panamint Valley Crater Rd	1.4	1,770'	2,290'	H	440
Reilly Road	1.7	1,852'	2,006'	P	447
Wingate Road	20.0	1,045'	1,425'	P	313-314
Key: P=Primitive (2WD) H=Primitive (HC) F=Primitive (4WD)					

north along the west side of the mid-valley and ends at the Trona limestone quarry (which is still active).

Besides these impeccably asphalted and utterly unchallenging highways, where the scenery has the uncanny habit of whizzing by as a blur, Panamint Valley can be discovered along several long primitive and graded roads, some easily passable with a sedan, others best tackled with a stronger vehicle. The northernmost one is the Big Four Mine Road. From Highway 190 it follows the east side of the valley north about 6 miles and ends not far below the Big Four Mine. Level and smooth enough for a passenger car, it is a great road to rough it the easy way, and the starting point of several hikes described in this book.

The Nadeau Trail is the valley's wildest dirt road. Built in 1877 to haul silver out of the valley, it parallels the scenic front of the Argus Range for more than 20 miles. It eventually hooks up with the Defense Mine Road, which continues north to Highway 190. Although long sections are suitable for a standard-clearance vehicle, high clearance (and four-wheel drive at places) is needed to make it from end to end.

The two primitive roads in the southern basin—the Indian Ranch and the Wingate roads—offer unhurried backcountry driving. For 32 miles they wind along the Panamints and command majestic open views. The graded Indian Ranch Road skirts the valley's east side south to the ghost town of Ballarat. Here the Wingate Road takes over and continues south for many miles down to the China Lake Naval Weapons Center (closed to the public). The northern third of the Wingate Road is regularly oiled by the C. R. Briggs Mine. The rest of it is a bone-rattling washboard, but it is usually negotiable with a standard-clearance vehicle down to the Goler Canyon Road.

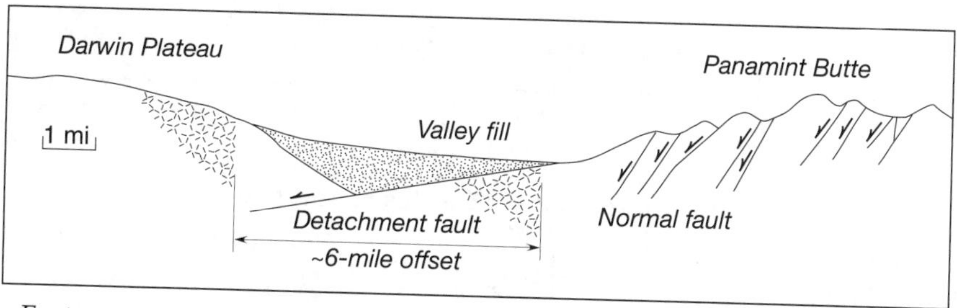

East-west cross-section of northern Panamint Valley showing the directions of motion along the Hunter Mountain Fault Zone.

Geology

Like most valleys in the Basin and Range province, Panamint Valley is what structural geologists call a "pull-apart" basin. It was formed by extensional movements along the Hunter Mountain Fault Zone, a major fault system that traces the entire east side of the valley along the foot of the Panamint Range. This system of faults has witnessed complex motions in all directions: northward on a strike-slip fault, downward on a normal-slip fault, and westward on a detachment fault. The opening of Panamint Valley, which began about 3 million years ago, is believed to have been caused mainly by movement along the detachment fault. Think of it as a giant slide that dips gently west from the foot of the Panamint Range under the valley and extends under Darwin Plateau and the Argus Range on the valley's west side. The fault block west of the fault has been slipping west and slightly down on this detachment plane, while migrating north relative to the Panamint Range. The widening gap between the two fault blocks was gradually filled by alluvia ripped from the blocks by erosion. Because the angle of this detachment fault is low (see figure above), the downward slip has been relatively small: drill holes in central Panamint Valley encountered less than 400 feet of valley fill before hitting bedrock. But motion in the horizontal direction has been far more substantial. The northward slip has been clocking about 0.1 inch *per year*. This may seem puny, but after three million years the offset between matching rock formations on opposite sides of Panamint Valley is as large as 6 miles! The small transverse faults that cut across some valley fans attest that this process is still very much active today.

At the north end of Panamint Valley, the Hunter Mountain Fault Zone angles northwest along Hunter Mountain, then follows the west side of Saline Valley at the foot of the Inyo Mountains. So as the Panamint and Argus ranges were being pulled apart to make room for Panamint Valley, the same fault was also pulling apart the Inyos and

Suggested Hikes in Panamint Valley

Route/Destination	Dist. (mi)	Elev. gain	Mean elev.	Access road	Pages
Short hikes (under 5 miles round trip)					
Ash Hill tufa	0.6	60'	1,690'	H/0.4 mi	435-436
Ash Hill tufa (loop)	2.9	310'	1,790'	H/0.4 mi	435-436
Ballarat (loop)	0.6	10'	1,070'	Paved	442-444
North Panamint Playa					
highway to Lake Hill	2.4	0'	1,540'	Paved	427-430
Onyx Mine	0.3	~40'	2,860'	Graded	527-528
Panamint Valley Crater	1.5	570'	2,030'	Graded	440
Post Office Spring	0.6	30'	1,060'	Paved	444-446
Reilly (loop)	1.2	440'	2,700'	P/2.8 mi	447-450
Warm Sulfur Springs				Graded	
loop	4.7	30'	1,040'		436-440
northern trail	1.3	10'	1,040'		436-440
southern trail	1.0	20'	1,040'		436-440
Intermediate hikes (5-12 miles round trip)					
Lake Hill loop	5.4	40'	1,550'	Graded	430
Panamint Valley Dunes				Graded	
highest dune	3.8	1,130'	2,010'		421-426
loop	9.1	1,650'	2,120'		421-426
North Panamint Playa				Paved	
highway to north end	5.3	~10'	1,540'		427-430
Long hikes (over 12 miles round trip)					
North Panamint Playa				Paved	
highway to dunes	9.3	1,170'	1,700'		427, 421

Key: P=Primitive (2WD) H=Primitive (HC) F=Primitive (4WD)
Distances: one way for out-and-back hikes, round-trip for loops
Elev. gain: sum of all elevation gains on round-trip or loop hike

the Last Chance Range to create Saline Valley. The two valleys were created simultaneously, like twins united by the same umbilical cord.

Archaeology

The prehistoric people who inhabited Panamint Valley have left behind a unique legacy of artifacts called stone alignments—giant figures drawn on the ground, usually on valley fans, by methodical

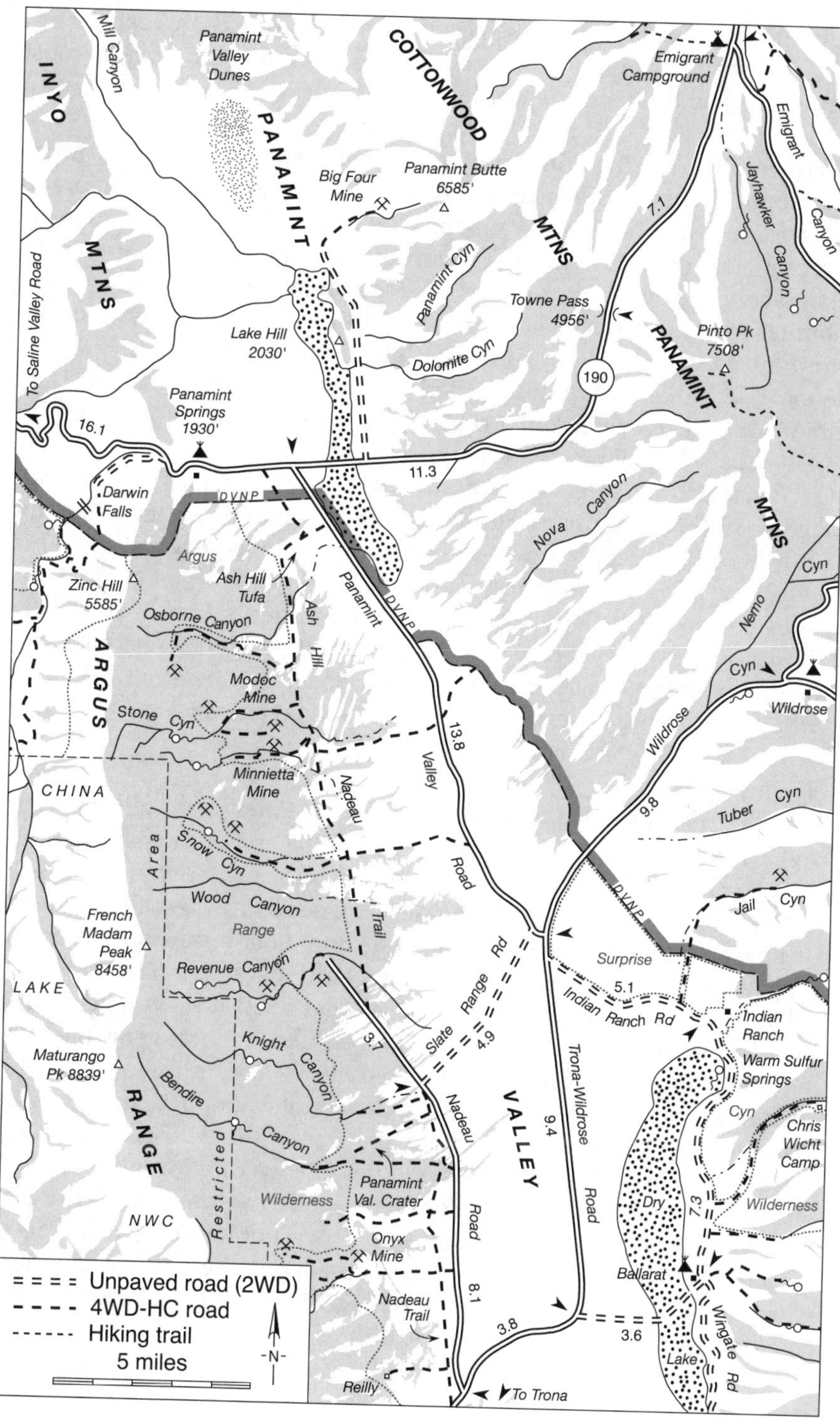

Mill Canyon
Panamint Valley Dunes
COTTONWOOD
INYO
PANAMINT
MTNS
Emigrant Campground
Emigrant
Big Four Mine
Panamint Butte 6585'
Jayhawker Canyon
Canyon
7.1
Panamint Cyn
Towne Pass 4956'
Pinto Pk 7508'
Lake Hill 2030'
Dolomite Cyn
190
To Saline Valley Road
Panamint Springs 1930'
16.1
11.3
Darwin Falls
DVNP
Nova Canyon
Argus
Zinc Hill 5585'
Ash Hill Tufa
Ash Hill
Panamint
Nemo
Cyn
Osborne Canyon
ARGUS
Modoc Mine
Wildrose
Stone Cyn
13.8
Valley
CHINA
Minnietta Mine
Nadeau
9.8
Tuber Cyn
Area
Snow Cyn
Road
Wood Canyon
Jail Cyn
French Madam Peak 8458'
Range
Trail
Surprise
Revenue Canyon
5.1
LAKE
Indian Ranch Rd
Indian Ranch
Slate Range Rd
4.9
3.7
Warm Sulfur Springs
Maturango Pk 8839'
Knight Canyon
Trona-Wildrose Road
RANGE
Bendire Canyon
VALLEY
9.4
Cyn
Chris Wicht Camp
Restricted
Panamint Val. Crater
Wilderness
Dry
7.3
NWC
Onyx Mine
Ballarat
Unpaved road (2WD)
4WD-HC road
Hiking trail
5 miles
N
8.1
Nadeau Trail
3.8
3.6
Wingate Rd
Lake
Reilly
To Trona

placement of rocks or cairns. Whether they represent an abstract figure, as is most common, a human being, or an animal, what is most impressive is their sheer size: they extend anywhere from tens of feet to over 100 yards. Stone alignments are rare. Only a few sites are known to exist in the multi-million acres of Death Valley. A few others are found from Owens Lake and Ash Meadows down to the Colorado River and Baja California. Panamint Valley stands out for hosting the largest and most concentrated occurrences in the West. We are uncertain about the age and purposes of stone alignments. In Death Valley, similar structures have been estimated to be between a few hundred and 2,000 years old. In historic times, elsewhere in the country Shoshone Indians have made offerings at stone-alignment sites. They might have been ceremonial centers, or some sort of record, perhaps trail maps. We may never know.

Panamint Valley is *big*. Without a serious clue, your hope of finding one of these enigmatic figures is dismal at best. Even if you do not find them, the very knowledge of their existence is exciting. This awareness adds meaning and mystery to this valley and enhances our appreciation of it. On every hike, the alignments lurk around like ghosts, out of sight yet constantly watching. If you run across an alignment, remember how precious it is. Do not upset the stones. Treat it with the reverence deserved by all things sacred and ancient.

Hiking

What is most pleasant about hiking in Panamint Valley is that much of it is nearly level and easy—and at the end of the day, you can indulge in the luxury of a sit-down dinner at nearby Panamint Springs. The following sections describe some of the valley's most striking destinations, including an assortment of springs and unusual geological features. None of them requires a long drive on nasty roads. All you need is a passenger car, and you get to spend less time on the road and more on your feet. A few longer hikes to local gems are also included, in particular to the extensive dry lake known as North Panamint Playa, and to the remote Panamint Valley Dunes. There is also ample room for backpacking trips—across the wild northern valley, or down historic Nadeau Trail. If you are looking for more, try the salt flats west of the Wingate Road, the southern extension of the Big Four Mine Road, or the small dunes southwest of Indian Ranch. These are all superb destinations. Do not attempt any of them in the summer, when the whole place turns into a furnace. You will find it much more comfortable from October to mid-April.

▪

THE PANAMINT VALLEY DUNES

Lost at the far end of the valley, ringed by beautiful and desolate mountains, the Panamint Valley Dunes are among the most remote dunes in the park. It is close to 4 level desert miles to get to them, but the walking is easy and the scenery is so grand that it will entice you to go on. About 250 feet tall and unusually steep, the dunes are an exhilarating playground, and they command superb views of Panamint Valley.

General Information

Jurisdiction: Death Valley National Park
Road status: Roadless; access from graded road
Highest dune: 3.8 mi, 1,090 ft up, 40 ft down one way/easy
Panamint Dunes loop: 9.1 mi, 1,650 ft up loop/moderate
Main attractions: Isolated dunes, valley-floor hiking
USGS 7.5′ topo map: The Dunes
Maps: pp. 425*, *419*

Location and Access

The Panamint Valley Dunes are at the north end of Panamint Valley, on the fan below Hunter Mountain. The easiest way to get to them is to hike from the Big Four Mine Road. This road starts 4.5 miles east of Panamint Springs, which is 0.3 mile east of the dry lake's eastern edge. Drive this graded road 5.8 miles to the first sharp right bend and park. The dunes are visible a few miles to the north-northwest.

Geology: The Footprints of Moving Dunes

The Panamint Dunes are moving. In this seemingly unchanging landscape, geologists managed to find clear evidence of their imperceptible migration. Because of their location part way up an alluvial fan, the dunes form a local barrier across the fan's sloping surface. During a flashflood, debris flows—boulders, gravel, sand, and silt—washed down from Hunter Mountain normally spread out over a wide area of the fan. However, the portion of a debris flow intercepted by the dunes collects against the dunes' up-fan side and forms a low, flat-topped bench, much like water impounded behind a dam. Flows strong enough to reach as far down as the dunes occur infrequently, perhaps every few centuries. During this hiatus, the dunes continue to be herded up the fan by the wind, going right over the debris bench

Panamint Valley Dunes

and leaving it behind as a mark of their passage. Subsequent flash-floods create other benches, higher up the fan, but the older benches are protected from them by the screen of up-fan dunes.

Like giant footprints, at least 15 benches record the steady progression of the dunes across the fans at the north end of Panamint Valley, and they tell us much about the dunes' history. By mapping the location of the benches, one can retrace the migratory path of the dunes and identify their original location. By dating the benches, one can infer the dunes' age and their rate of travel.

Up until about 9,000 years ago the valley was flooded under Lake Panamint. The dunes formed at least 6,000 years ago near the shoreline of the drying lake, about half a mile northwest of today's playa. They were likely built with sand particles wind-blown off the desiccating lake playa. Since then they have migrated about 4 miles north-northwest, at an average speed of 2.8 feet per year. The benches also tell us something about the shape of the dunes: when debris flows pile up against the dunes, they mold the dune's up-fan side and record their outline like a cast. Like today's dunes, about 6,000 years ago the Panamint Valley Dunes were star dunes. Since star dunes do not move nearly this fast, the Panamint Valley Dunes must have migrated mostly during wind regimes that transformed them into more mobile forms, such as barchan dunes.

The dunes are still moving. As they reach higher up the increasingly steep fan, the wind will gradually lose its battle against gravity and they will move more and more slowly. A few thousand years from now, the Panamint Valley Dunes will reach their final resting place, near the foot of Hunter Mountain.

Route Description

The approach. This is a pure desert walk, across sandy, sparsely vegetated flats. Your target is in full view the whole time, but it is far away and it gets closer very slowly. The local plant community is a typical low-desert mix of creosote and bursage. In 1996, this area was hit by a nasty parasite called dodder—also known as devil's guts. Dodder attaches itself via tiny suckers to a plant and ensnares it in a fishnet of bright orange threads that lives off the juices of its host and often dehydrates it to death. By 1999 the dodder was all gone, but square miles of fan cover had been turned into a devastated field of scrawny, leafless plants.

In the spring, quite a few flowering plants add bolts of color to the landscape, including evening primrose and desertgold. None is as striking as the desert prickle poppy. You will have to be patient: it is just about the last plant you will get to before all vegetation finally gives out, where the sand mantle first swells into dunes. When in bloom, this blue-green, thistle-like plant graces the sandy slopes with a dazzling belt of large white flowers, their papery petals fluttering in the slightest breeze.

Wildlife is fairly abundant, if you are willing to think small. You may even spot a few animals you have never seen before, like sand-dwelling bees. Their burrow openings are just wide enough for a single bee to crawl through. They swarm over large areas, aimlessly it seems, producing an unceasing drone. They left me alone, but I wondered whether they are always this complacent. At least three species of grasshoppers also live here, each one beautifully matched to its surrounding. Near the road, where the fan is mostly brown to black cobbles of lava, they are brownish. Much larger grasshoppers, up to 2 inches long, live a little further out. When on the ground they are mottled gray and white, matching the dominant granitic rocks of the fan. In flight, their wide blue wings merge with the sky. In the dunes the grasshoppers are smaller and the color of sand.

Other locals blend in remarkably well. Once in a while a zebra-tailed lizard will dart out of nowhere, scared silly by what may be its first encounter with a human being. These creatures must hold some sort of lizard record for speed. They run with such amazing swiftness and their skin is so pale that it is hard for human eyes to track them. You are not even sure you actually saw anything moving. If you manage to track one for long enough, you will see that it runs on stretched legs, sometimes only on its hind legs, its black and white tail curled high over its back. They stop almost as swiftly—literally on a dime.

Larger animals, too, inhabit or visit these hostile flats: wrens, sparrows, ravens, cottontail rabbits, snakes, even an occasional coyote or wild burro. One day in early summer I was checked out on several occasions by Costa's hummingbirds. While I was crouched in the meager shade of a creosote, one of them parked in midair 3 feet from my face, hovered for a few seconds, then proceeded to describe a half circle around me, in those sudden little skips hummingbirds do, slowly inspecting the red trim of my pack. Then it landed on the high branch of a nearby creosote and kept me company for several minutes.

The dunes. The sand apron surrounding the dunes is extensive. In the summer, crossing it will seem like a good fraction of eternity. But the dunes are worth the wait, the heat, the sweat, and the warm canteen water. Besides their aesthetic appeal, there is something special about the Panamint Valley Dunes. Perhaps it is their improbable location, high up against a fan, surrounded by a stunning ring of deeply chiseled mountains. Or it might be their isolation, miles from asphalt and steel, at the far end of a lonesome valley. Or is it the virgin sand, often free of human beings and footprints?

The main source of sand is probably the quartz monzonite exposed in the Panamint Mountains and Argus Range. A good part of the north-valley fill is made of chunks of these formations shed by the mountains over the last few million years. For thousands of years, the dominant southerly winds have been relentlessly blowing quartz particles up the long floor of Panamint Valley and building sensual waves of sand.

The Panamint Valley Dunes are relatively small in extent, covering less than one square mile. There are four main dunes, all of them star dunes with multiple slipface ridges resulting from variable wind directions. They are surrounded on all sides by a choppy sea of smaller dunes. Disposed in a circular arrangement, the main dunes are partly linked by razor-sharp ridges with unusually deep and steep sinks on both sides. The highest dune is the easternmost one, and the closest. Trudging from its summit to the other three and back makes an exhilarating loop. Negotiating the ridges is like walking a tight rope—there is a deep void on both sides and not much substance in the middle. When at the bottom of a sink, you are trapped in a well of sand,

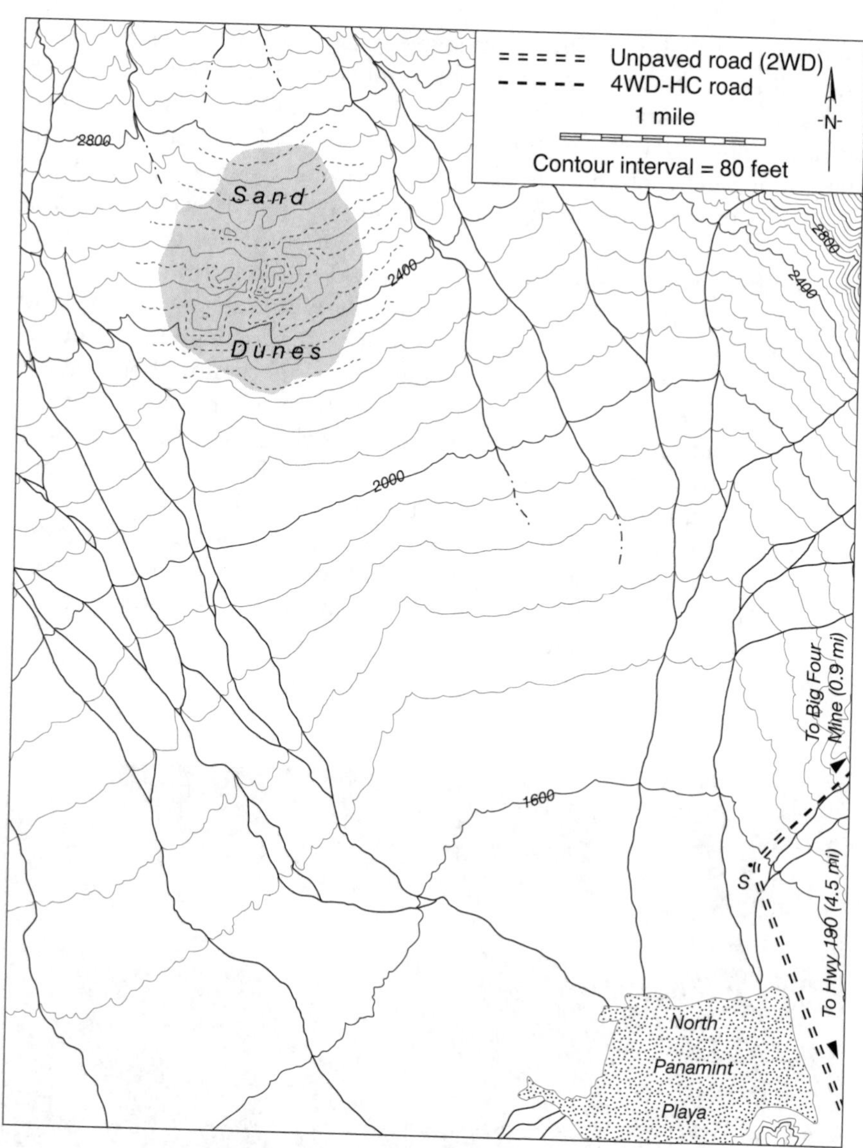

The Panamint Valley Dunes	Dist.(mi)	Elev.(ft)
Big Four Mine Road	0.0	1,570
Edge of dunes	3.4	~2,320
Summit of highest dune	3.9	2,660
Summit of furthest dune	4.5	2,650

staring up at smooth slopes streaked with swirls of black magnetic sand. It gives the area a strange look, almost too artistic for nature, perhaps what it would have looked like if Georgia O'Keefe had put it on canvas. The views from the high points extend straight down the length of Panamint Valley, overlooking the valley's dark Lake Hill and long, sinuous playa. The highest mountain on the east side of the valley is Telescope Peak, nearly 30 miles away and 8,400 feet higher. Across from it stands the Argus Range, and to the north of this range sprawls the barren volcanic mesa of the Darwin Plateau. Turn around and you will be looking up at Hunter Mountain, dusted with conifers.

On your way back, look for some of the debris-flow benches left behind by the moving dunes. A few of them are right among the dunes, in particular up against the up-fan side of a small whaleback dune near the northwest corner of the dunes. The most conspicuous benches are down on the sand-free fan. They are the most prominent topographic features on the fan, roughly aligned along a south-southwest direction and easiest to spot when heading back from the main dunes. They have nearly flat, smooth tops with short but steep down-fan slopes, and they stretch across the fan for up to 100 yards.

■

Panoramic view of Panamint Valley's dunes and north playa from Saline Valley Road near South Pass

NORTH PANAMINT PLAYA

Explore this ancient lake bed by either driving the primitive road that parallels it or hiking its nearly level surface: in all your walking you will not gain more than a few feet of elevation. You are in for spellbinding scenery, soil lacerated with billions of fractal cracks, earthquake-induced trenches, and an alien-looking island the size of downtown San Francisco that slid down the side of a mountain.

General Information

Jurisdiction: Death Valley National Park
Road status: Roadless; access from paved or graded road
Lake Hill loop: 5.4 mi, 40 ft up loop/easy
Trans-playa hike: 5.3 mi, 0 ft up, 10 ft down one way/moderate
Main attractions: Valley-floor hike on a dry lake bed, geology
USGS 7.5' topo maps: The Dunes*, Panamint Springs*, Nova Canyon
Maps: pp. 425, 429*, *419*

Location and Access

Stretching north-south for about 9 miles and 1 mile at its widest, the North Panamint Playa covers much of the floor of northern Panamint Valley. It is easily accessible on foot from Highway 190, which crosses it near its mid-point starting 3.5 miles east of Panamint Springs; and from the Big Four Mine Road, which parallels its northern half on the east side. This graded road begins on Highway 190, 4.5 miles east of Panamint Springs. For the Lake Hill loop hike, drive it 2.4 miles north to the southern tip of Lake Hill.

Route Description

The playa from Highway 190. Hiking the North Panamint Playa is a treat only the desert can offer. For miles the terrain is reduced to one of the purest landforms on Earth—a fantastically level plain of dry mud punctuated with isolated pockets of desiccated vegetation. There is an hypnotic, contemplative quality to walking across such repetitive terrain, where every step is identical to the previous one. The jagged outline of Lake Hill puncturing the playa's horizon is an arresting sight, like a shipwrecked alien vessel. In the spring, the edges of the playa are often densely covered with primrose, desertgold, and goldeneye. The improbable sight of this bright yellow mist floating ethereally across the landscape is one of the desert's sweetest surprises.

The playa is made of a 500-foot pile of sediments deposited in Lake Panamint, the vast body of water that filled Panamint Valley off and on over the last 3 million years. In wetter times, increased snow melt in the Sierra Nevada caused Owens Lake to overflow and fill a chain of lower basins—China Lake, Searles Valley, Panamint Valley, and finally Death Valley. As the global climate fluctuated, so did the number and size of the lakes. For most of the past one million years, Searles Valley was the terminus of the chain. It thus became the recipient of most of the chain's sediments and salts, eventually accumulating the 3,300 feet of lacustrine deposits that support today's large evaporite extraction industry at Trona. In the last 1.3 million years, Panamint Lake was replenished at least on four occasions when Searles Lake spilled over into Panamint Valley, and it dried up completely at least once. At its fullest, it covered a huge area—about 300 square miles—down to a depth of 950 feet. Its last high stand occurred sometime between 55,000 and 95,000 years ago. By 8,000 BC it was almost gone.

This was not the lake's last word. Every decade or two, unusually heavy rains bring it back to life. For a few weeks the playa is flooded under several inches of water, and vehicles have to crawl along Highway 190 to ford the ephemeral reincarnation of Lake Panamint.

The surface of the playa is still actively filling with wind-blown particles from the surrounding ranges. It is composed mostly of silt (75%), with a little clay (20%) and very fine sand (5%). Because evaporation far exceeds precipitation, these sediments are strongly desiccated and shrink. When they locally reach their shrinkage limit, the soil

North Panamint Playa

	Dist.(mi)	Elev.(ft)
Playa		
Highway 190	0.0	1,540
South end of Lake Hill	2.4	1,541
North end of playa	5.3	1,543
Panamint Valley Dunes	9.3	2,660
Lake Hill loop		
Road at south end of Lake Hill	0.0	1,555
Edge of playa	0.35	1,542
Lake Hill (gap between hills)	2.2	1,542
North end of Lake Hill	2.9	1,542
Back along Big Four Mine Rd	5.4	1,555

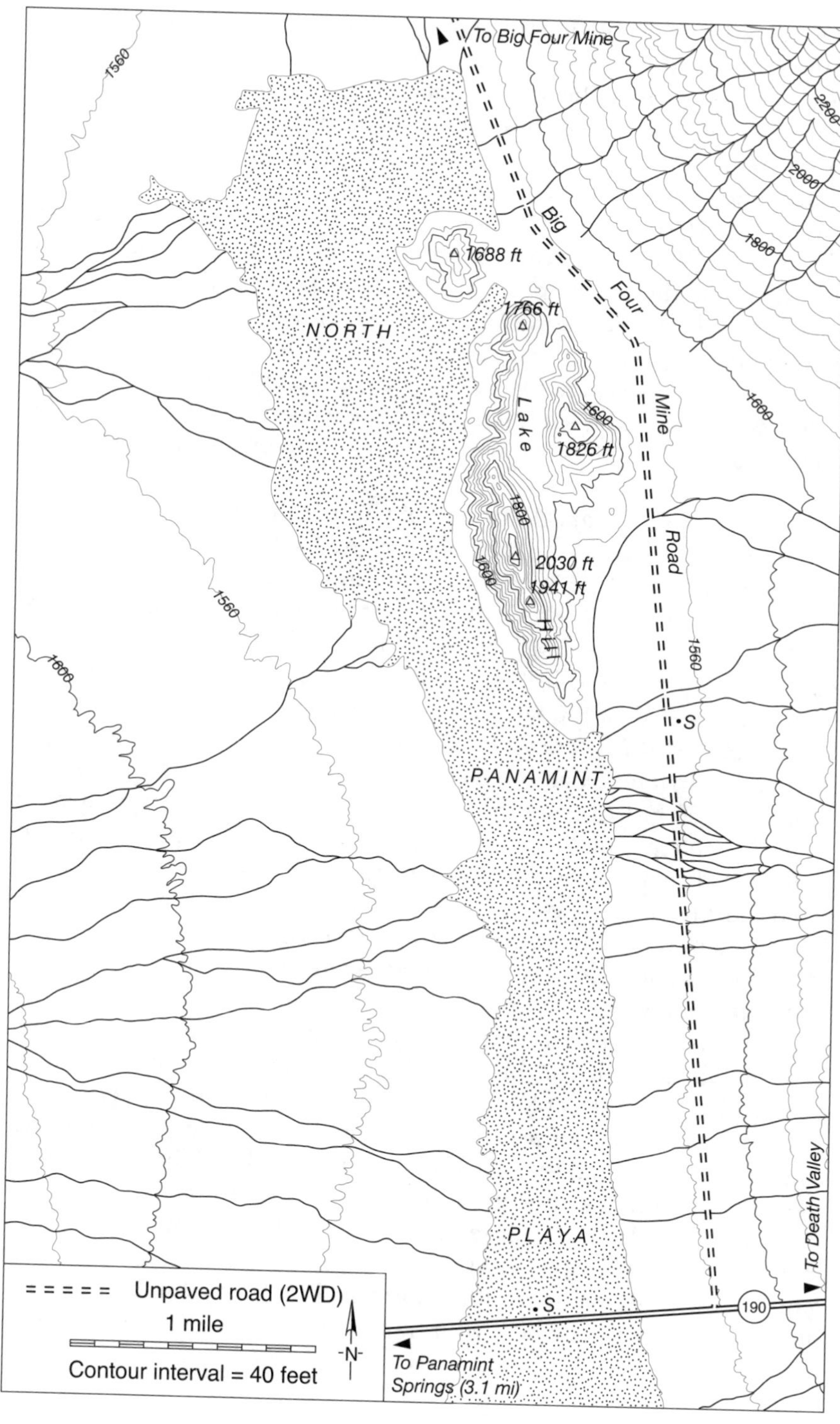
To Big Four Mine
1560
2200
2000
1800
1600
Big Four Mine Road
1688 ft
1766 ft
NORTH
Lake
Hill
1826 ft
1800
2030 ft
1941 ft
1560
1600
S
PANAMINT
PLAYA
S
190
To Death Valley
To Panamint Springs (3.1 mi)
Unpaved road (2WD)
1 mile
N
Contour interval = 40 feet

ruptures. The most obvious sign of desiccation is the playa's billions of mud cracks and flakes, which are due to the drying out of the top few inches of sediments. The soil is frequently cracked into polygons up to 2 feet across, subdivided into smaller patterns that are themselves latticed with even finer cracks. Desiccation structures also occur on a much larger scale, so large that you may well miss it.

Over periods of years the soil dries up and contracts deep beneath the surface. When it ruptures, it produces spectacular trenches several feet wide and deep and up to 100 yards long. Some of them form when an earthquake shakes the valley. Trenches fill with sediments and may survive only a few months. Yet they remain clearly visible for years. The long lines of vegetation growing on the playa are mostly former trenches which, being slightly moister, have been colonized by plants. The long, slight depressions are relict tracks of swollen-shut trenches.

The Lake Hill loop. From the Big Four Mine Road, hike west to the south end of Lake Hill, then north along the hill's impressively dissected western wall. This unexpected island stranded in the middle of the valley is a chunk of mostly Ely Springs Dolomite that was once part of the Cottonwood Mountains 3 miles to the east. It slipped down to its present location in the late Pliocene or early Pleistocene, as a result of repeated earthquakes along a low-angle gravity fault.

Around 10,000 years ago Panamint Lake had split into two separate body of waters, one 200 feet deep in the southern valley, and the other only 20 feet deep in the northern valley. Lake Hill was then an island. Native populations lived near the lush marshes that flourished around it. The area was then livened by aquatic birds. They had mastered the fine art of carving stone tools out of basalt quarried locally. They may also have been the creators of the valley's giant stone alignments. The light-colored tufa coating the western base of Lake Hill are one of the many signs left by the lake's passage. The filled-in trenches on the short fans surrounding Lake Hill were dug by geologists to analyze the valley's pluvial history. There is one at the southern tip of Lake Hill, about 230 feet long, and two more at the northwestern tip. A few feet beneath the surface, they uncovered a thin layer of dark, peaty soil that formed when the playa was submerged. It still holds pollen of the sedges and cattails that grew at these prehistoric marshes.

After 2.3 miles you will reach the 200-yard wide gap between the main hill and the smaller northern hill. You can return either via this gap or by continuing around the northern hill. If you climb Lake Hill, do it on the west side, where your tracks will be hidden from the road.

■

THE NADEAU TRAIL

Built in 1877 by Remi Nadeau to provide access to the rich Modoc Mine, the Nadeau Trail is the longest primitive road in Panamint Valley and a wonderful playground for discovering this beautiful valley leisurely. Though not as wild as some—it is never more than a few miles from pavement—this desert track is seldom traveled and provides a gratifying sense of isolation, as well as an opportunity to visit many mines and canyons in the nearby Argus Range.

General Information

Jurisdiction: Bureau of Land Management
Road status: Access from paved road
Main attractions: Long primitive valley road, scenery, history
USGS 7.5′ topo maps: Slate Range Crossing, Maturango Peak SE, Maturango Peak NE, Revenue Canyon, Panamint Springs
Maps: pp. *319**, *419*

Location and Access

The Nadeau Trail follows the west side of central Panamint Valley roughly in a north-south direction near the foot of the Argus Range. It starts on the Trona-Wildrose Road at Slate Range Crossing, the pass between Panamint and Searles valleys, and ends 26 miles north at the Modoc Mine, in the Argus Range. It is best to drive it northbound, away from the sun. Start from the pass, 7.4 miles south of the Ballarat Road (or about 14.5 miles north of Trona). The primitive road that branches off on the east side *at* the pass is the Nadeau Trail, signed P 105. On the valley floor, much of the Nadeau Trail is surprisingly smooth and can be driven with a standard-clearance car. But to drive all of it requires good clearance, and four-wheel drive at a few spots.

History: Remi Nadeau's Freight Empire

The Nadeau Trail is named after freighter Remi Nadeau, one of the many unsung heroes of the Death Valley days. Although seldom acknowledged, freighters played a vital role in the prosperity of remote mining communities by providing economical transportation to haul out their ore and bring in supplies. Born in Quebec in 1821, Nadeau was a stocky Frenchman who built flour mills while helping raise his family of four children. Energetic and restless, he moved from New Hampshire to Chicago, then Minnesota, until in 1860 he decided to leave his family to seek fortune in the West. The heavy freight traffic out of Salt Lake City impressed him so much that when he arrived in Los Angeles in the fall of 1861, he bought a wagon and six mules and jumped into the freighting business. This was the start of a prestigious career. Over the next 20 years, Nadeau forged a successful freighting empire that eventually dominated the eastern California market. There is hardly a mine worth the name that didn't resound with the bells of his teams. Nadeau's teamsters hauled merchandise from LA to Salt Lake City and as far as Montana, freighted borax for Searles Valley, and silver for Darwin, Resting Springs, and Ivanpah. In 1875-1876 they made headlines freighting Panamint City's 400-pound silver ingots all the way across the desert to the railroad station at Mojave.

The main catalyst for Nadeau's prosperity was Cerro Gordo. In 1868, shortly after sending funds to his wife and family for their passage to California, he heard of Cerro Gordo's fabulous silver bonanza and landed his first large contract with the owners. Except for a short hiatus in 1872-1873, until 1881 Nadeau transported all of Cerro Gordo's huge production to San Pedro and Mojave, accumulating in the process a sizable personal wealth. The arduous 230-mile journey was an extraordinary undertaking that employed up to 80 teams of 14 to 22 mules drawing enormous custom wagons the size of boxcars.

The Modoc Mine, over in the Argus Range, was another of his successes. In 1876, after promising silver ore bodies were discovered there, Nadeau seized the opportunity and contracted with the mine owners to handle their bullion. To reduce travel time, in the spring of 1877 he had a large crew of Chinese immigrants build the shortest possible access road from Searles Valley to the Modoc Mine—which would later be named the Nadeau Trail. The completed road went straight up Panamint Valley, hugging the Argus Range to shave precious miles, then cut west to the mine. It was indeed so straight that it earned the nickname of Shotgun Road. By the end of 1876, Nadeau had already delivered $400,000 worth of ingots to Mojave. Nadeau's fees were probably around $50 per ton, so that his road was paying back a tidy $500 a day—and he was picking up extra cash by also hauling charcoal from Wildrose Canyon's kilns to the Modoc smelters.

Nadeau retired from freighting in 1883. After braving the wild West for 22 years, he moved back to the sleepy village of Los Angeles, but until his death in 1887 his entrepreneurial spirit never let go. He planted southern California's first sugar beet field, then the world's largest vineyard and barley crop. Not all of it was a frank success, but it launched the first wave of large-scale farming in LA County. Nadeau's penchant for grand enterprises culminated with the financing of the first four-story hotel in Los Angeles, an elegant building with the town's first elevator. The Nadeau Hotel remained LA's most reputable accommodation into the next century, and it hosted for years the first stars and celebrities of the budding LA glitz.

Route Description

The first stretch is a breathtaking introduction to Panamint Valley. From the pass, the Nadeau Trail, still supported by the original retaining walls of volcanic cobbles laid down by Nadeau's Chinese laborers, drops along the Slate Range's precipitous ledges. Far down the open slope, the immense valley unfolds for miles between towering ranges, looking much the same as it did a few million years ago. The roadway is rocky and steep, reinforcing the sense of adventure. Shortly after reaching the valley, it cavorts across the wide wash of Water Canyon, crosses the Trona-Wildrose Road, then slips into the wild again.

For the next 20 miles you are immersed in the desert. On one side the 11,000-foot front of the Panamint Mountains across the valley; on the other, closer by, the stratified walls of the Argus Range; in the middle the one-lane road, a vast alluvial plain coated with a thousand shades of green and gray—and nothing else. We are lucky that such a road has survived our civilization's unspoken conspiracy to pave the Earth. Rather than zooming down the highway at video-game speed, this one-lane byway gives us a chance to discover an empty valley at

The Nadeau Trail

	Dist.(mi)	Elev.(ft)
Slate Range Crossing	0.0	~2,930
Trona-Wildrose Road crossing	3.3	2,000
Reilly Road	4.4	1,852
Onyx Mine Road	6.9	2,095
Bendire Canyon Road	9.85	1,838
Panamint Valley Crater Road	11.45	1,770
Knight Canyon Road	11.75	1,750
Merges with Nadeau Road	12.0	1,730
Leaves Nadeau Road	14.6	1,885
Snow Canyon Road	18.2	2,357
Merges with Minnietta Road	21.2	2,380
Minnietta Road (west)	21.4	2,358
Stone Canyon (mouth)	23.2	3,015
Lookout	26.0	3,580

Twister scooping up dust off Panamint Valley's southern playa

an unhurried pace. It transports us back to the turn of the century, when this was the only kind of road there was. As the road cuts across swarms of minor drainages, your car noses in and out of innumerable dips, as on some endless roller coaster. It is a long and slow drive; time itself seems to be suspended. If a car comes the other way—a rare event—someone will pull over to make room for the other vehicle. You might roll down your window and exchange greetings, or step outside to swap desert tales, and maybe make a friend. Occasionally you will come across an unmarked side road that wanders off toward the mountains. Together, they give access, often in just a handful of miles, to a trove of minor treasures—mining relics, backcountry cabins, tunnels sparkling with ore, oases and flowing creeks. These hidden destinations are often the reason for driving the trail. But even if we never get to see them, their very presence adds a sense of mystery to the ride.

The Nadeau Trail ends with a bang at the rich silver mine that put it on the map, high on the spectacular brow of Lookout Mountain. Here too, getting there is not the main objective. The highlights of the ride are open space and solitude. To fully enjoy it, you must be content with simple pleasures—the smell of creosote, a glimpse of a cactus, a rabbit bounding between shrubs, cloud shadows drifting across the valley, the aesthetic appeal of a particular alignment of summits. Or visions of Nadeau's wagons inching their way on this very road one and a half century ago, creaking under the sheer weight of silver.

■

TUFA, CRATER, AND SULFUR SPRINGS

If you poke around a place as vast as Panamint Valley long enough, you are bound to turn up minor treasures, some of them far away, others within sight of a well-traveled road. This section describes a few of my favorites—a delightful spring called Warm Sulfur, a little-known crater, and the vestigial tufa deposits from an immense lake that still filled the valley just 10,000 years ago.

General Information
Jurisdiction: Bureau of Land Management
Road status: Roadless; easy access from graded and primitive roads
Ash Hill tufa: 2.9 mi, 310 ft up loop / very easy
Warm Sulfur Springs: 4.7 mi, 30 ft up loop / easy
Panamint Valley Crater: 1.5 mi, 530 ft up, 40 ft down one way / very easy
Main attraction: Springs, desert salt lake, salt flat, tufa, botany, geology
USGS 7.5' topo maps: Ballarat, Jail Canyon, Panamint Springs, Maturango Peak SE
Maps: pp. 437*, 439*, *419*

Location and Access

The three sites described here are located on the perimeter of Panamint Valley and reached by short walks from a graded or primitive Road. Refer to each individual site for exact location and access.

Route Description

Ash Hill tufa. Not all of the desert's wonders are grand and magnificent. This one is, in fact, precisely the opposite. What first drew me to it is a series of small, cream-colored outcrops at the north end of Ash Hill that I kept seeing while driving through the valley. With a little research, I found out that others had noticed them too and identified them as tufa, a young rock formation brought to fame by Mono Lake.

Like stalactite, marble, and chalk, tufa is almost pure calcium carbonate, in this case calcite and aragonite. It forms under curious circumstances—by the action of springs submerged under a desert lake. If the spring water has traveled through limestone, it contains calcium carbonate, and when it enters the alkaline lake, the carbonate precipitates as tufa. Little by little, a mound of tufa forms around the spring's outlet. Algae growing on its surface help fix new calcium onto it. Over time, the mound can evolve into a spire, sometimes more than 150 feet high, as spring water is fed upward through the spire's hollow core and deposits tufa higher and higher. The spires normally remain under water—until the lake subsides or dries up.

Ash Hill is one of several localities in Panamint Valley where tufa is exposed. They occur at elevations between 1,600 and 2,150 feet—around the high-water mark of prehistoric Lake Panamint. Compared to the 12,000-year-old tufa in nearby Searles Valley, they are all strongly weathered, hence older. To understand their origin, two ingenious geologists analyzed their chemistry and found that they contain traces of uranium and thorium. By measuring the relative abundance of these elements' isotopes, they were able to determine that Panamint Valley's tufas probably represent a single generation formed during the same high stand of the lake, between 55,000 and 95,000 years ago. This finding sheds precious light on the local pluvial history: the time span between complete fillings of the valley was at least 55,000 years, long enough for complete erosion of earlier tufa.

To get to the Ash Hill tufa, drive the Panamint Valley Road 1.6 miles south from Highway 190 (5.8 miles north from the Minnietta Road) to a primitive road on the west side. In 0.6 mile it reaches the Defense Mine Road. Continue west (straight) on this high-clearance road and park after 0.45 mile, at the very northern tip of Ash Hill, where a short ramp drops to the left into a wash. The closest tufa mound is visible 250 yards south of this wash. A few hundred feet long and up to 10 feet high, it consists of large chunks of tufa sharpened by wind and rain. Half a dozen mounds occur in the next 0.6 mile southeast along the base of Ash Hill, as well as scattered tufa coatings on basalt boulders. They are the best preserved tufas in the valley, although all the spires have collapsed and they pale in comparison to the towering Trona Pinnacles in Searles Valley. The scattered holes in the mounds, roughly circular and up to three feet across, are the cores through which spring water welled up from the bottom of the lake.

While searching for more, you may end up at the wide gap through Ash Hill about a mile south of the road. This is the mouth of Osborne Canyon. To make a loop hike, go up this gap to the Defense Mine Road, then return north along this scenic road to your vehicle.

Warm Sulfur Springs. These pretty springs are scattered at the foot of the Panamint Mountains, less than a couple of miles south of Indian Ranch. From the Ballarat store drive the Indian Ranch Road 5.45 miles north to just after a left bend, where the road is closest to the mountain and right next to a large grove to the left. Coming from the north, this point is 6.4 miles south from the Trona-Wildrose Road.

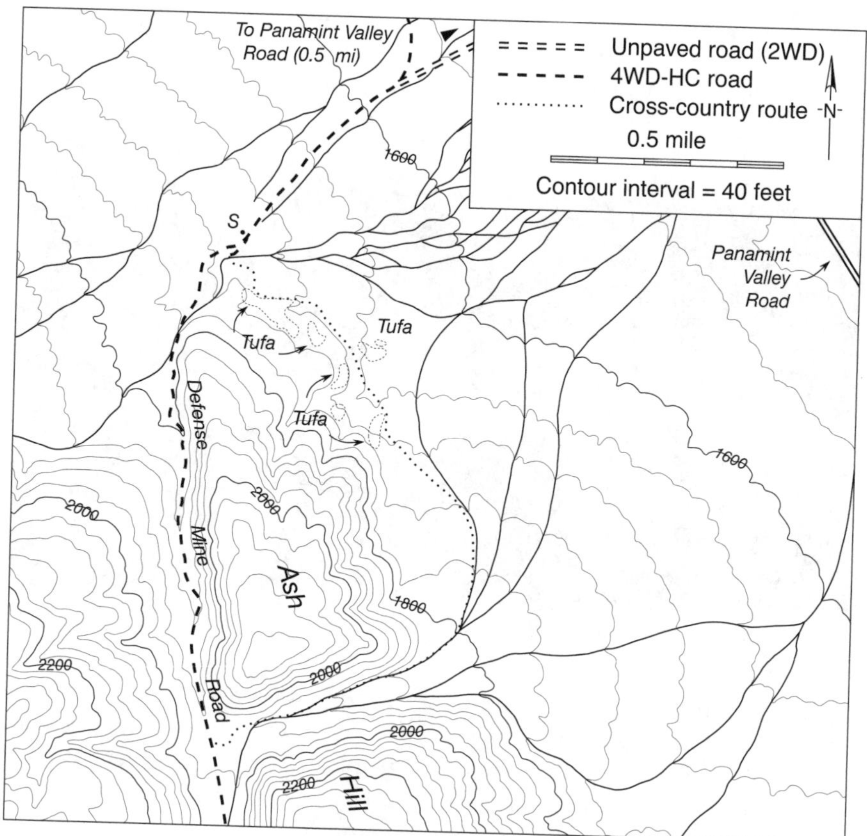

Ash Hill Tufa		
	Dist.(mi)	Elev.(ft)
Defense Mine Road	0.0	1,710
Northernmost tufa	0.2	1,700
Southernmost tufa	0.7	1,660
Defense Mine Road	1.7	1,925
Back to starting point	2.9	1,710

This is Warm Sulfur Springs, a series of seeps that rise from a fault at the abrupt base of the mountains to the east. The water, which is usually neither warm nor sulfurous, flows and collects into a pond a little further north, and in two shallow lakes in the depression to the west. Just below the road, the water supports one of the largest marshes in Panamint Valley. The vegetation forms a dense mat of cattail,

Flooded salt flats at Warm Sulfur Springs

grasses, and rush soaked in spring water. The marsh is too thick to penetrate. To explore this area, consider instead the scenic hike around the sink, an excellent area for photography. Two burro trails go part way around this roughly circular depression, about 1.5 miles across. The rest of the way is cross-country (see map).

The trail starts right at the road, on the west side. This is not much of a trail: a burro track barely wide enough for walking is more like it. There are in fact many crisscrossing tracks; follow the main one, and expect that you will occasionally take a longer way around on a parallel trail. The main trail skirts the southeastern edge of the sink to the vestiges of the wooden fence that once enclosed the marsh, follows it briefly, then gradually veers west. The muddy ground is so saturated with salt that it supports only pickleweed and salt grass, among nature's most salt-tolerant plants. The trail goes by a succession of small groves that feral burros use as rest areas. Most of the trees are screwbean mesquite, some of them loaded with mistletoe. The two small lakes at the bottom of the sink, visible all along this hike, are surrounded by a playa of nearly pure salt. Their shorelines are lined with distinct bathtub rings, formed by seasonal fluctuations in the water levels. To protect the shores from unsightly footprints, please do not walk near the lakes. Bring binoculars to observe the coots and other aquatic birds that sometimes wade in the ponds.

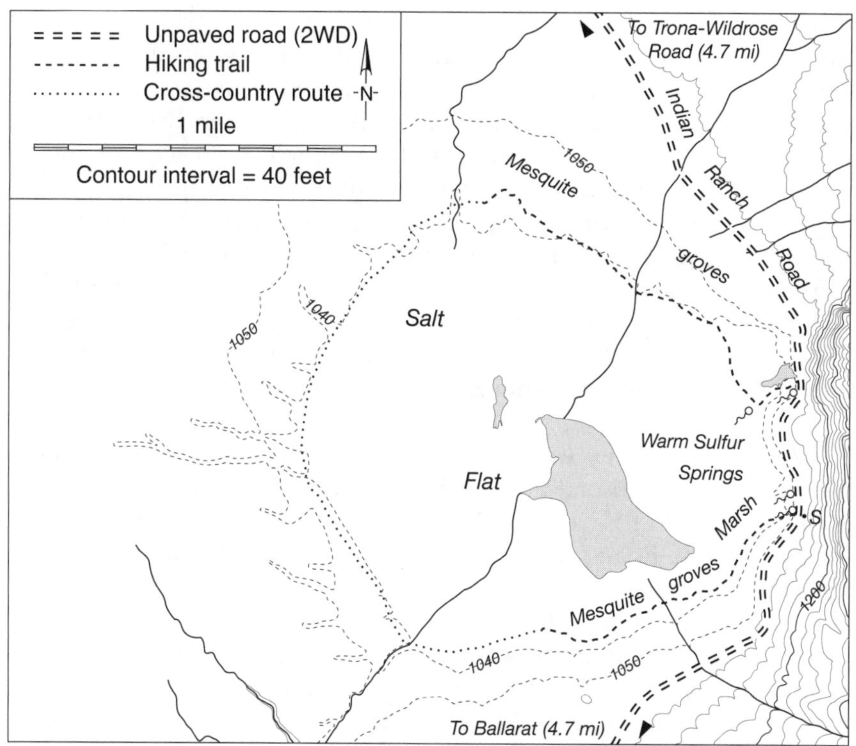

Warm Sulfur Springs		
	Dist.(mi)	Elev.(ft)
Indian Ranch Road	0.0	1,045
West end of southern trail	1.0	1,025
West end of northern trail	3.0	1,035
Back to Indian Ranch Road	4.3	1,040
Back to starting point	4.7	1,045

The trail ends at the northwest end of the large, westernmost mesquite grove, on the edge of the depression. You can turn around and retrace your steps, but you would miss the best. Continue westward instead, *around* the sink (it is tempting to cut north across the sink, but please don't, or your footprints will mar the slushy salt for years). For the next 2 miles, as you circumvent the sink's shallow rim, you will be walking on crunchy, salt-impregnated ground carpeted with pure stands of salt grass. The salt gives this desolate landscape a crisp luminosity. Some of the narrow washes on the sink's west side are coated with salt crystals. Your eyes are repeatedly drawn to the impressive wall of the Panamints to the east and the dissected face of the Argus Range across the valley. This hike is particularly exhilarating on clear winter days, when most of the continent is locked in wintery torpor and the pale sun spells out the silent promise of spring.

Three quarters of the way around the sink, you will reach the much larger grove of low mesquite that blankets its north rim. Between here and the road the grove is crisscrossed by burro trails. Follow the widest trail as it wanders along the grove's southern edge, splitting repeatedly to sneak under the trees. It ends back at the Indian Ranch Road, at the northernmost of the two ponds.

Panamint Valley Crater. This unusual geologic feature is on Bendire Canyon's broad alluvial fan, at the base of the central Argus Range. To get to it, drive the Nadeau Road 7.8 miles north from the Trona-Wildrose Road (or 0.3 mile south from the Slate Range Road) to the Knight Canyon Road on the west side. Take this road 0.1 mile to the Nadeau Trail, turn left, and go 0.3 mile south to the Panamint Valley Crater Road on the right. Drive this road 1.35 miles to a side road on the left, which ends in 150 yards, within a stone's throw of the crater's crumbling edge. With a standard-clearance vehicle, you can get to the Panamint Valley Crater Road, but this road soon crosses a rough wash that requires good clearance, as well as four-wheel drive for lighter vehicles. If you cannot make it, walk the road; it is worth it.

The Panamint Valley Crater is a nearly circular depression 230 feet across and 30 feet deep, neatly scooped out of the fan's alluvia. Unlike an impact or a volcanic eruption, it shows no evidence of upturned soil layers or raised rims. The shaft at the bottom was dug in the 1960s by the Naval Ordnance Test Station in an attempt to elucidate the crater's mysterious origin. The shaft's toppled headframe lies nearby, together with the ruin of the wooden ramp used to hoist the overburden over the rim. The study failed to turn up any evidence of volcanism, metallic cosmic debris, or bits of shipwrecked UFO. The most likely interpretation is that water erosion created a large underground cave in the limestone that probably underlies the fan. The crater was formed when the cave became too large to support its own roof and collapsed. It may be tempting to climb down the shaft's long ladder, but think again. Getting stuck at the bottom of a 130-ft shaft at the bottom of a crater at the bottom of an isolated desert valley is not the world's most enviable position.

■

BALLARAT

Beautifully situated at the foot of the majestic Panamint Mountains, the historic ghost town of Ballarat is one of the highlights of Panamint Valley. Once a throbbing supply and social center for the numerous gold and silver mines that flourished up in the mountains, Ballarat is now a vivid reminder of the area's colorful past. Visitors enjoy wandering through its adobe buildings, wooden cabins, and quiet cemetery, taking a stroll to its unexpectedly lush spring, or simply camping under the stars with the ghosts of old timers before taking another adventurous ride into the Panamints.

General Information

Jurisdiction: Bureau of Land Management
Road status: Easy access on graded road
Ballarat: 0.6 mi, 10 ft up loop/very easy
Post Office Spring: 0.6 mi, 30 ft up, 30 ft down/very easy
Main attraction: Ghost town, mining history, spring, salt flats
USGS 7.5′ topo map: Ballarat
Maps: pp. 445*, *319, 419*

Location and Access

Ballarat is located on the eastern edge of central Panamint Valley. To get to it, drive the Trona-Wildrose Road to the Ballarat Road, which is 9.4 miles south of the Panamint Valley Road (or 3.8 miles north of the Nadeau Road). This oiled road cuts northeast across the South Panamint Playa and ends after 3.6 miles at Ballarat's store. An alternative scenic route is the Indian Ranch Road, which is signed and graded. It starts off the Trona-Wildrose Road 0.4 mile south of the Panamint Valley Road. The mileage to Ballarat is 11.9 miles.

History

Optimistically named after the famous gold center of Ballarat in southeastern Australia, Ballarat flourished between around 1890 and the years preceding World War I as a lively supply and entertainment center for prospectors and miners working claims in the Panamint Mountains. At its apogee, it boasted three general stores, a boarding house, a jail, and even a school and a post office. The one institution most glaringly missing was a church, an oversight Ballarat made up for with a disproportionate number of saloons. At one time it was a large enough community to serve as the government seat of southern Inyo County. A stagecoach then connected it to the nearby mining towns of Lookout and Darwin, and points beyond.

Ballarat prospered until around 1905, when the best and most accessible ore deposits started playing out and mining gradually slowed down. By 1917 the post office had closed down. Over the next few years, the town gradually spiraled down to the noble status of ghost town. Local mining never came anywhere near amassing the fabulous wealth in gold of its Australian namesake, but Ballarat did leave its mark as the historic pulse of the Panamint Mountains.

Route Description

Ballarat. Ballarat's setting is nothing short of dramatic. As you approach it across Panamint Valley's perfectly level salt flats, it glitters on the far edge of the valley like a Lilliputian village lost in an immense wilderness. Its doll houses are dwarfed by the sheer volume of the Panamints looming nearly 10,000 feet right behind it. The general store, located just north of the junction between the Ballarat Road and Wingate Road, is the town's main building and hub, the place where most visitors stop first to check out the scene. The storekeeper has changed several times over the years, but they have all been quite knowledgeable about the area, and they always have the latest scoop on the state of local roads. The current keeper is Rocky Novak, a long-time local and occasional miner who moved here after his cabin at Chris Wicht Camp burned down (see *Surprise Canyon*).

Store hours are highly variable. With a little push from Murphy's law, chances are it will be closed when you need it the most—in the middle of a scorching day, just when you were starting to fantasize about that dew-beaded, ice-cold drink, or on a frigid winter evening when you were hoping to warm up by the store's roaring wood stove. The store does carry limited but welcome basic supplies, from canned food to candies, soft drinks, bottled water, maps, and books. Out in the back, a few tools are available for vehicles in distress.

Today Ballarat is a mere ghost of its former self. It is privately owned by a few families, most of whom, for reasons difficult to comprehend, have opted to spend their short stay on Earth in southern California rather than here. It is sad that although it has been a state historical site since 1949, Ballarat has aged much faster than it should have due to vandalism and lack of stewardship. Of its dozens of original cabins, only a few are still standing today. Gravity and wind are continually conspiring to claim new casualties, and there have been insufficient efforts to salvage what is left.

Old cabins at Ballarat (2008)

The best way to visit Ballarat is to park near the store and stroll around. The historic town covers about 40 acres south and west of the store (the prefabricated buildings behind the store are private property and off-limits). The green truck Dodge Power Wagon across the road from the store is said to have belonged to a member of Charles Manson's "family" when they lived in Goler Canyon in the 1960s. The white stars on the inside of its roof were left by the family to mark their passage. The small wooden building southeast across the Ballarat Road is the jail, which was restored in 1997. The crumbling adobe walls along the Ballarat Road west from there rank among the town's oldest ruins. They probably date from the 1890s. The only one still standing is a particularly awkward kluge of adobe, metal, and wood, the cabin of Frank "Shorty" Harris. A famous prospector with a flair for gold, although he never hung onto it long enough to get rich. The center of town used to be just a block north. The two cabins that still stood there in 2008 are now reduced to floor boards.

Ballarat's cemetery is a five-minute walk north, past the barren lot of the campground. Surrounded by a wrought-iron fence, it has two long rows of graves, most of them mere swells in the ground. There is little record of who is buried here. Only a few graves have a tombstone, and even fewer bear a name. The earliest recorded death dates from 1908. The most recent and prominent grave is that of Charles Ferge, also known as Seldom Seen Slim. A prospector during Ballarat's heyday, Seldom Seen Slim hung on after mining subsided in 1917 and remained Ballarat's only resident for 50 years. A stout independent and lifelong recluse, he never struck it rich but managed to scrape up a living in this sun-scorched valley he called "the suburbs of hell." When asked whether he ever got lonely, he was known to say: "Me lonely? Hell no! I'm half coyote and half wild burro." When he died in August 1968 at age 86, the last of the valley's single-blanket jackass prospectors, his funeral was televised around the country.

The large cleared area at the northwest corner of town is Ballarat's campground. Trailers, motorhomes, and tents alike can set up residence here for a modest fee. Register at the store and enjoy—most of the year—a peaceful night under crisp starry skies.

Reflections of the Argus Range in the lake south of Post Office Spring

Post Office Spring. Just south of Ballarat there is a luxuriant spring, poised in arrogant defiance on the fringe of the barren flats of the South Panamint Playa. On a hot summer day, when shimmering waves distort the horizon, you might doubt your senses at the sight of green trees and sparkling ponds. This improbable haven is Post Office Spring, one of only two sizable springs on the floor of Panamint Valley. In spite of its proximity to a road, it is a pleasant place to watch water perform its magic on the desert land.

To get there, walk or drive the Indian Ranch Road to its junction with the oiled cutoff south of town. A rutted dirt road continues south,

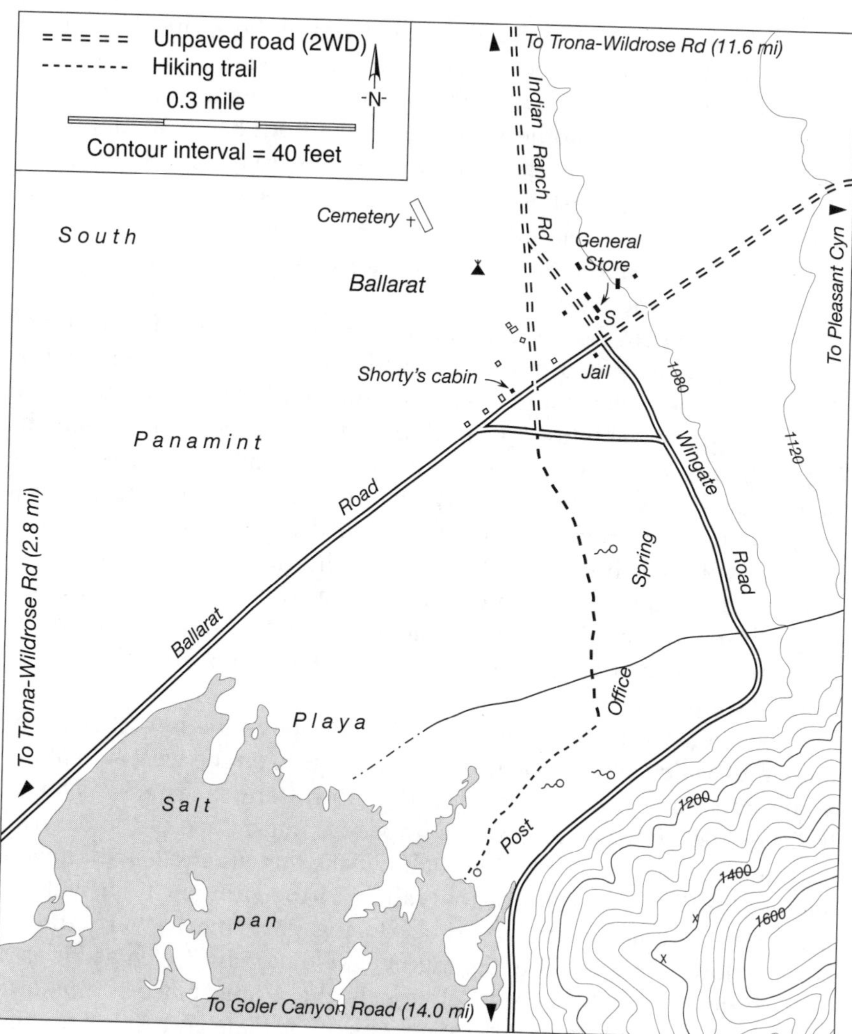

Ballarat		
	Dist.(mi)	Elev.(ft)
General Store	0.0	1,075
Jail	0.05	1,075
Shorty's cabin	0.15	1,065
Cemetery	0.4	1,065
Back to store	0.6	1,075
Post Office Spring (road's end)	1.05	1,055
Post Office Spring (lake)	1.15	1,045

past pockets of mesquite, 0.3 mile to the heart of the spring. The grove at the end of the road is the largest. The story goes that it was named Post Office because in the late 1800s outlaws used its relative shelter to post messages for each other in the trees, without being spotted from the town. The trees are mostly honey mesquite, up to 12 feet tall, many of them heavy with mistletoe. The downed trees and stumps are the remains of salt cedar and athel, two encroaching exotic species of the tamarisk family that the BLM and NPS are struggling to eradicate, here and throughout the West.

To explore Post Office Spring, from the end of the road take any of the many narrow burro trails that head southwest along the edge of the spring. The valley's immense mud and salt flats stretch out to the west. The ground is hardened mud, damp even after weeks of scorching heat, and coated with tiny white crystals of salt. Only salt-tolerant plants can survive in the strongly alkaline soil. The mid-size bushes are pickleweed; a crushed segment of their fleshy stems exudes a faint smell of salt. The short tufts of grass are salt grass, and the bunches of tall, slender blades are sacaton grass. The trails soon reach a long, soggy marsh of cattail, as tall and blond as wheat. A main trail crosses the marsh, passes by a rusted well casing, then ends after 0.2 mile at the edge of the salt flat.

You are, at this point, less than 12 feet above the lowest point in Panamint Valley, which is about 5.7 miles south, on the west side of the South Panamint Playa across from Big Horn Canyon. This is as far as the trail goes. Further progress is impeded, not by one of the desert's customary obstacles, but by the shallow lake that attempts, with mixed success, to fill the bottom of the valley. In the summer it shrivels to fragmented pools of syrupy brine. During particularly wet winters, surface flows replenish it to a genuine lake that may stretch as far as 1 mile south. So much water at obviously the wrong place strains our credulity. The ponds hold rare reflections of the Slate and Argus ranges across the valley. A few fortunate animals take advantage of this slender refuge in the midst of a sere landscape. It is not uncommon to hear frogs croaking in the marsh, to spot aquatic birds drifting on the lake, to run across the odd rabbit, unsure of its whereabouts, or the odd coyote stalking the odd rabbit.

■

REILLY

This pre-1890s historic site, still little known, is one of the hidden nuggets of Panamint Valley. Its sprawling ghost town of sturdy stone houses, massive gold mill, and extensive tunnels are beautifully situated in the boulder-strewn foothills of the Argus Range, at the high end of a deep alcove commanding dramatic views of the Panamints. Between searching for the ruins and pondering its many mysteries, this site will keep anyone even mildly interested in local history entertained for hours.

General Information

Jurisdiction: Bureau of Land Management
Road status: Hiking on trails; access via primitive road (2WD)
Reilly: 1.2 miles, 440 ft up loop/easy
Main attractions: A historic ghost town and mill, silver mine, scenery
USGS 7.5′ topo map: Maturango Peak SE
Maps: pp. 449, *419*

Location and Access

Reilly is at the western edge of central Panamint Valley, at the foot of the Argus Range a few miles north of the pass into Searles Valley. To get there, drive the Trona-Wildrose Road to the Nadeau Trail, which is 3.1 miles north of the pass, or 0.5 mile south of the signed Nadeau Road (200 feet past a power line). Take this dirt track 1.1 miles north to the Reilly Road on the left, at a broad low point in the road. Drive this road 1.7 miles west to a junction. Park at this junction and walk the very short distance south to the site, on either fork. This route is fairly smooth and usually drivable with standard clearance.

Route Description

Silver was said to have been discovered here in 1875. Not much happened until 1882, when promoter Charles Anthony sold the claims to a New York investor by the name of Edward Reilly. Reilly formed the Argus Range Silver Mining Company, and sold stock for Anthony to run the mining operations. By October 1882, Anthony started the construction of a 10-stamp mill and hired miners and other employees to run the town, mill, and mine. At one time as many as 60 people worked and lived here. The town, erected below the mines, had several stone buildings, a boarding house to put up some of the employees,

Main stone buildings at Reilly

a general store, and several stables and corrals. A post office opened in January 22, 1883. Reilly spent $40,000 to run a pipeline from Water Canyon, 5 miles to the south. Setting up everything cost Reilly and individual investors $200,000. The mill was in operation in September. Between October 1883 and February 1884, it churned out $21,500 worth of silver bullion—about what the Modoc Mine was producing in a day! The mine closed its doors a year later, never to open again.

The stealth ghost town of Reilly is truly one of a kind. Aside from Ballarat, it is the largest and best preserved in Panamint Valley. I inventoried over two dozen structures, anything from rock-lined tent sites to elaborate houses with walls eight feet high, scattered in the scenic setting of plump granitic boulders that dot the Argus Range foothills. The most conspicuous house is just above the apron at the end of the side road. There are two smaller ones behind it, and three more concealed among the boulders above it. Walking down the foot trail to the south, or up the two rock-strewn washes it crosses, will reveal many more. The local granitic rock is unusual. It is part of a tiny pluton called Quartz Monzonite at Anthony Mill exposed over only 120 acres. It contains an abundance of anhedral (a crystal with no plane faces), and beautiful large crystals of pink feldspar and perthite.

What makes this mining town particularly fascinating is that its history is so nebulous. After a while you start feeling the weight of its

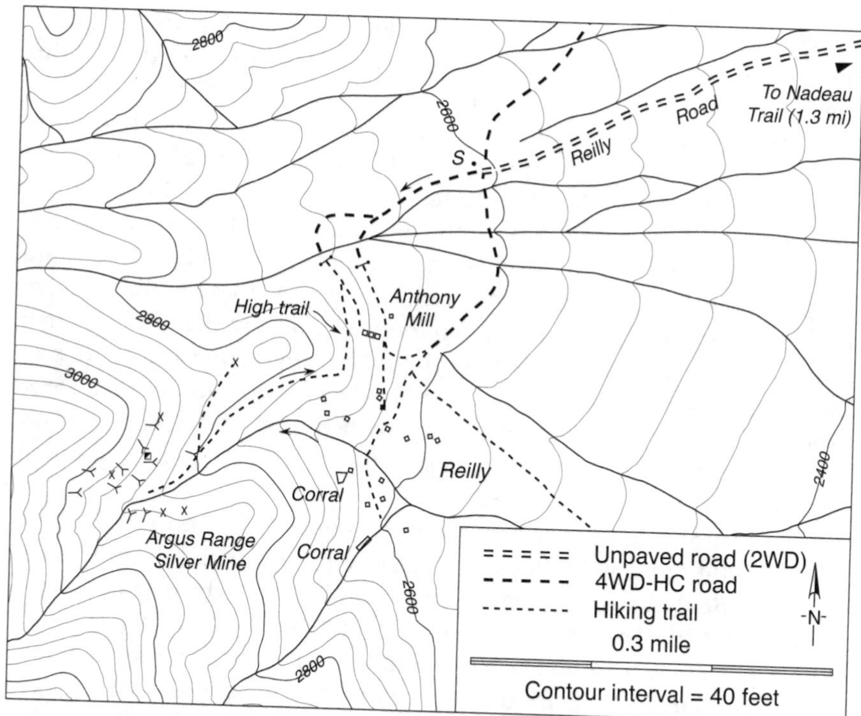

Reilly		
	Dist.(mi)	Elev.(ft)
Junction	0.0	2,602
Anthony Mill	0.2	~2,680
Reilly (south corral)	0.5	2,620
Lower workings via wash	0.8	2,880
Upper workings	(0.1)	~2,940
Back via high trail and mill	1.2	2,602

mystery. You wish you could unlock some of its secrets—and to some degree you can. These crumbling structures vary greatly in design and provide touching hints about the miners' lives. Some houses are comparatively spacious, up to 12 feet across, with well-built doorways and windows, and sometimes even a flight of stairs. Others are barely big enough for a mattress. Someone with even more modest aspirations closed off a low overhanging boulder with a few rocks and called it home. Most houses originally had a wooden roof; today, only one partial roof remains. Interestingly, many have a fireplace. Were winters colder than today? The interior of the large house at the lower end of the trail is decorated with two small niches. Were they used for lighting, for ornaments? Not all structures were dwellings. Some were used for storage, others were outdoor fireplaces. There are also two large corrals around the lower wash. The builders showed great imagination in utilizing what little this inhospitable land had to offer. Many buildings were erected against a large free-standing boulder for added support, which explains the town's erratic layout. The building stones are roughly hewn local granite. The walls, often over two feet thick, were not mortared, yet the stones were mated so carefully that they are free of gaps and have survived a long time. You might find indications of the town's age. I estimated its earliest occupation to at least 1887, which would make it contemporary with the nearby Minnietta and Modoc mines. Look for other clues. Listen to the stones. They relive their lives in what they tell you.

The large walls looming north of the ghost town and visible from miles are the ruins of Anthony Mill—a rare piece of pre-1900 gold mining equipment. It was erected on three split levels, each supported by a huge stone wall. The largest one, 40 feet long by 12 feet high, is as massive as a medieval rampart. Finely crafted with large blocks of quarried granite, it shows little damage after over one century of neglect. The mill tailings were impounded at the foot of it. On the edge of the tailings there is a small arrastre with cylindrical walls of corrugated iron. The wooden posts that supported its gears are still there, and so are the dragstones, polished to a smooth finish by countless passages around the arrastre. Its presence here is a little puzzle. Did it predate Anthony Mill? Or was it installed after the main mill was dismantled, perhaps by a lone miner reworking the old tailings?

The old diggings of the Argus Range Silver Mine are up in the short canyon to the southwest. The short trail, partly washed out, at the end of the upper road climbs to it. The tunnels are arranged in a horseshoe around an open area in the middle of the canyon wash. There are eight of them, some at wash level, others higher up on the north slope and reached by faint trails. Collectively, they rank among the most diverse and complex workings in the Argus Range. Some inclined tunnels are hundreds of feet long and fork at multiple levels, leading down to shafts, raises, and chambered galleries. Roof pendants are supported by original pine logs. Some walls are still pockmarked, a few feet above the floor, with the shallow niches where the miners propped their candles.

■

— 10 —

Darwin Plateau and The Argus Range

The region covered in this final section is the long western margin of northern and central Panamint Valley, which consists of the Argus Range and the Darwin Plateau. These two sub-regions are dramatically different. The Darwin Plateau to the north is a wide and subdued high plateau sprinkled with low desert hills. It is an austere region, vast and eerily empty, mantled with defiant armies of Joshua trees. Scorched in the summer, icy cold in the winter, it is comparatively devoid of valuable minerals and was shunned by hard-rock miners. Preserved today as part of Death Valley National Park, it attracts only a handful of desert aficionados, who revel in its solitude.

In contrast, the Argus Range is a true mountain range, a massive ecological island that stretches all the way down to Searles Valley. Although lower than the facing Panamints by nearly half a mile, it is still an impressive range. Crowned by Maturango Peak (8,839'), it towers nearly 7,000 feet above the valley, its flanks dissected by deep canyons. Bursting with minerals, it produced some of the region's most famous historic mines. The high country is part of the China Lake Naval Weapons Center (NWC) and off-limits to the public. The foothills between the NWC and the valley are preserved as the Argus Range Wilderness, managed by the BLM. This wilderness stretches along most of the range, from just south of Panamint Springs all the way down into Searles Valley. Visitors come here mostly to four-wheel the canyon roads and visit the mining relics that stud the foothills. The roadless backcountry holds some of the easiest hikes out of Panamint Valley.

Suggested Backcountry Drives on Darwin Plateau & Argus Range					
Route/Destination	Dist. (mi)	Lowest elev.	Highest elev.	Road type	Pages
Anton and Pobst Mine Rd	6.9	5,595'	6,580'	H	463-466
Cerrusite Mine	4.3	5,595'	6,580'	H	463-466
China Garden Spring	7.3	2,120'	3,780'	F	481-482
Copper Queen Mine Road	2.7	5,576'	6,315'	H	463-464
Defense Mine Road	7.0	1,149'	3,800'	F	491-492
Fairbanks Mine	2.0	4,990'	5,600'	F	480
Knight Canyon Road	2.3	1,725'	2,530'	H	521
Kopper King Cabin	4.9	1,976'	4,160'	H	528
Lee Flat Road	7.0	5,249'	6,220'	P	459
Lee Mine Road	1.0	5,182'	5,300'	P	467-468
Minnietta Cabin	5.1	1,700'	2,820'	H	503
Modoc Mine	8.8	1,149'	3,970'	F	497-498
Onyx Mine Road	2.8	1,976'	2,850'	H	527-528
Revenue Canyon Road	1.9	2,315'	3,070'	H	515
Shepherd Canyon Road	3.1	1,976'	2,930'	H	527
Snow Canyon Mill	7.3	1,603'	3,800'	F	510
Thompson Canyon	6.3	1,700'	3,410'	H	503
Key: P=Primitive (2WD) H=Primitive (HC) F=Primitive (4WD)					

Access and Backcountry Driving

The main access roads to the Darwin Plateau are Highway 190, which cuts east-west along the south end of the plateau, the Darwin Road, the southern portion of the Saline Valley Road, and the Lee Flat Road. The best backcountry drives on the plateau are on these last two roads and on the only two mining roads in the Nelson Range, at the plateau's northern edge.

The Argus Range is also fairly accessible, being closely paralleled in Panamint Valley by the Nadeau Road (paved) and the Nadeau Trail (primitive). All the main canyons are accessed by short mining roads that take off to the west and have been cherry-stemmed out of the wilderness so that they can continue to be explored by car. If you are into four-wheeling, these roads are ideal for short day trips into desert canyons. The upper reaches of some of these roads are in the wilderness, in many cases because they have been washed out, and they are closed to vehicles. BLM signs clearly mark the wilderness boundary.

Geology

The mountains that border the west side of Panamint Valley have had a tumultuous history of sedimentation, faulting, and volcanic and plutonic activities, reflected in their complexity and geological diversity. During most of the Paleozoic, they were the site of a thick accumulation of carbonate sediments in a shallow sea. Deposition stopped in the middle Triassic, when the onset of volcanism from western Nevada to the Mojave Desert uplifted and drained the sea. Tectonic instabilities started profoundly altering the local terrain in the Permian. They grew stronger through the Triassic into early Jurassic time, often associated with volcanism. In the middle Jurassic, as a side effect of the emplacement of the huge Sierra Nevada batholith to the west, a large granitic batholith known as the Hunter Mountain Pluton intruded the region, reaching as far north as the Inyo Mountains. A second one, the Maturango Peak Pluton, squeezed in 22 million years later, in the late Jurassic. These two plutons now form the hard crest of the Argus Range. In the latest Jurassic, major structural deformations took place along a northwest-trending fault called the Argus Sterling Thrust Fault. As a result of compressional failure of the crust, all along this fault the Maturango Peak batholith was shoved eastward over older formations. Mile-size slabs of Paleozoic limestone and Mesozoic volcanic rocks were metamorphosed to marble and mylonite. The final touch took place between 8 and 5.3 million years ago, when volcanism smothered the region under lava and ash, especially on the Darwin Plateau. A few million years ago, renewed tectonism snapped the land into fault blocks to produce the Argus Range's current topography.

Most of the Argus Range canyons still bear the mangled scars left by the mighty Jurassic thrust fault. As you drive or hike up a wash, first come the Paleozoic sedimentary strata, tilted but virtually undisturbed. Then you cross into the Hunter Mountain batholith and the terrain changes abruptly, to hard bluffs and angular benches of rusted granite. The thrust fault itself is unfortunately much further, mostly off-limits inside the NWC. The exception is Shepherd Canyon, where if you trudge far enough up the canyon trail, somewhere between the spring and the NWC boundary you will go right over it.

Snow, springs, and wildlife

Being closer to the Pacific Ocean than most local ranges of comparable elevation, the Argus Range receives a larger amount of precipitation. Snow blankets its highest summits every winter, and on wet years the snow line reaches below 4,000 feet. Most main canyons have one or more springs with permanent water, although generally little of it. The exception is Darwin Canyon; its stream is one of the strongest in the region. All springs are relished by wildlife and therefore contaminated, the smaller ones heavily. Purify all spring water if you must drink it. In part because of the availability of water, feral burros are common throughout the Argus Range and the Darwin Plateau. Free of predators, they have proliferated to the point where it is hard *not* to spot one. Birds are also fairly common, especially in Darwin Canyon.

The Darwin Plateau also gets snow, although less frequently and in lesser amounts. There was in recent history a blatant exception: for a few days in February 2001 the plateau was blanketed with snow up to a foot deep, offering astounded visitors visions of what this area might have looked like in the Pleistocene. Chances are that this is not what you will find. The Darwin Plateau is relatively dry, and most of the canyons draining it into Panamint Valley have no springs.

Petroglyphs, Nelson Range

History: The New Coso and Lookout Districts

In historic times, the Argus Range had spectacular silver deposits that produced some of the region's earliest and most lucrative mines. The uncontested star was Darwin, at the north end of the range. Founded in 1874 following a silver discovery on nearby Ophir Mountain, it quickly became a real mining town, with a population of 1,000 and 150 buildings, families and births, outlaws and murders. The area was organized as the New Coso District and eventually had several smelters and well-developed mines, including the Defiance, Sterling, Independence, and Lucky Jim. Between 1875 and 1883, the Defiance alone yielded $750,000 in silver and gold, not counting huge amounts of lead. Mining slowed down in the 1890s, when the best ore became exhausted, but it continued for over 100 years, with large sporadic bursts at the turn of the century, during World War I, and after World War II. Today, the long, towering tailings by the entrance to Darwin bear witness to the tremendous activity some of these mines sustained over the years. By the 1950s the total production of the New Coso District had reached over seven million dollars.

The Lookout Mining District, just over the crest on the eastern slope of the Argus Range, was also rich silver country, and one of the most prolific in the Death Valley region. The mine that started it all was the Modoc. Discovered in 1875, it stood out from the outset as the district's most promising. Its neighbor to the south, the Minnietta Belle Mine, looked almost as good; it was even hailed as "equal to any mine in the county." Eventually, every major canyon on this side of the range had a mine, if not several. The heart of the district was Lookout, a town famous for its lofty location overlooking Panamint Valley. It was the site of two smelters that treated the ore from the Modoc and other local mines. The district enjoyed a sporadic but long and productive life. By 1890 the Modoc had pulled $1.9 million in silver and lead. The Minnietta eventually brought in close to $1 million. Here also, in the 1890s many of the mines became idle. But over the next century, every so often a lucky miner would uncover a new high-grade pocket and production would jump up. This happened in 1916 at the Minnietta Mine, in 1926 at the Hughes Mine, and in the 1950s at the Defense Mine. As recently as the 1980s, when the price of gold was skyrocketing, a newly discovered gold vein at the Windless Mine was so unbelievably rich—around 200 ounces per ton—that the miners lugged the rocks in backpacks 2 miles down a mule trail to the nearest road!

The last mine to close down was the Little Mack, renamed the Golden Eagle, in Thompson Canyon. Its two owners, John and Karl, worked it for a few years before they packed up and left in the spring of 1998. It was not uncommon to run into them, either hoisting ore out of their tunnel with the winch mounted on the front of their 1940s army truck, or treating themselves to dinner at Panamint Springs. Listening to these two old timers share the invaluable knowledge of the local history they had accumulated over the years was a rare treat.

Hiking

For hikers, the main redeeming feature of the Argus Range is ease of access. All the main canyons have a road, most of which are short. Instead of having to drive for an hour or more to get to the starting point of your hike, here you are done with the driving and on your feet in typically less than half an hour, which means more daylight to explore. The upper reaches of most canyons being inside the Naval Weapons Center, the highest available elevations are not far above 6,000 feet, the terrain is not too steep, and hiking is easier. The downside is that peak climbs do not abound, although several are suggested in the following sections near the north end of the range, and on lower satellite peaks elsewhere. There are other perks. The canyons are deep

Suggested Hikes on Darwin Plateau and in the Argus Range					
Route/Destination	Dist. (mi)	Elev. gain	Mean elev.	Access road	Pages
Short hikes (under 5 miles round trip)					
China Garden Spring	0.8	150'	3,080'	P/7.4 mi	486
Darwin Falls (lower falls)	1.0	310'	2,610'	Graded	482-483
Darwin Falls (upper falls)	1.2	470'	2,630'	Graded	484-486
Darwin Peak	0.8	710'	5,650'	P/1.8 mi	480
Defense Mine	0.9	820'	3,970'	F/2.7 mi	492-494
Galena Peak	0.8	1,200'	7,130'	H/4.4 mi	464-466
Golden Eagle Mine tram	0.4	310'	2,740'	H/0.9 mi	506
Golden Lady Mine loop	2.1	970'	4,130'	F/7.1 mi	513-514
Imlay Mine (upper tram)	2.2	1,400'	4,340'	F/2.7 mi	496
Knight Cyn lower spring	1.9	850'	2,960'	P/2.3 mi	522
Kopper King Mine	0.8	910'	4,430'	H/4.9 mi	528
Lee Flat cutoff	1.9	90'	5,350'	Graded	462
Lee Flat loop	3.7	100'	5,320'	Graded	462
Lee Mine loop	1.0	100'	5,260'	H/1.0 mi	467-468
Lookout trail loop	3.8	1,370'	3,130'	P/4.0 mi	500-502
Lookout via China Wall Tr.	1.7	1,370'	3,180'	P/4.0 mi	500
Maltese Peak	0.8	440'	5,310'	H/1.0 mi	470
Mine Peak	2.3	1,850'	3,090'	H/1.0 mi	534-536
Minnietta (ghost town)	0.4	120'	2,760'	H/1.1 mi	506-508
Minnietta Mine	0.5	430'	3,010'	H/1.1 mi	504-505
Nile Spring	2.4	1,030'	3,390'	H/3.1 mi	532
Ophir Mountain	0.9	540'	5,780'	P/2.0 mi	477-478
Revenue Canyon					
Big Four Mill (shafts)	1.2	550'	2,980'	P/1.1 mi	516-517
Copper King Mine tunnel	1.2	720'	3,380'	F/1.9 mi	518
North Fork's lower spring	1.0	580'	2,970'	P/1.1 mi	520
Upper spring (head)	2.1	1,400'	3,770'	F/1.9 mi	518-520
Shepherd Cyn Springs loop	1.8	470'	3,360'	H/4.2 mi	528-529
Snow Canyon springs	1.0	720'	4,160'	F/7.3 mi	514
St. George Mine loop	3.6	1,510'	4,360'	F/7.1 mi	511-513
Thompson Canyon gorge	0.9	630'	3,710'	H/2.4 mi	508
Upper Thompson Springs	1.7	1,590'	4,060'	H/2.4 mi	508
Zinc Hill	2.3	1,970'	4,520'	F/5.3 mi	488-490

Key: P=Primitive (2WD) H=Primitive (HC) F=Primitive (4WD)
Distances: one way for out-and-back hikes, round-trip for loops
Elev. gain: sum of all elevation gains on round-trip or loop hike

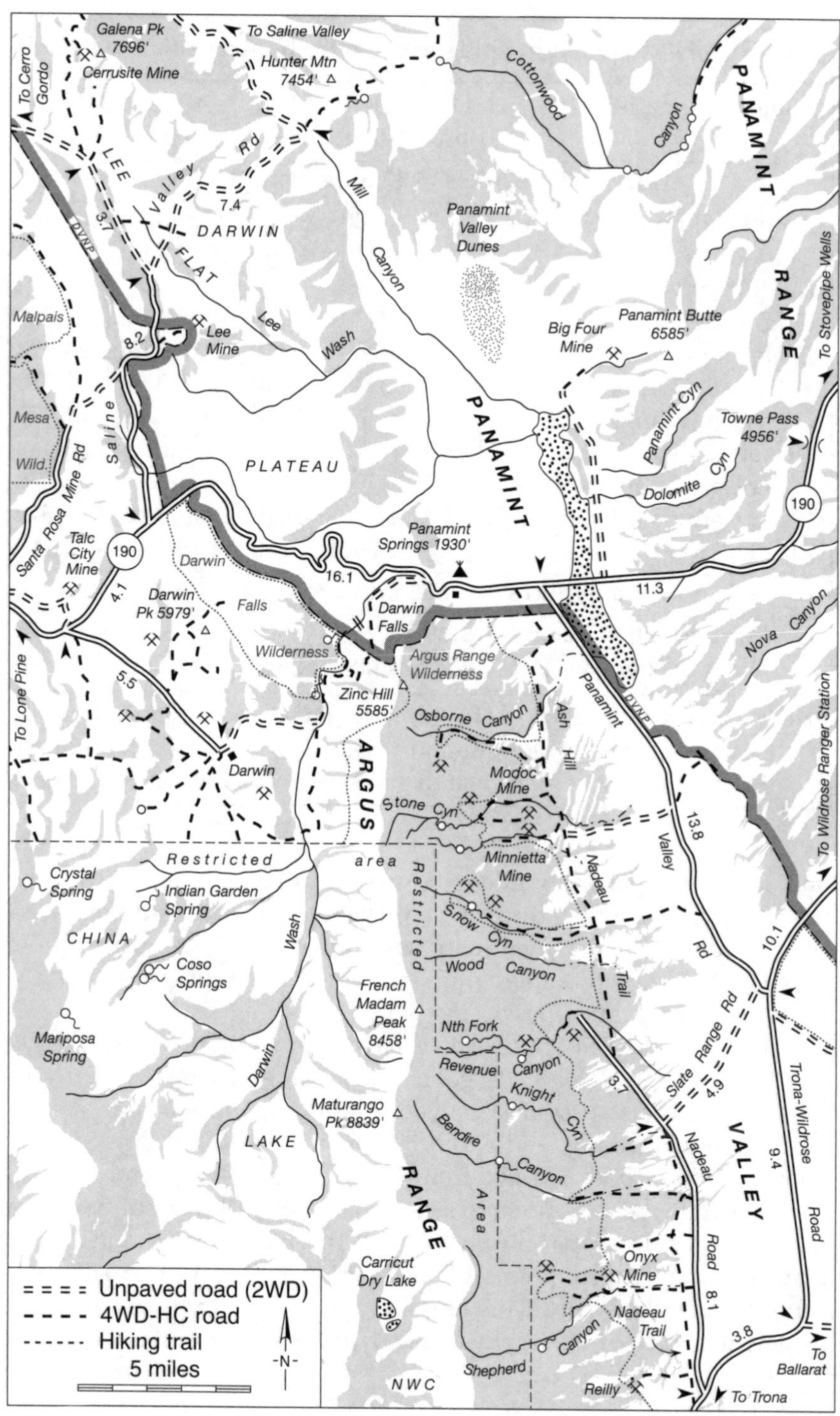
Galena Pk 7696'
Cerrusite Mine
To Saline Valley
Hunter Mtn 7454'
To Cerro Gordo
Cottonwood Canyon
PANAMINT RANGE
LEE Valley Rd
7.4
3.7
DVNP
DARWIN FLAT
Mill Canyon
Panamint Valley Dunes
Lee Wash
Malpais
Lee Mine
8.2
Mesa Wild.
Saline
Santa Rosa Mine Rd
PLATEAU
PANAMINT
Big Four Mine
Panamint Butte 6585'
Panamint Cyn
Towne Pass 4956'
Dolomite Cyn
To Stovepipe Wells
190
Talc City Mine
Darwin Falls Wilderness
Panamint Springs 1930'
16.1
11.3
Darwin Pk 5979'
4.1
Darwin Falls
Argus Range Wilderness
Nova Canyon
To Lone Pine
5.5
Zinc Hill 5585'
Osborne Canyon
Ash Hill
Panamint Valley Rd
To Wildrose Ranger Station
Darwin
ARGUS RANGE
Modoc Mine
Stone Cyn
13.8
Restricted area
Crystal Spring
Indian Garden Spring
Minnietta Mine
Nadeau Trail
CHINA LAKE
Snow Cyn
Wash
Coso Springs
Wood Canyon
10.1
French Madam Peak 8458'
Mariposa Spring
Nth Fork
Revenue Canyon
Slate Range Rd
4.9
3.7
Darwin
Knight Cyn
Trona-Wildrose Road
Maturango Pk 8839'
Bendire Canyon
VALLEY
Nadeau Road
9.4
Area
Carricut Dry Lake
Onyx Mine
8.1
Nadeau Trail
3.8
Shepherd Canyon
To Ballarat
NWC
Reilly
To Trona
Unpaved road (2WD)
4WD-HC road
Hiking trail
5 miles
N

Suggested Hikes on Darwin Plateau and in the Argus Range (Ctn'd)					
Route/Destination	Dist. (mi)	Elev. gain	Mean elev.	Access road	Pages
Intermediate hikes (5-12 miles round trip)					
Anton and Pobst Mine Road	5.9	1,480'	6,100'	Graded	463-466
Darwin Wash overlook	4.2	2,410'	4,940'	F/2.7 mi	496
Knight Canyon					
Lower viewpoint	3.5	1,730'	3,350'	P/2.3 mi	521-523
Narrows	3.7	1,780'	3,370'	P/2.3 mi	523-524
Upper viewpoint	4.7	2,540'	3,640'	P/2.3 mi	521-523
Lee Wash (Plunge Pool Fall)	2.5	560'	5,040'	H/2.3 mi	471-472
Nelson Cabin	4.3	910'	5,950'	Graded	463-464
Water Canyon (first spring)	2.9	790'	2,710'	Graded	537-538
Water Canyon (fifth spring)	5.4	1,770'	3,110'	Graded	537-540
Zinc Hill loop	5.7	2,090'	4,650'	F/5.3 mi	488-490
Long hikes (over 12 miles round trip)					
Lee Wash to canyon mouth	8.9	3,260'	3,920'	H/2.3 mi	472-476
Lee Wash to Highway 190	17.0	4,000'	2,870'	H/2.3 mi	472-476
Key: P=Primitive (2WD) H=Primitive (HC) F=Primitive (4WD) Distances: one way for out-and-back hikes, round-trip for loops Elev. gain: sum of all elevation gains on round-trip or loop hike					

and scenic, yet generally tame and free of impassible falls—with the notable exception of Bendire Canyon. The mining roads and trails are a plus for people disinclined to cross-country hiking. And the whole range is studded with mines, mills, and other interesting mementos of the range's rich mining past.

Hiking on the Darwin Plateau is an altogether different experience. Road access is also generally good, and poking around the flats and hills on foot is also easy. The canyons that drain into Panamint Valley are roadless and long, and exploring them takes a full day. So here there is a bit of both worlds, from easy strolls to long aerobic treks. Almost everywhere the scenery is dominated by Joshua trees, a feature that sets this area apart from most of the park. While out on the plateau, you might run into cattle wandering aimlessly. If you do, stay calm. Breathe normally. This area is covered by a pre-park grazing easement, and cows are legally allowed. Just leave the beasts alone.

■

LEE FLAT

Rimmed with wrinkled hills and graced by the distant peaks of the Inyo Mountains, Lee Flat boasts one of the largest and most striking Joshua tree forests in the northern Mojave Desert. Discover this beautiful area by taking a scenic drive on its graded roads, by four-wheeling or hiking beat-up roads to abandoned mines and historic sites in the nearby ranges, or by ambling through this signature landscape of Joshua trees and cacti.

General Information

Jurisdiction: Death Valley National Park
Road status: Hiking on old road; easy access from graded road
Lee Flat Cutoff: 1.9 mi, 80 ft up, 0 ft down one way / very easy
Lee Flat loop: 3.7 mi, 100 ft up loop / very easy
Main attractions: Extensive Joshua tree forest, flora, easy walks
USGS 7.5' topo maps: Lee Wash*, Santa Rosa Flat*, Nelson Range*, Jackass Canyon
Maps: pp. 461*, 457

Location and Access

Lee Flat is a high-desert valley on the Darwin Plateau, midway between the Argus Range and Saline Valley. It is easily reached by driving the Saline Valley Road 8.2 miles north from Highway 190 to the wide Y-junction at the south edge of Lee Flat. Over the next 2 miles the right fork (Saline Valley Road) crosses the width of Lee Flat. The left fork (Lee Flat Road) follows Lee Flat lengthwise several miles to near its north end. These two roads are graded and suitable for passenger cars. Although both are scenic, the Lee Flat Road goes through the densest forest on the west side. If you have time, explore the mining roads near the north end of Lee Flat (see *The Nelson Range Mines*). This is open range. Pay attention to cattle, which often roam freely.

Route Description

Cocooned by the Santa Rosa Hills to the west and the Nelson Range to the east, Lee Flat is a special place, spacious and luminous. On a sunny day, its inviting openness and immense sky inspire a deep sense of freedom and a rejuvenating peacefulness. Its Joshua tree woodland covers more than 4,000 acres of valley floor, and it spills generously over the surrounding hills in all directions. The entire area

Lee Flat's Joshua tree forest

is suffused with an odd timelessness, what one would expect on distant planets, where such alien landscapes no doubt abound. I have camped here many times, often at the end of the long solitary drive from home, pushing it all the way here just for the elation of waking up the next morning in this otherworldly dreamscape.

You may find, as I often do here, that the open desert invites aimless ambling. If you do, park anywhere along the roads and start walking. This is a perfect place for a leisure stroll in the high desert, for bird watching, or to inspect the distinct flora of this transition zone. Distractions are so plentiful that you might find yourself often drifting off in a new direction, drawn by the silvery glitter of a decaying trunk, the fluorescent glow of a cholla, or the magenta splash of a beavertail

Lee Flat Road		
	Dist.(mi)	Elev.(ft)
Saline Valley Road (Y junction)	0.0	5,249
Cutoff road (west end)	1.7	5,390
Saline Valley Road crossing	(1.4)	5,321
Wilson Ranch	(1.9)	5,316
Copper Queen Mine Road	3.7	5,576
Anton and Pobst Mine Road	3.8	5,595
Pass into San Lucas Canyon	7.0	~6,220

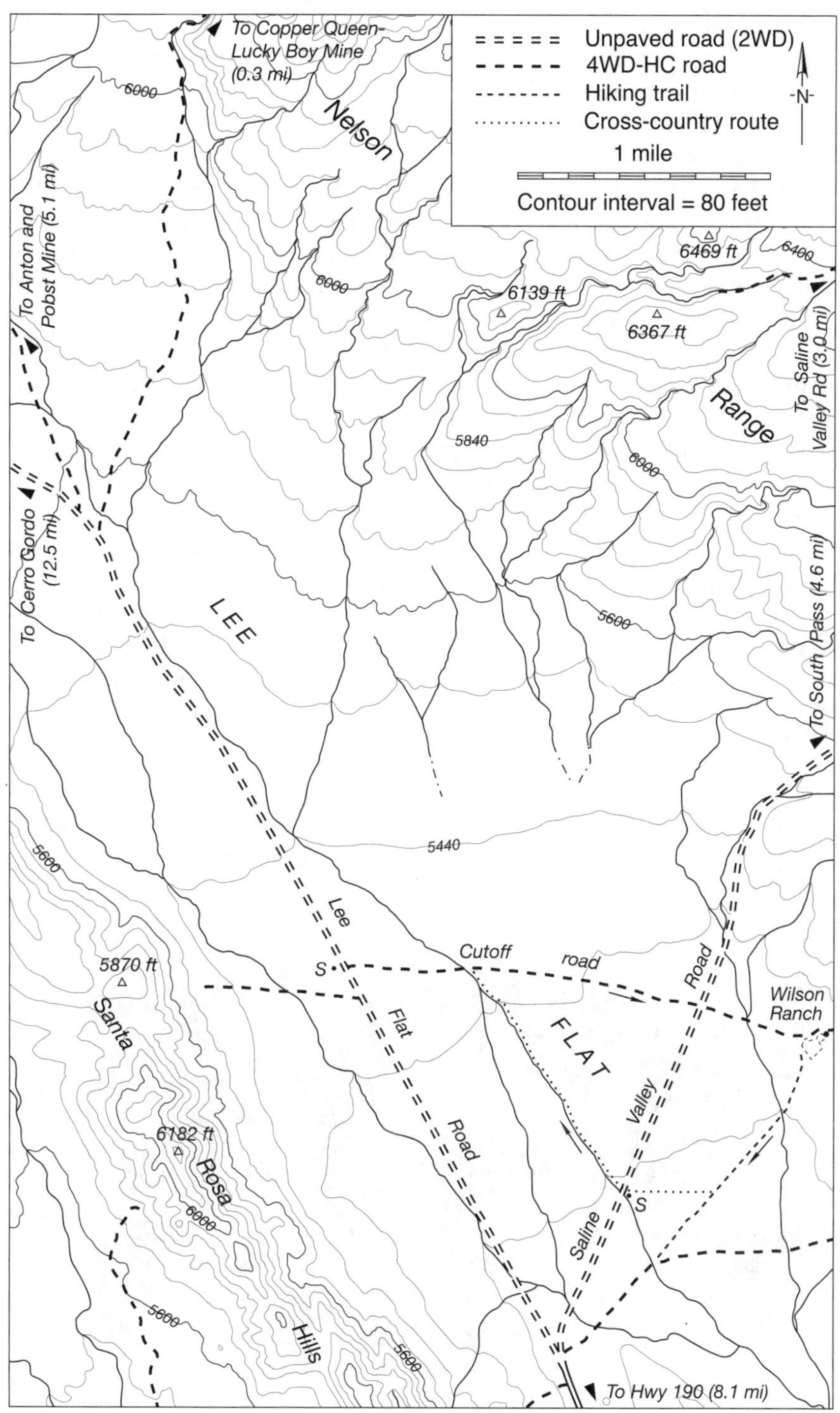
Unpaved road (2WD)
4WD-HC road
Hiking trail
Cross-country route
1 mile
Contour interval = 80 feet
N
To Copper Queen-Lucky Boy Mine (0.3 mi)
Nelson
Range
To Anton and Pobst Mine (5.1 mi)
To Cerro Gordo (12.5 mi)
To Saline Valley Rd (3.0 mi)
To South Pass (4.6 mi)
6469 ft
6139 ft
6367 ft
6400
6000
5840
5600
5440
LEE
FLAT
Lee Flat Road
Cutoff road
Saline Valley Road
Wilson Ranch
S
5870 ft
6182 ft
Santa Rosa Hills
To Hwy 190 (8.1 mi)

cactus. Just remember to keep track of where your car is parked, or after an hour of wandering you may have difficulty homing in on it!

For a more structured hike, consider one of these two routes. Park on the Lee Flat Road 1.7 miles from the Y junction, and walk the rarely used cutoff road, on the east side. It cuts east through the heart of the forest 1.4 miles to the Saline Valley Road, then goes on 0.5 mile to the water towers and corrals of Wilson Ranch, still in use today. To make a loop, start instead from the Saline Valley Road 0.75 mile from the Y. Follow the wash that runs north-northwest, parallel to the Lee Flat Road. It goes by the area's largest Joshua trees. In 1.1 miles it will take you to the cutoff road, which you then follow to the ranch. At the southwest corner of the corral, take the abandoned road that heads southwest 0.7 mile, then cut a beeline west back to your vehicle. These very easy walks cross gently sloping sandy terrain studded with chollas, spiny menodora, and countless Joshua trees of all sizes and shapes, some boasting thick crowns over 20 feet high.

Lee Flat may hold a weather record of sorts: it is often surprisingly cold. Besides the high elevation and openness, the main culprit is the frequent winds that seem to come straight from Alaska. I remember many visits wearing just about every piece of clothing I owned and still feeling the bitter cold. Unless you have a thing for pain, this is no place for a winter stroll. But if it is summertime and the brutal heat of the lower valleys is getting to you, think Lee Flat.

■

Nelson Cabin at the Cerrusite Mine

THE NELSON RANGE MINES

If you enjoy exploring isolated areas by car or on foot, don't pass up on these two scenic byways, which climb through Joshua-tree country to remote corners of the Nelson Range. They give access to several lead and copper mines loaded with colorful minerals, and to spectacular viewpoints and a peak overlooking Lee Flat and Saline Valley. Along the way you will find a pleasant backcountry cabin and excellent spots for summer camping in the cooler high desert.

General Information

Jurisdiction: Death Valley National Park
Road status: Hiking on old mining roads; high-clearance access roads
Cerrusite Mine: 4.3 mi, 910 ft up, 0 ft down one way / easy-moderate
Anton & Pobst Mine: 5.9 mi, 1,010 ft up, 470 ft down one way / moder.
Main attractions: Hiking on old roads, Joshua trees, vista points, mines
USGS 7.5' topo map: Nelson Range
Maps: pp. 465*, *137, 457*

Location and Access

The two mining roads described here are on the southern slope of the Nelson Range. They are the only open roads in this range. The Copper Queen Mine Road branches off the Lee Flat Road 3.7 miles north of the Saline Valley Road (or 12.9 miles from Cerro Gordo). The Anton and Pobst Mine Road starts 0.1 mile farther north. Both roads are compacted sand at lower elevation, but a little rocky higher up. You will need to come here with a high-clearance vehicle, or walk.

Route Description

The mining roads. Although little known, these two old roads cross some of the finest scenery in the western Death Valley region. The whole way they traverse a healthy community of Joshua trees, cacti, and spiny shrubs, the northern extension of the vast forest that mantles Lee Flat. The trees grow so densely that they crowd the narrow roadways, creating at places a genuine forest atmosphere. If your car cannot make it, it is definitely worth the hike, especially overnight. The local mines are interesting destinations. The Copper Queen Mine is at the end of the lower road (2.7 miles). The Anton and Pobst Mine Road, longer and more scenic, gives access to several mines. To get to the Cerrusite Mine, look for the side road on the right, at a high point

3.5 miles out. After 0.4 mile this side road forks: continue straight to the Nelson Cabin at the Cerrusite Mine (0.25 mile), or left to the Pinion Extension Mine (0.2 mile). The Anton and Pobst Mine is at the very end of the main road (5.9 miles).

The Copper Queen Mine. Located in a shallow gulch lined with dark basaltic boulders, this mine and its gutted camp are the least scenic of the lot. But the tunnels are the most complex, and ore is so abundant that the last stretch of road is practically paved with chrysocolla and malachite! Worked by San Diego owner Homer Stuck from 1969 to 1999, the main tunnel explored a nearly vertical vein of milky quartz up to 6 feet wide. A good deal of it has been carved out, leaving behind a giant slot braced by logs that reaches tens of feet above and below the tunnel floor (beware of the two deep shafts!). Cavities in the walls are thickly coated with chrysocolla, malachite, azurite, limonite, cinnabar, jasper, and hematite, and the tailings are equally colorful.

The Cerrusite Mine and Galena Peak. Long before reaching this mine you will see the tin roof of its well-kept cabin winking among the Joshua trees up on the mountainside. The Nelson Cabin, as it is occasionally called, is a typical miner's mansion, an old-fashioned shack of plywood and concrete with a roof sloping down to high glass windows. It is furnished with a table and chairs, a wood stove, and a few amusing gadgets. The cabin log recounts the adventures of exalted visitors who stayed here overnight, in snow or blissful heat, to enjoy the peacefulness and the sprawling views of Lee Flat. Although the cabin is neat and tidy, mice take up residence in it more often than humans, and hantavirus is a concern. Pitch a tent on one of the level spots nearby instead; I can't make any guarantees, but you may live longer.

The Cerrusite Mine was operated by several generations of miners, until as recently as 1996. It had some decent ore: in the late 1930s, when Panamint Valley mining veteran William Reid owned it, he was getting up to $25 per ton, mostly from silver. To reach the mine, continue 0.2 mile past the cabin to the lowest tunnel. Just beyond it, at the far end of the road, a trail winds up 500 yards past five more tunnels, some of them collapsed, and a shaft. The second tunnel is shored with lumber frames and terminated by a steep winze sparkling with argentiferous galena. In some tunnels the galena was altered to cerussite—which was later altered to "cerrusite" by a poor speller when the mine was named. The old wooden headframe and winch at the 25-foot shaft, further up the trail, attest to the mine's advanced age. If you have a couple of hours to spare, scramble past the upper end of the

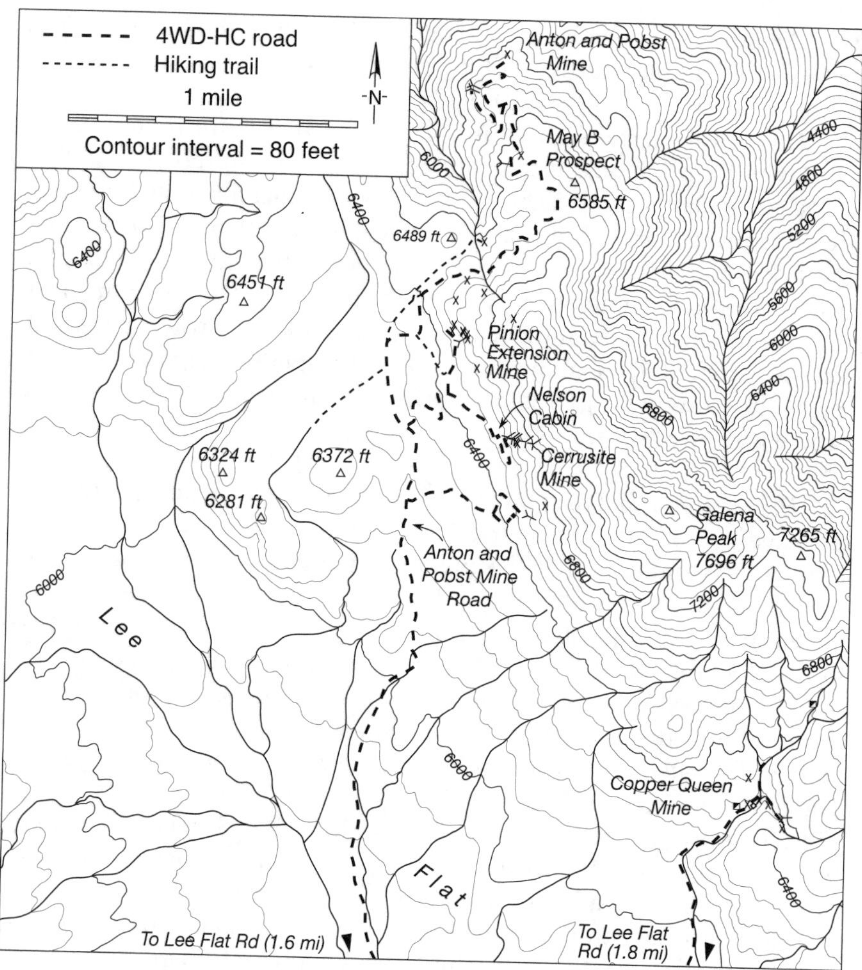

The Nelson Range Mines		
	Dist.(mi)	Elev.(ft)
The Copper Queen Mine Road		
Lee Flat Road	0.0	5,576
Copper Queen Mine	2.7	~6,315
The Anton and Pobst Mine Road		
Lee Flat Road	0.0	5,595
Junction to Cerrusite Mine	3.5	~6,290
Cerrusite Mine (lower tunnel)	(0.85)	6,580
Viewpoint on ridge	5.4	~6,315
Anton and Pobst Mine tunnels	5.9	6,125

trail 0.8 mile to Galena Peak, the highest summit in the Nelson Range (7,696'), for sumptuous views of the entire region.

The Pinion Extension Mine. Here the treats are reversed: the workings are minimal but they are peppered with a profusion of minerals, particularly garnet. This property was in fact formerly known as the Birdspring Garnet Mine, and an unsuccessful attempt was made in the 1980s to market this semi-precious stone. There are no trails: park below the southernmost working, which is the mine's only adit (turning around past this point is tedious), and work your way up the hillside in search of the shallow cuts. They all display varying amounts of malachite, turquoise, galena, calcite, and a profusion of dark reddish-brown garnet crystals.

The Anton and Pobst Mine. This historic copper property, first reported around 1903, was the area's richest. Lone Pine discoverers John Anton and David Pobst owned it for many years. There is no record to substantiate their production, but in 1916 a lessee put a dozen miners on the job and shipped 37 tons of copper, or about two thirds of all the copper known to have come out of Saline Valley!

The mine was exploited on two levels. At the far end of the road, the right fork drops to the lower level, an open cut mineralized with beautiful striated crystals of dark-green epidote in snow-white quartz. The left fork circles 0.3 mile down to the main level, where two short tunnels were punched into a 20-foot cliff. The cliff is generously brushed with colorful strokes worthy of an impressionist palette. The grays are silver-lead minerals and chalcopyrite. The ochres are limonite, probably from the oxidation of pyrite. The greens and blues are copper ore, including malachite sprinkled with brown garnet crystals. The long tailing that spills down the mountain below the workings is full of these pretty minerals.

But you don't need a fondness for rocks to enjoy yourself here. Perched on the high crest of the Nelson Range, the mine commands magnificent views of southern Saline Valley. The most dramatic site is the sharp ridge just before the final split in the road. To the north and west the land drops precipitously into the abysmal depths of Saline Valley, dark and mottled like a mortal wound in the Earth. You may well spot a few old acquaintances pinned against this grand tableau—the Racetrack, Corridor Canyon, Big and Little Dodd springs, or the Blue Jay Mine. In the summer, this is a first-class camping spot, cool, awesome, and wild, far away from everything.

■

THE LEE MINE

With its large primitive silver mill from the 1870s, this easily accessible mine is an important historic site. If you poke around, you will find touching clues about its operation and resuscitate, for a few moments, the ghosts of its ghost town. This short walk among scenic open hills studded with Joshua trees can be extended by climbing nearby Maltese Peak, a stack of fossiliferous Paleozoic limestones that commands sweeping vistas of the Panamint Valley area.

General Information

Jurisdiction: Death Valley National Park
Road status: Hiking on roads and cross-country; HC access road
Lee Mine loop: 1.0 mi, 100 ft up loop / very easy
Maltese Peak: 0.8 mi, 410 ft up, 30 ft down one way / easy
Main attractions: a historic silver mine, an easy peak climb, fossils
USGS 7.5' topo maps: Lee Wash*, The Dunes, Panamint Springs
Maps: pp. 469*, *179, 457*

Location and Access

The Lee Mine is in the Santa Rosa Hills, a short ride from Highway 190. From the highway drive the Saline Valley Road north 5.9 miles, where it crests the Santa Rosa Hills. The inconspicuous primitive side road that drops to the right is the Lee Mine Road. Drive it 0.95 mile to a fork at the foot of the Lee Mine's large mill to the right, and park. This road has a steep down grade with embedded rocks starting 0.25 mile in; it requires high clearance, and four-wheel drive coming back up. If you are driving a sedan, either park at the small open space on the right 0.2 mile from the Saline Valley Road and walk the rest, or try the north access road, which is smoother. It starts off the Saline Valley Road 1.1 miles further north. Turn right on this road. In 0.7 mile it ends at a right angle into the Lee Mine Road. The mill is 0.35 mile to the left.

Route Description

Lee Mine loop. This mine is very old: its earliest developments were probably contemporary with Darwin's original discovery. It was active mostly in the 1870s through around 1888, when lead ore rich in silver was shipped out. Afterwards, Lee Mine was operated off and on for many decades by numerous owners and lessees, who mostly squeezed out left-over silver, lead, and zinc from the old workings and tailings. The ore was actually fairly rich; in the 1950s it still assayed nearly 100 ounces of silver per ton. But, somehow, since its heyday Lee Mine probably produced less than a thousand tons.

Of Lee Mine's many past structures, the largest one that remains today is its grand silver mill. About 35 feet tall and 50 yards wide, it is a giant staircase of three tiered levels carved into a steep hillside of massive limestone and complemented with long stone walls. The ore was conveyed to the mill's highest level on a road that comes in from the left, then crushed to a powder. The concrete pilings that supported the stamp mill and mill tailings rest at the bottom of the mill. The shell of a water tank lies nearby, twisted like a Möbius strip. Still fairly well-preserved, this site is a fine example of the region's early silver mills. To spare this important historic structure, do not climb on its walls or taluses, but instead use the three narrow access roads that lead into it.

The Lee Mine sits in a luminous wilderness of low, barren hills haunted by armies of small Joshua trees. From the mill it can be visited along the half-mile loop road that circles around it (see map). From the mill take the right fork in the road (south). The first side road on the left ends shortly at two prominent rock mounds. This was the heart of the mine. It has several open shafts, connected underground by a contorted network of galleries that wander up and down and split over and over again in their educated search for silver. One of them starts with a cavernous opening. The long inclined tunnel that produced much of the ore is just past the mounds. Its tilted rail spur is still in place. An ore car was pulled out of the tunnel by a hoist, now long gone. The wooden posts poking out of the mounds are the ruins of the trestle that supported the rail on which the car delivered the ore. The ore bodies occurred in small parallel lenses along fractures in Tin Mountain Limestone. They contained hemimorphite, cerargyrite, galena, and bindheimite, and a little copper—azurite, chrysocolla, and native copper. Some of these minerals, as well as jasper and chalcedony, are scattered on the area's many dumps.

A short distance south are the ruins of a mining camp, marked by a bullet-ridden Chevrolet station wagon. A side trail on the right wanders to a long narrow trench with a sturdy retaining wall. Further on, other short side roads lead to other mining sites. Each one has something to show. There are gutted transistor radios, metal drums, old chairs, water heaters, mangled couches, ladders, can dumps, and defunct appliances. When you are done, close the loop along its northern leg, past the decaying exoskeleton of another vintage automobile, its chrome still shining in the desert light. All the shafts are open and deep. Be extremely careful, and do not walk around after dark.

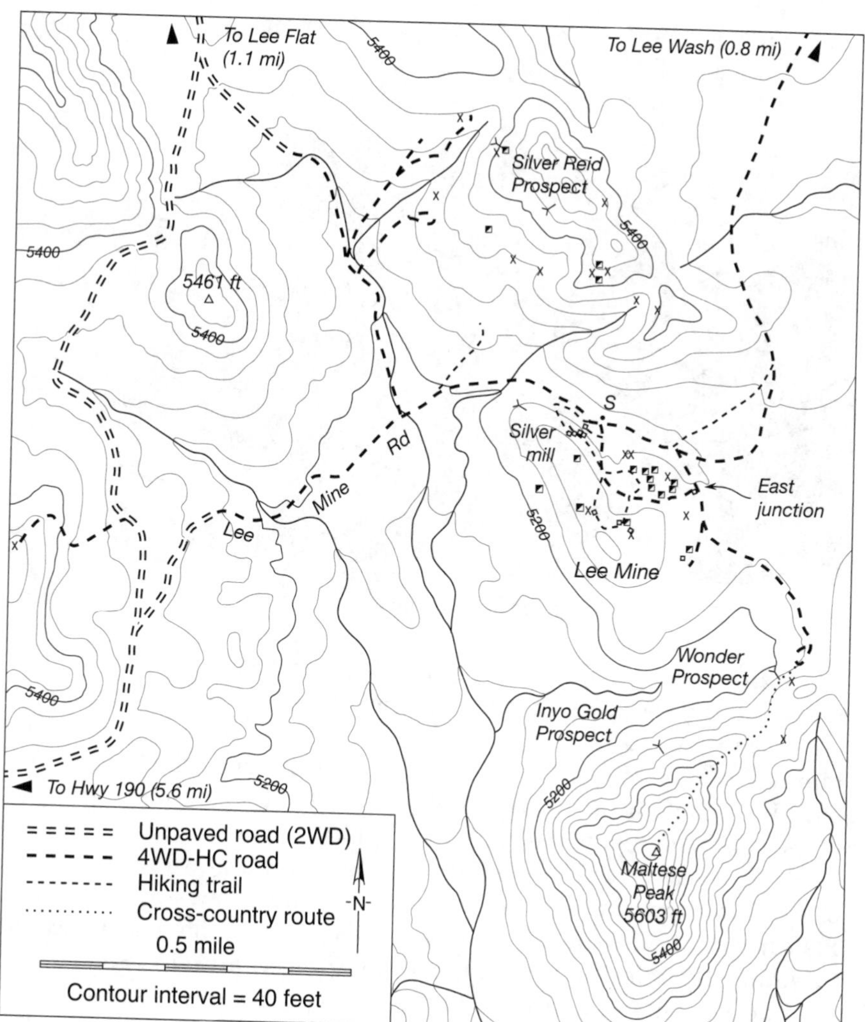

The Lee Mine

	Dist.(mi)	Elev.(ft)
Silver mill	0.0	5,220
Inclined shafts	0.1	5,260
Stone ruin	0.2	5,290
East junction	0.5	5,240
Return to mill on loop	(0.2)	5,220
End of road / Wonder Prospect	0.9	5,240
Maltese Peak	1.3	5,603

Silver Mill at the Lee Mine

Maltese Peak. Also known as Jack Gunn Peak, this isolated hill rising sharply southeast of the Lee Mine area is a great little summit to climb, and a good reason to stop by, even if you have no interest in mines. From the mill, either drive or walk the main road 0.4 mile to its end. Then contour the hillside southwest to the low saddle at the base of the peak, and follow the hill's open spine 0.4 mile to the summit.

It is an easy climb, on consolidated ground and low outcrops cleaved into natural staircases, with expansive views over Darwin Plateau and the Panamint Valley area. The hill is a tilted sequence of three mostly Mississippian formations (Tin Mountain Limestone, Perdido Formation, and Lee Flat Limestone), a sharp alternation of light to dark gray limestones, white marble, and brown siltstone. The first transition is unmistakable: in literally one step you cross over from white marble to gray limestone, a switch resulting from a major environmental change that took place exactly 347 million years ago. Each stair in the outcrops exposes a page in the Mississippian history. Some pages are teaming with ancient life—the white round spots of corals, more rarely the thin spiral of a snail. The most exciting is the crisp broken stems of sea lilies, a marine invertebrate that lived at a time when there were 393 days in a year and no mammals on land. This little mountain gives us not only a broad view of the region, but also a clandestine glimpse into its distant past.

■

LEE WASH

Lee Wash is, to say the least, a misnomer: it is not a wash but a true canyon, and a mighty one at that. Running over 8 miles from end to end, it is a spectacularly colorful volcanic gorge, more tortuous than any canyon this length in the region. The price is matched to the reward: it is a 3-mile hike just to get to it, and to see it all takes a long day. But what wildness it holds! Expect falls, narrow passages, finely chiseled outcrops, waterworn bedrock, secret side canyons, and towering perpendicular walls of massive congealed lava.

General Information

Jurisdiction: Death Valley National Park
Road status: Cross-country hiking; high-clearance access road
Plunge-Pool Fall: 2.5 mi, 20 ft up, 540 ft down one way/easy
Lee Wash: 8.9 mi, 50 ft up, 3,210 ft down one way/strenuous (Class 2)
Main attractions: a silver mine, a long, colorful, windy gorge, geology
USGS 7.5′ topo maps: Lee Wash*, The Dunes, Panamint Springs
Maps: pp. 469*, 475*, *179*, *457*

Location and Access

Lee Wash is one of several main roadless canyons that drain the Darwin Plateau eastward into northwestern Panamint Valley. The easiest starting point to hike to it is the Lee Mine. From Highway 190 drive the Saline Valley Road north 5.9 miles. At this point the road crests the Santa Rosa Hills, and an inconspicuous primitive side road drops to the right. This is the Lee Mine Road. Drive it 1.05 miles to just past a right bend embellished by the decaying exoskeleton of a vintage automobile. Look carefully for a faint road splitting off to the left. Drive this side road 1.3 miles to a high point at the rim of Lee Wash (high clearance is required). The road continues 0.3 mile down to the canyon wash, but its grade is so steep and rough that even with a four-wheel drive it is difficult to get back up. Park at the top of the grade instead.

Route Description

The upper canyon. Lee Wash takes a while to show its true colors. For the longest time, it meanders lazily across the extreme southeast corner of Lee Flat, past platoons of frozen Joshua trees. Nothing much happens; you will have to be patient. If it is late spring or summer, the high point may be the occasional splash of crimson of penstemon or

Indian paintbrush. Yet it is an interesting sensation to walk through this repetitive landscape that changes only very slowly, along a wash so imperceptibly tilted that it is difficult to tell which way is down.

The monotony ends after 1.4 miles, at the head of the gorge. In minutes you find yourself sinking below the surface of the plateau in sudden steps, climbing down polished bedrock, 5, 10, 40 feet at a time. Over the next 0.8 mile the wash is interrupted by five major falls and numerous low boulder jams and chutes. The first fall, about 25 feet high, is made of two polished chutes back to back, carved at the head of a short defile hemmed in by pillars of basalt. At the top of this fall there is a good display of mangled aa lava resting on smooth pahoehoe lava. The next fall, 25 feet high, is a series of hard steps in sub-vertical bedrock, and the one after that a 15-foot wall spanning the width of the canyon. These falls can be easily climbed—with care—but the next one is an 18-foot overhang at the head of short narrows, impassable in almost anyone's book. Fortunately, the fall and narrows are circumvented by a game track on its north side.

The fifth and final fall, Plunge-Pool Fall, is another matter. Encased between sheer walls, it leaves no alternative but climbing. Although only about 35 feet high, it is extended downward by a 12-foot circular pothole sunk into the sand at the foot of the fall. So when standing at the top of the fall, 50 feet of nothing but fresh air separate your eyes from the bottom of the pothole. This fall can be climbed down on its left side, where it is not quite vertical. Every move is easy, but the rock is friable and treacherous, it is quite exposed, and a fall from high up would result in death, if not worse. Bring a rope, and select the boulder on which to attach it carefully, as many of them are loose. Unless you have a rope *and* experience, do not attempt this climb. Look for a bypass instead, or turn around.

A sizable river once flowed through Lee Wash. It was not long ago, likely in the late Pleistocene, when glaciers smothered the high Sierra and local precipitation was higher. Vestiges of its passage are still ubiquitous—polished boulders, carved bedrock, undercuts at the base of the canyon walls. For 0.1 mile below Plunge-Pool Fall, which is the steepest section, the river flow was strong enough to transport and polish a long chaotic field of boulders, tedious to cross. Because Lee Wash drains a large area, including the southern flanks of the Nelson Range and almost all of Lee Flat, flashfloods occasionally create more modest incarnations of this former river. The deep pothole at the base of Plunge-Pool Fall was excavated by one of these recent streams as it rushed over the fall and spawned a waterfall that pounded the wash below. Small boulder dams also impede the stream's flow and create cascades that scoop out shallow depressions at their base. Coated with silt, up to 10-feet deep, many of these fossil river holes are still plainly visible, and a heavy cloudburst will turn them into ephemeral pools.

The central gorge. The eastern edge of the Darwin Plateau, including the drainage crossed by Lee Wash, is made of extensive volcanic flows reaching 600 feet in thickness. They were formed fairly recently, mostly during the Pleistocene and perhaps also the Pliocene, when belching volcanoes coated the land with layer upon layer of lava and ash. Lee Wash, Rainbow Canyon, and several nearby gorges were carved right through this volcanic phantasmagoria. As you walk down canyon, the volcanic events exposed in the walls become older. In a brilliant symphony of colors, layers of deep-red cinder and gray

Sculpted narrows below the first fall in Lee Wash

olivine basalt alternate with tuff-breccia filled with volcanic bombs, and with the most diverse palettes of neatly layered lapilli tuffs, yellow to orange, pink, and vermilion.

What makes exploring this kaleidoscopic canyon even more appealing is its delightfully serpentine path, reminiscent of the canyons of the Colorado Plateau. From head to fan, Lee Wash folds upon itself dozens of times, in tight bends, bends within bends, and long oxbows that throw you right back near your starting point. These contortions force us to discover this ever-changing place leisurely, almost voluptuously, one twist at a time. At half a dozen places the gorge tightens to short constrictions. In the deepest narrows, you slither along the base of soaring, strikingly banded purple walls, staring up at smooth slices of time. Elsewhere, you gaze off in the near distance at fluted bluffs splashed with punk streaks of mauve and apricot.

A surprising variety of birds kept me company throughout the gorge. Ravens were, as usual, most entertaining. They lingered overhead, or used thermals to fashion a roller coaster for themselves and carry out playful acrobatics. Just when I was concentrating on climbing down the tricky fifth fall, they startled me by materializing overhead and crying out in passing. Was it a friendly warning of danger, or a cheer in anticipation of me turning into cold buffet? I ran across several chukars, so close that I could count their shoulder striations. I interrupted the midday nap of three great horned owls, who flew down canyon and landed on a nearby spur. When I reached them I stopped and took a long look at their stiff bodies, 30 feet away, while they stared back with bored indifference. It may have been the first human sighting in this canyon in owl's memory.

Lee Wash

	Dist.(mi)	Elev.(ft)
Top of grade/rim of Lee Wash	0.0	5,360
Lee Wash	0.25	5,190
First fall (start of gorge)	1.5	5,110
Fifth fall (Plunge-Pool Fall)	2.5	4,840
Deepest narrows	4.3	4,130
Main side canyon	6.0	3,300
High fall at end of side canyon	(1.7)	~4,240
Mouth	8.9	2,200
Highway 190	17.0	1,575

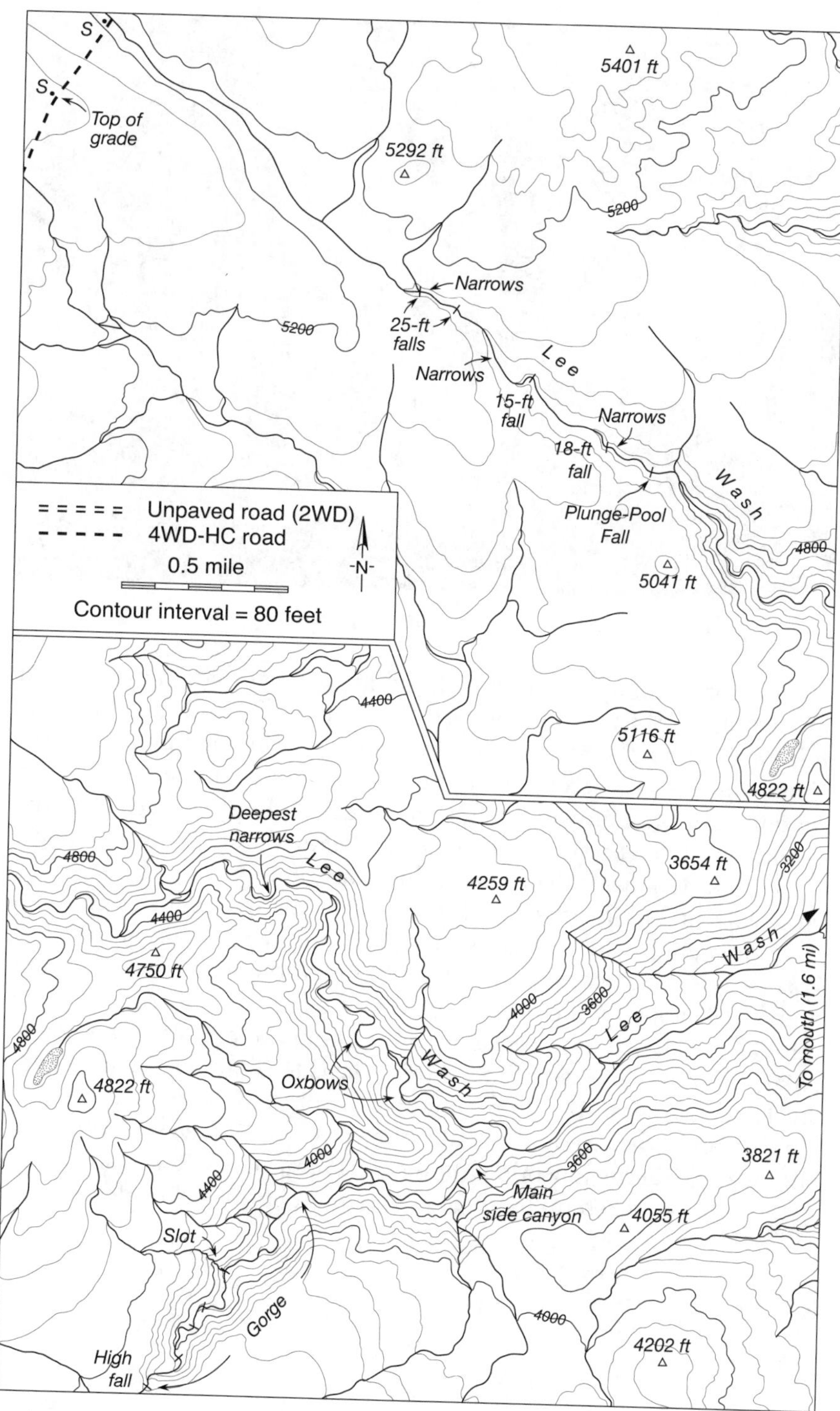
S
S
Top of grade
5401 ft
5292 ft
5200
Narrows
25-ft falls
5200
Narrows
Lee
15-ft fall
Narrows
18-ft fall
Plunge-Pool Fall
Wash
4800
5041 ft
===== Unpaved road (2WD)
- - - - 4WD-HC road
0.5 mile
-N-
Contour interval = 80 feet
4400
5116 ft
4822 ft
Deepest narrows
Lee
4800
4259 ft
3654 ft
3200
4400
4750 ft
Wash
To mouth (1.6 mi)
4800
4000
3600
Lee
Oxbows
Wash
4822 ft
4000
4400
3600
3821 ft
Main side canyon
4055 ft
Slot
Gorge
4000
High fall
4202 ft

Volcanic walls along the deep central gorge

The lower canyon. Lee Wash has only one main side canyon, but it is a whole world in itself, every bit as convoluted and tantalizing as Lee Wash. It bursts into view on the south side, framed by pink cliffs. If time allows, give it a try. Its upper half is a deep, rugged, and colorful gorge. About halfway though the gorge, starting 1.2 miles from the confluence, the wash is interrupted by several high falls, the last one a major drop that seals the canyon. There are, here too, awesome walls, dark slots, and more little secrets than can be discovered in a day.

Below the main side canyon and all the way to its mouth, Lee Wash is wider but just as colorful, unrolling through denuded hills and domes. It ends with a bang, on the bright edge of Panamint Valley, in full view of the valley's sensuous dunes, immaculate playa, and eerie Lake Hill. A possible extension of this hike is to continue down the valley. Hike southeast to within a mile of the playa, where the ground is very smooth, then roughly south along the playa's western edge to Highway 190 at the junction with the Panamint Valley Road (~8 miles). Arrange to be picked up there, or at Panamint Springs 2.5 miles west.

■

DARWIN HILLS

Famous for their fabulously rich historic silver mines, the Darwin Hills at the northwest end of the Argus Range are a free-standing ridge of plump hills whose very names—Ophir Mountain, inspired by the fabled mountain of gold, and Darwin Peak, named after early explorer Darwin French—are an invitation to amble. These two easy peaks, each less than a mile and 700 feet up, offer a reflective way to acquaint yourself with the scale, beauty, and history of this little-traveled part of the desert.

General Information

Jurisdiction: Public lands (BLM)
Road status: Hiking on roads and cross-country; 2WD access roads
Ophir Mountain: 0.9 mi, 510 ft up, 30 ft down one way/easy
Darwin Peak: 0.8 mi, 620 ft up, 90 ft down one way/easy
Main attractions: Easy climbs, mining history, views of Darwin area
USGS 7.5' topo map: Darwin
Maps: pp. 479*, 457

Location and Access

To reach the Darwin Hills, from Panamint Springs drive Highway 190 west 17.9 miles to the signed turn-off to Darwin (this junction is 27.4 miles east from Olancha). Drive the paved Darwin Road southeast 3.6 miles to a dirt road on the left, at the bottom of a long grade. Ophir Mountain is the high point due east; Darwin Peak is 2 miles north of it. Follow this signed road (SE 30) 0.6 mile north-northeast to a fork (right), then 0.8 mile, up a gulch that winds east into the Darwin Hills, to a road signed SE 28 on the left. For Ophir Mountain, continue 0.55 mile on SE 30, past a side road on the left, to a rougher road on the right closed to motor vehicles. Park at this junction, or at the crest 0.1 mile further. For Darwin Peak, turn left on SE 28 and go 0.4 mile to the third side road on the right, signed SE 28A. This short side road is quite steep and rough; park at this junction and walk it instead. The other roads are fairly smooth hard-packed dirt free of crowns. With a little experience they can be driven with a standard-clearance vehicle.

Route Description

The road on Ophir Mountain climbs gradually across the steep flank of the mountain's northern brow. Here as throughout the Darwin

Hills, the terrain is smooth bulging swells with scant vegetation, mostly low dehydrated shrubs with a serious aversion to chlorophyll. Even cactuses are not fond of the place. The only ornaments are immature Joshua trees, few and far between, only the healthiest granted stubby branches. Wildlife is scarce, although there is little doubt that if you spend a few hours you will come into sight of a burro. The road ends in 0.55 mile at a road cut. A single-track path worn by hooves and very occasional boots picks up at the south end of it. About 0.3 mile long, it heads south, angles right up a low rise, and descends 25 feet to a saddle. It then climbs gently south on the east side of and just below the crest to near the summit, with a short loose slope at the very end.

Ophir Mountain is a fine observatory to take in the size and beauty of four major desert ranges—the Inyo Mountains to the north, the Coso Range to the west, the Argus Range to the east, and behind it, past the pale trench of Panamint Valley, the great Panamint Range itself. Mount Whitney towers to the northwest, its 11,000-foot east face in full view. At the base of Ophir Mountain's furrowed southern slopes lies the half ghost town of Darwin, its cluster of cabins and barracks reduced to toys by distance. One of the smallest towns in the desert, it boasts a population of about 50, not all full-time residents, more mine tailings than trees, and fewer services than on Mars. If you stroll through town, a resident may well materialize out of nowhere to greet you, like children in the Sahara, and lavish you with tall desert tales.

In this dramatic immensity the Darwin Hills seem oddly small and out of place, too far from the closest range. They owe their existence and location, as well as their mineral wealth, to the Coso Range. When the Coso Range batholith boiled up in the Cretaceous, it squeezed a pre-existing stack of Paleozoic strata into an open concave fold known as a syncline. The uplifted west end of the syncline became the Darwin Hills, its east end the northern Argus Range, and its bottom the broad valley drained by Darwin Wash that separates the two—the Darwin Hills are just an extension of the Argus Range. This same batholith also deposited the Darwin Hills' prodigious amounts of silver—8 million ounces—and heavy metals—125,000 tons—exhumed in historic times.

The rocks on Ophir Mountain, Darwin Peak, and most of the Darwin Hills' crest belong to the Keeler Canyon Formation. Deposited in shallow near-shore water in Pennsylvanian and Permian times, it consists mostly of limestone, pebble conglomerate, and calcarenite, a purée of mashed corals and shells. Colorful exposures crop out along the road and crest, auburn or nearly white, often deeply corrugated by the wind, finely striated or imprinted with beautiful eye patterns formed by bluish limestone flowing around oblong tawny inclusions.

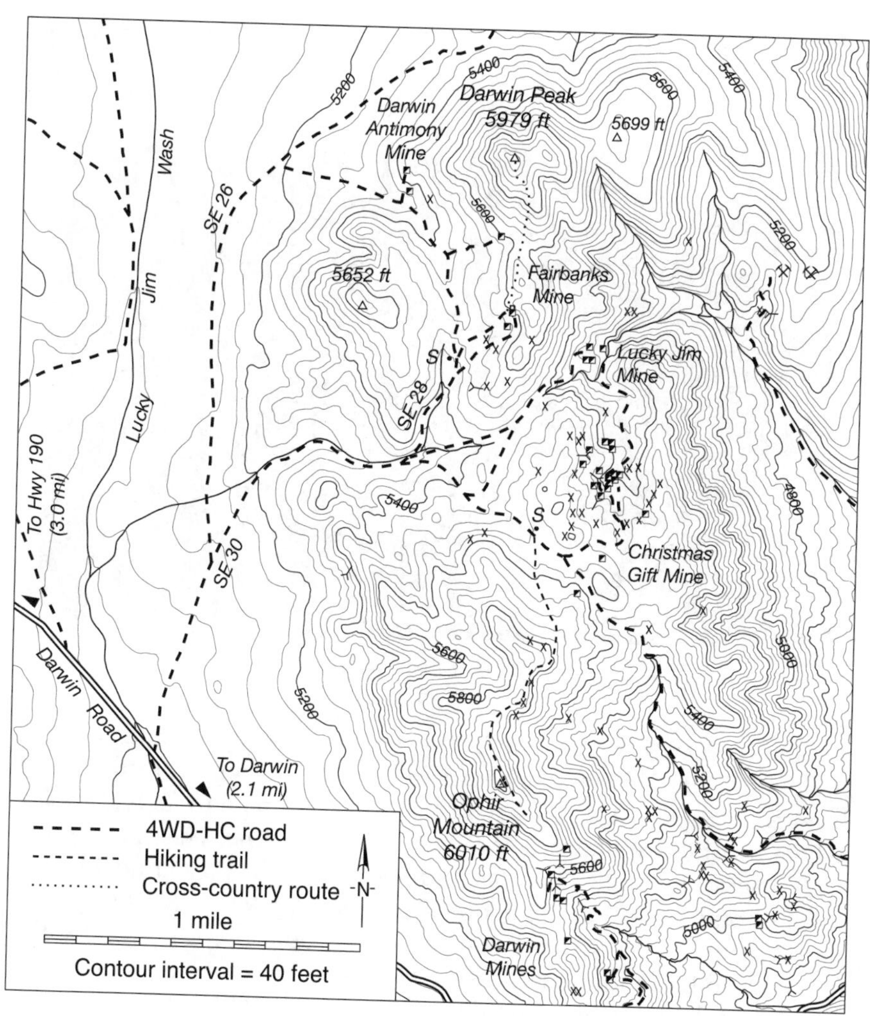

Darwin Hills		
	Dist.(mi)	Elev.(ft)
Trailhead on SE 30	0.0	5,525
End of road/start of trail	0.55	5,860
Ophir Mountain	0.9	6,010
Road junction (SE 28-SE 28A)	0.0	5,450
Top of SE 28A road	0.25	5,600
Saddle	0.5	~5,615
Darwin Peak	0.8	5,979

The historic mining town of Darwin from Ophir Mountain

On the Darwin Peak climb the vegetation, geology, and distance are similar but it is wilder because there is no trail. From the SE 28 road walk up the steep side road (SE 28A) 0.25 mile to its high point, where it curves right just before the Fairbanks Mine. Then head north over a set of low hills, and descend about 60 feet to a saddle. Darwin Peak's southeast shoulder looms up ahead, spiked with sharp outcrops. Aim for the left side of the lowest outcrop, then follow the shoulder to the summit, bypassing the higher outcrops on either side, whichever is less windy that day... Like on Ophir Mountain, the syncline's sheared rim was overturned by intense strains from the Coso Range batholith. The outcrops lean to the east, with their top side *older* than their bottom side. The climb is a little steep but easy, over sparse litters of limestone plates and occasional septarian concretions.

The summit of Darwin Peak is a mohawk of overturned blue-gray limestone. The views are much the same as on Ophir Mountain, minus Darwin but with the bonus of a sweeping panorama to the north of the burnt-sienna and blood-red volcanic ledges of Darwin Plateau and the perpendicular gash of Rainbow Canyon. After a winter storm, when a veneer of snow covers the desert summits and the Sierra Nevada are solid white, the spectacle is breathtaking.

■

DARWIN CANYON

Punctuated with idyllic waterfalls and irrigated by a lovely perennial creek, the deep narrows of Darwin Canyon are among the most lush and beautiful in the park. The short walk to the lower waterfall or through verdant China Garden Spring in the upper gorge are wonderful illustrations of the miracle of water in the desert. The more challenging climb to the upper waterfall is a gem for the experienced hiker.

General Information
Jurisdiction: Death Valley National Park, Darwin Falls Wilderness
Road status: Hiking on trails and cross-country; graded and dirt access
Upper Darwin Falls: 1.2 mi, 390 ft up, 80 ft down one way / Class 2
Upper gorge: 0.8 mi, 20 ft up, 130 ft down one way / very easy
Main attractions: Lush narrows, waterfalls, flora, birds, rock climbing
USGS 7.5' topo map: Darwin
Maps: pp. 485*, *419, 457*

Location and Access

This magical little place is at the north end of the Argus Range, a few miles west of Panamint Springs. Like the nearby town and several geographical features, it is named after Dr. Darwin French, who established a base camp here when he led his first prospecting expedition to Death Valley in 1850.

To access the lower canyon and Darwin Falls, from Panamint Springs drive Highway 190 west 1 mile to the graded Darwin Road on the left. Coming from the other direction, this junction is 6.9 miles east of Father Crowley Point. This road was part of Bob Eichbaum's original Death Valley Toll Road to Stovepipe Wells, which went through Darwin. It follows the wide bed of Darwin Wash 2.4 miles to a fork. Make a right and park 200 feet further at the turn-out just above the wash. A two-wheel-drive vehicle with standard clearance can easily make it this far.

To access the upper canyon, make a left at the fork. Continue 3.8 winding miles up along the side of Zinc Hill, then down to the wash of Darwin Canyon. This road requires good clearance (see *Zinc Hill*). At the wash, turn right at the junction and go 1.1 miles to China Garden Spring. The alternative is to go through Darwin. Make a left at the stop sign in town and go 7.4 miles down the graded, then primitive Darwin Road to the junction, then left 1.1 miles to China Garden Spring.

Natural History

One of the pleasures of Darwin Canyon is the wild diversity of its vegetation. The drier lower and upper canyons are vegetated with common desert plants, mainly cattle spinach, rabbitbrush, and four-wing saltbush. Many wild flowers grow here in the spring. The ones you are likely to see are prince's plume, globemallow, evening primrose, Mojave aster, phacelia, the showy desert prickle poppy, spotted langloisia, and bright-yellow monkeyflower. In contrast, the permanent creek in the mid-canyon supports a dense tree canopy and shrub understory. The dominant trees are Goodding willows; there are also a few cottonwoods. At places they are in fierce competition with salt cedar, a pest introduced from the Mediterranean. The creek bed is lined with water-loving plants—watercress, rush, cattail, wild celery, and beautiful stream orchis.

Expectedly, many bird species inhabit this ecological island, while others, like warblers, use it as a rest area during migration. The latest species count is around 80, from goldfinches to wrens, roadrunners, hummingbirds, swifts, sparrows, falcons, and red-tailed hawks. A few endangered species have also been spotted—yellow-breasted chat, loggerhead shrike, Cooper's hawk, and golden eagle. Even if you cannot identify them, look forward to their lively songs and chirps echoing off the walls and to the insects they feed on—butterflies, dragonflies, grasshoppers, and water striders. If you see a batrachian lazily hobbling along, it is either a red-spotted toad or a western toad. In fact, this may be the only place in the desert where they co-exist.

Route Description

The lower canyon. From the road, hike down to the broad wash and follow the developing trail 0.2 mile to a metal barricade (the site of the former parking area). Beyond it, the trail wanders up the open wash, mostly to the left of it. It is faint at places, but follow it carefully to avoid creating new tracks, as this place is heavily visited. The pipeline running along the west bank is diverting a portion of the creek flow down to Panamint Springs. In the colder months, the creek usually flows through this part of the open wash, but in the summer you will have to hike some distance to find it.

Lower Darwin Falls. After 0.8 mile, the canyon turns to narrows and the magic begins. Rabbitbrush and indigo bush abruptly leave the way to a shady world of willow, cattail, and rushes, and the desert silence to the enchanted sound of flowing water. On a scorching summer day, this cool oasis will strain your credulity. For a few hundred yards, the trail winds along the sun-dappled creek, under tall trees sheltered by the high-rising walls of the narrows. The local rock is a dark monzonite formed about 180 million years ago. Because its content in biotite, hornblende, and quartz vary from place to place, its aspect changes markedly throughout the narrows.

The vegetation is so dense that you will not see the first waterfall until the last moment. Here the creek leaps over a slanted wall and plunges 18 feet into a deep pool. Moss and maidenhair fern cling to the wet walls. Drizzle from the fall and the smell of moldering wood fill the air. The towering walls block the view in all directions but upward, creating a secluded environment, divorced from the desert.

Pool and cattail at Lower Darwin Falls

Upper Darwin Falls. Although most visitors turn around at this point, the best is yet to come—the upper waterfall. However, this hike is not for everybody. Getting there requires some climbing and is physically demanding. There is no trail, the route is not marked, and it is easy to get lost or stuck. Do not undertake it casually. To circumvent the first waterfall, climb the east canyon wall starting about 100 feet downstream of the pool. The idea is to reach just high enough to find a safe passage around the sheer wall that frames the waterfall. The optimum route goes something like this: a climb up a short cleft, a trail walk up a talus to a 10-foot wall of step-like rock, a walk along a broad, level slickrock ledge parallel to the creek, and finally a climb down a series of hard, angular rock steps that drop back to the creek like a giant stairway. This is only about 100 yards long, and the monzonite ledges are sturdy and relatively wide, but do not attempt it if you have a fear of heights. Many visitors fail to find this route and attempt the west side instead, but I have never found a way through on that side, and if there is one, it is much harder.

At the end of this bypass you are just below the base of the second waterfall. Its 5-foot plume of whitewater crashes noisily into a deep pool trapped between finely polished walls. The third waterfall, just behind it, tumbles 12 feet over the overhanging lip of a circular grotto. A short distance beyond, the narrows' walls loom vertically well over 100 feet, hiding from view the fourth and highest waterfall. To get to it, climb the steep rock talus on the north side of the creek. After gaining 40 or 50 feet of elevation, you will be level with a breach in the wall to your left. Walking through it will put you at the bottom of a majestic well of dark slickrock filled with the sounds of falling water. Tucked

Darwin Canyon

	Dist.(mi)	Elev.(ft)
Lower gorge (NPS)		
Parking	0.0	2,480
Lower Darwin Falls	1.0	2,760
Second and third waterfall	1.1	~2,790
Upper Darwin Falls	1.2	~2,820
Upper gorge (BLM)		
China Garden Spring	0.0	3,129
Spring head/trailhead	0.65	~3,045
End of trail	0.8	~3,020

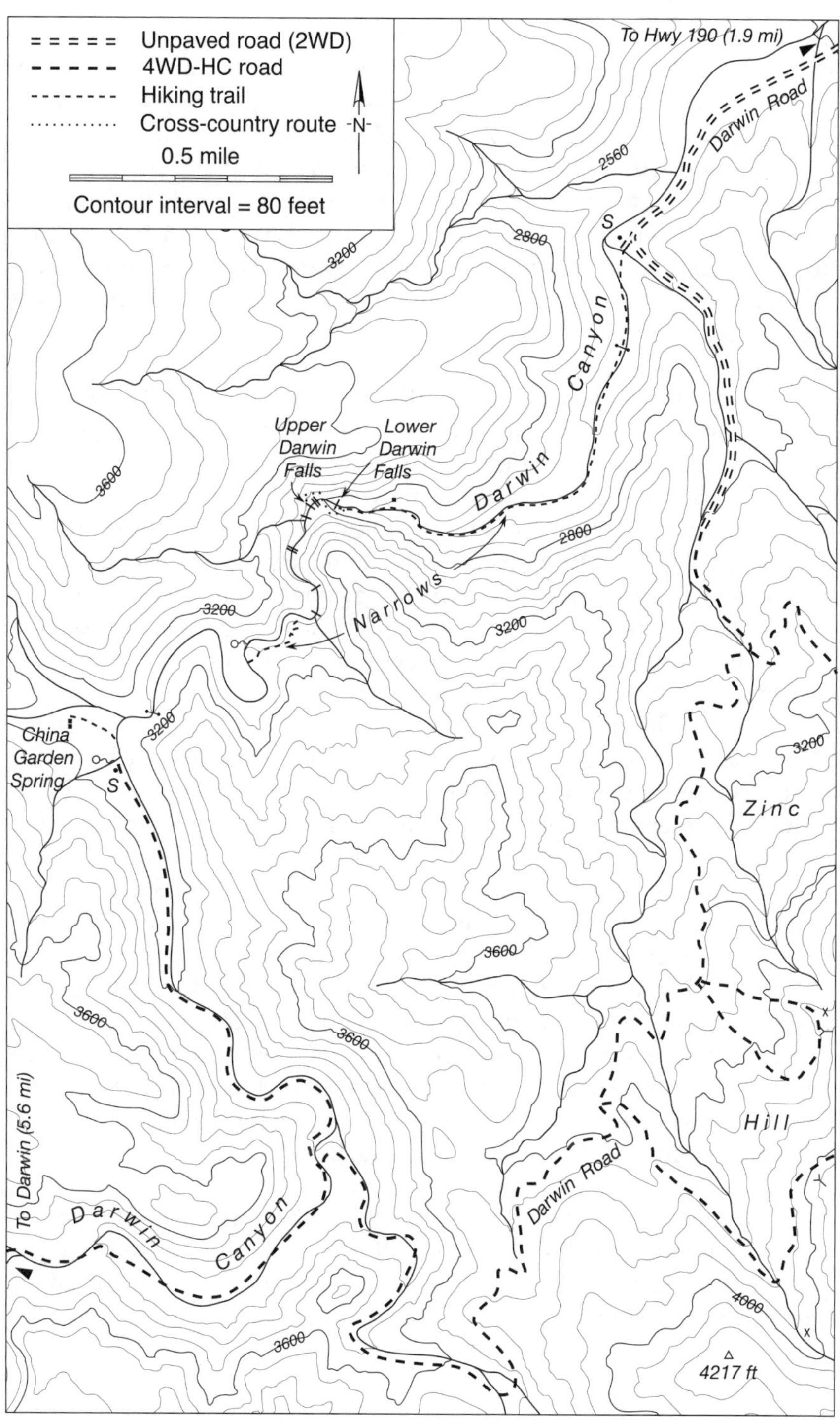

Unpaved road (2WD)
4WD-HC road
Hiking trail
Cross-country route
N
0.5 mile
Contour interval = 80 feet
To Hwy 190 (1.9 mi)
Darwin Road
2560
2800
3200
S
Darwin Canyon
Upper Darwin Falls
Lower Darwin Falls
3600
2800
Narrows
3200
3200
3200
China Garden Spring
S
3200
Zinc
Hill
3600
3600
3600
3600
Darwin Road
To Darwin (5.6 mi)
Darwin Canyon
3600
4000
4217 ft

away at the far end of it, Upper Darwin Falls glide in one unbroken ribbon 60 feet down a slender groove into a deep pool of cold water. This is perhaps the most beautiful waterfall in the park, a rare gem in an awesome site that will make you feel humble and small.

Climbing through the rest of the gorge to China Garden Spring can be done, and it is exciting, but it requires some technical climbing and it is not recommended by the NPS. Return the way you came instead. To see the upper end of this spectacular gorge, drive around to China Garden Spring and hike down from there through the BLM portion of the canyon.

China Garden Spring. As you drive down the dry and wide-open bed of Darwin Wash and approach China Garden Spring, you will be amazed once again by the power of water. Off in the distance, in the midst of an austere landscape of barren rocks, rise the improbable sight of a thick cluster of mature cottonwoods. Spend a little time at the spring. The large tin house, ore bin, and loading platform behind it are the remains of a small mill, which may have been used as a custom mill for local mines. The trees at the spring shade a derelict residential area, a tiny creek, and a pond of cool water with colorful and unexpected residents.

To get to the upper end of the gorge, hike down the wash below China Garden Spring. This part of the canyon is as uneventful as the lower canyon is action-packed. Barren hills compose a desolate background to an empty wash where gravel wins over vegetation. But not for long. After a few pronounced meanders, you will reach the head of the abundant spring that feeds Darwin Canyon's providential creek, and the scenery changes instantly. The wash is choked with trees and riparian vegetation so dense that further progress would be tedious at best. Instead, take the short high trail that bypasses the vegetation on the right (east) side. It ends after 300 yards, on the edge of a steep ravine, within earshot of the creek and waterfalls. You are now inside the park, so turn around to help preserve the core of this wonderful canyon. Take your time. There are fine viewpoints along the way to admire the dense selva that fills the gorge below.

Caution. More than ever, please respect this rare oasis. Stay on the trail. Do not step on the vegetation. If other visitors are sharing this place with you, respect their need for silence. When climbing, make sure no one is underneath you in case you dislodge a rock.

■

ZINC HILL

A century ago, when Zinc Hill was one of the state's largest zinc producers, the miners built trails all over the hill's inhospitable slopes to access the high country. The longest of these historic paths is still the best way to reach the mountain's highest summit, across impressively tall volcanic taluses looking out over the high Sierras. Expect a rough access road, surprisingly diverse geology, wild burros, stunning views from the stark summit, and a brisk workout.

General Information

Jurisdiction: Public lands (BLM)
Road status: Hiking on trails and cross-country; HC-4WD access road
Zinc Hill: 2.3 mi, 1,940 ft up, 30 ft down one way/difficult
Zinc Hill loop: 5.7 mi, 2,090 ft up loop/difficult
Main attractions: Mining trail, high views of Panamint Valley, mining
USGS 7.5' topo maps: Panamint Springs, Darwin
Maps: pp. 489*, *419, 457*

Location and Access

Zinc Hill is the northernmost main summit in the Argus Range, overlooking northern Panamint Valley. It is accessed from the Darwin Road, once the main thoroughfare connecting Death Valley to the town of Darwin and points west. This road starts on the south side of Highway 190, 1 mile west of Panamint Springs, or 29.7 miles east of Highway 136. Driving it is an adventure in itself. It starts as a broad washboard where even motor homes manage to creep their way to the popular Darwin Falls turnoff. Then it climbs out of Darwin Canyon and turns into a battlefield of rocks. The mountain that soon rises sharply 1,800 feet to the east is Zinc Hill. During the world wars it was extensively exploited for lead, silver, and gold, but its greatest wealth was zinc. The five side roads that branch off along the way lead to these historic mines. The second side road (SE 61), marked by twin ore bins and the stone ruins of a mill and camp, climbs to the Zinc Hill Mine. In the 1910s it was a full-fledged operation serviced by an aerial tramway, an inclined railway, and a mill. The access road is roughest just south of SE 61. Deep holes gape right below jagged bedrock; both high clearance and power are essential. After 5.1 miles the road reaches its high point. Drive 0.2 mile past it, to the right U-shaped curve at

Panamint Lake, Lake Hill, and the Cottonwood Mountains from Zinc Hill

the bottom of the steep grade. The way to Zinc Hill is the rough road that climbs on the left in the curve. Park at this junction.

Route Description

True to miners' general aversion to switchbacks, the old mining road goes straight up a narrow ridge, steep at first, then a gutter of sharp black lava. This area is mostly Pliocene basalt flows; the landscape has the typical looks of volcanic fields—dark, scantily vegetated, more desert-like than most. Absolutely nothing hints that it hides in its folds Darwin Canyon's sheer-walled gorge and luxuriant stream... After 0.75 mile the road crests at a four-way junction. A distinctive pointed hill with horizontal bands of white marble rises a short distance to the east. To its left there is a much taller slope of quartz monzonite outcrops and boulders. This is where the miners found this mountain's riches, at the contact between the marble and this pluton.

Two flat summits separated by a shallow saddle fill the horizon beyond the marble hill. The leftmost summit is Zinc Hill's high point. To get to the miner's trail that climbs almost all the way to it, stay on the main road 150 yards as it drops south to a wash, crosses it, and angles right. The trailhead, marked by a cairn, is 150 yards further again, on the left. If you cannot find it, return to the junction and take

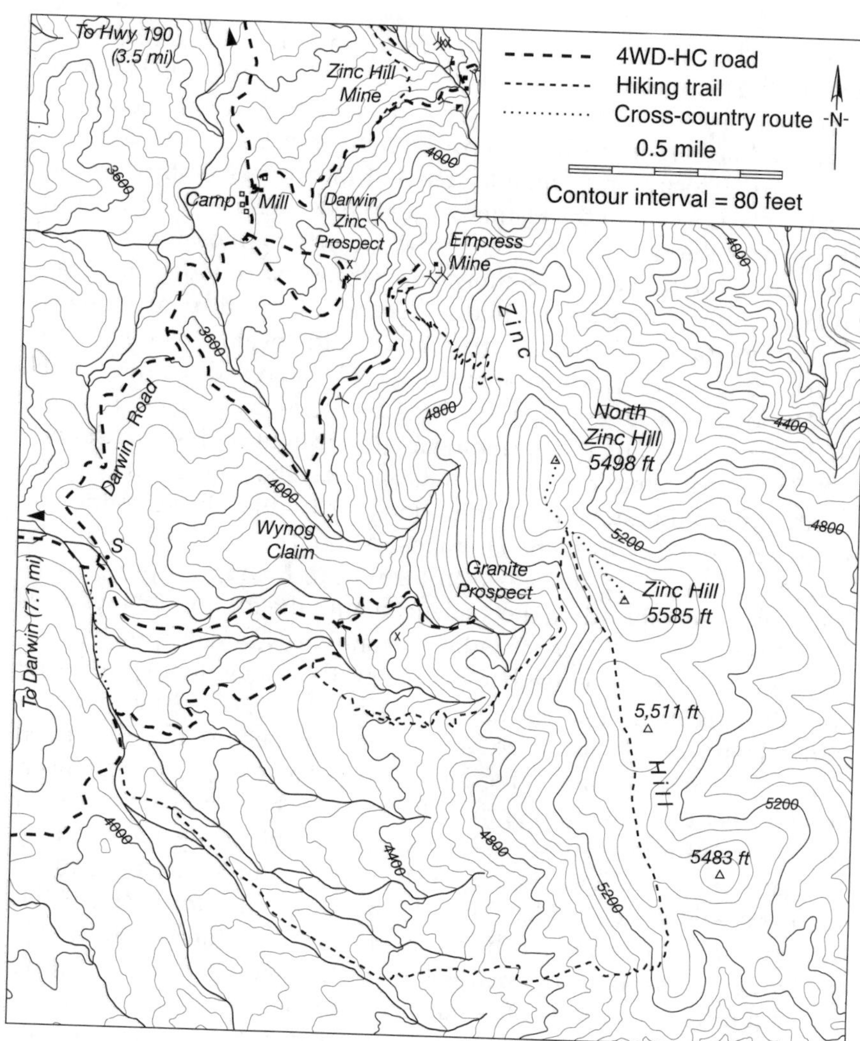

Zinc Hill

	Dist.(mi)	Elev.(ft)
Darwin Canyon Road	0.0	3,675
Junction at top of mining road	0.75	4,235
Mining trail (trailhead)	0.9	4,205
Saddle on crest	2.05	5,340
North Zinc Hill	(0.25)	5,498
Zinc Hill	2.25	5,585
Loop back via mining trail	5.7	3,675

the second road on the right. It winds up into the crooked ravine on the north side of the marble hill. Soon after the road ends below the Granite Prospect (0.5 mile), the wash splits. Scramble up the right fork to the saddle behind the hill, and pick up the trail 40-60 feet above it.

Narrow, rocky, and prone to frequent mood swings, this trail is a treat. It starts as a dim track among squat creosote bush. Rainwater has stripped its thin gravel cover, exposing underlying mosaics of smooth limestone. The trail climbs southeast toward a low rounded ridge, and follows its flank east for a while. Where the slope steepens it switchbacks three times, then angles right toward the peak. Beyond, the terrain is tall, steep, and unstable flows of broken reddish and black basalt, too rough to support anything but scrawny bushes. The trail traverses these giant slides unflinchingly, straight and at a sustained tilt. Below the summit, it readjusts its aim and shoots up to the saddle north of the summit. Since its inception, this trail has been trodden by more burros and coyotes than humans. Without it, the ascent would be unpleasant. With it you get into a rhythm, heart pumping, rocks crunching, steadily riding the avalanche until the ground finally levels off at the saddle on the crest, and Panamint Valley bursts into view.

This is a sight to remember. Far below, the valley floor spreads out for miles, its halo of dunes and long dry lake enclosed by immense alluvial fans. The Cottonwood Mountains loom behind it, their banded walls an open scroll displaying 300 million years of history. From nearly 4,000 feet up, Panamint Springs looks tiny. The two peaks on either side of the saddle, a short cross-country scramble away, offer equally spectacular views. Zinc Hill's highest summit to the south is a crinkled field of basalt, dark and bleak. In the other direction, North Zinc Hill is all granitic, a light-colored hump of rounded boulders artfully displayed on soft sand. It commands even better views of Darwin Plateau to the north, a sprawling aftermath of red volcanics. From anywhere the Sierra Nevada's formidable crest dominates the western horizon, from Olancha Peak to Mount Williamson.

This little trail has more to say. If you stay on it, it will take you on a grand tour of Zinc Hill. From the saddle it wanders south, across volcanic dregs, to a narrow, subdued ridge. Near the south end of the basalt flow the trail veers west and switchbacks down over nicely folded Paleozoic strata. At the foot of the mountain, it follows a straight low ridge for 0.7 mile to finally end, after 3.8 miles, back at the mining road not far below the upper trailhead. To complete the loop, walk the road north 500 feet to where it makes a right hook across a wash. Then hike down the wash 0.4 mile to your starting point.

■

STONE CANYON

Stone Canyon, a popular destination among four-wheelers on their way to Lookout, is an 800-foot-deep gash across the hard-rock spine of the Argus Range. In the roadless upper canyon, protected as a wilderness, hikers will enjoy several springs, a seldom-visited gold mine, beautiful rocks and falls, and a spectacular amphitheater. If you have a full day, you can hike back via the historic ruins of the Modoc Mine, high on Stone Canyon's south rim.

General Information

Jurisdiction: Bureau of Land Management, Argus Range Wilderness
Road status: Road in lower canyon (4WD/HC), roadless upper canyon
Defense Mine: 0.9 mi, 820 ft up, 0 ft down one way/easy
Imlay Mine: 2.2 mi, 1,400 ft up, 0 ft down one way/moderate
Darwin Wash overlook: 4.2 mi, 2,390 ft up, 20 ft down one way/moder.
Main attractions: Springs, mines, scenic canyon, viewpoints
USGS 7.5' topo maps: Panamint Springs, Revenue Canyon*
Maps: pp. 495*, 501*, *419*, *457*

Location and Access

Stone Canyon is in the northern Argus Range, north and west of Lookout Mountain. To get to it, drive the Panamint Valley Road 7.4 miles south from Highway 190 to the signed Minnietta Road on the right. Coming from the south, this junction is 6.4 miles north from the Trona-Wildrose Road. Drive this road west 3.6 miles over Ash Hill to the foot of a wide fan where the road merges with the Nadeau Trail, coming in from the left and signed P 105. Continue north 0.4 mile to the junction with the Nadeau Trail Cutoff on the left, at 10 o'clock. If you are driving a high-clearance vehicle, go northwest then west on the Nadeau Trail Cutoff 1.7 miles, along the base of Lookout Mountain, to the junction with the Defense Mine Road at the mouth of Stone Canyon. Otherwise go as far as you can and hike the rest of the way.

Route Description

Lower Stone Canyon. The lower part of Stone Canyon is a scenic and colorful gorge. The area past the first side canyon is framed by an impressive high wall on its north side, cleaved by two steep and narrow side canyons worth a closer look. Here as on the canyon fan, many flowering plants brighten the desert year-round. Even in the winter you may find mohavea, desert prickle poppy, and brittlebush still in bloom. In the spring many more plants join the show, including sacred datura, stingbush, locoweed, and beavertail cactus. Along the way there is a short constriction where the road is badly damaged and four-wheel drive and good clearance are mandatory.

After a wiggly mile, the Defense Mine Road reaches an open area and splits at a complicated four-road junction (see map). The road on the right is the Defense Mine Road. The road on the left climbs 0.45 mile to a saddle on the crest of Lookout Mountain and continues to the Modoc Mine (see *Lookout and the Modoc Mine*). The rougher road straight ahead, the original Nadeau Trail, ends up at the same saddle. The next 0.4-mile stretch of canyon is interrupted by four climbable falls, and it is off-limits to motor vehicles. It is possible to drive a little further up Stone Canyon by going up to the saddle, where a side road descends west to the wash and bypasses the falls. But it is rough, and the Argus Range Wilderness boundary is only 0.3 mile farther up the wash. Vandals periodically remove the boundary sign. So if you drive there, do not go by tire tracks; they are likely made by irresponsible drivers. Keep track of your mileage instead (the fine for driving into a wilderness approaches a king's ransom). If you came here to hike, it is just as easy to park at the four-road junction and start there.

The Defense Mine. From the four-road junction in Stone Canyon, the Defense Mine Road cuts north to a side canyon, then ascends its steep and narrow wash to the Defense Mine. This is one of the worst local roads still open to vehicles. When I was there the gaps between the boulders in the wash were wide enough to swallow a Greyhound bus; it is much easier to walk it. If you drive it, remember to stop at the usually unmarked wilderness boundary 0.25 mile up the wash. The road ends 0.4 mile further at a truck-loading area, just below the mine's spectacular ore-loading structure.

In spite of its modest appearance, the Defense Mine was fairly rich. It hosted a wealth of lead-copper-manganese minerals, including cerussite, cryptomelane, pyrolusite, bindheimite, linarite, caledonite, and brochantite. Its main ore was galena and coronadite, an uncommon black, fibrous oxide of lead and manganese. First discovered in the 1870s, in the heyday of the Modoc Mining District, this deposit was not exploited until the 1930s, when a few hundred tons of ore were mined from a small shaft. During World War II it yielded mostly lead, a strategic metal then essential for national security. In 1947, Lee Foreman, who had just cleaned out the Modoc Mine, and his partner William Skinner, purchased the mine and worked it every year until

Ore-loading complex at the Defense Mine in Stone Canyon

1957. They made a small fortune extracting at least 7,000 tons of ore rich enough to be shipped unrefined. The Defense Mine thus became the district's third largest producer, with a total production of about 3,200 tons of lead and 8 tons of silver worth 1.3 million dollars.

The massive ore-loading wooden structure at the bottom of the site is one of the largest in the region, and a precious piece of mining engineering from the 1940s. It was originally designed to service the lower tunnel, located 40 yards behind it. The loading structure has two parts, a long rail track that linked the tunnel to the chute, and the chute that dumped the ore into trucks parked under it. The tunnel, unusual for its length and high ceiling, is reached by scrambling up the rough wash at the foot of the chute. Sunk in 1949, it did not produce anything, but later on it was connected to the upper workings and used as a haulageway. The shack just outside the tunnel housed a workshop.

To access the mine's two higher levels of workings, strung out on the steep slope above the ore chute, climb the faint foot trail just to the left of the lower tunnel. The crosscut adit 125 feet higher up the slope is the upper level. It was driven 220 feet to a large ore body known as the 106 stope, now a dark and intricate cavern. Two raises connect it to the original glory hole above it. Deeper in, an inclined gallery drops 35 feet to the intermediate level, which exploited the Foreman ore body. This was the mine's richest: one large pocket yielded 4,400 tons of 25%

lead ore! The ore was mined with slushers and lowered to the loading area via the 540-foot cableway outside the adit. The glory hole from the 1930s is another 80 feet up the slope.

The mid-canyon. This part of the canyon is not too steep and is pleasant to walk, not particularly spectacular but scenic and ever changing. The first point of interest is the lower spring, on the south bank. Some years it is a profuse mass of greenery; at other times it shrivels to a hanging garden of ephedra and yellow grass vying for what little water oozes out of the mud. A little further, the ruin of a large, well-constructed stone house with thick walls rests on a low terrace. Next is Jack Gunn Spring. Named after the historic owner of the Minnietta Mine, it is the only perennial water supply for miles. A few inches of water usually fill the bottom of a 10-foot-deep vertical slit blasted into a rock wall. A stone ruin, a rusted tank, and scattered pipes attest to past exploitation of this spring for the Defense Mine. If you have binoculars, climb the opposite slope and stay still. It often takes only minutes before birds come flying in.

Windy and narrower, the next stretch of canyon is flanked by high walls of cleaved granite. The wash is punctuated by easy falls and slants, some of them finely carved in white marble. The biggest falls are bypassed by short manmade trails, some of them blasted into

Stone Canyon		
	Dist.(mi)	Elev.(ft)
Roadless canyon		
Four-road junction	0.0	~3,680
End of road/Wilderness bdry	0.7	4,190
Jack Gunn Spring	1.5	4,510
Imlay Mine Cabin	2.0	4,880
Imlay Mine upper tunnel	(0.15)	5,080
Upper canyon road (junction)	3.7	5,795
Darwin Wash overlook	4.2	6,052
Defense Mine		
Four-road junction	0.0	~3,680
Wilderness bdry	0.25	3,800
Ore chute	0.75	4,190
Glory hole	0.9	4,500

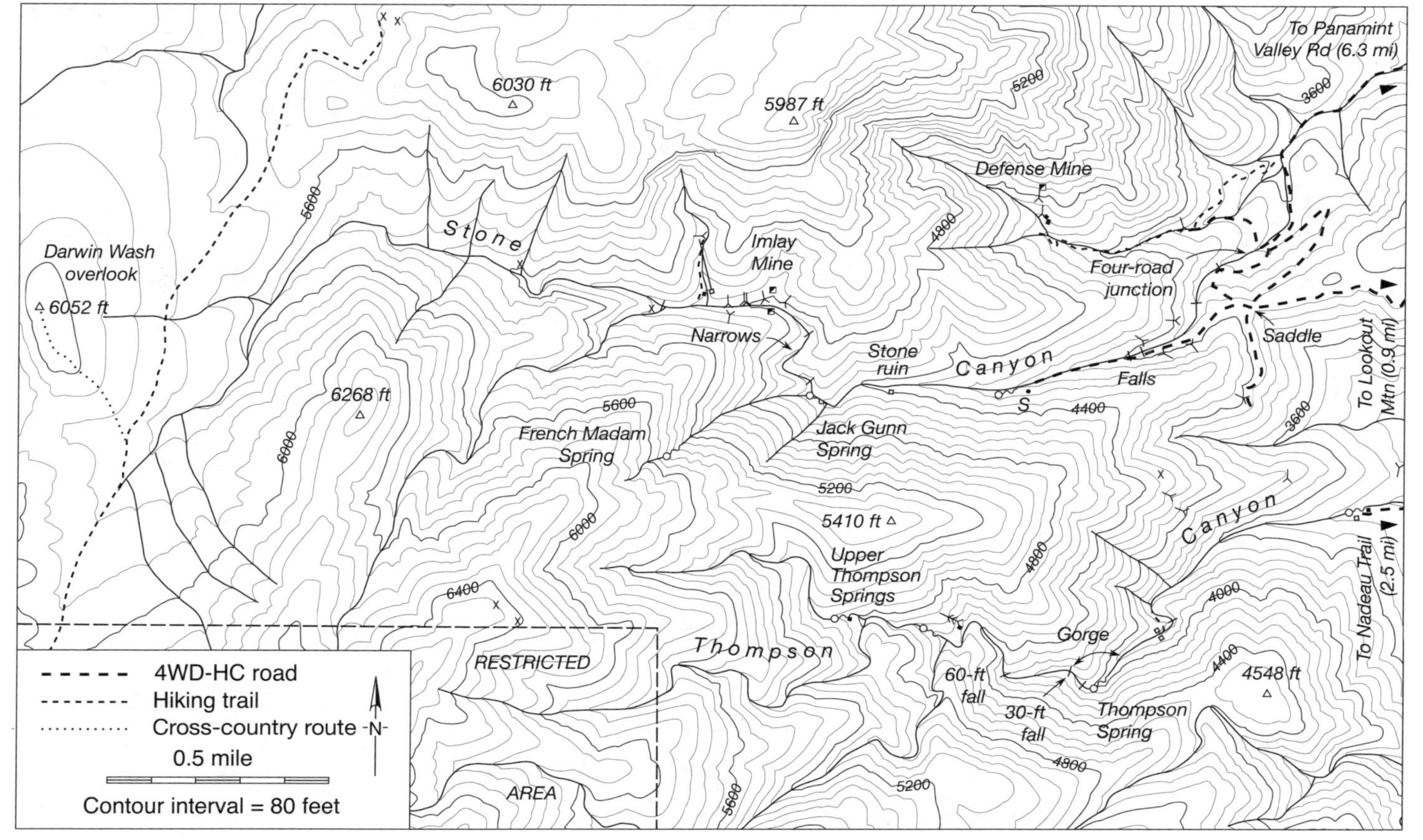
To Panamint Valley Rd (6.3 mi)
6030 ft
5987 ft
5200
3600
5600
Defense Mine
Stone
Darwin Wash overlook
6052 ft
Imlay Mine
4800
Four-road junction
Narrows
Stone ruin
Canyon
Saddle
Falls
To Lookout Mtn (0.9 mi)
6268 ft
5600
French Madam Spring
Jack Gunn Spring
4400
3600
6000
5200
5410 ft
6000
Canyon
Upper Thompson Springs
4800
6400
4000
To Nadeau Trail (2.5 mi)
Gorge
RESTRICTED
Thompson
4400
4548 ft
4WD-HC road
Hiking trail
Cross-country route
-N-
0.5 mile
Contour interval = 80 feet
60-ft fall
30-ft fall
Thompson Spring
4800
5200
AREA
5600

bedrock, for pack animals to access the mines. Wild burros very much enjoy the old haunts of their ancestors, perhaps drawn by the canyon's easy-going pace. From start to finish you share the nearly continuous trails that they have plowed in the gravel, often two parallel tracks, as if the burros use a different lane for uphill and downhill traffic.

The next point of interest is the Imlay Mine. Owned prior to the 1950s by Paul Imlay of Lone Pine, it has no production record. Its workings line the north side of the wash: five short tunnels and a 40-foot inclined shaft crowned by a crude headframe. The ore is iron and manganese oxides, with a little azurite and malachite, occurring as in white marble of the Lee Flat Limestone. The most interesting area is at the next side canyon, where an ore chute and a lonesome cabin with empty shelves guard the derelict property. The steep, rock-strewn trail behind the cabin is well worth the walk. It climbs into the side canyon to the upper tunnel, passing by a collapsed tramway tower and a stranded mine car before scooting under the tramway cable. Be careful: the 70-foot upper tunnel ends at a 15-foot shaft. The true prize is the scenery that opens up behind the tunnel, a vast amphitheater ringed by the sweeping curve of a sheer two-toned escarpment.

Although the name "Stone" is applicable to just about every canyon between here and Moab, Utah, it is particularly well suited to this canyon. Because it cuts through all three basic types of rocks (igneous, sedimentary, and metamorphic), its variety of "stones" is remarkable. One of them is jasper. A form of chalcedony, it outcrops at several places and it is a fairly common sight in the wash. Stone Canyon's jasper covers a broad spectrum of attractive colors, from yellow to mustard, cinnamon, and light green.

Upper Stone Canyon. In a range that has been mostly annexed for military purposes, the upper canyon offers the only easy route to the crest of the Argus Range, including a scenic viewpoint—Darwin Wash overlook. It is not too far: 1.7 miles beyond the Imlay Mine Cabin, after winding past a few falls and sculpted peaks, you will reach a junction with an abandoned road where the canyon opens up (elev. 5,795'). Do not bother going up the road (south): in a third of a mile it enters the China Lake Naval Weapons Center. Instead, hike north-northwest cross-country up the broad open ridge to the 6,052-ft dome (0.5 mile) for rare views of this forbidden desert. Below the dome's abrupt slope, the range tumbles down in rolling hills to the vast alluvial plain of Darwin Wash, backed in the distance by the sepia slopes of the Coso Range, and the high Sierras far beyond.

■

LOOKOUT AND THE MODOC MINE

Located on the narrow summit of a low mountain overlooking the valley, the Modoc Mine and its camp Lookout rank among the region's most scenic destinations. The Modoc Mine was one of the greatest local producers: between 1875 and the early 1890s, over one million dollars worth of silver came out of its two smelters. Getting there is half the fun, either by driving the rough access road to the mountain top or by hiking one of the short trails that burros used to transport charcoal up to the smelters. The mine's cavernous tunnel openings are impressive, the views are superb, and the stone ruins of Lookout moving tributes to early mining in Panamint Valley.

General Information

Jurisdiction: Private claims on BLM land
Road status: Hiking on trails; access via primitive road (2WD or HC)
Lookout via China Wall Tr: 1.7 mi, 1,350 ft up, 20 ft down one way/mod.
Lookout trail loop: 3.8 mi, 1,370 ft up loop/moderate
Main attractions: Historic silver mines, ghost town, panoramic views
USGS 7.5' topo maps: Panamint Springs, Revenue Canyon*
Maps: pp. 495*, 501, *419*, *457*

Location and Access

The Modoc Mine and its camp Lookout are high on Lookout Mountain, in the northern Argus Range. From Highway 190, drive the Panamint Valley Road 7.4 miles south to the signed Minnietta Road on the right. Drive this road 3.6 miles west to a junction, where it merges with the Nadeau Trail coming in from the left, signed P 105. Continue north 0.4 mile to the junction with the Nadeau Trail Cutoff on the left (see map). Lookout Mountain is the prominent mountain to the west. From this junction, there is a choice of two ways to get to the mine.

The first option is hiking the China Wall Trail. To get to it, turn left on the Nadeau Trail Cutoff and drive 0.35 mile to a junction. The left fork is the way to Lookout. It gets rapidly rough, so park at this junction. This starting point is accessible with a standard-clearance vehicle.

The second option is driving through Stone Canyon. Turn left also on the Nadeau Trail Cutoff, and follow it along the base of Lookout Mountain, northwest then west, 1.7 miles to the mouth of Stone Canyon. Continue up the canyon wash 1 mile to a fork, in a more open area. The road to the Modoc Mine makes a left, then in 100 feet a sharp

Main building at Lookout

left again, and climbs in one long switchback 0.45 mile to a saddle on the crest of Lookout Mountain. Turn left and continue east along the mountain crest. After 0.9 mile, the road splits. The right fork ends in 0.3 mile at the top of Lookout Mountain. The left fork ends in 0.7 mile at the Modoc Mine—watch near the end for the open shaft in the middle of the road! High clearance is required past the Nadeau Junction.

History

In April 1875, while Darwin and Panamint City were booming, a new silver bonanza was set off on the eastern slope of the Argus Range overlooking Panamint Valley. Prospector B. E. Ball discovered there an enormous lode assaying as much as 300 ounces of silver per ton and 50% lead. One of the first investors attracted by his find was Senator George Hearst—his son would later build Hearst Castle—who promptly bought the claims and formed the Modoc Consolidated Mining Company. Inspired by the fine views from the mine, the small camp that grew near it was named Lookout.

The ore occurred in large chambers and veins, and the tunnels quickly reached over 1,000 feet into the ground. Early on, the ore was teamed across the valley to the Panamint City smelters. In 1877, desert veteran Remi Nadeau, freighter for the Panamint and Cerro Gordo mines, expanded his business and built a rough trail along the eastern foot of the Argus Range for his mules to bring supplies to the mine (see *The Nadeau Trail*). Nadeau delivered Hearst's order for two 30-ton smelting furnaces, which were erected near the mine. First fired up in October 1876, the smelters produced around 10 tons of silver-lead bullion every day, worth several thousand dollars.

Ironically, one of Hearst's main difficulties was supplying the furnaces not with ore, but with charcoal to reduce the ore. Charcoal was initially obtained from pinyon pines harvested on the higher slopes of the Argus Range. By the end of 1876, this scant supply was nearly exhausted, and resourceful Hearst turned to Wildrose Canyon's timber belt, across the valley in the Panamint Mountains. Over the next few months, the Modoc company erected ten large stone kilns on the canyon floor (see *Wildrose Canyon*). Nadeau was hired again, this time to haul the charcoal to the Modoc Mine. In the meantime Lookout had kept pace with the boom. In May 1877, it boasted 30 or 40 wooden houses and stone buildings, three saloons, two general stores, and a bank. Three times a week a stagecoach ambled its way between Lookout, Darwin, and Panamint City. For a time the area was prosperous. By summer the furnaces had churned out over $600,000 worth of bullion. A year later the figure exceeded one million dollars.

For reasons not well understood, mining operations changed dramatically in the summer of 1879. Perhaps because it had run out of rich smelting ore, the Modoc company shut down its furnaces and the charcoal kilns. But there was still plenty of good ore. Just a few years later, the mine's early success sparked the creation of the Modoc Mining District, which encompassed the Modoc Mine and several rich neighboring properties such as the Minnietta Mine. Although the kilns were never used again, mining continued, albeit at a slower rate. New ore bodies were discovered, and by 1890 the Modoc Mine's production had reached around $1,900,000.

The mine was operated sporadically for many decades, up until fairly recently. Hopeful lessees periodically took advantage of surges in the price of silver and further explored its tunnels or scavenged its old tailings and smelter slags. The most profitable effort was led by Lee Foreman, of Panamint Springs. Between 1945 and 1947, he retrieved $450,000 of silver, mostly from the historic slags. By then the Modoc Mine had yielded around $2,400,000, which made it one of the richest silver mines in the Death Valley region.

Route Description

The China Wall Trail. In historic times, two shortcuts gave quick access to the Modoc Mine: the Pack Trail, built for pack animals, and the China Wall Trail, much steeper, for humans. Its namesake is the Chinese employees who built it, and likely also its construction: most of it was supported by curvy stone walls, reminiscent of the Great Wall of China. To get to it, from the road junction hike up the road generally southwest 0.45 mile to, then in, a steep canyon, to the foot of a tailing. Here as all over Lookout Mountain, the walls display the strikingly colorful bands of the Lost Burro Formation, bluish limestone alternating with white and iron-stained marble. At the top of the tailing are the broad platforms and remnants of machinery of the Lower Tunnel, one of the Modoc Mine's earliest workings. In spite of its small adit, it is impressive: it cuts a straight 1,800-foot bore into Lookout Mountain and sprouts more than 2,000 feet of drifts. It was originally dug in an attempt to intercept downward extensions of the rich upper ore bodies. Later on, it was—and still is—connected to level No. 2 by a 560-foot raise used as a giant chute to evacuate ore from that tunnel!

The China Wall Trail starts at the south end of the top platform, just before a cable anchored to the mountain. This narrow foot trail was built to last—and it did. Other than a small landslide and a litter of stones loosened by the local burros, it is essentially intact after 140 years. In 0.4 mile it switchbacks tightly 430 feet up the steep canyon slope to a saddle, where it joins the Pack Trail. The trail continues 0.15 mile up Lookout Mountain's more gentle northeast shoulder to join the end of the road at the Modoc Mine. The saddle commands the first of many gorgeous views of Panamint Valley.

The Modoc Mine. Continue west on the road; be very careful, as the area has several deep open shafts, including one *right in the middle of the road*. The Modoc Mine's tunnels are located along this stretch. The first one, up the slope, is reached by a short foot trail. An enormous chunk of its roof collapsed, creating a gaping cavern littered with boulders and the huge timber that once supported it. A faint trail climbs to higher tunnels—exercise caution, as it passes by deep shafts. The next tunnel, below the road, is level No. 2. Most of the Modoc Mine's production came out of its two split 500-foot tunnels. The Modoc Tunnel, about 600 feet long, is below the next bend in the road.

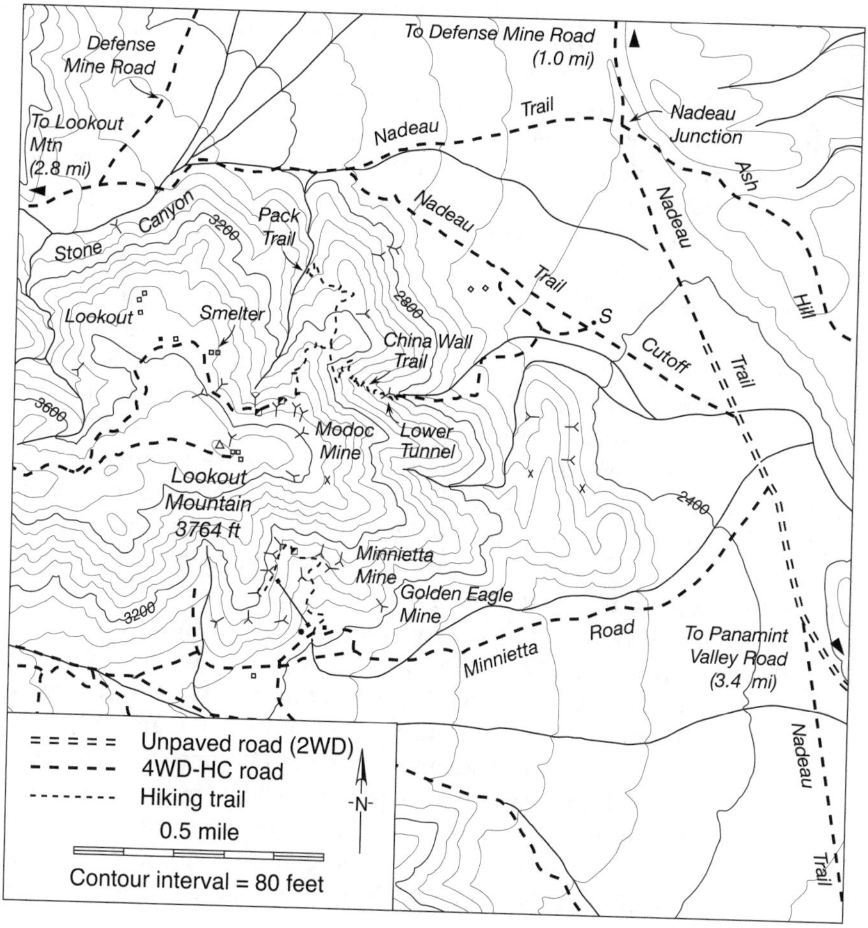

Lookout and the Modoc Mine	Dist.(mi)	Elev.(ft)
Nadeau Trail Cutoff	0.0	2,420
Lower end of China Wall Trail	0.5	2,840
Ridge/Jct with Pack Trail	0.9	3,270
Lower end of Pack Trail	(0.35)	~2,980
Nadeau Trail	(0.6)	2,750
Return via Nadeau Tr. Cutoff	(1.3)	2,420
Upper end of Pack Trail/Road	1.05	3,435
Modoc Mine's main tunnels	1.15	~3,280
Lookout (main building)	1.4	3,580
Lookout Mountain	1.65	3,764

The two long, superposed stone platforms on the right side of the road constructed into the steep slope just a little further is the site of the 1876 smelters. Here as along most local roads and trails, the ground is littered with pieces of slag, dense, black, pebble-size rocks with shiny conchoidal breaks. When the silver ore was treated at the Modoc smelters, the charcoal combined chemically with some of the ore to form this material, which was later washed down this side canyon. These bits and pieces are historically significant because they originated in part from Wildrose Canyon's famous charcoal kilns.

Lookout. Although it is one of the region's oldest ghost towns in the Death Valley region, Lookout still has five stone buildings and the ruins of at least two dozen more. The largest structure, right by the road past the smelters site, is a prime example of desert mining camp architecture in the 1880s. After well over a century of exposure to heat, sun, and cold, its two-foot-thick walls of carefully laid angular rocks and portions of its rafters and window frames still defy gravity. The small sunken structure on its east side is the remains of a scale.

From there it is a short walk up the road (or south on the broad ridge) to the top of Lookout Mountain. The origin of this name is instantly justified when you reach the wide, flat summit. It is indeed a spectacular lookout over the entire 75-mile length of Panamint Valley, from the pale dunes and dry lake in the northern basin to the southern basin's salt pan, all sprawled below the imposing Panamint Range. Lookout Mountain was so full of silver that there is a shaft even at its very top, as well as three stone buildings, still fairly well preserved, for the miners who liked their room with a view. The remoteness and harshness of this site speak to the endurance of the men who struggled here, decades ago, to harvest silver from the heart of the mountain.

The Pack Trail. To return a different way, hike back to the saddle and go down the Pack Trail. This is a nice, narrow foot trail, with strong retaining walls of angular rocks cemented with a crude mortar of mud and pebbles. As suggested by its historic name, it was meant for pack animals, which is why it is so much more level than the China Wall Trail. In 0.35 mile it switchbacks down to the wash of a narrow and curvy canyon. The trail's lower end is washed out; continue down waves of white-marble slickrock, then along the canyon's stony wash, to the canyon mouth. The Nadeau Trail, which runs just outside the canyon, and the Nadeau Trail Cutoff after it, will take you around the tip of the mountain back to your vehicle.

■

THE MINNIETTA MINE AND THOMPSON CANYON

The Minnietta Mine was one of the richest in the region, and today it remains one of the most interesting. It boasts some of the area's best-preserved historic remains, including a large wooden cabin, an aerial tramway, vintage relics, and its own ghost town. A steep road winds up the mountain to its impressive network of silver tunnels and shafts. Hikers in search of more remote destinations can explore nearby Thompson Canyon, which has several ruins, small springs with flowing water, and a nice granite gorge sprinkled with falls.

General Information

Jurisdiction: Private claims on BLM land, Argus Range Wilderness
Road status: Hiking on trails and cross-country; HC access road
Jack Gunn workings: 0.5 mi, 430 ft up, 0 ft down / easy–moderate
Minnietta: 0.4 mi, 0 ft up, 120 ft down one way / very easy
Upper Thompson Springs: 1.7 mi, 1,530 ft up, 60 ft down one way / mod.
Main attractions: Historic silver mines and camp, ghost town, springs
USGS 7.5' topo map: Revenue Canyon
Maps: pp. 501*, 507*, *419, 457*

Location and Access

The Minnietta Mine is on the southern slope of Lookout Mountain, in the northern Argus Range. From Highway 190, drive the Panamint Valley Road 7.4 miles south to the signed Minnietta Road on the right. Go 3.6 miles west, over Ash Hill, where the road veers north and merges with the Nadeau Trail. Continue 0.25 mile north to the Minnietta Road on the left. It climbs into Thompson Canyon 1.1 miles to a junction. The right fork goes 0.1 mile to the Minnietta Cabin. The left fork (Thompson Canyon Road) ends 1.5 miles up canyon at a stone cabin at the Argus Range Wilderness boundary. Up to the Nadeau Trail the Minnietta Road is graded. To the cabin it is rocky and barely passable with standard clearance. High clearance is required beyond.

History

The silver-lead deposits of the Minnietta Belle Mine, as it was then known, were located in 1876. Their proximity to the rich Modoc Mine, just on the other side of Lookout Mountain, promptly attracted a group of California investors, who raised $200,000 and put Richard Jacobs, one of the original discovers of Panamint four years earlier, in charge of the mine. As much as 20 feet thick, the Minnietta's ore bodies turned out to be exceptionally rich. Assays ran as high as 200 ounces of silver per ton and 50% lead—with a little gold to boot. By the end of 1876 Jacobs was erecting a 10-stamp mill and a pipeline from Thompson Spring, a few miles up in the mountains. The following May, Remi Nadeau's teams (see *The Nadeau Trail*) were hauling out the Minnietta's first silver bullion. To support the mining community, the small town of Minnietta sprang up on the canyon floor below the mill.

Despite these glowing promises, there were rough times ahead. In late 1877, after a few short months, production was so low that the mine had to foreclose. In 1878 it was taken over by its creditors, including Remi Nadeau and Mortimer Belshaw, co-owner of Cerro Gordo. Belshaw managed the mine for a while, with mixed success: by early 1881 Jacobs' mill had been hauled out and production had stopped.

The man who turned the Minnietta Mine around was Jack Gunn. Originally from Canada, Gunn had been a Confederate soldier, then a prominent figure at Bodie and a saloon keeper at Lookout. He acquired the mine in 1883 and diligently exploited it for 32 years—continuously until 1905, then intermittently until 1915. He reportedly harvested $500,000 in silver and gold, much of it from a stope that bears his name. The property remained in the Gunn family until the end of World War II. Up to a dozen miners at a time leased the mine's five claims. Between 1916 and 1920 two miners from Trona squeezed out 42,000 ounces of silver from the upper tunnels. In 1924 the old slag dumps and tailings were milled for leftover precious metals. The westernmost claim, variously called over time the St. Charles workings, Lead Mine, and Hughes Mine, produced $45,000 in 1926, then 120 tons of lead in the 1940s. Between 1949 and 1954 a mill reworked what was left of the historic tailings. Lessees were still giving it a try in the 1960s, and as late as 1991. All in all, the Minnietta Mine was active for the best part of 115 years, bringing in nearly one million dollars.

Route Description

The Minnietta Mine. The large Minnietta Cabin gives a good glimpse of the mine's later era. For many years the residence of the mine's superintendent—famous names like Richard Jacobs, Mortimer Belshaw, and Jack Gunn—it burned down in the 1930s and was rebuilt. It has a spacious living room with a make-shift stove pieced together from a drum, two bedrooms, a kitchen, and a small bathroom with an enamel tub. Maintained by volunteers, the Minnietta Cabin is furnished and usually fairly clean. It is used on a first-come, first-serve basis. The stone structure behind the cabin was the cold house. Its 30-

inch walls reportedly kept it cool enough in the summer to refrigerate milk! There were several other buildings nearby, including a blacksmith shop, but they are now reduced to mere foundations.

The Minnietta Mine has one of the largest collections of workings in the Death Valley region. The steep slopes behind the cabin are honeycombed with at least two dozen tunnels full of shafts, raises, caves, and stopes that total nearly a mile. They were divided in three groups so spread out that they partly overlap underground—the Cowshed and Jack Gunn workings, and the Hughes Mine. The best way to appreciate the magnitude of these developments is to hike the four-wheel-drive road that winds up behind the cabin.

The stocky wooden structure a short distance up is the mine's centerpiece—the lower terminal of its aerial tramway. This wonderful historic monument is well worth close inspection. The ore was lowered into its huge ore bin from the upper terminal, hanging 280 feet up the slope. The tramway's twin cables were extant until as late as 1998, when the BLM had them clipped to spare the aging structures. The fine tailings below the terminal mark the site of the stamp mill. Water from Thompson Spring was stored in the three nearby tanks.

Past the terminal, the road climbs past an antediluvian water truck, the slender terminal of a long waste-rock dump, then extensive retaining stone walls—before ending at an interesting, equally ancient steam engine. Just before the end of the road, a short side road on the right zigzags up to the Cowshed workings. Its two shafts dropped to two levels with extensive stopes. Here as elsewhere on Lookout Mountain, the ores were flat tabular bodies localized near a local thrust fault. They contained high-grade argentiferous galena and cerussite, as well as cerargyrite (silver chloride) and pyrolusite (manganese oxide).

The Jack Gunn workings, visible higher up to the west, were the Minnietta's bread and butter. To get to them, from the end of the road scramble up the rock-strewn ravine 100 feet to a trail on the left, and follow it 500 feet south to a wide inclined tunnel with a floor of rough lumber. This is the Merritt Incline. At the bottom of this 400-foot gallery, some 150 feet down, the ore was loaded in a mine car and pulled up to the surface using the wooden hoist that still stands outside the incline. The hoist's gas engine was housed in a tin shack that now rests way down the tailing. From the hoist the ore was hauled by rail to the upper tramway terminal, located a little further. With its intact wheel, cable arrangement, and funnel-shaped ore bin, this terminal is an interesting study in early mining engineering. Just past it, a steep side trail climbs 50 feet to the Jack Gunn stope, marked by a long metallic chute—the mine's largest producer.

The cabin and lower tramway terminal at the Minnietta Mine

The Hughes Mine, 0.3 mile up canyon on the main road, does not have as much to show, but the mine visible from the road east of the cabin is just the opposite. Historically known as the Little Mack, it produced some gold in the 1930s, and was worked again as the Golden Eagle in the late 1990s. Its tramway cables still connect the complex lower terminal, an awkward hybrid of concrete and steel, to the upper terminal way up the mountain. A trail winds up to its well-preserved pad, rusted chute, and ore bin, and the rail tracks that emerge from the 250-foot tunnel. Although it is not much of a climb, the mine commands unobstructed views of the entire Panamint Mountains.

Minnietta. From the vantage points of the mines, if you look south into the wash of Thompson Canyon, you may spot the ruins of Minnietta, the town that supported all this mining activity in the 1870s. It is an easy walk to it from the cabin: head southwest down the road 0.1 mile to the canyon road, cross it, and follow the old track south across the wash. The ruins are scattered along the next 0.3 mile. The town had a few stores, a saloon, dozens of residences, and, for a brief time, a post office. Here as at nearby Reilly, the ruins are all different. Some of them have 4-foot walls; others are camouflaged in the weeds. There are five-room houses and single-room shacks, a house built around a boulder, and spacious corrals. This is a moving place to

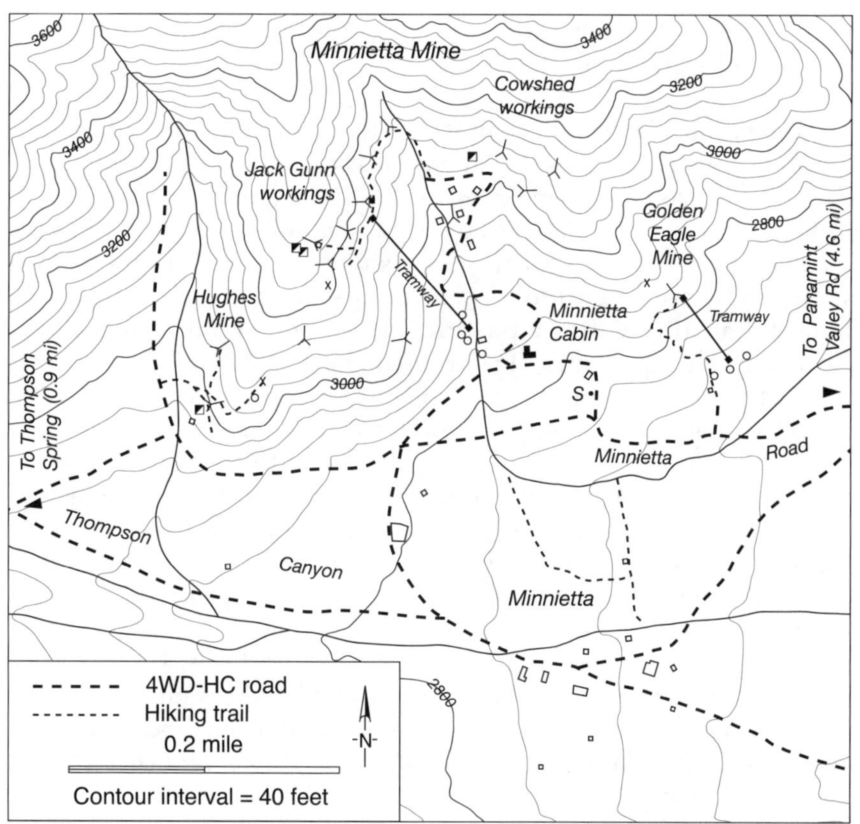

The Minnietta Mine and Thompson Canyon		
	Dist.(mi)	Elev.(ft)
The Minnietta Mine		
Minnietta Cabin	0.0	2,820
to Jack Gunn workings (upper)	0.5	3,250
to Golden Eagle Mine	0.4	2,850
to Minnietta	0.4	2,700
Thompson Canyon		
Road's end (old camp)	0.0	3,410
Thompson Spring (gorge)	0.9	4,000
60-ft fall	1.1	4,230
Fork	1.6	4,785
Upper Thompson Springs	(0.1)	4,880
China Lake NWC (off-limits)	2.2	5,700

visit, littered with the leftovers of a departed society, slowly returning to dust under the eternal desert sun.

Thompson Canyon. Back in the early days of the Minnietta Mine, the area at the end of the canyon road was the camp of a few mines in the upper canyon. The stone cabin, a sturdy construction with a part of its lumber roof still in place, is now the last building standing. There is a collapsed tin shack nearby, and a stone arrastre. The camp was strategically located next to a good spring—the two water holes sheltered by healthy willows past the cabin. They hold water, albeit cloaked with unappetizing algae, even in the dry season.

Past the camp Thompson Canyon quickly turns into a tight V, with steeply inclined walls rising over 1,000 feet. It is rarely visited, yet it is a delightful place,, filled with little secrets and new perspectives at every bend. The canyon is permeated with Thompson Spring, which is a series of closely spaced seeps distributed along a 1-mile stretch. Water surfaces here and there as random bits of creek, muddy puddles, and even a few cascades. At one seep, on the south side, a pipe pokes out of a soggy bank at eye level. Water used to gush out of it, until the pipe finally rusted itself shut in the mid-1990s. The road has long since been supplanted by an erratic and brushy path maintained by the thriving burro population. Where the trail vanishes, which is often, you hop on boulders, bushwhack through rabbitbrush, or graze the canyon's rocky edges.

Thompson Canyon has several stone ruins, including two shelters facing each other across the wash, and a crude square construction on the south side of the wash. This was the lower terminal of a cableway; its cables still hang down the opposite canyon wall. A vague trail winds up to the historic workings higher up. The long segments of 2-inch steel pipe lining the wash are the remains of the Minnietta Mine's pipeline. They will entice you to move on, thinking every time they end that you have reached the pipeline's intake, only to find moments later that they go on, deeper into the canyon.

In less than a mile the walls steepen and converge into a narrow, angular gorge of dark monzonite. In the spring, it is a treat to pause in its refreshing shade and listen to the restful sound of the creek. There are a few falls along the way. All of them are easy to bypass or climb, except for the last one, not too far before the upper spring and the Naval Weapons Center boundary. About 60 feet high, it is a serious obstacle. It took me a while to find the trick to circumvent it, but what I discovered beyond made my day.

■

SNOW CANYON

With a tally of more than 60 mine tunnels and shafts and a plethora of mills, cableways, ore bins, mining camps, and tailings, Snow Canyon is a mecca for mine enthusiasts. Both four-wheelers and hikers can get a kick out of searching for the dozens of roads and foot trails that wind across the canyon slopes to these forgotten nuggets, including at the St. George and Golden Lady mines.

General Information

Jurisdiction: Bureau of Land Management, Argus Range Wilderness
Road status: Hiking on trails and cross-country; access on 4WD roads
Golden Lady Mine: 2.1 mi, 970 ft up loop / moderate–difficult
St. George Mine: 3.6 mi, 1,510 ft up loop / moderate–difficult
Snow Canyon springs: 1.0 mi, 720 ft up, 0 ft down one way / easy
Main attractions: Historic gold and silver mines, mining trails
USGS 7.5' topo map: Revenue Canyon
Maps: pp. 513*, *419*, *457*

Location and Access

Snow Canyon is the first major canyon south of the Minnietta Mine, in the central Argus Range. The inconspicuous Snow Canyon Road branches off the Panamint Valley Road 3.2 miles south of the Minnietta Road (or 3.2 miles north of the Trona-Wildrose Road). It is a fairly good road up to the beat-up rocky grade at the first wash crossing just inside the canyon, at an elevation of 2,970' and 5.5 miles from the paved road. It takes high clearance and four-wheel drive to make it over this rough spot. Otherwise park before the crossing and walk.

Snow Canyon is loaded with shafts, none protected. Many are right by the trail. Be very careful. Do not hike or drive here at dark.

History: The St. George Mine

Located in the heart of Snow Canyon, the St. George Mine witnessed a long history of intermittent exploitation. What made this property attractive was that the ore outcropped in wide, well-defined, and rich quartz veins. Over the years, a succession of operators exploited it for gold, lead, silver, and even a little copper. The earliest recorded activity goes back to 1883, when gold was actively mined and a five-stamp mill was erected. In the 1890s, the Argus Gold Mining Company was working four tunnels and treated the ore at a new five-stamp 750-pound steam-powered mill. Twenty years later, the mine had been renamed the Merry Christmas. The Snow Canyon Mining and Milling Company was producing lead ore worth $11 per ton. Two aerial tramways and another mill were installed, this one with five 1,000-pound stamps and powered by gas. In the mid-1930s the property became the St. George Mine, after the name of one of its best claims. Lessees developed several workings, including the St. George Shaft, which carried up to $25 of gold per ton. These bursts of mining continued off and on until the 1980s, but other than the high-grade ore of the 1880s, production was probably minimal.

Route Description

The Snow Canyon Road. Typical of the Argus Range, Snow Canyon cuts a deep swath through smooth, steep hills. It looks deceptively like a box canyon: wide for a couple of miles, it pinches down in the distance and seemingly disappears. If you hike the canyon road, you will find that its modest grade is easy to walk. In the spring, many species of flowers grow right along it. The less common local stars are spotted langloisia, larkspur, desert prickle poppy, and desert mat, a beautiful, tiny plant that well deserves its other name of purple mat.

The first point of interest is the stone ruins of the Golden Lady Mine Camp, 7.0 miles from the pavement, on the north side. Large stone corrals, several feet thick and tens of feet long, are clustered in the wash, as well as a few houses, a stone arrastre, and platforms that once supported tents or cabins. At the end of the canyon road, 0.25 mile further, is the more recent three-story Snow Canyon Mill. It is the canyon's largest structure. The ore was loaded into the hopper at the top of the mill and fed into the milling machinery housed in the corrugated steel building below it, which recently collapsed. The attached shed was the maintenance shop. The vats and powdery tailings below the mill are the remains of a small processing plant.

To test your four-wheeling skills, try driving the two mining roads. Return to the Golden Lady Mine Camp and take the road that ramps up behind it. After 0.1 mile, it forks at a wide turnout. The rocky road on the right drops lopsided into a wash, then climbs a steep ridge to the Golden Lady Mine (0.4 mile). If you think this one is bad, try the other road to the St. George Mine. Deeply gouged and rocky, it is one of the most precipitous mining roads I have had the fortune to walk. In 1 mile, it ascends 1,300 feet to the canyon rim, and its steepest pitch tops the 40% mark. Most drivers bail before the ore bin marked "Saddle Mining Co." about half way up, at a nasty boulder stuck in soft sand. To see the St. George Mine, you will likely have to walk.

The three-story mill in Snow Canyon

The St. George Mine. There are two ways to hike to this mine: the road mentioned earlier and the trail. The trail starts in the wash of the side canyon right behind the Snow Canyon Mill (see map). Unless you can drive to the Saddle Mining Company ore bin, I recommend the trail. It is more gradual, and it passes by all the mine's attractions. The only difficulty is that two of the three trail junctions are tricky to find going up. Hiking the road has its disadvantage too: it is extremely steep and slippery. Coming down, I had to use the cable anchored along its steepest grade to rappel! Nothing is easy. Since the road and the trail join at two places (the ore bin and the upper shafts), several itineraries are possible. Make your own, based on what seems easiest.

Here are the general trail directions. From the Snow Canyon Mill, follow the trail up the narrow wash 320 yards to the first left bend. Go another 75 yards and search among low boulders for a trail climbing off to the right (east). It winds up past tunnels, headframes, and tons of mining junk to the road 50 yards below the ore bin. The trail resumes just to the left of the ore bin (if you drove up to here, this is where you want to pick it up). It passes under the ore bin cable and cuts across the canyon slope. The second tricky junction is 0.3 mile out, in a right bend (at this point you are a little lower than a wooden mill visible to the west-northwest). The main trail continues 0.5 mile to the shafts; the fainter trail on the left ends in 0.3 mile at the historic camp.

The historic camp is one of Snow Canyon's oldest sites. The wooden mill is a complex structure of patinated lumber. A little further, the tiered concrete foundations of another mill lie below the trail. Its dumps of drusy quartz sparkle with metallic glance (of course the flecks of gold aren't gold, but fool's gold and chalcopyrite). The trail ends shortly at a singular camp sheltered between rocky walls and a high fall. It has a one-room stone house, a well-constructed tent platform, a corral, and the customary junk. A commodity more precious than gold oozes out of the collapsed tunnel by the camp and pools in a shallow pond where burros gather for a drink.

The two deep timbered shafts and the long trench right by the upper part of the main trail were the mine's main producers. Ore from horizontal tunnels in the main shaft was dropped through raises to a nearby tunnel, then trammed in ore cars and cabled to the mill. There is another shaft and a trench further up, just before the trail joins the road. Here you are on the rim of Snow Canyon, a barren high-desert mesa of expansive limestone slickrock sprinkled with granite boulders and thorny blackbrush. This is an eerie place, rolling away on three

Snow Canyon

	Dist.(mi)	Elev.(ft)
St. George Mine (trail-road loop)		
Snow Canyon Mill	0.0	3,800
Saddle Mining Co. ore bin	0.6	4,240
Trail junction to historic camp	0.9	4,500
Historic camp	(0.3)	~4,600
Main shafts	1.4	4,820
Trail-road T junction on crest	1.7	4,930
Saddle Mining Co. ore bin	2.2	4,240
Golden Lady Mine Camp	2.8	3,645
Back to Snow Canyon Mill	3.0	3,800
Golden Lady Mine (trail-road loop)		
Golden Lady Mine Camp	0.0	3,645
Turnout at road junction	0.1	3,690
End of road/start trail	0.5	4,000
Top of trail	1.1	4,600
St George Mine Road	1.2	4,565
Back to camp via road	2.1	3,645

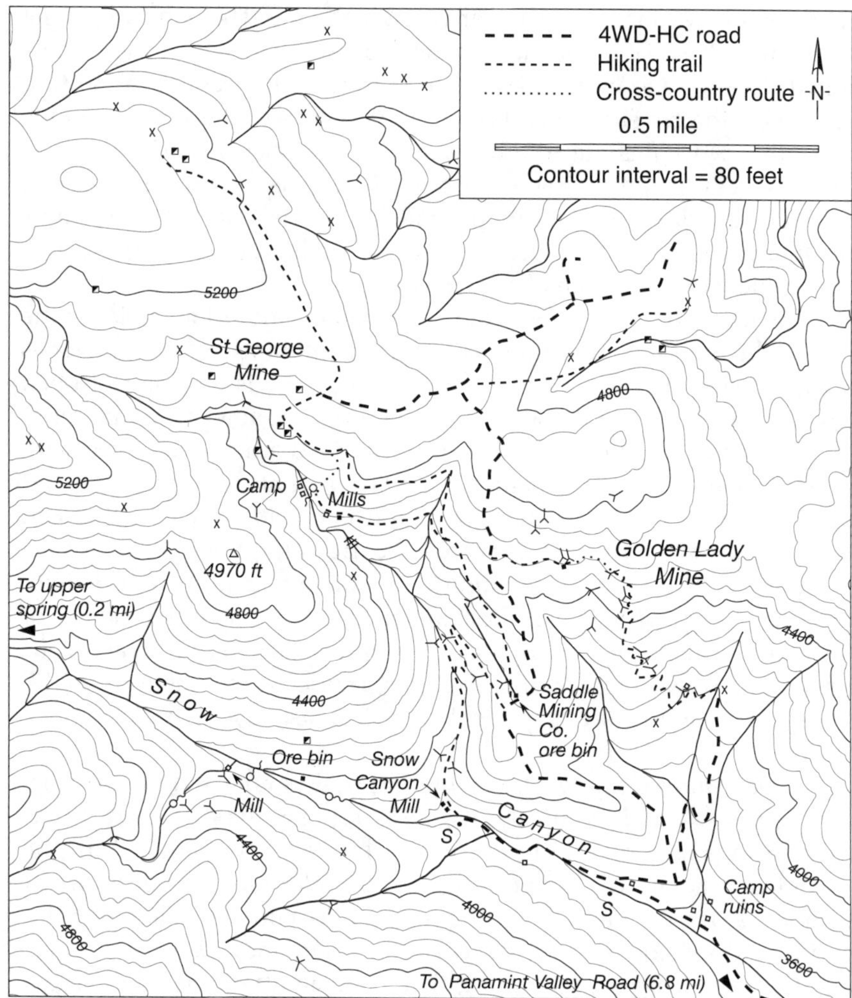

sides into precipitous canyons and dominated on the fourth side by French Madam Peak. Several trails wander north and east into upper Thompson Canyon, where many more workings are tucked away. If you like mines, you will enjoy looking for these forgotten sites.

The Golden Lady Mine. To visit this historic gold mine, drive or walk the mining road mentioned earlier. It dead-ends at the edge of a narrow trench-like ravine, 30 feet below a prospect covered with deep-blue copper minerals. Across the ravine, the mountainside is dotted with the pale tailings of the Golden Lady Mine's impressive array of tunnels, nearly all the way to the canyon rim. I counted seventeen, and there are likely more. There never was a road here. The only way to get to them is to walk the same narrow foot trails on which the miners toiled decades ago. Scramble down and across the ravine to the trail visible on the far side, then follow it 100 yards to the lowest tunnel. The other workings are roughly aligned in a northwesterly direction up the rocky slope. Crisscrossing mining trails zigzag up to them, intertwined with recent additions made by the descendants of the burros that did time at the mines. A good part of the fun is to explore this elusive network in search of all the workings.

The mood of this hike is set by the tunnels, mysterious holes in the face of the mountain, inviting yet fraught with danger. One tunnel has a gaping shaft right at its entrance. Another one is a cluster of open caves. Others are closely superposed across the same vein, like monstrous alien eyes. Almost all tunnels have caved adits or are lined with piles of fallen rocks. This is nature's warning that they are brittle and unsafe. Stay out of them. The good stuff is outside anyway. You will find a rock shelter, a burnt-out cabin, a curious rail track made of steel pipe, a dislocated ore chute, mining monuments, and, if it all fails to impress you, great views of the Panamint Mountains. From the top of the trail you may find a cross-country route west across treacherous rock faces to two more tunnels. A short trail connects them to the St. George Mine grade (see map), which you can use to loop back.

Upper Snow Canyon. If the mining trails sound too demanding, try the easy short hike up the roadless upper canyon instead. It has four springs and several mine ruins. The first spring is just up the wash from the Snow Canyon Mill. In the cooler months a little water wanders along the gravel. It will guide you to a pool of cold water lingering in the shade of a shallow cave concealed under tall rabbitbrush. On the way to the second spring there is a small mining site marked by a well-preserved wooden ore bin on stilts, on the north embankment. It was once connected to the shallow shaft on the ledge just above it by a slender ore chute. The second spring is a low tangle of greener vegetation, usually dry. Mosey on to the thick rock foundations of an early mill, at the mouth of the next side canyon south. Its small floury tailing came from the four partly collapsed tunnels beyond it. There is also a spring in this side canyon. The fourth spring is 0.6 mile further up the wide, brush-covered wash. It takes a little bushwhacking to get there, but it is worth it. The local flora of lupine and prince's plume can be exuberant. Even with modest luck you are likely to spot some of the locals as well, especially chukars and burros.

■

REVENUE CANYON

In one single hike through this surprisingly diverse canyon, you will get to sample many wonders of the desert—a lush spring, a wild gorge with neatly banded fossiliferous walls, the ruins of a gold mill, mine tunnels and mineral-rich dumps, forgotten trails climbing to sweeping vistas, and eventually, if you trudge far enough, narrows coursed by a tiny creek. The walking is easy, along an old mining road, and except for a little bushwhacking in the narrows, anyone in reasonably good shape should be able to make it and enjoy it.

General Information

Jurisdiction: Bureau of Land Management, Argus Range Wilderness
Road status: Hiking on roads and cross-country; 4WD access road
Copper King Mine: 1.2 mi, 720 ft up, 0 ft down one way / easy
Upper spring: 2.1 mi, 1,400 ft up, 0 ft down one way / easy–moderate
North Fork spring: 1.0 mi, 580 ft up, 30 ft down one way / easy
Main attractions: Scenic canyon, gold, copper, and silver mines
USGS 7.5′ topo map: Revenue Canyon
Maps: pp. 519*, *419, 457*

Location and Access

Revenue Canyon is easy to spot: its mouth is marked by the large white stockpile of the Trona limestone quarry, at the foot of the Argus Range below Maturango Peak, the range's highest summit. To get to it, from the Trona-Wildrose Road drive the Nadeau Road 11.8 miles to its north end at the quarry's gate. The quarry was recently reactivated and is closed to the public. Follow the primitive road to the right of the gate. It circles counterclockwise along the property's fence 1.05 miles to a junction in the wash of Revenue Canyon, just inside the wide canyon mouth. The road on the right ends in 0.25 mile just inside the canyon's north fork. The most interesting route is straight ahead into the main canyon. A high-clearance vehicle is needed to drive the 0.9 mile to the Argus Range Wilderness boundary sign. The rest is on foot.

Geology: Mapping Ancient Earth

From head to mouth, Revenue Canyon cuts through a continuous sequence of six Paleozoic sedimentary formations more than a mile thick. The formations get younger up canyon, starting in the Devonian (Lost Burro Formation) at the quarry and ending in the Permian

(Owens Valley Formation) at the end of the road. They were all deposited in the same ocean, but over such a long time—150 million years—that they witnessed very different environments. The Paleozoic seas were teeming with life, and most of these formations bear fossils—corals, crinoids, brachiopods, fusilinids, and dozens of others. The Keeler Canyon Formation, a neatly bedded sequence of gray limestone from the Late Pennsylvanian, is particularly interesting. It crops out just inside the wilderness area, and elsewhere in the region, but here it contains odd anomalies—sheets of silt, swirls of carbonate sands, coarse sedimentary material, and lenses of conglomerate. With their habitual wisdom, geologists read the past in this minutia as easily as we scan our morning paper. The silt tells them that the ocean was fairly quiet, perhaps offshore from a low coastal shelf. The sands hint of marine currents, the coarse sediments of nearby mountains being eroded, and the conglomerates of storms dumping the byproducts of erosion into the sea. This area was submerged not too far from shore. The Inyo Mountains, where this same formation is more uniform, were under deep-sea water. So it is that we can map ancient coastlines, reconstruct landscapes, trace rivers, and visualize atmospheric perturbations that occurred 300 million years ago. When you visit Revenue Canyon, you may not recognize the dusting of silt or the storm deposits. But the awareness of their existence may keep you intrigued, as subtle reminders of the constant presence of the past

Route Description

Lower Revenue Canyon. Revenue Canyon and Knight Canyon, its close neighbor to the south, drain the same slope of Maturango Peak and cut through the same formations. Expectedly, they are fairly similar. Both canyons start with a dramatic gorge, reach the plutonic core of the Argus Range, and eventually wiggle through narrows drained by a tiny creek. They also have cultural similarities—the road, the wilderness status, the mines and associated ruins. One of the appeals of this hike is the opportunity to gauge how well the mountain cloned these twins. The main differences are the ease of hiking and the mines—Revenue Canyon wins on both counts.

The scenic lower gorge is austere and wild. All along its windy course, its richly contrasted formations of banded sedimentary rock soar hundreds of feet to the saw-toothed peaks that crown the canyon rims. Most formations are fossiliferous. The Tin Mountain Limestone, on the south wall past the quarry, is known for its abundant silicified corals. The Lee Flat Limestone, in the gorge just beyond it, has large crinoid stems up to one inch across. The Keeler Canyon Formation,

Banded sedimentary walls along Revenue Canyon

next in line up to the mill, contains both, plus brachiopods. At several places, the narrow wash is lined with short slickrock cliffs of massive marble, white to blue-gray, smooth enough for technical climbing.

If you are driving, park at the BLM wilderness boundary post and continue on foot to the Big Four Mill, in the middle of the tight U-bend 0.3 mile up canyon. It has a cableway, a large ore bin about to collapse, four concrete cyanide vats, the ruin of a cabin, and a water tank. The water was piped from the lower spring, 450 yards up canyon, in the 8-inch steel pipelines scattered in the wash. The mill treated gold-bearing ore extracted from two groups of workings. The first one is high up the sheer facing slope. The short trail to it starts across from the cabin. Still in decent shape, it works its way steeply to two shafts. Both are record deep: the stone I dropped into the main one bounced off hidden scaffoldings before hitting bottom so far down that I never heard the final echo. The archaic contraption anchored on the rock spur above it served as both the headframe and the upper tower of the cableway.

The second group of workings is high up on the south rim. The well-defined trail that leads to it is the best deal in the lower canyon: there is no better place to appreciate the grandeur of the gorge you just crossed. To find it, from the concrete vats walk 370 yards up canyon to the middle of the next bend (left). The trail starts at the southern edge of the wash, by a 2-foot steel rod stuck in the ground. It winds up to a low bench, then to the prominent ridge to the south. If you cannot find it, look for the bleached lumber of a collapsed cabin on the bench (the trail passes right by it) or hike cross-country to the ridge, where the trail is unmistakable. Sample at least a little of it: even its lower reaches offer excellent views of the gorge and Pinto Peak across the valley. Up on the billowing canyon rim, the trail gets dimmer, and you may not find the mine's shaft and shallow prospect, but the views of southern Panamint Valley are almost always there.

The Copper King Mine. The abandoned road winds along the canyon bottom another 0.8 mile and ends in the vicinity of the four long and crooked tunnels of the Copper King Mine. This area is loaded with interesting tidbits, some easy to find, others—and this is the fun part—not so easy. By the time you have exhausted the local trails, you will have seen sparkling peacock ore and malachite, the ruin of an old stone mill, a prospect hole bursting with green copper minerals, a tailing coated with aragonite and galena, a spring-fed creek cascading over a series of low falls, and a curious stone house just large enough for a single bed. Have fun, but stay away from the tunnels: they are filled with noxious sulfur fumes and blind shafts.

The Revenue Canyon Creek. Beyond the mine you step into another world. The road vanishes, the canyon narrows, the walls steepen,

Revenue Canyon

	Dist.(mi)	Elev.(ft)
Junction in wash	0.0	2,700
Spring in north fork (head)	(1.0)	3,250
Wilderness boundary (park)	0.9	3,070
Big Four Mill	1.2	3,255
Twin shafts	(0.2)	3,480
Lower spring (head)	1.4	3,380
Upper shaft	(1.1)	4,260
Road's end/Copper King Mine	2.0	3,670
20-foot fall	2.3	3,980
Upper spring	2.9	4,465
China Lake NWC (off-limits)	3.6	4,980

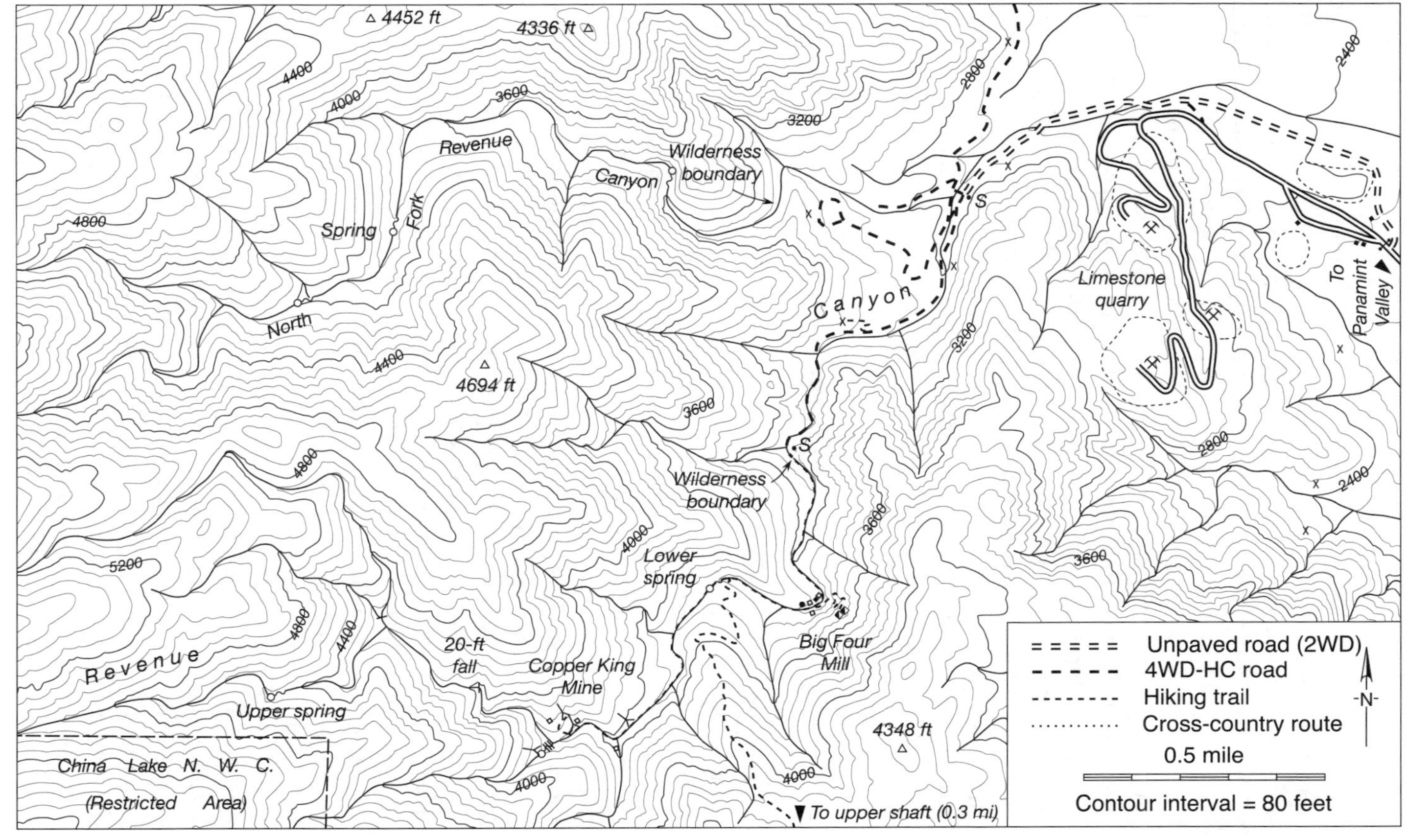
4452 ft
4336 ft
Revenue
Canyon
Wilderness boundary
Spring
Fork
North
4694 ft
Canyon
Limestone quarry
To Panamint Valley
Wilderness boundary
Lower spring
Big Four Mill
20-ft fall
Copper King Mine
Revenue
Upper spring
4348 ft
China Lake N. W. C.
(Restricted Area)
To upper shaft (0.3 mi)
5200
4800
4400
4000
3600
3200
2800
2400
Unpaved road (2WD)
4WD-HC road
Hiking trail
Cross-country route
N
0.5 mile
Contour interval = 80 feet

and a slender creek miraculously materializes along the wash. That so little water can cause such profound changes is hard to believe. You suddenly find yourself surrounded by polished slickrock, by the tiny sounds of running water, and by plants that normally have no business in the desert—fern, mosses, thistle, and cattail. Rust-colored monzonite walls rise all around, as if to shelter this rare trove from the rest of the world. The creek originates from the upper spring, one mile up this sinuous passage. Not much of a creek: it carries maybe a gallon per minute in a good winter, far less in the summer. It does not even spend much time above ground. Water surfaces only in the vicinity of the multiple boulder jams and bedrock exposures in the wash, which dam up the subterranean flow and force it out. It drips in sheets over these natural dams, oozes out of embankments, trickles over rock ledges. A few steps down canyon the wash is dry again.

Expect a little workout. Bushwhacking is unavoidable, mostly at the occlusions, which are wet and choked with rabbitbrush. One of them, a long, 20-foot wall of white granite blocks, takes a bit of climbing. But thankfully, these narrows are more open and less vegetated than in Knight Canyon, and hiking is easier. The rough burro trail that lopes along much of the way also comes in handy.

The head of the upper spring is a long thicket of rabbitbrush sunk into an abrupt 90° bend in the wash. In the late spring and early summer, it is surrounded by colorful penstemon and unusually large lupine in bloom. In another 0.7 mile, past the first Joshua trees, is the unmarked boundary of the China Lake Naval Weapons Center. Turn around before you get in trouble.

North Fork of Revenue Canyon. This fork has three springs. Most people will find that the last two are not worth getting all scraped up, but the first one is pretty and easy to reach. From the junction in the lower canyon, walk the rocky, high-clearance road or the canyon wash itself 0.5 mile west up the north fork to the wilderness boundary post, then 0.4 mile through a narrow stretch of polished marble and stratified limestone. In the spring, chia, fiddleneck, and many of the common local flowers brighten the wash. The lower spring is a skinny oasis cradled in a tight bend—low mesquite trees on one side, willows on the other, a flooded patch of grass and tule in the middle. The metal pipeline suspended across the grass once diverted water all the way from the upper spring down to the quarry. It was abandoned decades ago. On a warm day, it is enjoyable to rest in the spring's sparse shade and refreshing humidity.

■

KNIGHT CANYON

Knight Canyon is the longest and deepest canyon in the Argus Range Wilderness, and one of the most exciting. An abandoned mining road runs conveniently along most of it, which makes hiking unusually easy. Besides the company of wild burros, the main attractions are creek-fed springs, panoramic side roads climbing to derelict mines, and a small mining camp. The highlight is definitely the third and of course furthest spring, trapped in a tight granitic gorge filled with a little creek and lush riparian vegetation.

General Information

Jurisdiction: Bureau of Land Management, Argus Range Wilderness
Road status: Roadless; access via primitive road (2WD)
Lower spring: 1.9 mi, 840 ft up, 10 ft down one way / easy
Narrows and upper spring: 3.7 mi, 1,770 ft up, 10 ft down one way / mod.
Upper viewpoint: 4.7 mi, 2,450 ft up, 90 ft down one way / difficult
Main attractions: Springs and creeks, narrows, vistas, trails, mines
USGS 7.5' topo maps: Maturango Peak*, Revenue Canyon
Maps: pp. 525*, *419, 457*

Location and Access

Knight Canyon drains the eastern slope of Maturango Peak, just south of Revenue Canyon. To get to it, drive the Nadeau Road 7.8 miles north from the Trona-Wildrose Road (or 0.3 mile south from the Slate Range Road) to the Knight Canyon Road on the west side, a primitive road covered with white gravel. Drive it 2.3 miles to its end at a gate just inside Knight Canyon (make a right at the first junction, and a left at the second one). The gate marks the boundary of the Argus Range Wilderness. Park and walk on. The Knight Canyon Road is graded; it is a breeze even with a standard-clearance vehicle.

Route Description

The lower canyon. Knight Canyon starts right away as a deep open gorge hemmed in by massive slopes of Paleozoic strata. The most impressive area is the high, conspicuously striated southern wall a short distance into the wilderness. These rocks belong to a Permian sequence of sedimentary rocks known as the Owens Valley Formation. It is composed of dozens of long, thick, alternating layers of limestone, shale, and sandstone, stacked from the wash all the way up to the canyon rim. These giant strata give the lower canyon an artificial texture and contribute to much of its scenic appeal. Each stratum is a time marker, like a tree ring. Since this sedimentation took about 40 million years, each of its approximately 50 strata represents a modest 800,000-year slice of time. If you walk up to the south wall and touch any portion of it, your fingertip will cover only about 400 years of earth history—something like one heartbeat of eternity.

The old road provides an easy path up the canyon. Should it get washed out in the future, remember that at all three forks the main canyon is to the right. Erosion and vegetation are slowly turning the road into a single-track trail, kindly maintained by the local burros. They are so numerous that you would have to be unlucky not to see one. Signs of their presence are ubiquitous, including enough manure to fertilize all of Ridgecrest's gardens.

The lower spring. Around the second fork, marked by a fallen metal gate, Knight Canyon becomes shallower. Sedimentary rocks are gradually replaced by sweeps of quartz monzonite. It is part of the Hunter Mountain Pluton, the Middle Jurassic formation that makes up the hard spine of the Argus Range. The next couple of miles are dotted with points of interest, starting with the lower spring. To get to it, you will have to bushwhack through 300 yards of oversized rabbitbrush and get your feet wet splashing through the spring's runoff. The head of the spring is wedged against the low, rocky, south wall. A couple of large red willows shade a shallow depression. When it is filled with water, the pond is fringed with cattail and grass. Although barely wide enough for a normal human rear end, this is a pleasant spot to rest.

The middle spring and mines. The mid-canyon is dotted with the remnants of gold mining from the 1940s. A little past the lower spring, a side road on the right climbs to a short tunnel guarded by a steel door, which was most likely used as a safe to store rich ore and other valuables. Further up canyon, a 1946 yellow tractor sits regally in the center of what was the mining camp. The camp is now reduced to

Red willows at Knight Canyon's lower spring

odds and ends—a toppled water tank, a decaying workbench, a huge boiler of flaking rust. When I was there, the camp's only visible resident was a resourceful rodent squatting in a metal hopper. About 75 yards past the camp, a second side road on the right climbs to a main tunnel, just inside the next drainage north. The side road continues to the canyon rim, at a spectacular viewpoint of Panamint Valley. The middle spring is 0.6 mile further up canyon, in the next pronounced right bend. Below the road, a hefty creek rushes noisily through thickets of rabbitbrush. At this point the road is overgrown and partly flooded, and a little bushwhacking is in order again.

At the third major fork, the road dips in and out of the main canyon and veers left into a side canyon, then climbs 1,000 feet to a mine tunnel. The upper viewpoint just below it is a befitting conclusion to a beautiful trail, offering sweeping vistas of the canyon, of the chiseled slopes of the Argus Range, and Panamint Valley beyond. From there, you may want to explore the long side canyon that the trail crosses just before reaching the viewpoint. It winds down tightly and has two springs, and it offers an off-beat alternative return route.

The narrows. The upper canyon, starting on the right at the third fork, is Knight Canyon's greatest payoff and the place you will want to see. Over the next 0.4 mile, the wash wiggles through a tight gorge of vertical granite faces, 40 feet at its narrowest and much deeper than it is wide. A lively perennial creek gurgles through it, among a crowded cover of rush, cattail, and rabbitbrush. Except for a short track at both ends, there is no trail through here; you simply immerse yourself in it. You will need to pick your way carefully, mostly along the western wall. At places progress gets difficult, with some moderate bushwhacking and splashing through the creek. But it is a beautiful and imposing passage, pleasantly cool in the summer, the kind of hidden playground only desert canyons seem to hold. Lupine, globemallow, and Mojave thistle decorate the canyon bottom. Countless cracks in the walls have gathered soil particles and become hanging nurseries filled with tufts of grass and calico cacti. In the early summer, the cacti's bright red blossoms shine against the rock face like torches in an ancient temple. Past the left bend the passage widens a little. Progress is a little easier, along slickrock benches that require occasional scrambling. The gorge ends just past the next bend, at a sprawling tangle of low mesquite trees that marks the head of the spring.

At the next left bend the canyon forks again, in a desolate landscape spiked with the first Joshua trees. This is the approximate boundary of the China Lake NWC. Only burros are allowed beyond, in either fork.

Postscript. As luck had it, I first visited Knight Canyon on February 2, 2000—the day it rained that year. The drizzle slowly evolved into hard wind-driven rain, and the year-to-date rainfall jumped to a whole quarter of an inch. Every peak was festooned with

Knight Canyon

	Dist.(mi)	Elev.(ft)
End of road/gate	0.0	2,530
Lower spring	1.9	3,360
First side road	2.2	3,505
Camp/second side road	2.35	3,580
Lower viewpoint	(1.15)	4,200
Middle spring	2.95	3,860
Third fork/start narrows	3.3	4,035
End of road/upper viewpoint	(1.45)	4,890
Upper spring/end narrows	3.7	4,290
China Lake NWC boundary	4.2	~4,545

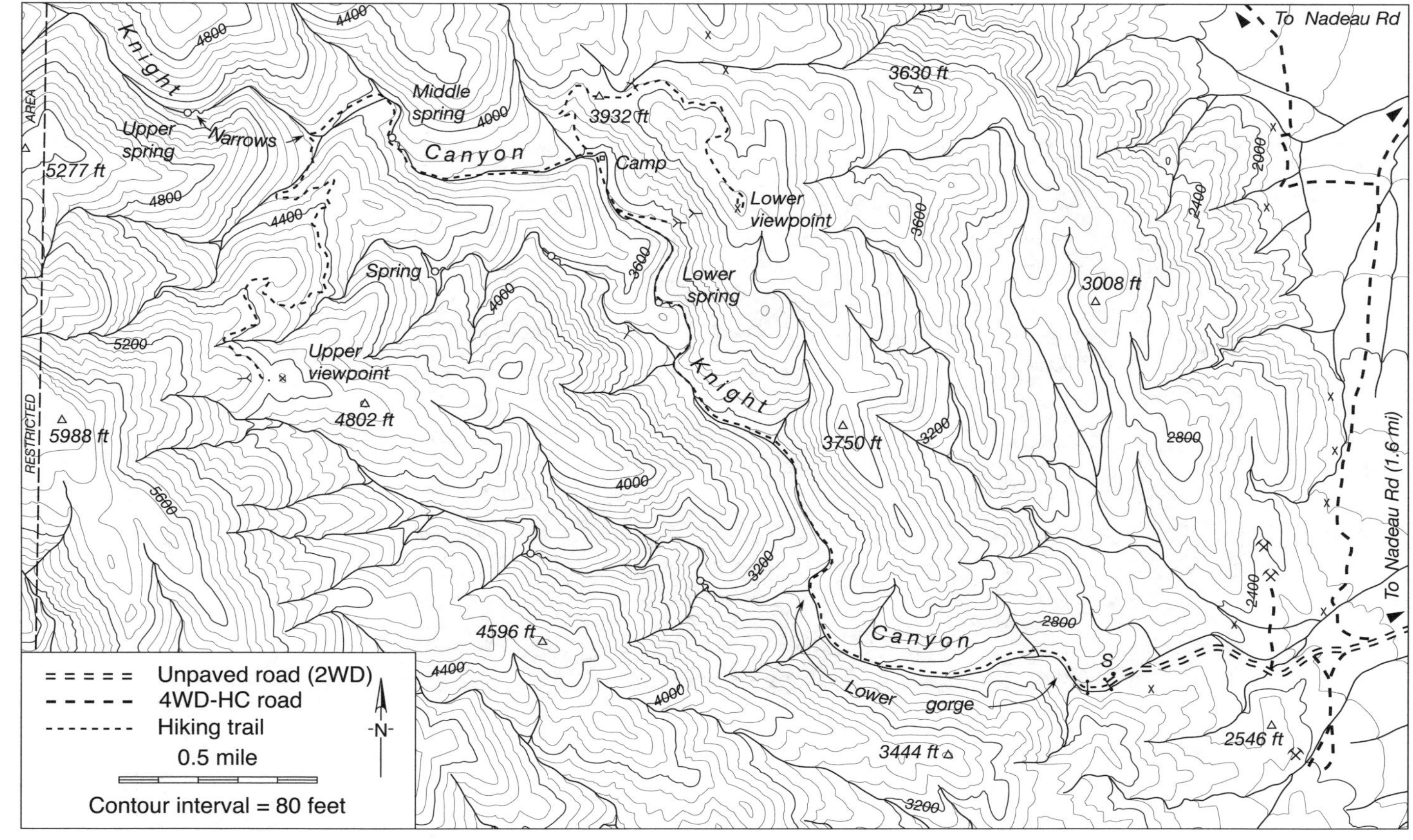
RESTRICTED AREA
5277 ft
Knight
Upper spring
Narrows
Middle spring
Canyon
3932 ft
Camp
3630 ft
To Nadeau Rd
Lower viewpoint
Spring
Lower spring
3008 ft
Upper viewpoint
4802 ft
5988 ft
Knight
3750 ft
4596 ft
Canyon
Lower gorge
3444 ft
S
2546 ft
To Nadeau Rd (1.6 mi)
5600
5200
4800
4400
4000
3600
3200
2800
2400
2000
Unpaved road (2WD)
4WD-HC road
Hiking trail
0.5 mile
N
Contour interval = 80 feet

its own coterie of clouds. In the upper canyon, it was snowing. Knight Canyon kept me so entertained that nightfall occurred three full hours ahead of schedule. I returned in darkness, clutching a flashlight in one hand, an umbrella in the other, and reached my car soaked to the bone. I had not had so much fun with water since floating down Zion National Park's Virgin River in an inner tube.

■

Stone ruins below Nile Spring, in Shepherd Canyon

SHEPHERD CANYON

Though not the most spectacular, Shepherd Canyon is a scenic drainage with expansive views of the Panamint Mountains where you can drive or walk to a profusion of small attractions. Treat yourself to the region's only onyx mine, to an azurite mine with a neat little cabin, to an easy loop hike to springs and colorful volcanic narrows, or to a longer hike into the Argus Range Wilderness up the historic Shepherd Canyon Road, where stagecoaches once bounced on their way to the silver fields of Panamint City.

General Information

Jurisdiction: Bureau of Land Management, Argus Range Wilderness
Road status: Hiking mostly on old roads; access via primitive road
Kopper King Mine: 0.7 mi, 810 ft up, 100 ft down one way/easy–moder.
Nile Spring: 2.4 mi, 1,030 ft up, 30 ft down one way/easy
Shepherd Cyn springs loop: 1.8 mi, ,470 ft up loop/easy
Main attractions: Azurite and onyx mines, springs, historic road
USGS 7.5' topo maps: Maturango Peak*, Maturango Peak SE
Maps: pp. 531*, 457

Location and Access

Shepherd Canyon is in the central Argus Range, roughly west of Ballarat. From the Trona-Wildrose Road, drive the paved Nadeau Road 3.2 miles north to the graded Onyx Mine Road on the left. Follow this road 1.4 miles to a fork. To get to the Onyx Mine, bear right (the wash crossing soon after requires high clearance) and go 1.4 miles. To get to Shepherd Canyon, at the fork bear left instead on the fainter Shepherd Canyon Road. After 1.7 miles, the road was neatly clipped at a vertical 10-foot embankment, the work of a violent flashflood around 2000. Park here, as the next 0.7 mile of road to the wilderness is mostly gone.

Route Description

The Onyx Mine. Onyx, like agate and other forms of chalcedony, is nearly pure silica—the main constituent of common glass. What makes it an attractive gemstone is its impurities: they give onyx its characteristically straight, parallel, and colorful bands. Although onyx is widely distributed, Panamint Valley has the region's only onyx mine. Discovered in 1925, this deposit was worked off and on until at least the 1950s and delivered a few hundred tons of gemstone.

The mining camp at the end of the graded road, once relatively sizable, is gone. The extensive concrete foundations supported what was probably a small gem cutting factory. Such facilities use high-speed blades powered by electric motors, which may have been mounted on the three large concrete blocks. The large quantity of water required to lubricate and cool the blades was piped from upper Shepherd Canyon and stored in two tanks that stood on the hill to the west. White boulders of onyx, partly diced, lie near the facility. Old equipment is slowly rusting on the small quarry just east of the camp. Onyx was also quarried on the low knoll 0.3 mile north. There are beautiful pieces and cuts of banded onyx, red to brown, cream, and green.

The Kopper King Mine. The Kopper King Mine Road is the road that heads west from the Onyx Mine. Drive it 2.15 miles, turning right at the junction after 0.2 mile. It follows a small wash into progressively taller and steeper hills, until it squeezes through a short, tight defile just before reaching the Kopper King Cabin. This mine was owned and exploited for azurite by John A. Gage of Alta Loma, California, from 1964—he was then in his mid-fifties—to 1981. After he stopped mining, the plywood cabin where he lived remained padlocked and fairly well protected for years. It was re-roofed by Friends of Briggs Camp in the late 1990s, then adopted by Friends of Kopper King Cabin in 2002. The cabin is furnished with two beds, a couch, a table, and chairs. There was even a small stash of firewood waiting to be fed into the funky stove, and a roll of toilet paper in the nearby outhouse.

One hundred yards up canyon, a trail on the left climbs to the Kopper King No. 1, a wide, collared shaft over 130 feet deep. Its tall tailing is covered with large chunks of azurite and other blue-green secondary copper minerals. Beyond, the canyon runs into a tight constriction with a 10-foot fall carved in quartz marbled with ochre and vermillion. A foot trail bypasses it on the west side. The tailing of the second shaft is at the top of the fall. From the shaft's timbered collar, a rickety ladder drops tens of feet into musty darkness. The upper tunnel is on the north rim; a foot trail on the right, past a second fall, climbs 0.2 mile and 200 feet to it. The third shaft is in the first side canyon on the right. All workings display colorful copper ore. In the late spring this whole area is blanketed with Indian paintbrush, lupine, globemallow, golden evening primrose, tackstem, and penstemon in bloom. The rocky outcrops are sprinkled with Mojave fishhook cactus.

The springs loop hike. To get to the starting point of this nice and easy loop hike on the north side of Shepherd Canyon, from the Onyx

Mine camp drive the Kopper King Mine Road 1.25 miles west to the entrance into a canyon and a smaller road on the left. Follow it 0.2 mile to a high point. The road drops to a wash, but the bottom is washed out and turning around there is a pain, so just park at the high point.

Hike down the grade 0.1 mile to its lower end at a wash, then down the wash 60 yards to a narrow foot trail cut in the south bank. This trail will take you in 0.2 mile to the first spring, a dense grove of mesquite draping a 40-foot cliff and graced by a couple of palm trees. Burros enjoy bedding here, no doubt drawn by the great views of the Panamints. At the foot of the spring, water sometimes drips into a dark pool under a thicket of cattail. The trail wanders on down the edge of a mesquite-lined gulch, following a disjointed pipeline. In 0.25 mile it reaches a second spring, this one just big enough to support one stubby palm tree. The dilapidated trailer next to it was once the heart of a small camp. The remains surrounding it recount in touching detail the story of the forgotten hermit who lived here in the 1970s. The trailer is tiny, but its veranda, now collapsed, and its flagstone patio and stone fireplace, added a little living space. A curious concrete structure was sunk in the hillside next to it. Was it a hot tub? A shower? Look also for the corral, and the sunken water trough. It would have been pleasant to rest under the full-size salt cedar behind the trailer, watching birds fly in and out of the birdhouse that hung from it, enjoying the views of the open canyon slopes sprawling below.

To complete the loop, walk down the wash below the camp, then look for a segment of road at its mouth and follow it generally north as it zigzags up across low hills (see map). This road connects to the next side canyon north. Follow the canyon wash uphill a short distance to and through colorful narrows in purple-gray volcanic ash. The upper end of the narrows is interrupted by a 15-foot fall. It is more impressive than difficult, but just in case, there are a couple of easy routes to circumvent it on the south side. The road where you parked is just 250 yards up the wash beyond the fall.

The Shepherd Canyon historic road. This canyon is named after John Shepherd, a prominent pioneer who homesteaded from 1863 to 1904 in the Manzanar area, in Owens Valley near Independence. He, his brother James, and their families, raised cattle, horses, and mules, and grew vegetables, hay, and grain. They sold these precious commodities, as well as wood logged in the mountains, to Cerro Gordo, Darwin, and other local mines. John Shepherd also freighted ore from the mines to San Pedro, and brought back supplies to Owens Valley. Their relationship with the local Paiutes, tense during the 1860s, gradually warmed up as the Shepherds provided labor and shelter to the natives. By the mid-1870s, the ranch employed up to 30 Paiutes for manual labor. In time, the Shepherds' fairness and sympathy to the Indians earned their respect and devotion. The ranch had the first two-story house in Owens Valley, an elegant nine-room Victorian mansion with running water, fountains, and marble statues. For years it was a center of social activity and a stopover for wayfarers and teamsters traveling between Bishop Creek and Mojave.

The Shepherds were also road builders. From 1874 to 1875, the two brothers hired indigenous labor to build the first road from Keeler, on Owens Lake's shore, to Darwin and Panamint Valley. It was originally operated as a toll road to transport farm products and livestock. The road through Shepherd Canyon was also built under John Shepherd's supervision. It was then part of a much longer wagon road that connected Owens Valley to Panamint Valley through the Coso Range and the Argus Range. After its completion in November 1874, stagecoaches took fortune seekers over it twice a week to Panamint City.

Shepherd Canyon

	Dist.(mi)	Elev.(ft)
Kopper King Mine		
Kopper King Cabin	0.0	4,140
Shaft No. 1	0.1	4,220
Shaft No. 2	0.25	4,350
Shaft No. 3	0.7	4,850
Springs loop		
High point on side road	0.0	3,515
Upper spring	0.4	3,510
Lower spring/Camp	0.55	3,330
Fall in narrows	1.6	3,390
Back to high point	1.8	3,515
Shepherd Canyon historic road		
Shepherd Cyn Road (washout)	0.0	2,930
Wilderness boundary marker	0.7	3,170
Stone ruins	2.1	~3,760
Nile Spring (head)	2.4	3,905
China Lake NWC (off-limits)	2.45	3,955

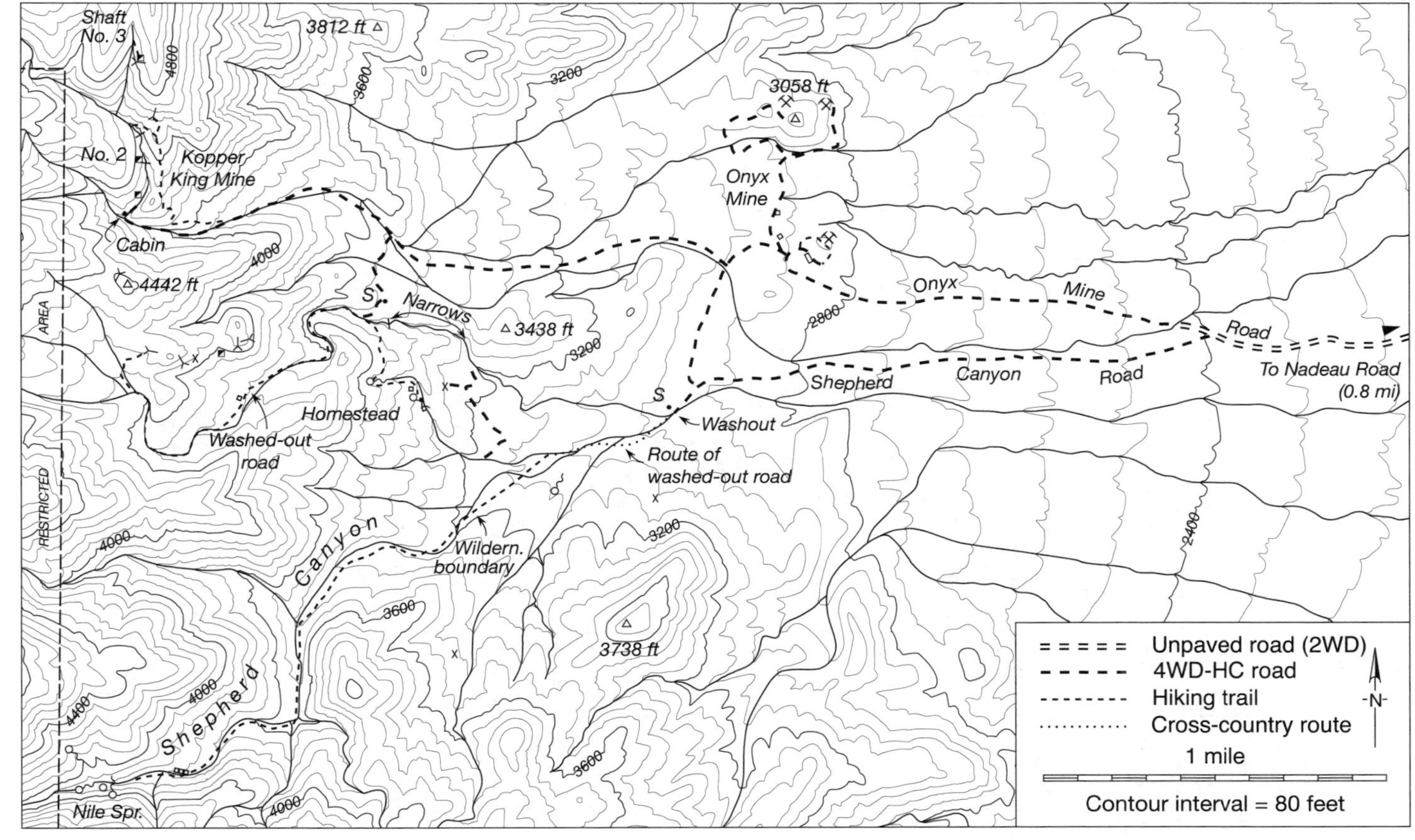
RESTRICTED
AREA
Shaft
No. 3
No. 2
Kopper
King Mine
Cabin
4442 ft
3812 ft
4800
4400
4000
3600
3200
3058 ft
Onyx
Mine
Narrows
3438 ft
Homestead
Washed-out
road
Washout
Route of
washed-out road
Wildern.
boundary
Shepherd
Canyon
3738 ft
2800
2400
Onyx Mine Road
Shepherd Canyon Road
To Nadeau Road
(0.8 mi)
Nile Spr.
Unpaved road (2WD)
4WD-HC road
Hiking trail
Cross-country route
N
1 mile
Contour interval = 80 feet

This hike explores a portion of this historic road, first through the lower canyon, then to a water hole once known as Nile Spring. From the end of the road, follow the wash up canyon. At first the canyon is wide open and surrounded by low wrinkled hills. Long tongues of polished conglomerate, stripped bare by flashfloods, display fine mosaics in the wash. Off in the distance, eerie alignments of stone monuments protrude from the barren hills, as jagged as the teeth of giant carnivores. These are the weathered remnants of long vertical quartz veins that slice across the canyon. The wash forks several times; use the map to identify the main wash, or follow the deeply rutted segments of road that parallel the wash on the low banks.

Shepherd Canyon is most scenic area past the wilderness boundary marker. The wash circles around the prominent peak in the near distance. The surrounding hills gradually morph into higher slopes, then into true canyon walls. This is a soft, bright landscape, dotted with granite boulders smoothed by a hundred centuries of erosion. The granite is peppered with garnet, as blood red as rubies, and apple-green crystals. Unusually large specimens litter the wash. The miles of black plastic pipe that line the way were deployed by the Onyx Mine to harvest water from Nile Spring. Coveys of quails often hide in the low shrubbery, and they may startle you with their loud synchronized takeoff. You might spot a motionless burro staring at you with unblinking eyes. In the evening, the declining sun torches the hills to a coppery gold and carves shadows along their every wrinkle.

A few hundred yards below the head of Nile Spring, the canyon tightens into a narrow gorge. On the north bench are the ruins of three rock structures, the largest one erected against a tall granite boulder. Its style suggests that it predates 1900; it may have been a station where stagecoaches traveling to Owens Valley stopped for water before the long haul across the Argus Range. Up until the late 1990s, the wash past the ruins was clogged with rabbitbrush and willows. At the spring outlet, 350 yards up canyon and 60 feet up the south wall, cold water gushed in vigorous spurts out of a pipe in the ground. The discharge irrigated green grass and ephedra, and gathered below in a tiny creek. The flashflood around 2000 erased this rare desert sight. Only the well 100 yards further up canyon still had water, which trickled out of its crushed plywood casing and spawned a rivulet all of three strides long. This is routine misfortune in the life cycle of a desert spring. Given enough time, Nile Spring will return to its full glory. The boundary of the Naval Weapons Center is 100 yards past the spring. A large yellow sign will remind you that you must turn around.

■

MINE PEAK

In the middle of the Argus Range stands a little-known summit called Mine Peak, girdled indeed by mines—gold, iron, and pumice—some dating back to the 1870s. It makes for a good little climb into a designated wilderness haunted by wild burros, most of it up a mining road blasted into vivid volcanic rocks. The whole route commands glorious vistas of Panamint Valley and the iconic, nearly two-mile-high western scarp of the Panamint Range.

General Information
Jurisdiction: Argus Range Wilderness (BLM)
Road status: Hiking on trail and cross-country; 2WD dirt access road
Mine Peak: 2.3 mi, 1,790 ft up, 60 ft down one way / moderate–difficult
Main attractions: Volcanic geology, views of Panamint Mountains
USGS 7.5′ topo maps: Maturango Peak SE, Slate Range Crossing*
Maps: pp. 535*, *319*

Location and Access

In its heyday, when the Modoc Mine needed iron-ore flux for its smelters, it turned to a small iron deposit conveniently located just down the road, at the foot of Mine Peak. The property, then known as the Hoot Owl Mine, had a lens of massive hematite and magnetite that met all of its needs. Enough ore was even left behind for another 8,000 tons to be shipped during World War II, then in 1959. Around the 1950s a circuitous road was built to develop a quarry on associated claims higher up the mountain. The quarry road, now within the Argus Range Wilderness, is the least difficult route to climb Mine Peak.

To get to the quarry road, drive the Trona-Wildrose Road 3.1 miles north from the pass between Searles Valley and Panamint Valley (Slate Range Crossing) down the switchbacks to the primitive Nadeau Trail on the left. Coming from Panamint Valley, this is 4.3 miles south of the Ballarat Road (half a mile past the paved Nadeau Road, paralleled by a small power line). Go 100 yards north on the Nadeau Trail to a road on the left. Follow it 0.75 mile to the smaller quarry road on the left. Turn left and go 0.2 mile to a small wash crossing, where the quarry road starts climbing steeply into the range. Park here, as the remaining 0.2 mile to the wilderness boundary is very rough. All along these roads Mine Peak is visible to the west, then southwest. There is a washout 0.4 mile from the Nadeau Trail that requires good clearance.

Route Description

From the valley the quarry road climbs along the steep side of a transverse ridge that buttresses the Argus Range. It switchbacks tightly three times, then shoots up a sustained 20% incline. Carved into solid rock with dynamite and steel blades, the rough grade hangs between blown-up cliffs on one side and a long drop on the other. When walking on its sharp edge, there is an astounding perspective in the vertical depth and breadth of the ridge's precipitous flank. Huge volumes of blasted rocks were unceremoniously shoved over the edge, a manmade landslide of boulders in stasis that spills down to a wash hundreds of feet below. The ridge is all volcanic, a colorful suite of andesite ranging from light gray with inclusions of pale plagioclase, to merlot sprinkled with black biotite crystals. Some road cuts are strikingly bicolored, one half blue-gray, the other a palette of purples laced with white calcite. Erosion and gravity reign supreme over the road. After a heavy downpour, the narrow erosional trench that runs along it channels a stream so energetic that the road's demise seems to be its sole mission in life. In normal weather the foot-deep trench is an awkward yet easier path than the rest of the road, as slippery as marbles.

This is a donkey's paradise—low human visitation, no NPS forced retirement program, and an asylum protected by military secrecy within trotting distance should things get out of hand. From valley to summit *Equus asinus* droppings are everywhere, in isolated clumps where an animal pooped on the go, in well-fertilized plots at their favorite hangouts. With binoculars you might spot a few of them, motionless mocha specks standing stoically under the sun down below among the valley shrubs. In a face-to-face encounter a shy burro will run away, stop, then turn broadside to check you out. Accustomed to occasional cars in the valley, on Mine Peak a burro will more likely stare at you with unflinching eyes that dare you to come one step closer.

After a mile the grade reaches its apex 720 feet below Mine Peak. There it angles left, levels off, and moseys on half a mile to a fork at the edge of the quarry. The left fork descends into the quarry, a mess of haulageways bladed into the mountainside. After all the roads and all the damage, unlike the Hoot Owl Mine this area turned out a superb failure—there was nothing up here to harvest. In the middle of this devastation the one structure left is an incongruous wooden outhouse, a farcical memorial to the money that was flushed down the toilet.

The right fork pushes on to a pass just above the quarry, then drops in sheer switchbacks into Water Canyon—a longer but scenic alternative return route. Mine Peak is just up the ridge northwest from the pass, but a spur bristling with vertical outcrops blocks the way. The

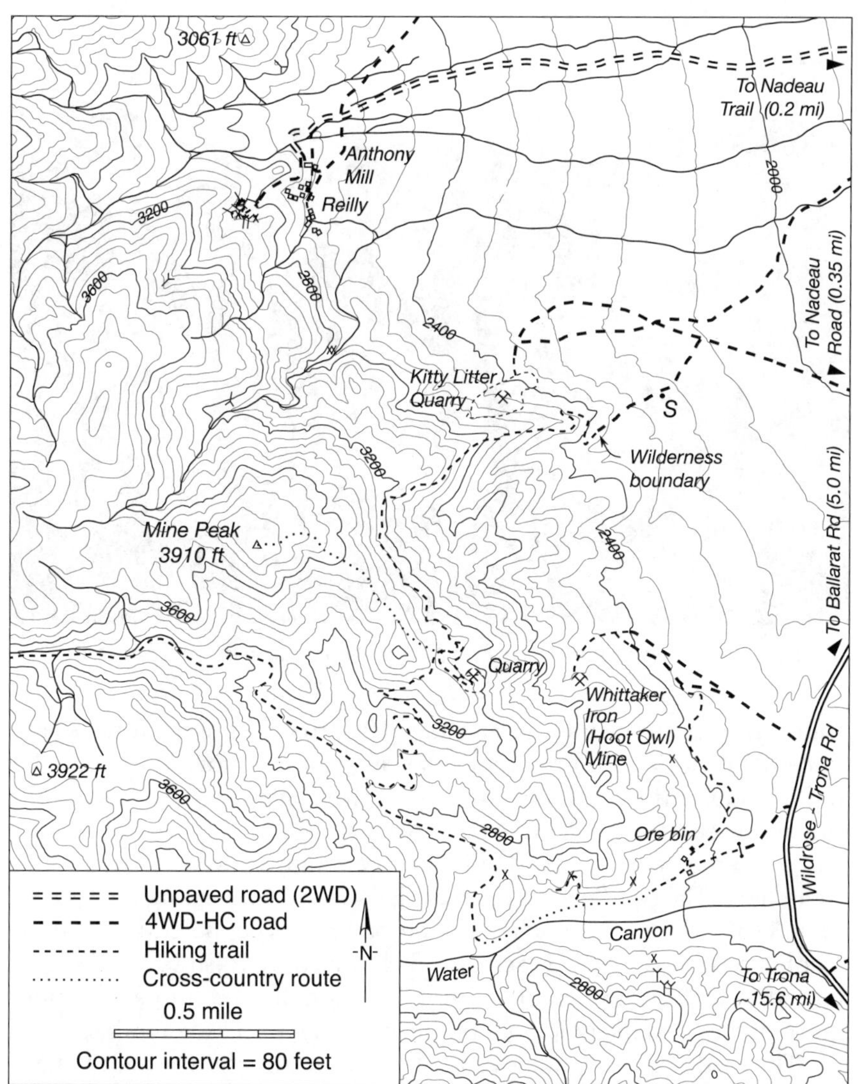

Mine Peak		
	Dist.(mi)	Elev.(ft)
Foot of mountain/grade	0.0	2,180
Top of grade (left bend)	1.05	3,190
Junction at quarry	1.55	3,310
Saddle on crest	1.85	3,500
Mine Peak	2.3	3,910

Manly Peak, South Panamint Playa, and Water Canyon from Mine Peak

spur can be circumvented by starting 200 yards west of the fork, where three tall historic claim monuments stand not far above the road. The route is straightforward, northwest past these markers up across a hillside to the saddle just north of the rocky spur. The slope is mostly dirt and scattered rocks, occasionally steep enough to want to hold onto something. The saddle is an open bridge of land connecting the spur to Mine Peak. The final stretch is up a broad ramp peppered with wind-stunted scrubs, cottontop cactus, and chunks of reddish basalt. When I visited in October the whole mountain had morphed into a sweeping green of new shoots fooled out of dormancy by unseasonal rains.

The road, the crest, and eventually the summit deliver increasingly wide-open views of Panamint Valley, its delicate dunes at one end, the ghost of its Ice-Age lake at the other, the skyscraping Panamint Mountains behind it. Someone familiar with this vast range will recognize dozens of places tucked in its giant pleats of stone—peaks named Tuber and Pinto, the wiggly crack of South Park Canyon, the pale fish-shaped imprint of the Hall Canyon Pluton, and the little green spot of Warm Sulfur Springs below Surprise Canyon. This sight is a vivid reminder of what we have been fortunate to visit, and of how much we have yet to discover.

▪

WATER CANYON

Water Canyon is special. Not just because of the water—every major canyon in the Argus Range has some—but because of the profusion of large springs. There are a total of about 30, running from dry pockets of greenery to long ribbons of water-loving plants flushed by year-round streams. Most of the well-watered springs are confined along the two-mile course of one tight and twisted side canyon. Guarded by falls and inextricable vegetation, often flooded and punctuated by waterfalls, this is the place you will want to see.

General Information
Jurisdiction: Argus Range Wilderness (BLM)
Road status: Cross-country hiking; 2WD primitive access road
First Spring: 2.9 mi, 770 ft up, 20 ft down one way / easy
Fifth Spring: 5.4 mi, 1,720 ft up, 50 ft down one way / strenuous
Main attractions: Extensive springs, pools and streams, wild burros
USGS 7.5' topo maps: Slate Range Crossing,* Homewood Canyon
Maps: pp. 539*, *319*

Location and Access

When you drive to Panamint Valley from Trona, over Slate Range Crossing and down the tight curves into the valley, the broad wash that you cross at the foot of the range is Water Canyon. On the far side of the wash, 2.0 miles from the pass, take the graded road on the left. Coming from the north, this is 5.4 miles south of the Ballarat turnoff. Drive this road 0.2 mile to its end at a barricade of boulders, and park.

Route Description

Directions to the first spring are quite simple. Walk into the Argus Range Wilderness on the continuation of the access road, past the ruins of a 1960s homestead and an ore bin (0.15 mile), then up the roadless wash to a lone conical outcrop 20 feet tall in the middle of the wash (2.25 miles). Angle right into the obvious side canyon on the north side of the outcrop. The first spring is 0.5 mile up the side canyon.

Water Canyon does not seem like a likely place for water. Snaking lazily between tall desert hills, its broad wash is covered with shrubbery as dry as if it had not rained in years. Yet the reason these plants are alive *is* water. Winter storms, slow and protracted, regularly recharge the groundwater that they rely on. Summer floods, though often devastating, dump huge volumes of nutrient-rich slurry laden with mud and torn plants that irrigate and nourish the topsoil. Such a flood came through Water Canyon around 2019. It spared the old-growth rabbitbrush on higher areas of the wash, but all along the lower active channel it deposited a coating of pale sediments. Two years later, large patches of fertilized wash had been converted into rabbitbrush nurseries, dozens of seedlings of the same size that all sprouted at the same time. Local plants were given a new lease on life.

Gently sloped and scoured clean, the active channel is easy hiking ground, and the scenery a constant attraction. At the wash's edges, the walls come right out in mangled Paleozoic ranks. There are pillars of dolomite, pale sweeps of limestone, and bluffs of purple-veined quartzite. A thick layer of gray ash caps a nearby summit. In the fall, the cover of rabbitbrush in bloom fills the canyon with light. Other shrubs add pleasing shades of green—cheesebush, sacred datura, and pygmy cedar so pine-green that they surely robbed all the water. Here too burros are in heaven. Protective of their springs to a fault, they will snort loudly from quite some distance to scare off human intruders.

The side canyon could not be more different. The wash is narrow, littered with boulders small and large, and crammed between steep rock walls. Then comes the first spring, a 50-yard strip of baccharis and tall willows that overwhelms the canyon bottom. It takes a little bush-whacking to cross it, past a couple of puddles fouled by burros. It is a restful spot, filled with bluish shadows, livened by birds and the sound of the trees' leaves shivering in the breeze.

The first obstruction is just past the first spring. It is a 10-foot polished chute flushed by a veneer of water and capped by a gigantic overhanging chokestone (Class 5). The easiest bypass is a Class-2 climb up a stair-like wall on the left at the head of the spring, followed by a safe traverse on a shelf, and a down-climb just past the top of the fall.

This first fall is the gateway into another world. For the next 2.5 miles the canyon is a narrow serpentine passage, most of it occupied

Water Canyon

	Dist.(mi)	Elev.(ft)
End of road	0.0	2,370
Side canyon	2.4	2,910
First spring (start)	2.9	3,095
Second spring (head)	3.5	3,320
Fifth Spring (head)	5.4	4,020

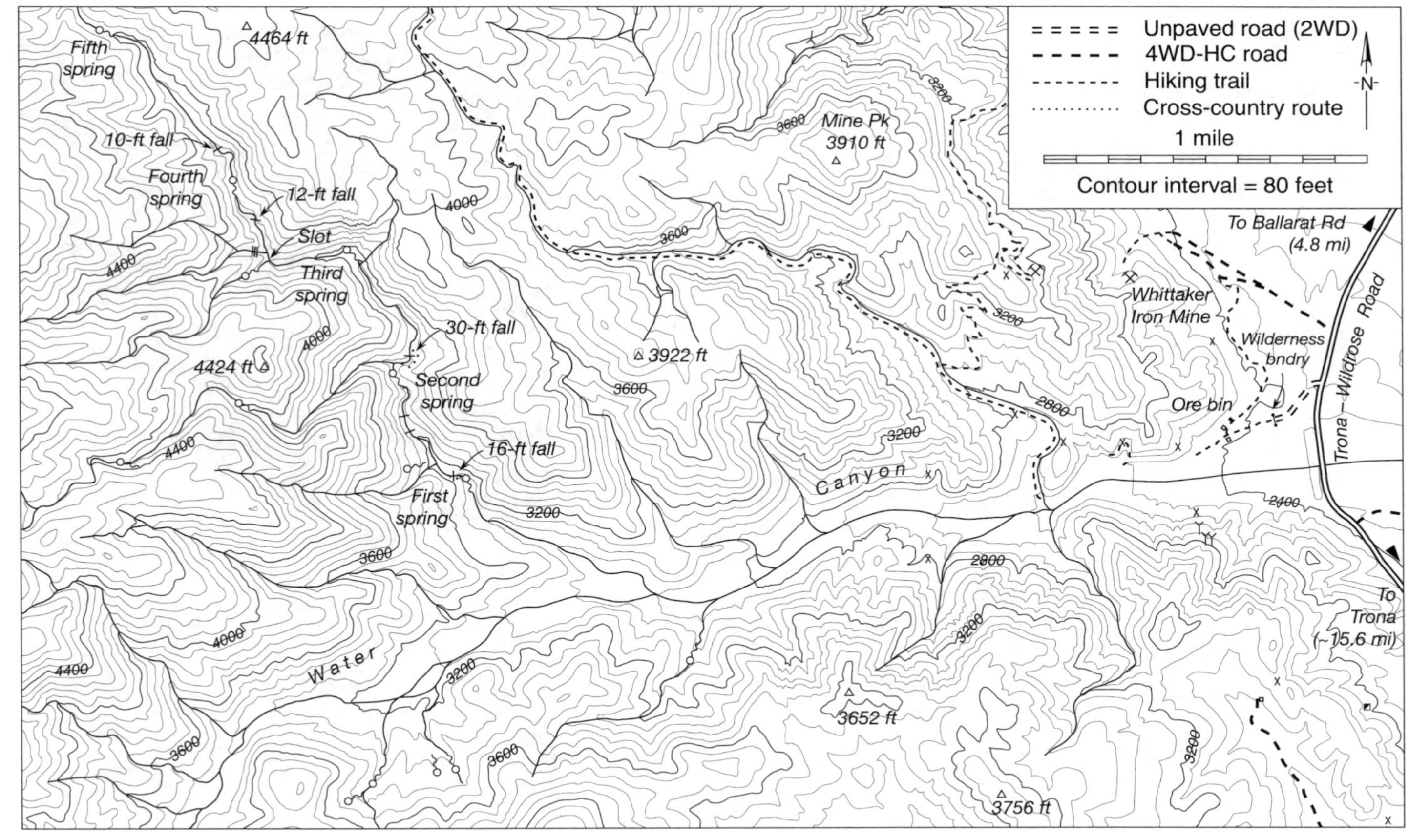
Fifth spring
4464 ft
10-ft fall
Fourth spring
12-ft fall
Slot
Third spring
30-ft fall
4424 ft
Second spring
16-ft fall
First spring
3922 ft
Mine Pk
3910 ft
Canyon
Water
3652 ft
3756 ft
Whittaker Iron Mine
Wilderness bndry
Ore bin
To Ballarat Rd (4.8 mi)
Trona – Wildrose Road
To Trona (~15.6 mi)
Unpaved road (2WD)
4WD-HC road
Hiking trail
Cross-country route
1 mile
Contour interval = 80 feet
N

Second spring in main side canyon of Water Canyon

by thick vegetation, so slow-going that it seems endless. There are falls, a slot, crooked narrows weaving between interlocked buttresses, thickets of cattail and baccharis under the canopy of willow. This is where Water Canyon's hidden water lies, in exiled pools sealed off from the world by natural obstacles. Finding these secret pockets of water is an intense source of enchantment. First comes a second of surprise, then the elation of discovery, and soon the urge to reach down and touch. Just above the first fall a half a dozen pools are cupped in bedrock and gravel hollows. The water comes not from furious floods but from the slow underworld, rain and snow melt that has percolated through the mountain and resurfaced at small faults. Purged of sediments, it is crystal clear, as cold as a cave, and deep enough to swim. Further on, there are more pools, waterfalls, and braids of flowing water concealed under the vegetation frenzy. They show up without warning, and each time they trigger the same excitement.

This is rough terrain. The baccharis is often too thick to cross, and the tree branches start near the ground and crowd each other. Bypasses on the low rims are generally too arduous. Even the burros stay clear. The best option is often to creep along the narrow rubbly space between the walls and the springs. When all fails you push your way through the vegetation, water to your ankles, branches slapping your thighs. This is sometimes what it takes to find water in the desert.

■

BIBLIOGRAPHY

Further reading

Bryan, T. S., and B. Tucker-Bryan. *The Explorer's Guide to Death Valley National Park*. 4th ed., Boulder, Co.: University Press of Colorado, 2021.

DeDecker, M. *Flora of the Northern Mojave Desert, California*. California Native Plant Society, Spec. Pub. No. 7, 1984.

Digonnet, M. *Hiking Death Valley*. Palo Alto, Ca.: self-published, 2007.

Ferris, R. S. *Death Valley Wildflowers*. Death Valley, Ca.: Death Valley Natural History Association, 1983.

Foster, L. *Adventuring in the California Desert*. San Francisco, Ca.: Sierra Club Books, 1997.

Ganci, D. *The Basic Essentials of Desert Survival*. Merrillville, Ind.: ICS Books, Inc., 1991.

Glazner, A. F., A. G. Sylvester, and R. P. Sharp, *Geology Underfoot in Death Valley and Eastern California*. 2nd ed., Missoula, Mt.: Mountain Press Publishing Company, 2022.

Greene, S. *Death Valley Book of Knowledge*. New York: iUniverse, Inc., 2009.

Hart, J. *Hiking the Great Basin*. San Francisco, Ca.: Sierra Club Books, 1981.

Jaeger, E. C. *Desert Wild Flowers*. Stanford, Ca.: Stanford University Press, 1969.

MacMahon, J. A. *Deserts*. National Audubon Society Nature Guides, New York: Alfred A. Knopf, Inc., 1997.

Mann, W. J. *Guide to the Remote and Mysterious Saline Valley*. Vol. 4. Barstow, Ca.: Shortfuse Publishing Co., 2002.

Mitchell, R. *Death Valley SUV Trails*. Oakhurst, Ca.: Track & Trail Publications, 2001.

Moore, M. *Medicinal Plants of the Desert and Canyon West*. Santa Fe, New Mex.: Museum of New Mexico Press, 1989.

Munz, P. A. *Introduction to California Desert Wildflowers*. Revised Edition, Edited by D. L. Renshaw and P. M. Faber. California Natural History Guides, 74, 2004.

Taylor, R. J. *Desert Wildflowers of North America*. Missoula, Mt.: Mountain Press Publishing Company, 1998.

Zdon, A. *Desert Summits*. 2nd ed. Bishop, Ca.: Spotted Dog Press, Inc., 2006.

Sources

Anderson, S. P., and R. S. Anderson. "Debris-flow benches: Dune-contact deposits record paleo-sand dune positions in north Panamint Valley, Inyo County, California." *Geology* 18, No. 6 (1990): 524-527.

Aubury, L. E. "The Copper Resources of California." *Cal. St. Mining Bureau Bull.* 50, 1908.

Belden, L. B., and M. DeDecker. *Death Valley to Yosemite: Frontier Mining Camps and Ghost Towns*. Bishop, Ca.: Spotted Dog Press, Inc., 2000.

Burchfiel, B. C., K. V. Hodges, and L. H. Royden. "Geology of Panamint Valley—Saline Valley Pull-Apart System, California: Palinspastic Evidence for Low-Angle Geometry of a Neogene Range-Bounding Fault." *J. of Geophys. Res.* 92, No. B10 (1987): 10422-10426.

Chalfant, W. A. *The Story of Inyo.* Stanford, Ca.: Stanford University Press, 1953.

Clark, W. B. "Gold District of California." *Cal. Div. of Mines and Geol. Bull.* 193, 4th printing, 1979.

Close, T. J. "Mineral resources of the Inyo Mountains Wilderness Study Area, Inyo County, California." *U. S. Bureau of Mines Open File Rept.* MLA 18-85, 1985.

Collier, M. *An Introduction to the Geology of Death Valley.* Death Valley, Ca.: Death Valley Natural History Association, 1990.

Crum, S. J. *The Road On Which We Came: A History of the Western Shoshone.* Salt Lake City, Ut.: University of Utah Press, 1994.

Crawford, J. J. "Mines and Mining Products of California." *Annual Rept. of the State Mineralogist* 12 (1894): 21-141; 13 (1896): 32-185.

Davis, E. L., and C. Raven. *Environmental and Paleoenvironmental Studies in Panamint Valley.* San Diego, Ca.: Contributions of the Great Basin Foundation No. 2, 1986.

DeDecker, M. *White Smith's Fabulous Salt Tram.* Morongo Valley, Ca.: Sagebrush Press for the Death Valley '49ers, Inc., Keepsake No. 33, 1993.

Dietz. R. S., and E. C. Buffington. "Panamint Crater, California, not meteoritic." *Meteoritics* 2, No. 2 (1964): 179-181.

Eric, J. H. "Copper in California." *Cal. Div. of Mines and Geol. Bull.* 144 (1948): 238-275.

Fiero, B. *Geology of the Great Basin.* Reno, Nev.: University of Nevada Press, 1986.

Fitzpatrick, J. A., and J. L. Bishop. "Uranium-Series Dates on Sediments of the High Shoreline of Panamint Valley, California." *U. S. Geol. Survey Open File Rept.* 93-232, 1993.

Fletcher, H. "Mines and Mineral Resources of Portions of California." *Annual Rept. of the State Mineralogist* 14 (1915): 1-974.

Fletcher, H., E. S. Boalich, W. B. Tucker, E. Hughenin, and C. A. Logan. "Mining in California During 1920." *Annual Rept. of the State Mineralogist* 17 (1921): 273-305.

Gale, H. S., "Salines in the Owens, Searles, and Panamint Basins, Southeastern California." *U. S. Geol. Survey Bull.* 580 (1914): 251-323.

Gale, H. S. "Salt, Borax, and Potash in Saline Valley, Inyo County, California." *U. S. Geol. Survey Bull.* 540 (1914): 416-421.

Greene, L. W., and J. A. Latschar. *Historic Resource Study: A History of Mining in Death Valley National Monument.* Denver, Co.: National Park Service, 1981.

Hall, W. E. "Geology of the Panamint Butte Quadrangle, California." *U. S. Geol. Survey Bull.* 1299 (1971): 1-67.

Hall, W. E., and E. M. MacKevett, Jr. "Geology and Ore Deposits of the

Darwin Quadrangle, Inyo County, California." *U. S. Geol. Survey Prof. Paper* 368, 1962.

Hall, W. E., and H. G. Stephens. "Economic Geology of the Panamint Butte Quadrangle and Modoc District, Inyo County, California." *Cal. Div. of Mines and Geol. Spec. Rept.* 73 (1963): 1-39.

Hanks, H. G. "Borax Deposits of California and Nevada."*Annual Rept. of the State Mineralogist* 3 (1883): 1-111.

Hunt, C. B., and D. R. Mabey. "Stratigraphy and Structure, Death Valley, California." *U. S. Geol. Survey Prof. Paper* 494-A, 1966.

Johnson, B. K. "Geology of a Part of the Manly Peak Quadrangle, Southern Panamint Range, California." *Univ. of Cal. Pub. in Geol. Sci.* 30, No. 5 (1957): 353-424.

Lingenfelter, R. E. *Death Valley and the Amargosa: A Land of Illusion*. Berkeley, Ca.: University of California Press, 1986.

Lydon, P. A. "Sulfur and Sulfuric Acid." *Cal. Div. of Mines and Geol. Bull.* 176 (1957): 613-622.

Lynton, E. D. "Sulphur Deposits of Inyo County, California." *Cal. J. Min. of Mines and Geol.* 34 (1938): 563-590.

McAllister, J. F. "Geology of Mineral Deposits in the Ubehebe Peak Quadrangle, Inyo County, California" *Cal. Div. of Mines and Geol. Spec. Rept.* 42 (1955): 1-63.

McHugh, E. L., R. S. Gaps, J. D. Causey, and C. M. Rumsey. "Mineral Resources of the Saline Valley Wilderness Study Area, Inyo County, California." *U. S. Bureau of Mines Open File Report* MLA 16-84, 1984.

McKee, E. H., J. E. Kilburn, J. H. McCarthy, J. E. Conrad, R. J. Blakely, and T. J. Close. "Mineral Resources of the Inyo Mountains Wilderness Study Area, Inyo County, California." *U. S. Geol. Survey Bull.* 1708-A, 1985.

Merriam, C. W. "Geology of the Cerro Gordo Mining District, Inyo County, California." *U. S. Geol. Survey Prof. Paper* 408, 1963.

Miller, J. M. G. "Glacial and Syntectonic Sedimentation: The Upper Proterozoic Kingston Peak Formation, Southern Panamint Range, Eastern California." *Geol. Soc. Am. Bull.* 96, No. 12 (1985): 1537-1553.

Miller, J. M. G. "Tectonic Evolution of the Southern Panamint Range, Inyo and San Bernardino Counties." *Cal. Geol.* 40, No. 9 (1987): 212-222.

Moore, S. C. *Geology and Thrust Fault Tectonics of Parts of the Argus and Slate Ranges, Inyo County, California*. Doctoral dissertation. Seattle, Wa.: University of Washington, 1976.

Murphy, F. M. "Geology of the Panamint Silver District, California." *Economic Geology and the Bull. of the Soc. of Economic Geologists* 25, No. 4 (1930): 305-325.

Murphy, F. M. "Geology of a Part of the Panamint Range, California." *Rept. of the State Mineralogist* 28 (1932): 329-356.

Murphy, R. *Desert Shadows*. Distributed by Sagebrush Press, Morongo Valley, Ca., 1993.

Nadeau, R. *Ghost Towns and Mining Camps of California*. Los Angeles, Ca.: The Ward Richie Press, 1965.

Nadeau, R. *The Silver Seekers*. Santa Barbara, Ca.: Crest Publishers, 1999.

Norman, L. A., and R. M. Stewart. "Mines and Mineral Resources of Inyo County, California." *Cal. J. of Mines and Geol.* 47 (1951): 17-223.

Page, B. M. "Talc Deposits of Steatite Grade, Inyo County, California." *Cal. Div. of Mines and Geol. Spec. Rept.* 8, 1951.

Palazzo, R. P. *Darwin, California*. Lake Grove, Or.: Western Places No. 16, 1996.

Palmer, T. S. *Place Names of the Death Valley Region in California and Nevada*. Morongo Valley, Ca.: Sagebrush Press, 1980.

Peterson F. F. "Holocene Desert Soil Formation under Sodium Salt Influence in a Playa-Margin Environment." *Quaternary Research* 13 (1980): 172-186

Raven, C. *Landscape Evolution and Human Geography in Panamint Valley, Perspectives for Future Research*. San Diego, Ca.: Contributions of the Great Basin Foundation No. 1, 1985.

Sagstetter, B., and B. Sagstetter. *The Mining Camps Speak*. Denver, Co.: BenchMark Publishing of Colorado, 1998.

Sampson, R. J. "Mineral Resources of a Part of the Panamint Range." *Rept. of the State Mineralogist* 28 (1932): 357-376.

Schweig, E. S., III. "Basin-Range Tectonics in the Darwin Plateau, Southwestern Great Basin, California." *GSA Bull.* 101 (1989): 652-662.

Smith, G. I. *Late-Quaternary Pluvial and Tectonic History of Panamint Valley, Inyo and San Bernardino Counties, California*. Doctorate dissertation. Pasadena, Ca.: Cal. Inst. of Technol., 1976.

Smith, G. I., and W. P. Pratt. "Core Logs from Owens, China, Searles, and Panamint Basins, California." *U. S. Geol. Survey Bull.* 1045-A (1957): 1-62.

Taylor, G. C. "Mineral Land Classification of the Eureka-Saline Valley Area, Inyo and Mono Counties, California." *Cal. Div. of Mines and Geol. Spec. Rept.* 166, 1993.

Travis, N. J., and E. J. Cocks. *The Tincal Trail: A History of Borax*. London: Harrap, 1984.

Tucker, W. B. "Mining in California." *Rept. of the State Mineralogist* 22 (1926): 453-539.

Tucker, W. B., and R. J. Sampson. "Mineral Resources of Inyo County." *Cal. J. of Mines and Geol.* 34 (1938): 368-500.

Tucker, W. B., and R. J. Sampson. "Inyo County." *Cal. J. of Mines and Geol.* 36 (1940): 22-28.

Wallace, W. J., and E. Wallace. *Digging into Death Valley's History: Three Studies in Historic Archaeology*. Ramona, Ca.: Acoma Books, 1981.

Waring, C. A., and E. Huguenin. "Mines and Mineral Resources of Alpine County, Inyo County, and Mono County, California." *Annual Rept. of the State Mineralogist* 15 (1917): 25-129.

Wrucke, C. T., S. P. Marsh, G. L. Raines, R. S. Werschky, R. J. Blakely, D. B. Hoover, E. L. McHugh, C. M. Rumsey, R. S. Gaps, and J. D. Causey. "Mineral Resources and Mineral Resource Potential of the Saline Valley and Lower Saline Wilderness Study Areas, Inyo County, California." *U. S. Geol. Survey Open File Rept.* 84-0560, 1984.

■

INDEX OF DESTINATIONS

This section compiles the destinations covered in this volume, categorized by types of attraction and activity. Each entry is keyed to the main page (occasionally two pages) where it is found in the book; the subject might continue in subsequent pages. An asterisk marks a site that can be reached by car or by a short stroll from a car.

Geology and minerals

Ghost towns, camps, and cabins

Joshua tree forests

Mining and milling structures

Mine tunnels, shafts, and quarries

Narrows

Peak climbs

Rock climbing

Salt lakes and dry playas

Sand dunes

Springs and creeks

Valley-floor hikes (*see also* Sand dunes, Salt lakes and dry playas)

Views (*see also* Peak climbs)

Waterfalls

Woodlands (conifers)

INDEX

Regular numbers indicate entries in the text; italic numbers indicate entries in a map; and boldface numbers indicate main entries.